ACTING

Graphic Illustrations
Ellis M. Pryce-Jones
University of Nevada, Las Vegas

wcb

Wm. C. Brown Company Publishing
Dubuque, Iowa

ACTING In Person and in Style

Third Edition

Jerry L. Crawford
University of Nevada, Las Vegas

All text and visual credits start on page 508.

Co-authored in the original edition with Joan F. Snyder

Library of Congress Catalog Number: 82–83543

ISBN 0-697-04234-0

Printed in the United States of America
10   9   8   7

To actors
everywhere and to my
students—past, present,
and future . . .
. . . and, of course,
again and again to "you."

A book on acting presents to any reader a very special challenge. First of all, most of us interested in acting begin by believing we don't need any help. What we need is a stage and an audience. After all, we do plenty of acting in our daily lives, putting on "acts" all over the place: in our living rooms (in fact, all over the house!), in our churches, in our schools, even in our own private rooms. Secondly, most of us who take up acting have already had some encouragement either from ourselves or from those around us who have seen us perform in some dramatic event: a play, a skit, a gala, a class party, a church social, a vaudeville evening, or possibly even an amateur night. The point is that many people say, "Why study acting?" After all, acting should be fun, or acting is a gift and you either have it or you don't, or acting can't be studied any more than talent can be learned. My advice to you, the reader of this book, is to discard all those myths that gossip, rumor, and misinformation have contributed to the attitudes toward acting in this nation. In their place, I would advise you to substitute some famous words written by actors who *know* about their craft of acting, words such as the following: acting is believing: respect for acting: technique of acting: the paradox of acting. And probably the most important single idea to keep in mind is *an actor prepares,* a fact that became the title for one of Stanislavski's great books on the art of acting.

For an actor to prepare, an actor must respect the special task of *acting on a stage.* Acting in life is not the same as *performing* on a stage, and that difference is crucial. One need not prepare in order to act in life. One needs to prepare completely in order to act *successfully* on a stage. To be truthful on a stage when one knows from the beginning that the actor is "pretending" to be truthful is a great paradox and a great challenge. This book attempts to orient you to that challenge and it does that job with vigor, honesty and scope. In many ways you are in for a special treat. The exercises in this volume, the information, and the understanding that is communicated to you, the reader, will inevitably help you comprehend the job you have chosen to introduce to yourself. And choosing is very important for the preparation of an actor.

A great acting teacher, Stella Adler, tells her classes that "imagination is in the choice." Miss Adler means that a person's making a choice from a variety of options indicates the quality of imagination the person possesses. For instance, your life and mine have been packed with choices. The level of imagination we have exercised in our lives is reflected in those choices. So in acting. An actor prepares by developing a huge array of options from which he or she chooses the most appropriate. This book provides you abundantly with the material with which to develop the habit of a great number of options. In fact it seems to me that one of the purposes of the book is to help you, the reader, cultivate the ability to create a lot of possibilities and then to act on the choice you think most fitting. This book has the power to nurture that ability in you. I envy you your first trip through this volume and encourage you to journey carefully. This book will provide you with excellent direction. And if there is one principle in the world that your education should teach you it is that "if you don't know where you are going, any road will take you there." Take this trip deliberately with goodspeed and good luck.

Howard Stein
Columbia University
New York City

Some of life's great joys come with renewal efforts. The Third Edition of this book has already brought me great joy through the satisfaction of improved material, improved photographs, and, above all, fresh personal insights. I have discussed this phenomenon of "learning from your own book as you rewrite it" with such good friends, colleagues, and authors as Robert Benedetti, Robert Cohen, Howard Stein, Barry Kyle, Gerry Freedman, and others. After wrestling with the theory and practice of the art of acting through this edition, the greatest insight of all is that one never stops learning. Naturally, one wants to share this experience with students and colleagues. After nearly thirty years of occupation in theatre, I realize how much my students have taught me, and how much my colleagues have taught me. Thus, I suppose this Third Edition is my continued effort to make some sort of return to those students and those colleagues.

My coauthor on the first edition of this book was Joan Snyder. At that time, Joan was a colleague of mine on the theatre staff at the University of Nevada, Las Vegas. In 1977, Joan left our staff to pursue a career in acting and directing. Accordingly, I have written the revised editions of *Acting in Person and in Style* alone. Obviously, the book retains some of Joan's and my mutual efforts. It is with respect, gratitude, and affection that I acknowledge Joan's contribution. Her former students and I wish her every success in her venture in theatre.

A Special Note to Female Performers and Readers

It is traditional theatre practice to refer to both male and female stage performers as "actor" when making general reference to such artists. However, when specific persons or situations arise, we naturally use the term "actress" when referring to female performers. Such is the usage applied in books written about acting and the theatre, and such is the usage applied in this Third Edition. Generally, "actor" refers to both male and female performers whenever you encounter the term throughout this book. At times you will note specific reference to "actress." The circumstances under description dictate the use. To deviate from this traditional practice would often create a very awkward syntax and, of course, extend the length of this book. Accordingly, I ask for the understanding and acceptance of traditional usage on this point from all of my readers. We must remember that *actor* is a professional term *intended* for its inclusive application to male and female; to constantly separate usage to *actor and actress* would in fact be sexist usage. We no longer say poet/poetess or sculptor/sculptress. The correct non-sexist terminology is *actor*, a fact recently pointed out to me by a leading editor in a leading publishing house who just happened to be female.

This book is again designed to assist with the training of the developing actor at the college and university levels. The earlier editions proved that the book can also be helpful to the secondary student as well as to the aspiring professional working alone or in studios.

Acting in Person and in Style approaches actor training through the concept of personalization. *Personalization is a process whereby the actor discovers and explores in himself characteristics, qualities, and attitudes which are legitimate dimensions of the role he is creating.* Such work contributes to relaxation and confidence by keeping the actor free of forced emotional and characterization work early in rehearsals. A believable, natural foundation of activity is promoted.

In addition to the concept of personalization, Part I discusses traditional acting techniques (generally rooted in the principles of Stanislavsky), including relaxation, breathing, body dynamics (movement), concentration, sensory awareness, emotion, imagination and improvisation, voice, speech and language, character work in *scenes* extracted from plays, auditioning (for both traditional plays and musical plays), role analysis, rehearsal and performance. Part I is designed to service one to two semesters of beginning acting courses, or, one to three quarters of beginning acting courses. Part I will also serve a variety of time lengths in private and professional studios.

The more extensive additions to Part I in the Third Edition involve Chapters Seven, Eight, and Nine. New material is included on Voice Placement, Diphthongs, Dialects and Regional Accents, Seven Steps to Preparing a Scene for Performance in a Class, Laboratory, or Studio, Musical Theatre Auditions, Cold Reading, Agents, Contracts, Unions, and Interviews.

The more extensive additions to Part II in the Third Edition involve expansion of the discussion on the concept of "style," on the concepts of non-realistic styles, on the concepts of Brecht and Epic Theatre, on the concepts of Absurdism, and, of course, on contemporary drama, theatre, and styles.

Part II discusses theories and history related to the styles of acting, proceeding chronologically from Fifth Century B.C. Greece to the present. The chapters on style combine vital theatre history, personalization, and the specifics of each style under study. A number of users of the earlier editions noted how valuable the book was as a supplementary source for beginning theatre history, dramatic literature, and introduction to theatre courses.

Other important features of Part II include prechapter quotations which establish the spirit of the style discussed in each chapter, an actor checklist for every style under consideration, recommended roles and plays for practice and study, and suggested readings (both of the latter have been considerably expanded and updated in the Third Edition). In addition to the twenty-seven scenes from famous plays originally reprinted in the book for practice in acting, the Third Edition adds *five* new scenes from contemporary dramatic literature, including two recent Pulitzer Prize scripts and, for the first time in this book, two scenes from contemporary musical theatre.

Part II (styles) remains intended for use only after completion of the work on beginning acting given in Part I. Style should not be encountered until an actor is at least a year or more into training.

The Third Edition benefits from another new Foreword written by Howard Stein, one of our nation's most distinguished educators and theatre administrators. Many users praised the accurate and illuminating perceptions stated in Howard's earlier Forewords; I believe they will find his new Foreword still more rewarding.

Following the advice of many users, the Third Edition again carries separate introductions to Part I and Part II. (The Part I Introduction includes a concise history of the art of acting. The Part II Introduction offers a succinct analysis of the complex term and concept known as "style.")

In earlier editions, Appendix A (detailing instructions for play analysis) received enthusiastic support from users. Accordingly, it is revised and reprinted in this edition.

Appendix B (a discussion of important experimental theatre groups), also well received in earlier editions, has been updated and expanded.

Appendix C, so warmly received by actors and coaches/directors across the country, is retained and expanded with special thanks to my friends and colleagues, Robert Benedetti and Barry Kyle. Their "contributions" came in the form of informal conversations while we worked together at a UCLA theatre festival, and during workshops/critiques.

Perhaps no appendix in this book has been so well received as has Appendix D, the "Short Form Role Analysis Document." Countless actors have written to me or approached me to express gratitude for this little document which aids the actor's work in role analysis. Prompted by the urging of my UNLV theatre colleague, Larry Kuhl, both "poorly done" and "well done" *samples* of this document are added in the Third Edition to further guide the work of the actor.

The Third Edition contains many practical *exercises* in acting in every chapter. These exercises have all been proven in the classroom, and, without exception, each exercise has been expanded in this edition.

As noted, "Suggested Readings" and "Suggested Characters and Plays for Scene Work" have been extensively expanded and updated.

The book concludes with a glossary of theatre terms (nearly doubled in size over previous editions) and an index.

Many users of the earlier editions pointed to the economic and convenience advantages gained from adopting this text. The breadth and depth of the book permit it to be used in as many as four or more courses of study in acting. Thus, the student can remain with a consistent system of study for two or more years with a single outlay of expense. Of course, the book also works well as a supplementary text. When this is the case, users find that it best complements material offered by Robert Benedetti, Robert Cohen, Charles McGaw, and Uta Hagen. In other words, *Acting in Person and in Style* is a highly flexible handbook for any actor engaged in any study of this art.

Finally, the Third Edition again benefits from new and exciting graphic illustrations by my esteemed colleague, Ellis M. Pryce-Jones. The work of Ellis in the earlier editions received broad commendation from critics and users. And, perhaps most striking of all, the Third Edition contains a vast increase in the quality and number of photographs by first-rate professional photographers. Dozens of new photos range from exercise photos to production shots from plays produced in the United States and London, ranging from top professional theatres to top regional and university theatres. Almost no "local" or "home" production photos remain. The result is not only a visual gain, but increased educational impact through the depiction of exercises, styles, and production values.

Every attempt has been made to sustain the writing style of the earlier editions, focusing upon a conversational, but lively mode.

One always marvels at how errors slip into books despite careful effort and several proofreaders. Hopefully, the Third Edition is finally free of all errors in dates, facts, and printing. However, should you locate any, please drop me a line to benefit my work with future revisions.

Acting for Fun! Recreational Acting

I wish to call attention to a special opportunity which this book offers. While the *focus* of this material is necessarily directed to the serious actor or student actor, one who is or probably will be pursuing a professional career, the entire body of content in *Acting in Person and in Style* lends itself very well to the person who would rather study acting for "fun," that is, for recreational purposes. This includes, of course, the so-called "community" theatre actor, and the person who wishes to "take one course" or "audition once or twice" or "accept a role once or twice." To utilize this book to their advantage, such people need to concentrate on the theories and the exercises, particularly in Part I, and utilize Chapter Eight with special emphasis. To these people, I extend my gratitude and my best wishes for "happy experiences in acting"—have fun!

A Special Note to Creative Dramatics Instructors and Directors of Children's/Youth Theatre

The theory and exercises in the Third Edition have been designed to aid the work of creative dramatics instructors and directors of children's theatre. Chapters One through Seven are particularly well suited to this purpose, albeit certain exercises in Chapter Five dealing with emotion probably should be deferred until later years (such as "affective memory/emotional recall"). The final decision on which theory and exercises to utilize and how to adapt that material to suit specific circumstances rests quite appropriately with the instructor/director. Depending on the experience and maturity of the group, Chapters Eight through Ten and all ten style chapters may also be well utilized with children and young adults. I encourage creative dramatics instructors and children's/youth theatre directors to try the Third Edition in their work. I think they will be pleased with the results.

Suggested Filmography

Note is also made of the helpful addition of a Filmography to each of the style chapters (chapters 11–20) in Part Two of the Third Edition. The suggested selections represent valuable visual and aural sources for the actor in the study of style.

My basic premise remains that no book actually "teaches" acting. This view is shared by my friends Robert Benedetti, Robert Cohen, and others who coach actors and write books on acting. Such a book is merely another tool, another aid to the highly personal and complex work of the actor. No one system, no one book can do it all. The actor should derive whatever possible from all sources, written and human. Finally, I continue to adhere to the fundamental credo concerning the art of acting: "What works, works!"

I am grateful to the following people who so generously gave of their time, professional ability, or inspiration in my writing of the Third Edition of this book: Ellis M. Pryce-Jones; Howard Stein; Robert Benedetti; Barry Kyle; Delmar D. Hendricks; Gerry Freedman; Nancy Vunovich; Salem Ludwig; Linda McCollum; Julie and Todd Tjaden; Leslie Hrusch; W. Scott Whisler; Paul C. Harris, Jr.; Larry Kuhl; Tom Prewitt; Bob Burgan; Fred Olson; John Unrue; Rick Romito; Teresa Gilmore; Grey Schmidt; Frank Gagliano; Don Finn; Ron Willis; David Young; Edward EmanuEl; Terry Miller; Lee and Jean Korf; George Gunkle; Edgar Swift; Joseph Falzetta; Glenn Casale; Martin Oltarsh; Patricia Lewis; Elizabeth Lindsay; Betty Vaughan; Philip Wm. McKinley; Elana McKinley; Joan and Jerome Snyder; JoAnn Johnson Patton; Cathie Fowler; Mary Brubaker; Selma Luttinger; Bob Freedman; Chuck and Cleo Lown; Carrie Freeman; Aden Ross; Phyllis Durham; and Jimmy Sturtevant.

Again, lasting gratitude and affection to Pamela Monakee, a very special actress.

Finally, and above all, thanks to my wife, Pat, and our three children, Mitchell, Vali, and Keli.

Thanks to the following people for assisting with the acquisition of photographs: Ruth Pearson; Al Muller; Jean Korf; Bob Dillard; Rebecca Renfroe; Rob Hill; Frank Gagliano; Irene Cory; Jo Bowman; Marilyn Holt; David Thayer; Robert N. Burgan; Jackie West; Alan Schneider; Barry Kyle; Deborah Weiner; Robert Benedetti; Sandy Robbins; JoAnn Johnson Patton; Fred Adams; Gary M. McIntyre; Scott Phillips; Jack Wright; Ralph E. Taylor; Robert Loper; Weldon Durham; Larry Clark; Lyle Dye, Jr.; Steve Archer; Margaret Spear; Leonard Leone; Carole Brandt; and Gene Feist.

Very special thanks to UNLV professional photographer, Randy Tunnel, for his excellent work with actors Teresa Gilmore and Grey Schmidt in creating exercise photographs for Part I.

Special thanks to Todd Tjaden for research work with filmographies, and to Julie Tjaden for filmography manuscript preparation.

Particular thanks are also extended to the wonderful people at Wm. C. Brown Co., Publishers, from the earlier years and Richard Crews, Twila Sears, Karen Gilligan, Susan J. Soley, and Sharon A. Easley, to more recent times and Pat Schmelling, Sharon R. Mueller, Mavis Oeth, and Kevin Kane. Last and, therefore, above all, my "Third Edition" appreciation and gratitude goes to my Editor, Louise Waller, who not only lightened the professional task, but made the entire experience with **wcb** and its production staff fulfilling and fun.

Jerry L. Crawford
University of Nevada, Las Vegas
Las Vegas, Nevada

Acting: I
In Person

Introduction to Part I
"In Person" On the Art and Nature of Acting

Acting "is forever carving a statue of snow." So stated Lawrence Barrett, nineteenth-century American actor. It has also been said that the actor is at once the piano and the pianist. And They have said acting is being; acting is believing; acting is feeling; acting is doing; acting is becoming; acting is illusion; acting is technique; acting is instinct; acting is craft; acting is creative; acting is reacting; acting is rehearsing; acting is game; and so on.

Traditionally and historically, acting has been associated with mimicry, exhibitionism, and imitation. The eighteenth-century French actor Francois-Joseph Talma declared that acting demanded "unusual sensitivity and extraordinary intelligence." Acting is based on the presentation of "emotion," which is defined as human feeling manifest as impulses toward open action. It follows that the actor must understand the working of the human personality and feeling. The key problem in acting is whether the actor should project the *illusion* of an emotion or genuinely feel that emotion. (Even if a role demands the portrayal of a mechanical robot, that robot will be imitating *human* behavior.) People have always found it difficult to define acting because the appreciation of it is greater than the understanding of it. Despite that difficulty, theorists and practitioners of the art of acting can come to grips with certain skills, processes, and disciplines germane to acting and performance.

What is the reply when the young aspiring actor asks, "What is acting?" Primarily, acting is a person behaving honestly, truthfully, economically, and comfortably in front of other people in a place used for theatrical presentation. Usually an actor performs a role written by a playwright; occasionally he performs improvisationally, that is, without a script. No matter what role or character the actor is called upon to create, or what activity he is asked to perform, his person and personality are on public view and frequently exhibit what is typically private behavior. Such work demands physical and vocal skill or craft, emotional stability, alert thinking, freedom of behavior, and confidence and trust in one's self and one's fellow actors.

One approach to the study of acting is to progress through theory and exercise work and to go rather quickly into what is popularly called "scene and role creation." Such an approach is designed to train the actor almost exclusively for the performance of roles written in a script by a playwright. While much of contemporary theatre is indeed of this nature, much of it is also improvisational. In improvisational theatre, a play script may evolve out of acting exercises. For example, Megan Terry's *Viet Rock* developed out of improvisational acting. It therefore follows that training in present-day theatre must be broader than it was in the past. Today, the actor must be capable of traditional performance of a written role as well as of improvisational stage behavior that can best be likened to modern dance or even gymnastics and acrobatics—at times with dialogue and at times without it. In improvisational theatre, the actor-performer also uses *himself* as a basis for creation of a performance. In both written and nonwritten theatre work, the task of the actor should be based upon economical, honest, and truthful use of himself and thereby eliminate much of the artificiality which pervades most acting.

The concept of personalization will be discussed again and again in this book and made specific in terms of its use in training, rehearsal, and performance.

Personalization has always been a feature of acting. Thespis, the acknowledged first actor of Greece in the sixth century B.C., undoubtedly used his entire person to the best of his ability in performing his roles. Dramatic theorists, actors, and directors have usually discussed the problem of how to utilize the actor's person in role creation and performance. Accordingly, it is necessary to review briefly the more important theories of acting to assist the actor in understanding personalization.

One of the earliest and most significant organized statements on the theory of acting was made by an eighteenth-century French theoriest, Denis Diderot, in his essay *The Paradox of Acting*. Diderot clarified the famous paradox of acting, namely, that in order to move an audience the actor must remain unmoved. From Thespis to present times, this paradox remains the central problem of acting. How much genuine feeling, if any, must an actor express to move an audience? Diderot knew that at times actors will feel and create believable emotion. However, he also knew that actors could not possibly sustain such creation over long periods of repeated performance. Inevitably, emotion would appear artificial. This fact led Diderot to the realization that actors had to have training and certain skills to create the illusion of believable emotion. While Diderot did not provide a program of training for actors, we are indebted to him for one of the first clearly organized statements of the problem.

A nineteenth-century French teacher, Francois Delsarte, extended the influence of Diderot with respect to training and skills. Delsarte attempted to formulate laws of speech and gesture through diligent observation and study. Valuable and correct though some of his work was, it ultimately led to rigid and mechanical acting techniques.

Near the turn of the nineteenth century, the Russian actor and director Konstantin Stanislavski developed a thorough system of actor training. After Stanislavski's death, his protege, Yvegeny Vakhtangov, refined and completed the system. Stanislavski dedicated himself to the central problem of stimulating the actor's creativity. He based his system on lengthy and careful study of the actor's mind and emotion. He emphasized the use of observation, imagination, intuition, affective memory (sensory and emotional recall), combined with intensive vocal and physical study (these terms are defined in Chapter Sixteen and the Glossary). The concept of advanced psychology implicit in Stanislavski's work was heavily influenced by the French psychologist Theodule Ribot who in 1890 described the term *affective memory*.

The post-Stanislavski period has been marked by a variety of refinements of previous theories. Perhaps the most important contributions in this century have been made by Antonin Artaud, Bertolt Brecht, and Jerzy Grotowski. Artaud and Brecht were concerned with aesthetics. Grotowski is concerned with methods.

Artaud, a French actor and director, explained his theories in his essay "Theatre of Cruelty." Artaud believed that actors needed to develop an extreme use of gesture and sensory response in order to communicate psychologically with an audience rather than through words. He believed in assaulting the senses of his audiences through a variety of physical and emotive stage behavior, typified by violence and hysteria. Artaud labeled the actor "an athlete of the heart." He believed there was a kinetic or emotional relationship between the organic life of the actor and his audience. (Later, Grotowski was to refute this point by asserting that Artaud's aesthetics led to stereotyped or caricatured acting.) For further discussion of Artaud, see Chapter Nineteen.

Brecht, a German playwright and director, was probably the most influential theorist since Stanislavski. He labeled his plays "epic realism" and published his acting theory under the title "Small Organum for the Theatre." The term *epic realism* relates to both his plays and his acting theory. *Epic* refers to the ancient narrative poem used by Homer. The epic play of Brecht is rambling and episodic in structure. It stresses narration and singing as well as dialogue. Brecht also attempted in his plays to de-emphasize emotional impact for the sake of the intellectual message. He believed in intermingling historic events and persons with modern events and persons. He called this technique "historification." Brecht's acting theories stressed the use of overt theatrical techniques to "alienate" or "make-strange" all dramatic activity, thereby reducing emotional impact upon the audience while increasing intellectual reaction. However, with certain characters in his plays Brecht was receptive to the kind of emotion advocated by Stanislavski. For example, the role of Mother Courage in the play of that name by Brecht demands acting which has an emotional effect upon the audience. For a detailed discussion of Brecht, see Chapter Eighteen.

Finally, Grotowski, a contemporary Polish director, has made efforts to rediscover the elements of the actor's art. Grotowski rejected Stanislavski because he believed that the Russian permitted natural impulses to dominate the actor. Grotowski rejected Brecht because he thought Brecht was too concerned with the construction of the role for its intellectual impact. To Grotowski, the actor is merely a person working artistically in public with his body. In a sense, the actor publically offers himself to the audience. The Grotowski system involves years of physical, emotional, and vocal training and inordinate concentration for the total commitment necessary to achieve a state of "trance." The actor searches for signs which express the sound and movement impulses between dream and reality. Through these signs the actor develops a special system of psychoanalytic language of gesture. Grotowski's criticism of Artaud concerning acting that leads to stereotype is a criticism that can also be leveled at his work in the Polish Laboratory Theatre. Grotowski's theatre reveals little emotion and as a result has gained little public favor. For further discussion of Grotowski, see Appendix B.

As noted, the theories just described will be referred to again and expanded in later sections of this book. All or any of these theories may be used with personalization to assist an actor in successful performance. It is my belief that no one system or theory is correct or advisable. Intelligent actors draw from all theories or any theory that assists them in role creation or performance. What works, works! However, personalization is always basic to the training discussed in this book.

Acting: In Person and In Style begins at the logical point of departure in the training of the actor: with the actor's person. The initial step involves the actor's becoming comfortable with himself, or in his learning how to use relaxation as the first acting tool.

As Howard Stein stated to you in his Foreword to this book, "Take this trip deliberately with goodspeed and good luck."

Relaxation 1

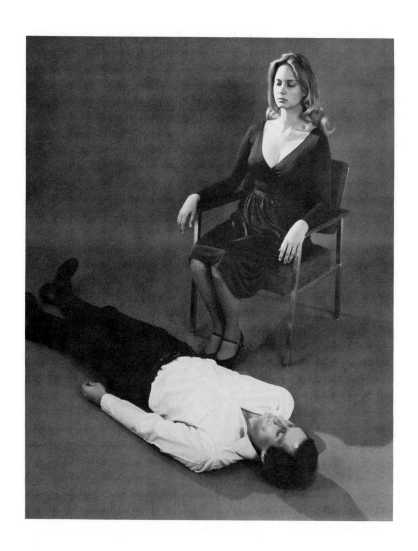

Teresa Gilmore and Grey
Schmidt demonstrate the
two basic positions of
RELAXATION: sitting
and reclining.
Photograph by Randy
Tunnel.

The first step in an actor's training program in personalization or self-exploration involves the concept of relaxation. By relaxation I do not mean passivity; relaxation is rather a positive condition whereby an actor finds emotional, mental, and physical freedom. To relax is to become less tense; the removal of excessive tension is a healthy pursuit for everyone, and is essential for the actor.

When awake, we are in what is called a conscious state. This means that we are mentally active. Relaxation is invaluable to the conscious state because it can enhance perception, thinking, physical activity, and emotional stability.

Relaxation is also invaluable if we are to probe the subconscious. The level of mental operation not yet present in consciousness is called the subconscious. The subconscious state of mind may be likened to that which is forgotten or lying dormant in an unopened memory bank. While the actor is constantly functioning in a conscious state, he is frequently called upon to probe the subconscious. Probing the subconscious means to activate forgotten or suppressed experiences into remembered events. Relaxation is also invaluable to this process. (Note: Do not confuse the *sub*conscious with the *un*conscious. The unconscious is a state lacking consciousness; a state lacking awareness, such as the state of sleep. The subconscious is beneath our aware, awake, conscious state.)

Exercises for Relaxing

People relax in different ways. Some people relax by reading; others, by playing golf, tennis, or handball. Actors use a variety of relaxing methods as warm-up and preparation for both rehearsal and performance. Some of these methods are group activities, while others are private, individual exercises. For example, a favorite group method of relaxation for actors is to stand in a circle and execute basic calisthenics. Simplistic vocal drills are also used in this situation. At times actors sit in a circle and play concentration and word games. Occasionally, they stand or sit in a circle and hold hands or put their arms around one another's waists. They hum or sing together or merely relax in silence with the trusting comfort of group harmony sustaining their relaxation. Individually, relaxation is often managed by reclining and concentrating on one's breathing or on one's skeletal structure. Some actor's actually doze or sleep to relax, but I do not advocate this because it leads to passivity. Some actors like to "run" lines with another actor as preparatory relaxation. Still others enjoy jogging around a spacious area. Meditation of one kind or another is also practiced by actors as a form of rehearsal and performance relaxation. One to two minutes of silent relaxation just prior to entrance on stage is important for all actors. Eventually an actor must discover an individualized and effective way to relax. However, there are certain theatre exercises which are especially designed to assist everyone in the process of relaxing.

Exercise 1 Step 1 Body Alignment

Initial activity prior to any form of acting work, including preparation for relaxation, requires doing some basic arching and extending exercises to make the body limber. Just as an athlete or dancer avoids pulling muscles, so must the actor. Hence, begin this exercise by slowly and carefully stretching and extending the arms, legs, torso, and neck muscles. Shake your limbs; massage stiff or sore spots; get physically loose! Now, how to relax? Recline on a firm surface, preferably on a clear floor. (Obviously, the exercise is more comfortable on a firm floor covered by a clean rug or carpet.) After you have reclined, it is absolutely imperative that you do not speak. Silence is the beginning factor in relaxing the mind and body. The next task is to remove general thought processes, which is difficult. When awake one has a natural tendency toward chaotic thinking. As you recline, begin by focusing on one thing and one thing only. For example, concentrate upon your right big toe. Ideally, move your thoughts from one part of your body to the next, lingering on each to concentrate on that part. In other words, a focused single thought can get the mind as relaxed and generally free of thinking as is possible; to go beyond this is to fall asleep and thereby destroy the purpose of actor relaxation which is positive and relatively energized. Your heels should be touching the floor, with the remainder of the foot at ease upon your heels. Rest the calves of your legs on the floor without strain or tension; your thighs should be in similar repose. The buttocks should be comfortable, not drawn or tense in any way. The two spinal curves of your neck and the small of your back should be aligned, meaning basically straight with the lower half of your torso. The back of your head and the back of your body should rest comfortably without strain or control, thus permitting the abdominal muscles to relax naturally. Your shoulders should be slightly rounded and not pressed against the floor; your arms should be at your sides, resting naturally on the floor or surface and not crossed or in any way reclining upon your body. Your hands should rest lightly upon the surface or floor, probably with the fingers naturally curled under a bit because stretching or extending the fingers tends to create some tension for most people.

Body alignment

The self-exploration or personalization system of acting begins with the simple reclining exercise just described. The body functions best when muscle tension is released. Tension can be released either by suggestion (i.e., being asked or directed by someone to relax, which works for some people, but not for many), by conscious effort (i.e., willing it oneself, which is also difficult), or by manipulation (i.e., moving the area of tension such as wiggling a tense foot, which nearly always works). The common areas of tension are the base of the back of the head and the neck, the small of the back, the hands and shoulders, and the calf-to-foot area of the legs. Once muscles are relieved of tension, actors are free to explore each physical area of the body separately and make inroads into the subconscious where emotions lie dormant.

Exercise 1 Step 2 Body Exploration

Begin by doing Exercise 1, Step 1, again. Exploration of the body should begin at one end of the body and progress to the other. Start by concentrating on the tips of your toes. Wiggle them and become acutely aware of them. Next transfer your concentration to the soles of your feet, then to the heels, and on to the ankles, calves, knees, thighs, hips, buttocks, abdominal area, rib cage, chest, shoulders, biceps, elbows, forearms, wrists, hands, and fingers. Now shift to the rear of the body at the base of the spine, move up the back to the neck, and around to the jaw, mouth, nose, cheeks, ears, eyelids, eyebrows, forehead, and top of the cranium. Imagine you are rolling your body into the top of your head in the manner that a sardine or coffee can lid is removed by coiling a metal key around a binding metal tape. After a few seconds, mentally release your body or unroll it in your mind to its full length. This action should actually provide physical release or relaxation from the mental stimulus.

Exercise 1 Step 3 Relaxation and Breathing

Step 3 in relaxation involves organic breathing. The term *organic* refers to that which is organized or arranged as a system of related parts. *Organic breathing* means that the entire body is systematically coordinated with breathing (a detailed exploration of breathing mechanics is given in chapter 7). If you have completed Steps 1 and 2, you should be automatically breathing organically. At this point the mind must make a final contribution by actually concentrating upon the breathing. You must think about the attempt to memorize how your breathing *feels.* Concentrate upon the movement of the body in the area of the diaphragm (see figure p. 62), abdomen, rib cage, and chest. Most breathing is flawed because of tension. Accordingly, since most beginning actors are overly tense, most breathing is incorrect and adversely affects speaking, movement, and emotion.

Now come to your feet, move around, and properly align your body posture in such a way that it perfectly duplicates your reclining position. Similarly, your memory and concentration must re-create the exact way you were breathing while lying down. At this point you are truly in the actor's basic position of positive relaxation.

While most actors prefer the reclining position for relaxation, others prefer a sitting position. Both ultimately lead to relaxation while standing.

Exercise 2 Relaxation and Sitting

Place a comfortable chair in an area free from other objects. Normal room illumination should prevail, with no strong light upon the chair. Ideally, the chair should have armrests and a firm back and seat. However, the back and seat should be minimally padded for basic comfort. Sit in the chair with your feet resting comfortably on the floor. Remove your shoes if this aids your comfort. Rest your elbows on the armrests. Your hands should dangle naturally off the front end of the armrests. If there are no armrests on the chair, merely let your hands rest on your lap. Your head should recline backward until it comfortably rests on the top of the chair. However, if resting your head on the

Relaxation and sitting

back of the chair causes too much passivity, merely hold it comfortably up-right. Adjust your body position accordingly to become comfortable. Close your eyes and concentrate upon your breathing. Move and adjust areas of tension. Remain in this silent, comfortable position for a minimum of three minutes. To test your relaxation, another actor should approach you and lift each of your arms by the wrist and drop them, move your legs by wiggling the knees, and roll your head from side to side. Any resistance in these areas will indicate tension. When tension is discovered, adjust your body position to a more comfortable one and relax in silence, concentrating on your breathing for two or three more minutes. When you are totally relaxed, your body will be limp and mobile. Remember that true relaxation never leads to sleep.

Exercise 3 "The Swim"

Recline on the floor (ideally, on a clean rug or carpet) in the position of proper body alignment on your back. Imagine that you are floating in a large, cool, clear swimming pool. Gently and slowly pretend to swim backward using the "backstroke." Lift each arm up and to the rear while lifting and kicking each

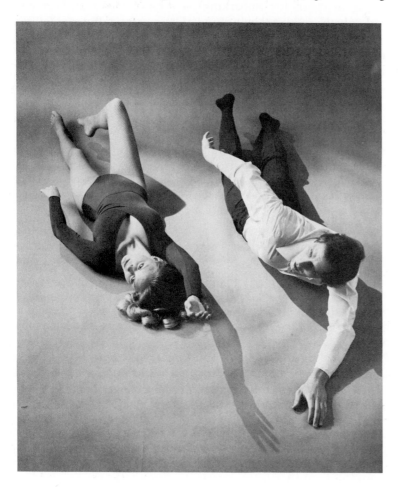

Teresa Gilmore and Grey Schmidt demonstrated the RELAXATION exercise: "The Swim." Photograph by Randy Tunnel.

leg. After a full minute, relax and rest, concentrating on your organic breathing. Then roll on to your stomach. Imagine that you are swimming forward by gently and slowly moving each arm up and forward while lifting each leg in a swimmer's kick. Turn your head from side to side as you do when you are swimming. After a full minute, relax and "float" in your pool, enjoying the sense of relaxed weightlessness which accompanies easy floating after a vigorous swim.

Stage Fright, the Actor's Malady

Relaxation exercises are basic to overcoming the main malady or problem of the beginning actor. Acting necessitates speaking and behaving in front of other people, activities which usually create excessive nervous tension. The popular label for this tension is "stage fright."

Although the term *stage fright* refers to the fear that takes place when an individual is on stage, it is the same human problem one has when soloing a plane, appearing for an interview, attending an important meeting, competing in sports, or embarking on a dangerous trip. Fear becomes harmful only when we become afraid of being afraid. We may fall into the trap of thinking normal behavior is abnormal; such thinking produces more energy than we need. Excess energy becomes inordinate tension and manifests itself through trembling legs, twitching knees, fidgety fingers, facial grimacing, shifting weight from leg to leg, aimless walking, and breathiness. All these events are signals that we are self-conscious, that is, are unusually aware of being watched and listened to. We become self-conscious because we are aware that someone is judging us. We think our appearance, manner, intelligence, emotions, and movement are threatened. The natural instinct is to become defensive. The automatic response action is to withdraw mentally and physically—to become guarded. The result is usually artifical behavior which, of course, deteriorates an actor's effectiveness and believability. Unnatural behavior is in direct opposition to personalization, which is based on comfort, naturalness, and believable behavior.

Fear is also harmful when we do not know why we are afraid. We should therefore ask: What in me is being threatened? Is the threat real? What can I do to deal with the threat? If we know what is being threatened and admit the fact, we may be better equipped to cope with the threat.

Stage fright in its wider sense is not unique to actors; it is common to public performers ranging from basketball players to musicians to well-established stage and screen personalities.

Perhaps the most surprising and hopeful thing to note here is that emotional tension or anxiety in study, rehearsal, or performance is not necessarily an unfavorable condition provided that it does not become excessive and create the conditions just described. Some tensions prepare the body for better physical and mental effort. The body recognizes the presence of an urgent situation and prepares itself accordingly. The adrenal gland pumps adrenaline into the system; when adrenaline reaches the muscles, vitality is restored and reaction time is enhanced. The body releases larger quantities of sugar into the bloodstream, giving it greater ability to cope with physical problems. Breathing quickens as more oxygen is absorbed, and carbon dioxide is expelled more rapidly. As the pulse rate also quickens, more blood arrives at the muscles, the heart, the brain, and the central nervous system. The blood and the excess oxygen combine to make the brain capable of thinking with greater clarity, perceptiveness, and quickness; the muscles are capable of performing greater physical effort; and, finally, the central nervous system is capable of reacting more quickly. These distinct physiological changes make the body perform at a higher level of alertness than under normal conditions. *Constructive* tension, then, can assist one emotionally.

Exercise 3   Relaxation and Stage Fright

Place two or three small objects in the middle of a large area. Included might be an apple, a set of keys, and a cup. Take a standing position. Align your body using Exercises 1 and 2 until you are relaxed. Concentrate upon your breathing. When you feel relaxed, shift your concentration to one of the objects and walk to it. Pick up the object and examine it thoroughly. Return the object to the floor and finish walking across the room. Repeat this exercise until you do it with full confidence and without any of the nervous tensions described in the discussion of stage fright.

Object-related, goal-oriented physical activity is a key factor in the elimination of stage fright. It is related to a principle to be learned early in acting, namely, the principle of single beat or single intention acting. A good actor learns to do one thing at a time on stage—one specific task is attempted at a time. Later, when you have developed further, you can learn to do several things at once. If Exercises 1 and 2 are mastered, Exercise 3 should be executed without producing fear, self-consciousness, or stage fright. If excessive tension is suffered doing Exercise 3, return to the first two exercises and practice them as a preparatory technique to all stage activity.

Relaxation is the heartbeat of acting. Single intention activity is the heartbeat of relaxation. Master single intention activity and relaxation now.

Suggested Readings

Alexander, F. Matthias. *The Ressurection of the Body.* Edited by Edward Maisel. New York: University Books, 1969.

Behenan, Kovoor T. *Yoga: A Scientific Evaluation.* New York: Dover Publications, 1937.

Bergler, Edmund. "On Acting and Stage Fright," *Psychiatric Quarterly Suppl.* 23 (1949):313–19.

Bloomfield, Harold H., M.D., Cain, Michael Peter, and Jaffe, Dennis T., *TM* (*Transcendental Meditation) Discovering Inner Energy and Overcoming Stress.* New York: Delacorte Press, 1975.

Clevenger, T., Jr. "A Synthesis of Experimental Research in Stage Fright." *Quarterly Journal of Speech* 45 (1959): 134–45.

Goffman, Erving. *The Presentation of Self in Everyday Life.* New York: Anchor, 1959.

Hagen, Uta (with Haskel Frankel). *Respect for Acting.* New York: Macmillan, 1973.

Pavlov, I. P. *Conditioned Reflexes.* New York: Dover Publications, 1927.

Ullman, Liv. *Changing.* New York: Knopf, 1977.

Body Dynamics 2

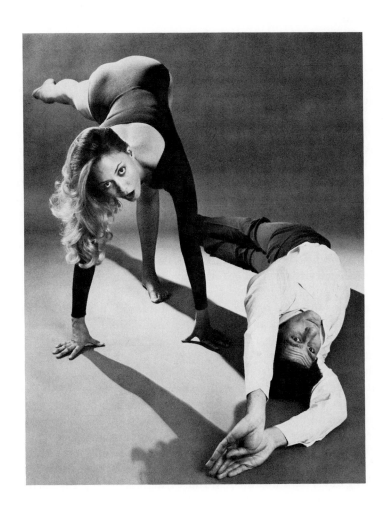

Teresa Gilmore demonstrates BODY DYNAMICS: "The Cat" Exercise; Grey Schmidt demonstrates BODY DYNAMICS: "The Stretch" Exercise. Photograph by Randy Tunnel.

A person relaxed is a body relaxed. An actor works best in a state in which his muscles are free of tension. In other words, an actor's energy must be under control, Chapter 1 guides the actor toward an understanding of how to relax—the initial step in personalization. A natural extension of that step involves working with both internal and external muscular energy, usually referred to as movement, or body dynamics.

Personalized Body Dynamics

Begin this work by performing a simple exercise.

Exercise 1   The Fist

Align your body in the standing position. Make a fist with one of your hands and then spread your fingers; the fingers, being extended, will energize by themselves. Now let the fingers move toward one another. Your muscular activity will flow easily. Try the exercise several times; you will feel the natural change from energy to lightness.

The fist

Body dynamics or movement sensitizes an actor to a specific flow of energy. By becoming aware of muscular activity, actors can be conscious of what is happening to their energy. In Exercise 1, activity of the fist and fingers is natural and immediate. Note that no thought or emotion colors the quality of action. Action is relatively pure. Emotional involvement, if it occurs at all, is instinctive—that is, occurs on its own. Repeat the fist exercise until you feel emotional involvement of any kind. At that point, immediately stop the exercise. It is important to keep the exercise in a pure state of mental awareness of muscular activity. Later you will learn how to combine physical activity with emotion.

The relaxation and fist exercises are designed to eliminate muscular tension. Breathing should be organically correct in order to free the actor to respond naturally to physical needs. Movements should be simple and unaffected; they should be naturally personalized, that is, honestly, truthfully, the actor's *person* or self. The body should perform as an unbroken unit or in what some acting teachers call *gestalt* (see Glossary).

The natural, undirected movement of the body must be shaped; that is, an actor must use body energies effectively. Movement must have some control or shape to it, in terms of both form and function. Relaxation will activate internal body movement in a natural and comfortable manner. A more difficult process is shaping or controlling external body movement.

The body performs a variety of natural external movements every moment of a waking day. I have heard Dr. Moshe Feldenkrais, the great teacher of movement and awareness, refer to such actions as "parasitic movements," or, those which are habitual. For example, we stretch, yawn, shake, shrug, wiggle, fidget, and scratch; on a slightly more complicated level, we stand, sit, and walk or run. We also perform a variety of highly complex and individualized movements such as driving cars, lifting objects, and making things. The comfortable personalization of these everyday, every-moment movements becomes the initial task in shaping the dynamics of the body. Stretching, yawning, and shaking must be shaped or controlled truthfully before an actor can begin imitating activities demanded by a playwright, a director, or an artist-leader.

Begin by examining basic body movements on which might be called an average day.

Exercise 2   Everyday Fun: Habitual Body Dynamics

From a standing, aligned position, perform the following everyday, fun activities: wiggle your nose; wiggle your ears; shrug your shoulders; reach and scratch your back; shuffle your feet; yawn; make large, silly grins.

Exercise 3   The Stretch

Assume the reclining position described in Exercise 1 in chapter 1 (p. 9). Follow the same procedures until you are in a relaxed state. Close your eyes for a few moments. When it seems suitable to do so, open your eyes as you do when you awaken on an average morning in your life. From this point on, the exercise will shape or control your external movements. Slowly stretch your right arm into the air, moving it past your ear and extending it to the floor behind you. Stretch the arm to the fullest possible extension. Repeat the same movement with your left arm. Now stretch both arms simultaneously above your head. Try to feel the elongated muscular pull in your arms. Begin to arch the small of your back in an upward motion, continuing to stretch to the point where the entire back is raised off the floor, with your shoulders touching the surface. Your neck will automatically leave the floor, as will part of your head. At the same time, be aware that your legs have a tendency to leave the floor. You should feel a slight pull in the muscles of your legs. Slowly lower your body to the floor. Once again, stretch your right arm over your head, but this time stretch your right leg as well, being careful not to let either the arm or the leg leave the surface of the floor. Repeat the same process with the left arm and leg. Now reverse the process: stretch your right arm and left leg and vice versa. Now stretch both arms and both legs simultaneously.

Lift your head and body slightly off the floor, rolling on to the right side. Arch your back by allowing both arms and legs to form something resembling a half-moon or half-arc. Hold for the count of five. Again relax to a fully reclining position on your back; repeat the exercise on the left side.

Now roll over on your stomach. Lift your right leg off the floor and stretch. Repeat the movements with the left leg. Lift your right arm; stretch; lift the left arm; stretch. Lift both arms and legs off the floor simultaneously and hold for the count of five. Repeat the exercise, but this time lift your head off the floor and hold for a count of five. Now recline and relax again.

A final and vital exercise in the fundamental personalization of both internal and external body dynamics is the "cat" exercise, a standard indispensable exercise employed by many actors and most acting teachers.

The cat

Exercise 4   The Cat

Begin from the reclining stomach position of Exercise 3. Extend both your arms away from the body, forming a T (your head should be turned on either the left or right side). Slowly bring your hands in and up to your body, palms flat on the floor, very near your underarms. At the same time, point your toes toward the floor. Begin to lift your body on to the weight of your arms and toes, arching your back and neck as much as possible. Bring your legs into your body by walking on the toes and balls of the feet toward your hands, arching your back to a greater and greater degree. When you feel that you cannot walk any farther, stop. Raise the right leg high into the air and lift your head up. Stretch and lower the leg. Repeat this action with the left leg. Walk your legs away or backward from your arms, decreasing the arch in your back. Let your body descend to the floor and relax. Slowly curl yourself into a ball, holding your body very tightly by clasping your hand and arms around your knees as you lie on your side. Release your body from the ball, stretching every muscle in your body including those tiny muscles in your face by forcing a large, artificial cat yawn. As you are releasing your body, try this yawn at least three times.

Exercise 5   The Shakeout

Recline on your back and slowly begin to shake your body; increase the intensity of the shaking until you can shake no further. Stand up and shake your body again. At the point at which the shaking is most vigorous, begin to bounce lightly into the air off the balls of the feet. Your first bounces should be easy and relaxed. Increase the height of the bounces until you feel you are tiring.

Exercise 6   The Swing and Hit

Stand for a moment in a relaxed position. Now swing your body from side to side and in half-circles, beginning with the arms and then the head, shoulders, upper torso, waist, hips, and legs. Try simultaneously swinging as much of your body as possible. Evolve this swinging exercise into a striking or hitting exercise with the arms, hands, and fists. Strike at space with all parts of your body. Hit the air with your arms, head, chest, legs, chin, ears, and so forth. When you have used every part of your body, collapse your entire body to the ground in a naturally shaped and comfortable fall.

The swing and hit

Exercise 7   Additional Body Exercises

1. Come to your feet. Try to fill the space around you by stretching horizontally as far as you can. Trying to make yourself as wide as possible, stretch from side to side.

2. Try to make yourself as thin as possible. Concentrate on being narrow.

3. Try to make yourself as short as possible. Concentrate on decreasing your vertical height.

4. In an exercise which will slowly relax your entire body, make yourself very tall by stretching your arms toward the ceiling. Slowly start to relax your body, beginning with the fingers, then the arms, neck, shoulders, chest, abdomen, and so on. Let your body fall forward in a hairpin manner until the upperpart is hanging limply. The only tension should be in the legs and thighs.

Alternate between the stretching toward the ceiling and the hanging positions.

5. Sit on the floor with your legs crossed in front of you in a comfortable erect position and eliminate all tension. Fall forward at the waist in the manner of a rag doll, letting your head dangle as far down as possible. Alternate between sitting erect and falling forward.

6. Imagine you have a metal band around your chest. Attempt to stretch the band by means of vigorous expansion of the trunk of your body.

7. To achieve a new physical position, squat with the head dropped forward and the arms dangling between the knees. Your buttocks should not touch the floor.

8. Stand straight, with your legs together, and bend forward from the waist in a rag-doll position. Bounce slowly, trying to touch the palms of your hands on the floor. Be certain your head is inclining toward the chest.

9. Vigorously rotate your trunk from the waist upward.

10. Rotate the head slowly in a circular fashion, changing directions if you feel dizzy. This exercise should be performed very slowly, starting at your front, then side, back, other side, and front again. Be careful to keep the shoulders and the remainder of the body motionless.

11. In order to warm the balls of your feet, stand in an aligned body position. Jump eight small jumps with the heels together and the toes apart. Make sure that your heels touch the floor on every jump. Bend the knees as you land. Repeat the jumps with the feet apart. Combine the two steps so that you do sixteen jumps, alternating feet together, then apart.

12. Keep both legs straight throughout this exercise. Extend your right leg back, pointing the toes. Keep the back lifted as you lower the body. The back leg will come off the ground. Take four counts to do this. Keep the head in line with the rest of the body. Place your hands on the floor and try to lift the back leg higher. Keeping the back lifted, return to the starting position. Repeat the exercise using the other leg.

13. Become very rigid or stiff in the manner of a robot or toy soldier. Walk in short, stiff steps and movements back and forth as though on parade.

14. Pretend you are a delicate figurine in the shape of a dancer or an acrobat, balanced precariously on a pedestal. Strike your pose and hold it motionless for one or two minutes.

Diligent repetition of the exercises described in this chapter, based upon solid understanding of the reasons for doing them, can accomplish the initial step of personalization necessary for a beginning actor. Additionally, invent exercises to suit your particular needs. This work may encompass several weeks, and can help one master the invaluable process of relaxation and body control.

Space Awareness Exercises

Comfortably aware of internal and external energy, the actor should now examine his relationship with the space he occupies.

If an actor is to become aware of the space he occupies, he must begin by again establishing a state of personal relaxation.

Exercise 8   Drifting

When you are relaxed, come to your feet and begin to walk slowly about the room. Concentrate initially on your breathing; as you walk, periodically check for undesirable tension in the arms, neck, and shoulders. Be certain your knees are flexing easily and naturally. Wiggle your third and fourth fingers on each hand, which will relax those areas. Remain silent; make no physical or visual contact with other persons. Permit your eyes to drift aimlessly to avoid running into people, but do not focus on anything or anyone. Keep your mind occupied with your breathing. As you move, your body is automatically molding your space by moving into it; that is, it is filling empty air with your mass, as well as making waves and abstract impressions in the air around you. In order to perceive your own energy and mass as it imprints itself upon space, first try to perceive the "space molding" that occurs from the impact of other people as they walk past you. Turn your mind from concentration upon your breathing to conscious search for the feeling of the waves in space from others walking by you. If you really concentrate, you can actually feel their energy in space as it strikes you.

Now shift your concentration to your own total energy and body. You should begin to feel or perceive your own space. A sense of lightness will ensue; every movement will take on new sensitivity. Your body will feel increasingly weightless, without mass. Instead of an awareness of walking, you will have a feeling of moving and floating, a distinctly different perception.

The first benefit reaped from self-perception in space is a sense of physical and mental freedom. The body will be instinctively more graceful and the mind unburdened. This exercise can eventuate beyond the classroom, rehearsal room, or stage into a perception of the variety of spaces one occupies in all everyday living experiences.

Exercise 9   Eye Contact

As you move with the awarenesses just described, begin to make eye contact for a few seconds with other people. It is vital to remain silent during this eye contact, but any other natural reaction such as smiling or nodding should be permitted. However, if you find these reactions distracting, and if they begin to create tensions or self-consciousness, eliminate eye contact and return to concentration upon your own space or breathing. Later, again try eye contact with others. Eventually, comfortable, relaxed eye contact should occur.

Visual contact with others expands one's perception to the energy and bodies of others. (Later this exercise will serve as the foundation for physical interaction. I will return to this factor when I discuss trust and related points in chapter 4.)

Exercise 10 Room Observation

> After having established eye contact with other people in the room, turn your attention to the room itself and all inanimate objects within it. Observe the room carefully, but do not touch anything (touching objects comes later). Study each wall, window, door; note their location, shape, texture, color, and so on. Similarly, observe every object. Extend your perception into the atmosphere of the room. Does mood connotation emanate from contrasting light and dark patterns? Conclude the exercise with a group discussion of observations.

Note that all work to date has been accomplished without a role or character being involved. Your person has been sufficient. Personalization has carried us through work with relaxation and movement or body dynamics. The actor should now focus upon the technique of *concentration*. If mastery of the skills presented in chapters 1 and 2 have not been accomplished, it is advisable to repeat some of the previous exercises or to invent new exercises before advancing to the skills described in chapter 3.

Suggested Readings

Alexander, F. Matthais. *The Resurrection of the Body.* Edited by Edward Maisel. New York: University Books, 1969. Dell Publishing Co., 1971.

Aubert, Charles. *The Art of Pantomime.* New York: Benjamin Blom, 1970.

Bernhardt, Frederica, and Edwards, Mrs. Vernon. *How to Fence.* Dubuque, Iowa: Wm. C. Brown Company Publishers, 1961.

Birdwhistell, Ray L. *Introduction to Kinesics.* Washington, D.C.: Foreign Service Institute, 1952.

————. *The Kinesic Level in the Investigation of the Emotions.* New York: International Universities Press, 1963.

————. *Kinesics and Content: Essays on Body Motion Communication.* New York: Ballantine Books, 1972.

Broby-Johansen, R. *Body and Clothes,* trans. Erik I. Friis and Karen Rush, New York: Rheinhold, 1968.

Cage, John. *Silence.* Middleton, Conn.: Wesleyan University Press, 1961.

Davis, Bridget Iona. *Releasing into Process: Joan Skinner and the Use of Imagery in Dance.* M.A. Thesis in Dance, Graduate College, University of Illinois at Urbana-Champaign, 1974.

Davis, Martha. *Understanding Body Movement: An Annotated Bibliography.* New York: Arno Press, 1972.

Dell, Cecily. *A Primer for Movement Description: Using Effort-Shape and Supplementary Concepts.* New York: Dance Notation Bureau, 1970.

Directory of Theatre Movement Specialists. UCTA/ATA "The Theatre Movement Program," Contact Jennifer Martin, University Theatre, Iowa City, Iowa, 52242.

Fast, Julius. *Body Language.* New York: Pocket Books, 1971.

Feldenkrais, Moshe. *Awareness Through Movement: Health Exercises for Personal Growth.* New York: Harper & Row, 1972.

Gordon, Gilbert. *Stage Fights: A Simple Handbook of Techniques.* New York: Theatre Arts Books, 1973.

Grotowski, Jerzy. *Towards a Poor Theatre.* New York: Simon & Shuster, 1968.

Hall, Edward T. *The Silent Language.* Greenwich, Conn.: Fawcett World Library, 1959.

Hobbs, William. *Stage Fights, Swords, Firearms, Fisticuffs, and Slapstick.* New York: Theatre Arts Books, 1967.

Hutchinson, Ann. *Labanation.* Boston: Little, Brown & Co., 1969.

King, Nancy. *Theatre Movement: The Actor and His Space.* New York: Drama Book Specialists/Publishers, 1971.

Kline, Peter and Meadows, Nancy. *The Theatre Student; Physical Movement for the Theatre.* New York: Richard Rosen Press, 1971.

Knapp, Mark L. *Nonverbal Communication in Human Interaction.* New York: Holt, Rinehart & Winston, 1972.

Laban, Rudolf. *The Mastery of Movement.* 3d ed. Rev. and enlarged by Lisa Ullman. Boston: Plays, Inc., 1971.

——— and F. C. Lawrence. *Effort.* London: Macdonald and Evan, 1947.

Lessac, Arthur. *Body Wisdom. The Use and Training of the Human Body.* New York: Drama Book Specialists, 1978.

Lidtstone, R. A. *Fencing: A Practical Treatise on Foil, Epree and Sabre.* London: Witherby, 1952.

Lifar, Serge. *Lifar on Classical Ballet.* London: Allan Wingate, 1951.

Logan, Gene, and McKinney, Wayne C. *Kinesiology,* Dubuque, Iowa: Wm. C. Brown Company Publishers, 1970.

Martin, John. *Introduction to the Dance.* New York: W.W. Norton, 1939.

Moore, Sonia. "The Method of Physical Action." *Tulane Drama Review,* Summer 1965, pp. 91–94.

Oxenford, Lyn. *Design for Movement.* A textbook on stage movement. New York: Theatre Arts, 1952.

Pamphlet on Fencing. Washington, D.C.: American Association for Health, Physical Education, and Recreation, n.d.

Penrod, James. *Movement for the Performing Artist.* Palo Alto, Calif.: National Press Books, 1974.

Pisk, Litz. *The Actor and His Body.* New York: Theatre Arts Books, 1976.

Rubin, Lucille S., Ed. *Movement for the Actor.* New York: Drama Book Specialists, 1979.

Scheflen, Albert E. *Body Language and Social Order.* Englewood-Cliffs, N.J.: Prentice-Hall, 1972.

Scheflen, A. E. "The Significance of Posture in Communication Systems." *Psychiatry* 27 (1964): 316–31.

Shawn, Ted. *Every Little Movement.* A book about Francois Delsarte. 2d. ed. Brooklyn: Dance Horizons, 1963.

"A Study of the Specificity of Meaning in Facial Expression." *Quarterly Journal of Speech,* October 1938, pp. 424–36.

Thornton, Samuel. *Laban's Theory of Movement.* Boston: Plays, Inc., 1971.

White, Edwin, and Battye, Marguerite. *Acting and Stage Movement.* New York: Arc Books, 1963.

Wolff, Charlotte, *A Psychology of Gesture.* Translated by Anne Tennant. 2nd ed. London: Methuen & Co., 1948.

Concentration 3

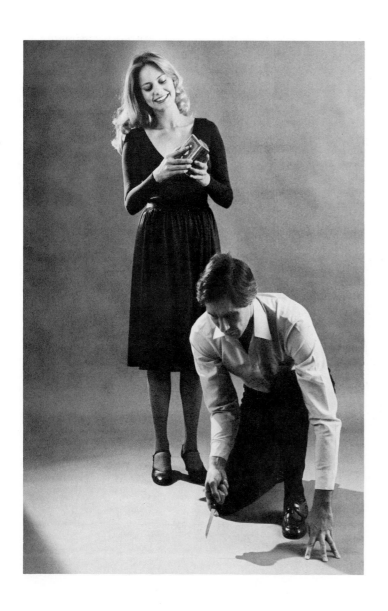

Teresa Gilmore demonstrates CONCENTRATION: Exercise 10, "Small Object;" Grey Schmidt demonstrates CONCENTRATION: Exercise 4, "The Minefield." Photograph by Randy Tunnel.

Aside from positive relaxation and physical discipline, concentration is probably the most important skill in the art of acting. *Concentration* is exclusive attention to what actors are doing, seeing, hearing, and feeling on stage. Concentration is also vital to offstage preparation and discipline. Concentration can be said to be the complete application of self to task.

Concentration is often the most abused technique of acting, in spite of the fact that it is the most important concept leading to interesting, dynamic, and believable performance on stage. Spencer Tracy once defined acting as simply learning lines and concentrating. Stanislavski placed great stress on concentration in referring to circles of attention for actors. By this he meant that actors must limit attention to separate parts of the stage established by objects. There are small, medium, and large circles of attention depending upon what the actor wants to include within his perimeter. An actor also has to learn to redirect attention from one circle to another. In beginning training, actors often have a tendency to let minor interruptions and random thoughts constantly break or disturb their concentration. They may hear airplanes flying over the building, voices out in the hall, and people talking in the theatre. An actor may find his mind wandering to thoughts of where he is going after class or rehearsal. Note the almost irresistible urge to look out at the audience, at the teacher, or at the director. Lack of eye contact between actors on stage is the clearest indication that they are not concentrating. Concentration requires self-discipline and total dedication to the task at hand.

An actor who is not concentrating has a tendency to *go up* with his lines, which means going blank or forgetting lines. Failure to concentrate

Exemplary and intense stage concentration: Nancy Donohue and Stephen Joyce in *The Runner Stumbles* by Milan Stitt. At the Hartman Theatre, Stamford, Connecticut, directed by Austin Pendleton.

leads to mistakes in blocking or movement patterns. It also leads to imprecise execution of stage business (*stage business* is defined as small, detailed actions of the body, often of the hands, such as handling a cane or smoking a cigarette). Above all, failure to concentrate on stage can result in an unmotivated and emotionally empty performance. It takes total concentration to focus the body energies and develop mental acuity to the point necessary to create believable emotion. Failure to concentrate offstage may cause an actor to miss an entrance or be late for it. Similarly, failure to concentrate offstage can result in distracting conversations that may disturb other performers who are on stage or about to enter.

Concentration to Enhance Personalization

Concentration is a skill which is best developed through rehearsal and performance experience as an actor. However, a beginning actor can gain immeasurable skill in concentration through execution of the following exercises. Remember that exercises are valuable only if faithfully repeated every day, just as a musician practices his instrument daily and a dancer exercises his body daily. Also note that these exercises are designed to enhance personalization. In other words, they are preparatory to acting in a role created by a playwright.

Exercise 1 Centers of Tension

Concentrate on and touch the following centers of tension in your body: the back of the neck, the sinus areas over the eyes, the small of the back, the calves of the leg, the soles of the feet, and the hands.

Exercise 2 Textures

Concentrate on the textures, materials, and objects worn on your body. With full concentration you can become aware of the differences in textures.

Exercise 3 Mirror

Stand facing another actor. Designate one as leader and one as follower. Without touching, the leader performs slow and precise body movements, gestures, and facial expressions. The follower imitates every movement of the leader precisely. As the exercise develops, you will note that you and your colleague will blend into simultaneous activity if you are using full concentration. Change roles without breaking concentration.

Exercise 4 The Minefield

Imagine that the room or stage is a field hiding one active land mine buried beneath the surface of the ground. Crawl on your hands and knees over the field searching with full concentration for the hidden mine. "Probe the ground" with an imaginary bayonet in the manner of a soldier; use the tips of your

The mirror

fingers to search for the "trip wire" which protrudes out of the ground from the mine. Search until your concentration is broken with the futility of the search, or until you are certain you have located the mine.

Exercise 5   Listening

Stand or sit perfectly still. Close your eyes. Concentrate on identifying all sounds you hear. After three minutes, explain to your fellow actors exactly what sounds you heard.

Exercise 6   The Flower

Curl into a ball on the floor. Concentrate on being a particular kind of flower seed. When you feel motivated to do so, begin to grow until you reach full blossom. This activity is directly related to what Stanislavski called "focus of attention." In this instance, the focus relates your body to an animate object.

Exercise 7   The Circle and Word Game

Sit in a circle with your fellow actors. One actor speaks a single word. The actor immediately to his left repeats the word aloud and adds another word from his natural association with the first word (for example, *green* followed by *grass*). The actor to the left of the second speaker repeats both words and adds a third. This process continues around the circle for as long as all words spoken aloud can be repeated by each actor. When an actor loses concentration and forgets a word, he must drop out of the circle. This exercise becomes an enjoyable game as it strengthens the power of concentration.

Concentration on Particulars

The following exercises will assist you in learning to focus full attention on particular tasks, both real and imaginary.

Exercise 8   Barefoot Walk

As you move, concentrate on imagining that you are walking barefoot on the following kinds of surfaces: wet grass, mud, hot sand, gravel, broken eggshells, waxed floor, and thick carpet.

Exercise 9   Weather

As you move, concentrate on imagining that you are walking in the following kinds of weather conditions: rain, snow, heat, hail, and wind.

Exercise 10   Small Object

Choose an object small enough to fit in your hand such as a comb. Concentrate on the object. Examine it thoroughly. Using concentration, become physically involved with the object and use it in four different ways. For example, rub it on your skin, touch it to your face, put it between your toes, and balance it on your head.

The flower, showing closed to full bloom (this exercise can be done from a rising position to a fully standing position).

Exercise 11 Puppet

Begin this exercise by walking around the room with your own natural rhythm, letting your arms swing naturally. Gradually, concentrate on your arms and legs being stretched by strings pulled by the hands of a person above you (i.e., an imaginary puppeteer). React to the pulling of your arms and legs with puppetlike motions.

Exercise 12 Halving Your Body

Think of your body not as a total entity, but as a mass divided in half. For example, concentrate on the idea that your upper half is separate from your lower half, or that your right side is separate from your left side. Once you have divided your body in half, think of the two halves as opposing forces. For example, the upper half of your body is happy, and the lower half of your body is sad; or one eye is intelligent and the other eye is stupid. Move or react in a state of happiness, sadness, anger, and drunkenness.

Exercise 13 Separate Emotions in the Body

Choose an emotional reaction and focus it on one particular part of your body: for example, your head is laughing. Choose other parts of your body and create different emotional reactions. Now perform the exercise using two different parts of the body simultaneously responding to an emotional reaction: for example, your arms are bored and your toes are happy.

Exercise 14 Concentration and Breathing

From a standing, aligned position, concentrate on organic breathing with focus on the area of the diaphragm. Inhale a large amount of air through your nostrils into the lungs and hold it for five seconds. Exhale slowly. Next inhale a large amount of air through your mouth into the lungs and hold it for five seconds. This time exhale slowly while observing a watch or clock to note how long it takes to expend all your breath. (Use a watch or clock with a second hand or digital second numbers.) Repeat this exercise until concentration and repetition permit you to expend enough air to last sixty seconds. Note that it may take several weeks or months to achieve this goal, but with a few minutes practice each day it can be accomplished. Cigarette smoking usually inhibits progress with this exercise. (Note: it may help you time the exhaling process if you make a small humming sound as you release your breath.)

The following story demonstrates how powerful concentration can be as a fundamental acting technique.

It is told that when actor Sidney Poitier met Spencer Tracy for the first time on the movie set of *Guess Who's Coming to Dinner?* Poitier was not prepared for the intense concentration of Tracy. Entering the room in their first filmed scene together, Tracy looked up at Poitier and delivered a line with forceful concentration. Poitier froze and went *up* or blank, and had to take several moments to prepare an equal level of concentration in order

Teresa Gilmore and Grey Schmidt demonstrate CONCENTRATION: Exercise 11, "Puppets." Photograph by Randy Tunnel.

to work comfortably in the scene with Tracy. Poitier later stated that he had never met an actor with such penetrating concentration as that of Tracy. The example to note from this story is that successful illusion of reality can best be accomplished through total concentration. Tracy's concentration was so complete that Poitier had to match it to do the scene successfully.

Good life habits become good stage habits. In daily life, practice full concentration on seeing, hearing, saying, and doing. Personalize on the stage; everyday living better equips us to exercise full concentration as actors.

Suggested Readings

Benedetti, Robert L. *The Actor at Work.* rev. ed. Englewood-Cliffs, N.J.: Prentice-Hall, 1978.

Boleslavsky, Richard. *Acting: The First Six Lessons.* New York: Theatre Arts Books, 1938.

Hunt, Douglas, and Hunt, Kari. *Pantomime: The Silent Theatre.* New York: Atheneum, 1968.

McGaw, Charles. *Acting Is Believing.* 3d. ed. New York: Holt, Rinehart & Winston, 1975.

Roberts, J. W., *Richard Boleslavsky: His Life and Work in the Theatre.* Ann Arbor, Michigan: UMI Research Press, 1981.

Rockwood, Jerome. *The Craftsmen of Dionysus.* Chicago: Scott, Foresman & Co., 1966.

Rolfe, Bari. *Behind the Mask.* Oakland, California: Persona Products, 1977.

Sensory Awareness 4

Teresa Gilmore and Grey
Schmidt demonstrate
SENSORY AWARENESS:
Exercise 12, "Specific
Touching." Photograph
by Randy Tunnel.

Another important aspect of personalization is working with the environment, with the sensory system, and with other actors.

The actor's environment is defined as his total working space and all external matter within that space. Therefore, the building, room or theatre, all scenic elements, and all objects including other people constitute the actor's environment. Actors should relate to and be familiar with their environment in order to humanize their acting. They relate to their environment through their senses. The five senses are seeing, touching, hearing, tasting, and smelling.

Sight Perception

The initial step in developing sensory awareness involves awareness of the room or theatre. Begin with visual perception. Normal vision implies that one sees clearly with or without glasses or contact lenses. It also implies that one is not color blind. However, the sense of sight involves more than looking at something clearly. To an actor, sight perception includes careful mental notation of what he sees. Actors should visually and mentally register what they see in their environment in order to relate to it better and to recall it later.

Exercise 1   Seeing Far and Near

Stand in a central location and visually examine every aspect of the room from the ceiling to the walls and all objects and people in it. Take all the time you need and register in your mind all that you see. Later, move about the room and visually examine everything at close proximity. Again register in your mind all that you see. Later, if there is time, discuss your visual examination. Note what others saw that you did not see.

Touch Perception

When an actor becomes visually familiar with the room and its objects, the next step is to begin the process of perception through the sense of touch. Touch perception involves physical contact of any part of the body against or upon any other matter. Touch implies tactile sensory awareness through physical contact. The mind helps interpret the sensory experience of touch.

Exercise 2   Room and Object Contact

Begin by touching walls, furniture, and objects with the fingers and hands. Initially, touch only the room proper and its inanimate objects. Do not touch other actors. Interpersonal touch comes at a later stage of development. Proceed slowly and methodically, attempting to elicit internal as well as external sensitivity as you touch things. After the initial response with the hands, close your eyes and repeat the process. Now feel the objects with the side of the face, nose, chin, and so on. For example, the entire body should be pressed against a wall to gain total perception of it. Do not overlook any object in the room, using both open-eye and closed-eye touch perception. Your tactile response should clarify the difference in surfaces and textures of objects.

Exercise 3   Touch Recall

As another exercise in concentration and simple sensory recall, sit in a relaxed position, close your eyes, and vividly recall both visual and touch perception of the entire room and all its objects.

Exercise 4   Touching While Blindfolded

Move around the entire room with a blindfold over your eyes. Touch the room and objects again. Note the quantity and quality of information you have retained from the previous exercises. Without consciously doing so, you will discover that you have memorized the location, shape, and texture of many, if not all, the objects. During the blindfold-touch exercise in an acting class at the University of Nevada, Las Vegas, one of the actors spontaneously removed a small box from its place on a table and perched it on his head. Other blindfolded actors, having previously examined the box, returned for it and immediately perceived its absence. A slight furor resulted as the actors searched for the missing box with total sincerity and silent concentration. The experience demonstrates how conscious and complete touch perception can become for an actor.

Exercise 5   "Blind" Experience

Sit with your fellow actors and discuss the impact of being blindfolded during Exercise 4. Note the variety of experiences shared: fear, giddiness, terror, isolation, loss, and the increased power of the other four senses when one is removed. (In a lab experience at The Actor's Studio in New York, actor Eli Wallach told me and other actors and writers that he frequently begins a day with several minutes of "blind" experiences while he goes about his early morning routine. Pretending he is blind sharpens his sensory awareness.)

Smell Perception

Smelling is perceiving through olfactory nerves to obtain the scent or odor of something. Smelling is strictly a sensory experience. It cannot reveal the shape or quality of things. Effective smelling is only possible when the nose, sinus, throat, and chest cavities are clear or free from congestion.

Exercise 6   Detecting Odor

At a designated time and day, each actor should bring a single object into the room with a particularly distinctive aroma or odor. The object must be concealed in a sack or bag (a plastic bag is best because it is relatively odorless). Blindfolds are once again used by everyone because sight remains the most predominant sensory experience available and, in this instance, you should

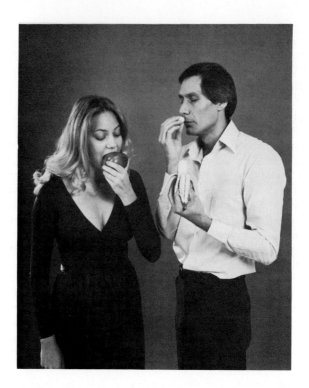

Teresa Gilmore and Grey Schmidt demonstrate SENSORY AWARENESS: Exercise 6 and 7, "Smelling" and "Tasting" freshfruit. Photograph by Randy Tunnel.

restrict it. The sacks should be opened and placed in a line; thus, you will not have to touch objects in order to smell them. Move from sack to sack, smelling deeply and registering the smell in memory. When everyone has completed the exercise in silence, blindfolds should be removed and the smell of each object clarified and explored through discussion.

Taste Perception

Tasting is perceiving the flavor of something by touching with the tongue, utilizing the taste buds. Effective tasting is only possible when we are healthy, particularly without sinus problems, head congestion, or colds.

Exercise 7   Tasting

On a designated time and day, convert the sense-of-smell exercise (Exercise 6) into a sense-of-taste exercise, using a variety of fruits. Each actor must bring a minimum of three different kinds of fruit. The fruit should be arbitrarily exchanged. Taste the three pieces of fruit in sequence and register those tastes in your memory. When everyone has completed the exercise in silence, the taste of each object should be clarified and explored through discussion. (Note: Exercises 6 and 7 can be combined into a single exercise.)

Hearing Perception

Hearing is perceiving sound through the ear mechanism. Effective hearing is possible only when the mechanism is in a healthy condition, unaffected by congestion or injury.

Exercise 8 Hearing

Everyone sit in a relaxed position. Either close your eyes or use a blindfold, whichever is most comfortable for you. Begin by trying to "listen" to silence (note that hearing is an automatic response, whereas listening requires mental concentration upon what you are hearing). Can you hear it? Your first perception will probably be that you cannot because your concentration will focus upon *any* sound. Do not resist listening to the sounds. Try to perceive precisely what is making the sounds and register them in memory. Occasionally you will note with delight that there are moments without sound and you will actually "hear" silence. After a comfortable duration of time, open your eyes and clarify and explore through discussion what you have heard. (Note: your coach or instructor can heighten this exercise by inserting several unique sounds into the experience. For example, he or she might whistle; tear a piece of cardboard; utter a low growl; and so on.)

Life Experience and Your Art

Having now completed exercises in sensory perception, you should be ready to turn to new exercises involving personalized observation and experiences related to sensory awareness. The sensory perception exercises extend an actor's creative development in relaxation, concentration, and observation. A common mistake made by some beginning actors is to leave all this work in the classroom, rehearsal studio, or theatre. Because of its personalization base, the art of acting cannot be professionally developed or maintained in a vacuum of time and place. Rather, the art of acting through personalization is another kind of life experience. It follows that the actor should extend the perceptions and awarenesses developed in the previous exercises into every waking moment. Initially extension must be practiced consciously whenever circumstances permit. Naturally, the details of occupation, family, and private life may not allow practicing these exercises frequently. However, if an actor insists upon some planned exercise work during his everyday life, eventually his subconscious perceptions may automatically continue without his being overtly aware of the fact. This is another way of saying that consciously and subconsciously an actor should be constantly intermingling his life experiences with the practice of his art. Like a sponge or a giant antenna, an actor should attract and select stimuli which will enrich the artist and the art.

Exercise 9 Verbalizing Personalized Observation and Experience Concerning the Senses

After achieving a state of relaxation, select a vivid personal experience concerning one or more of your five senses and relate the story to your colleagues. Do not select an experience of unusual emotional intensity. Select an important but simple and comfortable experience rather than one which in any way might create tension or embarrassment for you. For example, you might relate the story of how at an important job interview you failed to hear a key question and you gave a strange response which lost you the job. As you relate your experience, you should recount it not only verbally, but also nonverbally. While some will be forgotten, any minor, comfortable feelings and sensations you experienced should be recalled and *may* even be re-created by movement or gesture if you tell the story well. Do not attempt to re-create such feelings and sensations, but do not suppress them if they are generated honestly. The value of this exercise lies in its extension of personal contribution to the art of acting. In other words, it contributes to honest self-revelation or a kind of unzipping of oneself. Provided that you avoid intense emotional recollection at this stage of development, you need not fear this exercise as being amateurish psychotherapy. While an aspect of psychology is always involved in acting, it is important to note that therapeutic benefit is incidental or subsidiary. (Later in your development and work you will note that this exercise can serve as a foundation for use of the technique called "affective memory.")

Exercise 10 Combining the Senses

Select a favorite and easily transported object which you consider a kind of extension of yourself in your environment. Take a relaxed position in front of your colleagues and show the object to them. As you do so, describe the object in detail, carefully noting how it feels, smells, sounds, looks, tastes, where you got it, when you got it, and generally what it means to you in terms of both utility and sentiment. Your honest comfort with this object should be demonstrated without any conscious effort. Once again, the exercise is valueless if you leave it in the realm of a classroom experience. You must take this exercise into your world of everyday existence. Become totally aware of all the objects you handle or engage. The result will be increased sensory awareness.

Sensory Awareness through Interpersonal Contact

Finally, and perhaps most important, sensory awareness involves interaction with other people. In order to work with other people, we must trust them. However, before we can trust others, we must trust ourselves. Trust means possessing an honest confidence in ourselves and inspiring the same in others. The exercises previously encountered should have begun to increase self-trust. They should have increased awareness of self-trust and of the environment, emotions, senses, observations, and experiences. The actor should be more confident now of his sense of reality; that is, to use a psychological term, the actor should have a better grasp of personal identity.

The personalization theory necessitates that the actor confront and accept his personality and life experiences, using his strengths confidently and coping with his weaknesses with equal confidence. It follows that the actor should now be ready to engage the personality, reality, and identity of other people.

Exercise 11   Engaging Other People with Trust

Begin by creating a state of relaxation. Walk about the room with awareness of yourself in space. When you are comfortable, permit eye contact with every person you pass; remain silent and walk slowly. Without forcing the action, begin to casually touch the other persons as you pass them, either on the hand, arm, or shoulder. Eventually, you may find a natural instinct to pause and hold on to a person's hand or arm for a moment. If this occurs, give in to the instinct provided that it is honest and comfortable for both of you (note that the latter is not an obligatory direction; if the instinct does not arise, do not force it). Those of you who do stop to linger a moment upon physical contact may also note the instinct to explore the other person's face visually. Follow that instinct if it occurs. Similarly, visual exploration may lead to a natural desire to touch the other person's face. Again, if both of you are honest, trusting, and comfortable, permit the facial touching. Progression to this point may take several hours of several days, depending upon the confidence and trust factors of the people involved. As trust grows, the touch exploration may extend to the hands and other but not all parts of the body. (Exercise 11 is complete when you have accomplished physical contact with all other actors.)

Because our society is extraordinarily conscious of group therapy and Freudian psychology, the question arises as to how intimate touch perception will become in Exercise 10. The first answer to the question is obviously that it will be as extensive as trust and confidence permit. However, since there will be individuals capable of *total* body contact in this exercise, artistic discretion and public taste enter the picture. In other words, restrict touch perception at the point that it becomes private or sexually intimate. Later, if role creation in a play demands some kind of sexual physical contact, Exercise 10 can be reintroduced in a closed rehearsal under the supervision of a director or artist-leader. In no circumstances should this kind of work be permitted without that supervision because of the artistic necessities of craft and control involved. An objective and trained observer is needed to assist an actor in determining what works as art as opposed to what is merely self-indulgent. If for any reason Exercise 11 fails to accomplish trust through the sensory awareness of comfortable physical contact, use Exercise 12. However, Exercise 12 should be directed and controlled by close supervision, if it is used at all, in order to restrict inordinate or embarrassing behavior.

Exercise 12 Specific Touching

Sit with your colleagues in a line of chairs and relax. The person at the left end of the line rises and faces the person next to him. Select some specific physical area of the person's *face, head,* or *hands* to touch and examine, basing your selection on the most natural instinct you have for touching that person in those areas. For example, you may have always wanted to touch a person's hair, chin, lips, or hands. This exercise will permit you to do so with comfort and trust. Proceed down the line of actors until you have made specific physical contact as just instructed with every person. As the first person performing the exercise moves past two or three people, the next person may rise and begin specific touching. Eventually all of you will be engaged in the activity. Comfortable and directed physical contact heightens sensory awareness and increases trust between actors. Exercise 12 is an effective preparation device for all theatrical performance work, as well as an invaluable training device in beginning acting.

Exercise 13 Touching People Without Seeing and the Trust Circle

Begin walking freely about the room again, but this time move very slowly with the eyes gently shut or blindfolded. The inevitable result of this movement will be gentle physical collisions with other people. To avoid injury, remember to move at a slow pace. Again, you must remain silent. Upon collision with another person, freeze. The point of mutual physical contact should be sustained as though you were glued together at that point. Resume movement together, moving cautiously enough to maintain the point of adhesion. Obviously, collisions will increase until a connected mass of human beings is created. Group movement will be increasingly cumbersome. For example, various levels of attachment will occur with some people moving on their knees, others on their hands and knees, and so on, depending upon whether the collision caused them to drop into such position. The value of this exercise lies in its extension of ensemble or group trust. When the entire group is connected, it forms into a circle with members on their feet, facing toward a mutual center with each arm locked around the small of the back and waist of the person on either side. With your eyes still closed, permit any natural instinct from the unit to sway from side to side. A rhythm will result. The instinct to make a small humming sound may arise in this "trust circle." To demonstrate the trust, follow any instinct to lean far backward or forward, provided that your weight or balance does not break the circle. You will find you are comfortably supported by the unit without danger or fear of falling or collapsing. When a harmonious unit is firmly established, open your eyes and continue any natural instincts toward swaying, weaving, leaning, humming, or even singing. Later at some point of comfortable silence, permit one member of the group to break from the circle and stand in the center as the circle reunites. The person in the center closes his or her eyes as the other members of the circle drop their arms to their sides. When you are the one in the center, and you feel the urge to totally trust the others, fall into space in any direction without fear of landing on the floor, knowing full well that members of the circle will catch you safely and return you to an upright position. After you have fallen comfortably several times, return to the circle while another member of the group replaces you.

The trust circle

Continue the exercise until all of you have experienced the trust that accompanies falling without fear. While there may be tension early in this exercise among some members of the group concerning awkward or embarrassing physical contact, it will rapidly disappear with both the trust and fun involved in the falling action. This is particularly true because the contact, no matter where it is made, is extremely brief and usually involves support from several people at the same time. Women often fold their arms across their chests to aid trust when falling and being caught. (Incidentally, it should be obvious that good personal hygiene increases trust and confidence in group activity.)

Exercise 14 The Growth and Deterioration of Man

Extend your small catching circle into a very large one with plenty of space between one another to avoid collision in the following group exercise. Assume a human fetal position upon the floor and through your own pantomimic invention be "born" and "begin to grow." Let your growth progress into early infancy; move from reclining to crawling and then to standing and into toddling. Pass into childhood, adolescence, and young maturity. Continue through the "stages of Man" by physically moving around the stage until you reach middle age and, eventually, old age. Remain silent throughout this exercise, except for vocalization sounds such as crying, laughing, coughing, grunting, and so on. For example, to physicalize early childhood you might act out skipping rope and similar activities. For adolescence, you might imitate lighting a cigarette. For young adulthood, you might march as though in the army; at middle age, you might walk slower and do calisthenics with some difficulty, sit as though watching television, and so on. For old age, you might hobble on a cane or sit and stare blankly. This lengthy exercise should culminate in final deterioration leading to death. Throughout this exercise permit your instincts, confidence, and trust to carry you into any natural movement, physical interaction with others, and sound making. The exercise concludes in the position of the repose of death.

Personalization includes total sensory awareness of the self and the objects and people of one's personal environment. Hopefully, this awareness will increase with conscientious execution of the exercises given in this chapter.

Suggested Readings

Chekhov, Michael. *To the Actor on the Technique of Acting.* New York: Harper & Brothers, 1953.

Ghiselin, Brewster, ed. *The Creative Process.* Berkeley: University of California Press, 1954; Mentor Books, 1955.

Lewis, Howard R., and Streitfeld, Harold S. *Growth Games.* New York: Bantam Books, Inc., 1972.

McCaslin, Nellie. *Creative Dramatics in the Classroom.* 2nd ed. New York: David McKay Co., 1974.

Ward, Winifred. *Playmaking with Children.* 2nd ed. New York: Appleton-Century-Crofts, 1957.

Way, Brian. *Development Through Drama.* London: Longmans, Green & Co. Ltd., 1969.

Weissman, Phillip. *Creativity in the Theatre.* New York: Dell, 1966.

5 The Roots of Feeling: The Body and Emotion

Teresa Gilmore and Grey
Schmidt demonstrate
THE BODY AND
EMOTION: "Contrasting
Emotions" (unhappiness
and happiness).
Photograph by Randy
Tunnel.

Most people go to the theatre for an emotional experience. Whether they are conscious of it or not, they have a desire to witness and vicariously experience heightened emotional activity. People enjoy sharing emotions with others. At the very least, people find release from their own emotions by sharing feelings with performers. Naturally, many people also go to the theatre for an intellectual experience. However, as Aristotle stated in the fifth century B.C., meaningful dramatic thought is emotionally based; that is, ideas and concepts usually follow emotional dramatic action rather than precede it. For example, the plays of a highly philosophical playwright such as George Bernard Shaw are effective on stage only when the author's ideas are projected from characters involved in emotional crisis. When his characters lecture, an audience is less involved.

Defining Emotion

Fundamentally, emotion is feeling. For example, fear, anger, happiness, boredom, and grief are all emotions. When the mind enters into feeling or emotional experience, it usually suppresses, channels, or frustrates the feeling. Often when emotional control is needed, it is the mind that brings control.

Emotions are primarily manifested in human beings in a physical way. Literally, *emotion* means "outward movement," which implies impulse toward open action. In everyday life, emotions cause the release of frustrations and anxieties in physical ways. If we are angry enough, we may throw something or hit something. If we are unhappy enough, we may shed tears and cry. If we are delighted by something or happy enough, we may laugh. All of these physical actions help clarify emotional conditions and hence increase perception of ourself.

In order for an emotion to be projected or even for an emotion to be experienced, some kind of internal physical response must be activated in the actor. On stage, emotion is best projected to and understood by the audience through *physical action*. More often than not, mental activity suppresses, dissipates, or controls emotion rather than generates it. This is precisely why people say to an angry person, "Sit down and think about this; be calm and get control of yourself." On stage, an actress says the line "I'm furious with you!" dozens of times without making the audience believe it if she relies only on the words and thought. The audience will only believe an actress is "furious" when her physical actions and vocal accompaniment so demonstrate. (The ramifications of vocal accompaniment are discussed in chapter 7.)

The relationship of emotion to physical response is clarified in a famous theory developed by William James and C. G. Lange near the turn of the nineteenth century. The basic point of the theory is that body activity and emotional activity are analogous. In other words, the activity of our muscles is emotional activity. Stanislavski and most modern theorists and practitioners of the art of acting are familiar with the James-Lange theory.

In chapter 2 the exercises and discussion concerning body activity or movement are directly related to this theory (i.e., emotional internal muscular activity creates external physical action).

To test the ability to transform emotion and internal muscular activity into external physical action perform the following exercises.

Exercise 1 Breathing Alone

Sit quietly, close your eyes, and concentrate on your breathing; do not think about any emotions or experiences. Concentrate on the breath entering and leaving your lungs. Be aware of the shifting emotions which accompany your breathing.

Exercise 2 Breathing with a Partner

Sit on the floor and face a partner. Breathing is the only way you may shape the emotions communicated between you. (What happens to you as you explore this work? Will you stay in a human form? Do whatever is necessary to explore a full range of emotions as a result of breathing. You may vocalize sounds and noises, but no words.) Let the breathing become angry, erotic, happy, and so on. Combine this exercise with "The Mirror" exercise (see Chapter 3, page 25): two people breathe as one as a leader runs a gamut of "emotional breathing."

Emotion and Objects

Emotion is usually tied to physical activity, and most physical activity is usually tied to use of objects. Most of us instinctively relate to our environment to demonstrate or release emotion. For example, if we are furious, we usually hit a table or a wall or throw something; fury rarely stops with shouting.

When weeping, most of us lean or hold onto another person, a pillow, a handkerchief, or the sleeve of a garment.

When laughing, we slap our own leg, someone else's arm, and clap our hands together.

When afraid, we often clutch objects. The student sitting before a professor trying to explain why an assignment is not finished may fidget with a pencil, a coin, or a paper clip.

The study of emotion begins by personalizing. We live in a world of objects, most of which are inanimate. For example, we wear a wristwatch, shoes, clothing. We write with a pen and pencil. We drive an automobile and eat with utensils. The interesting philosophical or psychological question arises, Do any of these objects become an extension of you? An infant is totally comfortable without clothing until he is habitually forced to wear it. At a very young age, he learns that he must wear clothing in public to be socially acceptable. Early in life most children learn to attach themselves to a favorite object, usually a blanket, bottle, or toy. In our society favorite objects of children include such things as Snoopy, spaceships and space people (note the *Star Wars* and "E. T." craze), Superman, Spiderman, miniature trains, cars, airplanes, dolls, and baseball and football trading cards. (Take a moment to check your own fetish, that is, object of special devotion. Is it that guitar, that automobile, or that purse?) We instinctively develop personal ways of handling these objects. We store them in particular places and carry or wear them in special ways.

An actor is also inextricably tied to the objects of his environment, be it a stage setting, a classroom, or a rehearsal studio. If there is a table in that environment, he will relate to it even if he never touches it; he will do this by avoiding the table, which becomes a reverse aspect of relating to it.

Actors must carefully select objects to help demonstrate emotions on stage. Physical activity with objects can project the nature and degree of emotion more effectively than anything spoken. A playwright and a director automatically provide performers with many of these objects. (For example, a bouquet of roses should be used by Happy, Linda, and Biff in act 2 of *Death of a Salesman* by Arthur Miller.) However, the inventive actor provides additional objects to fully create character and emotion. If the performance is improvisational without a written script, objects and physical environment are even more important to the performer in the clarification and demonstration of emotion. In an improvisational theatre performance, a simple chair might provide several emotional possibilities. For example, as an obstacle to movement an actor may throw the chair aside with fury or exhilaration. The emotional point will be clearly made by the action with the object.

Actors and actresses are usually individualistic when selecting objects to demonstrate emotion; however, they should try to select things which are universally recognized as being related to an emotion and its physical manifestation. For example, the handkerchief is universally related to crying. For a comic or unusual object-emotion relationship, an actress might cry into a peculiar object such as a dishrag. Role and play analysis will assist in appropriate selection. (Role analysis is discussed further in chapter 10 and play analysis is discussed in Appendix A.)

For familiarity in handling objects related to emotions, perform the following exercises.

Exercise 3   Emotional Opinion

Select a partner and take a comfortable, seated position opposite one another. One of you introduces a subject and asks a question about it which requires an emotional opinion as a reply, such as, "Do you like the President of your country—why or why not?" Respond to your partner's answer with an opposite point of view. Pursue the argument to intense emotional commitment. Each partner must force the other to be very *specific* in the argument. (Limit the exchange to three minutes.)

Exercise 4   Emotional Reactions

One at a time, each member of the group takes an isolated position in front of the others. At random, group members speak honest but emotional opinions at the person which the individual must react to with honest comments; for example, a group member might say, "I've always disliked the way you wear your hair;" another person might say, "I've always liked the way you smile, but I think you dress very sloppily." Someone else might say, "I think you have a very large nose." The exercise is only valid and valuable if group members are honest with their praise, criticism, or observation. The person reacting should instinctively do so with comparable honesty. (As always, the instructor provides the control factor in an emotional exercise which possesses risk.)

Exercise 5   Words to Create Feelings

Select one of the following words and explain to your colleagues why the sound, spelling, and texture or "feeling" of the word accurately reflects the emotion or experience which the word represents:

> love   hate   fear   grief   joy
> agony   terror   misery   nervous
> giddy   tedious   lust   hilarity
> obnoxious   sickening   painful
> heat   cold   disgust   desire

(Can your discussion lead to the actual feeling or expression of the emotion?)

Exercise 6   Ambivalence

Ambivalence is an emotional quality involved with desiring something and rejecting it at the same time: for example, a person on a strict diet loves ice cream and is offered a chocolate sundae. The emotional response is ambivalent; that is, the person is caught between equally desirable choices.

Select a recent personal experience in which you had ambivalent feelings about something. Describe the experience in detail; is the emotion recreated? (If possible, recreate the situation with use of appropriate objects.)

Exercise 7   Fear of Height

Your instructor or his designate should lead the class to the top of a high building or structure such as to the top of a grid in a theatre. Note the nature of your emotional reactions the higher you get and the closer you get to the edge of the precipice. Be extremely careful not to fall or unnecessarily endanger life. When you have returned to the ground, note the additional emotional changes within you. Describe all the emotional activity you have undergone.

Exercise 8   Loss and Grief

Select an object that was a gift from someone now dead or gone out of your life forever. Bring the object to class and describe the person who gave you the object. Discuss their personality characteristics as well as the way they looked and behaved. Permit your emotions about the departed person to flow freely.

The exercise should create a strong sense of personal loss and grief, or a specific emotion/feeling about that person, as well as the object.

Exercise 9 Laughter

Everyone sit in a circle and remain silent. Let your eyes wander from person to person. Do not suppress any urge toward giddiness, giggling, or laughter. Do not force such responses, but permit them to flow freely if the natural urge strikes you. If you are inclined to do so, join in the laughter. This exercise should permit infectious, spontaneous laughter, using other people as the object stimulus. (Ignore any person who seems to deliberately resist the group laughter. The exercise is a success when everyone joins in naturally.)

Exercise 10 Love

Bring a portrait or photograph of someone you love to class. Sit in a chair facing the class and look at the photograph awhile. Relate to the class why you love this person; describe what it is about the person that brings you happiness and love.

Exercise 11 Anger

Describe to the class what you usually do when you are genuinely angry. Pantomimically and verbally demonstrate how you behave when angry.

Exercise 12 Terror

Describe to the class your most terrifying personal experience. Pantomimically and verbally demonstrate how you behaved; if you screamed, demonstrate the scream; and so on.

Dormant Emotion

Another important source of emotion remains to be explored—the emotion either forgotten or suppressed in the subconscious. Such emotion rests there in the fashion of a dormant volcano or seed. This store of emotion can perhaps be understood best through the metaphors of the volcano and the seed.

The earth holds several inactive or dormant volcanoes; that is, their active eruption has ceased. However, scientists have proved that deep within the recess of a volcano lies hot lava and potential explosive activity. Nature can provoke a dormant volcano into activity, or man can do it through use of explosives. Similarly, we may stand in the midst of a seemingly barren and dry desert, convinced that no plant or animal life exists there. A mere five-minute thundershower will stimulate seed and animal life to colorful and dynamic activity.

Old friends meet: intense love and happiness! Chev Rodgers and David Tabor in *Seed from the East* by Geraldine Lust, directed by Martin Oltarsh. At the Theater for the New City, New York.

Dormant emotion resides within each of us at all times. Fears, rules, laws, mores, guilt, desires, and hosts of other conditions force us to terminate certain emotional experiences. We often try to forget them. For example, most people develop or learn the fear of death. If one is consistently conscious of the emotional fear of his own death or the death of loved ones, one might very well experience a nervous breakdown, go insane, or behave in unusual and possibly destructive ways. Consequently, most human beings confront the reality of death through religion on a conscious level or through unconscious suppression of mortality. Like the dormant volcano or desert seed, suppressed emotion lies deep within us and is a continually potential source of eruption. In everyday life, most people have no occasion to deliberately activate that potential. Most people are satisfied and happier keeping many emotions dormant. However, the actor cannot afford that luxury. The personalization theory of acting utilizes dormant emotion, along with objects, as one of the primary sources, if not the primary source, of emotional stimuli. The longer we live, the more emotional experiences will be stored in our dormant "bank." If actors are to draw upon that bank, they may use what is commonly called *emotion recall*, or what Stanislavski called "affective memory." Stanislavski's concept focuses upon recalling events previously experienced. To do this, an actor must remember a specific experience vividly, attempting to recall what was done and said with as much of the original intensity as possible. (Note: no attempt should be made to recall the feeling or emotion itself; emotion often follows naturally by simply recalling the activities of the event.) The memories of the physical and verbal activity may create the desired emotion needed in an analogous situation in a play. The actor then substitutes the emotion of the life experience in the given circumstances of the play. The result can be very believable emotion on stage.

To illustrate the effectiveness of using dormant emotion, or affective memory experience, I cite a true story of an actress performing the role of Irina in Anton Chekhov's play *The Three Sisters*. Near the end of the play, Irina's fiance, Tusenbach, is killed in a duel with Solyony. Irina must receive the news of his death and cry. In early rehearsals the actress attempted the crying sequence strictly through use of mechanical technique. Upon hearing of the death, she took a handkerchief from her pocket, sat on a chair, collapsed her head upon her arms on the table, and shook physically, while emitting vocal sobs. The effect was not believable.

During the next week of rehearsals, the director assisted the actress with "affective memory." Through discussion, the director discovered that several years earlier the actress had lost her brother in a car accident. Her brother had been run over and killed in the street. The girl's memory of *what happened* was vivid and painful. She was able to recall the *activities* of the experience intensely. Recalling this memory immediately prior to acting Irina's reaction to the death of her fiance produced a very believable emotion, far more effective than the mechanical work of the previous week. The actress recalled the circumstances that occurred when she learned her brother had been killed. She sat down on a chair quietly and stared straight ahead. Her eyes glistened; her voice choked with feelings from within her. From effective memory, she created a believable emotion. The audience shared the experience, believed it, and was moved by it.

The following exercise will aid in the development of emotion recall. It is a very important exercise in preparation for later acting work in scenes and plays. However, if the exercise is unsuccessful, discretion should indicate postponing it until the actor has attained a more advanced state of development.

Exercise 13   Tapping Your Dormant Emotion
(This exercise is an extension of Exercise 9 in chapter 4.)

Begin by creating your own state of relaxation. When you are totally relaxed, come to a comfortable seated position on the floor or on a chair. Eliminate all body tension. The time necessary for you to relax and select an experience may be extensive, and may try the patience of any observers. Everyone must contribute to the aura of concentration and relaxation by maintaining silence. Development of art and craft necessitates this kind of discipline.

Select an important experience from your past in which you can vividly recall the circumstances of the experience. You may select experiences which occurred five to ten years ago. It is best to avoid selecting a recent experience (e.g., one year or less). The further away the experience, the more dormant the emotion.

Once the experience is vividly recalled, describe it in detail for the class. Do not explain what emotions you felt; rather, focus solely on the circumstances of the experience. In other words, vivid recollection of physical and verbal activity will trigger the internal nervous and muscular systems necessary to activate dormant emotion. Consequently, as you recall and verbally explain what happened to you, it is highly probable that the original emotion

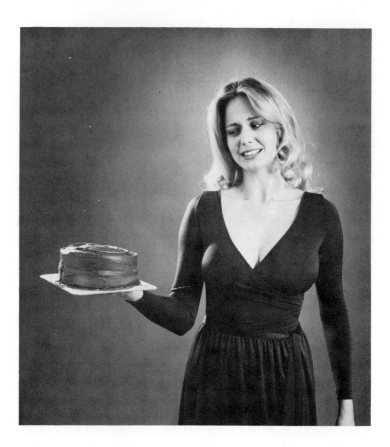

Teresa Gilmore demonstrates THE BODY AND EMOTION: Exercise 6, "Ambivalence" ("I want the cake, but I also want to hold my weight right where it is!"). Photograph by Randy Tunnel.

will erupt or grow again. Do not be upset if this exercise is not immediately successful. It can be repeated or postponed to a later point of development. Emotion recall is a complex and difficult technique. Since the technique is rooted in the personalization factor, you may require several attempts at affective memory to succeed. Also, a coach, an instructor, or a director should be present to guide you in the event excessive emotion is released.

Exercise 13 takes time, patience, dedication, skill, and a climate of trust within the group. Above all, it takes a willing and cooperative actor. One must have the courage to explore highly personal experience in public—experiences which have been heretofore suppressed in secrecy. The necessary *aspect* of "couch" psychology or group therapy must be accepted by all participants and naturally will be enhanced by the training and skill of the instructor. If an actor is not willing to explore dormant emotion in this way, the experience should be waived. Also, the instructor or coach is free to use or not use Exercise 13. Someone trained in psychology should be located to assist with the exercise.

Grey Schmidt
demonstrates THE BODY
AND EMOTION: Exercise
8, "Loss and Grief" (Lost
in thought holding a
photograph of his
deceased father.)
Photograph by Randy
Tunnel.

Even successful completion of Exercise 13 will not *guarantee* continued skill with affective memory. However, introduction of this skill in the first year of training can permit an artist to extend work with this complex process for two or more years. Hopefully, personalization will refine the tool throughout an acting career.

Projecting Experience

Projecting experience is another valuable technique to use in the creation of believable emotion on stage. Projecting experience means mentally perceiving emotional experiences which will unquestionably or probably occur in the future. The best example of such experience is death. It is a fact of mortal existence as we know it that life will terminate in death. Therefore, when past experience is insufficient to create a believable emotion, projection of future experience may stimulate emotional response. For example, the actress discussed earlier in the role of Irina might not have had a past experience of death vivid enough to use as affective memory. She might then use the projected death of a loved one such as the death of her father to assist in the creation of grief.

Projecting experience implies use of imagination and improvisation, acting techniques described in chapter 6. However, it should be noted that the projected death of a parent is not imagination; it is a fact. Death is not a fantasy. It is inevitable.

Exercise 14   Projecting Death

Relax in a chair on stage. Think of a living relative who is particularly close to you. For example, your father, mother, brother, or sister. Mentally project the death of the relative. Describe the circumstances of the death and funeral. (If your emotions become acute or excessive, stop the exercise.) Do not be alarmed by the seemingly maudlin or painful nature of this exercise. It is a proved and effective acting technique when handled maturely and efficiently.

While emotion is a physical or body activity, the nuances of its expression are greatly aided in the theatre by the ability to project the subtleties of one's personal emotional experiences.

Powerful emotions unleashed! Stephen Joyce and Nancy Donohue in *The Runner Stumbles* by Milan Stitt. At the Hartman Theatre, Stamford, Connecticut, directed by Austin Pendleton.

Suggested Readings

Berne, Eric. *Games People Play*. New York: Castle, 1964.

————. *What Do You Say After You Say Hello: The Psychology of Human Destiny*. New York: Bantam Books, Inc., 1973.

————. *Transactional Analysis in Psychotherapy*. New York: Castle, 1961.

Darwin, Charles. *The Expression of the Emotions in Man and Animals*. London: John Murray Publishers, 1872.

Davitz, Joel R., and Davitz, Lois Jean. "Nonverbal Vocal Communication of Feeling." *Journal of Communication* 11 (1961):81–86.

Dittman, A. T. "Relationship Between Body Movements and Moods in Interviews." *Journal of Consulting Psychology* 26 (1962):480.

Esslin, Martin. *An Anatomy of Drama*. New York: Hill and Wang, 1976.

Goffman, Erving. *Interaction Ritual*. New York: Anchor, 1967.

————. *Strategic Interaction*. New York: Anchor, 1972.

Harris, Thomas A. *I'm OK—You're OK*. New York: Avon Books, 1969.

James, William. "What Is Emotion?" *Mind* 9 (1884):188–204.

Koffa, K. *Principles of Gestalt Psychology*. New York: Harcourt, 1935.

Lange, Carl G., and James, William. *The Emotions*. Facsimile of 1922 ed. New York: Hafner Publishing Co., 1967.

Marowitz, Charles. *The Act of Being*. New York: Taplinger Publishing Co., 1978.

Moore, Sonia. *The Stanislavski System*. New York: Viking Press, 1974.

Morris, Eric. *Being and Doing. A Workbook for Actors*. Los Angeles: Whitehouse/ Spelling Publications, 1981.

Morris, Eric, and Hotchkis, Joan. *No Acting Please*. Los Angeles: Whitehouse/ Spelling Publications, 1979.

Perls, Frederick; Hefferline, Ralph F.; and Goodman, Paul. *Gestalt Therapy: Excitement and Growth in the Human Personality*. New York: Dell, 1951.

Wagner, Arthur. *The Drama Review*, Summer 1967 and Spring 1969. (Eric Berne theories related to acting.)

Woodbury, Lael J. "The Externalization of Emotion." *Educational Theatre Journal*, October 1960, pp. 177–83.

6 Imagination and Improvisation

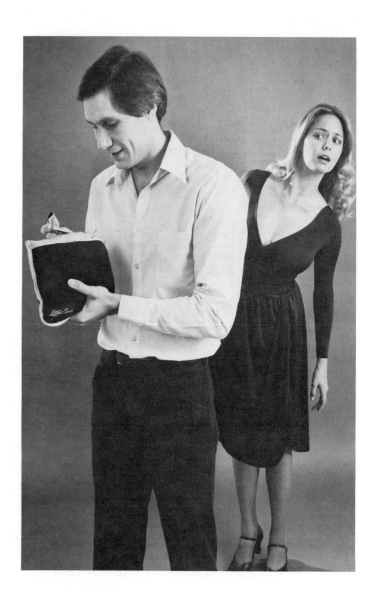

Teresa Gilmore and Grey
Schmidt demonstrate
IMAGINATION AND
IMPROVISATION:
Exercise 10, "The Theft."
Photograph by Randy
Tunnel.

Experiences, observations, and environment provide most of the emotional stimuli needed to perform effectively in the theatre. However, playwrights invariably create unusual and intense emotional situations requiring stimuli beyond these usual avenues. The most obvious example of this is found in *Oedipus Rex* by Sophocles. Probably no actor will be able to use specific, one-to-one personal experience, observation, or environment to create the correct emotional state of Oedipus when he discovers he has married his own mother and fathered children with her. The agony of despair and anguish in the man at the moment of that discovery usually requires use of imaginative stimuli.

Imagination

What is meant by *using imagination?* Imagination is the process of creating or inventing mental images or experiences. Everyone is born with a natural instinct for imagination, but relatively few people consciously develop the process as a skill. An actor and actress must consciously work to cultivate imagination. Children are particularly adept at vividly imagining things. In some instances, children actually create imaginary playmates, brothers, and sisters. As we grow older, this process is referred to as *daydreaming.*

Imagination! Actor, costume designer, makeup designer combine efforts: *The Book of Job*, Everyman Players. Irene Corey, designer.

The sign over the door at the Joe Bernard Acting Studio in Las Vegas, Nevada repeats the sign found in the late Lee Strasberg's Actor's Studio in New York: "Enter ye here, all who dare to dream." Stanislavski said that an actor must learn to dream by use of his imagination. Dreaming for an actor must be directional; that is, it must have an artistic purpose to it. This distinguishes everyday imaginative dreaming from creative imagination for artistic purposes. For example, a young actress in an acting class (performing Exercise 1 given in this chapter) indulged in totally aimless, stream-of-consciousness fantasizing, without any direction to her story about an object. She and her listeners were only confused because of the lack of clarity and believability in her wandering story. Imagination must be channeled to a climatic conclusion in order to provide truth and believability in acting.

The rigors of formal education and increased maturity tend to stifle the daydreaming process. However, daydreaming is never totally eliminated because psychologists have proved that all people daydream or fantasize in highly imaginative ways during part of both waking and sleeping hours of each day. Escape and sexual fantasies are rampant among members of modern society. The task of the actor is to channel imaginative instinct into constructive acting training, role creation, and stage performance. How does the actor train this instinct?

Exercise 1   Imagination and an Object

Establish a personal state of relaxation, concentration, and correct breathing. When you have created this condition by application of selected exercises from chapter 1, accept a personal object from one of your colleagues such as a purse, ring, or watch. Examine it in great detail. It is crucial that the object be totally foreign to you, and if it is not, return it and accept another object from someone else. Let your creative imagination work upon the object. Imagine in specific detail where it came from originally. That is, where was it made and by whom? Imaginatively trace the object on its journey to the person you received it from and relate the story verbally to the other actors. Next, using your knowledge and observation of the person who gave it to you, no matter how limited that knowledge and observation may be, imagine a highly emotional experience involving the object and that person and also relate it to the group. (The entire verbal part of Exercise 1 should be managed within 3–5 minutes per person.)

Exercise 2   Impromptu Imagination Work

Another exercise in rapid, spontaneous imagination work involves reacting *immediately* with verbal stories to *impromptu* (i.e., spontaneous or unrehearsed) questions or situations. For example, the following questions and situations may be used by the instructor or your colleagues to stimulate your imaginative response. Respond to the following situations by telling a 3–5 minute imaginative story, doing so as though you had actually experienced the situation described (it is crucial that you accept this exercise with total sincerity and believable involvement when you are either questioning or responding):

1. Your doctor informs you that you have pernicious anemia and have less than three weeks to live. Describe how you will spend the next three weeks.

2. You are talking to your mother. If you could be anyone in the world, past, present, or future, who would you be? What would you do?

3. You are awakened in the middle of the night by a totally unrecognizable sound in the next room. You and your sister listen carefully. Describe the sound and what you do.

4. You and your father receive an airmail special delivery letter postmarked from a foreign city. Describe the message in the letter.

5. On the day of your marriage, your mother tells you that your real father (who lives in another city) will not be able to walk down the aisle with you because he is in a federal penitentiary. How do you respond and what do you do?

6. You are about to be married when you learn from your brother that your former husband, believed killed in the war, is alive and returning to you. How do you react and what do you do?

7. You are about to give birth to your first child when you learn from your sister that your husband is having an affair with your best friend. How do you react and what do you do?

8. You are only one year away from retirement from a twenty-five-year job when your employer is forced to terminate you. How do you react and what do you do?

Imaginative theatre! Tony Papenfuss as Scrooge in *A Christmas Carol* at the Mark Taper Forum in Los Angeles. Directed by John Dennis, adaptation of the Charles Dickens classic by Doris Baizley.

9. At the conclusion of a divorce, you learn from your two teenage children that they wish to leave you and live with their father. How do you react and what do you do?

10. Recently married, you move happily into a new apartment, only to learn from your landlord that your in-laws have rented the apartment below yours. How do you react and what do you do?

11. You and your brother attend the reading of your father's will. To your amazement, your father leaves you nothing in the will. How do you react and what do you do?

12. You have been having an affair and cheating on your mate. You decide to confess; you return home to learn from your brother that your mate had discovered your affair and committed suicide. How do you react and what do you do?

13. You and your child go outside to pick up the morning newspaper and find your pet kitten has been killed by a car in the street. How do you react and what do you do?

14. You have not seen your sister for twenty years. You open the door and she is standing there. How do you react and what do you do?

15. You walk into your brother's room unannounced and discover him standing in front of a mirror in a dress, high heels, and a wig, singing a Judy Garland song. How do you react and what do you do?

Freely using your imagination, invent or create similar questions and circumstances as additional exercises for you and your colleagues. Whenever possible, try to use highly emotional circumstances such as are found in dramatic literature.

Stanislavski once said, "Spectators come to the theater to hear the subtext. They can read the text at home." Stanislavski was referring to the meaning which lies behind the playwright's dialogue, that is, the *subtext*. He noted that imagination was a key factor in creating valid subtext for a role (subtext is discussed in detail in chapter 10). The preceding exercises can assist in stimulating and developing imaginative skills. Conscious use of imagination can make an actor more alert to the world around him, both on- and off-stage. Imagination can permit an actor to think on any theme or develop any idea. It can aid in understanding the past and future life of characters by providing details often omitted by the author. A trained imagination is precise and logical. It permits actors to execute actions instinctively and naturally.

Imagination is particularly vital to the use of an important acting-training technique known as *improvisation*.

Improvisation

Improvisation is (a) imagining and creating a very brief plot or story and implementing it with unplanned and unrehearsed action and dialogue. Improvisation is also (b) imagining and creating subtextual material related to a script into unplanned and unrehearsed action and dialogue. Finally, improvisation is (c) rehearsing a scripted scene by relying on the

Teresa Gilmore and Grey
Schmidt demonstrate
IMAGINATION AND
IMPROVISATION:
Improvising a Comic
Dance. Photograph by
Randy Tunnel.

subjects, issues, purposes and intentions of the scene to imagine and create
the action and dialogue, thereby refraining from use of the author's action
and dialogue.

In executing an improvisation, usually two or more actors are involved. The technique of improvisation is important to actors for three particular reasons: (1) as an aid in working with simple actions and
characterizations and in evolving varied emotions, motivations, voice projection, and body movements; (2) in development of subtext or enhancing
it; and (3) as a technique to implement the script and specific roles when
some of the original spontaneity of character or environment is lost (points
2 and 3 are discussed in chapter 10). Plots for improvisation can be found
in plays or created with original words and actions.

Improvisation obligates the actor to use imagination in the practical application of his skills. It provides a means to integrate the techniques of relaxation, movement, concentration, sensory awareness, and emotions. Improvisation permits maximum use of personalization in a flexible and individualized manner. Although the voice is used in improvisation, the intricacies of voice training for the stage are not necessary for successful improvisation work that stresses personalization. Use the voice as naturally and comfortably as possible in improvisation. The developing actor cannot be expected to think about too many things at one time. Energies should be concentrated on relaxed, physically free action and emotion.

Particularly in the 1960's and 1970's, improvisation evolved into total theatrical performance. The Living Theatre, the Open Theatre, and other groups developed a distinct art form in which a script evolved or was created through rehearsal and performance rather than merely serving as a seminal point of departure. Playwrights such as Megan Terry and Jean-Claude van Itallie have published scripts *after* groups of actors have processed them through improvisation into a form permitting publication. These theatricals are guided by an *artist-leader* rather than by a director. This person often performs with the actors in addition to guiding their work. Julian Beck, Joseph Chaikin, and Jerzy Grotowski are leading examples of contemporary artist-leaders. Improvisational performances do not lend themselves to interpretation by performers outside the group because they are a special, improvised product of that particular group and are stamped with only one interpretation—the one each audience sees. Contemporary politics and social conditions are best suited to this work. Improvisational theatre is very much like a *living newspaper*. When a standard story such as a Greek myth or the Frankenstein fiction is used, it is reworked completely through improvisation.

Many contemporary directors use improvisation as the main activity of early play rehearsals. This is particularly true of "organic" directors who actively promote actor creativity and exploration early in rehearsals as opposed to prescribing blocking and business during this period of time. Thus, improvisation contributes to movement patterns (traditionally called, "blocking") and to meaningful textual and subtextual investigation. Rather than following textual dialogue/stage directions and the commands of the director, the actor is encouraged to immediately abandon the text and improvise every scene in the play one or more times (see "c" above). Then, when the actor returns to the text, activity and subtext provided by the improvisation should be richly in evidence. (These improvisations must be tied to the single word subjects or issues of the textual scene, such as "jealousy," "envy," "revenge," and so on, or to reference made to offstage or prior action.)

How does an actor use improvisation as a beginning acting technique during his early training period? He selects a contemporary political or social topic of interest to him and his group and answers the following questions. What kinds of people (usually stereotypes) are involved? Where does the action take place? What specific important actions are involved?

Why was this topic selected? What point is to be made? (Each improvisation must have a goal or objective because achievement of the goal determines when the improvisation concludes.)

A *minimum* of discussion about the improvisation should be used prior to performing it. The questions should be answered without overintellectualizing the characterization, overplanning the story, or structuring the action meticulously. The improvisation should be "put on its feet" as soon as possible. Once it is in progress, aimless chatter should be avoided, and words should be used economically. Words should contribute only to the flow of action. The scene should be kept moving by having several possibilities of action in mind. Improvisation should not be used to entertain an audience, except in *special* circumstances, such as a group organized to perform improvisations in public. The actors should be sensitive to the feelings and changes in attitude of their partners. If choices are made, they should be performed naturally without contrivance.

Exercise 3   Individual Improvisations

Return to the 15 situations described above in Exercise 2, "Impromptu Imagination Work;" divide your group into partners and perform the situations as improvisations. (The goal of each improvisation is met when the situation prompts one of the actors to exit, or when the instructor/coach stops the improvisation.)

Exercise 4   Group Improvisation

Create a topical and universal group improvisation. One of you acts as the president of the United States arriving for dinner at a group therapy session. Perform the improvisation according to the suggestions just mentioned. The goal of the improvisation is met when the president is convinced that he should join the session.

Exercise 5   The Revival Meeting

One of you is a fiery minister in a religious revival tent. Most of you are zealous believers. Create a revival meeting in which the goal is the conversion to religion of everyone in the room.

Exercise 6   The Audition

Two of you are roommates in New York City, struggling to become professional actresses. You have each auditioned for the same major role in a new play. One of you learns that you have been awarded the role. The goal of the improvisation is met when the other actress is told by her roommate who was cast.

Exercise 7   The Enlistment

Two of you are father and teenage son. The father wants the son to accept a scholarship at the local university. The son has secretly enlisted in the army. The goal of the improvisation is met when the son admits to the father what he has done.

Exercise 8   The Pregnancy

Two of you are a young married couple. You are poverty-stricken. The wife learns that she is pregnant, and knows they cannot afford to have the baby. The goal of the improvisation is met when the wife declares the pregnancy to her husband.

Exercise 9   The Withdrawal

You have been cast in a small, but important role in a play. You just learned that you can have a larger role in another play. Confront the director of the first play and ask for permission to withdraw from that production. The goal of the improvisation is met when the true reason for the withdrawal is confessed.

Exercise 10   The Theft

You accidentally observe your brother taking money out of your purse. Leave and then enter again, examine your purse, and announce the loss of money to your brother. Finally, confront him with what you saw. The goal of the improvisation is met when the brother admits his guilt and returns the money.

Create or invent other improvisations according to this format.

Imagination and improvisation enhance personalization during beginning work as an actor. These techniques provide further stimuli in the development of your skills.

Suggested Readings

Barker, Clive. *Theatre Games.* New York: Drama Book Specialists, 1977.

Burger, Isabel B. *Creative Play Acting.* 2nd ed. New York: Ronald Press Co., 1966.

Chilver, Peter. *Improvised Drama.* London: BT Batsford Ltd., 1967.

Dezseran, Louis John. *The Student Actor's Handbook.* Palo Alto: Mayfield Publishers, 1975.

Elkind, Samuel. *Improvisation Handbook.* Glenview, Illinois: Scott, Foresman, 1978.

Glenn, Stanley L. *The Complete Actor.* Boston: Allyn and Bacon, Inc., 1977.

Held, Jack P. *Improvisational Acting.* Belmont, California: Wadsworth, 1970.

Hodgson, John, and Richards, Ernest. *Improvisation.* New York: Grove Press, Inc., 1974.

McCaslin, Nellie. *Creative Dramatics in the Classroom.* 2nd ed. New York: David McKay Co., 1974.

Mearns, Hughes. *Creative Power: The Education of Youth in the Creative Arts.* New York: Dover Publications, 1958.

Mitchell, Roy. *Creative Theatre.* New York: Benjamin Blom, 1969.

Slade, Peter. *Experience of Spontaneity.* New York: Fernhill House, 1969.

Spolin, Viola. *Improvisation for the Theatre.* Evanston, Ill.: Northwestern University Press, 1963.

Ward, Winifred. *Playmaking with Children.* 2nd ed. New York: Appleton-Century-Crofts, 1957.

Way, Brian. *Development Through Drama.* London: Longmans, Green & Co., 1969.

7 Voice, Speech, and Language

Teresa Gilmore and Grey
Schmidt singing: VOICE,
SPEECH, AND
LANGUAGE. Photograph
by Randy Tunnel.

Words and Meanings

Words are abstract symbols representing people, places, and things. While people are capable of some communication without words, verbal and written thoughts are our primary ways to communicate meaning.

Words are meaningless abstractions until our experiences define what the words represent. For example, when we hear or see the word *chair*, our mind automatically connects the object and the word. Experience has clarified that objects constructed with seats, backs, arms, and legs and used to sit upon are usually called chairs. However, isolated words provide no meaning past the identification or labeling of single objects, places, or things. Words placed together in sentences provide thought and more complex meaning because they form a context (or overall structure of the various parts). In the theatre, the playwright is predominately responsible for organizing words into meaningful context. Occasionally, in improvisational theatre, actors are called upon to perform that task. It follows that they must be reasonably trained in reading skills and comprehension.

In order to speak well on the stage, an actor must develop certain mechanical vocal skills. These skills include breathing correctly; producing adequate sound; using pitch, range, tone, resonance, and timbre to create vocal quality; using inflection, intensity, rate or tempo, emphasis, pause, and rhythm to create vocal variety; using articulation, pronunciation, projection, phrasing, voice placement and context effectively—all to reinforce the words physically.

Breathing

As discussed in chapter 1, correct breathing is directly related to correct posture and relaxation. Breathing is necessary to the life process because oxygen removes waste products from the body, particularly carbon dioxide. Air is taken into the lungs and processed through the bloodstream. Inhalation and exhalation are the central factors involved in breathing. We are able to breathe through both the nose and the mouth. Air travels down the *trachea* or windpipe into the bronchial tubes and reaches the lungs. The size of the chest cavity enlarges, creating a partial vacuum. The air inhaled fills this vacuum and expands the lung sacs. An important muscle called the *diaphragm* located between the lower chest cavity and the upper abdominal cavity contracts due to the pressure of the air reaching the base of the windpipe. This muscular expansion forces the ribs up and out. When we exhale, the process is reversed. The diaphragm relaxes and resumes a dome shape. The process reduces the size of the chest cavity and compresses the lungs. As a result, air is driven out of the lungs, through the air tubes, past the *larynx* (where sounds are produced), and out of the body through the nose and mouth (see diagram, p. 62).

Making Sound

In the upper part of the trachea or windpipe, there are two membranes called the *vocal cords.* These vocal cords are located behind the soft palate (the upper, back part of the mouth). The area housing the vocal cords is called the *larynx* (the upper part of the trachea). These membranes serve as a bridge for the breath stream as it flows in and out of the mouth. As breath is taken in, the vocal cords spread apart and allow the passage of

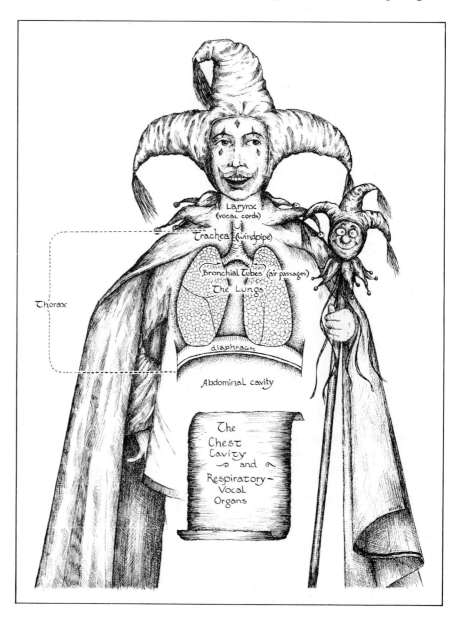

air. They close during the act of swallowing. The space between the open membranes is called the *glottis*.

When we decide to speak, the brain sends a message, or *nerve impulse*, to the vocal membranes and causes them to close. Breath comes from the lungs through the *bronchial tubes* and trachea into the larynx and builds up pressure behind the closed vocal membranes. When the pressure is strong enough, breath is emitted through the vocal cords and vibrates with rapid speed. The vibrating membranes send out waves which produce sound. The sound waves are located in and around the vocal membranes in the larynx. Hence, we may speak when we stop breathing, and we may breathe when we stop speaking.

Exercise 1 Diaphramatic Breathing—Correct Breathing

Stand in a relaxed position with good posture (i.e., posture which is a replica of your body position when you are reclining flat and relaxed on your back). Open your mouth and inhale deeply while holding the palms of your hands against your rib cage. You should feel your abdominal muscles expand your rib cage up and out. Hold your breath for a count of five and release it slowly through the mouth. You should feel your rib cage deflate (your diaphragm muscle will relax).

Exercise 1 can be extended by increasing the amount of air taken in; concurrently, the lung capacity will increase, which aids in breath retention. For example, large amounts of air in the lungs are needed for speaking verse, particularly Shakespearean iambic pentameter. Practice breath control and retention by timing the duration of breath exhalation in the diaphragmatic breathing exercise. The goal should be a minimum of sixty seconds of continual breath exhalation without having to take in new air. It follows that actors should not smoke and, of course, should keep the body in excellent physical condition.

Perform the following exercises for the development of good breathing:

Exercise 2 Breathing and Laughing

Since laughing promotes special breathing problems, begin by vocalizing a highly artificial laugh such as *ha-ha, ho-ho.* Check the action in your abdominal muscles. Your artificial laughter and that of others may lead you into group laughter. This is a desirable goal because then you can check the action of your breathing under honest conditions.

Exercise 3 The Alphabet

Practice projecting the alphabet. Repeat the exercise daily to increase the number of letters you can project without having to take in new breath. Then repeat the exercise calling and extending the sound of each letter as though trying to create an echo. Use all your breath on each letter. The effect will be tantamount to singing. (Incidentally, every actor should take singing lessons if at all possible, if only for breath development.)

Exercise 4   Question Responses

Select a partner at random and take turns asking important questions (for example: Are you married? Do you believe in God?) which require direct and simple answers, probably only yes or no. Notice that inhalation of breath is the first part of your responding action. Without forcing, try to increase the amount of inhalation with each response. This exercise can aid you in developing the habit of adequate inhalation of breath before you speak any unit of speech.

Exercise 5   Sounds

Practice breathing correctly as you project the following sounds:
1. *HAH h-h-h-h!*
2. *HAY a-a-a-a!*
3. *HEE e-e-e-e!*
4. *HOO o-o-o-o!*
5. *HI i-i-i-i!*

Exercise 6   Tongue Twisters

Practice the following difficult phrases and sentences individually and as a choral group; increase tempo or speed as you repeat the exercise:
1. Red leather, yellow leather.
2. Big bad bears bleed blue blood.
3. Rubber baby buggy bumpers.
4. Fuzzy Wuzzy wasn't fuzzy, was he?
5. Peter Piper picked a peck of pickled peppers.
6. Sally Sue sells seashells by the seashore.
7. Slippery snake, slithery snake.
8. Thistles whistle as missiles sizzle.
9. Cora Clayworth cooked curly cabbage in copper kettles.
10. Oliver Oodle toodled the stroodle as he strolled with his poodle.

Vocal Quality

Vocal quality refers to the way the voice sounds to the ear in terms of pleasantness or unpleasantness and includes consideration of pitch, range, tone, resonance, and timbre.

Pitch and Range

Pitch is how high or how low the voice sounds. Range is the distance measured in notes between the lowest and highest pitch of the comfortable speaking voice of an actor. An effective stage voice uses both high and low pitch, but probably modulates between the two much of the time. The potential range of most of us is as much as eight notes, but we tend to use only three or four notes.

Exercise 7   Pitch

Practice reading each of the following sentences with consistently high pitch and then with consistently low pitch. Finally, read the sentence aloud with modulated pitch between high and low, but slightly on the low end of the scale.

MACBETH   Tomorrow and tomorrow creeps in this petty pace from day to day.
Macbeth by William Shakespeare

BERNARDA   I have to let them feel the weight of my hand.
The House of Bernarda Alba by Federico García Lorca

BRICK   Wouldn't it be funny if that was true?
Cat on a Hot Tin Roof by Tennessee Williams

Exercise 8   Range

To increase the notes in your vocal range, practice the following:

1. Sing the traditional musical scale:
   Do, re, mi, fa, sol, la, ti, do
2. Speak the following sentence aloud and correspond each note of the musical scale with a word in the sentence:

MACBETH   Life's but a walking shadow, a poor player.
Macbeth by William Shakespeare

Tone, Resonance, and Timbre

Tone refers to the quality of vocal sound and includes resonance and timbre which refer to a specific tone quality such as high, low, nasal, harsh, shrill, gutteral, and so on. Resonance is the proper amplification of tone. It relies upon the openness and flexible adjustment of the mouth and throat cavities. Resonance contributes to tone through the vibrating quality of the voice resulting from the proper use of the resonators (i.e., the throat cavity; the mouth, tongue, teeth; the nasal cavities; and the sinus cavities). If an actor wishes to improve his resonance, he may do so by practicing clear pronunciation, middle-register pitch, and clear projection of sound. Timbre reflects the peculiar or distinctive character of vocal tone—for example: squeaky, hoarse, mellow, and gravelly. A popular misconception holds that an actor must have a "pleasant, deep-sounding voice," or what used to be called a "radio voice." Actresses were supposed to have a somewhat higher, but mellow voice. The correct conception is that any tone quality can provide an effective acting voice if it is clear, well projected, and understood. Unusual tone quality such as gutteral or shrill can be highly useable and advantageous on stage. Tonal quality is not as important as *how* the voice is used.

Exercise 9 Tone, Resonance, and Timbre

1. To develop your resonance and timbre, prepare to speak by opening the mouth and throat. Now close the lips and produce the sound \ m \ as an easy hum at your medium-pitch level. Center the tone in your nasal cavities, but feel the vibrations at the front of the face and in the lips. Sustain your breath while making a sound. Repeat the exercise with the sounds \ n \ and \ng\. Now combine \m\, \n\, and \ng\ with vowel sounds. For example:

m-ah, m-o, m-u, m-a, m-e
n-ah, n-o, n-u, n-a, n-e
ng-ah, ng-o, ng-u, ng-a, ng-e

2. Intone a continuous series of vowels, changing smoothly and without break from one to the next: for example, \ oo\ as in *ooze*, \ o\ as in *ode*, \ aw\ as in *all*, \o\ as in *odd*, \ aw\ as in *alms*, \ ow \ as in *ounce*, \ a \ as in *add*. Control your breath during the sequence, opening the mouth freely to achieve maximum resonance.

3. Create an unusual vocal timbre such as nasality (e.g., force the sound into the nasal cavity). Speak several sentences from Exercise 6 aloud in nasal tone. Repeat the exercise without the nasality and note the difference between unpleasant and pleasant vocal timbre.

Vocal Variety

The ability to modulate or vary voice within a pleasant tone range creates a flexible vocal variety, as opposed to a monotone. A flexible voice creates vocal variety by effective use of inflection, intensity, rate or tempo, pause, and rhythm.

Inflection

Inflection is the rise and fall in pitch of the voice. Actors use inflection to shade feeling and meaning.

Exercise 10 Inflection

Practice reading the following sentences aloud providing a variety of inflections to shade feeling and meaning:

1. Were everyone for whom he did some loving service to bring a blossom to his grave he would sleep tonight beneath a wilderness of flowers.
   "At His Brother's Grave" by Robert Green Ingersoll

2. You shall not press down upon the brow of labor, this crown of thorns, you shall not crucify mankind upon a cross of gold.
   "Cross of Gold" by William Jennings Bryan

3. We have nothing to fear but fear itself.
   First Inaugural Address, Franklin Delano Roosevelt

4. Though passion may have strained, it must not break, our bonds of affection.
   First Inaugural Address, Abraham Lincoln

Intensity

The strength of feeling involved in the quality of speaking combined with manner determines the intensity of the voice. Intensity is the controlled vocal energy which reflects emotional tension.

Exercise 11   Intensity

Practice reading the following sentences with varying levels of tension and intensity generally applying increased or strong intensity:

1. The passage of these resolutions will show more clearly, more decisively, the deep indignation with which Boston regards this outrage.

   "Murder of Lovejoy" by Wendell Phillips

2. Crush the wretch. (Voltaire)

   "The Scholar in a Republic" by Wendell Phillips

3. Yesterday, December 7, 1941—a date which will live in infamy—the United States of America was suddenly and deliberately attacked by the Empire of Japan.

   "Declaration of War Against Japan," Franklin Delano Roosevelt

4. All they that take the sword shall perish with the sword.

   Matt. 26:52

Rate or Tempo

The speed with which one speaks determines rate or tempo.

Exercise 12   Rate or Tempo

Practice speaking the following sentences aloud with varied rate or tempo:

1. What are you going to do about that?

   Anonymous

2. Wally whirled westward with a winning way.

   Anonymous

3. [Speak] not as a Massachusetts man, nor as a Northern man, but as an American [man].

   Seventh of March Speech, 1850, Daniel Webster

4. Their foot shall slide in due time.

   Deut. 32:35

5. They are as great heaps of light chaff before the whirlwind; or large quantities of large stubble before devouring flames.

   "Sinners in the Hands of an Angry God" by Jonathan Edwards

Emphasis

Emphasis refers to the amount of stress, force, or vocal weight placed upon a particular word or words within a sentence to provide coloration and variety to the delivery. Proper use of emphasis greatly enhances meaning.

Exercise 13 Emphasis

Practice reading the following material aloud using different levels of emphasis on those words you consider important:

1. congratulations
   farewell
   good morning
   shut up
   come here
   never mind
   sensational
   terrible
   why not?

2. Let me pay the tribute which it is only just that I should pay to some of the men who have been, I believe, misunderstood in this business.
   "For the League of Nations" by Woodrow Wilson

3. Yet, after all, it may be best, just in the happiest, sunniest hour of all the voyage, while eager winds are kissing every sail, to dash against the unseen rock, and in an instant hear the billows roar, a sunken ship.
   "At His Brother's Grave" by Robert Green Ingersoll

4. Man thinking must not be subdued by his instruments. Books are for the scholar's idle times.
   "The American Scholar" by Ralph Waldo Emerson

5. The actions and events of our childhood and youth are not matters of calmest observation. They lie like fair pictures in the air.
   "The American Scholar" by Ralph Waldo Emerson

Pause

A brief suspension of the voice, or a hesitation in speech, is called a pause. We use pauses for emphasis, to divide thoughts, to permit a listener time to understand a point, to increase curiosity, and to breathe. In writing, commas, along with dashes, semicolons, and colons, denote the use of pauses. Periods usually indicate a full stop or a lengthy pause.

Exercise 14 Pause

Practice reading the following sentences aloud using appropriate pauses, indicated by punctuation or by your judgment or intuition:

1. We, too, have our religion and it is this: Help for the living—hope for the dead.
   "At a Child's Grave" by Robert Green Ingersoll

2. The loved and loving brother, husband, father, friend died where manhood's morning almost touches noon, and while the shadows still were falling toward the west.
   "At His Brother's Grave," by Robert Green Ingersoll

3. There was—there is—no gentler, stronger, manlier man.

"At His Brother's Grave" by Robert Green Ingersoll

4. With malice toward none, with charity for all, with firmness in the right as God gives us to see the right, let us strive on to finish the work we are in, to bind up the nation's wounds, to care for him who shall have borne the battle and for his widow and his orphan, to do all which may achieve and cherish a just and lasting peace among ourselves and with all nations.

Second Inaugural Address, Abraham Lincoln

Rhythm

The alteration of silence, sound, strength, and weakness in speech determines rhythm. Do not confuse rhythm with tempo or rate, which are parts of rhythm. Rhythm does not necessarily imply timing; it is rather a matter of accenting syllables. We create a rhythm when we speak as we combine pitch, range, inflection, intensity, rate, pause, and emotion.

Exercise 15   Rhythm

Practice reading the following material aloud, bringing your mind and emotions to bear in order to create a rhythm of speech:

1. O, what a noble mind is here o'erthrown!
The courtier's, soldier's, scholar's, eye, tongue, sword;
The expectency and rose of the fair state,
The glass of fashion and the mould of form,
The observed of all observers, quite, quite down!

OPHELIA, in *Hamlet* by William Shakespeare

2. Help me do the job in this autumn of conflict and campaign; help me do the job in these years of darkness, of doubt and of crisis which stretch beyond the horizon of tonight's happy vision, and we will justify our glorious past and the loyalty of silent millions who look to us for compassion, for understanding and for honest purpose.

Acceptance Speech, Adlai Stevenson

Articulation and Pronunciation: Vowels, Consonants and Diphthongs

Articulation refers to the correct utterance of sounds, particularly the clear speaking of vowels, consonants, and diphthongs. When people refer to speaking with good diction, they really mean using clear vocal articulation. Clear and accurate *articulation* leads to correct *pronunciation* of words. Pronunciation includes correct utterance of vowels and consonants with the proper accent on syllables. For example, the word *picture* is often mispronounced as the word *pitcher* \ pich-er \ when the consonants *c* and *t* are not struck. *Vowels* are soft sounds such as \ā\, \ē\, \ī\, \ō\, and \ū\. *Consonants* are often hard sounds, such as \d\, \t\, \b\, and \k\. They are also vibrating sounds, such as /m/, /n/ and /z/. Consonants are interpreters which make words intelligible, musical, varied, and energetic. While vowels are all voiced and give difficulty to few speakers, consonants are both voiced (such as, /g/, /d/, /n/, /b/, /w/, and /v/) and unvoiced (such as, /t/, /f/, /h/, /p/, /s/, and /k/). Voiced and unvoiced consonants utilize different means of vocal production, thereby causing difficulties for many speakers. Vowels provide melody to words and aid vocal rhythm, while consonants mostly provide emphasis. Misuse of consonants cause many errors in pronunciation. *Diphthongs* are compound vowel sounds produced by combining two simple vowels, such as "ou" in the word, "loud." Proper use of diphthongs is crucial to good speech and good stage vocal work.

The best way to learn proper pronunciation is to examine the structure of a word in a dictionary and to hear it pronounced correctly. Also the study of phonetics will assist in learning how to pronounce words correctly. The proper study of phonetics requires extensive time and detailed instruction by a qualified expert. Phonetics, like stage dialects, extends beyond the confines of a chapter on stage voice, speech, and language. Special symbols, diacritical marks, and the phonetic alphabet must be learned in the examination of words and the process of voice production. (For example, the phonetic symbol [æ] keys to the letter "a" in the word, "at" [æ+].) For further, detailed study, I refer you to books in the Suggested Reading list at the conclusion of this chapter (especially, see work by David Jones, Lyle Mayer, Charles Thomas, and Claude-Merten Wise).

Exercise 16   Articulation and Pronunciation of Difficult Words

Practice proper articulation and pronunciation of the following words which are often poorly articulated or mispronounced:

probably	zoology	throw	preferable
company	fat	vehicle	photo
athletic	can't	Saturday	burial
no	sure	pitcher	statistics
tenth	potato	homage	egg
get	tongue	pseudo	Pete
loose	because	that	water
comparable	just	often	lose
library	when	nose	February
Wednesday	what	guard	root
Tuesday	where	picture	pieced
asked	can	unanimity	Washington
decision	and	tomato	orange
Grandma	lend	poor	couldn't

Also practice the following short sentences and brief phrase which likewise are often poorly articulated or mispronounced:

Have you eaten?
Didn't you?
ladies and gentlemen
It keeps recurring.
Anyway, I think so.

Sing out, Voices! Tony Award winner, Ron Holgate, (c), leads the male singers in the hit musical, *Shenandoah*, at "At Evening" Theatre in Elmsford, New York. Directed by Lyle Dye, Jr. Sets by Michael Bottari, costumes by Ron Case.

Exercise 17   Consonant Drill

Practice striking consonants clearly in each of the following words:

fume	humdrum	zone
unison	zoom	flip-flop
imbibe	cobbler	omnipresent
lollipop	omnipotent	straggler
stockade	sound	unique
zig-zag	recognized	hugged
Antartic	packed	soothe
stopped	writhe	schtick
fifths	sixths	rouge
Oshkosh	beige	dungheap
garage	menage	engaged
hanged	pledged	husbands
itched	witchcraft	physicists
swords	precincts	whistle
when (pronounced,	wigwam	piano
"hwen")	terrorist	reread
wormwood	nature	needle
you	condone	
pure		

Exercise 18   Linking Consonants

Practice connecting final consonants into vowels and with nonrelated consonants:

breathe in	over all	catch on
run off	get out	boil over
what for	ask not	has been
take time	back with	that's bad

Exercise 19   Diphthong Drill

Practice clear use of diphthongs in the following words (beware of strong "r's" which will create two syllables and distort the word):

pear	pour	peer	poor
moist	row	sew	my

Projection

When he is dealing with spoken words, sentences, and thoughts, the foremost task of the actor is to speak loudly and clearly enough to make the audience both hear the words and understand the meaning behind the words of the playwright. The point also holds for nonscripted theatre activity if improvisational dialogue is involved. The most believable characterization work, the finest emotional creativity, and the most striking personality projection will not suffice if the entire audience cannot hear and understand an actor. Note the distinction between hearing and understanding. First of all, the voice must be heard; that is, the sound of the voice must be fully projected to everyone listening. Second, the audience must understand what it hears. For example, a strong, loud voice may carry sound to the back of a 2,000-seat auditorium, but if that sound is slurred or if words are pronounced incorrectly, the sound will be unintelligible. Effective vocal projection is directly related to good breathing as defined earlier in this chapter. Do not confuse projection with yelling or with speaking loudly. Even a *stage whisper* can be heard and understood at the rear of a large theatre if the actor is "projecting from the diaphragm," that is, using the entire breathing and vocal mechanism to project sound correctly. Projection is fundamental to acting and any kind of verbal performance. When an actor has difficulty with projection on stage, two specific techniques are recommended. First, practice speaking using a consistent tone. (Add vocal variety later, after the consistent tone is heard by listeners in all regions of the theatre or performance area.) Second, practice effective pronunciation and articulation. Use these two practice techniques without attempting characterization or emotion. Accordingly, mechanical skill and control of projected sounds, words, and sentences should improve.

Exercise 20 Projection

To improve your projection, practice speaking to a friend or teacher in a large auditorium or outside in a public place such as a park. Your friend or teacher should move from place to place as you practice conversing, reading, or reciting. Use a consistent tone with effective articulation and pronunciation. Resist the temptation to yell. Remember, projection is rarely a matter of loudness. It is rather a matter of sending the voice up and out clearly. Use any of the material given in the preceding exercises to practice projection. Be certain that your rate or tempo is not too rapid. In fact, an effective technique in projection includes deliberately slowing down at times. *Projection is also aided by refraining from excessive movement of the head while speaking.*

Voice Placement

The great voice teacher, Arthur Lessac, has described proper "voice placement" simply as that voice used with a lack of effort. One of the best ways to learn your correct voice placement is to practice exercises in which you deliberately use *poor* placement! This requires effort and quickly demonstrates through contrast how your voice should feel when you use it in a relaxed, normal, and natural way (hence, the *correct* way or the correct placement). Poor placement may include deliberate stammering, slurring, nasal effects, speaking through stiff lips, "curling" one side of your mouth and speaking just through that side, monotone expression, "waving" the voice up and down as though singing off-key, speaking through clenched teeth, speaking with a gutteral roughness, speaking with a high, squeaky pitch, hanging and moving your head as you speak, slumping grotesquely as you speak, sniffing-coughing-belching as you speak, "whining" as you speak, using a mock crying or sobbing noise as you speak, speaking with insufficient breath, speaking as you inhale or exhale, speaking while doing a physical exercise, and so on.

Exercise 21 Poor Voice Placement to Learn Good Voice Placement

Practice each of the improper uses of voice placement described above, using the following speeches from a famous dramatic character who "slaughtered" the English language:

"Illiterate him, I say, quite from your memory."
" 'Tis safest in matrimony to begin with a little aversion."
"Never say more than is necessary."
"I know you are laughing in your sleeve."
"He is the very pineapple of politeness!"
"If I reprehend anything in this world, it is the use of my oracular tongue, and a nice derangement of epitaphs!"
"An apothecary should never be out of spirits."

Mrs. Malaprop
The Rivals (1775) by
Sir Richard Brinsley Sheridan

Repeat these sentences with a lack of effort, relying solely on a natural speaking voice with clear articulation. You should subsequently locate good voice placement.

Phrasing and Context

Phrasing is speaking two or more words which comprise a pattern of thought or a unit of sense. Playwrights provide material which actors use for phrasing. Improvisational performers phrase their own dialogue. Effective use of all the vocal skills learned in this chapter enhance an actor's individual phrasing. At times, the author's material is altered and meaning is shaded by the quality of vocal skills applied to the phrasing by the actor. Phrasing is inextricably linked to context.

Context refers to the possibilities of meaning for each word in each sentence and extends to the possibilities of meaning for each sentence within each paragraph (or speech) in a play. To discover context an actor must understand the placement of each speech within each scene and, in turn, within an entire play. Proper analysis of character, thought, and structure in a play will permit an actor to determine how best to phrase dialogue. For example, Hamlet's famous line "To be or not to be, that is the question . . ." has almost infinite possibilities for vocal phrasing. How actors phrase that line determines their interpretation. The line can be spoken flatly with no feeling or delivered as a question, superimposing new punctuation on it. Phrasing the line flatly without feeling connotes despair and suicide. Phrasing the line as a question connotes bewilderment concerning the nature of death as it relates to action. If the former contextual phrasing and interpretation are used, vocal work stresses slow rate, extensive use of pause, precise accents, and low, modulated, resonant tone to help evoke a somber mood. If the second contextual phrasing and interpretation are used, vocal work stresses rapid rate, infrequent use of pause, softer accents, and a higher, intensified, and less resonant tone to help evoke an excited but confused mood.

The importance of contextual understanding cannot be overemphasized if we are to apply effective phrasing and vocal technique in the theatre. The clearest and most pleasant speaking voice is rendered worthless if words and speeches are not placed into context.

Exercise 22 Phrasing and Context

1. Practice phrasing the following three words with as many different interpretations as possible:

   avalanche of hate

2. Now practice phrasing the three words within the context of a full sentence:

   What an avalanche of hate you've thrown on my heart.

3. Finally, practice phrasing the sentence within the context of a complete dramatic speech:

> BERNARDA I saw the storm coming, but I didn't think it would burst so soon. Oh, what an avalanche of hate you've thrown on my heart. But I'm not old yet. I have five chains for you and this house my father built. So not even the weeds will know of my desolation.
>
> *The House of Bernarda Alba* by Federico García Lorca

Physical Reinforcement of the Verbal

Verbal communication with an audience may be clearly heard and understood and still not be interesting or dramatic. Most vocal work on stage requires visual and emotional reinforcement and accompanying physicalization to elevate it above the level of information. Word meanings are not always precise; even when they are, they may be mundane. How do actors refine meanings to make them precise and how do they make the mundane interesting? They can accomplish much of this by using physical reinforcement of speech. Such reinforcement can enhance meaning and provoke interest.

Used discreetly and appropriately, physical hand gestures, facial gestures, and gestures from any part or all of the body can contribute immeasurably to vocal work on stage.

Teresa Gilmore and Grey Schmidt demonstrate physical reinforcement of vocalization. Photograph by Randy Tunnel.

Adding physical activity to reinforce words can also help clarify imprecise meaning. For example, imagine that a young man is talking to his mother in the living room. He wants to use the family car. The mother is convinced by the argument and calls the father into the room. She glances up at her husband, turns smilingly to her son, and says, "We've decided you can have the car tonight." The father, observing that she is looking at the son when she speaks, glances confusedly around and asks, "Who's 'we'?" The mother points to the father with one hand and touches herself with the other hand. Anyone watching now knows the identity of "we." On the stage, this type of physical clarification often makes words precise. Actors in plays are continually gesturing and pantomimically reinforcing language. An actor may have a line such as "He was this tall." Obviously the actor must pantomimically demonstrate how tall the man was if the line is to have any precise meaning. Also, actors must create something beyond clichéd gesture in striving for ways to physicalize.

Physicalizing with the hands, the face, or any part or all of the body can rarely be directed by a playwright, a director, or an artist-leader. Physicalization is fundamentally the actor's responsibility. Physicalization can rarely be superimposed on an actor; it should come from within, from personal needs and motivations. Personalization is vital to individual physicalization. Later, personalization can be intermingled with the needs and motivations of a *character* if a script is involved. Of course, it is the responsibility of the director to help actors see the possibilities for physicalization.

All physicalization must emanate from a center or primary energy source of a person. That is, the right arm cannot just pop out from the shoulder on its own and do something. A unified activity must be operative. In physicalization a part always functions within a whole. The process is organic. Naturally, character and emotion are included in that whole. In other words, character, emotion, energy, mind, and body all combine to create appropriate, dramatic physical behavior that reinforces speech. (For example, the next time you have a strong emotional experience, recall exactly what you did physically immediately upon its conclusion. You may discover how emotion was vented through physical behavior as it reinforced what you said.) Again, a word of caution concerning excessive head movement when speaking. The clearest speakers usually move very little.

Exercise 23 Physical Reinforcement of the Verbal

Memorize the following material and practice delivering it with a variety of appropriate physical activities including hand, face, and body gestures. Try to use physicalization to explicate meaning, clarify motivation, and reinforce emotion.

THE DEVIL   In the arts of peace Man is a bungler. I have seen his cotton factories and the like, with machinery that a greedy dog could have invented if it had wanted money instead of food. I know his clumsy typewriters and bungling locomotives and tedious bicycles: They are toys compared to the

Maxim gun, the submarine torpedo boat. There is nothing in Man's industrial machinery but his greed and sloth: his heart is in his weapons. This marvellous force of Life of which you boast is a force of Death: Man measures his strength by his destructiveness.

"Don Juan in Hell" from *Man and Superman*
by George Bernard Shaw

Dialects and Regional Accents

As with phonetics, voice training in special *dialects* and *regional accents* require concentrated, lengthy study under the instruction of a qualified expert in such work. For example, Californian Jerry Blunt, now retired, is one of America's foremost experts in the specialized area of vocal training. His books, *Stage Dialects* and *More Stage Dialects*, with accompanying tapes, provide a rich resource for the study of dialects. While extensive explication of stage dialects should only be undertaken in advanced training in acting, a fun exercise is introduced here to "whet the appetite" of the young actor.

Exercise 24   Stage Dialects for Fun

Everyone has heard various vocal dialects and regional accents through association with family and friends, travel, and listening to good actors as they perform on the stage, film, and television. Relying strictly on memory, raw imitation, and instinct, try the following dialects and accents on the speeches printed below (note where you seem to have surprising success, as well as where you are obviously far afield; these notations may serve you well when you one day begin specific training in this fun and challenging endeavor):

American Southern	Russian	Australian
French	Welsh	New York City
English cockney	Mexican	Utah
Swedish	American Indian	Greek
Hebrew/Yiddish/Jewish	Chicano	Polish
Irish	Caribbean (Puerto	African
German	Rican)	Boston
British	Arabian	Ozark
Oriental	Chicago	Oklahoma
Scottish	Southwest (Texas	Cajun
Italian	Panhandle)	(Others of your choice
	Midwest (Iowa/	or familiarity)
	Missouri)	
	East Indian	

"I believe there are more instances of the abridgement of the freedom of the people by gradual and silent encroachments of those in power than by violent and sudden usurpations."

James Madison
Speech in the Virginia
Convention, June 16, 1788

"Fie, fie upon her!
There's language in her eye, her cheek, her lip,
Nay, her foot speaks; her wanton spirits look out
At every point and motive of her body."

Ulysses
Troilus and Cressida by
William Shakespeare

Continued practice and extension of the exercises in this chapter should provide a sound basis for an effective speaking voice in the theatre. Serious students of acting practice vocal exercises daily as part of their habitual professional routine.

Suggested Readings

Andersch, Elizabeth; Staats, Lorin; and Bostrom, Robert. *Communication in Everyday Use.* 3rd ed. New York: Holt, Rinehart & Winston, 1969.

Anderson, Virgil. *Training the Speaking Voice.* New York: Oxford University Press, 1961.

Bachner, Loris. *Dynamic Singing.* New York: Hill & Wang, 1944.

Balk, H. Wesley. *The Complete Singer-Actor. Training for Music Theater.* Minneapolis: University of Minnesota Press, 1977.

Bairstow, Edward C., and Greene, Harry Plunket. *Singing Learned From Speech.* New York: St. Martins, n.d.

Bender, J. F. *NBC Handbook of Pronunciation.* New York: Crowell, 1955.

Berry, Cicely. *Voice and the Actor.* New York: MacMillan, 1973.

Blunt, Jerry. *Stage Dialects.* San Francisco: Chandler Publishing Co., 1967 (with accompanying tapes).

———. *More Stage Dialects.* New York: Harper & Row, 1980 (with accompanying tapes).

Brigance, William N., and Henderson, Florence, *A Drill Manual for Improvising Speech.* New York: J. B. Lippincott Co., 1939.

Buehler, E. Christian, and Linkugel, Wil. *Speech Communication.* New York: Harper & Row, 1969.

Chriest, Fred M. *Foreign Accent.* Englewood Cliffs, N.J.: Prentice-Hall, 1964.

Craig, David. *On Singing On Stage.* Riverside, New Jersey: Schimmer Books, 1978.

Denes, Peter P., and Pinson, Elliot N. *The Speech Chain.* Garden City, New York: Doubleday, 1973.

Dodds, George. *Voice Placing and Training Exercises.* New York: Oxford University Press, 1927.

Eisenson, Jon. *Voice and Diction.* 3d ed. New York: Macmillan Co., 1974.

Fairbanks, Grant. *Voice and Articulation Drillbook.* New York: Harper & Row, 1940–61.

Hahn, Elise, et al. *Basic Voice Training for Speech.* New York: McGraw-Hill, 1957.

Hall, E. T. *The Silent Language.* Garden City, N.Y.: Doubleday & Co., 1959.

Herman, Louis, and Lewis, Margaret. *Manual of Foreign Dialects.* New York: Theatre Arts Books, 1958.

———. *American Dialects.* New York: Theatre Arts Books, 1947.

Jones, Daniel. *An Outline of English Phonetics.* London: Albert Saifer, 1957.

Kenyon, John S. and Knott, Thomas A. *A Pronouncing Dictionary of American English.* Springfield, Mass.: Merriam, 1944.

Lee, Charlotte. *Oral Communication.* Boston: Houghton Mifflin Co., 1959.

Lessac, Arthur. *The Use and Training of the Human Voice.* New York: Drama Book Specialists/Publishers, 1967.

Linklatter, Kristin. *Freeing the Natural Voice*. New York: DBS Publishers, 1976.

Machlin, Evangeline. *Speech for the Stage*. New York: Theatre Arts Books, 1970.

Mayer, Lyle V. *Fundamentals of Voice and Diction*. 3rd ed. Dubuque, Iowa: Wm. C. Brown Company Publishers, 1968.

Powers, Leland. *Practice Book*. Boston: Thomas Groom & Co., 1913.

Reid, Cornelius L. *Voice: Psyche and Soma*. New York: J. Patelson Music, 1975.

Rubin, Lucille S. *Stage Voice Training in the London Schools*. Unpublished mimeograph document, 1978. (Author: c/o Voice Faculty, Circle-in-the-Square, New York.)

Thomas, Charles. *Phonetics of American-English*. New York: Ronald Press, 1958.

Thompson, D. F., and Meltzer, L. "Communication of Emotional Intent by Facial Expression." *Journal of Abnormal and Social Psychology* 68 (1964):129–35.

Tolch, Charles J. "The Problem of Language and Accuracy in Identification of Facial Expression." *Central States Speech Journal*, February 1963, pp. 12–16.

Trusler, Ivan and Ehret, Walter. *Functional Lessons in Singing*. Englewood-Cliffs, N.J.: Prentice-Hall, 1960.

Turner, J. Clifford. Foreward by British actress Peggy Ashcroft. *Voice and Speech for the Theatre*. London: Isaac Pitman & Sons, 1950.

Vetter, Harold J. *Language Behavior and Communication*, Itasco, Ill.: F. E. Peacock Publishers, 1969.

Wise, Claude-Merten. *Applied Phonetics*. Englewood Cliffs, N.J.: Arc Books, 1963.

(NOTE: for valuable pamphlets and information related to voice science, performance, and medicine, write to:

> The Voice Foundation
> 320 Park Avenue
> New York, New York 10022
> Telephone: (202) 688–1897)

(SPECIAL NOTE TO SINGERS AND MUSICAL THEATRE PERFORMERS: I especially recommend careful study in David Craig's book, *On Singing On Stage*. Craig is one of the foremost specialists in this field, a coach of unique talents and skills. His students are numbered among the leading stage performers in the world theatre. His book explicates many of his theories and exercises, such as how to use improvisation and pantomime to dramatize both text and subtext in song lyrics. Craig's working studio is in Los Angeles, California.)

8 Scene Study and Practice: Character Work in Scenes from Plays

Teresa Gilmore and Grey
Schmidt demonstrate
SCENE STUDY AND
PRACTICE: CHARACTER
WORK IN SCENES
FROM PLAYS.
Photograph by Randy
Tunnel.

The exercise activity now graduates from work in basic acting techniques to work with the collaborative artist known as the playwright who provides the basis for most dramatic characterization. To create characterization an actor should analyze what the author has written using a detailed procedure known as *role analysis*. Role analysis is best applied to the creation of a complete role in a one-act or full-length play meant to be performed before an audience (role analysis is treated in detail in chapter 10). Work with a character in an extracted scene is less detailed because in class or studio experience one need use only five to ten minutes of the author's written role.

This chapter will provide two efficient, proven approaches to scene study; one approach involves work with four basic acting techniques. The second approach involves following seven simple steps of scene preparation. Both of these approaches are similar and comparable; you may combine elements of both approaches or try each and decide which approach best serves your individual needs.

Selecting a Scene from a Play

Selecting an effective cutting from a play for scene practice is often a difficult task. Many scenes are available in published form in most bookstores (the Suggested Readings at the end of the chapter lists some of the popularly used scene books). If you use a library copy of a play as the acting script, do not mark in it. If a scene is extracted or cut from a play, make certain that it is at least five to ten minutes in length and that it is a manageable scene relatively complete within itself. Select a scene that seems to have interesting character work and emotional content within your current state of development (an instructor or coach can assist in assessing that development). Generally avoid intensely emotional scenes because an extracted form usually provides insufficient time to build much emotion. Select a character within your present basic age range and physical characteristics. Later in more advanced work it will be possible to select characters outside your age and physical type. It is also preferable to select a scene from a modern realistic play and to advance later to nonrealistic and classical styles. Select a play from personal knowledge of dramatic literature; if your experience in this respect is limited, ask your instructor or coach for recommendations (sample scenes in realism are provided in chapter 16 and at the end of this chapter, and recommended characters and plays for scene playing are given at the end of all chapters on style). It is usually a good idea to select scenes with two characters for beginning work.

Four Techniques to Prepare a Scene

Four basic techniques suffice to create a character for an extracted scene: personalization, visualization, pantomimic dramatization, and character motivation. These techniques aid in creating a sufficiently believable character. A more important aspect of scene acting is to practice the acting skills learned to date such as movement, emotion, observation, imagination, use of past experiences, use of the senses, work with objects, improvisation, and vocalization. Acting in an extracted scene requires only moment-to-moment performance skill, with minimal reference to the entire role in the complete play. Full-scale role analysis is an intellectual process, entailing research and study as discussed in chapter 10. There is a time for an actor to be a thinker. However, in initial character work in scenes the actor should also rely upon an intuitive factor and upon the exercise skills learned to this point. He should learn to trust the moment-to-moment action of a scene. He should also learn to trust character relationships in brief scenes. Were actors to do all the intellectual work involved in analysis of a complete role in preparation for a role in an extracted scene, that intellectual work would probably hinder rather than help—he might be thinking rather than doing. Later, with scene practice accomplished, he will be better equipped to do extensive intellectual work and apply it to a complete role without losing the intuitive physical and emotional effort necessary to effective acting. To put it another way: It is well to learn to walk before you run.

(l) Personalization and Character in a Scene

Basic fundamentals again apply. Relaxation and effective breathing are paramount if you are to comfortably approach initial work with author characterization. Remember, for the most part the role will be the *person* of the actor. Character development based on role analysis of a complete play is virtually impossible in most five-to-ten-minute scenes. Accept this fact and utilize personalization with confidence and comfort. An exercise in personalization should assist you in preparing for character work in scenes.

Exercise 1 Human Contact from Personal Resources

Two actors create an improvisation in which neither actor is to speak without making physical contact with the other one. Every time a new line of dialogue or new thought is introduced, a corresponding physical contact should be made by each actor. Only the actor who introduces the vocal line is to make the physical contact. Vocal sounds and noises do not necessitate physical contact.

This exercise is rooted almost totally in honest personality characteristics and automatically develops close communication between actors. It also provides a creative base for characterization because vocalizing requires some intellectual structuring related to instinctive physical activity. Mixing the vocal and the physical in this exercise increases dramatic tension onstage. This exercise relates personal activity to the rudiments of dramatic activity; that is, it relates the actor's *person* to the dramatic situation and conflict, thereby providing the roots of characterization.

Exercise 2   Autobiography

Sit in a relaxed manner with your scene partner. Take turns relating a short autobiography in which you explain where you were born, the various places you have lived, where you received your education, how many people are in your family, the nature of your career goals, and so on. The more you know about one another, the better you can personalize when you begin the scene work.

(II) Visualization and Character in a Scene

Visualization refers to a character's appearance including both the physical being and the dress. While the actor's person provides automatic visualization for much of the character in a scene, the playwright usually obligates an actor to add other visual elements to enhance basic characterization. For example, a character may be required to limp due to a physical deformity in one leg, as is true of Laura in Tennessee Williams' *The Glass Menagerie*. Similarly, a character such as Howard in Arthur Miller's *Death of a Salesman* may be obligated to wear a business suit.

An interesting use of visualization is for an actor to imaginatively relate himself and his role to the characteristics of an inanimate object. For example, he could observe the tall, clean lines of a Greek vase and incorporate such characteristics into his posture, movement, and activity. This technique is beneficial, for example, in portrayal of a king or queen or a head of state.

It is similarly helpful to use selected characteristics of animal behavior in visualizing a character in a scene. Try to use an animal with characteristics analogous to the role under study. For example, the crude, snorting activity of a pig as it eats in a feedlot might provide visual characteristics for activity in a boorish eating scene.

In Exercise 3 the elements of visualization just described are combined to provide valuable preparatory training to character work in a scene. Remain flexible and imaginative throughout this exercise.

Exercise 3   Visualization: the Animal and the Auction

Recline on a firm surface and establish relaxation and effective breathing. Concentrate only on a specific animal image such as an elephant and its physical attributes and movement (be certain that you select an animal you are familiar with, one that will not require extensive research). When the animal image is vivid in your mind, rise to your feet and begin moving about in the manner of the animal you selected. Place emphasis on bone structure, rhythm of movement, and facial expressiveness. After a period of time, the instructor will ask you to stop your animal movement and take a relaxed standing position. Walk comfortably in your own manner; then subtly add key characteristics of your animal to your activity. Emphasize bone structure, rhythm, and facial expression again, but try to wed them to your own attributes, dropping out the more excessive imitative factors. You may also use noises or sounds made by the animal.

Teresa Gilmore and Grey Schmidt demonstrated Exercise 3: "Animal Postures" (utilizing animals as a basis for visualization of character). Photograph by Randy Tunnel.

Later your instructor will announce your arrival at a specific place in the room or theatre to attend an auction of furniture and household goods. All of you are to be bidders at the auction. The auctioneer is imaginary. Each of you bids on an object with your private concept of what is being sold. You have the discretion of continuing the bidding, withdrawing from it, or concluding it with certainty that you have purchased the object. The vocal and physical work you have done with your animal should be apparent in your manner as you bid.

As you continue to bid, discard the animal characteristics and assume the characteristics of the object being sold. For example, if you are bidding for a short, squat cast-iron cooking pot, emulate similar physical characteristics as you bid.

Exercise 4   You, a Photo, and Your Character

Locate a photograph of a person who seems to resemble your concept of the character you are going to create; sit in front of a mirror and study your face and the photo. Adjust your hair and expressions to match the photo. Use this study to assist your early scene practice.

(III) Pantomimic Dramatization and Character in a Scene

Pantomime and *mime* are specialized kinds of theatre performances or exercises and are considered in their proper place in chapter 12, Commedia Dell'Arte. *Pantomimic dramatization*, as it is used here as a beginning acting technique in scene work in the class or studio, implies more than *pantomime*, which is action without words (what used to be called *dumb show*) and more even than *mime*, which is the imitating of scenes from life (usually as travesty or satire and usually without dialogue). *Pantomimic dramatization* is used here to refer to the process of discovering, creating, and using personalized physical action, or business, as it relates to objects. Effective pantomimic dramatization enriches, vitalizes, and adds distinction to the visual and physical impact of actors and their roles. The physical action may come from any part of the body or from all of it. For example, imagine an actress performing Blanche DuBois in Tennessee William's *A Streetcar Named Desire.* In a particular scene, Blanche breaks into sobbing hysteria following verbal and physical abuse from Mitch. Most young actresses have difficulty playing this scene believably. Pantomimic dramatization can greatly assist the effectiveness of acting this scene. Specifically, the actress could clutch a large pillow to her body, bury her face in it, and rock slowly from side to side. This clear visual action could be far more effective than artificial sounds of sobbing and violent screaming. The actress may not have to make a sound, or at best a muffled one into the pillow, to project the correct emotion.

Pantomimic dramatization requires an actor to use his imagination to determine what to do physically and visually while on stage. Exercise 5 assists you in learning how to arrive at that determination (pantomimic dramatization is used again in chapter 10 in developing role creation in a complete play).

Exercise 5   Pantomimic Dramatization and Characters

Select a role in one of the following scenes. Discover and create personalized physical action or business related to objects used in the scene. Write a list of all created action; then practice the scene and incorporate your pantomimic dramatization.

Elma and Grace   opening scene, Act I
   Bus Stop by William Inge
Laura and Jim   Scene viii
   The Glass Menagerie by Tennessee Williams
Willy and Linda   opening scene, Act II
   Death of a Salesman by Arthur Miller
Maggie and Brick   opening scene, Act I
   Cat on a Hot Tin Roof by Tennessee Williams
Biff and Happy   bedroom scene, Act I
   Death of a Salesman by Arthur Miller
Millie and Madge   opening scene, Act II
   Picnic by William Inge

Mel and Edna   beginning of Act II, Scene i
   Prisoner of Second Avenue by Neil Simon
George and Martha   opening scene, Act I
   Who's Afraid of Virginia Woolf? by Edward Albee

Exercise 6   Pantomimic Dramatization and Masks

Buy or make one or more facial masks which represent a variety of unusual human countenances. Sit in front of a mirror and study each mask. Create an imaginary autobiography for each mask. Practice pantomimic dramatization which seems appropriate to each mask and its autobiography. (Note: the term "autobiography" is used rather than "biography" to motivate you to link the mask to your own life, thereby aiding the factor of personalization.)

(IV) Motivation and Character in a Scene

The fourth element for successful acting in scenes is discovering or inventing valid motivations, or reasons, wants, needs, and desires, for everything done on the stage. The character should not seem to be arbitrary; that is, the audience should be able to recognize the purpose behind the behavior of the character. At times, the motivating factor will have occurred at some point in the play prior to the scene being performed. However, because it is generally not necessary to analyze the role in the complete play to perform effectively in a scene, the actor may have to invent appropriate motivation for some of the action. At other times, the motivation may be within the scene itself (incidentally, when a role in a complete play is analyzed, motivation is established in the same two ways: by situations provided in the script and by invented factors not readily apparent in the play; i.e., subtext). This procedure simplifies the acting task by restricting analysis to the perspective of an extracted scene. To further assist your work involved with motivation and character, I have devised what I call a "Short Form Role Analysis Document." Students in my acting classes use these to great advantage. A sample of this short form may be found in Appendix D.

Note: Instructors and actors who prefer a more extensive approach to role analysis in extracted scenes, naturally are privileged to apply all of the procedures described in chapter 10 to this work in scene acting. (See the seventeen steps of role analysis.) Also, you may wish to use some of the *scene combing* techniques described in chapter 10 in your work with extracted scenes. For example, playing *opposite values* is an effective motivation and emotion technique to use in extracted scenes. If the script clearly calls for anger, play love or happiness as the emotion in place of it. In other words, determine the motivation and its related emotion and reverse the values. The purpose of this technique is to avoid rigidly setting a motivation and an emotion too early in rehearsal. The technique also permits further exploration of motivational and emotional values in a character prior to their final selection for performance. Beginning stage performers frequently become stymied in the middle of a rehearsal period and need fresh or revitalized motivation. Playing opposite values is both fun and a beneficial technique for revitalization. It is helpful in classroom and studio scene acting, as well as in regular production rehearsal of a complete play.

Exercise 7 aids in the discovery and invention of motivation as preparation for scene work.

Exercise 7   Motivation

The entire group takes a position onstage, standing or seated as desired. The dramatic situation is that the group is locked in a room for an indefinite period of time and must pass the time waiting for release. No one may wait in total silence; as often as possible speaking must be included in the improvisational exercise. Your task is to find ways to pass the time without saying or doing things arbitrarily. In other words, all activity (both physical and vocal) must be truthfully and honestly motivated. Your instructor is to observe this improvisation carefully and may drop a person from the scene if that person appears to be "acting" or "performing without motivation." This exercise requires intense moment-to-moment concentration. The dramatic situation provides the possibility for motivational discovery. It also provides enormous possibility for invented motivation. The exercise concludes when the instructor has either removed everyone from the activity because of unmotivated work, or when the instructor announces that the waiting period has ended. (Note that this exercise also enhances work in believable and truthful stage activity.)

Exercise 8   Motivation through Understanding of the "Other" Character

Sit with your scene partner in a relaxed manner. Explain to your partner what you know about the character your *partner* is performing; explain what you think your partner's character *wants* in the scene and *why* he or she wants it. Your partner then reciprocates. When each is finished, comment on the observations heard. Are they correct and revealing? Why or why not?

Seven Steps to Heaven: A Simplified Approach to Preparing a Scene for Performance in a Class, Laboratory, or Studio

Another or second approach to preparing a scene for performance in a class, laboratory or studio involves seven simplified steps which can lead to a happy or "heavenly" conclusion. Before trying these steps, the actor should first observe a few fundamental "guidelines." (a) Read the entire play from which your scene is selected. (b) It is a good idea to do each of the steps a minimum of sixty minutes. (Use about two hours for Step 4.) (c) Keep a personal log or diary of all rehearsals and performances. This will aid you in your "homework" and in your post-performance evaluation. (d) Complete a "Short-Form Role Analysis Document" after completion of Step 4 (see Appendix D). (e) Do not *force* line memorization and do not try to learn lines at the very beginning of the rehearsal period. Let the lines become assimilated into memory over the initial half of the rehearsal period. (f) Do not over-structure and "set" blocking or movement patterns too early in the rehearsal period. Let the movement evolve naturally out of your behavior and activity as you work with simplified representations of furniture and hand properties. (g) Use costume and hand prop items from the beginning of rehearsals; at least, use facsimiles of actual props. Avoid pantomimic work which becomes an art in itself and usually mitigates against naturalness and believability.

The Seven Steps:

1. Accomplish information read-throughs of the scene, using as many as are needed, but at least two or three. Do not exert "effort" or try to "act" the scene at all; do not *work* for characterization or emotion, rather relying on any that might naturally result from your own person. Simply gather information and facts from the text and discuss these with your partner. (What time of day and season is it? What is the weather like in the scene? What is your character wearing? What has happened just prior to this scene? And so on.)

2. Accomplish several "communion" read-throughs of the scene (e.g., "communion" in the sense of intimate inter-personal communication). Use maximum eye contact even if it necessitates reading slowly and paraphrasing. Touch your partner whenever it seems comfortable and natural to do so.

3. Improvise the scene in your own words with free movement and activity. This is a "talk-and-walk-through" rehearsal. You should reveal all the information you learned in Step 1. Focus on covering all the subjects and issues used in the scene by the playwright. Do not consciously try to use the actual lines from the script, although occasionally you may be amazed at how many lines are already becoming part of your memory.

4. Freely explore the scene with script in hand. This process is called "organic combing" or searching for fresh ways to perform each moment of the scene. For example, perform the scene many times with a *single intention* each time. That is, perform it once concentrating solely on the weather and climate. Another time try eating and drinking something throughout the scene; perform it in a value *opposite* to that which seems to be called for in the script (if it is a love scene, perform it as a hate scene, and so on); practice all entrances and exits in several different ways; reverse roles with your partner and see what revelations occur; play music as you do the scene and compare the scene with a painting, sculpture, dances, and so on. Perform drills bearing on all special problem activity in the scene (such as, vocal dialects; limps and handicaps; kisses and love activity; slaps and fighting; nudity; violence; special object and hand prop work; and so on). (Remember, after Step 4, complete the "Short-Form Role Analysis Document;" refer to Appendix D.)

5. Set the movement patterns and set all "business" (some directors call this "setting the blocking" and "scoring" or orchestrating/finalizing all hand prop activity). Make final character and emotion decisions (choices and discarding).

6. Perform the scene several times without interruption to accomplish a sense of fluidity, a flow, or a "rhythm" (e.g., a smooth combination of tempo or speed and timing with the proper mood and emotional work). All simplified "technical" items are now realized, such as minimal use of performance costumes, props, furniture, and makeup (if used, which is rare in scene practice). Stage lighting is also rarely used in scene work. Step 6 involves full use of characterization and emotion.

7. Perform a couple final "polish" runthroughs of the scene (ideally with someone observing, taking and giving notes). "Preview" the scene in front of a few persons, if possible. Thereafter, perform the scene in front of a class, audience, instructor, or coach. Ideally, the performance (or performances) is followed by a written self-evaluation in your log. Any revisions in the "Short-Form Role Analysis Document" are accomplished. Finally, the class, audience, instructor, or coach may discuss and evaluate the performance and offer suggestions for further work.

A Word of Caution

While personalization is the free use of the self as far as is honestly and comfortably possible, and while it includes close interaction with other actors during the scene or play, it does not mean that actors must make intimate emotional commitment with fellow players. A friendly, cooperative manner is vital in acting, but in-depth offstage, personal involvement with colleagues usually creates obstacles to believable onstage work. Noted actor, Dustin Hoffman, who uses personalization so well as an actor, makes the latter point:

I always play it cool. I never get involved with anybody while I'm making a movie or doing a play. And I mean anybody. There's no question that you're bound to lose out if there are emotional commitments; people saying "Oh, let's not do it this way, let's do it this other way." People can use friendship as a lever to get you to alter what you believe in. So when I'm making a movie I don't socialize with the cast. I don't go to dinner with them. After the day's work is done I go home. . . . But suppose I'd just done a picture with a girl? I don't think you should go out and have an affair with a girl just because you're doing a love story with her. You know what? If you've been doing it in a hotel room, you aren't saving it for the camera, and on film your big love scene looks like a frozen fish dinner.[1]

1. Tom Donnelly, "Hoffman Makes His Minor 'Papillon' Role Major," *Las Vegas Review-Journal*, 9 January, 1974.

In effect, Hoffman is saying in rather stark terms that personalization is not a license for undisciplined, self-indulgent behavior. It is a system of acting and an approach to role creation and performance.

Personalization will rarely take an actor completely through the creation of a role. At some point, he will be unable to produce or perform an emotion or action. Some kind of traditional acting technique is needed. Such techniques as observation, imagination, emotional-sensory recall (dormant emotion), pantomimic dramatization, and improvisation have all been discussed; any one or all of these techniques can be put to use as part of or an extension of personalization.

A major misunderstanding frequently exists among directors and performers concerning "personalization" and "organic activity." The misunderstanding occurs when directors or performers believe that personalization should carry actors completely into performance without benefit of commanded direction of any sort. Personalization and organic activity do *not* imply *total* freedom and nondirection. Rather, the terms imply a restricted period of time early in rehearsals during which the actor may become comfortable and freely express movement and actions. *The actor is not forced to create character and emotion or learn lines and blocking too soon.* By all means, a director should and must guide and eventually refine or even command certain aspects of performance as rehearsals progress to the halfway point or beyond. The coaching staff at the Actor's Studio in New York is particularly adept at promoting and guiding personalization and organic activity. At the New York Studio, I observed Lee Strasberg, Frank Corsaro, Vivian Nathan, Salem Ludwig, Ellen Burstyn, and Eli Wallach, among others, guiding actors through such work. Many of our leading directors promote creativity through personalization and organic techniques. Gerald Freedman, Barry Kyle, Robert Benedetti, and Marshall W. Mason are four such directors. The work of each man has been influential upon me and many others.

Standard Acting Terms

As rehearsals progress toward performance, knowledge of standard terms related to acting and the physical theatre become necessary. The following terminology and definitions are given here for the actor's convenience and assistance during rehearsal of characters in scenes. Note that some of the terms are defined further in the Glossary at the end of this book.

Acting Area

The traditional proscenium stage is generally divided as shown in the accompanying diagram.

The traditional arena stage (central stage) is generally divided according to the accompanying diagram.

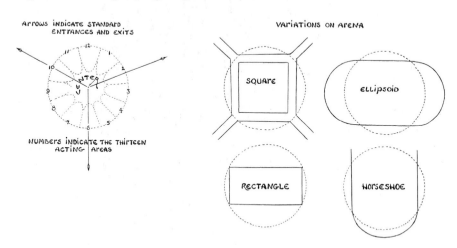

The basic acting areas of arena staging.

Acting Positions

Full-front The actor faces the audience fully. This is a very strong position, but can be sustained for long periods of time only in nonrealistic plays and musicals.

Full-back The actor stands with his full back to the audience. Used for special dramatic effect, the position is also very strong, but should generally be sustained only for brief periods of time.

One-quarter The actor stands in a quarter turn away from the audience, usually facing another actor. This is a strong position, but less so than full-front. The position increases in strength when the actor makes the one-quarter turn toward the audience rather than away from it. This position can be sustained for the longest period of time in realistic plays.

Profile or One-half Turn The actor stands facing either right or left with his profile in view of the audience. Rarely a strong position, this stance is also used for comic effect.

Three-quarters In this position the actor nearly turns his full back with less than one side of his head and a shoulder toward the audience. This is the weakest of the five basic acting positions.

Rehearsal Terms

Stage Business Small, detailed actions of the body (often the hands) such as drinking from a cup, lighting a cigar, mopping the brow, and so on.

Properties Physical objects used on stage by the actor. The term is usually shortened to *props*. There are four classifications of props:

1. Hand props: Small objects which actors can carry or handle onstage such as books, drinking glasses, and the like.
2. Personal props: Items on the actor's person such as eyeglasses, jewelry, key chain, and the like.
3. Costume props: Costume accessories such as fans, gloves, handkerchiefs, and the like.
4. Stage props: Major objects related to the physical scene such as stools, pillows, lamps, furniture, and the like.

(The four classifications are interchangeable, depending on how the props are used.)

Ad lib From the Latin *ad libitum* ("at pleasure"), the term applies to lines supplied by the actor when they are lacking in the script, but desired in the production (or lines invented when the actor has forgotten the memorized lines).

Aside A line onstage directed to the audience which is not supposed to be heard by other characters.

Build An increase in speed or volume in order to reach a climactic theatrical moment.

Cue The last word or words of a speech or the end of an action which indicates the time for another actor to speak or move.

Drop The drop in volume on the last word or words of a speech.

Pickup Cue A direction given to actors to avoid undesirable time lapses between lines or action.

Top Delivery of a line or lines with more volume and intensity than the line preceding it or them.

Terms Related to Movement or Blocking

If personalization works correctly, little or no marking of the script in terms of movement or blocking will be necessary. However, blocking may be marked in the script at an early rehearsal. Following are some of the commonly used notations.

Terms for Proscenium Stage

D	Downstage (forward; toward audience)
U	Upstage (back; away from audience)
L	Stage left (any area left of the performer when facing the audience)
R	Stage right (any area right of the performer when facing the audience)
C	Center stage (the approximate middle of the acting area)

(Variations should be self-evident. For example, *UL* indicates upstage left of the acting area.)

Terms for Arena or Central Stage

C	Center stage (the approximate middle of the acting area—the thirteenth area)
Twelve o'clock	Arbitrarily established point of the acting area analogous to the number twelve on a clock (all other eleven acting areas are designated from that point according to the numbers on a clock).

Additional Movement or Blocking Terms

X	Cross (stage)
XC	Cross center (stage)
XDL	Cross down left (stage)
XDR	Cross down right (stage)
XUL, XUR, UDC, etc.	

(A downward arrow ↓ may indicate "sit" and an upward arrow ↑ "rise.")

Short phrases can also be marked in the script, such as "close book," "slap him," and so on.

Example

"O, woe is me—XDR

Fall—T'have seen what I have seen, see what

↓ to Knees   I see!" ↑ Rise—run off DL

OPHELIA in *Hamlet* by William Shakespeare

A Last Comment Concerning Final Rehearsals and Performance of the Scene

As noted earlier, stage properties and furniture in scene study and practice should be kept to a minimum; it is not advisable to spend time and energy creating a believable scenic environment. In scene practice the audience accepts that the focus is upon the actor, with only essential scenic elements provided. These factors also hold true for costuming. What costuming is necesssary can probably be provided from personal wardrobes. Also, basic properties and furniture are usually available as part of standard classroom or theatre rehearsal items. Occasionally, actors may have to provide these items as well. In many instances it is acceptable to use substitute facsimiles for properties. Normal room illumination or basic area lighting are sufficient for scenes. Actors in classes often must be content with general room illumination or what is called in the theatre "work lights" (meaning nonspecialized illumination). Generally, if music and sound effects are necessary or desired, actors must provide them by bringing a tape recorder or phonograph. Care must also be taken to provide adequate rehearsal time for the person who operates the equipment. As a general rule, stage makeup is not used for scene practice. Audiences for scene performances usually come from the class or acting company. Occasionally, friends, relatives, and other students and faculty or other theatre artists in the company are invited to view a scene performance.

As noted earlier, after a scene is performed before an audience, standard practice is usually to have an informal critique or response from the instructor, director, or coach. Sometimes peers or colleague actors contribute to the response. Additionally, many instructors provide specific written evaluation of scene work, which should complement your self-evaluation. While scene study and practice are invaluable to the beginning actor, it is never abandoned by most successful actors. Many such artists return again and again to a studio or laboratory to explore problems, "stretch" their talents, experiment, and "freshen" their fundamental skills. (Members of the Actors Studio do this regularly.) Learn a positive approach to scene study and practice and sustain it through your entire career.

Suggested Readings

Barlow, Judith E. (Ed.) *Plays by American Women: The Early Years.* New York: Avon, 1981.

Cohen, Lorraine. (Ed.) *Scenes for Young Actors.* New York: Avon, 1973.

Cosgrove, Frances. (Ed.) *Scenes for Student Actors.* Vol. V. New York: Samuel French, Inc., 1942.

Elkind, Samuel, ed. *32 Scenes for Acting Practice.* Glenview, Ill.: Scott, Foresman & Co., 1972.

———. *30 Scenes for Acting Practice.* Glenview, Ill.: Scott, Foresman & Co., 1972.

———. *28 Scenes for Acting Practice.* Glenview, Ill.: Scott, Foresman & Co., 1971.

Emerson, Robert, and Grumback, Jane. (Eds.) *50 Speeches From The Contemporary Theatre.* New York: Drama Book Specialists, 1976.

Grumback, Jane, and Emerson, Robert, (Eds.) *Actors Guide to Scenes.* New York: Drama Book Specialists/Publishers, 1973.

———. *Actors Guide to Monologues.* New York: Drama Book Specialist/Publishers, 1972.

Handman, Wynn (Ed.). *American Scenes for Student Actors.* New York: Bantam, 1978.

Lass, Abraham H. and Levin, Milton. (Eds.) *A Student's Guide to 50 American Plays.* New York: Pocket Books, 1969.

Olfson, Lewy, ed. *50 Great Scenes for Student Actors.* New York: Bantam Books, Inc., 1970.

Schulman, Michael, and Mekler, Eva. (Eds.) *Scenes For Student Actors.* New York: Penguin Books, 1980.

Southern, Richard. *Proscenium and Sight Lines.* London: Faber & Faber, 1939.

Steffensen, James L., Jr., ed. *Great Scenes from World Theatre.* Vols. 1 and 2. New York: Avon Books, vol. 1, 1965, vol. 2, 1972.

Sullivan, Victoria, and Hatch, James. (Eds.) *Plays By and About Women.* New York: Vintage, 1974.

The Glass Menagerie

by *Tennessee Williams*

*from
scene i*

Characters	Tom Wingfield Amanda, his mother Laura, Tom's sister
Scene	An alley and the Wingfield apartment, St. Louis.
Situation	Tom, narrator of the play and a character in it, introduces this play from his memory involving the fantasy and real worlds of his crippled sister, Laura, and his mother, Amanda.

TOM   Yes, I have tricks in my pocket, I have things up my sleeve. But I am the opposite of a stage magician. He gives you illusion that has the appearance of truth. I give you truth in the pleasant disguise of illusion.

To begin with, I turn back time. I reverse it to that quaint period, the thirties, when the huge middle class of America was matriculating in a school for the blind. Their eyes had failed them, or they had failed their eyes, and so they were having their fingers pressed forcibly down on the fiery Braille alphabet of a dissolving economy.

In Spain there was revolution. Here there was only shouting and confusion.

In Spain there was Guernica. Here there were disturbances of labor, sometimes pretty violent, in otherwise peaceful cities such as Chicago, Cleveland, Saint Louis . . .

This is the social background of the play.
(*music*)

The play is memory.

Being a memory play, it is dimly lighted, it is sentimental, it is not realistic.

In memory everything seems to happen to music. That explains the fiddle in the wings.

I am the narrator of the play, and also a character in it.

The other characters are my mother, Amanda, my sister, Laura, and a gentleman caller who appears in the final scenes.

He is the most realistic character in the play, being an emissary from a world of reality that we were somehow set apart from.

But since I have a poet's weakness for symbols, I am using this character also as a symbol; he is the long delayed but always expected something that we live for.

There is a fifth character in the play who doesn't appear except in this larger-than-life-size photograph over the mantel.

This is our father who left us a long time ago.

He was a telephone man who fell in love with long distances; he gave up his job with the telephone company and skipped the light fantastic out of town . . .

The last we heard of him was a picture post-card from Mazatlan, on the Pacific coast of Mexico, containing a message of two words—

"Hello—Good-bye!" and no address.

I think the rest of the play will explain itself. . . .

(AMANDA's *voice becomes audible through the portieres*)

(LEGEND ON SCREEN: "OÙ SONT LES NEIGES")

He divides the portieres and enters the upstage area. AMANDA *and* LAURA *are seated at a drop-leaf table. Eating is indicated by gestures without food or utensils.* AMANDA *faces the audience.* TOM *and* LAURA *are seated in profile. The interior has lit up softly and through the scrim we see* AMANDA *and* LAURA *seated at the table in the upstage area.*

AMANDA (*calling*) Tom?

TOM Yes, Mother.

AMANDA We can't say grace until you come to the table!

TOM Coming, Mother. (*He bows slightly and withdraws, reappearing a few moments later in his place at the table*)

AMANDA (*to her son*) Honey, don't *push* with your *fingers*. If you have to push with something the thing to push with is a crust of bread. And chew—chew! Animals have sections in their stomachs which enable them to digest food without mastication, but human beings are supposed to chew their food before they swallow it down. Eat food leisurely, son, and really enjoy it. A well-cooked meal has lots of delicate flavors that have to be held in the mouth for appreciation. So chew your food and give your salivary glands a chance to function!

(TOM *deliberately lays his imaginary fork down and pushes his chair back from the table.*)

TOM I haven't enjoyed one bite of this dinner because of your constant directions on how to eat it. It's you that make me rush through meals with your hawk-like attention to every bite I take. Sickening—spoils my appetite—all this discussion of—animals' secretion—salivary glands—mastication!

AMANDA (*lightly*) Temperament like a Metropolitan star! (*He rises and crosses downstage*) You're not excused from the table.

TOM I'm getting a cigarette.

AMANDA You smoke too much. (LAURA *rises*)

LAURA I'll bring in the blanc mange. (*He remains standing with his cigarette by the portieres during the following*)

AMANDA (*rising*) No, sister, no, sister—you be the lady this time and I'll be the darky.

LAURA I'm already up.

AMANDA Resume your seat, little sister—I want you to stay fresh and pretty—for gentlemen callers!

LAURA I'm not expecting any gentlemen callers.

AMANDA (*crossing out to kitchenette. Airily*) Sometimes they come when they

are least expected! Why, I remember one Sunday afternoon in Blue Mountain—
(enters kitchenette).

TOM   I know what's coming!

LAURA   Yes. But let her tell it.

TOM   Again?

LAURA   She loves to tell it.

(AMANDA returns with bowl of dessert.)

AMANDA   One Sunday afternoon in Blue Mountain—your mother received—
seventeen—gentlemen callers! Why, sometimes there weren't chairs enough
to accommodate them all. We had to send the nigger over to bring in folding
chairs from the parish house.

TOM *(remaining at portieres)*   How did you entertain those gentlemen callers?

AMANDA   I understood the art of conversation!

TOM   I bet you could talk.

AMANDA   Girls in those days *knew* how to talk, I can tell you.

TOM   Yes?

(IMAGE: Amanda AS A GIRL ON A PORCH, GREETING CALLERS)

AMANDA   They knew how to entertain their gentlemen callers. It wasn't enough
for a girl to be possessed of a pretty face and a graceful figure—although I
wasn't slighted in either respect. She also needed to have a nimble wit and a
tongue to meet all occasions.

TOM   What did you talk about?

AMANDA   Things of importance going on in the world! Never anything coarse or
common or vulgar. *(She addresses* TOM *as though he were seated in the vacant
chair at the table though he remains by portieres. He plays this scene as though
he held the book.)* My callers were gentlemen—all! Among my callers were
some of the most prominent young planters of the Mississippi Delta—planters
and sons of planters!

*(TOM motions for music and a spot of light on AMANDA. Her eyes lift, her face
glows, her voice becomes rich and elegiac.)*

(SCREEN LEGEND: "OÙ SONT LES NEIGES")

    There was young Champ Laughlin who later became vice-president of the
Delta Planters Bank.

    Hadley Stevenson who was drowned in Moon Lake and left his widow
one hundred and fifty thousand in Government bonds.

    There were the Cutrere brothers, Wesley and Bates. Bates was one of my
bright particular beaux! He got in a quarrel with that wild Wainwright boy.
They shot it out on the floor of Moon Lake Casino. Bates was shot through
the stomach. Died in the ambulance on his way to Memphis. His widow was
also well-provided for, came into eight or ten thousand acres, that's all. She
married him on the rebound—never loved her—carried my picture on him
the night he died!

    And there was that boy that every girl in the Delta had set her cap for!
That beautiful, brilliant young Fitzhugh boy from Greene County!

TOM   What did he leave his widow?

AMANDA   He never married! Gracious, you talk as though all of my old admirers
had turned up their toes to the daisies!

TOM   Isn't this the first you've mentioned that still survives?

AMANDA   That Fitzhugh boy went North and made a fortune—came to be known
as the Wolf of Wall Street! He had the Midas touch, whatever he touched
turned to gold!

And I could have been Mrs. Duncan J. Fitzhugh, mind you! But—I
picked your *father!*

LAURA   (*rising*)   Mother, let me clear the table.

AMANDA   No, dear, you go in front and study your typewriter chart. Or practice
your shorthand a little. Stay fresh and pretty!—It's almost time for our
gentlemen callers to start arriving. (*She flounces girlishly toward the
kitchenette.*) How many do you suppose we're going to entertain this
afternoon?

(TOM *throws down the paper and jumps up with a groan.*)

LAURA   (*alone in the dining room*)   I don't believe we're going to receive any,
Mother.

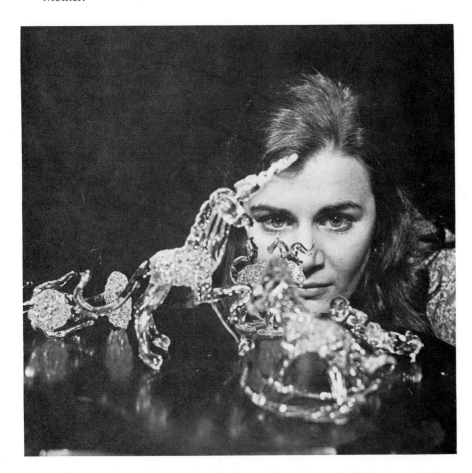

The Glass Menagerie by
Tennessee Williams.
Suzanne Collins as Laura
at The Seattle Repertory
Theatre. Directed by Dan
Sullivan.

AMANDA (*reappearing, airily*)   What? No one—not one? You must be joking! (LAURA *nervously echoes her laugh. She slips in a fugitive manner through the half-open portieres and draws them gently behind her. A shaft of very clear light is thrown on her face against the faded tapestry of the curtains.* MUSIC: "THE GLASS MENAGERIE" UNDER FAINTLY. *Lightly*) Not one gentleman caller? It can't be true! There must be a flood, there must have been a tornado!

LAURA   It isn't a flood, it's not a tornado, Mother. I'm just not popular like you were in Blue Mountain. . . . (TOM *utters another groan.* LAURA *glances at him with a faint, apologetic smile. Her voice catching a little.*) Mother's afraid I'm going to be an old maid.

THE SCENE DIMS OUT WITH "GLASS MENAGERIE"

MUSIC

(*END*)

Death of a Salesman
by *Arthur Miller*

from
Act I

Characters

Willy Loman, a salesman, past 60 years
Charley, his friend and neighbor, in his 60s
Ben, Willy's dead brother returning to inhabit his fantasies, in his 60s
Biff, Willy's oldest son, age 34 years
Hap, Willy's other son, 32 years
Linda, Willy's wife, in her 50s

Scene

The kitchen of the Loman home in Brooklyn.

Situation

An exhausted Willy has returned from his sales job on the road in New England. Confused over the loss of love from his oldest son, his economic problems, and the decline of his effectiveness, Willy's mind wanders in and out of the past and the present. His neighbor Charley joins him for a late-night game of cards to sooth and quiet him.

Death of a Salesman by Arthur Miller. James Edmondson as Willy and Anne Krill as Linda at The Oregon Shakespearean Festival. Directed by Robert Loper. Scenery by Jesse Hollis. Costumes by Jeannie Davidson. Lighting by Richard Riddell. Photograph by Hank Kranzler.

WILLY   I'm awfully tired, Ben.

(BEN's *music is heard.* BEN *looks around at everything.*)

CHARLEY   Good, keep playing; you'll sleep better. Did you call me Ben?

(BEN *looks at his watch.*)

WILLY   That's funny. For a second there you reminded me of my brother Ben.

BEN   I only have a few minutes. *(He strolls, inspecting the place.* WILLY *and* CHARLEY *continue playing.)*

CHARLEY   You never heard from him again, heh? Since that time?

WILLY   Didn't Linda tell you? Couple of weeks ago we got a letter from his wife in Africa. He died.

CHARLEY   That so.

BEN *(chuckling)*   So this is Brooklyn, eh?

CHARLEY   Maybe you're in for some of his money.

WILLY   Naa, he had seven sons. There's just one opportunity I had with that man . . .

BEN   I must make a train, William. There are several properties I'm looking at in Alaska.

WILLY   Sure, sure! If I'd gone with him to Alaska that time, everything would've been totally different.

CHARLEY   Go on, you'd froze to death up there.

WILLY   What're you talking about?

BEN   Opportunity is tremendous in Alaska, William. Surprised you're not up there.

WILLY   Sure, tremendous.

CHARLEY   Heh?

WILLY   There was the only man I ever met who knew the answers.

CHARLEY   Who?

BEN   How are you all?

WILLY *(taking a pot, smiling)*   Fine, fine.

CHARLEY   Pretty sharp tonight.

BEN   Is Mother living with you?

WILLY   No, she died a long time ago.

CHARLEY   Who?

BEN   That's too bad. Fine specimen of a lady, Mother.

WILLY *(to* CHARLEY*)*   Heh?

BEN   I'd hoped to see the old girl.

CHARLEY   Who died?

BEN   Heard anything from Father, have you?

WILLY *(unnerved)*   What do you mean, who died?

CHARLEY *(taking a pot)*   What're you talkin' about?

BEN *(looking at his watch)*   William, it's half-past eight!

WILLY *(as though to dispel his confusion he angrily stops* CHARLEY's *hand)*   That's my build!

CHARLEY   I put the ace—

WILLY   If you don't know how to play the game I'm not gonna throw my money away on you!

CHARLEY *(rising)*   It was my ace, for God's sake!

WILLY   I'm through, I'm through!

BEN   When did Mother die?

WILLY   Long ago. Since the beginning you never knew how to play cards.

CHARLEY (*picks up the cards and goes to the door*)   All right! Next time I'll bring a deck with five aces.

WILLY   I don't play that kind of game!

CHARLEY (*turning on him*)   You ought to be ashamed of yourself!

WILLY   Yeah?

CHARLEY   Yeah! (*He goes out.*)

WILLY (*slamming the door after him*)   Ignoramus!

BEN (*as* WILLY *comes toward him through the wall-line of the kitchen*)   So you're William.

WILLY (*shaking* BEN's *hand*)   Ben! I've been waiting for you so long! What's the answer? How did you do it?

BEN   Oh, there's a story in that.

(LINDA *enters the forestage, as of old, carrying the wash basket.*)

LINDA   Is this Ben?

BEN (*gallantly*)   How do you do, my dear.

LINDA   Where've you been all these years? Willy's always wondered why you—

WILLY (*pulling* BEN *away from her impatiently*)   Where is Dad? Didn't you follow him? How did you get started?

BEN   Well, I don't know how much you remember.

WILLY   Well, I was just a baby, of course, only three or four years old—

BEN   Three years and eleven months.

WILLY   What a memory, Ben!

BEN   I have many enterprises, William, and I have never kept books.

WILLY   I remember I was sitting under the wagon in—was it Nebraska?

BEN   It was South Dakota, and I gave you a bunch of wild flowers.

WILLY   I remember you walking away down some open road.

BEN (*laughing*)   I was going to find Father in Alaska.

WILLY   Where is he?

BEN   At that age I had a very faulty view of geography, William. I discovered after a few days that I was heading due south, so instead of Alaska, I ended up in Africa.

LINDA   Africa!

WILLY   The Gold Coast!

BEN   Principally diamond mines.

LINDA   Diamond mines!

BEN   Yes, my dear. But I've only a few minutes—

WILLY   No! Boys! Boys! (*Young* BIFF *and* HAPPY *appear.*) Listen to this. This is your Uncle Ben, a great man! Tell my boys, Ben!

BEN   Why, boys, when I was seventeen I walked into the jungle, and when I was twenty-one I walked out. (*He laughs.*) And by God I was rich.

WILLY (*to the boys*)   You see what I been talking about? The greatest things can happen!

BEN (*glancing at his watch*)   I have an appointment in Ketchikan Tuesday week.

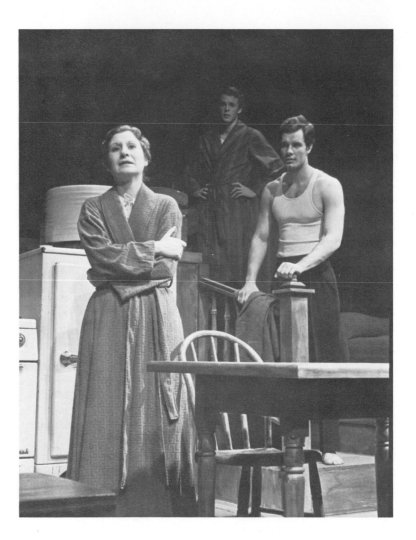

Death of a Salesman by Arthur Miller. At Illinois Wesleyan University. Directed by Carole Brandt. Tom Gaitch is Biff; Linda Sterline is Linda; and T. Ronald Nison is Hap. Scenic and Lighting design by Max Culver.

WILLY No, Ben! Please tell about Dad. I want my boys to hear. I want them to know the kind of stock they spring from. All I remember is a man with a big beard, and I was in Mamma's lap, sitting around a fire, and some kind of high music.

BEN His flute. He played the flute.

WILLY Sure, the flute, that's right!

(New music is heard, a high, rollicking tune.)

BEN Father was a very great and a very wild-hearted man. We would start in Boston, and he'd toss the whole family into the wagon, and then he'd drive the team right across the country; through Ohio, and Indiana, Michigan, Illinois, and all the Western states. And we'd stop in the towns and sell the flutes that he'd made on the way. Great inventor, Father. With one gadget he made more in a week than a man like you could make in a lifetime.

WILLY   That's just the way I'm bringing them up, Ben—rugged, well liked, all-around.

BEN   Yeah? *(to BIFF)* Hit that, boy—hard as you can. *(He pounds his stomach.)*

BIFF   Oh, no, sir!

BEN   *(taking boxing stance)*   Come on, get to me! *(He laughs.)*

WILLY   Go to it, Biff! Go ahead, show him!

BIFF   Okay! *(He cocks his fists and starts in.)*

LINDA   *(to WILLY)*   Why must he fight, dear?

BEN   *(sparring with BIFF)*   Good! Good boy!

WILLY   How's that, Ben, heh?

HAPPY   Give him the left, Biff!

LINDA   Why are you fighting?

BEN   Good boy! *(Suddenly comes in, trips BIFF, and stands over him, the point of his umbrella poised over BIFF's eye.)*

LINDA   Look out, Biff!

BIFF   Gee!

BEN   *(patting BIFF's knee)*   Never fight fair with a stranger, boy. You'll never get out of the jungle that way.

(END)

9 Auditioning

Teresa Gilmore and Grey
Schmidt demonstrate
AUDITIONING: "Smiling
and Ready to Audition."
Photograph by Randy
Tunnel.

At only one time does an actor find it relatively easy to gain a role or to become involved in a performance activity. This happens when he is given one of those opportunities in an acting class or a studio. There, he is simply assigned a part or is asked to participate in a related activity or he arbitrarily makes a selection. Thereafter, actors must compete. Competition is a necessary aspect of any acting career. As many actors as are available determine the range of selection possible for any given role or activity. There is always someone who can do the role as well as you; in some instances, better and more experienced people will challenge you. However, there are always people less capable of achievement than you. Be prepared to accept rejection or defeat and to return with resilience and renewed determination. Playwright Eugene O'Neill said that perseverance and good luck are the key factors to success in the theatre. When actors use phrases such as the "big break" and "being in the right place at the right time," they are using catch phrases for good luck or good fortune. The shear volume of actors striving for achievement in the field automatically indicates that even high-quality talent will be overlooked in the scramble and competition for roles and jobs. Without question, no matter how good an actor is, he is also going to have to be lucky. Have no illusions about this fact. It is relatively true that "good contacts" are invaluable. Rarely, if ever, will such a contact *keep* an actor working, but that contact might increase his chances of getting the opportunity to work. The most classic misunderstood concept related to good contacts is the infamous myth of the casting couch. The connotation in that phrase is obvious, but generally incorrect. The so-called casting couch is neither necessary nor valid in terms of constant work in the theatre any more than in any other walk of life. The favors implied in such activities are no more valuable or invaluable than having a mutual friend establish a contact. An actor should never attempt to offer anything less than his skill, dedication, and experience as the selling features of himself as an actor. While an actor should take advantage of honest, ethical contacts to assist him in gaining work opportunities, he should never sacrifice his personal integrity.

The term *tryout* is generally used in the theatre to denote securing of a role by reading aloud from the script before a director, a producer, or an author. The term *audition* is generally used in the theatre to denote securing of a role by presenting prepared, memorized, and rehearsed material before a director, a producer, or an author. To simplify matters, throughout the following discussion *audition* will be used rather than *tryout*. Note however that the discussion applies to both terms.

How to Audition

I am indebted to J. Gordon Greene for making major contributions to the following material.

How does an actor best approach an audition? Since organization of auditions is a function of the director (and occasionally of the producer or

Call board

playwright), an actor participates as a performer. Following are some direct, basic suggestions for actors when they audition.

1. If you are auditioning for a written role, read the play in advance.

2. If you are auditioning for a specific part, practice key speeches for that role in advance. It is usually not necessary to memorize speeches unless audition directions call for it. What is desired is sufficient familiarization in order to permit glancing out at the audience occasionally.

3. Be extremely disciplined and courteous at auditions. Be punctual and be attentive to all directions and requests. Be totally silent except when you are asked to speak. Most directors become irritated by actors who stand or sit around chattering with other people at open auditions. It is also wise to avoid unnecessary commentary or discussion with the director, who is bound to be completely occupied. Any attempt at idle chatting is usually viewed as a device for gaining favor or special consideration. Be cooperative, but not aggressive.

4. If the audition is open, listen carefully to the competition as it may be beneficial to hear other interpretations. However, if you are particularly impressed by someone, it is generally best not to change your interpretation. Rather, use the other audition as stimulation to do an even better job with your audition. Do not imitate anyone else's work.

5. Avoid falling into the trap of self-criticism. If you strive for perfection, even one verbal error, for example, can lead to inordinate self-criticism and collapse of an entire audition. Reflection and self-evaluation should occur after the audition is completed. During the audition, remain flexible and good-natured no matter what happens.

6. How much emotion should an actor reveal at an audition? Again, personalization is the key to the answer. If the role and scene demand intense emotion, provide as much as your person can honestly project, but do not force emotion. Forcing inevitably leads to artificiality. Personal naturalness and comfort should be the guides. For example, it is said that Dustin Hoffman usually provides considerable, but natural and honest, emotion at an audition. However, once he has been cast, he reverts immediately to several weeks of relaxed, comfortable personalization during rehearsal. Remember that an audition is usually a heightened emotional experience. Unless the role calls for truly unusual emotional intensity, the audition situation may provide enough energy that you need not worry or think about creating emotion.

7. When casting is announced, be understanding and cheerful whether you are cast or not. It is juvenile and destructive to allow disappointment to affect progress for any length of time. The only thought an actor should have is what, where, and when is the next audition. It is particularly meaningless to second-guess casting decisions. To do so is to indulge in debilitating emotionalism. It is the surest sign of unprofessionalism, and it invariably gains nothing but the possible disfavor of a director and your colleagues. Learn this lesson at the first unsuccessful audition.

Pages 108 to 113 in this book were adapted from J. Gordon Greene, "The Actor Auditions," *Southern Theatre* 16, Fall 1972 and Winter 1973.

Types of Auditions

Auditions will be either open or closed. In an open audition any interested person may participate. Traditionally, also at an open audition actors may watch other actors perform. In a closed audition the general public is usually excluded, and the audition privilege is limited to specific people and groups. Traditionally, at a closed audition actors may not watch other actors perform. In these auditions, actors are usually called at a specific time, and the length of the audition time is rigidly controlled.

Auditions are usually divided into two categories: specific and general. For example, at a specific audition, an actor might audition only for Hamlet, or only for Hamlet and Laertes. At a general audition the actor auditions for any role, and the director has the privilege of casting him in any role he wishes. Further, a general audition may be for membership in an acting company or group rather than for a specific role or play. For example, when auditioning for a summer stock group or repertory company, the actor may perform one or more short prepared audition pieces to demonstrate his general ability.

Selecting an Audition Piece

When an actor selects personal audition pieces, it is vital for him to select cuttings which best reveal the range of his *personal* acting abilities. Following are some direct suggestions to assist you in choosing selections from most classical and realistic plays:

1. Generally remain wthin your own basic age range and physical type. While everyone complains about type casting (see Glossary), the practice is used almost exclusively in the professional theatre and much more often than is admitted in educational theatre. How can you best function within the limitations of that concept? Above all, careful, critical understanding of yourself is essential. First, you know how old you are; your age range will generally not vary as a type beyond ten years on either side of your age, provided that you are at least twenty-six or twenty-seven years old (at eighteen years of age most actors cannot perform the role of an eight-year-old child). You also know your height, weight, and general physical characteristics. Painful though it may be, do not have illusions about yourself. For example, if you are not the correct age and physical type to perform Helen of Troy in *The Trojan Women*, do not audition for the role.

The most frequently used actor categories or types include the following:

Leading man—age range from twenty-five to forty years; height from five feet ten inches to six feet two inches; relatively attractive; not overweight; pleasant voice; good posture.
Leading lady—age range from twenty-five to forty years; height from five feet four inches to five feet eight inches; relatively attractive; not overweight; pleasant voice; good posture.

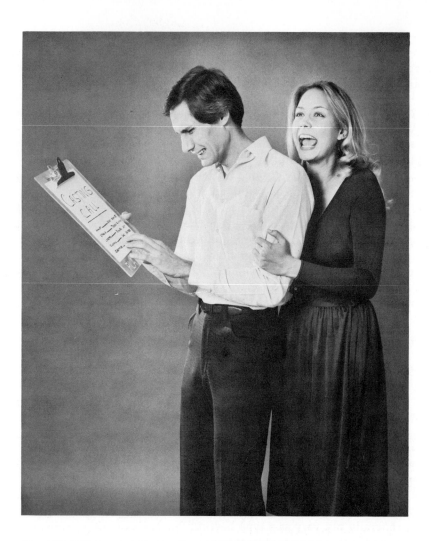

Teresa Gilmore and Grey Schmidt demonstrate joy and agony at the moment of reading a casting notice. Photograph by Randy Tunnel.

Juvenile male—younger version of the leading man, except shorter; age range and appearance fifteen to twenty years.

Juvenile female (ingenue)—younger version of the leading lady; may be shorter; age range and appearance fifteen to twenty years.

Character men and character women— all shapes and sizes; age range and appearance usually forty years and beyond; vocal and physical eccentricities common.

2. Select characters with whom you can identify. It will strengthen your audition if you have some understanding and emotional identification with the character you are portraying. However, this does not mean that you must have experienced what the character has, nor does it mean that you must be a great deal like the character. You do need to have empathy or sympathy for the character because that will help you identify better.

3. Select modern realistic plays for audition unless there are specific directions to the contrary. The requirements for speech and movement of modern plays are usually more immediately comfortable to a young actor than are classical or nonrealistic styles of acting.

4. If your audition permits time for more than one selection, try to provide offerings with distinct rhythmic contrasts. In other words, if one piece is serious or tragic, the other should probably be light and comic.

5. It is preferable not to select a character for an audition that demands a heavy vocal dialect or accent unless there are specific directions to the contrary. One reason for this is that it is difficult to do accents and dialects well and also to suit the concept of the people hearing you. Also, you do not want to risk having an accent or dialect misinterpreted as your own. Finally, because accents and dialects are largely a matter of mechanics, most directors will be more impressed by confident character work than with vocal techniques.

6. When you construct or cut a selection, it is best not to splice several different speeches together to make one excerpt. If another character is speaking to the character you are performing, that character's speeches can be eliminated and with slight alteration you can usually link you own character's speeches together as one excerpt. Avoid linking a speech from act 1 with a speech from act 3. Constructions like this are usually confusing, and transitions are difficult. In addition, the rhythm of the speech is sacrificed.

7. Extremely intense and climactic moments rarely make good audition selections unless the actor has sufficient time to build to those moments in a believable manner. An effective audition is usually complete within itself. When the requirement is to be extremely brief (e.g., two minutes is the usual time limitation), material should be selected for its unity and character nuances.

8. It is absolutely essential to time your selections carefully and finish within the time limitations. Discipline is vital. Excellent auditions have been ruined by self-indulgence.

Practical Suggestions

Here are important suggestions concerning how to dress for and how to conduct oneself at an audition.

1. You should generally dress for an audition in a comfortable, clean manner. The question arises, Should you dress appropriate to the attire of the character? The answer is in a reasonable way yes—with qualifications. Dress similarly to the attire of the character only for auditions for modern plays. If you are auditioning for the role of a truck driver, jeans, boots, and flannel shirt would be appropriate. If the role is a business woman, a tailored suit would be good. Obviously, if the role is selected from a historical play, you should not attempt to dress in period costume. In this instance, wear neat, but neutral clothing such as slacks and sweater (wear basic blue,

gray, or brown colors). For women, a dress (or skirt and blouse) with simple lines and neutral colors is favored over slacks or jeans. While the latter are popular and acceptable, most directors need to see the legs of an actress because more plays require women to wear dresses than pants. Hair should be well groomed and kept out of the face of both men and women. Shoes and clothing should fit well and never hinder quiet, natural movement. Do not wear shoes with platform heels which adversely affect balance and movement. Also, unless necessary for a character type, do not wear tennis shoes or sandals. Shoes or boots are best for both men and women. Generally, it is important not to overdress and thereby have to compete against your own appearance. On the other hand, *overly* casual dress is not desirable.

2. Be certain to establish your name clearly. Use the phrase "My name is. . . ." These first three nonessential words tune the listener into catching the important phrase, your name. If your name is unusual, spell it. If you have an audition number, announce it with your name.

3. Quickly determine the size of the room in which you are auditioning and adjust your vocal projection accordingly. If the listeners are at the rear of a large auditorium, you must amplify considerably. If they are only a few feet from you, do not blast them out of their seats. A cardinal rule, If you err, do it slightly on the loud side.

4. Never apologize for your appearance or physical condition (such as a head cold). If you have a cold, it will be obvious and understood. Concentrate upon the character. Do not fuss with yourself, the room, or the properties. Most auditions do not permit the use of props except for a chair. Remember personalization and do not push for artificial intensity. Use yourself to the best advantage no matter what character you are reading.

5. Repeat your name and number with warmth and sincerity before leaving the audition area and say, "Thank you." It is important to leave an impression of confidence.

The Callback

Few actors are cast on the basis of one audition. Hopefully they are asked to return for a callback session. The callback may be for another reading or for a prepared performance, or it may be an interview (or all). The second reading or performance reveals more depth and usually more time is allotted. A callback generally permits an actor to discuss interpretation and other matters with the director—a distinct advantage over an open audition where the actor usually should not attempt discussion. Concerning the interview, answer all questions directly, economically, and honestly. Never lie or stretch the truth to gain an impression. Directors and producers are adept at spotting lies. They may believe that if an actor lies in an interview or on a résumé, he may lie or cheat at other things such as punctuality or reliability. If high school is your sole acting experience, so state and without apology. Finally, do not attempt to impress the interviewer by babbling on incessantly. Respect his time and simply offer him your photograph and a typed résumé of your acting experience. Never fail to thank the interviewer.

A recent sharp black-and-white photograph should be attached to the résumé. Eight-by-ten inch prints are preferred. There are firms in large cities which produce one hundred such photographs for under one hundred dollars. Gloss-finish is preferred to matte-finish photographs because they reproduce better for publicity purposes. A single pose is preferred to a composite, a simple head shot is preferred to a full-length pose, and a natural, unretouched photo is favored over a glamour picture. A final caution concerning photographs: Never use ultradramatic poses because they connote amateurism. Use an informal unpretentious pose.

In acting, a cardinal rule is that a résumé never exceeds one page regardless of the length of experience. As roles accumulate, an actor becomes more selective as to which ones he lists. Learn to cite only representative roles and major credits and rarely more than fifteen or twenty. A half-dozen solid roles are more impressive than thirty small ones. The résumé should be neatly typed and easily read. If you have acquired an agent, the agent's and the agency's name or logo usually appear at the top or the side of the résumé (see the sample résumé on page 115 provided by actor Jimmy Sturtevant). If you have no agent, merely list your own name at the top of the resume (see the sample résumé on page 117 provided by actress Pamela Monakee). List your name, full address, and telephone number near the top. Most actors in urban centers utilize an answering service or recording machine to take messages. This is the number you should list on your résumé. Next, list your height, weight, hair color, eye color, and all professional unions to which you belong. Current practice is to eliminate listing your age, age range, and marital status, although some actors still choose to do so. Under *Training* list schools, degrees, workshops, and well-known acting coaches under whom you have worked. Note any special training (such as, voice, mime, improvisation, fencing, dance, and so on). Under the section labeled *Acting Experience* list just the significant roles you have played, play titles, theatres, theatre locations, and directors if they are well known (list latest roles first). List *Television*, *Radio*, and *Film* credits (if any) separately. Under *Special Talents or Abilities* list only activities, sports, hobbies, or interest which generally reinforce the art of acting, such as musical instruments played, western riding, sports played, and the like. Because putting together an effective résumé is expensive and time-consuming, leave extra room at the top for changes of address and telephone number, plus empty space at the bottom to add recent credits and keep the résumé up-to-date.

An actor should never let the brief time allotted him for an audition mislead him into thinking that a director will not be able to recognize his ability. Ethel Barrymore once commented, "Well, if they've got any talent, you can tell it in a minute; and if they don't, it'll seem like an hour."

Musical Theatre Auditions

Auditioning for a musical theatre production requires the same procedures of preparation detailed above plus the preparation of a song to sing and, at times, a dance. A few pertinent guidelines follow.

1. Select a song within your vocal range.

2. Prepare the song through careful rehearsal with a piano accompanist and, if possible, a singing coach.

3. Do not select a "signature" song which is well known due to its rendition by a famous singer (such as "People," well established by Barbra Streisand).

4. Select a song within the style and concept of the musical play under audition, but not from the actual play. For example, a song from *Godspell* might do well to use at an audition for *Jesus Christ Superstar*. This procedure will premit you to escape the situation of singing a song from the play under audition contrary to the manner in which the director may plan to have it sung.

5. However, it would be wise to be *familiar* with one or two songs from the actual play being auditioned in the event the director asks you to try one.

6. If possible, bring your own accompanist to the audition. If this is not possible, try to find out who will be playing at the auditions, contact the person, and try to arrange a rehearsal with the person. If this fails, ask if you may work for one or two minutes with the accompanist prior to singing the actual audition.

7. Be certain that you take a few seconds to "warm-up" your voice prior to the audition.

8. Unless specifically asked to do so, avoid singing acappella (unaccompanied) or with taped music. *Never* sing to a tape which has singing on it; use only instrumental tape music.

9. You may have only a few seconds to sing and make an impression; therefore, be certain you sing a song which has a strong opening lyric.

10. Be certain that you act and perform the song; just singing it well is usually insufficient. For specific work on this crucial factor, see David Craig's excellent book, *On Singing On Stage.* Improvisation and pantomime work are vital to the rehearsal of any song.

11. The factors of dress and appearance apply as described above in regular auditioning.

12. Dance auditions are usually separate from singing auditions and are conducted by the production choreographer. Most dance audition notices carry very specific instructions as to type and requirements (e.g., dress, shoes, music, and so on). However, as a general principle, prepare something within your ability and scope as a dancer; warm-up properly; if possible, use your own piano accompanist or use clear, appropriate recorded instrumental music; execute fundamentals particularly well which will indicate that you are trainable and directable; again, be certain that your initial movements are strong and impressive, and, if permitted to execute an

Sample Photo, Actor

JIMMY STURTEVANT

Professional actor Jimmy Sturtevant: A Sample of a Proper Professional Photograph for Casting Distribution.

(213) 463-7300

JIMMY STURTEVANT

HEIGHT: 5'6"
WEIGHT: 130
HAIR/EYES: BROWN

JACK ROSE AGENCY/ DOROTHY DAY OTIS 6430 SUNSET BLVD., SUITE 1203 HOLLYWOOD, CA 90028
TALENT AGENCY

FILM

HELLNIGHT (starring)	COMPASS INTERNATIONAL PICTURES	TOM DESIMONE
THE COMPETITION	COLUMBIA PICTURES	JOEL OLIANSKI

TELEVISION

QUINCY	UNIVERSAL PRODUCTIONS	RAY DANTON
QUINCY	UNIVERSAL PRODUCTIONS	SAM EGAN
SHIRLEY	UNIVERSAL PRODUCTIONS	BOB BRINBAUM
HELLO LARRY	TAT	ALAN RAFKIN
ONE DAY AT A TIME	TAT	ALAN RAFKIN
ANDROCLES AND THE LION	PBS	DON JACOBS
COMMERCIALS UPON REQUEST		

THEATRE

STOP THE WORLD I WANT TO GET OFF	LITTLECHAP
JESUS CHRIST SUPERSTAR	SIMON
GODSPELL	CHORUS
ROMEO AND JULIET	BENVOLIO
PETER PAN	MICHAEL & CHECCO
OLIVER	ARTFUL DODGER
YOU'RE A GOOD MAN CHARLIE BROWN	SCHROEDER
HAPPY BIRTHDAY WANDA JUNE	PAUL
WIZARD OF OZ	COWARDLY LION
ROAR OF THE GREASEPAINT	THE URCHIN
OUR TOWN	WALLY
ANDROCLES AND THE LION	ANDROCLES
RAGS TO RICHES	MARK
THE HOBBIT	BOMBER

TRAINING

VOICE - 5 YEARS; DANCE - BALLET AND JAZZ 2 YEARS; PIANO - 2 YEARS
UNIVERSITY OF NEVADA YOUTH THEATER - 6 YEARS
JUDY BAYLEY REPERTORY THEATRE - 3 YEARS

CURRENTLY STUDYING ACTING WITH GORDON HUNT; IMPROVISATION WITH GARY AUSTIN;
VOICE WITH AURTHUR JOSEPH; AND JAZZ DANCING WITH JOE TREMAINE

SPECIAL ABILITIES

SINGS; DANCES; PIANO; TENNIS; RACQUETBALL; SWIMMING; SOCCER; BASEBALL; FRISBEE;
RIDES WESTERN; ROLLERSKATING; COMPOSES ORIGINAL MUSIC

Sample Photo, Actress

Pamela K. Monakee

Professional actress
Pamela K. Monakee: A
Sample of a Proper
Professional Photograph
for Casting Distribution.

Sample Résumé, Actress

RESUME

PAMELA KATHRYN MONAKEE

Actress

Age:	22	Telephone:
Height:	5'7"	
Weight:	115 lbs.	Mailing
Hair:	Light Brown	Address:
Eyes:	Dark Brown	

STAGE

Twelfth Night .... Viola
(Judy Bayley Theatre, Las Vegas, Nevada)

FILM

The Fish That Saved Pittsburgh .... day player

TELEVISION

Commercial (national), Montgomery Ward ...... featured
("Beauty Week"--Perfumes)
Internship, Vega$, 1979 .... acting/production

TRAINING

University of Nevada, Las Vegas (UNLV) .. acting classes
Tutoring/coaching/resource actress ...... with Jerry L.
Crawford
author, **Acting in Person and in Style** third edition
(Roles: Maggie, **Cat On A Hot Tin Roof**; Honor, **The Wager**)
Ohio University/Youngstown University ..... psychology

AWARDS AND HONORS

"Outstanding Acting Debut, City of Las Vegas, 1979" Las
Vegas, Nevada, Charles Supin, critic, Las Vegas **Review Journal**
"Best Female Performance, City of Las Vegas, 1979", Chip
Mosher, critic, Las Vegas **Sun**

Teresa Gilmore and Grey
Schmidt demonstrate
"Selling That Song!" The
Musical Theatre Audition.
Photograph by Randy
Tunnel.

entire routine, have an equally strong, impressive finish. If you are one of
the few asked to perform a song and dance in the same audition, carefully
combine the principles discussed above for the song and dance and execute
as cleanly and confidently as possible. Be especially careful to let the song
dominate slightly and avoid dance tempos which render you breathless.
Obviously, the singer/dancer in the theatre must be in top physical condition.

Gordon Hunt and Michael Shurtleff have provided contemporary actors with particularly helpful written material relative to the special art of
auditioning. You are urged to consult the excellent books written by these
men (see *Suggested Readings* at the end of this chapter).

Cold Reading

In the professional theatre, more auditions are based on "cold reading"
than on prepared material. That is, the director, producer, or author hands
you a script and asks you to read from a designated point. However, rarely
is an actor asked to do this *instantly*; usually you are given "a few minutes"
to "look over the material." This is the crucial time for the experienced or
wise auditioner. Use this time to read through the material once or twice
to become familiar with syntax, style, and punctuation. Make no major decisions on *how* to read the material. Next look at the material to try and

understand what is happening to your character in the situation. Finally, ascertain a sensible idea on what is happening to the character emotionally. Do not try to "pose" or "assume an attitude" relative to the character. Rely on personalization, common sense, and read the audition piece as clearly and well as you can based upon your two to three minute study of it. Thus, the key point to note about "cold auditions" is that few auditions are truly "cold." The good actor has *practiced* or studied the art of "cold or sight reading" and "warms" to the given material within a couple minutes. Do not rely on faking or forced acting. Do not develop one, set "cold reading" style and try to use it in any situation. Be yourself and rely on common sense and your own good instincts. Glance up sufficiently to create some eye contact with your listener or fellow-actor. Perhaps use some sensory recall and try to communicate honestly and personally. Do not try to give a "performance" or "become" the character. Be as confident and sincere as possible and read with communicative meaning.

Agents, Contracts, and Unions

Eventually good actors are located by agents. Selecting an agent is as vital as selecting a career. Ask others in the profession about the quality and reputation of particular agents, or seek the counsel of trade unions. Actors can seek an agent by leaving a photo and resume with an agent and by asking for an interview. In general practice, actors in the film and television industry must have an agent, especially in the sprawling city of Los Angeles. In New York, the aspiring stage performer need not have an agent in the early years of work.

Contracts are generally complex and beyond the business skills of most actors. An actor who has reached the point in his career in which contracts are involved has usually acquired an agent to handle the contracts. If not, it is advisable to consult an attorney or experienced friend prior to signing any contract.

Obtaining membership in theatrical unions usually comes with increased experience, time, and, of course, professional employment. *Actor's Equity Association* (AEA or Equity) and *Screen Actor's Guild* (SAG) are the two most crucial unions for actors. Membership in these unions is the mark of the established professional. Other unions include *Screen Extras Guild* (SEG), *The American Guild of Variety Artists* (AGVA), *The American Federation of Television and Radio Artists* (AFTRA), and *The American Guild of Musical Artists* (AGMA). The AFL-CIO charters all these unions together as *The Associated Actors and Artists of America.*

The Interview

Finally, the most important thing an actor may do outside auditioning is participating in interviews. The actor interviews for casting, to obtain an agent, to negotiate with unions, and so on. The key rule to follow for a successful interview is to conduct yourself with courtesy and honesty. "Be yourself." However, do not parade your eccentricities. If waiting in a room or office, use the time to practice a seated relaxation exercise, read through likely audition material, and generally concentrate on positive matters germane to the task at hand. Do not "fuss" with yourself or engage in frivolous conversation and activities with others. In the actual interview, use the standard minute or two of "small talk" to relax and establish good communication—eye contact, warmth, and courtesy. Answer all questions clearly and honestly. Never compromise your integrity or person in any way, but be pleasant even when being firm. Do not volunteer extraneous stories or anecdotes. Provide facts and honest reactions. Follow directions as efficiently and effectively as possible, especially relative to an audition. Do not "plead" a case, apologize, or seek special favors or requests. At the conclusion of the interview and/or reading, thank the person or persons involved and leave. On your way out, also thank any secretary or supervisor in the outer office or area. Such persons may have unknown influence on the ones actually conducting the interview or audition. If you have questions, keep them brief and to the point; if they do not provide you with an opportunity to ask questions, save them for the secretary or the person designated to supervise the interview or audition. Later, do not dwell on the experience. Assess it briefly and note what you learned from it. Be patient about any response from the interview or audition and get busy looking for the next experience.

Interviews and Auditions With Companies Using Non-Scripted Material

Obtaining a position in a preformance group devoted to improvisation and work without script is usually made by personal application and interview. Good recommendations and contacts are invaluable here. Audition may or may not be used, depending upon the nature of the group. If you are interested in joining this kind of group, write to the group or preferably go directly in person.

Auditioning is a perennial affliction of the art of acting—exciting, tormenting, heartbreaking, and rewarding. Always vulnerable, always hopeful, the actor by necessity returns to audition again and again. Following the tenets of this chapter can at least provide an actor with confidence to meet the experience and can enhance his opportunity for success.

Suggested Readings

Babcock, Dennis, and Boyd, Preston. *Careers in the Theatre.* Minneapolis: Lerner Publications, 1975.

Beil, Norman; Supnik, Paul; and Wagner, Paula. *The Actor's Manual. A Practical Career Guide.* New York: Hawthorn/Dutton, 1980.

Campbell, Douglas, and Devlin, Diana. *Looking Forward to a Career: The Theatre.* Minneapolis: Dillon Press, 1970.

Canfield, Curtis, *The Craft of Play Directing*. New York: Holt, Rinehart & Winston, 1963.

Cohen, Robert. *Acting Power*. Palo Alto: Mayfield Press, 1978.

————. *Acting Professionally*. 3d. Ed. Palo Alto: Mayfield Press, 1981.

Craig, David. *On Singing On Stage*. Riverside, N.J.: Schimmer Books, 1978.

Dalrymple, Jean. *Careers and Opportunities in the Theatre*. New York: E.P. Dutton, 1969.

Dean, Alexander, and Carra, Lawrence. *Fundamentals of Play Direction*. 3d ed. New York: Holt, Rinehart & Winston, 1974.

Engel, Lehmann. *Getting Started in the Theatre*. New York: Macmillan, 1973.

Farber, Donald C. *Actor's Guide*. New York: Drama Book Specialists, 1971.

Gallaway, Marian. *The Director in the Theatre*. New York: Macmillan Co., 1963.

Greene, J. Gordon. "The Actor Auditions." Part I. *Southern Theatre 16* (Fall 1972); Part 2. *Southern Theatre 16* (Winter 1973).

Horton, Louise. *Careers in Theatre, Music, and Dance*. New York: Franklin Watts, 1976.

Hunt, Gordon. *How to Audition. A Casting Director's Guide for Actors*. New York. Dramatist's Publishing Co., 1977.

Markus, Tom. *The Professional Actor: From Audition to Performance*. New York: Drama Book Specialists, 1978.

Matson, Katinka. *The Working Actor: A Guide to the Profession*. New York: Viking, 1976.

Moore, Dick. *Opportunities in Acting*. New York: Universal, 1963.

Morris, Eric. *Being and Doing. A Workbook For Actors*. Los Angeles: Whitehouse/ Spelling Publications, 1981.

Nahas, Rebecca. *Your Acting Career How to Break into and Survive in the Theatre*. New York: Crown, 1976.

Savan, Bruce. *Your Career in the Theatre*. Garden City, N.Y.: Doubleday, 1961.

Shurtleff, Michael. *Audition. Everything an Actor Needs to Know to Get the Part*. New York: Walker and Co., 1978.

Sievers, W. David; Stiver, Harry E., Jr.; and Kahan, Stanley. *Directing for the Theatre*. 3d ed. Dubuque, Iowa: Wm. C. Brown Company Publishers, 1974.

Welker, David. *Theatrical Direction: The Basic Techniques*. Boston: Allyn & Bacon, 1971.

Rehearsal and Role Analysis and Performance

10

Teresa Gilmore and Grey Schmidt demonstrate REHEARSAL AND ROLE ANALYSIS: "Reading and Discussing the Script." Photograph by Randy Tunnel.

Once an actor has auditioned and been cast, how does he begin role creation? And how does an actor utilize both personalization and traditional acting techniques (i.e., observation, imagination, improvisation, and so on) in rehearsal and performance?

Rehearsal

The initial rehearsals in most productions are devoted to *reading and play analysis, role analysis, production goals, organization, and discussion.* Except for role analysis, most of this material is handled by the director and his artistic staff. Although some directors provide written or verbal remarks on role analysis, many directors expect the actor to provide or initiate most of it. The following is an organized, precise, and practical approach to role analysis.

The Steps of Role Analysis

These steps have been refined through practical experience in actual productions.

1. *Read through the play for basic enjoyment and information.* (It is fun and helpful to read the *last* act *first* and progress toward the beginning of the play in like manner until the *first* act of the play is read *last.* This system will aid you in raising questions and reading for solutions/connections.)

2. *Do some basic reading and research on the playwright.* Succinct biographical sketches can be found in *Current Biography* (H. W. Wilson Co.), a reference found in most libraries. If the author is not listed in that publication, look him up in the card file or in *Reader's Guide to Periodical Literature* (H. W. Wilson Co.). It is probably not necessary to read a complete biography of the playwright if one or more are available, although you may wish to do so for an in-depth study. It is true that the script itself is sufficient for an actor to perform a role well. However, it is also possible that some meaningful insights into the life and other works of an author may prove helpful to role creation. For example, knowing the relationship between Tennessee Williams and his sister and other family members might prove very beneficial to an actor playing Tom in *The Glass Menagerie.* Furthermore, knowledge of a playwright and his works expands your general knowledge of theatre.

3. *Do some basic study or research on the era in which the play was originally written and produced.* A play set in Atlanta, Georgia, in 1950 has an entirely different social milieu than a play set in the same city in 1980. The most immediate sources of material of this kind are standard history textbooks, periodicals, and newspapers.

4. *Read the play a second time focusing your attention on your role.* Try to locate any and all aspects of the role which you think are similar to your person, personality, and behavioral characteristics. Be certain that you take notes on these personalization discoveries in order to utilize them in the

early part of your rehearsal period. Finding as many aspects of the role that are already like you decreases the chances for artificial or forced acting in the crucial preliminary stages of rehearsal. Personalization is the key to early comfort, relaxation, and believability. This is part of the process loosely called "letting the role come to you rather than your pursuing it." The notes you take during your second reading begin your personalization work.

5. *The director usually provides the next step in role analysis, namely, play analysis.* Play analysis refers to the understanding of the form, structure, and literal and metaphorical content of a play. It includes a basic understanding of the play's type, style, subject issues, theme and intellectual content, exposition, point of attack, conflict, major dramatic question, protagonist or central character, antagonist or opposing force, deciding agent, struggle and complications, major crisis or turn, climax, outcome or denoument, and character drives (most of these terms are defined in the Glossary). While play analysis is basically the responsibility of the director, an actor can enhance his work greatly by knowing how the play is made and how it works in terms of performance. Play analysis is particularly important to an understanding of the emotional builds and peaks of your role. Therefore, if role analysis is not provided by a director, a thinking actor does well to analyze the play for himself. However, play analysis is a complex process and one which lies somewhat outside the province of basic acting techniques. A basic approach to play analysis is outlined in Appendix A of this book.

6. *Take a blue pencil or ball-point pen and underline all physical action performed by your character directly in your script.* Include action directed to you by "stage directions" as well as action clearly implied by dialogue (in which case, you need to make a marginal note of what action you think is implied by the dialogue). The question arises as to whether the actor should follow all stage directions printed in the script. Some directors follow these directions closely, although they may realize that all of the directions are not from the author. Most printed stage directions are from a master production script of a professional company. The actor has the same discretion as the director; he can completely ignore the directions in rehearsal and performance, he can follow them faithfully, or he can use some and disregard others. Whichever course *you* follow, it remains important to underline the directions in order to grasp the overall action pattern of your character as indicated by the author or other producers. Armed with this knowledge, you can better decide whether to retain or disregard the printed stage direction.

7. *Take a red pencil or ball-point pen and make a D to designate major character "discoveries" in the margin of your acting script.* A discovery is any knowledge you learn about the character ranging from such simple matters as "Frank is a black American male" to "Ellen suffers from guilt at having run away from home twenty years before the beginning of the play." Insert a red arrow connecting the letter *D* in the margin to the precise line or action which reveals the discovery. At times, you may wish to add a brief sentence

The marked script of an actor performing the role of the Clown in Shakespeare's *Twelfth Night*. Notice the notes from the *Variorum*, the rehearsal schedule, and the sketch of Henry VIII's court jester. The pencil is an item actors too often forget, and should not!

or two beneath the *D* to clarify the nature of the discovery. In these instances, use phrases or simple sentences, not lengthy narrative.

8. *Visualize your character carefully*. Begin with any description offered by the author either through stage directions or from dialogue. Complete the description with your own understanding of the character. Obviously, this description necessarily utilizes many of your own physical characteristics. After all, you are performing the role, and personalization dictates that the role is you to some extent. While makeup and costume alter this factor, your fundamental physical characteristics remain at the base of the visual aspects of your character. It is particularly important to note any physical abnormalities of your character such as a crippled arm, a humped back, and so on. Be aware of how your character wears his or her hair. Does your character wear glasses? If your character bald? Does your character wear false teeth? Does your character have arthritis? Is your character hard-of-hearing?

Visualization includes careful understanding of how your character dresses; for example, is your character neat and well groomed or casual and slovenly? Is your character dressed in the latest style? Does your character favor certain colors? Know what kind of shoes your character wears because most movement will be affected by foot apparel. Also note what costume accessories your character uses such as jewelry, purses, handkerchiefs, hats, and so on. It is strongly recommended that you establish your visualization concretely by writing it out as a list.

Some actors complete character visualization by selecting an animal which in appearance, movement, or manner seems analogous to the role they are creating. For example, Marlon Brando used an ape as part of his visualization for the crude and savage role of Stanley Kowalski in Tennessee Williams' *A Streetcar Named Desire.* Select an animal analogous to your character and write out a description of the appearance, movement, and behavior characteristics of the animal, clarifying how those traits relate to your role. When you begin rehearsals, you may wish to consciously attempt some of the animal's movement and behavior to assist visualization. (A bird may also be used, but animals usually provide more humanlike characteristics.)

9. *Study your role carefully in terms of emotional behavior and personality traits.* In other words, examine your role in terms of its psychological factors. For example, is your character generally quiet, demure, and retiring or loud, flamboyant, and extroverted? Note the basic emotions engaged in by your character: fear, love, hate, anger, pride, desire, jealousy, envy, and so on. Conclude by writing a personality description of your character as a list of phrases and simple sentences.

10. *Select someone from life well known to you; the person should be analogous to your role.* Do an observation study of this person. Try to select a relative or friend. Do not let the person know you are using him for observation. Note visual and psychological characteristics in detail. Write a description of the characteristics and behavior from your life study.

11. *Discover and specifically define the motivational spine of your character or what is often called the character's MF, that is, motivating force.* The motivating force should be stated as one complete sentence including the action verb *wants*; for example, "Willy wants Biff to love him again." Be certain that the statement is specific and involves other characters whenever possible. Conflict exists between two or more people more often than it exists between people and things or between people and themselves.

12. *Make a list of the major beats of action carried out in the play or scene by your character.* A *beat* is the distance from the beginning to the end of an intention. For example, a card game between two men on stage encompasses a beat. Changing from one subject under discussion in a play to a different subject also constitutes a beat. (The smallest beat is any single line of dialogue. However, for a role analysis list, it is best to use "intentions" and "subjects" as beats.) Your list of beats should be constructed sequentially from the beginning of a play or scene to the end of it.

13. *Based on your understanding of the printed text, write a creative imaginary biographical list of major subtext events in your character's life prior to the time of the play.* This list should begin with the specific date of birth and astrological sign of your character, including a brief description of what the sign generally indicates. Knowing the significance of astrological signs is important to many people in contemporary society. However, if such knowledge is not of great significance to you, and the text does not indicate that it is significant to the character either, you may omit this point. Obtain

your character's birth date by subtracting the character's age from the year the play occurs; if the year of the play is not given, either use the present year or carefully select a year that seems sensible to the text. If your character's age is not given, use your own age *or* carefully select an age that seems sensible to the text. It is crucial that you restrict subtextual major life events to very important or traumatic events. Write these events as a list, not as a narrative. Do not let your imagination run wild and create subtext wholly out of keeping with your character and the play. *Subtext must always be justified by its relevancy to text.* If you have marked your textual discoveries well, noted your actions carefully, and thoroughly accomplished the textual work just described, you will rarely go astray in the process of creating *valid* subtext. For example, subtext might include such items as "had no formal education beyond second grade," "mother died when I was age thirteen," "went to work in coal mine at age fourteen," "father was an alcoholic," "fell in love for first time at age fifteen," "joined the army at age seventeen," and so on. Complete your subtext by creating a list of succinct subtext events related to text describing the major activities your character has undergone from the moment of rising from bed on the morning of act I to the exact moment you first enter the stage action.

14. *Create a brief list of subtext events for all offstage activity of your character following every exit made during the play,* concluding each offstage sequence at the moment your character enters the stage again.

15. *Create a brief list of major character idiosyncrasies, likes, and dislikes.* For example, "loves wine; hates meat; likes fish or fowl; suffers from insomnia; reads classical Spanish literature"; and so on.

16. *Maintain a rehearsal-and-performance log or diary concerning your work with your character.* No one but you and your instructor or director need ever read this log. The log should create a progressive and permanent record of your growth and development as well as of your disappointments and problems. Only experiences directly related to your role creation need be included. Note in the log all major events, changes, and experiences which affect your earlier role analysis.

17. *When the final performance of a scene or play is concluded, write a brief objective self-evaluation of final results of your work with the character in terms of role creation and execution of the part.*

Many directors use the second phase of rehearsals for *blocking the movement* of the characters. Often directors plan the blocking for the actor and dictate the movements at rehearsals. In these instances, you should mark all blocking in the script with a pencil, using the symbols learned in chapter 8 as a kind of shorthand. Later, as line memorization occurs and the script is no longer carried in rehearsal, the blocking patterns should also be memorized and become instinctive. However, some directors prefer to take a more flexible, organic approach to blocking. For a week or more such directors permit actors to move at will according to motivational instincts. Later, the director refines or polishes the movement. During either of these kinds of blocking rehearsals, it is advisable to use *personalization* for the sake of relaxation, comfort, and believability. In other words, an actor should not work immediately for characterization and emotion. Rather, he should use as much of his own person as possible in rehearsals to establish a comfortable base for later characterization work.

Following blocking and personalization rehearsals, most productions enter the period known as *work rehearsals.* These rehearsals are devoted to moment-by-moment coaching of actors by the director. Some directors use a technique known as *scene combing.* In these rehearsals a director permits actors to experiment in order to discover new values and character nuances. For example, a director may have an actor comb a scene by performing opposite values throughout; that is, when the script obviously calls for love, the actor performs hate; courage is displayed rather than fear; fear is used instead of courage. At times, directors have actors exchange roles in order to provide fresh insights into character. When they are working with a director who rigidly dictates all aspects of character development, an unwritten code of the theatre demands that actors oblige him. However, in these instances an actor has the right to question and discuss interpretation and, of course, to work privately (provided such work does not go directly against the intentions of the director). Remember that the theatre is a collaborative art, and in contemporary theatre the director usually has the final word on all aspects of production. Nonetheless, the wise director knows the actor is paramount in the production process because the actor communicates more directly with the audience than does any other theatre artist. Accordingly, a sensible director creates an environment which permits maximum actor creativity. During work rehearsals and scene-combing periods, both personalization and traditional techniques of role creation are used to advantage.

At what point does the actor turn to traditional techniques of role creation to complete what he is trying to accomplish with personalization? A skilled, understanding director can help you identify when to modify personalization and when to use traditional techniques. There are points of characterization which personalization cannot accomplish. In these instances, actors should turn to traditional techniques to handle a problem. These techniques include use of makeup and costumes, lighting, properties, physical mannerisms, observation, imagination, and improvisation. However, great acting usually does not begin with those techniques. It begins with the richness of the person! Technique follows rather than leads.

Following work rehearsals, most directors utilize a number of *run-through rehearsals.* The director no longer stops the action for coaching. He devotes these rehearsals to continuity and rhythm. The actors polish their earlier work. The director takes notes which are relayed to the actors after rehearsals to aid their polishing. (Many directors use a small tape recorder for these notes.) In professional theatre, notes are usually written/typed and given to the actor the next day.

Finally, *technical rehearsals* are used to implement scenery, lighting, properties, costumes, and makeup. These rehearsals culminate either in a

The Stage Artist and
Stage Makeup: "Before
and After."

preview performance before an invited audience or in the actual opening
of the production before a paid audience. Some directors continue to give
polishing notes or minor changes to actors during technical rehearsals and
performances. In these instances, honor the desire to continue improvement. Other directors choose to completely "give a show over" to actors
once performances have begun. Normally, the stage manager replaces the
director as the production supervisor once performances begin.

Incidentally, in most college and university theatre an established custom following the final performance of a production is that all actors assist
the technical crews in the *strike,* or dismantling and storing of all scenery,
properties, and costumes.

Discipline: Working with a Director or Artist-Leader

Whether they are creating a role in a traditional theatre experience or creating a performance with an improvisational group, the key factor (beyond
ability) required of actors by a director or artist-leader is discipline. What
does the term imply? Punctuality and reliability are implied. It is an excellent idea to arrive consistently fifteen minutes prior to all rehearsal calls.
This early arrival time should be used for preparation and warm-up. An
athlete cannot compete in an activity without first warming up with calisthenics. A singer cannot sing well without warming-up; a dancer cannot
dance well without warming-up; a musician cannot play an instrument well
without warming-up. Should an actor consider himself any less obligated?

An actor should not rehearse or perform without vocal, body, and mental exercises as a prelude to the rehearsal or performance. Warm-ups should be executed either as individual activity or as group activity. The latter frequently involves use of theatre games that focus on concentration and relaxation. Effective games include jumping imaginary rope in groups of four or five and playing catch with an imaginary ball. Word-repetition games whereby an actor says a word and each subsequent actor repeats that word and adds another, all the while repeating every word spoken before his turn, are also effective.

Reliability means consistent attendance at rehearsals. Legitimate illness and death in the family are probably the only valid excuses for missing a rehearsal. An actor should notify the stage manager or assistant director prior to the rehearsal of these circumstances. Reliability connotes dedication; in other words, it establishes an actor's reputation.

Discipline also establishes his rehearsal behavior. Poor discipline results in distracting chatter in the wings or auditorium, in missed cues or entrances, and absences from the theatre without the permission of the stage manager or assistant director. (Rarely should an actor bother the director or artist-leader by asking him for special consideration.)

An actor can best demonstrate good discipline at rehearsal by sitting quietly in the wings or auditorium, absorbing all activity. He can also accomplish good discipline by working with a colleague actor in the greenroom (i.e., actor waiting area) or other location in the theatre well away from the stage (provided that the stage manager or assistant director knows precisely where he is). Always plan economical use of offstage time at rehearsals because some directors fail to budget rehearsal time effectively.

Actors should never invite friends or relatives to a rehearsal or for a visit in the theatre (if someone is to meet you or pick you up, ask the person to come to the greenroom or door of the theatre at a specific time and wait for you there).

Another important aspect of discipline is how well actors cooperate with the technical staff and crews. For example, be punctual for all costume measurements and fitting sessions. After their use, return all hand or personal properties to the proper person or replace them in the location established for such items. Have respect for and stay out of the way of the activity of stagehands and crew members. Be particularly respectful and pleasant to the costume dresser if the complexity of your changes merit your having a dresser. If potential dangers or problems are noticed or if irritations or complaints develop, do not brood about them or gossip about them with colleague actors. Discuss them politely and openly with the stage manager or assistant director. If either one believes the problem merits it, the director will be brought into the discussion. However, any onstage problem should be discussed immediately with the director at the moment it occurs or following rehearsal (again, never take petty matters to a fellow actor, expand such matters out of proportion, or create rifts and dissention).

Theatre decorum provides a precise chain of command which should be rigorously followed. If an actor violates this decorum, creates dissention, or loses his temper, he gains the infamous label *prima donna*. Legitimate human behavior has its place in the theatre. If temper flares, let it, but end the episode quickly. There is no place in the theatre for holding a grudge or for self-indulgent behavior. (The precise chain of command for a particular production or performance is usually determined and announced by the director or artist-leader at the beginning of rehearsals.) Discipline is the heart of acting success because it demonstrates how to use one's ability for the benefit of group or ensemble harmony and achievement. Establish rigid, productive discipline in a constructive manner early in your training. Never deviate from a sense of discipline, especially when and if success and notoriety are achieved. Self-discipline is the mark of a professional artist.

Sustaining a Role or Performance

In educational theatre, actors will probably not encounter the problem of sustaining a role over a long period of time (unless they are fortunate enough to go on tour). However, performing in the professional theatre, repertory, and stock means sustaining an effective performance over several weeks, months, or even years. How does an actor sustain a fresh, spontaneous performance under such circumstances?

Improvisation is an effective technique to sustain role creation when spontaneity is lost. For example, an actress portraying Ophelia in a production of *Hamlet* was unable to create the appropriate emotion in the scene in which she explains Hamlet's mad appearance to Polonius. According to Shakespeare's script, the character Hamlet is not in the scene. To assist the actress with genuine visual and emotional recall, the director asked the actor playing Hamlet to *improvise* the unwritten scene with the actress playing Ophelia. The actor improvised all of Shakespeare's descriptions in carefully scored detail as the actress watched him and reacted to his improvisation. Later, the actress rehearsed the actual scene from the script with Polonius. Her description of Hamlet's appearance and behavior was charged with new emotional depth and believability.

Frequently, omitted or unwritten scenes in a play must be performed through rehearsal improvisation. It is an excellent technique and one that is all too infrequently used by actors and directors because it takes time and extra work. Insist on using the technique even if you must do it on your own, away from the theatre.

Other techniques for sustaining a role include spot rehearsals in which actors alter pantomimic dramatization, business, and movement.

Another interesting technique is to rehearse a problem scene by reversing roles with another actor. For example, two actresses playing Antigone and Ismene could exchange roles and a fresh viewpoint might result from the different interaction.

Teresa Gilmore and Grey Schmidt demonstrate actors in PERFORMANCE: Exercises and Rehearsal behind them, actors in costume and makeup perform before an audience on a stage with scenery, properties, and stage lighting. Photograph by Randy Tunnel.

If a scene is difficult, again try the rehearsal technique of using animal or bird mannerisms similar to those of your character (e.g., walk like an ape or strut like a peacock).

Still another technique is to rehearse the problem scene without dialogue relying strictly on pantomime or gibberish (i.e., nonsense sounds).

Playing opposite values is usually rewarding in revitalization of a role (see chapter 8).

It might also be effective to rehearse a scene in the dark with words only using no movement or business.

It is also a good idea to sit down with the play and read it again after performances have begun. Continuity will be increased and important factors may be caught which have been missed or for some reason have been eliminated (such as transitional words and specific stage directions).

Any type of fresh invention assists an actor in finding new life in a scene or moment gone dead.

As you conclude Part I of actor training, remember that there is no substitute for practice. All the theory in the world is useless if it is not applied. Merely reading this or any other book on acting is of little value if exercises are not practiced every day. An actor is no different from a musician or dancer. There will never be time to practice—an actor must make the time if he is a serious student of acting. Katharine Hepburn has perhaps said it best:

> A lot of hogwash is talked about acting. It's not all that fancy! When Nijinsky visited Chaplin on a set, Charlie was about to have a custard pie in his face and Nijinsky said, "The nuances! The miraculous timing!" And it's a lot of bunk. You laugh, you cry, you pick up a little bit, and then you're a working actor. It's a *craft!* You're out there desperately doing something you hope people will come and see. Nowadays directors, stars are constantly talking—pretentiously and a great deal more than they should—about their art. Talk, talk, talk, talk, *talk!* Spencer Tracy always said acting was "Learn your lines and get on with it," so does Larry Olivier, so does John Gielgud, and the great ones. . . . *Life's* what's important. Walking, houses, family. Birth and pain and joy—and then death. Acting's just waiting for a custard pie. That's all.[1]

In other words, there comes a time when intellectualizing and discussion must cease. Finally, acting is action—saying, listening, and doing! Acting is organic *reaction!*

With Part I of this book completed, you are now ready to pursue specialized study in the "styles" of acting.

Suggested Readings

Burton, Hal, ed. *Great Acting.* New York: Hill & Wang, 1967.

Chaikin, Joseph. *The Presence of the Actor.* New York: Atheneum, 1972.

Cole, Toby, and Chinoy, Helen K., eds. *Actors on Acting.* New York: Crown Publishers, 1949.

Funke, Lewis, and Booth, John E. *Actors Talk About Acting: Fourteen Interviews with Stars of the Theatre.* New York: Random House, 1961.

Green, Michael. *The Art of Coarse Acting.* New York: Drama Book Specialists, 1981.

Hindman, James, Kirkman, Larry, and Monk, Elizabeth. *TV Acting. A Manual for Camera Performance.* New York: Hastings House, 1981.

Hodge, Francis. *Play Directing: Analysis, Communication, and Style.* 2d. Ed. Englewood-Cliffs, N.J.: Prentice-Hall, 1982.

Kuritz, Paul. *Playing: An Introduction to Acting.* Englewood-Cliffs, N.J.: Prentice-Hall, 1981.

Lewes, George. *On Actors and the Art of Acting.* New York: Grove Press, 1957.

---

1. Charles Higham, "Private and Proud and Hepburn," New York *Times,* 9 December, 1973.

Marshall, Norman. *The Producer and the Play.* Rev. ed. London: Macdonald & Evans, 1962.

Matthews, Brander, ed. *Papers on Acting.* New York: Hill & Wang, 1958.

Osborn, Alex. *Achieving Characterization in Applied Imagination.* New York: Charles Scribner's Sons, 1963.

Redgrave, Michael. *The Actor's Ways and Means.* London: William Heinemann, 1953.

Stanislavsky, Konstantin. *Building a Character.* New York: Theatre Arts Books, 1936.

Strasberg, Lee. *Strasberg at the Actor's Studio.* Edited by Robert H. Hethmon. New York: Viking Press, 1965.

Strickland, F. Cowles. *The Technique of Acting.* New York: McGraw-Hill Book Co., 1956.

Styan, John Louis. *The Dramatic Experience.* London: Cambridge University Press, 1964.

Acting: II
In Style

Introduction to Part II
"In Style"

What is "style"? *Style* is a frequently misunderstood and misused word in the theatre today. For example, it is a common mistake to call any non-realistic play or theatre experience "stylized." It is as though that one highly general term encompasses all possibilities and thereby all nonrealistic theatre activity is swept "by one broom into one basket."

In recent years, scholars and artists of the theatre have attempted to define the illusive term, "style." For example, at its conventions and conferences, members of the American Theatre Association have created forums and meetings to address this matter. Roger Gross of the University of Arkansas, Fayetteville, among others, has provided valuable leadership in this work. Some of the ideas in this Introduction are indebted to remarks made in public forums by Professor Gross, as well as to such authors as Aristotle, Michel St. Denis, Francis Hodge, James H. Clay, and Daniel K. Krempel.

The achievement of style in the theatre, particularly in the art of acting, requires specific analysis. For example, many actors do not know that Realism is as stylized as Romanticism or Expressionism. Realism is a distinct style of play requiring a distinct style of acting, just as does Expressionism or whatever.

No matter the style required, the initial and central problem of an actor is to use personalization to establish comfort and familiarity with his role or activity. Then he must communicate the intentions of the playwright as revealed by the action and characters of the script or the theatrical activity. Language, mood, emotions, thoughts, and physical activity are all parts of personalizing and communication.

In his important book *Theatre: The Rediscovery of Style*, Michel Saint-Denis discusses how *style* is rooted in the form and content of the play, in its language, and in its place in the past, that is, in its historical period. Saint-Denis emphasizes that each style has its own reality based on the totality of the script and its historic period. According to Saint-Denis, this is the same as saying "the style is the man himself." In other words, the style of the play is not determined merely by its language, or by the social conventions of the period, or by the design of the scenery. The *total* play in historic perspective creates its style, that is, its particular reality.

In its simplest and earliest definition, the word *style* comes from the Latin word *stilus*, a pointed instrument used by the ancients in writing on wax tablets. The stilus made an imprint, a definition, into the wax and left its expression in either design or words. This indentation made a distinct, original, and sometimes artistic impression. We loosely attribute style to a person who is an artist or who is artistic. In this sense, any person can be an artist who is said to have style, from the lady who wears her fox fur elegantly to a sculptor welding a metal collage. Style represents not only a personal stamp, but also a mode of perception by the artist. He chooses a recognizable pathway from his intention to his execution and synthesizes the form and material into a living emotional or intellectual experience which is particular to him. When a literary or dramatic artist can compel his language to conform to his mode of experience, his communication with the audience will be more precise and, therefore, comprehensible.

It is true that a playwright sometimes manipulates his material to create his personal stamp or style. By degrees and by kind, he incorporates lifelike qualities into his characters. Within each play will be various departures from true-to-life representations.

There are two courses open to a playwright when he re-creates a particular reality in the theatre. If he chooses a representational technique, he brings a truthful image of life into the theatre which establishes and enhances the illusion of his reality. The actors appear to represent true life by being *oblivious* of the audience and interact only with each other. In representational drama, the audience is only permitted to "peek through an illusory fourth wall." The other avenue open to a playwright is to utilize the presentational technique which directs the actor to focus on the audience with *awareness* that it is there watching. This creates a different kind of reality, one which *includes* the audience within it.

Saint-Denis clarified that learning to act in any style means accepting the concept that an acting style is an organic outgrowth of a play. *Style in a theatre production is the truth or essence of the particular play being produced. Primarily, it is the author's particular view of truth or reality.* Even a distorted nightmare depicted on stage is truth and reality to its author. *Obviously, then, style is a direct result of the choices used by the artist in creating the art object.* (It was Aristotle who noted that *identity* is revealed primarily by choice.) *Thus, individual choices are made to create an object or form, controlled by the goals established by the artist, and the result of those choices and goals creates the particular style of the object, form, and artist. It follows that the task of any actor relative to the delineation of style is to understand and find ways to execute or perform the author's/character's choices accurately and with a truthful sense of inevitability.* This entire process is what Professor Gross and others have called "organic," that is, interconnected and fluid.

As Saint-Denis also explained, the style of a play is additionally a process which creatively reflects the mode of some particular era. The author mirrors the hopes, desires, and attitudes of the people living in his age. The playwright is motivated by current psychological, social, religious, and philosophical influences. He is further influenced by the architecture of the theatre, the climate and geography of the country, the technical means of production, the traditions of playwriting, the theories of acting, and the nature of the audiences who see his plays. When an audience is led to identify and accept the reality of the artistic statement, then the mode of presenting the truth of the author and his age becomes the dominant style of the period.

How can we delineate the truths of the past? Style is captured by presenting the author's reality in its own way, not by imposing our own or some other reality on it. Much of the truth of an age resides in the values, personal relationships, and insights into the human condition revealed by its literary and dramatic artists. Also, the prevailing mood, the aesthetic and sensory awareness, the scientific investigation, and the search for knowledge are expressed in an individualized manner by the playwright.

However, all the traditions of a particular age cannot be translated from generation to generation. We can only infuse acting with style by commanding our attention to the plays which in turn will lead us to the spirit of the author and his age. After all, the theatre is not life. The theatre represents life.

How can the actor arrive at an authentic appraisal of the playwright's personal stamp or style? In order for the actor to comfortably adopt the original style, he must first examine the dramatic form of a play, either tragedy or comedy, or their derivatives, melodrama, farce, tragicomedy, and other subforms. The reading of plays will help one develop an understanding of the basic classifications of the drama. In addition, study in play analysis can bring awareness of the basic essentials that relate form to the literal and metaphorical content of a play (see Francis Hodge for an in-depth study of play analysis, as well as James H. Clay and Daniel K. Krempel for a metaphorical approach to play analysis).[1] Play analysis (which is specifically a director's responsibility, but is invaluable also to an actor) involves study of a play's form, literal and metaphorical content, structure (e.g., plot, character, thought, dialogue, melody, and spectacle), and author's intention. Play analysis precedes style analysis, which is the final clarification of a play's particular reality and its means of expressing that reality (a detailed guide to play analysis is provided in Appendix A). See also the discussion of acting in style in John Harrop's and Sabin Epstein's book, *Acting With Style*.[2]

Your specific study of style beings with the great century of classical antiquity, fifth century B.C., in the country of Greece.

---

1. Francis Hodge, *Play Directing, Analysis, Communication and Style*, 2d. Ed. (Englewood-Cliffs, N.J.: Prentice-Hall, 1982); James H. Clay and Daniel K. Krempel, *The Theatrical Image* (New York: McGraw-Hill Book Co., 1967).

2. John Harrop and Sabin Epstein, *Acting With Style* (Englewood-Cliffs, N.J.: Prentice-Hall, 1982).

Classical Antiquity 11
Restraint

Man's life is a day. What is he?
What is he not? A shadow in a dream
Is man: but when God sheds a brightness,
Shining light on earth
And life is sweet as honey.

Pindar
The Pythian Odes

Never man again may swear things shall be
as they once were.

Archilochus
from *Ancient Gems in Modern Settings*

Pindar and Archilochus reflect the spirit of ancient Greece. Man was fated to be subservient to the gods, but in subservience he drew upon his free will and the sense of his own magnificence to create a civilization whose influence was to be with us always. Almost as though they knew this civilization would pass away, the ancient Greeks lived fully, and life was indeed "sweet as honey."

To Delphi by bus is a long, arduous ride through countryside that is at once beautiful, rocky, unfertile, and uninhabited. Sumptuous mountains stretch for miles around and sage covers the land. Although Delphi has many attractions, it is primarily the oracle that for centuries has drawn people to the shrine. After a climb from the road to the shrine, the Charioteer of Delphi is the first edifice to catch the eye. Another quartermile up the hill, the Temple of Athena and the Temple of Apollo stand blazingly in the afternoon sun. Weary tourists of every generation have walked the Sacred Way to face the oracle and ask for advice from Apollo. Possibly modern tourists also file past this once imposing monument seeking an answer to some impossible question. In ancient times, Delphi was Greece's central archive and seat of political intelligence and was the most sacred and powerful place in Greece. The oracle, as interpreted by the priests, wished to promote stability in government and religion. However, the priesthood strongly encouraged the orgiastic cult of Dionysus (the god of wine and fertility), who occupied the temple as alternate god in winter when Apollo was away.

Overview of Greek Tragedy

The origins of Greek drama are generally familiar, but extremely speculative. Few matters of scholarship are certain. Vase paintings, some extant plays, and writing fragments provide most of the available information. Greek drama probably evolved from the rites performed in honor of Dionysus by masked worshipers who danced and sang (e.g., Dithyrambs, or hymns to Dionysus) and worked themselves into a frenzy in order to lose their identity and merge with nature and gods. As drama slowly emerged from these ceremonies, it became more and more formalized. So, too, did the physical place evolve as a recognizable area for the presentation of drama. The very earliest *orchestra* or dancing place was probably a threshing floor worn smooth by oxen who trod grain upon it. Around the orchestra the *theatron* or seeing place developed where the spectators sat on the ground to watch the religious ceremonies. These earliest theatres were always built into a hillside to accommodate large numbers of people. Historical references are also made concerning the custom of having the actors change costumes in a tent or *skene* in a sacred wood nearby. As plays grew more complex, the actors were required to enter and leave the orchestra more quickly. Eventually a wooden skene, or scene house, containing dressing rooms and storage space was built directly behind the theatre for the actors. In time, painted set pieces were placed in front of this building

Dionysus! A Fifth Century depiction of the Wine-god, complete with wine-cup and ivy branch. The spirit of classical Greek theatre is epitomized in this depiction.

to represent scenery. These became more and more intricate with the evolution of the *proskenion*, or central playing area, and the scene building itself became merely a background structure. Wooden and later stone seats were added to the hillside.

The first actor of record was Thespis, who was also a playwright and production manager or precursor of the director. We have evidence that Thespis performed in the first dramatic-religious festivals in Athens around 534 B.C. He probably wore different masks to represent different characters and was the sole actor in a tragedy. These early plays used a chorus or group of singer-dancers who sang odes between the actor's speeches or dialogue.

The chorus served ultimately as character, narrator, participant, and ideal spectator. Only men were allowed to act in plays.

In tragedy, three great writers are noteworthy because of their exemplary work and their significant contributions to the development of dramatic art and theatre: Aeschylus (525–456 B.C.), Sophocles (496–406 B.C.), and Euripides (480–406 B.C.). In comedy, Aristophanes (ca. 448–ca. 380 B.C.) was probably the greatest Greek author of Old Comedy (meaning "early"). Later, another writer, Menander (ca. 342–292 B.C.), contributed significantly to the transition from Greek to Roman comedy.

Greek tragedy can be characterized as follows:

1. Use of a limited number of characters acted usually by one to three actors who changed masks to portray different roles. Most scholars agree that Aeschylus used a single actor in his plays; Sophocles, two actors; and Euripides, three or more.
2. Use of a singing-dancing chorus. It should be noted that Aeschylus emphasized the chorus in his plays and Euripides emphasized the actor, giving little attention to the chorus. Sophocles struck a balance of emphasis.
3. Use of iambic trimeter verse for dialogue and for choral odes.
4. Use of a superhuman hero in the plays of Aeschylus, usually a powerful mythological character whose will was continually subjugated to the higher impersonal power of the gods.
5. Use of refined, idealized characters with human problems (rather than religious themes) in the plays of Sophocles, centered on strong, forceful, vehement emotion with which the audience could easily identify.
6. Use of ordinary characters with everyday problems in which thought and emotion were unified in the plays of Euripides, providing the transition from old to new ideas and from religion-myth to human passion.
7. Use of sexual themes in the plays of Euripides to portray man's beginning struggle not with fate and the gods, but with society and his mind and emotions.

Beauty, truth, and grandeur were the objectives of the tragic writers. Greek verse is noble and poetic and stresses a measured cadence. Action is brief and straightforward and concentrates on a single point. Characters are present at any given time on the stage. The Greek authors carefully avoided indiscriminate realism or excessive violence in front of an audience; this action was performed offstage or told in the narrative (note the death of Ajax in Sophocle's *Ajax* and of Evadine in Euripides's *Suppliants*). Greek tragedy penetrates our feelings by its even flow of dialogue interspersed with passages of choral odes and subtle changes of metrical form enhanced by accurate vocal intonation.

Greek acting was characterized by the wearing of masks—large, serious masks for tragedy and somewhat more life-size but grotesque ones for comedy. Early in the development of Greek drama, simple slippers were used on the feet, and the actors may have also performed in bare feet. Later, thick wooden or cork shoes were worn. High shoes or boots called *cothurni* increased an actor's height to larger-than-life size. Long, flowing garments or short simple ones usually in brilliant colors, were used. Probably the masks were also very colorful. Later, a high headdress was frequently worn. (Highly simplified scenic equipment may have been available for performances, such as altars, statues, tombs, cranes, scenic prisms, and platforms.)

The exact style of acting in Greek tragedy remains uncertain. Scholars offer a number of theories from which we may determine the attributes of a typical classical Greek actor. We do know that acting was considered a craft by the classical Greek philosopher Socrates. To Plato, his protégé and another great philosopher, acting was something that could not, and should not, be learned. The extant play texts reveal that acting in tragedy called for simple, direct action—clear, controlled, and orderly. Some realistic actions are suggested in the plays, such as running, weeping, and falling on the ground. Conventional action was often necessary, as in the choral passages where lyricism and dance are prevalant. While we know that actors had to play many characters within each play and that men took female roles, it may be that females acted minor comedy parts. Although we know that a realistic or lifelike technique of acting was not employed totally by Greek tragic actors, performance of Greek plays today should not be devoid of identifiable human action. It is possible that actors created a sense of realism by discovering expressive and sympathetic characteristics and portrayed them in a somewhat idealized form. The total concept of characterization, then, was truthfulness in a somewhat larger-than-life impersonation.

Voice – Greek Tragedy

Acting techniques for the tragic Greek actor were very specialized due to the tremendous size of the physical theatre. The size can be calculated to be approximately the area of a football stadium and the number of spectators to range from 15,000 to 100,000. Acoustics in this bowl-shaped structure were good. Given a strong, resonant, clear voice, an actor probably did not exert excessive vocal effort. More than likely the emphasis was on vocal projection, not on increased volume. Perhaps actors were cautioned to deliver speeches with clear enunciation and heightened word emphasis. In effect, the impression created probably tended more toward a recitative or singing mode.

To perform Greek tragedy in present-day theatre, use strong vocal projection, heightened word emphasis, precise diction, and varied tonal qualities (singing a musical scale is an effective preparatory exercise for vocal work in Greek tragedy). Obviously you (and your director) should lessen or increase projection according to the size of the theatre. However, you should not de-emphasize the enunciative quality of Greek speech. You may encounter difficulty when working with Greek lyrical passages, especially in key emotional moments. When a long sentence is sustained, it is very difficult to maintain precise diction throughout the line. On the other hand, you also face the possibility of losing the emotional builds at the expense of achieving competence in projection and enunciation.

Exercise 1 The Voice—Greek Tragedy

1. Each actor sings a musical scale individually. Repeat the exercise as a choral group.

2. Practice speaking the following line individually as though chanting it in an echo chamber. Repeat the exercise singing the line. Finally, repeat the exercise and modify the recitative and sung experience into spoken delivery, but retain the larger-than-life quality of the first two deliveries. Repeat the exercise as a choral group.

> "Let every man in mankind's frailty
> consider his last day, and let none
> Presume on his good fortune until he finds
> Life, at his death, a memory without pain."

> Chorus, Sophocles
> *Oedipus the King*

3. Go outdoors to a large, enclosed patio or to a stadium; practice calling and greeting other actors at long distances. Try the speech from *Oedipus the King* in number 2 above.

Movement — Greek Tragedy

In keeping with the serious vocal tone of tragedy, the Greek actor had to carry himself with authority and confidence. Most of his movement was probably slow, majestic, and rhythmic. Movement must have been simplified and broadened to accompany the idealized characterization. Physical contact between actors was probably rare; more than likely the quality of restraint was accentuated by allowing great physical distance between characters. The long monologues in the plays would seem to indicate that body positions were mostly full-front, one-quarter, or profile. The manner of speaking was probably directed more toward the audience than toward other actors (i.e., presentational). Gestures must have been simple, large or even grand, flowing, and complete, emanating from the upper part of the body. They were probably conventionalized and immediately understood by audiences. It is unlikely that actors ever sat on the stage. It is likely that simple hand props such as a staff, sceptre, or sword were carried. At times, certain characters such as a chorus of furies might have carried lighted torches. We can assume that the gods carried their emblems (e.g., a lion skin and club for Heracles).

A Greek tragedy given in today's theatre would probably utilize many of the original Greek conventions. Once again, depending on the size of the theatre, begin from the Greek concept of simple restraint. Generally perform slow, suggestive, rhythmic movements and gestures. The presentational mode of acting should probably dominate, but not to excess. However, a sensible balance between presentational and representational interpretation should be achieved; for example, when one actor turns to respond directly to the audience, the other actor should usually focus on the speaker. Individualized physical movements should be kept to a minimum. While you may move more onstage than your classical Greek counterpart, you must be extremely careful to sustain controlled physical presence. Modern adaptations of the Greek acting style rarely execute a purist concept of the original style. More often than not, you may be required to sit, carry more hand properties than the original Greek style, and interrelate with other actors more (e.g., touch, stand close, and so on).

It is not known in what exact style the chorus performed its dance functions. Here, too, a modern adaptation might be more flexible than suggested by the traditional Greek chorus. Since we have no record of choral dancing except descriptions that date back to the early religious ceremonies honoring the god Dionysus (e.g., dancing with animallike frenzy), the key to dance adaptation is probably to use controlled, dignified, stately movement with shifting rhythmic patterns.

It is difficult to speak about movements and gestures without again referring to the subject of masks and costumes since they directly affect an actor's physical projection. In the early development of Greek drama, masks may have been made of lightweight linen, wood, or cork. The mask was placed over the head of the actor and undoubtedly gave depth and clarity to facial expression and head movement. (The mask had an open mouth which a few historians say could have amplified the human voice; however, most recent scholarship does not support this view.) The mask indicated the essence of the character—tragic by an expression of physical or mental suffering and happy by a smile or contented look. In general, the mask showed the specific emotional state of the character. Sometimes, the actor changed masks as the character changed moods or as he changed roles. However, it would seem that the mask could be manipulated by the actor to create shadows which in turn gave an illusion of changing expression. Later in the development of Greek drama, most tragic characters wore a headdress or a wiglike structure called an *onkus* which was not unlike headdresses worn in everyday life. Together, the mask and the headdress probably restrained flexibility of head movement.

The body garment of the later Greek periods must have presented a problem of mobility. A long-sleeved, ankle-length, heavily embroidered tunic, or *chiton*, was worn by the major characters. According to scenes depicted on vase paintings, other characters wore native dress such as a short tunic, mourning clothes, or ragged garments, all designed to represent the daily clothes of ordinary Greek citizens. Indications are that the chorus wore clothing prescribed by age, sex, and national and social status. Although the clothing in later periods must have been somewhat restrictive due to length and heaviness, this in no way indicates that the actors were unable to move. In fact, costumes remained remarkably similar to the everyday dress of the citizens and did allow freedom of movement and speech and rapid change of roles, particularly during early development of Greek drama.

The modern actor need be concerned only with wearing a costume that does not inhibit freedom of movement. It would be a mistake to use a garment and its accompanying decor (e.g., headdress, boots) that would constrict you in any great way. The main concern is whether masks should be worn in a modern adaptation. It is my suggestion that masks be worn only when close fidelity to the original Greek is desired; generally, I advise *against* use of masks in today's theatre in order to aid audience involvement. Instead, I suggest heightened, formalized makeup, applied to resemble remotely the look of a mask or half-mask. (See Irene Corey's designs in this chapter, page 150.)

Exercise 2 Movement—Greek Tragedy

1. All actors come to an aligned position on their feet, breathing comfortably in a relaxed state. Move through space in the manner of a slow-motion film or in the manner of moving through water or as a spaceman on another planet. Concentrate upon grace, rhythm, fluidity, and a sense of controlled restraint.

2. Repeat Exercise 1 using a modified tempo and permitting the slow motion to evolve into an acceptably believable or realistic tempo.

3. Practice various forms of stereotyped movement gestures which reflect emotional states, such as drawing one arm up slowly with the back of your hand in front of your eyes, your other hand protruding behind you, and your body slowly bending backward to indicate grief. As a welcoming gesture, slowly extend both arms forward and upward with the palms up; the head should elevate somewhat, and the entire body should come to its full height. Freely invent other kinds of movement gestures.

4. Costume yourself in any kind of long robe and/or cape with bare feet, slippers, or sandals, and practice moving with grace and fluidity. Incorporate the garments into your gesturing.

Music—Greek Tragedy

It is important to understand the major emphasis placed on musical accompaniment in the original Greek plays. In the beginning, use of music was light, to underscore choral passages. Later, music became more prominent, and actors used a variety of instruments including the flute, whose tone was similar to that of a modern oboe or clarinet, and the lyre, a stringed instrument used for special effects. A flute player probably preceded the chorus into the orchestra, and played music as an accompaniment to underscore the emotions described in the choral passages. Occasionally, music might have been used during the episodes or acted segments. Music was extremely important in choral interludes because it made the singing and dancing more harmonious. Additionally, it aided in building choral passages to a climax.

Repeat Exercise 2 to the accompaniment of the extant musical fragments titled "Delphic Hymn" and "Epitaph of Seikilos and Mandikiaw."[1] If this recording is not available in your school library, any recording utilizing flutes, drums, and string instruments played in relatively slow tempo will do.

Again repeat Exercise 2, but this time *create* "music" through hand-clapping, humming, and fingersnapping.

Character and Emotion — Greek Tragedy

Greek tragedy reveals the author's awareness of each character's underlying motives and justification for action and emotion, but not at the sacrifice of the lyric poetry of the verse.

The problems of a modern actor attempting to physicalize emotions in an ideal way, to maintain believability, and to achieve truthfulness in a Greek role are not insurmountable. Difficulty will arise if you overemphasize the physical aspects of style instead of maintaining a good balance of believable characterization grounded in the reality of the style. Examine the play for primary motivations and justifications, particularly those analogous or similar to yours in order to use personalization at the beginning of rehearsals; find the emotional builds within each scene; discover the intentions of the character as described by the playwright. At times you may encounter conflicting or paradoxical stylistic demands such as restrained versus heightened vocalization and movement. The solution is not to play one quality and eliminate the other. Modify both or adapt them to today's theatre, using both qualities in an appropriate mix of the restrained and the heightened. Role and play analyses will indicate to you when restraint should dominate the acting and when the acting should be heightened. For example, in the play *Oedipus* by Sophocles, the actor portraying Oedipus may effectively use restraint through modern, naturalistic emotion when Oedipus talks to his subjects about the plague early in the play. Oedipus is emotionally under control; he is a proud, majestic king whose voice and movement are characterized by precision and grace. Later in the play, when Oedipus discovers that calamity is the result of his own actions, greatly heightened emotion, vocalization, and movement should be used, including rapid tempo, strong volume, expansive physicalization, and bold movement. Most Greek playwrights of tragedy wrote to idealize and to transcend the emotions of the ordinary Athenian citizens and to challenge them by exciting their pity for and fear of the character. To use both restrained and heightened emotion in a Greek tragedy requires careful analysis and intense concentration. You will need to adapt your emotion from so-called real-life emotion to the larger-than-life conception of the tragic writer.

1. RCA Victor Album *History of Music in Sound*, vol. 1, "Ancient and Oriental Music," LM 6057.

Studies in makeup design, formalized to resemble the look of the classical Greek mask. Design by Irene Corey for Sophocles' *Electra*. Everyman Players, directed by Orlin Corey.

Exercise 3   Character and Emotion—Greek Tragedy

1. Examine each of the following phrases which depicts a single idea and emotional disposition. Establish an immobile physical position which typifies the essence of the emotion or idea. The face and entire body should express the idea or feeling. Once this is successfully accomplished, place the physicalization and attitude into motion through simple walking, sitting, and gesturing. After this is accomplished, invent a complete sentence of dialogue expressing the idea or emotion you are depicting. Memorize the sentence, and as you physicalize and move, vocalize the sentence with different tempos and a variety of expressions ranging from classical restraint to naturalistic intensity.

   1. Excessive pride
   2. Incestuous passion
   3. Obsessive revenge
   4. Martyred sacrifice
   5. Burial grief
   6. Insane frenzy
   7. Blind drunkenness

2. Select a partner and face one another in a standing position, one of you designated as "leader." Using the concept of the "mirror" exercise, mimic one another in the facial depiction of various emotions; repeat the exercise, but this time the "follower" should facially express a *contrasting* emotion to that depicted by the "leader."

Electra by Sophocles.
Everyman Players.
Directed by Orlin Corey.
Designed by Irene Corey.

Overview of Satyr Comedy and Old Greek Comedy (Aristophanes)

As the Greek tragic playwrights acquired a following in the fifth century B.C., festival officials required them to present a satyr play when they competed in the festivals. A satyr play was a short comedy which usually burlesqued a Greek myth. This afterpiece utilized a chorus of satyrs whose function was to satirize the seriousness of tragic stories by parodying gods, heroes, tragic dances, actions, conventions of acting, costumes, and scenery. The satyrs wore a goatskin loincloth with a phallus (comic imitation of the male sexual organ) in the front and a horsetail in the rear. They wore tight flesh-colored garments which ridiculed tragic costumes. Some characters wore masks with fixed size and expression. In the earlier satyr plays, the masks were not large. Later masks covered the entire head and were decorated with hair, beards, and ornaments. The chorus usually wore identical masks representing animals; the actors wore masks with set human expressions. Characters who did not wear masks, primarily the satyrs, had a snub nose, dark unkempt hair, a beard, and pointed ears, or they were bald and wore horns on top of their head. All action concentrated on lewd pantomime and general buffoonery.

Today we have only one complete satyr play, *Cyclops* by Euripides. It is a parody of the serious story found in the *Odyssey*. A modern actor would rarely be asked to act in *Cyclops*. However, if you choose to perform a scene from the play, you might refer to the discussion of Greek comedy on pp. 152-155 of this book, paying special attention to the sections on the use of physical action.

Greek comedy was offically supported by the State beginning in 486 B.C. (it may have been part of the festival City Dionysia in 501 B.C.). The first professional comedians probably made their debut onstage around 455 B.C., displaying their buffoonery and comic jests. The chorus consisted of twenty-four members whose function was to perform music and dance.

Old Comedy as exemplified by the works of Aristophanes differed from tragedy principally in subject matter and in approach. The stories were concerned with contemporary matters of politics or art or with revealing corrupt public and private practices such as sustaining foreign war and the practice of pedantic sophistry. Well-known politicians, philosophers, and playwrights also received a fair share of notoriety in the plays. Usually institutions and public figures were satirized or held up to ridicule for their beliefs or practices. Plot was entirely the invention of the playwright, and unlimited license was the rule. Greek comic plays provided a balance between exaggeration and believability. Caricature was the the prominent feature in character portrayal; however, roles of minor stature required closer fidelity to real life. These so-called low characters projected everyday emotional response. Hence, verisimilitude or fidelity to real life was vital in Greek comedy, although fantasy was occasionally intermingled (see *The Birds, The Frogs, The Wasps, The Clouds,* etc.).

Voice – Old Greek Comedy

Vocalization in Old Greek Comedy was undoubtedly much more lifelike than was vocalization in tragedy. Since the characters were often members of lower social status, everyday speech was necessary (the exceptions to this were characters such as gods and statesmen). Vocal variety, clarity of diction, and effective projection are standard techniques for successful vocalization of Old Comedy. Occasionally, singing is required as well. Lyricism and rhythm are important in line delivery.

Exercise 4 Voice—Old Greek Comedy

1. Practice the following speech individually and then collectively emphasizing vocal variety, clear diction, and effective projection.

Frogs   Brekekekex Koax Koax
            Brekekekex Koax Koax!
            We are the swamp-children
            Greeny and tiny,
            Fluting our voices
            As all in time we
            Sing our Koax Koax
            Koax Koax Koax

2. Repeat the exercise by *singing* it lyrically and rhythmically, both individually and collectively.

3. Practice various kinds of animal, insect, and bird sounds, calls, and noises. (For example, goats, wasps, geese, and so on.) Eventually turn these sounds into comic, "human" variations of the sounds, including the actual use of words which are easily formed by the sounds. (For example, "bad" from "baaa," "fuzz" from "bzzz," and "whack" from "quaa.")

Movement — Old Greek Comedy

The movement in Old Greek Comedy was mimetic, large or bold, and expressive of a character type; expression undoubtedly developed from highly exaggerated wild-animal movements adapted from religious dances and victory celebrations. Emphasis was probably on kicking the buttocks, slapping the chest or thighs, leaping, high kicking, running, spinning like a top, and beating other actors. Some scholars think that three to five major characters in the play joined the chorus to perform pantomimic tricks and stage business with gusto and fast-paced rhythm. The movement must have depended on the performer executing a variety of skills. Athletic and disciplined, the actors probably reverted to extensive physical action and body contact, relying heavily on farcical and satiric invention and the interpolation of song, dance, and comic acrobatics.

Although comic costumes provided the actor with freer movement, they were not necessarily standard or prescribed. As seen on vase paintings, actors usually wore short, tight-fitting tunics (chitons) over flesh-colored tights to give the illusion of partial nakedness. Nudity and ridiculousness were further emphasized by attaching a phallus to the costumes of most male characters. As in the satyr plays, a mask was a common accoutrement of the comic costume. However, masks were probably more specialized in function, depicting actual persons or representing animals, birds, insects, or exaggerated characteristics such as baldness, skinniness, and obesity.

When Greek comic acting is adapted for modern audiences, very little adjustment is needed. Personalization can again be used effectively in early rehearsals, particularly if you have an instinctive flair for comedy, timing, laughter, and a sense of humor. Major focus should be on the extensive use of physical action and body contact, with corresponding pantomimic business. This simply means to use as much burlesque or vaudeville activity as you can invent. Use music and dance, singing, and acrobatics to provide interpolation between dialogue as well as to punctuate comic lines. Play to the audience slightly more than to one another (e.g., presentational technique slightly dominates representational). Let movements and gestures be energetic, large, and rapid. Coordinate your movements with the satiric speeches to add stress and clarity to the thought. Respond to an emotion when it is appropriate, but do not indulge in the feeling, or tempo and pace will be sacrificed. Use costume to simulate nudity, and to provide an illusion of sexuality use a phallus, provided that it is used for comic exaggeration rather than as a sexual reality. Modern adaptation probably calls for limited, or no, use of Greek comic masks. However, it would not be incorrect to use masks occasionally for minor characters, particularly when the playwright calls for a caricature or portrait effect (e.g., the creation of an animal face or the creation of a known individual such as Socrates in *The Clouds*). Most important, you must be physically able to handle the demands of Greek comedy. A high energy level helps provide the correct rhythm to the play; vocal variety, clear diction, and projection aid in crystallizing satirical points, and a relaxed, well-toned physical posture allows for body control and agility.

Exercise 5   Movement—Old Greek Comedy

1. Repeat vocal Exercise 4, but this time concentrate on executing the following physical activities as you deliver the lines.
   1. Somersaults
   2. Cartwheels
   3. High kicks
   4. Handstands
   5. Leapfrog
   6. Pratfalls
   7. Comic hitting, running, and animallike dancing
   8. Juggling
2. Costume yourself in any kind of short, sack-like garment with or without a waistbelt, and bare feet, slippers, or sandals. Construct simplified comic "tails," "phallus-like clubs," and "grotesque masks." Practice slapstick clowning, buffonery, dances, and acrobatics.

Character and Emotion in Old Greek Comedy

Authors of comedy such as Aristophanes focused upon a single obsessive dimension of human character, utilizing it for stereotype or caricature (only occasionally did he create full-dimensional, believable human characters). Aristophanes also used animals, birds, and inanimate objects as character types to represent human beings. He mixed reality and fantasy and treated both in a satiric manner. Examples of his character types include the pompous statesman or philosopher (see Socrates in *The Clouds*), the frustrated lover (see Kinesias in *Lysistrata*), the vulnerable and effeminate god (see Dionysus in *The Frogs*), the comic bird (see Epops in *The Birds*), and the amusing slave or parasite (see Xanthius in *The Frogs*). The emotion depicted by these characters was frequently singular and obsessive. For example, Kinesias's sole interest was in sexual activity with his wife. Accordingly, character and emotion in Old Greek Comedy are much less complex to perform than in Greek tragedy. Emphasis must be on mechanical techniques, physicalization, voice, and movement as just described. However, personalization and a reality base should support all work with mechanics.

Also note that characters in Greek comedy often make abrupt changes from lyricism to broad farce (see *Lysistrata* as an example). Consequently, acting transitions simply are not provided in the script. This puts extra burden on the actor who often must create transitions or simply change activity without use of them.

Exercise 6   Character and Emotion—Old Greek Comedy

1. Invent one comic emotional characteristic for each of the character types in the list that follows. Establish an immobile physical position which typifies the essence or idea. Your face and entire body should express the essence of the idea or feeling. Once this is successfully accomplished, place the physicalization and attitude into rapid motion through fast walking, sitting, gesturing, tumbling, hitting, and falling. After these movements are accomplished, invent a complete sentence of dialogue expressing the idea or emotion you are depicting. (For example, for pompous statesman, the sentence could be, "I am a great king.") Memorize the sentence and as you move, vocalize the sentence with different tempos and a variety of expressions, ranging from larger-than-life size to modern, naturalistic detail.
 1. Pompous statesman
 2. Braggart warrior
 3. Passionate lover
 4. Effeminate god
 5. Comic bird
 6. Comic frog
 7. Comic wasp
 8. Comic cloud
 9. Comic slave
 10. Comic poet

2. Select a character from the list in #1 above. Perform an improvisational monologue in which you tell a comic story; depict a variety of emotions with comic expressiveness—all in the mode of the character you have created.

Transition—Roman and Medieval Drama

Greece attained its greatest influence during the fifth and fourth centuries B.C. Thereafter, military and economic difficulties eroded the power of Greece, while Rome became the dominant influence in the known world.

Roman Drama

Early Roman theatre utilized a crude form of improvised dialogue. Abusive and obscene, drama was given mostly at harvest and wedding celebrations. Favorite entertainment included chariot races, boxing contests, athletic games, and gladitorial contests in stadiumlike arenas. The dominate theatre form was the farce play. The farces were heavily influence by Old Greek Comedy and the so-called Middle or New Comedy of Menander, written during the Hellenistic period of the fourth century. Menander reemphasized the ordinary characters and farce typical of Old Greek Comedy. By

Roman mask.

the middle of the second century B.C., Rome produced its first major playwrights, Plautus and Terence. Plautus wrote comic farces whose plot devices and low-life characters were of minimal dimension. The plays of Terence were more genteel, and their content was more educational in purpose. Available evidence indicates that the Romans produced comedies and few if any tragedies in their theatre. However, Seneca did write several tragedies based on Greek models. These tragedies, while probably never produced, had major influence on Renaissance playwrights hundreds of years later (this influence is discussed in chapter 12).

In serious Roman drama, Seneca's characters, modeled after their classical Greek counterparts, were deeply emotional.

In Roman comedy, the characters were one-dimensional stereotypes, particularly in the plays of Plautus. Plautine farces usually depicted characters of a single emotional bent. The plays of Terence contained a more lifelike human dimension and the characters were of a slightly more complex emotional level.

Since Roman dramas are rarely produced in the modern theatre, and because the style of acting in these dramas is so closely allied to the Greek style, this style of acting is merely summarized here.

Acting Roman Drama

Acting in serious Roman plays was probably closely allied to oratory. Actors probably declaimed to the audience, using little vocal variety. Evidence from Quintilian and Plutarch indicates that meaning and thought were stressed in oratory rather than emotion and feeling.

In Roman comedy heightened vocal projection and close attention to comic patterns of speech are necessary. Increased emphasis on words and phrases will intensify the comic meaning.

Movement in serious Roman drama is best handled today by using the techniques explained in the Greek discussion of classical style, with some modification (i.e., less exaggeration in movement and gesture and less vocal size).

Roman comedy should probably be produced as originally presented—broad and lusty and with a large amount of physical contact between performers. Most of the material should be played directly to the audience (presentational). Again, dancing, tumbling, acrobatics, hitting, falling, running, and general slapstick behavior can be used effectively. Great emphasis should be placed on comic precision in the timing of business and dialogue. Many of the Old Greek comic properties such as clapboards, staffs, fans, money pouches, and so on should be used. As the guide to dress, use Roman period costumes. While masks were probably used in original Roman comedy, they are usually eliminated in present-day theatre and replaced with makeup. If you do use a mask, a half-mask might be appropriate.

Most of the acting style characteristic of Greek drama may be used (with modification) to perform Roman drama. The Roman theatre was important for vitality and entertainment, for perpetuating and adapting Greek drama, and for a heritage which Renaissance playwrights were to use effectively.

Medieval Drama

The power of the Roman empire diminished by the sixth century A.D. Invasions by nomadic barbarians and the influence of the Christian Church splintered Roman power and dispersed popular entertainment and theatre activity. Popular theatre was forbidden during the so-called Dark Ages or Medieval Ages which ranged generally from the sixth century well into the tenth A.D. Ironically, the Church helped revive theatre activity by introducing exchanges of dialogue in the form of *tropes* or hymns into the mass between the priest and the choir. Later, actual scenery and costumes were used to help teach moral and religious lessons to the common people who were uneducated and easily influenced by dramatic display.

As the activity became increasingly secular and involved more participants, drama moved out of the church itself onto the church steps and into streets and courtyards. The mystery plays (Biblical stories), miracle plays (stories of saints and martyrs), and morality plays (stories with moral precepts) were produced on a simple platform. In England these kinds of plays were performed on pageant wagons which were drawn by horses through the streets, stopping to perform as a crowd formed. Trade merchants formed guilds which sponsored and produced these religious plays in England and on the Continent.

Eventually, secular, or nonreligious, material became more important than religious material in the plays. Native farce comedy began to dominate theatre activity and was a major development in the transition from the religious plays to the great theatre of the Renaissance. Interludes, another transitional dramatic form, were also performed and were particularly enjoyed by nobles and rich merchants. Interludes were often performed by minstrels or jongleurs (strolling players) who were skilled in singing, dancing, and storytelling. Medieval theatre produced few known playwrights. Authorship was generally anonymous.

Acting Medieval Drama

Several Medieval plays are still quite actable today. *Everyman* (anonymous), *The Second Shepherds' Play* (anonymous), *Pierre Patelin* (anonymous), *The Iron Pot* by Hans Sachs, and the short biblical pieces of Hrosvitha the Nun, are among the most popular with audiences. If the limitations caused by negligible information on styles of Medieval acting are recognized, Medieval plays can be a valid acting vehicle if you begin by carefully defining your physical acting area. Since these plays were usually performed on a platform stage, adaptation of a Medieval play requires a similarly limited acting space. Generally, be careful not to perform on a large stage requiring a complicated set. Use smaller areas which limit movement and gesture. Rely essentially on strong, clear vocal work and vivid physicalization to project characterization. (Although characters are clearly and boldly drawn in Medieval plays, some subtle psychological traits, revealed primarily in monologues and isolated scenes, do exist.) Acting in Medieval plays should project a predominately lifelike quality. A study of occupational skills prevalent during the Middle Ages will provide insight into details of everyday life. Since most of these plays emphasize religious allegories and everyday activities (e.g., a monk at study, a carpenter at work, a mason laying bricks, a cobbler making shoes, or a tailor sewing clothes), the modern actor needs to give his character sufficient stage business to develop believable characterization. The rare emotional scenes in these plays make a relatively brief but important contribution to the play's action. Perform these emotions with a direct and simple honesty, whether comic or tragic. Be sincere without belaboring the emotion.

The vocal and physical rhythm of the plays should be expressed in a steadily fluid manner. If the play is written in verse, speak with extra clarity and directness. When comedy appears in the play (e.g., a henpecked husband or a cowardly shepherd), convey the appropriate wide range of comic responses with exaggerated vocal detail and physical action. You must accept archaic conventions when they arise: for example, falling asleep instantly and awakening the next moment. React believably to the entrance of unusual characters such as angels or God in a scene. Be prepared to sing and move with ease. Maintain a realistic base when acting real-life characters by projecting commonplace details of human behavior.

Translators and Translations and Adaptations

The key to successful dramatic presentation of Greek, Roman, and most Medieval drama is to use a quality translation by an effective translator. Most plays, particularly verse plays, are performed best in their original language. Greek and Latin plays are particularly difficult to translate into effective English. As a general rule, a wise director, producer, and actor compare several translations of a particular play before deciding which translation should be performed. In this manner you can better judge what reads well, sounds believable, and would seem to interest modern audiences. Some authorities believe the more modern or recent the translation, the better will be the version. In some instances this may be true. However, some nineteenth-century translators remain the most widely used in the theatre today. Another reliable method of determining a good translation is to check which translations are most frequently published in dramatic anthologies.

An adaptation differs from a translation in that it goes beyond language translation into major textual changes. Greek drama, particularly comedy, is frequently adapted as well as translated. For example, there is a version of *Lysistrata* by Aristophanes which has been adapted to an American hillbilly environment. *The Frogs* by the same author has been presented as a 1920 vaudeville production, has been staged in the Yale University swimming pool, and has been played in a boxing ring at the University of Iowa. *The Bacchae* by Euripides has been staged in the manner of the American "hippy" movement of the 1960s. Selecting a translation or an adaptation is primarily the director's decision, but is of course of major importance to the actor. Your familiarity with different translations and adaptations will greatly assist your development in the art of acting.

Suggested Characters and Plays for Scene Work

Aeschylus

Agamemnon, Clytemnestra, Cassandra
  Agamemnon
Orestes, Electra, Clytemnestra
  The Eumenides

Sophocles

Oedipus, Jocasta, Tiresias, Messenger
  Oedipus Rex
Antigone, Creon, Ismene, Nurse, Messenger
  Antigone

Euripides

Medea, Jason
  Medea
Hecuba, Andromache, Cassandra, Helen, Menelaus, Talthybius
  The Trojan Women
Electra, Orestes
  Electra
Phaedre, Nurse, Hippolytus, Aphrodite, Artemis, Theseus
  Hippolytus
Dionysus, Cadmus, Tiresias, Pentheus, Agave
  The Bacchae
Cyclops, Odysseus
  Cyclops

Aristophanes

Dionysius, Xanthias, Aeschylus, Euripides
  The Frogs
Lysistrata, Myrinna, Kinesias
  Lysistrata
Epops, Peithetairos, and Euelpides
  The Birds

Additional Suggested Characters and Plays for Scene Work

Plautus

Menaechmus I, Menaechmus II, Cylindrus,
Erotium, Sponge
  The Twin Menaechmi
Euclio
  The Pot of Gold
Pyrogopolynices, Philocomasium
  The Braggart Warrior

Terence

Phormio, Phaedria, Pamphila
  Phormio
Micio, Aeschinus, Demea, Ctesipho, Pamphila
  The Brothers

Seneca

Atreus, Thyestes, the Ghost
  Thyestes

Anonymous

Abraham, Isaac
  Abraham and Isaac
Mak, Gyll
  The Second Shepherd's Play
Everyman, Good Deeds
  Everyman

Stevenson

Gammer Gurton, Diccon, Dame Chat
  Gammer Gurton's Needle

Anonymous

Pierre Patelin
  Pierre Patelin

Hrosvitha

Paphnutius, Thais
  Paphnutius

Sackville and Norton

Any role
  Gorboduc

Udall, Nicholas

Ralph Roister Doister, Dame Custance,
Mathewe Merygreeke
  Ralph Roister Doister

Actor Checklist   *Greek Tragedy*

Voice

Heightened word emphasis; precise diction;
varied tone qualities; close to declamatory,
rhetorical, oratorical, lyrical, or sung mode
during the key emotional or lyrical movements.

Movement	Generally slow, suggestive, and rhythmic; rare use of sitting positions; rare use of physical contact with other characters; predominately presentational mode.
Gestures	Restrained, large, fluid, and complete; highly selective and mostly in the upper portion of the body.
Pantomimic Dramatization	Clear, appropriate, limited, and highly selective; rare use of hand props such as staffs, and emblems; use of full masks, half-masks, or makeup simulating a mask.
Character	Truthful, though somewhat larger than life; almost exclusively of high rank including gods.
Emotion	Complex and penetrating, particularly Sophocles and Euripides; clearly established and projected; somewhat larger than life; rooted in human psychology, particularly Euripides.
Ideas	Lofty, complex, clear; effectively theatricalized.
Language	Complex, clear, lyric, and rhythmic.
Mood and Atmosphere	Serious, restrained, lofty, passionate, and intense.
Pace and Tempo	Controlled, disciplined, rhythmic, and generally moderate to deliberate.
Special Techniques	Training in singing and dancing highly recommended, particularly for chorus members.

Actor Checklist *Old Greek Comedy*

Voice	Clear diction; projection with effective vocal variety.
Movement	Energetic, large, extensive physical contact with others; considerable use of sitting; balance of presentation and representational mode.
Gestures	Lifelike but expansive; detailed rather than selective; full use of the entire body.
Pantomimic Dramatization	Extensive interpolation of song, dance, and comedic acrobatics; wild-animal movements; adaptation of religious dances and victory antics, kicking, slapping, and so on; highly inventive use of half-mask or makeup.
Character	Exaggerated to level of caricature, particularly with chorus and minor characters; major characters somewhat closer fidelity to real life. Abrupt transitions.
Emotion	Singular obsession; somewhat more complex in some major characters.

Ideas	Satiric; emphasized; clear.
Language	Mix of prose and verse; generally lifelike.
Mood and Atmosphere	Humorous; unrestrained; common; grotesque; fun.
Pace and Tempo	Rapid to moderate; exuberant
Special Techniques	Singing, dancing, and acrobatic training highly recommended.

Suggested Readings

Allen, James T. *Greek Acting in the Fifth Century.* Berkeley: University of California Press, 1916.

———. *The Greek Theatre of the Fifth Century before Christ.* Berkeley: University of California Press, 1920.

———. *Stage Antiquities of the Greeks and Romans and Their Influence.* New York: Longmans, Green, 1927.

Aristotle. *Poetics.* Edited by A. Gudemen. Translated by Lane Cooper. Ithaca, N.Y.: Cornell University Press, 1928.

Arnott, Peter D. *Greek Scenic Conventions in the Fifth Century, B.C.* London: Oxford Clarendon Press, 1962.

———. *An Introduction to Greek Theatre.* London: St. Martin's Press, 1956; Bloomington, Ind.: Indiana University Press, 1963.

Bates, William. *Euripides. A Student of Human Nature.* New York: A. S. Barnes & Co., 1961.

Bieber, Margarette, *The History of the Greek and Roman Theatre.* 2d ed. Princeton, N.J.: Princeton University Press, 1961.

Butler, James H. *The Theatre and Drama of Greece and Rome.* San Francisco: Chandler Publication Co., 1972.

Casson, Lionel, ed. *Masters of Ancient Comedy.* Translated by Lionel Casson. New York: Macmillan Co., 1960.

Chambers, E. K. *The Medieval Stage.* 2 vols. London: Oxford University Press, 1963.

Cornford, Francis M. *The Origin of Attic Comedy.* London: E. Arnold, 1914.

Corrigan, Robert W. *Roman Drama.* New York: Dell Publishing Co., 1966.

Craig, Hardin. *English Religious Drama of the Middle Ages.* London: Oxford University Press, 1955.

Deardon, C. W. *The Stage of Aristophanes.* London: 1976.

Duckworth, George E. *The Nature of Roman Comedy.* Princeton, N.J.: Princeton University Press, 1952.

Flickinger, R. C. *The Greek Theatre and Its Drama.* 6th ed. Chicago: University of Chicago Press, 1960.

Frank, Tenney. *The Status of Actors at Rome.* New York: Russell & Russell, 1933.

Gaster, Theodor. *Thespis; Ritual, Myth and Drama in the Ancient Near East.* New York: Abelard-Schuman Ltd., 1950.

Goldberg, Sander M. *The Making of Menander's Comedy.* Berkeley: University of California Press, 1980.

Haigh, A. E. *The Tragic Drama of the Greeks.* New York, 1968.

Hamilton, Edith. *The Greek Way,* New York: W. W. Norton & Company, 1952.

———. *The Roman Way.* New York: W. W. Norton, 1932.

Helterman, Jeffrey. *Symbolic Action in the Plays of the Wakefield Master.* Athens: University of Georgia Press, 1981.

Kitto, H. D. F. *Greek Tragedy.* 2nd ed. London: Methuen & Co., Ltd., 1950.

———. *The Greeks.* Baltimore: Penguin, 1964.

Lawler, Lillian B. *The Dance of the Ancient Greek Theatre.* Iowa City: The University of Iowa Press, 1964.

Meade, Anna McClymonds. "The Actor in the Middle Ages." Master's thesis, Columbia University, May 1927.

Murray, Gilbert. *Euripides and His Age.* New York: Holt, Rinehart and Winston, 1913.

Nicoll, Allardyce. *Masks, Mimes, and Miracles.* New York: Harcourt Brace Jovanovich, 1931.

Norwood, Gilbert. *Plautus and Terence.* New York: Cooper Square Publishers, 1932.

————, ed. *Greek Comedy.* New York: Hill & Wang, 1963.

O'Connor, John B. *Chapters in the History of Actors and Acting in Ancient Greece.* Chicago, 1908.

Pickard-Cambridge, A. W. *Dithyramb, Tragedy, and Comedy.* 2nd ed., rev. by T. B. L. Webster. London: Oxford University Press, 1962.

Price, Jonathan (Ed. and Transl.). *Classic Scenes.* New York: Mentor, 1979.

Salter, F. M. *Medieval Drama in Chester.* Canada: University of Toronto Press, 1955.

Segal, Erich W. *Roman Laughter: The Comedy of Plautus.* Boston: Harvard University Press, 1968.

Southern, Richard. *The Medieval Theatre in the Round.* London: Faber & Faber, Ltd., 1957.

Webster, T. B. L. *Greek Theatre Production.* London: Oxford University Press, 1956.

Wickham, Glynne. *The Medieval Theatre.* London, 1974.

Young, Karl. *The Drama of the Medieval Church.* 2 vols. London: Oxford University Press, 1962.

Suggested Filmography

1. *Antigone.* 1961. Playwright-Sophocles. With /Irene Papas.
2. *Everyman.* 1913. Kinemacolor. Playwright-Anonymous.
3. *Oedipus Rex.* 1956. Playwright-Sophocles. Director-Tyrone Guthrie. W/ Douglas Campbell.
4. *Oedipus Rex.* 1967. Playwright-Sophocles. Director-Pier Paolo Pasolini. W/ Silvana Mangano.
5. *The Trojan Women.* 1971. Playwright-Euripides. With /Katharine Hepburn.

Oedipus The King

by *Sophocles*

Translated by William Butler Yeats

Characters Oedipus, King of Thebes
Jocasta, his Queen (discovered later to be his mother)

Scene The palace of King Oedipus.

Situation Oedipus has promised his people to remove the plague from Thebes by discovering the cause of the affliction, not realizing it is himself (he has unknowingly killed his own father and married his own mother). Oedipus believes his brother-in-law, Creon, and the soothsayer, Tiresias, are plotting against him by accusing him of incest and patricide. Jocasta encounters Oedipus. Oedipus expresses his fears and Jocasta tries to reassure him.

JOCASTA In the name of the Gods, King, what put you in this anger?

OEDIPUS I will tell you; for I honour you more than these men do. The cause is Creon and his plots against me.

JOCASTA Speak on, if you can tell clearly how this quarrel arose.

OEDIPUS He says that I am guilty of the blood of Laius.

JOCASTA On his own knowledge, or on hearsay?

OEDIPUS He has made a rascal of a seer his mouthpiece.

JOCASTA Do not fear that there is truth in what he says. Listen to me, and learn to your comfort that nothing born of woman can know what is to come. I will give you proof of that. An oracle came to Laius once, I will not say from Phoebus, but from his ministers, that he was doomed to die by the hand of his own child sprung from him and me. When his child was but three days old, Laius bound its feet together and had it thrown by sure hands upon a trackless mountain; and when Laius was murdered at the place where three highways meet, it was, or so at least the rumour says, by foreign robbers. So Apollo did not bring it about that the child should kill its father, nor did Laius die in the dreadful way he feared by his child's hand. Yet that was how the message of the seers mapped out the future. Pay no attention to such things. What the God would show he will need no help to show it, but bring it to light himself.

OEDIPUS What restlessness of soul, lady, has come upon me since I heard you speak, what a tumult of the mind!

JOCASTA What is this new anxiety? What has startled you?

OEDIPUS You said that Laius was killed where three highways meet.

JOCASTA Yes: that was the story.

OEDIPUS And where is the place?

JOCASTA In Phocis where the road divides branching off to Delphi and to Daulia.

OEDIPUS And when did it happen? How many years ago?

JOCASTA News was published in this town just before you came into power.

OEDIPUS O Zeus! What have you planned to do unto me?

JOCASTA   He was tall; the silver had just come into his hair; and in shape not greatly unlike to you.

OEDIPUS   Unhappy that I am! It seems that I have laid a dreadful curse upon myself, and did not know it.

JOCASTA   What do you say? I tremble when I look on you, my King.

OEDIPUS   And I have a misgiving that the seer can see indeed. But I will know it all more clearly, if you tell me one thing more.

JOCASTA   Indeed, though I tremble I will answer whatever you ask.

OEDIPUS   Had he but a small troop with him; or did he travel like a great man with many followers?

JOCASTA   There were but five in all—one of them a herald; and there was one carriage with Laius in it.

OEDIPUS   Alas! It is now clear indeed. Who was it brought the news, lady?

JOCASTA   A servant—the one survivor.

OEDIPUS   Is he by chance in the house now?

JOCASTA   No; for when he found you reigning instead of Laius he besought me, his hand clasped in mine, to send him to the fields among the cattle that he might be far from the sight of this town; and I sent him. He was a worthy man for a slave and might have asked a bigger thing.

OEDIPUS   I would have him return to us without delay.

JOCASTA   Oedipus, it is easy. But why do you ask this?

OEDIPUS   I fear that I have said too much, and therefore I would question him.

JOCASTA   He shall come, but I too have a right to know what lies so heavy upon your heart, my King.

OEDIPUS   Yes: and it shall not be kept from you now that my fear has grown so heavy. Nobody is more to me than you, nobody has the same right to learn my good or evil luck. My father was Polybus of Corinth, my mother the Dorian Merope, and I was held the foremost man in all that town until a thing happened—a thing to startle a man, though not to make him angry as it made me. We were sitting at the table, and a man who had drunk too much cried out that I was not my father's son—and I, though angry, restrained my anger for that day; but the next day went to my father and my mother and questioned them. They were indignant at the taunt and that comforted me—and yet the man's words rankled, for they had spread a rumour through the town. Without consulting my father or my mother I went to Delphi, but Phoebus told me nothing of the things for which I came, but much of other things—things of sorrow and of terror: that I should live in incest with my mother, and beget a brood that men would shudder to look upon; that I should be my father's murderer. Hearing those words I fled out of Corinth, and from that day have but known where it lies when I have found its direction by the stars. I sought where I might escape those infamous things—the doom that was laid upon me. I came in my flight to that very spot where you tell me this king perished. Now, lady, I will tell you the truth. When I had come close up to those three roads, I came upon a herald, and a man like him you have described seated in a carriage. The man who held the reins and the old man himself would not give me room, but thought to force me from the path, and I struck the driver in my anger. The old man, seeing what I had done, waited till I was passing him and then struck me upon the head. I paid him back in full, for I knocked him out of the carriage with a blow of my stick. He rolled on his back, and after that I killed them all. If this stranger were indeed Laius, is there a more miserable man in the world than the man before you? Is there a man more hated of Heaven? No stranger, no citizen, may receive him into his house, not a soul may speak to him, and no mouth but my own mouth has laid this curse upon me. Am I not wretched? May I be swept from this world before I have endured this doom!

CHORUS   These things, O King, fill us with terror; yet hope till you speak with him that saw the deed, and have learnt all.

OEDIPUS   Till I have learnt all, I may hope. I await the man that is coming from the pastures.

JOCASTA   What is it that you hope to learn?

OEDIPUS   I will tell you. If his tale agrees with yours, then I am clear.

JOCASTA   What tale of mine?

OEDIPUS   He told you that Laius met his death from robbers; if he keeps to that tale now and speaks of several slayers, I am not the slayer. But if he says one lonely wayfarer, then beyond a doubt the scale dips to me.

JOCASTA   Be certain of this much at least, his first tale was of robbers. He cannot revoke that tale—the city heard it and not I alone. Yet, if he should somewhat change his story, King, at least he cannot make the murder of Laius square with prophecy; for Loxias plainly said of Laius that he would die by the hand of my child. That poor innocent did not kill him, for it died before him. Therefore from this out I would not, for all divination can do, so much as look to my right hand or left hand, or fear at all.

OEDIPUS   You have judged well; and yet for all that, send and bring this peasant to me.

JOCASTA   I will send without delay. I will do all that you would have of me—but let us come in to the house. (*They go into the house.*)

Oedipus the King by Sophocles. James Barton Hill as Oedipus and Martin Molson as The Priest (up left) at The Hilberry Theatre, Wayne State University. Directed and scenic design by Richard Spear; costumes by Robert Pusilo and lighting by Gary M. Witt.

The Frogs
by *Aristophanes*

Translated by Dudley Fitts

Chorus of Frogs   *Characters*
Dionysos

Near the shore of a great river/lake separating the known world from the unknown   *Scene*
world below. Dionysos is onstage, resting.

The God, Dionysos, caricatured as rather effeminate and ineffectual, is on his way   *Situation*
to Hades to retrieve the poet Euripides from the dead and return him to earth to
raise the level of tragedy being written in Athens. At the river/lake known as Styx,
Dionysos encounters a chorus of frog creatures and engages in frivolity and crude
conflict.

KOMMOS: CHORAL EPISODE

(*The* ACCESSORY CHORUS *of* FROGS *is heard, offstage.*)

FROGS   Brekekekéx koáx koáx
      Brekekekéx koáx koáx!
  We are the swamp-children
                Greeny and tiny.
  Fluting our voices
          As all in time we
    Sing our koáx koáx
    Koáx koáx koáx
  For Dionysos
         Nysa-born
  On the Winey Festival
             When the throng
  Lurches in through his temple gate,
  Every man as drunk as a hake.
    Brekekekéx koáx koáx
    Brekekekéx koáx koáx!
DIONYSOS   My arse is sore, koáx koáx.
FROGS   Brekekekéx koáx koáx.
DIONYSOS   And you don't give a damn, koáx.
FROGS   Brekekekéx koáx koáx.
DIONYSOS   Go jump in the lake, koáx, koáx!
  Let's have a different tune, koáx!
FROGS   Different? What a
            Meddlesome fool!
  Pan and the Muses
         Love us, our whole
    Koáx koáx koáx
    Koáx koáx koáx

Draws down Apollo
                Golden-lyred:
Ours are the marsh-reeds
                God-inspired
That sing to his heavenly fingering
Their music with our own mingling
           Brekekekéx koáx koáx.

DIONYSOS   My hands are ablaze, my bottom's a wreck!
   In a minute or two you'll hear it speak.

FROGS   Brekekekéx koáx koáx!

DIONYSOS   Silence, you lily-pad lyrists, koáx!

FROGS   No, we must sing. The
        Sunshine will bring the
          Glint to the pools,
            The shimmer of reeds,
      And when Zeus descends
        In rain on our heads
           We'll leap with our friends
             And pipe from our souls
              Brekekekéx koáx koáx!

DIONYSOS   Brekekekéx koáx koáx!
   Come, that's enough!

FROGS   We've hardly begun!

DIONYSOS   I suppose you think that rowing is fun?

(A furious increase in volume and tempo to the end of the chorus.)

FROGS   Brekekekéx koáx koáx!

DIONYSOS   Brekekekéx koáx koáx!
   I wish you'd die!

FROGS   We'll swell up and cry
   Brekekekéx koáx koáx!
   Brekekekéx koáx koáx!

DIONYSOS   Brekekekéx koáx koáx!
   I can beat you at that koáx koáx!

FROGS   The devil you can, koáx koáx!

DIONYSOS   I will, by God, if it takes all day!
      Brekekekéx koáx koáx!
   Go and koáx yourselves away!
     KOAX KOAX *KOAX!* (*He breaks wind hugely; the* FROGS *are silent.*)
   There! That settles your damned koáx!

Commedia Dell'Arte 12
Regeneration

The snow dissolv'd no more is seen,
The fields, and woods, behold, are green,
the changing year renews the plain,
the rivers know their banks again. . . .
Horace
in *A History of Latin Literature*

The poetic description by Horace of the regeneration of a Roman spring may well be applied to a theatrical regeneration that occurred several hundred years later in Italy and elsewhere on the Continent.

A major form of theatre and style of acting, *commedia dell' arte*, regenerated dramatic activity in the sixteenth century. More than a transitional activity, the *commedia dell' arte* became a unique actor-oriented form of theatre. The term *arte* was used to signify professional artists. Commedia performances were improvisational and performed by traveling companies of actors. These companies frequently consisted of members of a single family, such as the famous Gelosi company. The origin of the commedia may be traced to the Atellan farce of Rome or possibly to the plays of Plautus and Terence. Emerging into prominence around the sixteenth century, the influence of the commedia would be important for over two hundred years.

Overview of Commedia Dell' Arte

Commedia was a comedy of intrigue using stock characters, often masked, and largely improvised dialogue based on a brief scenario. (Serious dramatic activity was limited during these years, favored only in erudite court or noble theatres. Commedia was the theatre of the masses.)

Plays were topical, drawn from the immediate time and place. Commedia used considerable pantomime. Speeches were added as an accompaniment to gesture, movement, and stage business. The accent in commedia was on visual performance. Actors were given a standard plot. Memorized lines were used only when they coincided with specifically outlined action. Comic stage business called *lazzi* and comic verbal jokes called *burla* were interspersed throughout the story to provide bits of stage fun or tricky comic turns (e.g., an actor might pretend his hat was filled with cherries, daintily eat them, flick the pits into another actor's face, and remark, "a pit in the eye is worth two in the hand").

Commedia scenarios were refined and performed again and again until the last half of the eighteenth century. The most successful plots concerned love and intrigues, disguises and deception.

Commedia dell' Arte masks on Commedia dell' Arte characters.

During its peak years, from approximately 1550 to 1650, about ten or twelve famous commedia dell' arte troupes traveled the Continent. Seven or eight men and three or four women comprised each group. Together they generally formed two sets of lovers, a servant girl, a captain, two zanni (comics), and two old men. Handsome and well-educated young men and women portrayed "straight" roles, usually romantic in nature; these characters were fashionably dressed and not masked. Other characters such as Pantalone wore tight-fitting red vests, breeches, stockings, and a black, ankle-length matching coat. Pantolone was always depicted wearing a brown mask with a hook-nose and having unkempt hair and beard. Dottore's costume always consisted of a long academic gown and a cap. Over the years these costumes were adapted slightly to current trends. Harlequin often shaved his head and wore a comic hat with a black mask. He carried a slapstick or clapboard; originally he wore a suit of colorful diamond-shaped patches. Capitano wore a comic version of a military uniform with lots of green braid; he wore colorful plumes on his hat. Comic female characters such as courtesans wore long, full-length dresses or skirts of current fashion; some were masked. Character roles required special physical traits to help define the older men such as Capitano, Pantalone, and Dottore. The servants or zanni (e.g., Arlecchino or Harlequin) needed to be physically agile and supple in order to project the ridiculous burlesque qualities of these clever comic characters.

Almost eight hundred commedia dell' arte scenarios exist in outline form today (a complete scenario is included at the close of this chapter). It is virtually impossible to obtain the actual quality of the commedia performance since we have little information concerning its execution. We know, however, that it took great physical skill and clown talent to act in commedia. Although this theatre developed without playwrights, its influence was felt throughout Europe and subsequently had tremendous impact on later actors and playwrights such as Moliere (see chapter 14).

Harlequin character in Commedia Dell' Arte.

Pantalone character in
Commedia Dell' Arte.

Voice

The key aspect of vocal training for commedia is mental acuity for line invention. In other words, it helps to be glib. However, your verbal invention must be relevant to the scenario or the contemporary situation under enactment. The essentials of good stage speech are vital to delivery. Clear articulation, effective projection, rapid tempo, and considerable vocal variety are most important. The presentational mode dominates, necessitating adroit comic timing and direct audience delivery. Establishing reliable verbal burle will greatly assist your ability to emphasize so-called punch lines of comedy.

Exercise 1   Vocal Dexterity and Mental Acuity

1. Recite individually the following comic tongue twisters aloud as rapidly and clearly as possible:

Red leather and mellow yellow make wet weather and jolly fellows.

Peter Piper picked a peck of pickled peppers; a peck of pickled peppers Peter Piper picked.

Following this format, invent and practice comic tongue twisters and punch lines.

2. Invent or recall and practice telling comic jokes aloud in under thirty seconds. Every actor must tell at least one joke (refrain from obscene or so-called dirty stories).

3. Using a current, local newspaper, glance over headlines and major captions. Quickly invent and tell comic one-line jokes about each headline and caption.

4. Print several unusual words on slips of paper and place them in a hat or bowl. Each person draws a word and immediately improvises a two–three minute comic story based on the word, regardless of whether the definition of

the word is known. (Later, comic fun can conclude this exercise by looking up the meaning of the words in a dictionary.) Suggested words: arbalest; besom; carillon; dado; escudo; flambeau; gewgaw; hamadryad; ichor; jute; kumquat; lintel; mesquite; nanny; Ouija; pariah; quoit; ribald; seism; toucan; uxorious; wildebeest; xebec; yucca; Zouave.

5. Select a series of famous morals or epithets and improvise four–five minute comic stories which illustrate and clarify imaginative origins of the morals or epithets. Suggested morals or epithets: "A bird in the hand is worth two in the bush." "Nothing succeeds like success." "Nothing ventured, nothing gained." "Pound wise and penny foolish." "He who hesitates is lost." "Never put off until tomorrow what you can do today." "He who laughs last, laughs best." And so on.

Movement

Without question, movement is the essence of successful acting in commedia. The style requires acrobatic ability, forceful, flexible and rapid activity, and, occasionally, gracefully executed dance movements. All of the farce activities of Old Greek and Roman Comedy again apply, with special emphasis on characteristic movements and gestures of stock characters. For example, Pantalone, the old, grumpy father, walks with a hunch using a cane. Capitano, the braggart soldier, struts about with his head held high using grand hand gestures, waving his plumed hat. Harlequin turns cartwheels and somersaults and dances about with great abandon.

Exercise 2   Movement

1. Invent and practice comic movement suitable to each of the following stock commedia characters:
   a. Pantalone, the old merchant, miser, or father
   b. Dottore, pedantic bore
   c. Capitano, braggart soldier
   d. Zanni (comic servant), Harlequin, Pulchinello, Brighella, Scaramouche, Scapin
   e. Fontesca, comic maid
   f. Young lovers (Innamorato—male lover;
      Innamorata—female lover)

2. Execute a combination or series of acrobatic techniques ranging from tumbling to juggling.

3. To the accompaniment of rapid, high-spirited music (guitars, drums, and flutes are preferable), invent spontaneous and collective group dancing. In the event that music is not available, this exercise can be great fun by improvising the music with the aid of crude instruments such as washboards and metal pipes, bells, wooden sticks or shoes, humming through a piece of paper placed over a comb, and so on.

4. Practice stereotypical movements standardly used in competitive sporting events (such as, the "left cross" and "right jab" of a prize fighter; the swing of a baseball batter and wind-up of a baseball pitcher; the jump-ball of a basketball player; the forward pass of a football quarterback; the serve of a tennis

player; and so on). Adapt each movement or activity into a comic action for the stage.

5. Practice the following "comic accidents" or lazzi (use real props or pantomime):

    a. Sit on a basket of eggs.

    b. Slip on a banana skin.

    c. Trip on a rug.

    d. Squirt water in your eye at a fountain.

    e. Brush your teeth with Ben-Gay.

    f. Carry a pie and fall into it.

    g. Drop ice cream on your lap.

    h. Spill hot coffee on your lap.

    i. Sit on a cactus.

    j. Look into a water hose and get squirted.

    k. Laugh and bite your tongue.

    l. Rinse your mouth with shaving lotion.

    m. Trip on your shoelaces.

    n. Get your tie caught in an electric beater.

    o. Hold sour milk in your cheeks while you look for a place to spit.

    p. Miss the nail while hammering and hit your thumb.

    q. Kick yourself in the shin while dancing.

    r. Pick a rose and get a thorn.

    s. Step on a tack.

    t. Slide down a pole and get splinters.

    u. Bite into a pearl in an oyster stew.

    v. Spray under your armpits with extra-strength hair spray.

    w. Get soap in your eyes as you search for a towel.

    x. Spill the bubble bath as you bathe in a tub.

    y. Walk barefoot on hot pavement.

    z. Kick a soccer ball which turns out to be a bowling ball.

6. Practice "comic retrievals" (lazzi) by attaching rubber bands, elastic, or string to a variety of personal objects, such as your cap or hat, a pencil, your purse, your billfold, keys, and so on; drop the object as if by accident and develop "comic retrievals."

7. Practice playing "invisible instruments" as lazzi. For example, play an invisible violin, tuba, flute, drum, piano, and so on. Your colleagues should dance to your "invisible instruments" and "silent music."

8. Study the comic pantomime and physical activities of famous clowns and comics; imitate their activities both individually and in groups. For example, study the specialty movement and business of Charlie Chaplin, Buster Keaton, Stan Laurel, Oliver Hardy, Bud Abbott, Lou Costello, The Three Stooges, The Marx Brothers, Red Skelton, and others.

9. Practice a variety of "safe comic fights" as lazzi. For example, pillow fights, feather fights, bubble fights, confetti fights, and so on.

10. Practice "duplicate comic activity" by performing a variety of routine activities with two (duplicate) items rather than one. For example, drink from two glasses at one time, eat with two forks at one time, smoke two pipes simultaneously, brush with two toothbrushes at the same time, comb your hair with two combs simultaneously, write with two pens in one hand at the same time, and so on.

Character and Emotion

Commedia characters were one-dimensional stereotypes, usually possessive and obsessive, in the tradition of Old Greek and Roman Comedy. Commedia characters differed from their ancient counterparts in that commedia activity was more presentational. Except when performance was repetitive, dialogue and action for commedia characters were almost totally improvisational, and character types were refined and inflexible.

Exercise 3 Character and Emotion

1. Utilizing the work in Exercises 1 and 2, create brief scenarios from the following situational ideas, identifying one actor for each stock character.

When you have completed discussing the scenario, each actor performs the stock character he selected within the context of the scenario. Act the scenario as an improvised play, keeping the performance under five minutes.

1. A man refuses his daughter's hand in marriage to a young cobbler in favor of an old schoolmaster.
2. A long-lost twin is reunited with his brother who is identical in appearance.
3. An old miser is cheated out of his money by a clever servant.
4. A man masquerades as a doctor of medicine to gain access to the wife of an old merchant.
5. A soldier returns from the wars to discover his sweetheart has been forced into a marriage with an old attorney-at-law.

2. To create bold, large character types and emotional attitudes, males should practice improvisational characterizations of stock female roles and females should do the same with stock male roles. Create a comic monologue for your "role reversal," depicting a wide range of emotions.

3. Assemble a variety of old clothes, hats, caps, shoes, and boots. Practice fast changes of headdress, outer garments, and footwear individually and as a group. With each change, affect a comic character and emotional trait suitable to that item of clothing.

4. This exercise should be a long-range assignment. Ideally, several weeks or even months should be used to develop this unusual and challenging exercise. Carefully study your features and physique in a mirror. Study your voice by listening to it on tape. Study your walk and habits by observing yourself on video tape. If you were to accentuate portions of your face, body, voice, walk, and habits for comic purposes, what would you choose and how would you manage the comic accentuation? Would you work with your nose? Ears? Chin? Stomach? Bosom? Legs? Your vocal *quality, pitch,* or *rate?* Your slow walk or your fast walk? The way you eat? Smoke? Drink? Laugh? Make your selections and develop a "comic character and emotion" appropriate to your choices. Over a period of time, carefully create a "comic or clown" character and appropriate scenario to present as part of a final, individual performance in this style. (Later, a group scenario can be invented to incorporate all the "clown characters.")

Transition—Tudor Drama

As the commedia developed and flourished in Italy and elsewhere on the Continent, Europe was prey to barbarism, sacrilege, and selfishness. Despondency was the prevalent mood. As early as the fourteenth century, the French poet Eustache Deschamps set the tone for the late Medieval period when he wrote:

> Why is our life so cruel and dark
> That men no longer speak to friend?
> Why does evil so clearly mark
> The monstrous government of Men?
> Compare what is with what is past
> And see how fraud and sorrow stand,
> While law and justice fade so fast
> That I know no longer where I am.
>
> from *The Horizon Book*
> *of the Elizabethan World*

The individual became engulfed in the tide of swelling institutional power. Man's life on earth lost meaning except as preparation for an afterlife.

Although Medieval institutions dominated, the spirit which sustained them eventually withered and died. The Holy Roman Empire was crumbling by 1400. Monarchs were subject to foreign invasions and international alliances. Throughout Europe, kingships were suffering paralysis. Economic, social, and political disasters seemed to be without end. Disease, death, suffering, and war took their toll on most of Europe. However, the picture of despair lessened somewhat in England with the presence of Henry VII, founder of the Tudor dynasty, who came to the throne in 1485.

Henry VII was part of the new breed of monarchs on the European continent. He worked to liberate royal government from ecclesiastical interference, enforced laws, promoted financial solvency, and achieved complete control over the nobility. The violent class turmoil in English life produced by the Wars of the Roses was beginning to settle into a less violent pattern of living in which middle-class gentlemen gained predominance.

In drama, this transitional period produced a combination of Medieval-like Interludes performed by professional actors and classically inspired plays written at universities and Inns of Court performed by students. History was a popular subject, as were Bible stories rewritten in a romantic style. School drama was influenced by the plays of Plautus, Terence, and Seneca, all of which were read or performed in Latin. Original plays were written in both Latin and English, imitating the Roman or classical models. The most popular school plays were *Ralph Roister Doister* by Nicholas Udall and *Gammer Gurton's Needle* by Stevenson. The first known English tragedy was *Gorboduc* by Thomas Sackville and Thomas Norton. Other original native drama combined elements of classical learning (e.g., use of mythological figures) and English low comedy (e.g., use of farcical types). Even prior to Shakespeare's arrival in London, the theatre was under the influence of sophisticated playwriting. In his play *The Spanish Tragedy*, Thomas Kyd revealed the influence of Seneca by use of the revenge motif in combination with supernatural reference and suspenseful plot. (Shakespeare's *Hamlet*, written later, resembled Kyd's play closely.) Christopher Marlowe's contribution was to perfect blank verse as a medium for drama in his play's *Doctor Faustus, Edward II, Tamburlaine the Great,* and *The Jew of Malta.* John Lyly wrote prose comedies with themes from mythology which significantly developed comic playwriting beyond the crude farces of the Tudor period. All playwrights accented the chronological approach to action, emphasizing stage violence, a blend of serious and comic elements, poetic imagery, soliloquy, and short scenes.

Acting Tudor Drama

The Tudor acting style was both conventionalized and basically realistic or unconventional. The major convention was the performing of all female roles by young male actors. Considerable emphasis was placed on realistic contemporary life and manners, especially in the comedies. Actors arrived at an essential truthfulness of what we would term *human psychology.* That is, they created fundamentally convincing characters. However, there are exceptions to realistic character portrayal in these plays. There are roles in Tudor plays which call for a nonrealistic or highly exaggerated acting style, especially the farces in which a bizarre mixture of dramatic and comic elements appear (e.g., mixing serious mythology and low slapstick comedy).

An important outgrowth of Tudor drama in the development of theatrical art was the attention paid to costuming. Following the lead of society, dress for stage use also became quite exaggerated. Men's robes were larger, longer, and more elaborate than during early Medieval times. Young men often dressed in short formfitting tunics, pulled in with a belt. Hose and pointed shoes were worn. Sleeves were ballooned and gathered at the wrist; others were long enough to trail on the ground. Women's bodices also became more formfitting, with pinched waists, and skirts were fuller and heavier. Accordingly, acting style in plays was affected. Walking in a fourteenth-century skirt required extensive knee action. When a curtsy was executed, the front of the skirt was lifted to allow an actor to bend to the ground and rise gracefully. The skirt was held out and the head was inclined slightly to one side or slightly forward.

The men had difficulty executing movements due to their padded breeches. Walking and standing were cumbersome matters. However, men usually walked with a vigorous stride and displayed an athletic physique. Bowing usually occurred in the third ballet position, with toes and knees turned out, the rear knee bent, and the rear heel slightly off the ground; the forward leg was straight with the weight evenly distributed on both feet. Wearing clothes was a pleasure for the Tudor gentleman. They were dedicated to showing off their legs and general attire.

Women, too, enjoyed elaborate display of clothing by keeping the torso straight and stiff, turning from the waist, and keeping the skirt in line with the shoulders. The head was poised to balance the headdress. The total physical effect of costuming, movement, bowing, and curtsying became a distinctive aspect of Tudor acting.

Late in the sixteenth century as the commedia dell' arte achieved prominence on the Continent, the limited but promising Tudor drama passed gradually into a new and distinct period in theatre activity and style—into the incomparable dramatic Renaissance of Elizabethan England—the age of William Shakespeare.

Suggested Characters and Plays for Scene Work

See any of the many extant commedia dell' arte scenarios. (Refer to Suggested Reading at the conclusion of this chapter for titles containing scenarios.)

Actor Checklist   Commedia Dell' Arte

Voice	Comic verbal invention and *burle;* clear articulation; effective projection; rapid tempo, considerable vocal variety.
Movement	Acrobatic ability; forceful, flexible, and rapid; occasional dance activity; balance of presentational and representational mode, with slight dominance of presentational.
Gestures	Stock character *lazzi;* considerable physical contact with others; lifelike but expansive; full use of entire body.
Pantomimic Dramatization	Extensive interpolation of song, dance, comedic acrobatics; highly inventive slapstick; use of full mask and half-mask on all characters except young lovers.
Character	Definitive types throughout; young lovers closest to real-life fidelity.
Emotion	Generally limited or one-dimensional; singular obsession.
Ideas	Satiric concerning local and contemporary references; generally light and fun-oriented; usually simple, love-triangle basis.
Language	Improvisational prose; generally memorized verse in songs.
Mood and Atmosphere	Humorous, unrestrained, common, grotesque, fun.
Pace and Tempo	Rapid to moderate; exuberant.
Special Techniques	Improvisational skill with dialogue and physical activity; singing, dancing, and acrobatic training highly recommended to relate comic stories.

Suggested Readings

Beaumont, Cyril V. *The History of Harlequin*. 1926. Reprint. New York: Benjamin Blom, 1967.

Craik, Thomas W. *The Tudor Interlude: Stage, Costume, and Acting*. Leicester: The University Press, 1958.

Disher, Maurice Wilson. *Clowns and Pantomimes*. New York: Benjamin Blom, 1968.

———. *Italian Comedy*. New York: Dover Publications, 1965.

Du Charte, Pierre. *Italian Comedy*. New York: Dover Publications, 1965.

Farley-Hills, David. *The Comic in Renaissance Comedy*. Totowa, N.J.: Barnes & Noble, 1981.

Herrick, Marvin. *Italian Comedy in the Renaissance*. Urbana: University of Illinois Press, 1960.

Lea, Kathleen M. *Italian Popular Comedy: A Study of the Commedia dell' Arte (1560–1620) with Special Reference to the English Stage*. 2 vols. 1924. Reprint. New York: Russell & Russell Publishers, 1962.

Nicoll, Allardyce. *The World of Harlequin*. New York: Cambridge University Press, 1963.

Oreglia, Giacomo. *The Commedia dell' Arte*. New York: Hill & Wang, 1968.

Rolfe, Bari. *Commedia dell' Arte: A Scene Study Book*. Oakland, California: Persona Products, 1976.

———. *Farces, Italian Style*. Oakland, California: Persona Products, 1978.

Salerno, Henry F., ed. and trans. *Scenarios of the Commedia dell' Arte Flaminio Scala's 11 Theatre Della Favole Rappresentative*. New York: New York University Press, 1967.

Sand, Maurice. *The History of the Harlequin*. 2 vols. 1915. Reprint. New York: Benjamin Blom, 1968.

Smith, Winifred. *The Commedia dell' Arte: A Study in Italian Popular Comedy*. New York: Benjamin Blom, 1965.

Suggested Filmography

See any of the films of the great comics/clowns, such as Charlie Chaplin, Buster Keaton, Stan Laurel, Oliver Hardy, Bud Abbott, Lou Costello, Jerry Lewis, The Marx Brothers, The Three Stooges, Red Skelton, and so on.

The Portrait

by *Flaminio Scala*

A Commedia dell' Arte Scenario

Translated from the French by Garrett H. Leverton

Characters	Vittoria	Flavio
	Piombino	Pedrolino
	Pantalone	Arlecchino
	Gratiano	Captain Spavento
	Isabella	Lesbino, *later Silvia*
	Flaminia	A Rogue
	Oratio	Nobles and Civilians

Place   Parma.

Time   Midsixteenth Century.

A troupe of actors were performing in Parma. According to the custom, the principal actress received many visitors, one of whom was a cavalier of the city named Oratio. During his visit the cavalier exhibited a locket in which was hidden the portrait of the very beautiful woman who had given him this locket. During the course of the conversation, the actress—Vittoria, by name—subtly removed the portrait from the locket before returning it, at the close of his visit. A few days later the husband of the beautiful woman came to see the actress. Vittoria, not knowing who he was, chanced to show him the portrait of his wife. The husband, Pantalone, was very much surprised, and at great length tried to persuade the actress to tell him the name of the man who had given her this portrait. Pantalone concealed the reason for his interest in the affair and returned to his home in a fury to inflict exemplary chastisement on his culpable wife. However, on arriving there, the wife gave so many good excuses in support of her innocence that she succeeded in appeasing his anger.

    The persons concerned in working out this situation are the actress, Vittoria, and her comrade Piombino; the two old men Pantalone and Gratiano; their wives, Isabella and Flaminia; and the wives's lovers, Oratio and Flavio. Pedrolino is valet to Pantalone, and Arlecchino to Captain Spavento. A young Milanese girl, disguised as a page, comes under the name of Lesbino to offer her services to the Captain, whom she loves.

Act I, Scene i

After the quarrel between ISABELLA and PANTALONE, her husband, over the portrait which was last seen in the hands of VITTORIA, ISABELLA begins to doubt ORATIO's love for her. She orders PEDROLINO to go to ORATIO and to demand from him the portrait which she had given him some time previously.

Scene ii

CAPTAIN SPAVENTO tells ARLECCHINO how through being obliged to assist in the play, he has fallen in love with the actress, VITTORIA. ARLECCHINO tells him he is wasting time.

Scene iii

Later, the CAPTAIN consents to take LESBINO as his page, after asking him many foolish questions about his bravery and his military talents.

Scene iv

From her window, FLAMINIA calls to ARLECCHINO and asks him to carry a letter to a cavalier named FLAVIO, whom she will meet at the place where she conducts her rendezvous with gentlemen. ARLECCHINO takes the letter and promises to deliver it to the one to whom it is addressed. FLAMINIA gives him some money and withdraws. ARLECCHINO regards FLAMINIA's window knowingly.

Scene v

Doctor GRATIANO, the husband of FLAMINIA, seeing ARLECCHINO with a letter in his hand and gazing at his wife's window, becomes suspicious, and demands to know what he is doing there and for whom the letter is intended. ARLECCHINO replies that a man named FLAVIO gave it to him to deliver to a lady. The DOCTOR takes the letter and raps ARLECCHINO with his cane.

Scenes vi to x

PANTALONE comes between the DOCTOR and ARLECCHINO. FLAVIO presents himself. GRATIANO, furiously angry, returns the letter to him. FLAVIO receives it with profound humility. The others depart and FLAVIO reads the letter in which FLAMINIA begs him to frequent the theatre no longer.

Scene xi

When PEDROLINO asks the return of the portrait of ISABELLA, ORATIO explains that it is impossible to return it to him because the locket is being repaired at the jeweler's. PEDROLINO smiles and asks him how long it has been since he has gone to the theatre, questions him about all the actors, and finally about the SIGNORA VITTORIA.

Scene xii

At this moment ISABELLA arrives. She dissembles at first, then asks for the return of the portrait. But ORATIO repeats the same story he had already told PEDROLINO. She calls him a traitor and tells him she knows about his love for the actress to whom he has given her portrait. In her anger, she commands PEDROLINO to follow her and she leaves refusing to listen to ORATIO. ORATIO bemoans his ill luck and blames the presence of the actors as the reason for all his trouble. He is particularly discourteous in expressing his opinion of VITTORIA who has tricked him so deceitfully.

Scene xiii

The CAPTAIN, hearing what ORATIO says about the actors, and particularly VITTORIA, comes to their defense. He argues that the theatre is a noble diversion and that the SIGNORA VITTORIA is an honorable lady. ORATIO, furious, calls him a liar and reaches for his sword. At this the CAPTAIN asks ORATIO if he wishes to fight a duel with him. ORATIO replies that he is ready. Then the CAPTAIN says he goes to write a letter which will remove from ORATIO the responsibility for his death in case he is killed, and will prevent the officers of justice from regarding him as an adversary. He asks ORATIO to do the same for him. Then he departs. ARLECCHINO observes that his master has the appearance of wishing to escape the affair. Thus ends the first act.

Act II, Scene i

VITTORIA, richly dressed, with gold necklaces and pearl bracelets, with diamonds and rubies on her fingers, engages herself through PIOMBINO to the DUKE OF PARMA, recalling the many courtesies which she was constantly receiving from the Parmesan nobility.

Scenes ii to v

PEDROLINO praises his master PANTALONE to VITTORIA. PANTALONE appears but he does not dare to approach the actress because he sees his wife at the window. PEDROLINO persuades PANTALONE that the actress is in love with him. PANTALONE, flattered, expresses the intention of giving her a present.

Scene vi

While ORATIO recounts to his friend FLAVIO the unfortunate history of the portrait, ARLECCHINO brings him the CAPTAIN's letter of remission from blame. ORATIO strikes him with his fist and rushes off to the theatre.

Scenes vii to xii

FLAVIO and PEDROLINO, and then FLAMINIA attempt to reconcile ISABELLA and ORATIO. ISABELLA softens but she declares that ORATIO shall get nothing from her so long as he does not return the portrait, and she forbids him, moreover, to go, himself, to negotiate for its return. PEDROLINO informs them how the two old men, PANTALONE and GRATIANO, are paying attention to the actress.

Scene xiii

Now the DOCTOR arrives. PEDROLINO pretends to be arguing with FLAMINIA and is saying: "How do I know whether your husband goes to the theatre or not?" FLAMINIA, entering into the deception, pretends to be jealous of her husband. When she has withdrawn, PEDROLINO tells the DOCTOR of his visit to the SIGNORA VITTORIA and of how she is in love with the DOCTOR. GRATIANO is enchanted.

Scene xiv

PIOMBINO greets the DOCTOR in behalf of SIGNORA VITTORIA. He begs him to take to the actress a silver pitcher and vase which she needs for a play which she is going to present. The DOCTOR replies that he will send these by PEDROLINO. PIOMBINO assures him that the actress is in love with him, and that because of him, she rejects the attentions of all the gentlemen who call on her at home or at the theatre. The DOCTOR is overjoyed and promises a reward to PIOMBINO.

Scene xv

The CAPTAIN talks with his page, LESBINO, about the passion which the actress inspires in him. LESBINO tries to turn him away from this passion which he

cannot make honorable. He asks him if he has never had another love. The
CAPTAIN replies that he had been in love, in Milan, with a very beautiful young
girl named SILVIA.

Scene xvi

ARLECCHINO interrupts his master to tell him that VITTORIA is waiting for him at a
nearby jeweler's. LESBINO, desperate, seeks to persuade ARLECCHINO that he
ought to kill him, LESBINO, because he has conceived the intention of killing his
master. ARLECCHINO beats and injures the page. FLAMINIA and ISABELLA intervene.

Scene xvii

Suspecting that LESBINO is a woman in spite of her male attire, they take her to the
residence of FLAMINIA. Thus ends the second act.

Act III, Scene i

VITTORIA and PIOMBINO go to dine at the house of a rich gentleman who gives them
magnificent presents. They congratulate themselves because of the custom of
making gifts to actors, a common custom in Italian cities and one which is
seldom neglected by persons of distinguished rank. VITTORIA confesses that she
laughs at all lovers who are not generous with her. PIOMBINO promises to
provide well for her old age.

Scenes ii and iii

PANTALONE comes to call on VITTORIA. She thanks him for the presents he has brought
to her and invites him to be present at the theatre for the opening of her play.
PANTALONE promises to be there. Presently FLAVIO arrives and the actress
detains him with engaging conversation.

Scene iv

But FLAMINIA sees them from her window. She is so angry that she goes out and
slaps FLAVIO in the face and then returns to her house. FLAVIO, putting his hand
to his smarting cheek, goes without saying a word. VITTORIA laughs heartily.

Scene v

PANTALONE who has been a witness to this *coup de théâtre* blames FLAMINIA for her
effrontery. He congratulates himself that he has such a modest and well-bred
wife. After these musings, he exchanges compliments with the actress. But
ISABELLA appears.

Scene vi

She reproaches her husband for being gallant with other women while neglecting
her. She lays all the facts before him and then adds that he does not deserve a
wife like her. Finally, as her anger increases, she attacks him and puts him to
flight. She turns to VITTORIA and tells her that if his honor does not prevent him
from compromising himself with an actress, then he will have to be taught how
to behave. ISABELLA then returns to her home. VITTORIA laughs and says that
wherever one finds a troupe of actors, there also will be found married women
with sour dispositions.

Scene vii

GRATIANO now arrives. "Behold, the other pigeon waiting to have his feathers
plucked," says PIOMBINO. The actress flirts with the DOCTOR. PIOMBINO reminds

him of the silver pitcher and vase which he has promised her. GRATIANO joyfully takes PEDROLINO with him in order to bring back these presents. The actors ridicule his stupidity.

Scene viii

ORATIO arrives and greets VITTORIA. He demands the portrait of ISABELLA. She replies, with a laugh, that she hasn't the slightest idea what he is talking about. Then she departs with PIOMBINO.

Scene ix

ISABELLA has seen ORATIO talking with the actress; she reproaches him for not keeping his promise. ARLECCHINO tells ORATIO that ISABELLA and FLAMINIA have taken his master's page away with them to their home, and are holding him there against his will. ISABELLA seizes the occasion to spite ORATIO and calls FLAMINIA, telling her to bring her new lover to the window. LESBINO appears and says to ISABELLA, "What do you wish of me, Signora?" ORATIO becomes enraged at the sight of this unknown person and withdraws, cursing ISABELLA.

Scene x

PANTALONE asks the reason for all this noise. ISABELLA says that ORATIO wished to take her page away from her. "And what do you want with this page?" PANTALONE asks angrily. Then ISABELLA tells the story of SILVIA, the Milanese girl. She then urges PANTALONE to go to the theatre, find the CAPTAIN and bring him back if possible. PANTALONE sees at once that this is the chance he himself needed in order to get to go to the theatre.

Scenes xi to xvii

The lovers begin to quarrel again. PEDROLINO observes that quarreling is a waste of time. Since their husbands are at the play which lasts for six hours, they could, therefore, use their time to much better advantage than quarreling. The lovers see the good sense in this remark and become reconciled. The valets try to decide on the best means to restore SILVIA to the CAPTAIN's good graces. The CAPTAIN appears.

Scene xviii

PEDROLINO tells the CAPTAIN that he will find VITTORIA at the home of PANTALONE. The CAPTAIN enters through the basement of the house where he comes upon SILVIA divested of her male attire.

Scene xix

The two valets, PEDROLINO and ARLECCHINO, are alone in the theatre. They sit on the floor and decide what they would say if the two old men were to return suddenly. At this moment in the scene there is some amusing pantomime. A rogue, carrying a lantern, sees the two valets. With many tears, he bemoans the fact that he has lost much money at cards. He does not have more than a dozen pieces of money left. The valets invite him to play with them. They play. The rogue wins the money and also the clothes of PEDROLINO and ARLECCHINO. He leaves them sitting on the floor in their shirts. The valets are very despondent.

Scene xx

A great tumult arises in the theatre. PANTALONE, GRATIANO and PIOMBINO rush in carrying VITTORIA. She begs them to protect her from the dangers of a brawl which has broken out because of her. These gentlemen brawlers—the *bravi*—pour in, their swords bared. They see VITTORIA, they seize her, and carry her out. PIOMBINO follows them with gestures of despair.

Scene xxi

PANTALONE and GRATIANO find themselves face to face with the valets who are clad only in their shirts. They ask them to explain what has happened. The valets invent an explanation and say that the crowd which just left the theatre, robbed them of their money and clothes. They add, philosphically, that although the theatre brings pleasure, it is also the source of numerous scandals. While they are indulging in these wise reflections, ISABELLA and FLAMINIA come in and ask their husbands why the play ended so soon.

Scene xxii

PANTALONE replies that a brawl interrupted it and that he has not seen the CAPTAIN. ISABELLA tells how they informed the CAPTAIN that he would find VITTORIA in the basement of their house, and that it is SILVIA instead of the actress who is waiting there for him. Fearing however, that the CAPTAIN, thus deceived might commit violence, they had asked ORATIO and FLAVIO to take the trouble to stay with them. PANTALONE and GRATIANO approve.

Scene xxiii

The CAPTAIN leaves the house swearing he has been betrayed. ORATIO and FLAVIO endeavor to calm him. PANTALONE and all the others intercede in behalf of SILVIA. The CAPTAIN listens. He admits that SILVIA is honorably born; that she is the daughter of a rich Milanese merchant; and that he loves her. This diabolical actress had so far bewitched him that he had forgotten poor SILVIA. But he returns to her and consents to marry her.

Scene xxiv

They bring in SILVIA and she learns that her lover returns her affection.

ISABELLA and FLAMINIA urge their husbands to stay away from the theatre, and instead to watch over their homes and the conduct of their wives. They reply that henceforth they will do as their wives ask. Everybody now goes to PANTALONE's home to celebrate the wedding of SILVIA and the CAPTAIN, and it is thus that the comedy of *The Portrait* ends.

13 Elizabethan and Shakespearean Style

Virtuosity

The Playgoers
In our assemblies at plays in London you
shall see such heaving and shoving, such
itching and shouldering, to sit by women—
such care for their garments, that they be
not trod on—such eyes to their laps that no
chips light in them—such pillows to their
backs that they take no hurt—such masking
in their ears I know not what—such giving
them pippins to pass the time—such
playing at footsaunt without carts—such
ticking, such toying, such smiling, such
winking, and such manning them home
when the sports are ended.

from *the schoole of abuse*
by Stephen Gosson

A goodly sport
Turner and Dun, two famous fencers,
played their prizes this day at the Bankside,
but Turner at last ran Dun so far in the
brain at the eye that he fell down presently
stone dead; a goodly sport in a Christian
state, to see one man kill another!

from the diary of John Manningham,
a law student in Elizabethan England

Gosson's description of a spirited, flirtatious London theatre crowd reveals the new mood of the Renaissance. Man for the most part was happy to be alive and lived every moment with zest. Manningham's entry indicates the intriguing mix of barbaric sports and activities within a Christian state. In a single day, the average Londoner could go to church, see a criminal mutilated and hanged on the London Bridge, and see a poetic play by William Shakespeare.

Overview of the English Renaissance in Theatre

The English Renaissance in theatre was dominated by a single genius: William Shakespeare, the poet of London from the town of Stratford-on-Avon. Any study of drama in the age of the great Renaissance of learning and progress following the Medieval period must focus upon this great English poet and playwright.

Three fundamental ideas of the period must be kept in mind with this focus. (1) The concept of *ego*. The majesty of man must be exalted! His intellect and ability were believed unmatched among living creatures. (2) The concept of *individuality*. Nothing seemed beyond the vanity and confidence of any Renaissance artist. (3) The concept of *virtuosity*. Man had multiple capability and breadth of vision; art was a business and man practiced the art well.

Shakespeare—The Man, The Theatre, The Art, The Acting

William Shakespeare, the dramatist, was melodic, free, and eratic in his verse. His plays possessed virtuosity. He was aware of space, of people— all kinds of people. With words, Shakespeare was capable of creating a "landscape." He was as brilliant, philosophical, and learned as any master musician of the Renaissance. In Shakespeare, genius and craft were welded in one incredible dramatist. He was the Michelangelo of playwrights.

Shakespeare wrote at least thirty-six plays within a short life span of fifty-two years (1564–1616). These plays and the Bible probably rank as the two richest sets of literary documents in the entire history of Western Man. Shakespeare accomplished all this having only what we would term an elementary school education, albeit equivalent to a modern secondary education.

How did it happen? How did such a man evolve? Why?

One must begin to find the answers in the Renaissance itself. When the Islam Turks (who lacked artistic interest) took Constantinople, the artists of the city escaped to Venice. There, a true revival of classical art and learning began. Thus, it was Italy, followed by England and Spain, that led the way out of the Middle Ages.

In England, Henry VIII built a strong Protestant nation which continued under Edward VI. Then, in 1558 the stingy but theatre-loving Queen Elizabeth I took the throne. Man became aware again of his "goodness," as well as of his "evil." Sir Francis Drake defeated "the invincible" Spanish Armada in 1588. England became a power and a glory, and her people developed a passion for their own history.

On the Continent in Spain and in Italy, similar impulses brought a flourishing of art, music, and drama led by writers such as Lopé de Vega, Calderon, and Niccolo Machiavelli. However, only England was able to produce a theatre genius of Shakespeare's magnitude.

As brief background, note that in fifteenth-century England actors were still considered vagabonds. However, by 1482 noblemen employed actors for local entertainment, and by 1572 actors were recognized legally when a statute requiring a license to act in plays was enacted. By 1574 all plays had to be approved for production by the Master of Revels. This form of control or censorship, which survived well into the twentieth century in England, provided both advantages for and limitations to the theatre.

Sponsorship of acting companies by noblemen in England increased, and the profession of acting was reborn, assisted greatly by the royal support of Queen Elizabeth who favored the activity. The strong Puritan element in England opposed the movement, but Elizabeth and the nobility triumphed, at least until well into the seventeenth century. Soon theatre was a prospering public concern. The great period of English Renaissance theatre dates from 1570 to 1620 (in 1642 the Puritans and the Commonwealth closed the theatres until the restoration of the throne to Charles II in 1660.)

King Lear by William Shakespeare. Anthony DeFonte as King Lear, Eric Hill as Earl of Kent, Donald Ilko as Duke of Albany, Christopher as Edgar, and Michele Farr as Cordelia at the Utah Shakespearean Festival. Directed by Howard Jensen. Photograph by Boyd D. Redington.

What were the key influences in the development of dramatic art in the Renaissance?

1. Schools and Universities. Formal educational institutions provided translations of Plautus, Terence, and Seneca. The English scholars wrote in imitation of these Roman classics and made a major contribution to dramatic activity.

2. The Inns of Court. Combined residences and training centers for lawyers developed, and there, too, classical drama was studied and imitated.

3. The heritage from English Medieval drama. Old farces, religious plays, and mixed forms of drama were studied. Portions of plays and techniques of writing were borrowed by Renaissance writers.

Certain key dramatists developed, all of whom had a decided influence on Shakespeare. Thomas Kyd, Christopher Marlowe, and John Lyly were all University Wits, or university scholar-artists, who wrote prior to Shakespeare. The youthful Shakespeare undoubtedly studied their work carefully and borrowed techniques, plots, and ideas. Later, literally dozens of fine playwrights developed to compete with Shakespeare, including such writers as Ben Jonson, Francis Beaumont and John Fletcher, John Webster, Thomas Dekker, and John Ford, among others. Marlowe, unusually adept at blank verse, and Jonson, skilled in comedy of humours (see Glossary), were particularly outstanding dramatists. However, for purposes of clarity

A Midsummer Night's Dream by William Shakespeare. John Rensenhouse as Oberon at the University of Wisconsin-Milwaukee. Directed by Barry Boys, scenery by R. H. Graham, costumes by Julie Jackson. Photograph by Alan Magayne-Roshak.

and continuity a study of the acting style of the period should concentrate on Shakespeare, the foremost dramatist of the time and probably unrivaled among playwrights.

The structure of the Elizabethan theatre must be noted before we examine Shakespeare, his work, and the acting style necessary to performance of his plays. While evidence concerning these theatres is incomplete, and while scholarly disputes have resulted, it is generally accepted that two types of theatres flourished. One was the open-air public theatre (such as the famous Globe), and the other was the indoor private theatre (such as the Blackfriars). Actually, general audiences could enter both theatres for a fee, but the indoor winter or private theatres tended to be frequented mostly by nobility and royalty. The size of the more popular outdoor or public theatres varied, ranging in seating capacity from 2,000 to 3,000 patrons.

The theatres were enclosed in part by three tiers of roofed *galleries* which formed the outside of the structure. A large central area, popularly called the *yard* or *pit*, was unroofed. The least expensive ticket placed the customer in the pit where he stood to watch a play; by paying more, he could sit in one of the galleries. The *stage* itself was about four to six feet in height and thrust forward from one of the sides, of the theatre (it is likely that the stage was portable or removable in most of the theatres, which permitted the theatres to be used for cruel sporting events such as bullbaiting and bearbaiting). The *roof* of the theatre was thatched with straw and wood; to the rear was an area similar to a small balcony called the "musicians gallery" where musicians sat and played instruments. It is fairly certain that one or more *trapdoors* were cut in the stage floor and that two large doors at the rear of the stage were used by actors to make entrances and exists. Probably a *pavillion* of some sort stood upon the rear center of the stage. The pavillion was more than likely hung with curtains which could be used to reveal new scenes of action in progress. It would seem that the theatre and stage just described permitted a rather continuous flow of dramatic action. There were probably no act or scene divisions in the playing of the scripts (most such divisions were added in later centuries by editors).

It is now believed that some minor scenery and stage machinery were utilized in Shakespearean, or Elizabethan, productions. Documented evidence exists of painted backdrops, rocks, trees, tables, and the like being kept at the theatre. Scenic effects resembled the freestanding three-dimensional units called mansions, popular during the Medieval period. However, they were probably more detailed than the sets used in Medieval drama. Elizabethans equipped their stage with such articles as trees, thrones, beds, scaffolds, barriers, prison bars, tombs, tents, caves, tables, and chairs. The large central area (the equivalent to the Medieval platea) could be localized. Set pieces were used when necessary or if they were available. Scenery was probably used when it suited the convenience of the actors, managers, and playwrights rather than to follow any principle of consistent scenic design. As knowledge of the court masques became public, and royalty became increasingly interested in acting troupes, theatre owners paid more attention to scenic spectacle.

The costuming utilized contemporary Elizabethan street and court dress, with no or very limited attempt at historical accuracy. From 1558 to 1642 costumes were identical to Medieval and Renaissance dress. Attention was paid to correct dress according to rank and to fanciful garments worn by ghosts, fairies, and witches, and traditional kingly attire was copied for such characters as Henry VI, Falstaff, and Richard III. The Elizabethans spared no expense in executing their costumes. Garments were costly and elegant, combining satin, silver, silk, and lace. Color for costumes depended on propriety: foresters wore green, shepherds wore white, royalty wore purple, friars wore brown. In essence, the stage was a glass of fashion—the epitome of the art of wearing clothes.

An Elizabethan acting company was composed of ten to twenty members. The chief actor in Shakespeare's company was Richard Burbage, an accomplished tragedian. Will Kemp was the leading comic actor. Approximately ten members of the company were "hired" men. The latter included doorkeepers, musicians, stagehands, and box office personnel, all of whom were paid flat salaries or wages and did not share in profits. There were also three to five boy apprentice actors in the company who played all the female roles (not until the Restoration and the eighteenth century were actresses permitted on the stage). Productions were given at about three o'clock in the afternoon, and natural daylight illuminated the action. A volatile and noisy audience ate and drank during a performance and cheered or jeered their approval or disapproval. As the play ended at twilight, the highly diverse audience dispersed for a drink in a local public house or retired to dinner and conversation. At the end of each performance, the actors sang, danced, and performed comic action, even though the play may have been a tragedy. The theatrical custom was to end the performance on a light, happy note and to send the audience away in a good humor.[1]

Modern adaptation of the original style of Elizabethan acting will probably be minimal, as opposed to the extensive adaptation needed for Greek and Restoration acting styles. The following discussion of language, voice, gestures, movement, pantomimic business, character, emotion, and spectacle provides you with the necessary tools to perform in the acting style of the Elizabethan period, be it in tragedy or comedy.

1. For further, more detailed discussion of the Elizabethan theatre and audience, see C. Walter Hodges, *The Globe Restored*, 2d Ed. (London: Oxford University Press, 1968); Alois Nagler, *Shakespeare's Stage* (New Haven, Conn.: Yale University Press, 1958); Alfred Harbage, *Shakespeare's Audience* (New York: Columbia University Press, 1961).

In a letter to Mrs. Patrick Campbell, George Bernard Shaw advised the actress, "When you play Shakespeare, don't worry about the character but go for the music. It was by word-music that he expressed what he wanted to express, and if you get the music right, the whole thing will come right."[2] Shaw's advice is well taken. An understanding of the verse and poetry in Shakespeare's plays is the key to development of all other acting concepts—character, emotional quality, rhythm, gesture, and movement. In line with the theory of personalization, reducing verse to simple ideas gives you more confidence with your interpretive ability and thus enables you to approach the roots of Shakespeare's reality which is different from your own only in the manner of utterance and degree of intensity. You need to separate ideas clearly to give the proper shape to the verse, which will give the poetry a pervasive "music."

The most common problem a modern actor encounters with Shakespeare's plays is to achieve complete character portrayal while trying to speak the lines effectively. The audience must be stirred by the nuances of the poetry. What you must remember is that character and poetry are inseparable. A study of the details and nuances and structure of the lines will enable you to reveal and portray a character in depth.

Verse-speaking should be based on an understanding of the structure of the verse. To accomplish this task, you must study the organized relationship of words and sounds. During Shakespeare's time, school boys were taught to recognize figures of speech and pronounce them rhetorically with accompanying gestures. Recognition of metaphor is crucial in this task. You cannot circumvent the fact that Shakespearean poetry must be elevated somewhat above a conversational mode to achieve lyricism and beauty. Elevation is aided by permitting the presentational mode to dominate delivery. You need not be confused by all this if you keep in mind the fact that unrhymed iambic pentameter or blank verse is the most malleable and adaptable of forms, open to variety and individuality of expression.

The verse is called *blank* because it allows both the speaker and the listener to anticipate rhymes when the rhythmical pattern is regular and the actor to emphasize sounds to reveal character and emotion.

An *iambus* is a foot of two syllables, a short or unaccented syllable followed by a long or accented syllable—brief, long, brief, long. The human heart, for example, beats in iambs, that is, in two recurring strokes—brief, long, brief, long. Breathing also occurs in iambic feet, outbreathing, inbreathing, with stress on the inbreathing because it takes longer and is consciously done, whereas outbreathing is automatic. Another analogy is the ticking sound of a metronome. The sound and movement of the metronome are measured. The rhythm never changes. The basic unit in a metronome is the *tick*. If you think of the basic unit of iambic pentameter as a *foot* (or two syllables) and establish that we must complete the utterance

2. Marowitz, Charles, *The Method as Means* (London: Herbert Jenkins, 1961), p. 77.

Much Ado About Nothing
by William Shakespeare.
JoAnn Johnson Patton as
Beatrice and John H.
Reese as Benedick at the
Utah Shakespearean
Festival. Directed by
Leslie Reidel. Photograph
by Boyd D. Redington.

Much Ado About Nothing
by William Shakespeare.
JoAnn Johnson Patton as
Beatrice, John H. Reese as
Benedick, Jesse Bennett as
Leonata, and M. Scott
Wilkinson as Don Pedro
at the Utah
Shakespearean Festival.
Directed by Leslie Reidel.
Photograph by Boyd D.
Redington.

An imaginative interpretation of *As You Like It* by William Shakespeare. At The Julliard School, New York. Directed by Norman Ayrton. (Photo by Susan Cook.)

of those two syllables by the time it takes the bar of the metronome to tick from one side to the other, then you will be speaking in correct rhythm. If you stress or accent either of the two syllables, you will reveal ideas and feelings. Correct pronunciation will result. An example follows:

⏑　／　⏑　／　⏑　／　⏑　／　⏑　／
Oh,₁what—oh,₂what—oh,₃what—oh,₄what—oh,₅what

Note that the mark ⏑ indicates the short or nonstress syllable; the mark ／ is the long or accented syllable. If you speak comprehensibly, you are using meter and accent, or you are scanning the poetry.

When working with a line of five feet (or iambs), with accent on the second syllable of each foot, you should take from two-to-four seconds to speak. The formalized lines taken together are called iambic pentameter. Sometimes Shakespeare deviated from iambic pentameter in order to surprise or heighten a dramatic situation. For example:

⏑　／　⏑　／　／　⏑　／　　　／
Though this be madness, yet there is method in't.

It is the task of the poet to decide the exact word or group of words to accent to express meaning or emotion. His designs are planned and carefully executed to produce intensity of expression.

Exercise 1 Iambic Pentameter

Read the following speech aloud with clear articulation and heightened projection, practicing correct iambic pentameter:

O, that this too too solid flesh
would melt,
Thaw, and resolve itself into a dew,
Or that the Everlasting had not fixed

The Merry Wives of Windsor by William Shakespeare. JoAnn Johnson Patton as Mistress Page and Michele Farr as Mistress Ford at the Utah Shakespearean Festival. Directed by Sabin Epstein. Photograph by Boyd Redington.

His canon 'gainst self-slaughter. O
God, God,
How weary, stale, flat, and unprofitable
Seem to me all the uses of this world!
    Hamlet Act I, scene ii

Notice the repetitive, heavy sound of the words in expressing Hamlet's wish to leave a world which disgusts him. There is an effective repetition of the word *too* in the first line and of *God* in the fourth line. The heavy repetition dramatizes the emotion. The iambic pentameter is altered from time to time to keep the pattern from sounding monotonous and the delivery from sounding too austere.

Shakespearean language also reveals that clauses are frequently short. For example, Lady Macbeth says:

The raven himself is hoarse
That croaks the fatal entrance of Duncan
Under my battlements
    Macbeth Act I, scene v

Pauses are stronger or more imperative; for example, in the prose exchange between Hamlet and Rosencrantz and Guildenstern, Hamlet says:

You were sent for, and there is a
kind of confession in your looks, which
your modesties have not craft enough to
color. I know the good king and queen
have sent for you.
    Hamlet Act II, scene ii

Transitions are abrupt; for example, the confrontation between Hamlet and Polonius in act 2, reveals such a transition:

POLONIUS   My lord, I have news to tell you.
HAMLET   My lord, I have news to tell you.
    When Roscius was an actor in Rome—
POLONIUS   The actors are come hither, my lord.
HAMLET   Buzz, Buzz.
POLONIUS   Upon my honor.
HAMLET   Then came each actor on his ass—
    Hamlet   Act II, scene ii

Questions and interjections abound; for example, in the same passage with Hamlet, Rosencrantz, and Guildenstern, Hamlet asks: "Were you not sent for? Is it your own inclining? Is it a free visitation?"

Imagery is frequently symbolic; for example, the rose is a symbol of youth and the lily is a symbol of purity. Shakespeare often used diverse images to illustrate a single idea. This quality increases the range of concepts and heightens the emotion (e.g., Hamlet's "To be or not to be" speech reveals a number of dramatic and diverse images).

Shakespeare often used the half-line in dialogue. A speaker ends his speech in the middle of a metrical line and another speaker takes the line up and completes it.

HORATIO   Friends to this ground.
MARCELLUS   And liegemen to the Dane.
    Hamlet Act I, scene i

You should note the atmosphere and mood of the scene in order to project the correct feeling of the lines. The illusion which the poet undertakes must be understood.

When speaking the verse, you should intone and stress the figures of speech to show the relationship of sound and meaning in the words. Learn to distinguish the words which are essential to expressing the individual figures of speech. You will use these figures to better express emotions and ideas. One of the most frequently encountered Shakespearean figures of speech is the "marching or climbing figure." In act 1 of *Richard III*, Richard says of the sickly king:

He cannot live, I hope and must not die,
Till George be packed with post horse up
to heaven.
    Richard III   Act I, scene i

At times you will see repetition of the same sound rather than a play upon different sounds. For example, in *Romeo and Juliet*, Romeo says to the Nurse:

Where is she? and how doth she and what
Says my concealed lady to our cancelled love?
    Romeo and Juliet   Act I, scene iii

Othello by William Shakespeare. James Avery as Othello and Joyce Harris as Desdemona at the Oregon Shakespearean Festival. Directed by Sanford Robbins. Scenery by William Bloodgood, costumes by Michael Olich, Lighting by Rovert Peterson. Photograph by Hank Kranzler.

Puns are words which play upon multiple meanings. They were considered a vital part of Elizabethan word usage. Shakespeare's plays abound in puns (e.g., the dying Mercutio in *Romeo and Juliet* remarks to Romeo, "Ask for me tomorrow, and you shall find me a grave man").

Another peculiarity of Shakespearean language is the *conceit*. The Shakespearean conceit is a piece of extreme, unusual, and often witty poetic imagination.

For example, consider these lines from Romeo and Benvolio in *Romeo and Juliet* in which Romeo discusses the qualities of love:

. . . O brawling love! O loving hate!
O any thing, of nothing first create!
O heavy lightness! serious vanity!
Mis-shapen chaos of well-seeming forms!
Feather of lead, bright smoke, cold fire, sick health!
Still-waking sleep, that is not what it is!
       Romeo and Juliet   Act I, scene i

Scene from *King Lear* by
William Shakespeare.
King Lear, Len Cariou;
the Fool, Nicolas Keprose.
The Guthrie Theatre,
Minneapolis, Minn.

These are conceits in which Shakespeare plays with opposites. Many of his conceits are shocking, melodramatic, and extreme and are usually rooted in the inner conflict of the character speaking the lines.

In his later and better plays, Shakespeare used conceits in an abstract way. In earlier plays, he merely listed apparent contradictions, while in *King Lear*, for example, the Fool's speeches to Lear are used very precisely as commentary on Lear's weaknesses.

Awareness of the conceit device helps to better understand character and to better speak the tricky, ear-challenging, and thought-challenging conceits.

Shakespeare often joined contrasting ideas to make an expressive, compressed statement of equivalence or opposition (e.g., Hamlet's line, "A little more than kin and less than kind").

In all the examples just given, meaning and emotion were integral to the structure of the pattern of sound. The most common sound pattern was *rhyme*, often used to end long speeches or scenes. Rhyme is created when the end sounds of lines correspond. (Other structures include *assonance*—likeness of sound in which the stressed vowel sounds are alike but the consonant sounds are unlike as in *main* and *came*; and *alliteration*—repetition of an initial sound, usually a consonant, in two or more words of a phrase as in "a fair field full of folk.")

When studying the figures of speech in Shakespearean verse, you should discover words designed to simultaneously produce calculated and special emotional reactions. Claudius's soliloquy in *Hamlet* at the end of act 3 is a case in point. The lines depict the sound of anguish:

Oh, wretched state! O bosom black as death!
O liméd soul, that struggling to be free
art more engaged! Help, angels! make assay!
Hamlet   Act III, scene iii

Or note the sensual and romantic lines spoken by Juliet as she waits for Romeo:

Lovers can see to do their amorous rites
By their own beauties; or, if love be blind,
It best agrees with night. Come, civil night,
Thou sober-suited matron, all in black,
And learn me how to lose a winning match,
Played for a pair of stainless maidenhoods.
Hood my unmanned blood bating in my cheeks,
With thy black mantle till strange love grow bold.
Romeo and Juliet   Act III, scene ii

Shakespeare was a master at selecting *the* word and sound to express mood. A classic example is the witches scene in *Macbeth* where supernatural mystery is vividly duplicated:

FIRST WITCH   When shall we three meet again?
In thunder, lightning, or in rain?
SECOND WITCH   When the hurlyburly's done,
When the battle's lost and won.
THIRD WITCH   That will be ere the set of sun.
FIRST WITCH   Where the place?
SECOND WITCH   Upon the heath.
THIRD WITCH   There to meet with Macbeth.
FIRST WITCH   I come, Graymalkin!
SECOND WITCH   Paddock calls.
THIRD WITCH   Anon!
ALL   Fair is foul, and foul is fair
Hover through the fog and filthy air.
Macbeth   Act I, scene i

The structure of Elizabethan language is fully realized when the pattern which emerges contains a rhythmic quality. The rhythm of a line is organic and is derived from the irregularity of the line. Each line usually has its own rhythm to give color, variety, and meaning. This rhythmic flow of sound is called *cadence* (do not confuse meter with rhythm; meter deals with feet and stresses, as in iambic pentameter). The rhythm of a line is punctuated by pauses called *caesura*. The pauses usually last the time it would take to speak ten syllables, which is indeed plenty of time to catch a breath.

Also note linguistic changes and modern alterations in word meaning as compared with the time of Shakespeare. It is important to study the original meaning of words (i.e., etymology—the additions and losses in vocabulary), semantics (i.e., alterations in meanings and associations of words), accidence and syntax (i.e., changes in inflection and construction of words to form phrases, clauses, and sentences), and phonological changes or equivalents.

A peculiar language situation developed during the Renaissance. Elizabethans loved to borrow phrases from foreign languages. Latin was favored by writers and served to enrich the English language. Latin words were either naturalized or added to the English language. Latin did not replace native words, but provided synonyms such as *wonder* and *admiration*, words derived from Latin. It follows that even a slight knowledge of Latin is a great advantage to the correct understanding of Elizabethan writers, especially when we consider that many Latin borrowings of the sixteenth century now have meanings different from the original. For example, the Latin sense of *apparent* no longer means visible or evident, and *intention* does not convey the idea of intentness. Some Latin forms such as the word *objectum* were later changed to conform to English spelling and accent.

French also supplied words and influenced changes in spelling. Commercial, religious, and architectural terms were adopted from the Spanish, Italian, and Dutch languages. Foreign influences on language provided unparalleled freedom of vocabulary and form. However, that freedom also produced confusion, and clarity and precision were often sacrificed. Nevertheless, the English language gained more than it lost by allowing in foreign importations. The number of compound words such as "homekeeping wits" was increased, and prefixes such as *dis-, re-,* and *en-* and suffixes such as *-ful, -less, -ness,* and *-hood* were introduced.

Perhaps the greatest problem encountered in the study of Shakespearean verse is not the deciphering of obsolete words, but the difficulty arising from the many times it is possible to get some idea of meaning, however imperfect it might be. It becomes a matter of missing exact shades of meaning and thereby misinterpreting the tone. The following Shakespearean words often differ from their present meaning:

a he
ability means, wealth
addition title
admiration wonder, care, anxiety
carry manage
conceit conception, idea
confusion overthrow, ruin
fellow equal
gear matter, stuff, thing, business
humour moisture, temperament, whine, caprice
modern common, ordinary
moe more
pregnant resourceful, apt, inclined
prevent anticipate, hinder

The foregoing analysis of Shakespearean verse and language in which the importance of relationships between words was clarified leads to a consideration of what is technically involved in speaking that verse and language. Once you have learned the details of emphasis, the technique usually becomes second nature. Do not aim solely at reproducing structural patterns because concentration on characterization will suffer. Elizabethan actors may not have had exact patterns or conventions for speaking on the stage, but they did adhere to general attitudes of speech. The actor needed a voice capable of tremendous range of tone and volume. The speaking style was partially influenced by the rhetoric of the Tudor period in that the Elizabethan actor was taught to heighten the simulation of emotion

Hal Proske as Prospero in The *Tempest* by William Shakespeare. Directed by Orlin Corey. Designed by Irene Corey. Everyman Players.

thus to move an audience. (An effective Elizabethan acting voice exhibits spontaneity and beauty of expression.) The speaking style was generally presentational. Verse necessitated a pattern of intonation which ran counter to the metrical pattern of stressed and unstressed syllables. The effect of the actor's delivery was musical, that is, well modulated. The voice was able to convey contrast among words, developing climaxes in tempo and rhythm. Thus, the vocal tone and emotional manner of the character were delineated more clearly. Emotion also played a part in producing the music of the line. Emotion gave color and life to the tones. (Be aware of which emotion is derived from a word or combination of words. An emotion may change just as the sense of a line changes.)

To perform Shakespeare's language you might do well to review Hamlet's advise to the players in act 3, scene 2. Hamlet warns the actors not to chant, whine, or elongate syllables: " . . . but if you mouth it, as many of our players do, I had as lief the town-crier spoke my lines." A fundamentally normal and controlled speaking voice is desired in delivery of Elizabethan prose. A natural vocal quality can best produce a melodic sound. I stated earlier that verse should be heightened somewhat above the conversational mode. However, when the verse is less passionate and emotional, a more natural or conversational mode may be effectively used. It is sometimes difficult for a modern actor to believe in the concept of a natural (as opposed to a declamatory) style of speaking Shakespeare because of the fear that the music of the verse will suffer. If the structural organization of the language is correctly analyzed, the music of the verse can still be maintained with natural speaking. *Natural speaking* means to speak the verse with a sustained tone, giving diaphragmic support and clear, accurate articulation. For example, many people slur the letter *r* when speaking. The partial loss of *r* in modern English works to the detriment of acoustical richness and energy. Pitch and length of tone can change quickly and abruptly. Vary your pace according to the needs of the lines. Modern actors often have a tendency to overintellectualize word analysis when speaking Shakespeare by assigning *each word* a definite emotion and objective. A more accurate technique is to let the sense of the whole sentence decide the emphasis on any given word. Elevate or emphasize some words in each sentence and allow the lines to flow. Rarely pause under the pretext of thinking words out, as actors often do in modern naturalistic plays.

Exercise 2   Voice

1. Study the following speech by Prospero from *The Tempest:*

You do look, my son, in a moved sort,
As if you were dismayed. Be cheerful, sir.
Our revels now are ended. These our actors,
As I foretold you, were all spirits and
Are melted into air, into thin air;
And, like the baseless fabric of this vision,

The cloud-capped towers, the gorgeous palaces,
The solemn temples, the great globe itself,
Yea, all which it inherit, shall dissolve,
And, like this insubstantial pageant faded,
Leave not a rack behind. We are such stuff
As dreams are made on, and our little life
Is rounded with a sleep. Sir, I am vexed.
Bear with my weakness. My old brain is troubled.
Be not disturbed with my infirmity.
If you be pleased, retire into my cell
And there repose. A turn or two I'll walk
To still my beating mind.

The Tempest   Act IV, scene i

Practice the speech aloud:

1. to establish the correct iambic pentameter rhythm.

2. to focus upon correct pauses and transitions.

3. to focus upon imagery, figures of speech, climbing figures, repetitions, conceits, and contrasting ideas.

4. to focus upon emotion and mood (be certain to check an Old English dictionary or a Shakespearean glossary to determine exact meanings of words).

In each of the foregoing exercise steps, utilize the best of the vocal characteristics learned in chapter 7.

2. As a lesson through deliberate error, read the Prospero speech above aloud once more and consciously adapt the speech to a very modern, naturalistic mode. That is, place pauses and punctuation where there are none, discard some words by murmuring them as though they were unimportant, and so on. This negative lesson may prove comical, but it should reveal the necessity to practice # 1 above again.

3. Practice comic vocal timing and a comedic manner by reading aloud the following prose selection:

MACDUFF: What three things does drink especially provoke?
PORTER: Marry, sir, nose-painting,
       sleep, and urine. Lechery,
       sir, it provokes, and un-
       provokes; it provokes the
       desire, but it takes away
       the performance: therefore,
       much drink may be said to be
       an equivocator with lechery. . . .

Macbeth   Act II, scene iii

Gesture and Movement

Elizabethan actors also used considerable gesture and movement to communicate what was being expressed in words. Gestures were occasionally conventional; they were undoubtedly also natural and precise, revealing the general disposition, humor, and state of mind of the character. The probable view among Elizabethan actors was that if a gesture was seen in daily life, its inclusion onstage was justified. For example, Richard Burbage, leading tragic actor in Shakespeare's company, probably noticed that Elizabethans frequently pointed a great deal with the forefinger; he undoubtedly used the gesture within a play if it was at all appropriate to the text and character. Perhaps this idea contrasts somewhat with the popular notion that in Shakespearean plays a heightened, elevated style of delivery necessitates use of conventional stereotyped gestures. A common misconception among many modern actors is to equate acting of Shakespearean drama with a system of external clichés. On the contrary, Shakespeare's characters exemplified truthful inner emotion, and action was suited to emotion and language. Elizabethans prided themselves on precise, explicit, heightened, and direct action that emanated from within an individual. Elizabethan stage acting surely demonstrated the same concept—expressing externally in a truthful manner what was felt inside.

As gestures acquired an appropriate, natural, though somewhat elevated appearance, so, too, did stage movements. Movements were characterized as full, fluid, and controlled. A consideration of the physical aspects of the Elizabethan stage and audience indicates the necessity to maximize all physical action. Since the acting areas were small and audiences were rowdy and loud, Elizabethan actors were trained in strong stage action such as fencing. The actor had to handle a heavy rapier in one hand and a dagger for parrying in the other. All fencing movements were highly calculated. Thrusting was accomplished at close quarters from the wrist and forearm and was usually aimed at the opponent's eye or below the ribs. In fencing, the actor had to achieve brutal reality to please the crowd. His training for theatrical fencing was highly rigorous and his physical coordination was excellent. Action was rapid and intensified.

The modern actor playing in an Elizabethan drama finds his stage movement immediately restricted simply because of the incredible weight of the costumes. It is commonly noted that Elizabethan clothes could "stand up by themselves." If we generalize the typical Elizabethan man as assertive, arrogant, and physically well toned, we create a picture of someone moving with confidence and vigor. However, he is attired in clothes that are difficult for us to wear. His doublet fits tightly to the body, the ruff fits stiffly around the neck, stockings reach to above the knee and are fastened up to the waistline by points or laces. Although physical action is startlingly limited within these confines, an actor must try to give the illusion of a rapid flow of movement. Continual practice in Elizabethan costume is the only solution for an actor who must be "swaggering and virile." Physical strength is further inhibited by the excessive padding under the garments which tends to throw modern actors completely off-balance.

Women also have their share of difficulty moving in costume. An immense amount of space is absorbed by the shape of the skirt (e.g., a bell-shaped skirt with a farthingale worn underneath, literally, a series of hoops which start at the waist and become progressively larger toward the ground). Moving through doors is awkward, approaching a chair and sitting in it pose problems, turning excessively is next to impossible, and hanging the arms at the sides is difficult. All stage movement must be taken in stride—no forced action or sudden moving. Women wear a long, tight bodice and tight *stomacher* (stiff front waist piece). They glide fluidly along the stage, holding the torso and head straight. (A wired ruff at the back of the head precludes excessive head movement; it also shields the face from the audience.) Hands can rest lightly on the top of the farthingale or strike a pose on top of each other, palms up, at the waist, or hands can be brought together at the waist with the thumbs on top and knuckles pointing down. Because of the stiff roll at the top of sleeves, underarms are held away from the body. Ladies usually carry a fan which is moved from the shoulder or from the wrist, depending on the cut of the costume. Fan movement usually involves the entire arm, not just the wrist, due to the tight-fitting sleeves.

Exercise 3   The Bow

Two types of bows and two types of curtsies should be learned to accommodate these important social customs used in most Elizabethan plays.

1. To execute a full or formal bow, stand with the feet astraddle in a normal standing position; withdraw either foot behind the other leg about 12 inches, turning the rear foot to form a 45-degree angle behind the other foot. The rear knee should now be bent. Remove the hat and drop that hand to one side or to the rear as you bend, or, depending on circumstances, leave the hat on your head as you bend; turn the other hand palm forward to the person being addressed. Lower the head toward the chest, and bend the back forward slightly.

2. A less formal version of this bow is to simply remove the hat while bending the head and back slightly forward. The feet remain astraddle. This bow was used for respect to peers or for hurried recognition, while the full or formal bow was used to address noblemen or royalty.

The Elizabethan bow.

Costume design for a "saucy" Elizabethan lady. (After executing the "less formal version of the curtsy.")

Exercise 4   The Curtsy

1. To execute a full or formal curtsy, rest the hands on top of the farthingale or skirt. Withdraw one foot behind the other several inches; bend both knees, the head, and the back. If you are addressing a queen, your body might bend to the point where you are sitting on the rear foot with the head inclined forward to the floor and the arms outstretched. To curtsy to one's peers usually bend the knees only 6 to 12 inches with the head slightly inclined.

2. A less formal version of this curtsy can be accomplished by lowering the head slightly and bending both knees a few inches with the feet in a straddled position. This curtsy was used for making quick acknowledgments or for entering or leaving a room.

Exercise 5   Pantomimic Greetings

Practice the following:

1. Greet another man with both arms extended while grasping one another simultaneously with both hands above the elbows or about the wrists.

2. Greet another woman by kissing her on the cheek as you meet.

3. One man extends his hand to a lady while walking by putting an arm forward at the elbow, palm down; the lady places her fingertips on top of his wrist or hand. As you walk by other couples, nod heads in informal greeting.

Using a course of movement in Elizabethan plays which is direct and decisive applies also to handling soliloquies (solo monologues) and asides (short addresses to the audience).

A popular opinion holds that an actor speaking a soliloquy must come downstage center to deliver his innermost thoughts directly to the audience. However, there is nothing sacred concerning the way an actor delivers a soliloquy. There is no special stage area where this intimate, intensive, and personal revelation must take place. Sometimes it may not be appropriate to address your character's thought to the audience at all, although the Elizabethan actor probably oriented much of his action in that manner. There are exceptions to the presentational directness of stage movements in every play including Elizabethan plays.

It is important to consider the appropriateness of the movement in the soliloquy and its effect on the character's emotions and thoughts. Modern lighting, for example, permits a soliloquy to be staged at any location onstage.

Exercise 6   The Soliloquy

Practice the following soliloquies by performing them at various stage locations, alternating direct presentation to the audience with self-reflective representational delivery. Invent your own movement and gestures.

> The spirit that I have seen
> May be the devil: and the devil hath power
> To assume a pleasing shape; yea, and perhaps
> Out of my weakness and my melancholy,
> As he is very potent with such spirits,
> Abuses me to damn me: I'll have grounds
> more relative than this: the play's the thing
> Wherein I'll catch the conscience of the King
> > HAMLET   *Hamlet*   Act II, scene iii

> How easy it is for the proper false
> In women's waxen hearts to set their forms!
> Alas, our frailty is the cause, not we!
> For such as we are made of, such we be.
> How will this fadge? My master loves her dearly;
> And I (poor monster) fond as much on him;
> And she (mistaken) seems to dote on me.
> > VIOLA   *Twelfth Night*   Act II, scene ii

The *aside* is an expression of thought spoken privately to the audience while other characters are present. Depending upon the circumstances in the play, the character may or may not move away from the other character or characters onstage. The actor delivering the aside may simply turn the body or face or change the voice. Asides can be spoken from all areas of the stage—from the rear to the front. An aside might be performed during action or other actors can *freeze* when the aside is delivered. It is not always believable to move away from other actors in an aside; however, the speaker *usually* remains stationary.

Exercise 7 The Aside

Practice the following asides using the various methods of delivery just discussed. Invent any necessary movement or gesture.

HAMLET Let her not walk i' the sun: conception is a blessing: but not as your daughter may conceive. Friend, look to 't.

POLONIUS (*aside*) How say you by that? Still harping on my daughter . . .

HAMLET . . . for yourself, sir, should be old as I am, if like a crab you could go backward.

POLONIUS (*aside*) Though this be madness, yet there is method in 't. . . .

Hamlet Act II, scene ii

TOBY . . . Therefore draw for the supportance of his vow. He protests he will not hurt you.

VIOLA (*aside*) Pray God defend me! A little thing would make me tell them how much I lack of a man.

Twelfth Night Act III, scene iv

Elizabethan actors were highly selective concerning the use of pantomimic business. Tragic plays did not require use of extensive and detailed stage business; conversely, comic plays tended toward use of highly inventive and extensive business. In tragedy, the Elizabethan audience loved to see an actor simulate running a sword through another actor's body or "tearing out his entrails." They cheered at the slight of hand. They wanted to see "real blood" (usually sheep's blood), which was put into a bladder with a hollow handle or slipped inside a white leather jerkin painted to look like human skin and punctured at the appropriate moment.

The play text itself will usually provide you with definite circumstances for stage business (e.g., knocking at a door, sword fighting, striking a bell, reading a book, holding a skull, holding a candle, etc.). Banquet scenes are frequently called for, as well as receptions, funerals, and *dumb shows.* Sometimes Shakespeare implied pantomimic business by mentioning the use of a book, dagger, or some other prop; at other times, more expansive physical action such as falling down was implied.

Note should be made concerning pantomimic dumb shows. These shows were performed in true commedia dell'arte style, using masks, appropriate costumes for stock characters, and detailed slapstick burlesque activities. Following the traditional Roman pantomime, no words were spoken. Movements were slow, precise, and exaggerated. For modern actors a dumb show should be truly improvisational. Later, the action can be set in order to perfect the precision of the pantomime.

Comedy permitted more flexibility in the use of stage properties and accessories; therefore, business was more inventive and detailed. Articles that a modern actor may utilize in comedy include handkerchiefs, keys, purses or notecases, letters, combs, and fans with mirrors hidden in them.

Costume properties can also be considered material for stage business. For example, gloves sometimes concealed "poison." Comedy often called for disguise—for example, adding a hood or a hat or a mask to cover the head and face. It is characteristic in comic plays for actors to consider the circumstances of a situation and create appropriate pantomimic business to add interest and heighten the humor.

Exercise 8   Dumb Show

Read and study the following dumb show performed by the players in *Hamlet*, act 3, scene 2:

Enter a King and a Queen very lovingly; the Queen embracing him. She kneels, and makes show of protestation unto him. He takes her up and declines his head upon her neck. He lays him down upon a bank of flowers. She, seeing

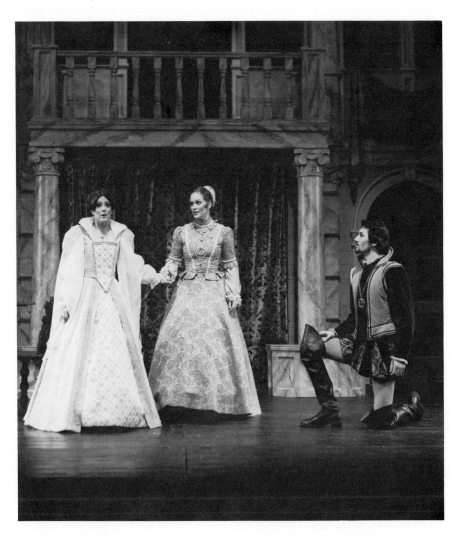

The Duchess of Malfi by John Webster. Barbara Acker as Duchess of Malfi, Dianne Winslow as Cariola, and Geoffrey Beauchamp as Antonio at The Hilberry Theatre, Wayne State University. Directed by Robert Emmett McGill. Scenic design adapted from the drawings of C. Walter Hodges by Russell Smith. Costumes by Jackie Durbin. Lighting by Gary Witt.

him asleep, leaves him. Anon comes in a fellow, takes off his crown, kisses it, pours poison in the King's ears, and exits. The Queen returns, finds the King dead, and makes passionate action. The Poisoner, with some two or three Mutes, comes in again, seeming to lament with her. The dead body is carried away. The Poisoner woos the Queen with gifts; she seems loath and unwilling awhile, but in the end accepts his love.

Exeunt

Form several casts of players and create the action called for in the dumb show. Improvise pantomimic dramatization as needed, including the use of any necessary props.

Character and Emotion

Shakespeare did not provide character description as many modern playwrights do. Nor did he provide many stages directions. It will be your and the director's responsibility to decide the quantity and quality of personality characteristics necessary for the development of character. Observe how the style of the speech affects the formality or informality of the person. You will often find that both qualities are fused. Although the formality does not necessarily mean a less natural performance, you must remain conscious of your character's emotions and actions. Again, the personalization technique permits you to rehearse the role first as if the character was you. The degree of realism will be determined by what the character says and how much he says. Natural acting orientated toward truthfully expressed emotion is essential to acting in an Elizabethan play, just as it has been in most plays throughout history.

Shakespeare's characters are extraordinarily well defined in the text and extremely varied and complex. The characters are usually multidimensional. The verse is an unusually sensitive gauge of the character's disposition and humour. Shakespeare's plays blend standardized fictional character types with well-known historical figures. Because Shakespeare's stories were usually based on existing stories or earlier plays, his characters retain a classical kind of clarity. A character comes from a definite place; he has traceable literary and historical progeny, fixed attitudes, indicative bearing, and pronounced temperament (e.g., think of Iago, Hamlet, Macbeth, and Falstaff). Shakespeare also utilized the Elizabethan society well by presenting the psychological and philosophical foundations prevalent in his milieu. Characters fit into a generic group whose behavior tends to conform to specific social classes. Shakespeare also differentiated characters within each class. For example, gentlewomen and ladies-in-waiting bore the signs of the upper class, yet they were given internal qualities and distinct characterization (e.g., Maria in *Twelfth Night* and Emilia in *Othello* may be portrayed as women of a certain social position in a particular social scheme and as highly individualized characters). Other generic types of characters were the messenger or servant and the clown. Their distinction lies in the particularized task required of them by the playwright. For example, these characters may affect the course of action (e.g., the Nurse in *Romeo and Juliet*); they may affect the plot (e.g., the Friar in *Romeo and Juliet*); they may sing (e.g., Feste in *Twelfth Night*); they may comment on character or situation (e.g., Reynaldo in *Hamlet*); they may plead or mock (e.g., the Fool in *Lear*).

The difficulty encountered in delineating character development in any play need not concern you unnecessarily if the character's state of being is clear at the beginning of the play. Character development will come organically out of the whole play. Shakespeare was particularly careful to base character motivation on the broad desires that all men might experience. As with the Greeks, it was a belief of the Elizabethan society that affections or emotions *should* be controlled by reason. When passions rule, disaster follows. Men are motivated by specific ends and universal emotions—greed, love, hate, revenge, and jealousy. Reason remains powerless before the volatile and pervasive nature of emotion which can destroy the moral and political world.

Shakespeare defined his characters more by their emotion than by their reason. *How* the character speaks is often more important than what is said. Often the poetry seems to consume the character. Rhythmic and melodic recitation affect the emotions of the character and may be heightened by

As You Like It by William Shakespeare. Barbara Bazaldua as Phebe and James Dierker as Silvius at The University of Missouri. Directed by Stephen Archer. Setting and Lighting by Lewis W. Stoerker. Costumes by Hazel Hall.

close physical proximity to the audience. It is through the verse that impressions of dignity, suffering, grandeur, and human significance are created. However, there is no need to portray Shakespearean emotion melodramatically or unconvincingly. The guide for today's actor is control and precision when handling Shakespearean emotion. Place your focus on the spoken word and the verbal display such as in soliloquies, orations, descriptions, repartee, and puns. Concentrate on emphasizing and elevating key words in sentences. Try not to "think the emotion out"; imagine the emotion of an actual person in a real situation. The outcome should result in contagious response of clear, disciplined, and appropriate emotion.

Exercise 9   Character and Emotion

1. Select a character from the list at the end of this chapter. Read the play and study the character with special focus on character development, character personality, and character emotion. Write a one-to-two-page paper in which you clarify what you learned from your study about the character and emotion. The paper should be read and discussed by your instructor and colleagues. Later you may wish to perform a representative scene or monologue to complete this exercise.

2. Practice creating emotional complexity in each of the following speeches:

IMOGEN: I would have broke mine eye-strings; crack'd them, but
To look upon him, till the diminution
Of space had painted him sharp as my needle,
    Nay, follow'd him, till he had melted from
The smallness of a gnat to air, and then
Have turn'd mine eye and wept.

Cymbeline   Act I, scene iii

ULYSSES: Time, hath, my lord, a wallet at his back,
Wherein he puts alms for oblivion,
A great-sized monster of ingratitudes:
Those scraps are good deeds past, which are devour'd
    As fast as they are made, forgot as soon
As done: perseverance, dear my lord,
Keeps honor bright: to have done is to hang
Quite out of fashion, like a rusty nail
In monumental mockery.

Troilus and Cressida
Act III, scene iii

Dance and Music

It is an historical fact that most Elizabethan men were excellent dancers. In addition, some men, especially the nobility, were accomplished musicians. Elizabethan society was exceptionally conscious of the role that music and dance played in helping formulate the temperament of the times. Execution of dances was skillful and intricate. Dancing became a test of quick intelligence and physical agility. Men took the lead in creating a pattern of steps. There are many extant Elizabethan dances which can be performed either before a play, during intermission, or after a play. Performances traditionally ended with a dance called the *jig*. This was a violent, spectacular dance with many intricate steps. Actors executed exaggerated leaps called *caprioles* and violent lifts of one's partner high into the air called *voltes*. Other known dances were the *Pavane* (after the peacock's pride of bearing), the *galliarde* (a lively, nimble movement), and the *alman* or *allemande* (German or heavy type of movement with the feet).

The richness of the Elizabethan period was fully exemplified by its music. Nearly everyone sang and performed. Class distinctions ceased to exist when it came to music. The most popular kind of music was the *madrigal*, a song written with up to seven parts. There were drinking songs and solo love ballads. Unfortunately, many of Shakespeare's songs have to be adapted to modern music because the original melodies are lost. However, most scholars believe Shakespeare considered music to be supportive, not dominant, in his plays. Music was created for effect, to underscore some point, to add character dimension, or to introduce scenery and characters. Occasionally instruments were played by stage characters to add color. Musicians were used in dumb shows for entrances and exits of special (usually royal) characters, to underscore alliterative verse or repetition of phrases, and to intensify emotional effects. Mad or insane people also were associated with music, for example, Lear and Ophelia. Music was used for moments of fantasy (e.g., *The Tempest* and *A Midsummer Night's Dream*). In general, music was classified into three groups: fanfares, dances, and songs. The instruments varied greatly, but the main ones were the virginal, the lute, the viola da gamba, and the recorder. We are most familiar with the lute and the recorder. The lute was similar in shape to a bowl and was slung across the shoulders by brightly colored ribbons. The strings were plucked, and it was used primarily to accompany singing of love songs. The recorder, a thin-sounding instrument, has regained popularity in recent times. The virginal was played by the ladies who plucked the strings with quills to actuate the keyboard. The viol (viola da gamba) was a stringed instrument suitable for chamber music. Flageolets or penny whistles were also used to produce a sweet, melodic tone. The hautboy, a reed instrument, was rather shrill and harsh. Horns were used for hunting music; trumpets and drums were used as "alarums" and "flourishes" to announce royalty. Violins, cornets, flutes, hautboys, drums, and flutes were traditionally used in dumb shows. Instruments might be grouped by families, or small mixed combinations of three or four instruments with or without voices. The organ was used by itself primarily. It was a small instrument consisting of flute pipes and beating reeds which produced a harsh sound.

Learning to dance to Elizabethan music is a highly specialized technique which should not be undertaken in a single acting exercise. Extensive study and practice with a trained choreographer or director are required (study references are given in Suggested Readings at the end of this chapter).

Music and dance in Shakespeare's plays should always be considered in the light of how clearly and appropriately they support character, action, and mood and should rarely be used as spectacles in their own right. Music and dance are only supportive and must never dominate or destroy the power of what is inherently Shakespearean in terms of brilliant verse and characterization.

Suggested Characters and Plays for Scene Work

Shakespeare, William

Hamlet, Ophelia, Claudius, Gertrude, Polonius, Laertes, Horatio, Ghost, First Gravedigger
   Hamlet
Othello, Desdemona, Iago, Emilia
   Othello
Romeo, Juliet, Mercutio, Nurse
   Romeo and Juliet
Anthony, Brutus, Cassius, Caesar, Calpurnia, Portia
   Julius Caesar
Richard III, Clarence, Lady Anne
   Richard III
Bottom, Puck
   A Midsummer Night's Dream
Shylock, Portia, Jessica
   The Merchant of Venice
Falstaff, Hotspur, Henry IV, Mistress Quickly
   Henry IV, Part I
Henry V, Katherine
   The Life of King Henry V
Rosalind, Jaques
   As You Like It
Malvolio, Feste, Sir Toby Belch, Sir Andrew Aguecheek, Viola, Olivia, Maria, Duke Orsino
   Twelfth Night
Lear, Edmund, The Fool, Gloucester, Goneril, Regan, Cordelia
   King Lear
Macbeth, Banquo, Macduff, Lady Macbeth, The Witches
   Macbeth
Antony, Cleopatra
   Antony and Cleopatra
Prospero, Caliban, Ariel
   The Tempest

Jonson, Ben

Volpone, Mosca
   Volpone
Morose, Epicoene
   Epicoene
Jeremy, Subtle, Dol Common
   Alchemist

Dekker, Thomas

Lacy, Rafe
   The Shoemaker's Holiday

Unique Shakespearean costume designs fully realized by Irene Corey. *A Midsummer Night's Dream* by William Shakespeare; Everyman Players; directed by Orlin Corey. The designs in this production were based on inspiration from various birds (as befitting the woodland setting). In photo *a*, Puck is based on the masked Tanager (performed by Randy Tallman); in photo *b*, Oberon is based on the Grouse with his fluffed ruff (performed by Allen Shaffer); in photo *c*, Peasblossom is based on an exotic and colorful talon bird (performed by Barbara McMillan).

Webster, John

Duchess of Malfi, Bosola
  The Duchess of Malfi

Marlowe, Christopher

Dr. Faustus, Mephistophilis, Wagner, Helen
  Tragical History of Dr. Faustus
Barabas, Abigail, Ithamore
  The Jew of Malta
King Edward the Second, Queen Isabella
  Reign of Edward the Second

Actor Checklist   Elizabethan and Shakespearean Style

Voice	Clear articulation; well projected; varied; slightly elevated tone.
Movement	Full and fluid; appropriate to character; slightly elevated but natural and comfortable; highly selective for tragedy; free and spontaneous for comedy; presentational delivery generally used in soliloquy and aside; representational mode dominates slightly in both tragedy and comedy.
Gestures	Use of full body; clear, fluid, and appropriate; slightly elevated; highly selective in tragedy; flexible in comedy.
Pantomimic Dramatization	Clear, appropriate; use of hand and costume props, particularly in comedy; highly selective for tragedy; highly inventive for comedy.
Character	Truthful and believable; clear; empathic, if appropriate; appropriate dimension.
Emotion	Complex and multidimensional; clear; disciplined; rooted in human psychology.
Ideas	Complex and clear; rooted in Renaissance and Elizabethan social, philosophical, and theological thought; effectively theatricalized.
Language	Often unusual vocabulary; clear and understandable; iambic pentameter rhythmically intact with interpretative freedom permitted; correct pronounciation; lyrical and musical when intended.
Pace and Tempo	Varied; rhythmic; disciplined.
Special Techniques	Specialized dancing and singing depending on context; specialized musical instruments when required; language requires unusual vocal dexterity; unusual attention to movement in costume.

Suggested Readings

Adams, John C. *The Globe Playhouse: Its Design and Equipment.* 2d ed. New York: Barnes & Noble, 1961.

Adams, Joseph Q. *Shakespearean Playhouses: A History of English Theatres from the Beginnings to the Restoration.* Boston: Houghton Mifflin Company, 1917.

Bartlett, John. *A Complete Concordance of Shakespeare.* London: St. Martin's, 1980.

Baxter, John. *Shakespeare's Poetic Styles: Verse Into Drama.* Boston: Routledge and Kegan Paul, 1980.

Beckerman, Bernard. *Shakespeare at the Globe, 1500–1609.* New York: Macmillan Co., 1962.

Bentley, Gerald E. *Shakespeare, A Biographical Handbook.* New Haven: Yale University Press, 1961.

Berry, Ralph. *Shakespearean Structures.* Totowa, N.J.: Barnes & Noble, 1981.

Brown, John Russell. *Shakespeare in Performance.* New York: Harcourt, Brace Jovanovich, 1976.

Campbell, Lily Bess. *Scenes and Machines on the English Stage during the Renaissance.* Cambridge: Harvard University Press, 1923.

Chambers, E. K. *The Elizabethan Stage.* 4 vols. London: Oxford University Press, 1923.

———, and Williams, C. *A Short Life of Shakespeare.* London: Oxford University Press, 1933.

Chute, Marchette. *Shakespeare of London.* New York: E. P. Dutton & Co., 1949.

Clurman, Harold. "Actors in Style and Style in Actors." New York *Times Magazine*, December 7, 1952.

Ellis-Fermor, Una. *The Jacobean Drama: An Interpretation.* 3d ed. London: Oxford University Press, 1953.

———. *Shakespeare's Drama.* Ed., Kenneth Muir. New York: Methuen, 1980.

Farnham, Willard. *The Medieval Heritage of Elizabethan Tragedy.* New York: Barnes & Noble, 1936.

Gibson, William. *Shakespeare's Game.* New York: Atheneum, 1978.

Glenn, Stanley L. *A Director Prepares.* Encino, Ca.: Dickenson and Co., 1973.

Granville-Barker, H. *Prefaces to Shakespeare.* 4 Vols. Princeton, N. J.: Princeton University Press, 1947.

———, and Harrison, G. B. *A Companion to Shakespeare.* New York: Doubleday & Co., 1960.

Gurr, Andrew. *The Shakespearean Stage, 1574–1642.* 2d. Ed. New York: Cambridge University Press, 1981.

Harbage, Alfred. *Shakespeare's Audience.* New York: Columbia University Press, 1961.

Hazlitt, William. *The Characters of Shakespeare's Plays.* New York: E. P. Dutton, 1929.

Hewitt, Barnard, ed. *The Renaissance Stage: Documents of Serlio, Sabbattini, and Furttenbach.* Coral Gables, Fla.: University of Miami Press, 1958.

Hibbard, G. R. *The Making of Shakespeare's Dramatic Poetry.* Toronto: University of Toronto Press, 1981.

Hodges, C. W. *The Globe Restored.* rev. ed. New York: Coward, McCann & Geoghegan, 1968.

Horst, Louis. *Pre-Classic Dance Forms.* New York: Kamin Dance Publishers, 1953.

Irvine, Theodoria. *A Pronouncing Dictionary of Shakespearean Proper Names.* New York: Barnes & Noble, 1947.

Jaggard, William. *Shakespeare Bibliography.* New York: Ungar, 1959.

Jorgensen, Paul A. *Redeeming Shakespeare's Words.* Berkeley, Ca.: University of California Press, 1962.

———. *Shakespeare's Military World.* Berkeley, Ca.: University of California Press, 1956.

Joseph, Bertram. *Elizabethan Acting.* London: Oxford University Press, 1951.

——. *Acting Shakespeare.* New York: Theatre Arts Books, 1969.

——. *A Shakespeare Workbook.* 2 Vols. New York: Theatre Arts Books, 1981.

Kernodle, George. *From Art to Theatre: Form and Convention in the Renaissance.* Chicago: University of Chicago Press, 1943.

Kirstein, Lincoln. *Dance.* New York: G. P. Putnam, 1935.

Knight, G. Wilson. *Principles of Shakespearean Production.* Harmondsworth, Middlesex, England: Penguin Books, 1949.

Kokeritz, Helge. *Shakespeare's Names: A Pronouncing Dictionary.* New Haven: Yale University Press, 1959.

——. *Shakespeare's Pronunciation.* New Haven: Yale University Press, 1953.

Nagler, A. M. *Shakespeare's Stage.* New Haven, Conn: Yale University Press, 1958.

Nevo, Ruth. *Comic Transformations in Shakespeare.* New York: Methuen, 1980.

Pitt, Angela. *Shakespeare's Women.* Totowa, N.J.: Barnes & Noble, 1981.

Prosser, Eleanor. *Shakespeare's Anonymous Editors: Scribe and Compositor in the Folio Text of 2 Henry IV.* Stanford: Stanford University Press, 1981.

Raleigh, Walter, et al., eds. *Shakespeare's England: An Account of the Life and Manner of His Age.* 2 Vols. London and Oxford: Clarendon Press, 1916–62.

Redfield, William. *Letters from an Actor.* New York: Viking, 1967.

Reese, M. M. *Shakespeare: His World and His Work.* 2d. Ed. New York: St. Martin's Press, 1980.

Robinson, Marion Parsons, Ed. *Scenes for Women from the Plays of Shakespeare.* Boston, Mass.: Walter H. Baker Co., 1967.

Rudnicki, Stefan, Ed. *Classical Monologues: 1 Shakespeare.* New York: Drama Book Specialists, 1979.

"Shakespeare: An Annotated Bibliography," *Shakespeare Quarterly (1924–19—).* *[SQ was originally called The Shakespeare Association Bulletin.]* Annual bibliography of writings about Shakespeare.

Shakespeare Survey: An Annual Survey of Shakespearean Study and Production. Cambridge: Harvard University Press, 1948.

Schmidgall, Gary. *Shakespeare and the Courtly Aesthetic.* Berkeley: University of California Press, 1981.

Schofield, Martin. *The Ghosts of Hamlet: The Play and Modern Writers.* New York: Cambridge University Press, 1980.

Schoenbaum, S. *Shakespeare The Globe and the World.* Oxford: University Press Folger Shakespeare Library, 1979.

Smith, Gordon Ross. *A Classified Shakespeare Bibliography.* University Park: Pennsylvania State University Press, 1963.

Smith, Irwin. *Shakespeare's Blackfriar's Playhouse.* New York: New York University Press, 1970.

Speaight, Robert. *Shakespeare on the Stage: An Illustrated History of Shakespearean Performance.* New York: William Collins Sons & Co., Ltd., 1972.

Sprague, A. C. *Shakespearean Players and Performances.* Cambridge, Mass.: Harvard University Press, 1953.

——. *Shakespeare and the Actors.* Cambridge, Mass.: Harvard University Press, 1945.

Thorndike, Ashley H. *Shakespeare's Theatre.* New York: Macmillan Co., 1960.

Watkins, Ronald. *On Producing Shakespeare.* 2d. ed. New York: The Citadel Press, 1964.

Webster, Margaret. *Shakespeare without Tears.* Greenwich, Conn.: Fawcett World Library, 1955.

Wickham, Glynne. *Early English Stages, 1300–1660.* 2 vols. New York: Columbia University Press, 1959–1962.

Suggested Filmography

1. *Chimes at Midnight.* British. (*Falstaff* in U.S.). 1966. Adapted from *Richard II, Henry IV, Pts. 1&2, Henry V, The Merry Wives of Windsor,* with narration from Holinshed's *Chronicles.* Playwright—Wm. Shakespeare. Director—Orson Welles. With Orson Welles.
2. *Cymbeline.* 1913. Thanhouser. Playwright—Shakespeare.
3. *Dr. Faustus.* 1967. Columbia. Playwright—Christopher Marlowe. Director—Richard Burton. With Burton, Elizabeth Taylor.
4. *Hamlet.* 1911. Danish. Filmed at Kronborg Castle, the scene of the original events. Playwright—Shak.
5. *Hamlet.* 1948. Universal-International. Playwright—Shak. Director—Sir Laurence Oliver. With Olivier and Jean Simmons.
6. *Henry V.* 1944. U. A. Playwright—Shak. Director—Sir Laurence Olivier. With Olivier.
7. *Henry VIII.* 1911. Filmed presentation of Herbert Beerbohm Tree's production. Playwright—Shak.
8. *The Merchant of Venice.* 1914. Universal. Playwright—Shak.
9. *A Midsummer Night's Dream.* 1935. Warners. Playwright—Shak. Director—Max Reinhardt and Wm. Dieterle. With James Cagney.
10. *Richard III.* 1956. London Films. Playwright—Shak. Director—Sir Laurence Olivier. With Olivier.
11. *Romeo and Juliet.* 1936. MGM. Playwright—Shak. Director—George Cukor. With Norma Shearer, Leslie Howard, John Barrymore.
12. *The Taming of the Shrew,* 1908. Biograph. Playwright—Shak. Director—D. W. Griffith.
13. *Throne of Blood.* 1957. (From *Macbeth.*). Playwright—Shak. Director—Akira Kurosawa. With Toshiro Mifune.
14. *The Winter's Tale.* 1910. Thanhouser. Playwright—Shak.
15. *The Taming of the Shrew.* 1967. Playwright—Shak. With Elizabeth Taylor and Richard Burton.

Hamlet
by *William Shakespeare*

from
Act III, scene i

Characters   HAMLET   Prince of Denmark
OPHELIA   daughter to Polonius, Lord Chamberlain of Denmark; beloved of
young Hamlet

Scene   Within the castle of Claudius, King of Denmark.

Situation   Hamlet, visited by the Ghost of his dead father, learns that his uncle Claudius
murdered his father. Walking within the castle, Hamlet contemplates the nature of
being, suicide, and death in a famous soliloquy. Encountering Ophelia, their love
revives for a few moments. However, suspecting her to be a pawn of her father
and the King, Hamlet violently denounces and rejects her.

Hamlet by William
Shakespeare. Christopher
Walken as Hamlet,
Jeannie Carson as
Gertrude, and Ted
D'Arms as Claudius at
The Seattle Repertory
Theatre. Directed by
Duncan Ross.

(*Enter* HAMLET)

HAMLET   To be, or not to be, that is the question:
        Whether 'tis nobler in the mind to suffer
        The slings and arrows of outrageous fortune,
        Or to take arms against a sea of troubles,
        And by opposing end them. To die, to sleep—   60
        No more; and by a sleep to say we end
        The heartache, and the thousand natural shocks
        That flesh is heir to. 'Tis a consumation
        Devoutly to be wished—to die, to sleep—
        To sleep, perchance to dream, ay there's the rub;   65
        For in that sleep of death what dreams may come
        When we have shuffled off this mortal coil
        Must give us pause—there's the respect
        That makes calamity of so long life.
        For who would bear the whips and scorns of time,   70
        Th' oppressor's wrong, the proud man's contumely,
        The pangs of despised love, the law's delay,
        The insolence of office, and the spurns
        That patient merit of th' unworthy takes,
        When he himself might his quietus make   75
        With a bare bodkin? Who would fardels bear,
        To grunt and sweat under a weary life,
        But that the dread of something after death,
        The undiscovered country, from whose bourn
        No traveller returns, puzzles the will,   80
        And makes us rather bear those ills we have
        Than fly to others that we know not of?
        Thus conscience does make cowards of us all;
        And thus the native hue of resolution
        Is sicklied o'er with the pale cast of thought,   85
        And enterprises of great pitch and moment
        With this regard their currents turn awry
        And lose the name of action.—Soft you now,
        The fair Ophelia.—Nymph, in thy orisons
        Be all my sins remembered.
OPHELIA   Good my lord,   90
        How does your honor for this many a day?
HAMLET   I humbly thank you, well.
OPHELIA   My lord, I have remembrances of yours
        That I have longed long to re-deliver.
        I pray you now receive them.
HAMLET   No, not I,   95
        I never gave you aught.
OPHELIA   My honored lord, you know right well you did,
        And with them words of so sweet breath composed
        As made the things more rich. Their perfume lost,
        Take these again, for to the noble mind   100
        Rich gifts wax poor when givers prove unkind.
        There, my lord.

65. *rub* obstacle (lit.,
    obstruction encountered
    by bowler's ball).
67. *coil* bustle, turmoil.

75. *quietus* settlement.
76. *bodkin* dagger;
    fardels burdens.

79. *bourn* realm.

86. *pitch* height.
87. *regard* consideration.

89. *orisons* prayers.

HAMLET   Ha, ha! are you honest?

OPHELIA   My lord?

HAMLET   Are you fair?   105

OPHELIA   What means your lordship?

HAMLET   That if you be honest and fair, your honesty should admit no
discourse to your beauty.

OPHELIA   Could beauty, my lord, have better commerce than with honesty?

HAMLET   Ay, truly, for the power of beauty will sooner transform honesty   110
from what it is to a bawd than the force of honesty can translate beauty
into his likeness. This was sometime a paradox, but now the time gives
it proof. I did love you once.

OPHELIA   Indeed, my lord, you made me believe so.

HAMLET   You should not have believed me, for virtue cannot so inoculate our   115
old stock but we shall relish of it. I loved you not.

OPHELIA   I was the more deceived.

HAMLET   Get thee to a nunnery. Why wouldst thou be a breeder of sinners?

I am myself indifferent honest, but yet I could accuse me of such things
that it were better my mother had not borne me: I am very proud,   120
revengeful, ambitious, with more offences at my beck than I have
thoughts to put them in, imagination to give them shape, or time to
act them in. What should such fellows as I do crawling between earth
and heaven? We are arrant knaves all; believe none of us. Go thy ways
to a nunnery. Where's your father?   125

OPHELIA   At home, my lord.

HAMLET   Let the doors be shut upon him, that he may play the fool
nowhere but in's own house. Farewell.

OPHELIA   O, help him, you sweet heavens!

HAMLET   If thou dost marry, I'll give thee this plague for thy dowry: be thou   130
as chaste as ice, as pure as snow, thou shalt not escape calumny. Get
thee to a nunnery, farewell. Or if thou wilt needs marry, marry a fool,
for wise men know well enough what monsters you make of them.
To a nunnery go, and quickly too. Farewell.

OPHELIA   Heavenly powers, restore him!   135

HAMLET   I have heard of your paintings well enough. God hath given you one
face, and you make yourselves another. You jig and amble, and you lisp;

138–39. *make your
wantonness your
ignorance* excuse your
wanton behavior with the
plea that you don't know
any better.
140. *moe* more.

you nickname God's creatures, and make your wantonness your
ignorance. Go to, I'll no more on't, it hath made me mad. I say we
will have no moe marriage. Those that are married already, all but   140
one, shall live. The rest shall keep as they are. To a nunnery, go. *(Exit.)*

OPHELIA   O, what a noble mind is here o'erthrown!
The courtier's, soldier's, scholar's, eye, tongue, sword,

Th' expectancy and rose of the fair state,
The glass of fashion and the mould of form,   145

Th' observed of all observers, quite quite down!
And I of ladies most deject and wretched,
That sucked the honey of his musicked vows,
Now see that noble and most sovereign reason
Like sweet bells jangled, out of time and harsh;   150
That unmatched form and feature of blown youth
Blasted with ecstasy. O, woe is me
T' have seen what I have seen, see what I see!

151. *blown* blooming.
152. *ecstasy* madness.

(END)

Hamlet by William Shakespeare. Sam Tsoutsouvas as Hamlet and Vos Call as The Ghost of Hamlet's Father at The Utah Shakespearean Festival. Directed by Fred C. Adams. Photograph by Boyd D. Redington.

Twelfth Night
by *William Shakespeare*

from
Act III, scene i

Characters   Viola
Clown (Feste)

Scene   In Olivia's garden.

Situation   The young maiden Viola, separated from her twin brother in a shipwreck, is dressed in disguise as a male. The Clown, servant to the beautiful Olivia, is leading Viola to a meeting with Olivia who has fallen in love with Viola, not knowing "he" is in fact a woman. The Clown and Viola engage in a typically Elizabethan exchange of wit.

(*Enter* VIOLA, *and* CLOWN [*with a tabor and pipe*].)

Ent. tabor: a small drum

VIOLA   Save thee, friend, and thy music! Dost thou live by thy tabor?
CLOWN   No, sir, I live by the church.
VIOLA   Art thou a churchman?
CLOWN   No such matter, sir. I do live by the church; for I do live at my house, and my house doth stand by the church.   5
VIOLA   So thou mayst say, the king lies by a beggar, if a beggar dwell near him; or, the church stands by thy tabor, if thy tabor stand by the church.

9. *chev'ril:* flexible kidskin

CLOWN   You have said, sir. To see this age! A sentence is but a chev'ril glove to a good wit. How quickly the wrong side may be turned outward!   10

12. *dally nicely:* play lasciviously

VIOLA   Nay, that's certain. They that dally nicely with words may quickly make them wanton.
CLOWN   I would therefore my sister had had no name, sir.
VIOLA   Why, man?   15

17–18. *since . . . them:* i.e., since men began to require bonds instead of trusting another's word in making bargains

CLOWN   Why, sir, her name's a word, and to dally with that word might make my sister wanton. But indeed words are very rascals since bonds disgraced them.
VIOLA   Thy reason, man?
CLOWN   Troth, sir, I can yield you none without words, and words are grown so false I am loath to prove reason with them.   20
VIOLA   I warrant thou art a merry fellow and carest for nothing.

23. *in . . . conscience:* as conscience is my judge

CLOWN   Not so, sir; I do care for something; but in my conscience, sir, I do not care for you. If that be to care for nothing, sir, I would it would make you invisible.   25
VIOLA   Art not thou the Lady Olivia's fool?
CLOWN   No, indeed, sir. The Lady Olivia has no folly. She will keep no fool, sir, till she be married; and fools are as like husbands as

29. *pilchards:* small fish of the herring family

pilchards are to herrings—the husband's the bigger. I am indeed not her fool, but her corrupter of words.   30

VIOLA   I saw thee late at the Count Orsino's.

CLOWN   Foolery, sir, does walk about the orb like the sun; it shines everywhere. I would be sorry, sir, but the fool should be as oft with your master as with my mistress. I think I saw your wisdom there.

VIOLA   Nay, an thou pass upon me, I'll no more with thee. Hold, there's expenses for thee. 35

(Gives a piece of money.)

CLOWN   Now Jove, in his next commodity of hair, send thee a beard!

VIOLA   By my troth, I'll tell thee, I am almost sick for one, though I would not have it grow on my chin. Is thy lady within?

CLOWN   Would not a pair of these have bred, sir? 40

VIOLA   Yes, being kept together and put to use.

CLOWN   I would play Lord Pandarus of Phrygia, sir, to bring a Cressida to this Troilus.

VIOLA   I understand you, sir. 'Tis well begged.

CLOWN   The matter, I hope, is not great, sir, begging but a beggar: 45 Cressida was a beggar. *(Viola tosses him another coin.)* My lady is within, sir. I will conster to them whence you come. Who you are and what you would are out of my welkin—I might say "element," but the word is over-worn. *Exit.*

VIOLA   This fellow is wise enough to play the fool, 50
And to do that well craves a kind of wit.
He must observe their mood on whom he jests,
The quality of persons, and the time;
Not, like the haggard, check at every feather
That comes before his eye. This is a practice 55
As full of labor as a wise man's art;
For folly that he wisely shows, is fit;
But wise men, folly-fall'n, quite taint their wit.

(END)

32. *orb:* earth
33–34. *I . . . mistress:* i.e., I would regret to think my mistress more foolish than your master.
35. *pass . . . me:* offer a duel
37. *commodity:* consignment
38. *one:* i.e., a man with a beard
40. *these:* coins
41. *use:* lending at interest
45. *begging . . . beggar:* a reference to the practice of "begging" the wardship of wealthy minors through the Court of Wards
47. *conster:* construe; explain
48. *welkin:* sky (element)
51. *craves:* requires; *wit:* intelligence
54. *haggard:* an untrained hawk
55. *practice:* craft
57. *wisely:* deliberately (to earn a living); *fit:* suitable

Twelfth Night by William Shakespeare. Linda Alper as Viola, Wayne Ballantyne as Sir Toby, Lawrence Paulsen as Sir Andrew, and Stuard Duckworth as Fabian at The Oregon Shakespearean Festival. Directed by Pat Patton. Setting by Richard L. Hay. Costumes by Deborah M. Dryden; Lighting by Richard Riddell. Photograph by Hank Kranzler.

14 Seventeenth-Century French Neoclassicism

Restraint Again

. . . Indeed, I think that it is much easier to soar with grand sentiments, to brave fortune in verse, to arraign destiny and reproach the Gods, than to broach ridicule in a fit manner, and to make the faults of all mankind seem pleasant on the stage. When you paint heroes you can do as you like.

Dorante in *School for Wives* by Moliere

. . . Aristotle laid down the rules of dramatic poetry, and Socrates, the wisest of the philosophers, did not disdain to speak of the tragedies of Euripides. We should like our works to be as solid and full of useful instruction as were those of antiquity. This might be a means to reconcile tragedy to a number of celebrated persons. . . who would undoubtedly cast a more favorable eye upon it [tragedy] if the dramatists endeavored to instruct as well as please their auditors, and so came nearer to the true end of all tragedy.

Racine in Preface to *Phaedra*

The Misanthrope by Molière!

Molière's delightful female character Dorante expresses the key problem confronting the comic playwright—how to reveal man's ridiculous nature, lower sentiments, and human faults in a humorous and, therefore, pleasant statement on a stage. Perhaps no comic playwright, with the possible exception of Aristophanes, Shakespeare, and Shaw, has succeeded in mastering this problem as well as the genius of the seventeenth-century French stage, Molière. Molière wrote a host of brilliant comedies with infinite dramatic variety. In tragedy, his chief counterpart, Jean Racine, in following the so-called new or Neoclassic bent, abandoned the flexible forms of Renaissance tragedy and returned to a restrained imitation of the ancient Greeks (refined through the influence of the Romans). Pierre Corneille in his plays also contributed to the reform of French tragedy, but the finest examples were those of Racine. The plays of Molière and Racine are the best for a modern actor to study when learning how to act seventeenth-century French Neoclassic drama.

Overview of French Neoclassicism (Seventeenth Century)

The period of French Neoclassicism (i.e., *New* Classicism) began in the third decade of the seventeenth century when Cardinal Richelieu became primate to King Louis XIV (the French often delete *Neo* from the name and refer only to the French *Classicism*). During this period France was flush with a fierce nationalism which spilled into the cultural heritage of the nation. In 1630 under the guidance of Richelieu, a revolution in the arts was forged whose pattern of cultural development was modeled on the Italian Renaissance and derived primarily from the work of Castelvetro, a

The Amorous Flea, A Musical Adaptation of *The School for Wives,* by Molière. Cynthia Dozier as Agnes and Erick Devine as Arnolphe at The Hilberry Theatre, Wayne State University. Book by Jerry Devine. Music and Lyrics by Bruce Montgomery. Directed by Robert T. Hazzard. Musical Director and Conductor: Philip Michael. Choreography by Nira Pullin. Scenery by Russell Smith. Costumes By Ellen Ryba. American College Theatre Festival finalist, John F. Kennedy Center for the Performing Arts, Washington, D.C.

sixteenth-century Italian scholar. Neoclassic drama began with the study of classical Roman plays in the late fifteenth century and continued with the writing of Latin imitations of classical works in the early sixteenth century, and its influence spread to French drama after 1550. The principle of Neoclassicism was dramatization of abstract concepts. Plays were concerned with ideas and their effect on human beings—ideas such as honor and dishonor, sin and innocence, loyalty and treachery, will and necessity, respect and contempt, authority and servility. In Neoclassic plays, the concept of verisimilitude (likelife quality) was paramount in exemplifying generalized ideals. French playwrights wanted the audience to see the "appearance" of reality—a world perceived by the senses, a particularized world which the playwright alowed to be seen. The classical unities of time, place, and action were strictly supported. The *unities* were attributed erroneously to Aristotle when actually they were misinterpretations of his writing by Italian Renaissance critics who studied Horace more than Aristotle.) Emphasis was on the universal aspects of character and situation. Character was synonymous with status, rank, and code of behavior. This concept of character became known as *decorum* or appropriateness of characterization. To Neoclassicists verisimilitude and decorum were essential to achieve complete universality in drama.

Neoclassic playwrights produced virile drama. Most plays were based on the models of Alexandre Hardy (ca. 1572–1632). Hardy was the innovator of the Alexandrine line, the basic verse used in Neoclassic drama (i.e., six iambic feet, with the caesure after the third foot). Romantic character dominated in his plays, whose trademark was a highly narrative elegiac style.

The first exponent of Neoclassic drama in France was Corneille (1604–1684). Corneille's use of simple characters and complex plots made him a highly popular playwright. *The Cid*, written in 1636, typified Corneille's use of a hero with an indomitable will. *The Cid* is perhaps most famous for having been the center of a controversy in the French Academy (formed in 1635 by Cardinal Richelieu to set cultural standards in France). Corneille's highly successful play was rejected by the Academy because it violated the unities. Subsequently, Corneille set out to write other plays which adhered to the Neoclassical rules of playwriting. However, they were singularly unimpressive as viable drama.

Jean Racine (1639–1673) was a much more impressive Neoclassic playwright. Racine's plays possessed a natural sense of order and good taste. He achieved the epitome of the Neoclassic style of tragedy in his plays—in effect, the Neoclassic form was truly an expression of his natural style of writing. His plays contained little external action. The drama resulted from internal psychological conflict centered on a single complex character. Racine de-emphasized the physical appearance of characters, emphasizing instead the psychological and moral states of the hero or heroine. Characters portrayed intense emotional depth which was manifested in great conflicts of passion and willpower (e.g., Phaedra). Human weakness and strength were exposed by simple dramatic passages. Departure from established decorum brought about the downfall of a character.

Comedy was very popular in France during the seventeenth century. True to the Neoclassic demands of the French Academy, Molière (christened, Jean-Baptiste Poquelin; 1622–1673) wrote plays that conformed to the classical ideal of having five acts and adhering to the unities. His plays were usually set in a drawing room (rarely out-of-doors). Molière created dramatic action through the impact of events on character, which in turn reacted and created new events for counterimpact (i.e., *Tartuffe*). Molière drew his characters from all levels of society. Psychology was the mainspring of his plays, exposing humanized and vulnerable man in a weakened condition. Molière was essentially a satirist devoted to truth. He used satire to expose the pretentions of the world while attempting to bring about change. It is important to keep in mind that Molière was a great admirer of the commedia dell' arte (he toured with a commedia troupe as an actor). Many characters in Molière's comedies were based on commedia types (for example, Harpagon in *The Miser* is a Pantalone figure). Molière's farces also borrowed from Plautus and Terence and from Spanish and Italian sources. Although he wrote other types of plays such as ballets and tragedies, Molière's appeal has endured strictly because of his comedies.

The major theatres of Paris included the Hotel de Bourgogne, the Theatre du Marais, and the Palais-Royal (first theatre in France to use a proscenium arch). Tennis courts were often converted into temporary theatres, with a simple platform for acting at one end of the court, while galleries and benches were placed on the sides and down the length of the court for spectators. The Hotel de Bourgogne was simply a long, narrow room with galleries on the sides and benches in front of a raised platform at one end. The Marais and Palais-Royal resembled the kind of theatres generally

Hume Cronyn as Harpagon in *The Miser* by Molière. Directed by Douglas Campbell. Designed by Tanya Moiseiwitsch. The Guthrie Theatre, Minneapolis, Minn.

The Bourgeois Gentleman in *The Bourgeoise Gentleman* by Molière.

used today. The spectators sat on a sloping floor or in one of the three gallery levels on the sides. Some people sat in the pit below the apron or upon the stage itself (thereby severely limiting the acting area). Scenic demands were simple, ranging from curtains and small three-dimensional units to painted representations of rooms, streets, and gardens. All scenic changes were executed in full view of the audience. Footlights as well as overhead lighting utilized candles and oil lamps. Poor lighting forced actors to play primarily downstage center. Movement was limited also by lighting and the spectators onstage.

Actors and actresses wore contemporary costumes except for well-known historic, fantastic, and allegorical characters. A variety of elaborateness prevailed in costuming, depending upon the character and the financial status of the acting troupe. Most characters wore long, full wigs. In a few plays the commedia influence resulted in the retention of masks by some characters. Costuming and contemporary dress were generally beautiful and elaborate, emphasizing lace, brocade, and other fineries (see illustrations and photographs in this chapter).

Voice — French Neoclassic Tragedy

The acting style in France during the seventeenth century was generally characterized as highly formal and conventionalized, with great emphasis on vocal recitation. The tradition for performing in plays by Corneille was that actors were to use grandiose recitation while standing rigidly in one place. On the other hand, for Racine's plays a less declamatory vocal delivery was necessary. Because Racine's characters explored the subconscious passions of the mind, the actor had to develop a new and fairly subtle naturalness in the voice. A trained voice is the key requirement for successful performance of Neoclassic French tragedy. The voice must vary with respect to passions and with differing parts of the classical oration; it also must vary with figures of rhetoric, unusual sentences, and unique words. Racine's art is a formal one contrived of human passion within strict linguistic limitations. In Alexandrine verse, recitation must achieve a balance of the rhymed couplet and the individual line. The line may or may not be broken in the middle by the caesure. The verse is "sculptured" to help compress passion into one major crisis. For example, Phaedra is a tormented woman trying to find a way to control her incestuous passion in act 4 as she speaks to Oenone:

> Hypocrisy and incest breathe at once through all I do. My hands are ripe for murder. To spill the guiltless blood of innocence. Do I still live, a wretch, and dare to face the holy sun, from whom I have my being? My father's father was the king of gods; My race is spread through all the universe.— Where can I hide? In the dark realms of Pluto? But there my father holds the fatal urn.
>
> *Phaedra* by Racine

Language is probably the most difficult problem in studying the acting style of Racine and Neoclassic French tragedy. The magnificent quality of his style with language can only be conveyed indirectly in English. Any translator of Racine begins by apologizing. Racine's language is considered to be the most nearly perfect example of purity of style of all French literature.

Alexandrine poetry was written in a twelve-syllable line of qualitative rather than quantitative verse, with a thirteenth unpronounced syllable permitted in a feminine line. The line was further divided into two hemistichs, with a caesura after the sixth syllable. Boileau-Despreaux, French dramatic critic, stated it this way for the actor:

Have an ear for cadence,
Always let your meaning, cutting off your words,
Halt at the hemistich, mark it with a stop.

There was also a requirement, extremely difficult to fulfill, that each line should terminate a logical sequence of thought with no carry-over to the next line. Such a carry-over, an *enjambement*, was considered a defect of style and a flaw in the writing. A kind of carry-over was allowed, in rare cases, for a special effect and was then called a *rejet*. A famous example of a successful *rejet* occurs in *Phaedra* in the scene between Phaedra and Hippolytus in the second act in which Phaedra makes five *rejets*. By use of this devise at precisely these points Racine called attention to the fact that Phaedra is distraught. She can no longer arrest her speech normally as a lady should. The five *rejets* which Racine used indicate to the audience that Phaedra is being carried away by her emotions.

The language of Neoclassic tragedy was aristocratic and removed from daily life. The poet spoke abstractly, with rarified elegance and great formality. Today this language is considered rather affected and is one of the difficulties in performing Neoclassic tragedy adequately for modern taste. A good English translation naturally accomplishes a great deal in making the verse palatable, but just as naturally also sacrifices much of the great beauty and meaning of the language in the process. However, awareness of the precision, beauty, and special effects as just described is a valuable part of an actor's training as he prepares to act Neoclassic tragedy.

Exercise 1 Voice—Neoclassic Tragedy

1. Practice the following selections aloud, emphasizing highly grandiose, declamatory delivery. Work to achieve balance of rhythm and rhyme. Try to achieve termination of thought in each line. Be highly selective in where you place emotion, inflection, and variety. Later repeat the exercise by modifying it to a level of what might be considered palatable or natural for contemporary audiences:

PHAEDRA Although you hate me, I shall not
complain, My lord: for you have seen me
bent to harm you.

You could not read the tables of my heart.
I've taken care to invite your enmity,
And could not bear your presence where I
dwelt.
In public, and in private, your known foe,
I've wished the seas to part us, and even
forbidden
The mention of your name within my hearing.
But if one measures punishment by the offense,
If only hatred can attract your hate,
Never was woman who deserved more pity,
My lord, and less deserved your enmity.

HIPPOLYTUS A mother jealous for her children's
rights
Seldom forgives her stepson. I know it,
madam.
Nagging suspicions are the commonest fruits
Of second marriage; and another wife
Would have disliked me just the same; and I
Might well have had to swallow greater wrongs.

Phaedra by Racine

2. Using the selection from *Phaedra* in #1 above, *sing* the speeches in an improvised tune. Try to create a serious, melodic, and fluid tune to assist you in grasping the level of grandeur inherent with in the style. Then repeat the speeches in regular speaking patterns, but utilizing a *stage whisper*. This may assist you in locating the delicate, psychological depths inherent within the style. Finally, attempt to combine vocal grandeur and delicate, psychological shadings into a rich and appropriate style of delivery.

Movement — French Neoclassic Tragedy

All movement in Neoclassic tragedy is confined by the linguistic demands of the playwright. That confinement requires that the actor achieve poetic and precise command of gestures and movements highly elevated to a larger-than-life level. The elevation should coincide with the formality of the words. Movement should be characterized by elegance and gracefulness of manner and bearing, reminiscent of the Classic Greek style. Modern actors can benefit greatly from studying the paintings of such seventeenth-century artists as Peter Rubens, Nicolas Poussin, and Charles Lebrun. These artists depicted the dress and costumes of the time well and also captured gestures and facial expressions which might be helpful. Movement was probably very limited on the seventeenth-century French stage because of the poor lighting, small acting area, and emphasis on language. The physical focus was on the upper portion of the body, particularly the face, hands, and arms. Naturally, in today's theatre more movement is employed in the staging. However, emphasis remains on voice and character. Modern directors employ more use of sitting positions and handling of properties than in the original style. Movement, sitting, and use of properties must be handled discreetly; it is a mistake to use a great deal of realistic activity in a Neoclassic French tragedy. Similar to the seventeenth century, selective use of hand and costume properties such as fans, handkerchiefs, staffs, canes, goblets, capes, swords, and so on, is advisable today. Movement was generally slow with rare physical contact with other characters. The presentational mode dominated almost exclusively in the original style, but is, of course, modified today.

Exercise 2 Movement—Neoclassic Tragedy

1. Perform the following action as a review of classical Greek movement which relates closely to Neoclassic movement.
   a. From an aligned position on your feet, breathe comfortably in a relaxed state. Move through space in a slow-motion manner concentrating upon grace, rhythm, fluidity, and sense of controlled restraint.
   b. Repeat the foregoing exercise in a modified tempo permitting the slow motion to evolve into an acceptably believable or natural tempo.
2. Locate a book on the history of art which contains photographs of paintings by Rubens, Poussin, and Lebrun. Create stage replicas of these paintings which depict posture and expressions similar to those seen in the paintings. Then put these "portraits" and "tableauxs" into graceful, restrained motion.

Character and Emotion – French Neoclassic Tragedy

Except for the psychology of their emotion, characters in Racine's plays were not realistically conceived. They are contained in a condition of artistic purity. We see very little of their daily routine; they seem not to sleep, eat, or drink. They speak with an elevated and artificial (meaning "contrived by art") language. Their soliloquies are rational pieces of literature or rhetoric. However, close examination reveals shivering emotion beneath the reason. That emotion was based on valid human psychology having full, rich motivation. An intelligent approach to character and emotion in French Neoclassic tragedy is to establish a believable characterization beginning with the use of personalization. The personalization is best used in this style only for the sake of comfort in early rehearsals. While the language will dominate, the style works best in today's theatre with believable characterization. The language in itself will keep the character and emotion at a necessary larger-than-life level.

Exercise 3 Character and Emotion—Neoclassic Tragedy

1. Invent and perform a series of improvisations in pairs in which you explore the levels of human psychology concerning the following character and emotional states. Be certain that a goal or objective is established for each

improvisation. For example, the goal of a *greed* improvisation might be: a wife discovers her husband has hidden a million dollar inheritance from her.

    a. Greed
    b. Ambition
    c. Incestuous love
    d. Pride
    e. Jealousy
    f. Grief
    g. Hatred
    h. Love

2. Using the eight emotions listed in the foregoing exercise, "overact" a highly contrived physical manifestation of each emotion; improvise a highly artificial verbal expression or phrase to coincide with your physicalization. Finally, use personalization to modify your previous effort in order to make the character and emotion palatable and believable, with some "elevation" lingering from the exaggerated work.

Voice—French Neoclassic Comedy

French Neoclassic comedy as exemplified by Molière was concerned with the manners and customs of the court and those persons who lived on the edge of the social life of the period. It was fashionable to be impious and licentious about serious subjects. Audiences probably enjoyed seeing their manners and customs mirrored. The focus of the acting style is on language, but due to the genius of Molière, equal focus comes to bear on character. Molière's plays conform to Neoclassic rules of structure and the unities; some of his plays were written in verse and others in prose. Rhythm and pace are crucial considerations when delivering Molière's comic lines.

His characters generally interacted rapidly. The vocal tempo is usually rapid and precise. Again it is necessary to check vocabulary carefully. Soliloquies and asides were frequently used. Unusually clear articulation, pronunciation, and projection are necessary to handle the rapid line delivery and varied language of Molière. Complex inflections and vocal variety are absolutely necessary in performing the language of Molière, who wrote primarily in Alexandrine couplets (some translators adapt his writing to prose at great damage to rhythm and lyricism).

Exercise 4 Voice—Neoclassic Comedy

1. Practice the following speeches for rapid delivery; comic repartee and inflection; clear articulation, pronunciation, projection; and variety. Perform entirely presentational; then modify and repeat the exercise with balanced use of representational and presentational modes.

CLÉANTE . . . You agreed of late
That young Valere might have your
daughter's hand.
ORGON I did.
CLÉANTE You've not postponed it; is that true?
ORGON No doubt.

CLÉANTE   The match no longer pleases you?

ORGON   Who knows?

CLÉANTE   D'you mean to go back on your word?

ORGON   I won't say that.

CLÉANTE   Has anything occurred
Which might entitle you to break your pledge?

ORGON   Perhaps.

Tartuffe   Act I, scene v, by Molière

MARIANNE   Oh, you turn my blood to ice!
Stop torturing me, and give me your advice.

DORINE *(threatening to go)* Your servant,
Madam.

MARIANNE   Dorine, I beg of you . . .

DORINE   No, you deserve it; this
marriage must go through.

MARIANNE   Dorine!

DORINE   No.

MARIANNE   Not Tartuffe! You know I think him . . .

DORINE   Tartuffe's your cup of tea,
and you shall drink him.

MARIANNE   I've always told you everything,
and relied . . .

DORINE   No. You deserve to be tartuffified.

Tartuffe   Act III, scene iii, by Molière

2. To enhance vocal rhythm, practice the foregoing speeches by improvising a tune and singing them. Try to create a light, rapid, and fun tune.

3. Repeat the same speeches above from *Tartuffe* and toss a tennis ball to your partner as you say the last word of each speech; the partner does the same in return. This exercise can enhance timing and cuing.

The Miser by Molière. Wayne Turney as Harpagon, Douglas Stark as Jacques, and Bruce Matley as Valere at The Hilberry Theatre, Wayne State University. Directed by Robert T. Hazzard. Scenery by Enoch Morris. Costumes by Daniel Thomas Field and Helen Markovitch. Lighting by Benjamin F. Levenberg.

The character of Tartuffe
in the play of that title by
Molière.

Movement — French Neoclassic Comedy

Two points must be kept in mind when movement in Molière comedy is discussed. One, when heavy commedia dell'arte influence is obvious, commedia acting style should dominate; for example, *The Physician in Spite of Himself*, a farcical short play by Molière, is frequently performed in the commedia style (commedia style is discussed in chapter 12). Two, a unique, elaborate acting style is necessary in most of Molière's character comedies because they are rich in social satire. His character and social comedies were rooted in precise, inventive activity, and therefore movement should be selective and rapid in tempo. A highly theatrical, presentational mode should be used. For example, movement should focus on firm stride and erect standing position or posture (weight resting on the back foot with the front foot forward and to the side). Men walked with virility and used elaborate finger gestures. Gestures were broad and punctuated by use of fluid movements of the wrist and hand. Maids and servants bounced and pranced a great deal; central female characters generally glided in a highly elevated and charming manner. Clothing generally emphasized the figure.

Unlike Neoclassic tragedy, there was considerable stage movement, particularly in the plays influenced by commedia. Bowing and curtsying were used frequently. Pantomimic dramatization was inventive, emphasizing facial grimacing and extensive use of hand and costume properties. Hands were usually held high to reveal lace cuffs. Personal objects were handled with flourish: handkerchiefs were waved between the fingers; fans were fluttered at crucial moments of anxiety, discovery, or flirtation; half-masks were deployed at gala public affairs and out-of-doors; canes and staffs were swung about for emphasis or humor; and snuff was taken by most characters, male and female. Snuff was usually a mixture of tobacco and dried herbs or powders and occasionally drugs. Snuff was used to attract attention. Its use was a matter of great ceremony and social custom. On a practical level, taking snuff usually caused one to sneeze, thereby cleaning the nasal passages. It also had a slightly intoxicating and pleasant effect. Most people of upper society carried a small box of snuff with them. A snuffbox was taken from the waistcoat pocket, tapped at the top to make the particles fall to the bottom, and a pinch was taken with the thumb and second finger and either applied to the nose and inhaled or placed on the back of the hand and sniffed. The cuffs were then shaken or snapped at with a handkerchief to remove any clinging particles of snuff.

The male bow was slightly modified from that used in the Renaissance. A gentleman stepped back, bent one knee, and placed his right hand over his heart while bending slightly. Some men used a more elaborate bow by bending more deeply and sweeping their hats behind them. The female curtsy used the same variations as the Renaissance, and the use of fans and handkerchiefs made the curtsies more elaborate.

Soliloquies and asides were handled basically as they were in Elizabethan drama (see chapter 13).

Exercise 5 Movement—Neoclassic Comedy

1. Review all steps of Exercise 2 in chapter 12 on commedia movement.
2. Practice the modified bows and curtsies just described.
3. Study and practice the following:
   a. Take snuff according to the directions given above (see *Movement— French Neoclassic Comedy*)
   b. Assume the male standing position with weight resting on the rear foot, the front foot forward and to the side. With arms extending slightly to the side, move rapidly about the stage with precision and elegance. If they are available, use walking staffs, canes, handkerchiefs, and costume properties (Execute these movements with considerable male virility.)
   c. Assume an elegant and graceful female pose. The weight should be balanced on both feet with the arms and hands extended away from the body. Move gracefully and rapidly about the stage with precision and elegance. If they are available, use fans, handkerchiefs, and costume properties.
   d. Using the speeches from *Tartuffe* in Exercise 4 above, create fun, lively dances to perform *as you deliver lines*.

Tartuffe by Molière. John Rensenhouse as Tartuffe and Edith Elliott as Elmire at the University of Wisconsin-Milwaukee. Directed by Nagle Jackson. Scenery by R. H. Graham. Costumes by Liz Covey. Photograph by Alan Magayne-Roshak.

Seventeenth-Century French Neoclassicism 237

Stock characters prevail in the plays of Molière influenced by commedia. In these plays, such as *The Doctor In Spite of Himself,* your main concern will again be with singular obsession and usually one-dimensional personality characteristics.

However, the genius of Molière is exemplified in his great character creations in the social comedies such as *The Misanthrope, Tartuffe,* and *The Would-Be Gentleman.* The central characters in these plays are multidimensional, complex, and rooted in human psychology. The humanity of Molière's characters permit effective use of personalization in early rehearsals and in some instances beyond. Full-scale role analysis is necessary to create these characters. Molière's brilliant language in both prose and verse provides the key to character delineation. His characters have biographical background, clear attitudes, and temperament. They represent clear facets of 17th Century society and current political, philosophic, and theological thought and run the gamut of human feelings. Molière characters are highly motivated by clear emotional hungers and desires. Your approach to these roles must be serious and in no way mocking, detached, or superficial. The wit and comic situation tend to render the characters ludicrous and humorous, although a serious point of view underlies the comic facade. Create a complete human being; take the roles seriously and reveal the various emotional desires which drive them such as greed, love, lust, avarice, and so on. If you play a role as though you or the character know you are humorous, you may destroy Molière's satire. The audience and other characters must recognize the ludicrous and comic element, but the actor and the character must not be aware of it. For example, Tartuffe in *Tartuffe* and Alceste in *The Misanthrope* are deadly earnest concerning their desires and problems. The situations Molière put them into, combined with his language and wit, turns the rich human characterizations into comedy. However, without detracting from foregoing points, it should be noted that Molière's characterizations are not totally natural. Behavior is altered; it is different from real life. It is magnified life.

Exercise 6   Character and Emotion—Neoclassic Comedy

1. Select a character from the list of Molière plays provided at the end of this chapter. Read the play and study the character, with special focus on character background, development, personality, and emotional hungers. Carefully identify the obsessive aspects of the hunger which ultimately render the character ludicrous or comic. Write a brief paper in which you clarify your study. After the paper is read and discussed, perform a representative scene or monologue to complete this exercise.

2. Using the character you selected in #1, Exercise 6 above, identify a stock commedia character type suitable as a stereotypical model for this character. Practice a speech from the play using a one-dimensional, commedia approach. Repeat the speech using the full-dimensional, personalization efforts reflective of the work done in #1 above, yet retaining the commedia factor as a foundation for the role.

Hume Cronyn as Harpagon and Zoe Caldwell as Frosine in *The Miser* by Molière. Directed by Douglas Campbell. Designed by Tanya Moiseiwitsch. The Guthrie Theatre, Minneapolis, Minn.

Music and Translations—French Neoclassicism

Most of Molière's plays called for use of some music and dance. For example, a form of ballet interlude was required in *The School For Husbands*. In seventeenth-century France orchestral music was usually quite lavish, ranging from chamber groups to complete stringed orchestras. Viols, lutes, and organs were popular, along with wind instruments. Choral singing was also enjoyed.

While Racine and French Neoclassic tragedy are only occasionally performed today, Molière's comedies remain among the most popularly produced plays in the theatre. Effective translations are difficult to find because the elegant French language and meter suffer greatly when transposed into English. In recent years, poet Richard Wilbur has written highly acclaimed translations of Molière plays including *The Misanthrope* and *Tartuffe*.

French Neoclassic acting styles were influential on the Continent. Their influence was also seen in England with the restoration of the crown in 1660. However, as discussed in chapter 15, the glory of the French style was modified and uniquely adapted and altered by the artists of the Restoration.

Suggested Characters and Plays for Scene Work

Molière

Tartuffe, Orgon, Elmire, Dorine, Marianne, Cléanté
  Tartuffe
Alceste, Célimène
  The Misanthrope
Harpagon, Cléanté, Marianne
  The Miser
M. Jourdain, Cleante, Covielle
  The Would-Be Gentleman

Scapin, Octavio, Leander
  Scapin
Sganarelle, Isabella, Valère, Ariste
  The School for Husbands
Argon, Angelique
  The Imaginery Invalid
Arnolphe, Agnes, Horace, Oronte
  The School for Wives

Racine, Jean

Phaedra, Hippolytus, Oenone, Theseus
  Phaedra
Andromache, Hermoine
  Andromache

Corneille, Pierre

Chimene, Don Rodrique
  The Cid

Actor Checklist   *French Neoclassic Tragedy (Racine)*

Voice	Clear diction; oratorical, rhetorical, and declamatory; well projected; varied; highly elevated; smooth and polished delivery; generally restrained except for *rejet* moments.
Movement	Highly restrained; elevated; appropriate; graceful; coordinated with linguistic demands; highly selective; presentational mode dominates; slow-to-moderate tempo, but accelerated at emotional moments.
Gestures	Selective; elevated; restrained except when emotion overcomes reason as in the vocal *rejet*; focus on the upper part of the body; rare use of sitting position.
Pantomimic Dramatization	Clear; appropriate; elevated; restrained; use of hand and costume properties; selective.
Character	Psychological; believable and truthful; clear; empathic, if appropriate; full dimension in Racine; somewhat larger than life.
Emotion	Rooted in human psychology; well motivated; at times larger than life; controlled until moments of outburst.
Ideas	Exemplify Neoclassic mandates of verisimilitude and decorum; focus on reason over emotion.
Language	Lyrical; controlled Alexandrine verse; aristocratic, removed from daily life; abstract; elegant; formal; precise; beautiful.
Mood and Atmosphere	Correct and clear in terms of being supportive of character and action; no mix of comedy; pure in its seriousness.
Pace and Tempo	Moderate to slow except for moments of high emotion.
Special Techniques	Verse complexity requires great vocal dexterity.

Actor Checklist   *French Neoclassic Comedy (Molière)*

Voice	Exaggerated melodic patterns and inflections; rapid but clear; smooth and polished line delivery; precise diction, particularly in verse.
Movement	Elegant; elevated; graceful; controlled; well-executed use of bows, curtsies, asides, and soliloquies; balance of presentational and representational mode; generally rapid tempo.
Gestures	Hand, head, facial dominate; clear; elevated.
Pantomimic Dramatization	Clear and highly inventive; extensive use of period costumes and props such as fans, staffs, handkerchiefs, half-masks, snuff, and so on.
Character	Major characters are well motivated, multidimensional, complex, and rooted in human psychology; clear background, attitude, and temperament; representative social facet clear; serious actor involvement.
Emotion	Complex and multidimensional in major characters; clear; at times obsessive; rooted in human psychology.
Ideas	Clear; satiric; witty; to correct social injustices.
Language	Witty; rhythmic, brilliant vocabulary, and rich imagery; correct pronunciation; lyrical and musical when intended.
Mood and Atmosphere	Clear in terms of comic satire, farce or repartee and wit, as script demands; supportive of situation, action, character; generally comic with serious undertones.
Pace and Tempo	Generally rapid.
Special Techniques	Wit and language demand unusual vocal dexterity; singing and dancing usually required of some characters; unusual attention to movement in costume.
For Commedia Influence	See chapter 12.

Suggested Readings

Chapman, R. A. *The Spirit of Moliere: An Interpretation.* Princeton, N.J.: Princeton University Press, 1940.

Fernandez, Ramon. *Moliere: The Man Seen Through the Plays.* New York: Hill & Wang, 1958.

Gossip, C. J. *An Introduction to French Classical Tragedy.* Totowa, N.J.: Barnes & Noble, 1981.

Gossman, Lionel. *Men and Masks: A Study of Moliere.* Baltimore: Johns Hopkins University Press, 1963.

Hubert, Judd D. *Moliere and the Comedy of Intellect.* Reprint of 1962 ed. New York: Russell & Russell, 1971.

Lancaster, H. C. *A History of French Dramatic Literature in the Seventeenth Century.* 9 vols. Reprint of 1942 ed. Staten Island, N.Y.: Gordian Press, 1966.

Lockert, Lacy. *Studies In French Classical Tragedy*. Nashville: Vanderbilt University Press, 1958.

Lough, John. *Paris Theatre Audiences in the Seventeenth and Eighteenth Centuries*. New York: Oxford University Press, 1957.

Palmer, John. *Moliere*. New York: Brewer & Warren, 1930.

Reiss, Timothy J. *Tragedy and Truth: Studies in the Development of a Renaissance and Neo-Classical Discourse*. New Haven: Yale University Press, 1980.

Schwartz, Isidore A. *The Commedia dell 'Arte and Its Influence on French Comedy in the Seventeenth Century*. Paris: H. Samuel, 1933.

Tilley, A. A. *Moliere*. Cambridge, Mass.: Harvard University Press, 1936.

Turnell, Martin. *The Classical Moment: Studies in Corneille, Moliere, and Racine*. Reprint of 1948 ed. Westport, Conn.: Greenwood Press, 1971.

Vinaver, Eugene. *Racine and Poetic Tragedy*. Translated by P. M. Jones. Manchester: Manchester University Press, 1955.

Wilcox, John. *The Relation of Moliere to Restoration Comedy*. New York: Benjamin Blom, 1964.

Wright, C. H. C. *French Classicism*. Cambridge, Mass.: Harvard University Press, 1920.

Suggested Filmography

1. *Phaedra*. 1910. Italian. Pathe. Playwright-Jean Racine.
2. *Tartuffe*. 1925. German. Ufa. Playwright-Moliere. Director-F. W. Murnau. With Emil Jannings.

Phaedra

by *Jean Racine*

Translated from the French by Robert Henderson

Phaedra, wife of Theseus and stepmother to Hippolytus
Hippolytus, son of Theseus and Antiope (Queen of the Amazons)

Characters

In Traezen, a town of the Peloponnesus.

Scene

The goddess Aphrodite hates Phaedre and implants in her a guilty passion for her stepson, Hippolytus. Thinking her husband, Theseus, is dead, Phaedre confesses her love to Hippolytus who, reviled and shocked, rejects her.

Situation

PHAEDRA   They tell me that you leave us, hastily.
    I come to add my own tears to your sorrow,
    And I would plead my fears for my young son.
    He has no father, now; 'twill not be long
    Until the day that he will see my death,
    And even now, his youth is much imperiled
    By a thousand foes. You only can defend him.
    And in my inmost heart, remorse is stirring,—
    Yes, and fear, too, lest I have shut your ears
    Against his cries; I fear that your just anger
    May, before long, visit on him that hatred
    His mother earned.
HIPPOLYTUS   Madam, you need not fear.
    Such malice is not mine.
PHAEDRA   I should not blame you
    If you should hate me; I have injured you.
    So much you know;—you could not read my heart.
    Yes, I have tried to be your enemy,
    For the same land could never hold us both.
    In private and abroad I have declared it;—
    I was your enemy! I found no peace
    Till seas had parted us; and I forbade
    Even your name to be pronounced to me.
    And yet, if punishment be meted out
    Justly, by the offense;—if only hatred
    Deserves a hate, then never was there woman
    Deserved more pity, and less enmity.
HIPPOLYTUS   A mother who is jealous for her children
    Will seldom love the children of a mother
    Who came before her. Torments of suspicion
    Will often follow on a second marriage.
    Another would have felt that jealousy
    No less than you; perhaps more violently.
PHAEDRA   Ah, prince, but Heaven made me quite exempt
    From what is usual, and I can call

Phaedra in *Phaedra* by Racine.

That Heaven as my witness! 'Tis not this—
No, quite another ill devours my heart!

HIPPOLYTUS   This is no time for self-reproaching, madam.
Perhaps your husband still beholds the light,
Perhaps he may be granted safe return
In answer to our prayers; his guarding god
Is Neptune, whom he never called in vain.

PHAEDRA   He who has seen the mansions of the dead
Returns not thence. Since Theseus has gone
Once to those gloomy shores, we need not hope,
For Heaven will not send him back again.
Prince, there is no release from Acheron;—
It is a greedy maw,—and yet I think
He lives and breathes in you,—and still I see him
Before me here; I seem to speak to him—
My heart—! Oh, I am mad! Do what I will,
I cannot hide my passion.

HIPPOLYTUS   Yes, I see
What strange things love will do, for Theseus, dead,
Seems present to your eyes, and in your soul
A constant flame is burning.

PHAEDRA   Ah, for Theseus
I languish and I long, but not, indeed,
As the Shades have seen him, as the fickle lover
Of a thousand forms, the one who fain would ravish
The bride of Pluto;—but one faithful, proud,
Even to slight disdain,—the charm of youth
That draws all hearts, even as the gods are painted,—
Or as yourself. He had your eyes, your manner,—
He spoke like you, and he could blush like you,
And when he came across the waves to Crete,
My childhood home, worthy to win the love
Of Minos' daughters,—what were you doing then?
Why did my father gather all these men,
The flower of Greece, and leave Hippolytus?
Oh, why were you too young to have embarked
On board the ship that brought your father there?
The monster would have perished at your hands,
Despite the windings of his vast retreat.
My sister would have armed you with the clue
To guide your steps, doubtful within the maze.—
But no—for Phaedra would have come before her,
And love would first have given me the thought,
And I it would have been, whose timely aid
Had taught you all the labyrinthine ways!
The care that such a dear life would have cost me!
No thread could satisfy my lover's fears.
I would have wished to lead the way myself,
And share the peril you were sure to face.
Yes, Phaedra would have walked the maze with you,—
With you come out in safety, or have perished!

HIPPOLYTUS   Gods! What is this I hear? Have you forgotten
    That Theseus is my father and your husband?
PHAEDRA   Why should you fancy I have lost remembrance
    And that I am regardless of my honor?
HIPPOLYTUS   Forgive me, madam! With a blush I own
    That I mistook your words, quite innocent.
    For very shame I cannot see you longer—
    Now I will go—
PHAEDRA   Ah, prince, you understood me,—
    Too well, indeed! For I had said enough.
    You could not well mistake. But do not think
    That in those moments when I love you most
    I do not feel my guilt. No easy yielding
    Has helped the poison that infects my mind.
    The sorry object of divine revenge,
    I am not half so hateful to your sight
    As to myself. The gods will bear me witness,—
    They who have lit this fire within my veins,—
    The gods who take their barbarous delight
    In leading some poor mortal heart astray!
    Nay, do you not remember, in the past,
    How I was not content to fly?—I drove you
    Out of the land, so that I might appear
    Most odious—and to resist you better
    I tried to make you hate me—and in vain!
    You hated more, and I loved not the less,
    While your misfortunes lent you newer charms.
    I have been drowned in tears and scorched by fire!
    Your own eyes might convince you of the truth
    If you could look at me, but for a moment!
    What do I say? You think this vile confession
    That I have made, is what I meant to say?
    I did not dare betray my son. For him
    I feared,—and came to beg you not to hate him.
    This was the purpose of a heart too full
    Of love for you to speak of aught besides.
    Take your revenge, and punish me my passion!
    Prove yourself worthy of your valiant father,
    And rid the world of an offensive monster!
    Does Theseus' widow dare to love his son?
    Monster indeed! Nay, let her not escape you!
    Here is my heart! Here is the place to strike!
    It is most eager to absolve itself!
    It leaps impatiently to meet your blow!—
    Strike deep! Or if, indeed, you find it shameful
    To drench your hand in such polluted blood,—
    If that be punishment too mild for you,—
    Too easy for your hate,—if not your arm,
    Then lend your sword to me.—Come! Give it now!—

(END)

The Misanthrope

by *Molière*

Act IV, scene iii   **Translated from the French by Henri Van Laun**

Characters   Célimène, a flirtatious lady of society
                    Alceste, the misanthrope, in love with Célimène

Scene   At Paris, in Célimène's house.

Situation   Alceste is bitter in his opposition to the superficial and hypocritical society of
                    Paris; yet he loves Célimène, a clever and scheming lady of that very society.
                    They meet in both love-play and conflict.

ALCESTE *(Aside)*   Grant, Heaven, that I may control my temper.

CÉLIMÈNE *(Aside)*   Ah! [*To* Alceste] What is all this trouble that I see you in,
   and what means those long-drawn sighs, and those black looks which you
   cast at me?

ALCESTE   That all the wickedness of which a heart is capable is not to be
   compared to your perfidy; that neither fate, hell, nor Heaven in its wrath,
   ever produced anything so wicked as you are.

CÉLIMÈNE   These are certainly pretty compliments, which I admire very much.

ALCESTE   Do not jest. This is no time for laughing. Blush rather, you have cause
   to do so; and I have undeniable proofs of your treachery. This is what the
   agitations of my mind prognosticated; it was not without cause that my
   love took alarm; by these frequent suspicions, which were hateful to you,
   I was trying to discover the misfortune which my eyes have beheld; and in
   spite of all your care and your skill in dissembling, my star foretold me what
   I had to fear. But do not imagine that I will bear unavenged this slight of
   being insulted. I know that we have no command over our inclinations, that
   love will everywhere spring up spontaneously, that there is no entering a
   heart by force, and that every soul is free to name its conqueror: I should
   thus have no reason to complain if you had spoken to me without dissembling,
   and rejected my advances from the very beginning; my heart would then
   have been justified in blaming fortune alone. But to see my love encouraged
   by a deceitful avowal on your part, is an action so treacherous and perfidious,
   that it cannot meet with too great a punishment; and I can allow my
   resentment to do anything. Yes, yes; after such an outrage, fear everything;
   I am no longer myself, I am mad with rage. My senses, struck by the deadly
   blow with which you kill me, are no longer governed by reason; I give way
   to the outbursts of a just wrath, and am no longer responsible for what I
   may do.

CÉLIMÈNE   Whence comes, I pray, such a passion? Speak! Have you lost your
   senses?

ALCESTE   Yes, yes, I lost them when, to my misfortune, I beheld you and thus
   took the poison which kills me, and when I thought to meet with some
   sincerity in those treacherous charms that bewitched me.

CÉLIMÈNE   Of what treachery have you to complain?

ALCESTE   Ah! how double-faced she is! how well she knows how to dissemble! But I am fully prepared with the means of driving her to extremities. Cast your eyes here and recognize your writing. This picked-up note is sufficient to confound you, and such proof cannot easily be refuted.

CÉLIMÈNE   And this is the cause of your perturbation of spirits?

ALCESTE   You do not blush on beholding this writing!

CÉLIMÈNE   And why should I blush?

ALCESTE   What! You add boldness to craft! Will you disown this note because it bears no name?

CÉLIMÈNE   Why should I disown it, since I wrote it.

ALCESTE   And you can look at it without becoming confused at the crime of which its style accuses you!

CÉLIMÈNE   You are, in truth, a very eccentric man.

ALCESTE   What! you thus out-brave this convincing proof! And the contents so full of tenderness for Oronte, need have nothing in them to outrage me, or to shame you?

CÉLIMÈNE   Oronte! Who told you that this letter is for him?

ALCESTE   The people who put it into my hands this day. But I will even suppose that it is for some one else. Has my heart any less cause to complain of yours? Will you, in fact, be less guilty towards me?

CÉLIMÈNE   But if it is a woman to whom this letter is addressed, how can it hurt you, or what is there culpable in it?

ALCESTE   Hem! The prevarication is ingenious, and the excuse excellent. I must own that I did not expect this turn; and nothing but that was wanting to convince me. Do you dare to have recourse to such palpable tricks? Do you think people entirely destitute of common sense? Come, let us see a little by what subterfuge, with what air, you will support so palpable a falsehood; and how you can apply to a woman every word of this note which evinces so much tenderness! Reconcile, if you can, to hide your deceit, what I am about to read. . . .

CÉLIMÈNE   It does not suit me to do so. I think it ridiculous that you should take so much upon yourself, and tell me to my face what you have the daring to say to me!

ALCESTE   No, no, without flying into a rage, take a little trouble to explain these terms.

CÉLIMÈNE   No, I shall do nothing of the kind, and it matters very little to me what you think upon the subject.

ALCESTE   I pray you, show me, and I shall be satisfied, if this letter can be explained as meant for a woman.

CÉLIMÈNE   Not at all. It is for Oronte; and I will have you believe it. I accept all his attentions gladly; I admire what he says, I like him, and I shall agree to whatever you please. Do as you like, and act as you think proper; let nothing hinder you and do not harass me any longer.

ALCESTE   (Aside)   Heavens! can anything more cruel be conceived, and was ever heart treated like mine? What! I am justly angry with her, I come to complain, and I am quarreled with instead! My grief and my suspicions are excited to the utmost, I am allowed to believe everything, she boasts of everything; and yet, my heart is still sufficiently mean not to be able to break the bonds that hold it fast, and not to arm itself with a generous contempt for the ungrateful object of which it is too much enamored. (To Célimène) Perfidious woman, you know well how to take advantage of my great weakness, and to employ for your own purpose that excessive, astonishing, and fatal love which your treacherous looks have inspired! Defend yourself at least from this crime that overwhelms me, and stop pretending to be guilty. Show me, if you can, that this letter is innocent; my affection will even consent to assist you. At any rate, endeavor to appear faithful, and I shall strive to believe you such.

CÉLIMÈNE   Bah, you are mad with your jealous frenzies, and do not deserve the love which I have for you. I should much like to know what could compel me to stoop for you to the baseness of dissembling; and why, if my heart were disposed towards another, I should not say so candidly. What! does the kind assurance of my sentiments towards you not defend me sufficiently against all your suspicions? Ought they to possess any weight at all with such a guarantee? Is it not insulting me even to listen to them? And since it is with the utmost difficulty that we can resolve to confess our love, since the strict honor of our sex, hostile to our passion, strongly opposes such a confession, ought a lover who sees such an obstacle overcome for his sake, doubt with impunity our avowal? And is he not greatly to blame in not assuring himself of the truth of that which is never said but after a severe struggle with oneself? Begone, such suspicions deserve my anger, and you are not worthy of being cared for. I am silly, and am vexed at my own simplicity in still preserving the least kindness for you. I ought to place my affections elsewhere, and give you a just cause for complaint.

ALCESTE   Ah! you traitress! mine is a strange infatuation for you; those tender expressions are, no doubt, meant only to deceive me. But it matters little, I must submit to my fate; my very soul is wrapt up in you; I will see to the bitter end how your heart will act towards me, and whether it will be black enough to deceive me.

CÉLIMÈNE   No, you do not love me as you ought to love.

ALCESTE   Indeed! Nothing is to be compared to my exceeding love; and, in its eagerness to show itself to the whole world, it goes even so far as to form wishes against you. Yes, I could wish that no one thought you handsome, that you were reduced to a miserable existence; that Heaven, at your birth, had bestowed upon you nothing; that you had no rank, no nobility, no wealth, so that I might openly proffer my heart, and thus make amends to you for the injustice of such a lot; and that, this very day, I might have the joy and the glory of seeing you owe everything to my love.

CÉLIMÈNE   This is wishing me well in a strange way! Heaven grant that you may never have occasion . . . But here comes Monsieur Dubois curiously decked out.

(END)

The Misanthrope by Molière. Richard Levine, Sam Tsoutsouvas, Michael Blazina, and Madelon Thomas at The Pioneer Memorial Theatre, The University of Utah. Directed by Keith Engar. Scenery by William S. Barber. Costumes by George Maxwell. Photograph by Robert Clayton.

A Modern Dress Version of *The Misanthrope* by Molière. English Version by Tony Harrison. Michael Mauldin as Alceste and Susan Melissa Hatfield as Eliante at The University of Missouri Summer Repertory Theatre Directed by Weldon B. Durham. Scenery by Patrick Atkinson. Costumes by James M. Miller. Lighting by Arthur Elliott Alvis, Jr.

15 Restoration Comedy

Vitality

Our Galleries too, were finely us'd of late,
Where roosting Masques sat cackling for a
    Mate;
They came not to see Plays but act their
    own,
And had throng'd Audiences when we had
    none.
Our Plays it was impossible to hear,
Confound you, give your bawdy prating
    o're,
Or Zounds, I'le fling you i' the Pit, you
    bawling Whore,
      Crowne   Epilogue to *Sir Courtly Nice*

Leaning over other ladies awhile to
whisper with the King, she rose out of the
box and went into the King's right hand,
between the King and the Duke of York;
which . . . put the King himself, as well as
every body else out of countenence. . . .
She did it only to show the world that she
is not out of favour yet, as was believed.
              Samuel Pepys *Diary*

Crowne's view of the boisterous and unruly theatre audiences of Restoration England typifies the excitement and vitality that characterized the revival of dramatic activity and the reopening of the theatres after their closing by the Puritans and Commonwealth government between 1642 and 1660. The accession to the throne of Charles II brought a fun-loving, woman-loving, theatre loving king to power. Dramatic activity flourished again. As Pepys notes, the king was a frequent visitor to London theatres. He and his entourage played many of the same flirtatious games in the royal box as did the aristocratic populace in the galleries and pit. Elegant dandies and fops (effeminate males) sat upon the stage itself to exhibit their clothing and other fineries.

Restoration drama was noteworthy primarily for its comedies, although authors such as John Dryden, Thomas Otway, and others produced some interesting serious plays categorized Heroic Tragedy. Dryden's *The Conquest of Granada* was a notable example, although his tragedy about Antony and Cleopatra, *All for Love*, has proved more stageworthy. Excessively bombastic and written in rhymed heroic couplets, the tragedies are rarely if ever produced in the contemporary theatre. Were they to be produced, directors and actors could well utilize the acting style employed in seventeenth-century French Neoclassic tragedy.

Overview of Restoration Comedy

Throughout the following discussion, I am particularly indebted to the work of Lyn Oxenford in *Playing Period Plays* and Charles A. Gildon in *The Life of Mr. Thomas Betterton* (see Suggested Readings at the end of this chapter for specific bibliographic information).

There are many similarities between theatre development in England and in France during the seventeenth and eighteenth centuries. Although the English Commonwealth under Cromwell suppressed plays and players from 1642 to 1660, theatre activity was not completely destroyed. Bandit actors and theatre managers provided a limited public with live "underground" entertainment. When Charles II was restored to the monarchy in 1660, the granting of theatre monopolies to William D'Avenant (Duke's Men) and Thomas Killigrew (King's Men) ensured competent management of plays, playwrights, actors, and theatres. Audiences attending the Restoration theaters (approximately 1660 to 1710) were predominately the aristocracy who demanded heroics in their tragedies and imitation of their own manners in their comedies.

Theatre structures in England were similar in style to the French theatres. Theatres were arranged in a semicircle ending in a gallery about midway in the auditorium. Most buildings provided a second gallery and a sloping pit with rows of seats arranged in a semicircle. The deep apron was backed by a raked stage whose depth from the front of the apron to the back wall was slightly less than half the total length of the building. The second Drury Lane theatre had four proscenium doors, two on either side of the apron with a box above each door (musicians usually sat in one of the boxes and spectators sat in the other box). In 1696, the apron was shortened by four feet and the downstage proscenium doors were converted into boxes. Additional benches were installed in the pit.

A feature of the French theatres not duplicated was the characteristic manner of moving scenery and producing scenic effect. On the Continent, scenery was moved by a pole-and-chariot system; in England a wing-and-backdrop system of sliding scenery was used. Grooves were inserted in the stage floor to receive the wing flats and shutters which formed the set. They were spaced to allow room between each set of scenes for placing furniture and assembling actors in a tableau. Sometimes scenes were cut out and set one behind the other to provide vistas and give the illusion of depth. Actors entered and exited through the proscenium doors. There was no act curtain; a front curtain was lowered and raised to begin and end the play. The audience never waited between scenes. The action was continuous due to the streamlined execution of scenery and the inclusion of songs and musical interludes between scenes.

Scenic demands for tragedies and comedies in seventeenth-century England were more elaborate than in France. Scenes were usually painted in perspective on wings, borders, and backdrops. However, the Neoclassic demand for universality was satisfied by the generality of the localized settings. As in France, few realistic set designs were needed for plays. The first move toward scenic realism came late in the eighteenth century (1771) when the scenic artist Phillip James de Loutherbourg was employed by the actor-manager David Garrick. Following the trend toward naturalism, Garrick removed all spectators from the stage (Voltaire accomplished the same thing in France).

The Restoration stage was generally lit poorly. Hooplike chandeliers obstructed the vision of the audience in the gallery seats. Oil lamps and candles were also used, and illumination was hazy. Later in the eighteenth century Garrick removed the chandeliers from the front of the proscenium and placed them in the upstage area, out of sight of the audience, which thus was given a clear view of the stage. Garrick was also able to illuminate the backstage area to heighten dramatic effects. In addition, he placed light behind the wings on a level with the actors, introduced lanterns and wall brackets as integral parts of the set, provided greater use of oil lamps, and used colored transparent silks to produce lighting effects in color.

Restoration comedy, or comedy of manners, was preeminent on the English stage from 1660 to approximately 1710. The English aristocracy were enthralled with the accurate imitation of their customs and manners mirrored on the stage. Restoration actors and actresses captured their audience with a flamboyant display of witty, bluntly sexual dialogue, boudoir intrigues, sensual innuendos, and rakish behavior. A narrow set of conventions entirely dominated Restoration comedy: constancy in love, especially in marriage, was a bore; sex should be tempting; love thrived on variety; genuine sexual feelings (e.g., sentimentalism) had no place on the stage.

The Country Wife by William Wycherley. Mary Benson as Lady Fidget and Woody Eney as Mr. Horner at The Hilberry Theatre, Wayne State University. Directed by Richard Spear. Scenery by Russell Paquette. Costumes by Vic Leverett and Helen Markovitch (executed by Helen Markovitch). Lighting by Gary M. Witt.

The Country Wife by William Wycherley. Dianne Hill as Mrs. Margery Pinchwife and John Napierala as Mr. Pinchwife at The Hilberry Theatre, Wayne State University. Directed by Richard Spear. Scenery by Russell Paquette. Costumes by Vic Leverett and Helen Markovitch (executed by Helen Markovitch). Lighting by Gary M. Witt.

In play after play, characters clashed with other characters in situations selected to produce love entanglements and intrigues. Dorimant, a character in Etherege's *The Man of Mode*, summarized the Restoration philosophy: "Next to coming to a good understanding with a new mistress, I love a quarrel with an old one."

Country life was considered boring. The clergy and professional men were treated with indifference or condescension. The most popular Restoration playwrights of the comedy of manners were William Wycherley, George Etherege, William Congreve, Thomas Shadwell, and John Vanbrugh. (George Farquhar was also a noted Restoration playwright, but one who might better be considered a "transition" author between Restoration and Sentimental Drama [see under Transition—Eighteenth-century Sentimentalism and Nineteenth-century Romanticism and Melodrama, later in this chapter].) These and many other comic authors proved once again that man was corruptible. The humor was in the satiric treatment of people who allowed themselves to be deceived or attempted to deceive others. Laughter was directed against the fop, the pretender at wit and sophistication, the old trying to be young, and the old man with a young and beautiful wife. For the most part, any standard of moral behavior was acceptable, but rewards and punishments were clearly meted out in accordance with the ability to achieve self-knowledge.

Prologues and epilogues were especially important in plays throughout the Restoration and well into the eighteenth century. Playwrights and actors-comedians continued the ancient stage tradition of introducing and concluding plays with special pieces, usually poetic, performed in a coarse, boisterous, hilarious manner.

The prevailing costume style in Restoration comedy was the contemporary dress of the late seventeenth and early eighteenth centuries. Every conceivable part of the human body was adorned. The actor wore a large-brimmed, plumed hat, a heavy periwig with curls over his forehead and down to his shoulders, a square-cut coat and a waistcoat hanging to the knees, wide, stiff cuffs and ruffles reaching to the knuckles, and ribbons on every available unmarked surface. The actress wore a gown with bell-shaped skirt and sleeves. A high mantilla and veil covered her head. Women were allowed to show their face, hands, and neck (and, of course, much of their bosom) when indoors. However, when appearing outside, ladies wore large hooded cloaks. As the years passed, men's tights revealed more muscular contour of the legs. Women's dresses became more clinging and revealed more of the female body. Sumptuous costumes were worn by heroes and heroines. Eye patches were seen regularly. Both sexes wore excessive makeup, false noses, beards, mustaches, powder, rouge, pencil, lipstick, and beauty patches. Obviously, little attempt was made at facial expression; to do so meant risking a cracked face.

Voice

In Restoration comedy the focus was unquestionably on brilliant, brittle, witty language, usually in prose. The style of Restoration acting was characterized by harmonious fusion of heightened oratory and rapid repartee. Vocal tone was important to denote emotional quality. For example, a soft and charming voice reflected love to an audience; a sharp, sullen, severe voice denoted hate or anger; a full, flowing, brisk voice denoted joy. English actors deliberately imitated the Parisian aristocratic style of address with its rich heritage from Molière. Phrasing and precise pronunciation were angli-cized and became the fashionable language of British upper society and aristocracy. Training in British schools included singing, dancing, posture, gesture, walking, and all the arts of deportment. Because of the spectators on the stage and the inadequate lighting, actors learned to use the downstage center portion of the apron area with proficiency and aplomb. Intricate vocal pauses and timing were developed. Vocal tempo was usually rapid. Articulation, pronunciation, and projection were clear and precise. Vocal asides and soliloquies (particularly in the prologues and epilogues) took on new dimension with the heightened presentational intimacy between performer and audience. Vocal inflection and variety were uniquely expansive.

Exercise 1   Voice—Restoration Comedy

1. Practice the following verses individually and then collectively stressing a variety of vocal tones. Repeat the exercise stressing precise phrasing, clear articulation, pronunciation, and projection. Repeat the exercise stressing pauses, timing, and rapid tempo. Finally, repeat the exercise stressing expansive vocal inflection and variety.

> King Charles, and who'll do him right now?
> King Charles, and who's ripe for fight now?
> Give a rouse: here's, in hell's despite now,
> King Charles!

> Who gave me the goods that went since?
> Who raised me the house that sank once?
> Who helped me to gold I spent since?
> Who found me in wine you drank once?

>> King Charles, and who'll do him right now?
>> King Charles, and who's ripe for fight now?
>> Give me a rouse: here's in hell's despite now,
>> King Charles!

> To whom used by boy George quaff else,
> By the old fool's side that begot him?
> For whom did he cheer and laugh else,
> While Noll's damned troopers shot him.

King Charles, and who'll do him right now?
King Charles, and who's ripe for fight now?
Give me a rouse: here's, in hell's despite now,
King Charles!

Anonymous English tune

2. Improvise a fast, lively, fun melody for the English tune in #1 above and practice singing it as an individual and within a group. Finally, incorporate exaggerated postures, gestures, and facial expressions to accompany the song and perform it as both a presentational solo and as a presentational chorus.

Movement

As originally staged, Restoration comedies were almost entirely presentational. Most movement was concerned with entering through the proscenium doors and exiting through the doors later. Much of the action took place downstage center on the apron. When adapting Restoration comedy to the modern stage, you and your director should not confine your action exclusively to the apron. You should probably utilize the area behind the proscenium arch in addition to the forestage. Movement in Restoration comedy should be characterized by highly elevated, graceful patterns. All physical activity should be precise and inventive. A wide range of uniquely conventional gestures must be employed. For example, in the Restoration theatre an actor would point to his head to indicate reason and to his heart to indicate love or passion, raise his eyes or hands upward when evoking the gods, or extend his arms forward, palms out, to indicate horror or surprise. An elaborate system of facial grimacing, winking, and smiling was used both for humor and for intimate communication to the audience.

The *fop* was a very fashionable character and the butt of much sarcastic humor. Actors playing fops minced, strutted, and performed myriad flourishing hand and facial gestures. Outlandish posturing and posing were employed in a static presentational position. Actresses flirted continually over and behind fans, half-masks, and handkerchiefs.

Bows and curtsies in the seventeenth-century French manner were used throughout a play and were directed to other characters as well as to the audience. When one character passed another, they frequently performed the *en passant* which was a slight bow from the waist with one foot sweeping in an arc around the other foot without losing the pace of the walk.

Taking snuff, a very popular social custom enjoyed by both men and women of society, was frequently performed on the stage. (Utilize the instructions for taking snuff provided in chapter 14, page 236.)

A gentlemen always kissed a lady's hand when leaving her. Men always held their hands high and away from their body to emphasize their lace cuffs, handkerchiefs, and ornate walking sticks and canes. This was done in a masculine and virile manner, except by fops. Men also swaggered elegantly in high-heeled shoes and relished their expansive movement. While controlled, these movements were vital and zestful. The women balanced enormous and outlandish hats upon their head. Most women carried a muff which was used not only for warming the hands, but also as a place to hide objects such as love letters. The women walked in slightly curved, graceful patterns, their dresses held slightly off the floor in a delicate manner.

In modern adaptation of Restoration comedy, more extensive use of pantomimic dramatization is necessary than in the original plays. For example, more furniture is used. Use of the sitting position is fairly common although women find it difficult to manage because of the size of the long, full skirts. Similarly, hand properties are used more frequently today. Drinking tea is a common example of this kind of activity. Movement in Restoration comedy is perhaps the most decorous and theatricalized of any stage movement in the history of theatre and reflects an affected, artificial manner almost without modern parallel. The possible exception is the exaggerated, satirical presentation of cocktail parties and events of so-called high society (e.g., recall the Ascot racetrack scene from *My Fair Lady*). However, beneath the externals of highly-elevated, stylized movement, characters should be portrayed who are realistically rooted in their society. That is, care must be taken not to reduce characters to the level of robots. While many characters were one-dimensional (often reflected in their names), moving and speaking artifically by today's standards, they nevertheless reflected real counterparts within their society. The skill of the playwrights was often reflected in the focus upon and accentuation of single traits of those realistic counterparts.

"The joy of taking snuff!"

Exercise 2 Movement—Restoration Comedy

1. Review and practice Exercise 5, chapter 14, page 237.

2. Organize and perform a group improvisation called "The President's Cocktail Party." Pantomine all activity in a highly exaggerated manner. Improvise dialogue and movement and overdo every action in an extremely decorous but theatrical way. An actor and an actress should be designated host and hostess, while everyone else arrives and participates. The improvisation ends when the president of the United States departs.

3. Repeat Exercise 2 above in the manner of a Restoration high-society party. Employ all available Restoration properties and costumes or facsimiles. The improvisation ends with the departure of King Charles II.

4. As described earlier in this chapter, practice bows, curtsies, *en passants*, taking snuff, wearing lace cuffs, flicking handkerchiefs, and walking with sticks and canes.

Character and Emotion

Many characters in Restoration comedy were notoriously one-dimensional, frequently caricatured by the implication in their name such as Snake, Lady Wishfort, Sir Fopling Flutter, Fainall, Lady Loveit, Sullen, Aimwell, Pinchwife, Manly, Lady Brute, Lady Fanciful, and so on. Characters were usually obsessed by a single emotional drive such as seduction, deception, gossip, greed, lust, and so on. *A major distinction between characterization in Restoration comedy and French Neoclassic comedy is the actor's sense of involvement with a character. Whereas serious involvement is necessary for playing most of the major roles in Molière, in Restoration comedy performance will probably be more successful if a certain level of detached objectivity is retained.* Even with personalization and subtextual role analysis, it is difficult to become involved with Restoration characters because of their lack of depth and subservience to plot situation and because of the mechanistic language. This is somewhat less true of the more intelligent Restoration characters such as Millamant and Mirabell in Congreve's *The Way of the World*. The question arises, How far does the actor take the sense of detachment or objectivity? Is everything an artificial mockery or put on? Actually, a highly-affected, theatricalized performance which appears to be a kind of comment on itself can be very effective in staging Restoration comedy. However, a more discerning director or actor probably will not carry the detachment to that extent. In other words, *the advice given for playing Molière's major characters may again be the best advice. Take your character and his emotional obsession or foible seriously enough for genuine human portrayal. Retain enough detachment to execute the role using the various stylistic mannerisms necessary to engage comic response.* Characters were not defined realistically, but created according to conventional decorum. Despite this, Restoration comic characters do possess an element of believability and natural emotion. However, more often than not, characters built on principles, as they tend to be in Restoration comedy, rarely create a true illusion of reality. Audiences enjoy the dramatic vitality of extremely witty characters and laugh at the foolishness of those who would be witty but are not.

Although the aristocratic manners of the time were "realistically" portrayed on the Restoration stage, it is a mistake to interpret late seventeenth-century *realism* as the word is defined today. In other words, what was represented on the Restoration stage was an exaggeration of what happened in life (albeit in a small section of society). The wit, repartee, precision of language, and elegance of manners were realistic *in terms* of appearance before the Restoration audience. Bawdy, sensual situations were not new to English drama. The only innovative ingredient was the realism of sensuality given by the appearance of women onstage. The inclusion of women allowed the dramatist greater freedom to develop situations which had heretofore been denied him. Sex play was a favorite aristocratic pastime. The female was displayed onstage for provocation (e.g., witness the many examples in Restoration plays of partial exposure of a female bosom or of a girl wearing breeches disguised as a boy). These sexual conventions simply mirrored the practices of society. Frequently, court ladies dressed as boys in order to arrange a rendevous with a lover. (Sexual flirtation was pursued just as vigorously in the auditorium among the spectators as onstage!)

Exercise 3   Character and Emotion—Restoration Comedy

1. Select a Restoration character from the list that follows and determine a singular emotional obsession apropriate to the implication in the name. Perform an improvised soliloquy in the manner of a Restoration prologue or epilogue in which you explain and pantomimically dramatize your emotional obsession, what you want, and how you are going to get it.

Sullen	Lord Plausible
Snake	Witwood
Lady Wishfort	Petulant
Scandal	Waitwell
Tattle	Foible
Mrs. Frail	Constant
Lady Pliant	Heartfree
Lady Fidget	Lady Fanciful
Mrs. Squeamish	Sir Novelty Fashion
Sparkish	Mr. Smirk
Pinchwife	Loveless
Horner	Sir Clumsey
Manly	Bull

2. Select a character from the list in #1 above. Locate the play in which this character is written. Select a long speech or two from your character's dialogue and practice singular emotional obsession for the character. Thereafter, expand that singularity through personalization and subtext.

Transition—Eighteenth-Century Sentimentalism and Nineteenth-Century Romanticism and Melodrama

The turn of the century (specifically, by 1710) saw the ushering in of sentimental treatment for both serious and comic material. By the beginning of the eighteenth century the number of people attending the theatre had increased (the population of Britain increased from six million in 1650 to ten million in 1800), and included many middle-class patrons. During the reign of Queen Anne (1702–1714) standards of decorum were higher. As interest in the court's activities lessened, middle-class self-awareness grew. No longer were theatre audiences predominately aristocratic. The purpose of sentimental drama was to show the middle classes the disparity between the real world and the ideal world. The sentimentalists believed that it was a part of Christian morality to see oneself as a moral paragon whose behavior was in many respects Christlike. Playwrights stressed the rewards of virtue and need for gentility. Great emphasis was placed on arousing sympathetic response to the misfortunes of others, and it was considered healthy to display emotion and to test one's virtues.

Opposition to the Restoration high comedy of manners came first from the playwright Colley Cibber in his play *Love's Last Shift* (1696). Shortly thereafter, other playwrights adopted the sentimental theme. Although George Farquhar is considered a Restoration author, his plays *The Recruiting Officer* and *The Beaux' Stratagem* delineated high moral standards for the middle class. Sir Richard Steele's *The Conscious Lovers* aroused kindly laughter and tears, as did Richard Cumberland's *The West Indian*. Sir Richard Sheridan's *The Rivals* and *The School for Scandal* pointed out the distinction between true virtue and pious remarks and satirized human shortsightedness and frailty. In Oliver Goldsmith's *She Stoops to Conquer* deviations from morality were punished and traditional Christian values were upheld. George Lillo in *George Barnwell: The London Merchant* exalted the merchant class and presented a central character who was weak and pathetic and thus established the first bourgeois tragedy.[1]

New comic forms provided alternate entertainment during the eighteenth century: for example, the ballad opera, exemplified by John Gay in *The Beggar's Opera* in 1728. John Rich created pantomimes in which dancing and silent mimicry were performed to musical accompaniment. Burlesque was written by Henry Fielding (*Tom Thumb*). These forms of theatre entertainment required detailed scenery and special effects. They were highly popular with the middle classes and much admired for their dance and music.

Later, the Licensing Act of 1737 placed all English drama under the regulations of censorship. The ballad opera and burlesques were replaced

---

1. It should be noted that Sheridan and Goldsmith attempted to break with sentimentalism and create brittle comedy in the Restoration style, but were only partly successful. Nonetheless, as examples of eighteenth-century comedy (sometimes called *baroque* or ornate) in the Restoration *tradition*, their work ranks high.

Wild Oats by John O'Keefe. Bruce Evers as Twitch, Mark Tymchyshyn as Rover, and Barbara Acker as Amelia at The Hilberry Theatre, Wayne State University. Directed by Robert Emmett McGill. Scenery by Jeffery R. Thomson. Costumes by Jackie Durbin. Lighting by Richard S. Latta. Regional American College Theatre Festival winner.

by the comic opera, a more sentimental play/entertainment utilizing music and comedy. Sheridan's *The Duenna* was in this vein, as was the work of John O'Keeffe (*The Poor Soldier* and *Wild Oats*.)

The prologue acting piece reached its height of popularity in David Garrick. The epilogue was more strategically important than the prologue. It literally "saved" the play. The epilogue was usually assigned to an actress; the prologue, to an actor. Both pieces were accompanied by stage business, by noisy encounters of actors at the stage doors, and by a plea to judge the play by emotion and not by reason.

During the middle and late eighteenth century, periodic attempts at acting reform toward a more natural or lifelike style were made. A number of individual actors began to revolt against the traditions and conventions of acting styles. This emphasis on the individual artist coincided with other theatre developments. Newly constructed theatres such as the Haymarket used a smaller apron—a feature which in the earlier years of the Drury Lane, Covent Garden, and other theatres had severely limited the actors' freedom of movement. With Garrick's reforms in lighting, actors were moving away from the apron and behind the proscenium. Realistic details were more vivid in the upstage areas against a more naturalistic painted backdrop. When the spectators were finally removed from the stage, actors could give their characters a more realistic base, and thereby could pay more attention to the play than to the audience. Eighteenth-century dramatists began to write about middle-class characters who were undergoing personality change. Granted, the writing was strictly sentimental and stressed the rewards of virtuous behavior. The character traits, however, were grounded in reality. Unfortunately, playwrights detracted from realistic detail by emphasizing disguises, surprises, and generally superficial characters.

Except for the modifications just mentioned, throughout the eighteenth century emphasis was on rant or cadence in theatrical speech. Rant produces declamatory monotone. In a declamatory style, the actor runs on with little regard for accent or emphasis. Passion is revealed by turgid vocalization or effeminate whine.

Actors studied ancient orations, moral philosophy, and paintings of the period to learn manners and to delineate passion. The study of passion was highly scientific and systematized. Accompanying gestures were copied from prints and paintings; for example, the hands were never raised about the head unless for some extraordinary occasion, and a woman had to veil her face when expressing grief. As late as 1744, acting style was entrenched in exaggerated characterization, cadence, rant, and traditional convention. (Garrick offered some reforms in these areas.)

However, in 1750, a change in theatrical speech somewhat supplanted cadence with natural speaking, and actors began creating specific characters. There was little sense of historical accuracy, but costumes were no

The Country Wife by William Wycherley. At The Seattle Repertory Theatre. Directed by Allen Fletcher. Actors (left to right) are Jacqueline Coslow as Mrs. Margery Pinchwife, Stanley Anderson as Mr. Pinchwife (seated), and Theodore Sorel as Mr. Horner (standing).

longer based strictly on current fashion. Perhaps the most famous actor to discard contemporary dress was Charles Macklin who made history by wearing historically accurate costumes in his portrayal of Macbeth. Thereafter, most actors leaned toward realistic propriety in costuming.

In Italy, a great eighteenth century writer, Carlo Goldoni, provided the world with several remarkable comedies in the best tradition of commedia dell'arte and scripted material combined. Goldoni humanized the commedia characters, abandoned masks, and improved stage speaking. His plays are witty, fun, and still play well on the modern stage. *The Servant of Two Masters* and *Il Campiello* are representative of his fine work.

The eighteenth century German playwright and critic, Gotthold Lessing, provided the foremost dramatic criticism of the period in his document, *The Hamburg Dramaturgy* (1767–1769). His influential plays include *Miss Sara Sampson* and *Minna von Barnhelm*. He also wrote a famous treatise on dramatic theory, *Laokoon*, an opposition to the Neoclassic aesthetic.

In the eighteenth century it was Denis Diderot, French encyclopedist, who above all argued against the limitations of Neoclassic drama. Diderot advocated reform in staging, in plays, and in acting and was instrumental in introducing the concept of the "fourth wall" in which the stage picture was filled with realistic detail and the audience peeked through an imaginary fourth wall to observe the action. His famous document *The Paradox of Acting* was revolutionary in articulating a philosophy of acting based on minimizing the actor's emotional involvement. Diderot believed that the

School for Scandal by Sir Richard Brinsley Sheridan. Directed by Larry D. Clark. Scenery by Patrick Atkinson. Lighting by Earl Stringer. Costumes by Jim Miller. Greta Lambert as Lady Teazle and Jerry Eisenhower as Sir Peter Teazle at The University of Missouri Summer Repertory Theatre.

Il Campiello a Venetian Comedy by Carlo Goldone, adapted by Richard Nelson. Lori Putnam as Lucietta with The Acting Company On Tour for the John F. Kennedy Center. Directed by Liviu Ciulei. Photograph by Martha Swope.

actor should feel nothing himself, but rather render the external signs of emotion in such a way as to convince the audience of the reality of the illusion (hence, the *paradox*)—an audience that is convinced it is seeing real emotion or feeling when in fact it is only the truthful *appearance* of reality. In an age when the acting style was still highly presentational and declamatory, Diderot's total insistence upon representational style brought adamant opposition from many critics and audiences. Diderot emphasized natural speech and pauses for thought and stressed use of lifelike gestures, pantomime, silence, and emotion. Diderot argued the revolutionary idea of conscious identification by the actor wth his character through the use of imagination and impersonation. While little heed was paid at the time, Diderot's theories on acting were preparation for the turn-of-the-century movement toward realistic and naturalistic styles of acting.

In the Western world the nineteenth century was largely a century of revolution and turmoil. After a century of emphasis on nature and reason, the nineteenth century, often called the Romantic Age, was an emotional, passionate time. The term *romance* implies emotional attractions, affairs of the heart, religious ideals, freedom, and strong emphasis on the needs of both the masses and the individual. This was the time of Napoleon and the French Revolution, a time in which the aristocracy was challenged by the middle and lower classes. It was as well a century of scientific innovation

She Stoops to Conquer by Oliver Goldsmith. Edith Elliott as Mrs. Hardcastle at the University of Wisconsin-Milwaukee. Directed by Sanford Robbins. Scenery by R. H. Graham. Costumes by Maura Smalover. Photograph by Alan Magayne-Roshak.

leading to the Industrial Revolution, to the evolutionary theories of Charles Darwin, and to the psychological insights of Sigmund Freud. In England, it was the era of the great Romantic poets such as Wordsworth, Coleridge, Byron, Shelley, and Keats; in Germany, of the poets and dramatists Johann von Goethe and Friedrich Schiller; in France, of the Romantic poet, novelist, and dramatist Victor Hugo; in America, of Henry Wadsworth Longfellow.

Romanticism encouraged men to explore the unreal world of fantasy in juxtaposition to the world of natural phenomena. Men believed in religious transcendentalism, or the affinity of man and spirit and of man and nature. The Romantics believed in the autonomy of inspired genius, the necessity of releasing the imagination, the spontaneity of intuitive feeling, the freedom of artistic expression, and a vision of nature as part of a unified cosmos. Romantic idealism culminated in the notion of organic growth and development arising from an interest in the past, particularly in the Middle Ages. In Germany the Romantic movement was called *Sturm und Drang,* or Storm and Stress. Goethe wrote both Romantic and Neoclassic plays such as *Faustus* and *Iphigenia at Tauris*. Schiller wrote *William Tell* in the Romantic vein. Goethe is considered one of the precursors of what is now called the director in the theatre. In his theatre at Weimar Goethe succeeded in classifying many acting techniques.

Movement toward Realism

During the eighteenth and nineteenth centuries, acting style in German theatre continued to move toward naturalness. Actors became interested in techniques of role creation and in disciplined vocal and emotional work. Acting style was moving closer to Realism (discussed in chapter 16). Part of the transition toward Realism was accomplished by changes in the content and structure of plays. August von Kotzbue wrote the first melodramas, which were a combination of music and drama in the form of a three-act play accompanied by a musical score.

Finally, in mid-nineteenth century, theatre in Germany reached a new level of supremacy with the achievements of Richard Wagner and, late in the nineteenth century, with the Duke of Saxe-Meiningen. Wagner advocated theatre as mythical music; he was devoted to dramatizing the ideal world. Conversely, Saxe-Meiningen aimed at producing lifelike pictorial illusions. Both of these men were among the first great directors. Saxe-Meiningen was instrumental in unifying theatrical production by using realistic costumes and sets and effective ensemble playing.

Rene Pixérécourt did for melodrama in France what Kotzbue had done for melodrama in Germany (a melodrama is a serious play in which good and evil are clearly separated, characters are simple, action is full of suspense, a double ending rewards virtue and punishes evil, and plot and characterization are frequently reinforced by music and physical properties). Pixpérécourt's melodramas paved the way for the rise of Romantic drama in France. In addition to Victor Hugo, Alexandre Dumas (pere) and Alfred de Musset also wrote important Romantic plays. French Romanticism was ultimately modified toward Realism by the end of the nineteenth century.

Eugène Scribe and Victorien Sardou contributed to the development of Realism (see chapter 16) in France by writing realistic plays which were tightly structured, or well made. The great playwright of early Realism, Henrik Ibsen, was greatly influenced by these plays.

Similarly in England the Romantic movement advanced toward realism. W. C. Macready, Charles Kean, and other actors were leaders in the development of increasingly realistic acting in the nineteenth century. They also helped introduce reforms in staging and costuming, along with J. R. Planché, Madame Vestris, Charles Mathews the Elder, and Charles Mathews the Younger. Madam Vestris also introduced the first realistic *box set* in England. The great English actors during these times included Sarah Bernhardt, Henry Irving, and Ellen Tree.

Across the Atlantic Ocean, the new United States imitated English drama, but produced some excellent actors and persons of the theatre such as Edwin Forrest, Edwin Booth, Clara Morris, Ada Rehan, and Joseph Jefferson III.

Acting in Romantic Plays and Melodramas

Nineteenth-century Romantic plays and melodramas are rarely performed in the theatre today. In present-day presentation of a Romantic drama, the style of acting should emphasize intense emotional expression; rhythmic, melodic, poetic vocal delivery in a highly elevated manner; and sweeping, flowing movements and gestures. Center stage should be used predominately, and the focus should be on the presentational mode. The overall impression of style should be an elevated version of the Elizabethan acting style.

If you are cast in a nineteenth-century melodrama (not to be mistaken for the kidded or mocked comic melodramas of cabaret theatre), your style of acting should employ the tenets of Realism described in chapter 16—in other words, lifelike character creation, predominately representational mode (except for asides), detailed pantomimic business, and natural speech and movement.

What is known as the beginning of modern drama and modern styles of acting was initiated in the late nineteenth and early twentieth centuries. The foundation of all current acting styles commences with a study of Realism and Naturalism.

Suggested Characters and Plays for Scene Work

Congreve, William

Millamant, Mirabell, Fainall, Mrs. Marwood
   The Way of the World
Valentine, Miss Prue, Sir Sampson Legend, Ben, Angelica
   Love for Love

Etherege, George

Dorimant, Bellinda, Lady Loveit, Sir Fopling Flutter
   The Man of Mode

Dryden, John

Antony, Cleopatra
   All for Love

Farquhar, George

Airwell, Archer, Bonniface, Cherry, Lady Bountiful, Dorinda, Sullen
   The Beaux' Stratagem

Wycherley, William

Marjorie Pinchwife, Horner
   The Country Wife
Manly, Olivia, Freeman, Widow Blackacre
   The Plain Dealer

Vanbrugh, John

Sir John Brute, Lady Brute, Lady Fanciful
   The Provok'd Wife

Gay, John

Macheath, Polly Peachum, Lucy Lockit
　　The Beggar's Opera

Goldsmith, Oliver

Kate Hardcastle, Marlowe, Tony Lumpkin
　　She Stoops to Conquer

Sheridan, Sir Richard

Sir Peter Teazle, Lady Teazle, Joseph Surface, Charles Surface, Maria, Lady Sneerwell
　　The School for Scandal
Mrs. Malaprop, Lydia Languish, Captain Jack Absolute
　　The Rivals

O'Keeffe, John

Twitch, Rover, Amelia
　　Wild Oats
All characters
　　The Poor Soldier

Additional Suggested Characters and Plays for Scene Work

Goldoni, Carlo

All characters
　　The Servant of Two Masters
All characters
　　Il Campiello

Goethe, Johann Wolfgang von

Goetz, Bishop of Bamberg
　　Goetz von Berlichingen
Doctor Faust, Mephistopheles, Margaret
　　Faust Part 1

Schiller, Friedrich

Mary Queen of Scots, Queen Elizabeth
　　Mary Stuart
William Tell, Gessler
　　William Tell

Hugo, Victor

Hernani, Dona Sol
　　Hernani

Dumas (fils), Alexander

Marguerite Gautier, Armand Duval
　　Camille

Rostand, Edmund

Cyrano de Bergerac, Roxanne, Christian
　　Cyrano de Bergerac

de Musset, Alfred

Camille, Perdican, Rosette
　　No Trifling with Love

Sardou, Victorien

Cyprienne, Des Prunelles, Adhemar
  Let's Get a Divorce

Buchner, Georg

Danton, Robespierre
  Danton's Death
All characters
  Woyzeck

Kotzebue, August

The Stranger
  The Stranger

Actor Checklist *Restoration Comedy*

Voice	Exaggerated inflection; rapid but clear; smooth and polished line delivery; precise diction; clear articulation and projection.
Movement	Elevated; exaggerated; elegant when appropriate; controlled; well-executed use of bows, curtsies, and asides; predominately presentational; generally rapid tempo; highly artificial for most characters (such as the fop).
Gestures	Hand, head, facial dominate; clear; elevated; exaggerated, especially for fops.
Pantomimic Dramatization	Clear; inventive; selective; extensive and elaborate use of period props and costumes: female headgear, fans, staffs, handkerchiefs, half-masks, snuff, jewelry, makeup, and so on.
Character	Often one-dimensional; extra dimension usually comes from intelligence and not from emotion; rooted in social mores, conduct, and foibles, representative social facet clear; actor involvement somewhat detached or objective.
Emotion	Usually single obsession; clear; nonsentimental; scheming and cynical.
Ideas	Clear; satiric; witty; cynical.
Language	Brittle; witty; rhythmic; brilliant vocabulary; correct pronunciation.
Mood and Atmosphere	Clear in terms of satire, repartee, and wit; supportive of usually cynical and flirtatious-sexual situation; some serious undertone with certain lead characters.
Pace and Tempo	Generally rapid.
Special Techniques	Wit and language demand unusual vocal dexterity; unusual attention to movement in costume.

Suggested Readings

Bernbaum, Ernest. *The Drama of Sensibility: A Sketch of the History of Sentimental Comedy and Domestic Tragedy, 1696–1780.* Cambridge, Mass.: Harvard University Press, 1915.

Brown, J. R., and Harris, B. *Restoration Theatre.* New York: G. P. Putnam's Sons, 1967.

Bryant, Arthur. *The England of Charles II.* London: Longmans, Green and Co., 1935.

Campbell, Lily B. "A History of Costuming on the English Stage between 1660 and 1823." *University of Wisconsin Studies in Language and Literature* 2(1918): 187–223.

Cunningham, C. W., and Cunnington, P. *Handbook of English Costume in the Seventeenth Century.* 2d ed. London: Faber, 1957.

Curtis, Mattoom. *The Book of Snuff and Snuff Boxes.* New York: Liveright Pub. Corp., 1935.

Dobree, Bonamy. *Restoration Comedy, 1660–1720.* London: Oxford University Press, 1924.

———. *Restoration Tragedy, 1660–1720.* London: Oxford University Press, 1929.

Downer, Alan S. "Nature to Advantage Dressed: Eighteenth Century Acting," *PMLA* (1943), 58:4 (part I), pp. 1002–37.

Durant, Jack D. *Richard Brinsley Sheridan: A Reference Guide.* Boston: G. K. Hall & Co., 1980.

Fujimura, Thomas H. *Restoration Comedy of Wit.* Princeton, N.J.: Princeton University Press, 1952.

Furst, Lilian R. *Romanticism in Perspective.* New York: Humanities Press, 1969.

Gildon, Charles. *The Life of Mr. Thomas Betterton.* New York: A. M. Kelley, 1970.

Henshaw, N. "Graphic Sources for a Modern Approach to Acting Restoration Comedy." *Educational Theatre Journal,* May 1968, pp. 157–70.

Highfill, Phillip H., et al. *Biographical Dictionary of Actors, Actresses, Musicians, Dancers, Managers, and Other Stage Personnel in London, 1660–1800.* Carbondale: Southern Illinois University Press, 1973-. (In progress.)

Holland, Norman N. *The First Modern Comedies: The Significance of Etherege, Wycherley, and Congreve.* Cambridge, Mass.: Harvard University Press, 1959.

Hughes, Derek. *Dryden's Heroic Plays.* Lincoln: University of Nebraska Press, 1981.

Joseph, Bertram. *The Tragic Actor.* New York: Theatre Arts Books, 1959.

Krutch, Joseph W. *Comedy and Conscience after the Restoration.* New York: Russell & Russell, 1949.

Lacey, Alexander. *Pixérécourt and the French Romantic Drama.* Toronto: University of Toronto Press, 1928.

Loftis, John, ed. *Restoration Drama, Modern Essays in Criticism.* London: Oxford University Press, 1966.

———, et al. *Revels History of Drama in English, Vol. 4:1660–1750.* New York: Barnes & Noble, 1976.

Lynch, James J. *Box, Pit and Gallery: Stage and Society in Johnson's London.* Berkeley: University of California Press, 1953.

MacCollum, John I., Jr. *The Restoration Stage.* New York: Houghton Mifflin, Co., 1961.

Matthews, Brander. *French Dramatists of the Nineteenth Century.* 5th ed. New York: Benjamin Blom, 1968.

———. *The Theatres of Paris.* London: Sampson, Low, Marston, Searle & Rivington, 1880.

Melcher, Edith. *Stage Realism in France From Diderot to Antoine.* Bryn Mawr, Pa.: Bryn Mawr College, 1928.

Milhous, Judith. *Thomas Betterton and the Management of Lincoln's Inn Fields, 1695–1708.* Carbondale: Southern Illinois University Press, 1979.

Muir, Kenneth. *The Comedy of Manners.* London: Hutchinson University Library, 1970.

Nicoll, Allardyce. *History of English Drama, 1600–1900.* 6 vols. London: Cambridge University Press, 1955–1959.

Oxenford, Lyn. *Design for Movement.* A textbook on stage movement. New York: Theatre Arts Books, 1952.

———. *Playing Period Plays.* London: J. G. Miller, 1957.

Palmer, J. L. *The Comedy of Manners.* New York: Russell & Russell, 1962.

Perry, Henry T. *Comic Spirit in Restoration Drama.* New York: Russell, 1962.

Reynolds, Ernest. *Early Victorian Drama (1830–1870).* New York: Benjamin Blom, 1965.

"The Romantic Movement: A Current Selective and Critical Bibliography." *English Literary History* (1937–49), Johns Hopkins Press; *Philological Quarterly* (1950–present) University of Iowa. Annual lists of publications.

Rowell, George. *The Victorian Theatre.* London: Oxford University Press, 1956.

Summers, Montague. *The Restoration Theatre.* London: Paul Trench, Trubner & Co., 1934.

Watson, Ernest B. *Sheridan to Robertson: A Study of the 19th Century London Stage.* Cambridge, Mass.: Harvard University Press, 1926.

Wilkenson, D. R. M. *The Comedy of Habit.* London: Universitaire Press, 1964.

Wilson, Garff B. *A History of American Acting.* Bloomington, Indiana: University of Indiana Press, 1966.

Suggested Filmography

1. *The Beggar's Opera.* 1953. British. Playwright-John Gay. Director Peter Brook. With Sir Laurence Olivier.
2. *Camille,* 1927. First National. Playwright Alexandre Dumas, fils. Director Fred Niblo. With Norma Talmadge.
3. *Cyrano de Bergerac.* 1925. Italian. Playwright Edmond Rostand.
4. *Cyrano de Bergerac.* 1950. United Artists. English. Playwright Rostand. Director Michael Gordon. With Jose Ferrer and Mala Powers.
5. *La Tosca.* 1911. French. Playwright Victorien Sardou. Director Andre Calmettes. With Sarah Bernhardt.
6. *The Rivals.* 1913. Kinemacolor. Playwright R. B. Sheridan. Director Theodore Marson. With Wm. Winter Jefferson, son of Joseph.
7. *The Robbers.* 1913. Edison. Playwright Friedrich Schiller. Director Walter Edwin.
8. *The School for Scandal.* 1912. Playwright R. B. Sheridan. Director Bertram Phillips. With Basil Rathbone.
9. *She Stoops to Conquer.* 1923. Universal. Playwright Oliver Goldsmith. Director Edwin Greenwood.

The Country Wife by
William Wycherley.
James Hooks as Dr.
Quack, William Kelsay as
Sir Jasper Fidget,
Katherine Parks as Mrs.
Squeamish, Mary Pat
Quintin as Lady Fidget,
and Michael Krause as
Mr. Horner in "The
China Scene" at The
University of Missouri
Summer Repertory
Theatre. Directed by
Larry D. Clark. Scenery
by Edward L. Gallagher.
Costumes by Linda
Conaway. Lighting by
Steve Ross.

The Country Wife
by *William Wycherley*

from
Act IV, scene iii

Lady Fidget
Horner
Mrs. Squeamish
Old Lady Squeamish
Sir Jasper
Quack
Pinchwife

Characters

Horner's lodging, London.

Scene

Horner passes himself off as a eunuch in London's elite society in order to gain easy access to the more enticing married women. In the famous "china" scene, he and Lady Fidget return from a bedroom escapade to engage with others in witty, sexual repartee.

Situation

(*Re-enter* LADY FIDGET *with a piece of china in her hand, and* HORNER *following.*)

LADY FIDGET   And I have been toiling and moiling for the prettiest piece of china, my dear.
HORNER   Nay, she has been too hard for me, do what I could.
MRS. SQUEAMISH   Oh, lord, I'll have some china too. Good Mr. Horner, don't think to give other people china and me none; come in with me too.
HORNER   Upon my honour, I have none left now.
MRS. SQUEAMISH   Nay, nay, I have known you deny your china before now, but you shan't put me off so. Come.
HORNER   This lady had the last there.
LADY FIDGET   Yes indeed, madam, to my certain knowledge, he has no more left.
MRS. SQUEAMISH   O, but it may be he may have some you could not find.
LADY FIDGET   What, d'ye think if he had had any left, I would not have had it too? for we women of quality never think we have china enough.
HORNER   Do not take it ill, I cannot make china for you all, but I will have a roll-waggon for you too, another time.
MRS. SQUEAMISH   Thank you, dear toad.
LADY FIDGET   What do you mean by that promise? (*Aside to* HORNER.)
HORNER   Alas, she has an innocent, literal understanding. (*Aside to* LADY FIDGET.)
LADY SQUEAMISH   Poor Mr. Horner! he has enough to do to please you all, I see.
HORNER   Ay, madam, you see how they use me.
LADY SQUEAMISH   Poor gentleman, I pity you.
HORNER   I thank you, madam: I could never find pity, but from such reverend ladies as you are; the young ones will never spare a man.
MRS. SQUEAMISH   Come, come, beast, and go dine with us; for we shall want a man at ombre after dinner.
HORNER   That's all their use of me, madam, you see.
MRS. SQUEAMISH   Come, sloven, I'll lead you, to be sure of you. (*Pulls him by the cravat.*)

LADY SQUEAMISH   Alas, poor man, how she tugs him! Kiss, kiss her; that's the way to make such nice women quiet.

HORNER   No, madam, that remedy is worse than the torment; they know I dare suffer anything rather than do it.

LADY SQUEAMISH   Prithee kiss her, and I'll give you her picture in little, that you admired so last night; prithee do.

HORNER   Well, nothing but that could bribe me: I love a woman only in effigy, and good painting as much as I hate them.—I'll do't, for I could adore the devil well painted. (*Kisses* MRS. SQUEAMISH.)

MRS. SQUEAMISH   Foh, you filthy toad! nay, now I've done jesting.

LADY SQUEAMISH   Ha! ha! ha! I told you so.

MRS. SQUEAMISH   Foh! a kiss of his—

SIR JASPER   Has no more hurt in't than one of my spaniel's.

MRS. SQUEAMISH   Nor no more good neither.

QUACK   I will now believe anything he tells me. (*Aside*) (*Enter* PINCHWIFE.)

LADY FIDGET   O lord, here's a man! Sir Jasper, my mask, my mask! I would not be seen here for the world.

SIR JASPER   What, not when I am with you?

LADY FIDGET   No, no, my honour—let's be gone.

MRS. SQUEAMISH   Oh grandmother, let's be gone; make haste, make haste, I know not how he may censure us.

LADY FIDGET   Be found in the lodging of anything like a man!—Away.

(*Exeunt* SIR JASPER FIDGET, LADY FIDGET, OLD LADY SQUEAMISH, *and* MRS. SQUEAMISH.)

(*END*)

The Country Wife by William Wycherley. Lynn Chausow as Mrs. Margery Pinchwife and Richard Iglewski as Mr. Pinchwife with The Acting Company On Tour for the John F. Kennedy Center. Directed by Garland Wright. Scenery by Jack Barkla. Costumes by Judith Dolan. Lighting by Dennis Parichy. Photograph by Diane Gorodnitzki (Martha Swope).

Realism and Naturalism 16

Selectivity and Photographic Detail

Zola descends into the cess-pool to take a
bath, I to cleanse it.

Henrik Ibsen
from Vera Mowry Roberts, *On Stage*
A History of the Theatre.

Details are also the thing in the sphere of
psychology. God preserve us from
generalizations. Best of all, avoid depicting
the hero's state of mind; you ought to try to
make it clear from the hero's actions. It is
not necessary to portray many active
figures. The center of gravity should be two
persons—he and she.

Anton Chekhov to his brother Alexander
from Ernest Simmons
Introduction to Russian Realism.

MR. STANISLAVSKI
AS VERSHININ IN
"THE THREE SISTERS"

"THE SEAGULL" –
INSIGNIA OF THE
MOSCOW ART THEATRE ——— Moist

As Chekhov revealed to his brother, the new dramatists at the turn of the century stressed mainly selective detail, not generalization—details whose origins were in human psychology and which emphasized the everyday reactions between men and women. Realists such as Henrik Ibsen carefully selected and arranged their material to create art which reflected social problems. Emile Zola, the French naturalist writer, went a step further into what might be described as scientific observation, revealing life in a seemingly indiscriminate, nonselective, photographic manner. At times this resulted in material which caught the "cesspool" or seamy side of life. No longer was drama restricted to artificial or contrived views of society and people.

The question arises, What were the distinctions between the plays of the realists (e.g., Ibsen) and of the naturalist (e.g., Chekhov and Zola)?

Read each of the following speeches aloud.[1] Compare them in terms of their lifelike qualities.

> For eight years I've been waiting patiently; I knew, of course, that such things don't happen every day. Then, when this trouble came to me—I thought to myself: Now! Now the wonderful thing will happen! All the time Krogstad's letter was out there in the box, it never occurred to me for a single moment that you'd think of submitting to his conditions. I was absolutely convinced that you'd defy him—that you'd tell him to publish the thing to all the world; and that then—
>
> Nora to Torvald *A Doll's House* by Henrik Ibsen

> Not only in two or three hundred years but in a million years life will be just the same; it does not change, it remains stationary, following its own laws which we have nothing to do with or which, anyway, we shall never find out. Migratory birds, cranes for instance, fly backwards and forwards and whatever ideas, great or small, stray through their minds, they will go on flying just the same without knowing where or why. They fly and will continue to fly, however philosophic they may become; and it doesn't matter how philosophical they are so long as they go on flying. . . .
>
> Tusenbach *The Three Sisters* by Anton Chekhov

Scrutiny of the two speeches immediately reveals a measurable alliance between these lifelike speeches. The revolt against Romanticism and melodrama in the late nineteenth century produced two distinct literary trends throughout Europe: Realism and Naturalism. The new dramatic styles demanded more inquiry and observation of playwrights. Critics as well as audiences desired more controlled, true-to-life characterization. The foregoing examples of dialogue serve to illustrate the subtle differences between the two dominant dramatic movements of the late nineteenth century.

The most notable quality of Nora's speech to Torvald is its orderly arrangement of thought. It is selective in vocabulary and it flows with logical

1. Nora's speech from *A Doll's House* by Henrik Ibsen. Translated by Eva LeGallienne. In *Landmarks in Modern Drama* edited by Charles Aughtry. Reprinted with permission of Random House, Inc., New York. Tusenbach's speech from *The Three Sisters* by Anton Chekhov. Translated by Constance Garnett. Reprinted with permission of Random House, Inc., New York.

intent. The lines are believable and truthful for purposes of characterization; however, they are slightly heightened and intensified above normal conversational tone. Although the playwright carefully selected the choice of words, his character is inwardly motivated. The style of the speech is *realistic*.

Tusenbach's speech is much closer to normal, reallife conversation. The emotional quality of his monologue causes immediate audience identification. Motivated thoughts and feelings are internalized, producing a truthful, believable quality. Incidental references are made as the logic flows in uneven and at times repetitive measures. In order to sustain his mood, an actor portraying Tusenbach may use silences and pauses as he speaks the lines. The style of the speech is *naturalistic*.

Overview of Realism

The movement toward Realism was allied with the origins of modern science. Instead of being based on emotional or mystic explanations, late nineteenth century theatre was based on natural, rational explanation as evidenced and experienced through the five senses. The work of the philosopher August Comte (1798–1857) was a primary influence on realistic thought. His philosophy was based on "positivism" as the key to knowledge. Positivism was the examination of all apparent things, of all one could see. Evidence was based on precise observation and experimentation; events were understood in terms of cause and effect. When Charles Darwin published *On the Origin of the Species by Means of Natural Selection* in 1859, his advanced theories concerning the influence of heredity and environment on man's behavior gave tremendous impetus to the dramatic community. Man became one of many objects worthy of scientific study. The individual was part of an evolutionary movement whose hereditary traits and environmental conditions determine his existence and explain his character. The theory of evolution strengthened the theory of human progress—individual and collective improvement became inevitable.

The realists observed man and his environment primarily through the five senses. Playwrights consciously set out to abandon antiquated techniques such as formula plays, surface characterization, romantic subject matter, and scenic splendor in favor of duplication of contemporary life. Although realistic plays were well constructed, they were not overly predictable in terms of cause and effect. Characters were based on reallife, three-dimensional human beings. Plots were concerned with the problems of daily life—the environmental and social forces that encroached on man. Scenery mirrored contemporary environment in an attempt to express external realism. The playwright exercised careful selectivity and control in arranging events within a play. All action was motivated to achieve truth and believability in character portrayal. Although a character's actions were usually impelled by thoughts, feelings, and environmental conditions, realistic playwrights tended to emphasize outward action more than inner

Hedda Gabler by Henrik Ibsen. Sus...nah York and Roxanne Hart at The Roundabout Theatre, New York City, Gene Feist and Michael Fried, Producing Directors.

psychology. Dialogue was significantly more conversational than, for example, the formal dialogue in plays by Scribe or Sardou. However, there was a tendency in realistic plays to heighten conversation at moments of high emotion.

Henrik Ibsen was the most representative playwright of the realistic school. A native of Norway, Ibsen gave Realism stature by writing plays with lifelike dialogue, settings, costumes, and stage business. However, the term must be qualified when it is applied to Ibsen. He did not copy reality in explicit detail. Because he was not interested in the raw material of life in the manner of a factual recorder, he became both a creative artist and a re-creative artist. His material was carefully selected and organized into a pattern of refinement, omission, and intensification.

Ibsen's themes suggest man's unending conflict between duty to himself and duty to others. His characters constantly try to achieve individual integrity. Although external action is somewhat static, his dialogue is tight, dynamic, and full of hints and allusions. Ibsen had a tremendous capacity for conveying the unspoken thought with emotional and mental undercurrents. In his realistic plays, Ibsen abandoned the aside and the soliloquy. Expository material was interwoven in cause-and-effect sequences.

Ibsen was flexible enough to explore many types of plays including historical-romantic studies (*The Pretenders*), poetic drama (*Peer Gynt*), realistic or thesis dramas (*A Doll's House, The Wild Duck, Ghosts, Hedda Gabler*), and symbolic plays (*The Master Builder*). His historic-romantic plays are militant in tone, inspired by his yearning for a better man and a better world. His poetic dramas are episodic, but impressive accounts of lofty ideals. Ibsen's realistic thesis or social-problem plays are perhaps most noteworthy for their convincing characters and dialogue, exciting and innovative social ideas, and realistic prose. His symbolic plays grope sensitively into mysticism. All of his plays blend art, morality, philosophy, and social considerations. Although Ibsen was basically a reformer and a fighter against the evils of society, his art has a warm feeling for life.

In England, the tenets of Ibsen's playwriting were emulated by Arthur Wing Pinero, Henry Arthur Jones, Sir James Barrie, John Galsworthy, and George Bernard Shaw. Shaw fused paradox and satire effectively. He had a devastating wit aimed at shattering established beliefs and false ideals. Shaw was a master of clever, brilliant ideas. Although he sometimes made his characters a mouthpiece for his own ideas, Shaw created vital characters who discovered themselves during a crisis. The message in a Shavian play rests on character development. Some of Shaw's most famous plays include *Major Barbara, Arms and the Man, Candida, The Devil's Disciple, Caesar and Cleopatra*, and *Man and Superman* (a combination of Romanticism and Realism).

The impact of Ibsen's realism was not felt specifically nor purely in all countries at the same time or in the same manner. Since most dramatic work in Europe was in the Romantic tradition, playwrights varied in immediate acceptance of realistic techniques.

In Ireland, the first effective realistic and poetic plays were the peasant dramas of Lady Gregory and the poet-playwright William Butler Yeats. In order to give Irish playwrights a "home," Lady Gregory and Yeats established the Abbey Theatre. Principal Abbey playwrights were John Millington Synge and, later, Sean O'Casey. The realism of Synge's modern dramas was infused with poetry shaped from Irish colloquial speech, Irish humor, and Celtic romanticism. Synge's realism was not inspired by that of Ibsen; it was unique because his poetic language was slightly elevated and the exhilaration of his characters was based firmly in the traditions of the Irish peasant class. *The Playboy of the Western World* and *Riders to the Sea* rank as two of the finest examples of early twentieth century drama. Synge was a great realist/naturalist with a poetic flair.

Playboy of the Western World by John Millington Synge. Tom Costello and Jennifer Blomfield McLaughlin at The Pioneer Memorial Theatre, The University of Utah. Directed by Marilyn R. Holt. Scenery by Herb Caldwell. Costumes by Callie Floor. National alternate winner, American College Theatre Festival.

In Hungary, Ferenc Molnar wrote several fine plays depicting the contemporary salon life of Budapest and early twentieth century European society. His plays reveal verbal beauty, detailed characterizations, irony, light humor, and romantic plots (his nineteenth century heritage). Chief among his works are *Liliom* (later adapted to the musical, *Carousel*) and *The Guardsman.*

In Russia, Nikolai Gogol introduced Realism to the stage. Gogol's most famous play was a satire on provincial corruption called *The Inspector General.* Although his character delineation was somewhat exaggerated and grotesque, Gogol was notable for having ushered in Realism to Russian drama at a time when other European countries were still struggling with Romanticism and melodrama. Ivan Turgenev (*A Month in the Country*) explored psychological realism further by portraying ordinary men with humor and understanding (Turgenev was actually a precursor of Naturalism). Alexander Ostrovsky's plays (such as *The Thunderstorm*) depicted Russian middle-class life in considerable detail. However, most Russian playwrights of early realistic drama sacrificed subtle characterization for external realism.

The Guardsman by Ferenc Molnar, English version by Frank Marcus. JoAnn Johnson Patton and Jesse Bennett at The Pioneer Memorial Theatre, The University of Utah, and at The Utah Shakespearean Festival. Directed by Fred C. Adams. Scenery by Gary M. McIntyre. Costumes by Barbara C. Cox. Photograph by Robert Clayton.

Overview of Naturalism

In 1873, Emila Zola proposed the first naturalistic doctrine in the preface to his play *Thérèse Raquin.* In his treatise Zola stated his determination to base dramatic work on scientific methods of observation. Zola foresaw man formulating laws of human conduct based on observation, analysis, and classification of facts in a manner similar to that of scientists. *Naturalism* was a philosophical theory dating back to the sixteenth century which proliferated during the early nineteenth century. In Naturalism nature was considered the first principle in the universe, even above God. During the eighteenth century, Rousseau used the term *naturalism* to describe his concept of a "return to nature." In the eighteenth century advocates of the Age of Enlightenment also also used the term as the basis for their spirit of inquiry. By the nineteenth century, Balzac, Flaubert, and the Goncourt brothers were already studying scientific methods. Zola's originality lay in the thoroughness of his scientific documentation and his choice of medical science as the inspiration for his literary work.

Zola's use of Naturalism was in rebellion against the sterotyped formula of morality and rhetoric fostered by the Romantic movement. In order to recapture truth in literature and drama, Zola attacked the conventions restricting the scope of the stage. He wanted to open the eyes of the public to the possibilities in new forms and new subjects. Zola prescribed lifelike scenery, costumes, and methods of acting. With the eye of a scientific observer, Zola wanted segments of life (*tranche de vie* or slice of life) to be represented onstage in exact duplication, as in a photograph. Scenery had to express the inner spirit of the play as well as the external details of its milieu. Action was simplified and lifelike. Characters were psychologically motivated and physiologically correct in appearance and manner. Environment was the primary influence on characters. Naturalistic plays did not present the logic of facts, sensations, or sentiments. For Zola, there was no difference between truth in the theatre and truth in life. Spectators were "invisible" to the actors. Although the public was invited to the theatre, they were required only to "peek through the fourth wall" to watch *life*, not a play. In theory, it was therefore permissable for actors to stand with their backs to the audience and speak with slovenly diction. The correct attitude for naturalistic actors was to *live* the life of the characters on stage rather than to *play* the role. Zola strove to make the vocabulary of language different for each class. Since language had to fit the character and situation, crudity was appropriate in sordid scenes. The total effect of Zola's naturalism was an attempt to reproduce photographic detail on the stage.

Most naturalistic playwrights were preoccupied with human maladies. Among the foremost naturalistic playwrights (in addition to Zola) were Henri Becque (*The Vultures* and *La Parisienne*), Gerhart Hauptmann (*The Weavers*), Arthur Schnitzler (*Anatol* and *La Ronde*), August Strindberg (*Miss Julie* and *The Father*), Anton Chekhov (*The Seagull, The Three Sisters, The Cherry Orchard,* and *Uncle Vanya*), Maxim Gorky (*The Lower Depths*), and Sean O'Casey (*The Plough and the Stars* and *Juno and the Paycock*).

The Lower Depths by Maxim Gorky. Rebecca Nibley as Vasilissa and Victor Love as Vaska Pepel at The University of Wisconsin-Milwaukee. Directed by David Chambers. Scenery by Bob McBroom. Costumes by Maura Smalover. Photograph by Alan Magayne-Roshak.

Contrasting views of *Miss Julie* by August Strindberg. (1) Stephen Schnetzler and Giulia Pagano at The Roundabout Theatre, New York City. Gene Feist and Michael Fried, Producing Directors.

Contrasting views of *Miss Julie* by August Strindberg. (2) JoAnn Johnson Patton as Kristen at The Oregon Shakespearean Festival. Directed by Elizabeth Huddle. Scenery by Richard L. Hay. Costumes by Jeannie Dividson. Lighting by Dirk Epperson. Translation by Jerry Turner. Photograph by Hank Kranzler.

Dissatisfaction with nineteenth-century theatre produced a growth of individual writers, directors, and scenic and lighting designers (electricity was then in use) dedicated to eliminating abuses on the stage—namely, the commercial managerial system, the "staginess" of productions, and the histrionic style of acting with its emphasis on star roles. After 1875, playwrights demanded characterization from actors beyond their technical repertoire. Nineteenth-century acting in the declamatory style was so solidly entrenched in Europe that it inevitably fell to the director and the scenic and lighting designers to nourish the realistic and naturalistic movements. Director André Antoine, founder of the *Théâtre Libre* (Free Theatre) in Paris, was the practical, innovative leader of the naturalistic movement, and Gordon Craig, Aldoph Appia, and Vsevolold Meyerhold were the leaders of innovative scenic and lighting design and staging, albeit much of it was in a non-realistic style (see Chapter 17).

Other new or little theatre movements occurred throughout Europe, paralleling Antoine's objectives (i.e., developing new writers and new acting styles). Otto Brahm's *Freie Buhne* in Germany, J. T. Grein's Independent Theatre in England, Lady Gregory's Abbey Theatre in Ireland, and, above all, Konstantin Stanislavski's Moscow Art Theatre in Russia gave impetus to theatrical experimentation and innovation. Stanislavski developed a system of acting techniques which became the foundation of all modern acting theory.

The evolution of realistic acting continued to vacillate between representational and presentational concepts until the emergence of Stanislavski and his partner Vladimir Nemirovich-Danchenko. Stanislavski's acting system was influenced by the work of the actor Mikhail Shchepkin. Shchepkin discovered that a natural speaking tone resulted in realistic characterization. Together with Gogol, Shchepkin urged actors to identify with the character being portrayed, to take on his identity, and to strive for truth and naturalness in speech and bodily movement. Character believability was further heightened by accurate study of the background of the role. It was Shchepkin who gave Stanislavski the motto for the Moscow Art Theatre: There are no small parts, only small actors. Although the playwrights Ostrovsky and Turgenev continued to develop the realistic style of acting, Stanislavski saw that even in the 1890s, realistic acting was still based on able elocution. During the last decade of the nineteenth century, Stanislavski and Danchenko were influenced by the work of the Duke of Saxe-Meiningen, an innovative German director who is often considered to be the first director in the theatre and notable for his emphasis on natural ensemble acting.

The policies of the Moscow Art Theatre, as described by Stanislavski (the artistic director) and Danchenko (the administrator), focused on the production of plays of distinction by both Russian playwrights and foreign writers and on the subordination of individual acting to the intention of the playwright. Careful attention to detail in scenic design and realistic characterization were prime considerations. A new rehearsal concept in which the cast studied plays in thorough detail, supervised by the director, was established. Rigid discipline was enforced throughout the rehearsal period.

Stanislavski's early efforts at theatre reform were directed against the style of acting noted for its shouting, rapid tempo, and exaggerated gestures and actions. Except for the few attempts at Realism mentioned earlier, theatrical productions prior to this time were notoriously contrived and stereotyped. Repertory offerings included light farcical plays whose only appeal was the Star in the lead role. Stanislavski's primary goals of reform were to discover a more realistic base for acting and to eliminate technical stage abuses. Early productions of the Moscow Art Theatre were more lifelike, perhaps even more realistic, than ordinary Realism—that is, super-realism or Naturalism. Stanislavski was dedicated to photographic duplication. Lighting and sound effects were essential to producing naturalistic sounds such as thunder, rain, wind, and ordinary sounds of daily life (e.g., birds singing, bells ringing, and dogs barking). Sound was used to reveal contrast or to heighten a significant moment. However, scenic detail, three-dimensional settings, and external facts were eventually *ov-er*emphasized.

It was not until he worked on three plays by Maeterlinck (*The Blind, The Interior*, and *The Unbidden Guest*) that Stanislavski began to search for still newer forms of expression. Realizing that impressionist paintings and music usually produced fantastic and imaginative evocations of the mind and heart, he studied the works of modern painters, sculptors, and composers. This knowledge led Stanislavski to repudiate his former dependence on the scene designer. He realized that inner truth could not be achieved merely by the scenic atmosphere of a play. He made the key discovery that emotions and feelings come from the actor and his person.

The tenets of style encompassing Realism and Naturalism are contained within the techniques of acting described by Stanislavski.

In 1909, Stanislavski set down his refined principles of acting, and his acting system became the foundation for all realistic and naturalistic acting of the twentieth century. The most profound question probed by Stanislavski was, How can an actor achieve a creative mood which would favor inspiration?

Voice

Stanislavski did not neglect cultivation of the actor's external techniques. All his actors received vocal training for intonation, inflection, use of pause, and tempo-rhythm. Stanislavski believed that an actor should study singing in order to learn how to use the whole vocal scale. He treated the front of the actor's face as though it were a *masque* with resonators, and he stressed natural speaking using good breathing technique, clear articulation, and excellent projection. He believed in a disciplined vocal instrument and very expressive speech. Simplicity and clarity created precise patterns of speech, rooted in natural movement and emotion. Stanislavski treated *words* as the physical side of action and images in the mind as the psychological side of action. Perhaps the most important contribution Stanislavski made to stage speech was his explanation that there are reasons why characters say words. The actor's task is to make the author's words his own. Thus, dialogue must have purpose if words are to be meaningful and have impact. The actor then uses his craft through intonation, enunciation, and expression to color vocal delivery imaginatively. Stanislavski believed that mechanical memorization ruined believability and created artificial vocal delivery. Stanislavski often said, "Treasure the spoken word." He knew that energetic language and vocal expressiveness stirred emotions. A word becomes a verbal action when the action is motivated by purpose. Therefore, speech influences character and emotion. Stanislavski knew that actors should analyze their speeches in order to deliver them logically and convincingly. He believed that speaking was acting. Stanislavski also knew that verbal action depends upon physical action (which will be discussed later).

Exercise 1   Voice

1. Sing the vocal scale repeatedly until it becomes instinctive. You should be capable of using the scale in a modified manner when speaking as well as when singing.

2. Think of the front of your face as a mask with resonators connecting the mouth and nose. Imagine you are in a canyon calling back and forth to your own echo. Call or sing such expressions as *Helloooooooooo, Farewellllllllll,* and *Where are Youuuuuu.* With conscious effort you should be able to actually feel vibrations in the resonating areas of your face.

3. Study the speeches by Nora and Tusenbach given at the beginning of this chapter. Determine the purpose or motivation for each idea in the speech and, if possible, for each word. When you have determined purpose, deliver the speech using imaginative, colorful intonation, pauses, and natural expressiveness. Finally, permit natural gestures to accompany your vocal delivery.

4. In your own words, paraphrase the ideas contained within the speeches by Nora and Tusenbach at the beginning of this chapter. Improvise the speeches in your own words. Then return to the actual text which should be richer and clearer to you.

Movement

Training the body in movement was an important part of the Stanislavski acting system. His actors worked for complete, graceful control of all physical activity. Stanislavski opposed the artificial mannerisms and mechanical gestures of most of the preceding acting styles. He believed that gestures should relate to inner experience. Stanislavski insisted upon movement that was motivated, honest, and logical. He stressed that actors must practice every day just as must musicians and singers. Both voice and body must be trained to the point at which they instantly express correct, external activity linked to and motivated by inner experience.

The significance of external form and physical detail was directly tied to correct costuming. Stanislavski recognized that costumes and properties were not extraneous or mere support items. They were rather an integral part of character, tied to motivation, action, and emotion.

Onstage, an actor must be physically free, attain muscular control and relaxation, and have limitless concentration.

Stanislavski believed in dance training for actors because he considered it important in increasing physical dexterity of both actors and musical theatre performers. Movement should be simple, vital, and natural. Movement is an actor's most intense means of expression.

An actor's whole physical being represents the character being interpreted. Stanislavski taught that an actor should always be "in character," should not recognize the audience, and should concentrate on producing an ensemble effect in production. Personalization was in effect the foundation for physical activity in the Stanislavski system. That is, after study and practice an actor's person united with the role until they *appeared* to be one and the same. Great art hides art. Stanislavski knew that the organic totality of an actor's personality and physical being was always at work in the art of role creation.

Exercise 2 Movement

1. Relax your body using any of the exercises described in chapters 1, 2, or 3.

2. Select music from Brahms, Debussy, Copeland, Ravel, or Stravinsky and as the music plays interpret the moods and rhythms of the music through improvised movement. In some instances the movement can become modern dance activity.

3. Sit down before a group. Conversationally and naturally relate an interesting personal experience. Animate your story with instinctive natural gestures, particularly of the face, hands, and upper portions of the body. When you have completed the story, discuss the gestures you have used. Listen carefully to any criticism concerning arbitrary, meaningless, or repetitive gestures. Relate another personal story and attempt to use more expressive, artistic, disciplined gestures without losing the natural, spontaneous, inner-motivated behavior.

4. Perform the following series of natural, everyday activities using as many parts of your body as possible to accomplish each task. You need not speak. Concentrate solely upon purposeful activity. Your entire organic being should focus upon your task. When necessary, pantomime the use of objects.

    a. Walk into a room, sit upon a chair, and remove your shoes.

    b. Enter a room, prepare a cold drink, and drink it.

    c. Brush your teeth.

    d. Pick up a newspaper and read it.

    e. Remove your makeup.

    f. Search an entire room for a lost key.

g. Move furniture from one location to another.

h. Put a series of things away on a high shelf.

i. Dance to imaginary kinds of music.

j. Fly a kite in a strong wind.

k. Jump rope; play kickball; play an imaginary game of softball, basketball, or touch football; imagine you are roller-skating or ice-skating.

l. Hold hands and create a chain of movement proceeding all over the room.

5. Sit silently and listen to every sound you can distinguish. Create a movement, walk, dance, or pantomime which reflects the activity and/or mood of the sound which motivates your activity. For example, the ringing of a bell might cause you to hop and tremble with joy or sorrow.

Character and Emotion

In his search to discover the inner truth of human feeling and experience, *Stanislavski urged his actors to personalize and display character motivation and emotion simply and naturally.* In addition to this role creation technique, Stanislavski suggested heavy reliance on intuition. In time, Stanislavski discovered that most of his actors were continuing to "act" rather than to behave naturally. The intuitive method, combined with background material from the play, produced only surface character. The actor was executing the appropriate walk, emotional state, and rhythm of speech, but the depth of true inner character was still missing. It remained for the tremendous influence of Anton Chekhov to bring that deep inner truth to the productions of the Moscow Art Theatre. Chekhov's plays required actors to use an extra dimension in character portrayal. The complexity of the writing demanded that actors seek the truth of their inner life and then

A scene from *The Cherry Orchard* by Anton Chekhov. At the Julliard School, New York. Directed by Alan Schneider. (Photo by Louisa Johnson.)

equalize that reality with their role. In seeking to liberate the deeper individuality of the actor, Stanislavski rose to the task Chekhov presented. Stanislavski helped his actors free their innermost feelings, moods, thoughts, and experiences. As you learned in Part I, one of the best techniques of role creation involves actor personalization. Stanislavski's actors strove to achieve expression of an inner image by awakening the subconscious from which flowed the outer image. The roots of the personalization theory of acting are imbedded in that striving.

One of the first steps in Stanislavski's process of using the actor's person as the foundation for role creation is the technique known as the "Magic If." Stanislavski thought that actors must believe in the possibility of events in their own life before they could believe in events onstage. He saw the value of transforming a character's aim into an actor's aim. An actor says to himself, "If I were the character *in this situation,* what would I do?" Providing the answer to the Magic If enables him to react to the unreal life onstage as if it were real. (Note: Stanislavsky did not say to ask yourself. "What would I do if I were the character?" He said, "If I were the character *in this situation,* what would I do?" The former can lead to artificial "acting"; the latter can lead to present- and future-oriented *activity.*) Stanislavsky's point concerning the Magic If and personalization is clear: always and forever, when you are on stage, you must play yourself. The *person* is at base in any role you play—*your* person.

Stanislavski believed the next step in role creation was to examine the given circumstances of a play including time and place of action, director's interpretation, setting, lighting, and sound effects.

Stanislavski also stressed concentration as the key to dynamic, believable performance onstage (see chapter 2). Concentration leads to truthful, believable, relaxed stage activity, which in turn leads to what Stanislavski called "communion" or interaction with other people. Both physical communion and psychological communion are necessary to accomplish action that is both realistic and naturalistic. (Also see the discussion of concentration and circles of attention in chapter 3, page 24.)

An important aspect of communion involves "adaptation" or adjustment. An actor must overcome many obstacles to achieve his goal, finding ways to adapt or adjust his activity or action to accomplish his goal. He asks himself: What must I do? Why must I do it? and How can I do it? Both personal adaptation and character adaptation are involved in acting. For example, if you are a woman playing a love scene with a man several inches shorter than you, the need for physical adaptation is obvious. The actors and director must find an adjustment to the problem, probably by seating both persons for the love scene. Similar, but more complex, characterization may demand that you sob convulsively. You must find a way to adapt to the demand and accomplish the behavior.

Finally, the actor focuses upon tempo-rhythm in execution of all aspects of a role. Correct speed and varying intensity of activity are identified and rehearsed. The tempo-rhythm is tied to the emotional and mood disposition of both character and actor in conjunction with the speed of speaking and moving.

Stanlislavski knew that the foremost method of expressing the truthful emotional life of a character was through observation, imagination, and use of the senses. An actor recalls and draws attention to each encountered object to discover its living substance. This method is known as affective memory or emotion memory (see chapter 5), a process by which the actor selects emotions from his living experiences analogous to those of his character and utilizes duplication of emotional sensations within the role (again, see chapter 5). Emotion recall leads to inspiration whereby an actor uses the best within himself and carries it onstage. The use of emotion recall varies according to the necessities of a play. In any event, when emotions are created in this manner onstage, they are usually alive and vital. (However, it should be noted that late in his life, Stanislavsky turned away from use of this technique.)

Stanislavski believed in thorough role analysis prior to onstage performance. The tenets of role analysis described in chapter 10 correspond closely to Stanislavski's concept of role analysis. Central to Stanislavski's theory was identifying what he called "the Super-Objective" and "the Through Line of Actions." The Super-Objective was the main idea or final goal of each performance. Some theatre artists call the Super-Objective the "spine" of the role. The Through Line of Actions is a logical mental line running through a role which an actor can trace in his mind. The Through Line of Actions guides the actor toward accomplishment of his Super-Objective. For example, all of the Through Lines of Actions by Willy Loman in *Death of a Salesman* lead to the Super-Objective of winning Biff's love again.

Exercise 3   Character and Emotion

1. The main exercise technique employed by Stanislavski in the practice of his theories focused on improvisation. Define the circumstances before performing actions. In the following, circumstances are defined for you. Using those circumstances, improvise what *you* would do *if* you were in each situation.

    1. You are in a small elevator when it becomes lodged between floors. What do you do?

    2. You arrive at the home of a civic leader on the wrong night for a banquet. What do you do?

    3. You receive word of the death of a beloved family member. What do you do?

    4. You are walking home late at night along a dark street. You think someone is following you. You learn you are in a blind alley. What do you do?

5. You are alone on your first solo flight as a pilot when you learn you have forgotten your maps, your radio is out, and your gas is low. What do you do?

6. You are waiting for a message concerning an operation performed on a beloved family member. What do you do?

7. Listen carefully to all sounds. React to each sound individually.

8. Treat the room as though it were a sunken submarine incapable of surfacing. What do you do?

9. You are in a cell awaiting execution. What do you do?

10. You are a criminal lawyer interrogating a prisoner about a murder. Relate to one another.

11. You are proposing marriage to someone. Relate to one another.

12. You are meeting a blind date. What do you do?

13. You are in a hurry, but you are at the rear of a supermarket line. What do you do?

14. You are waiting to meet a truant officer after having skipped school for a week. What do you do?

15. An alarm wakes you and you discover you are one hour late for an appointment. Establish the correct tempo-rhythm for what you do.

16. You are alone on the beach at sunset. Establish the correct tempo-rhythm for what you do.

2. Review each of the 16 circumstances in #1 above. Define your Super-Objective or spine for each circumstance and state it as a desire using the action

A scene from Nicolai Gogol's *The Inspector General*. Bob Balaban as Ossip at the Hartman Theatre, Stamford, Connecticut. Directed by Byron Ringland; scenery by Peter Harvey; costumes by Dona Granata; lighting by John McLain. (Photo by Dave Robbins.)

verb, "want." For example, "I want to escape the elevator through the small trapdoor in the ceiling."

3. Define a "Through Line of Action" for each of the circumstances in #1 above. For example; (a) I stand on the iron handrail in the elevator; (b) I push open the trapdoor; (c) I pull myself through the tiny trapdoor; (d) I shimmy up the cable to the floor above; (e) I force the door open to the hallway or I pound on the door for help; and so on.

The influence of Stanislavski has been continued through the work of such disciples and pupils as Eugene Vakhtangov, Richard Boleslavsky, Michael Chekhov, Lee Strasberg, Sonia Moore, and many others, particularly actors who study or have studied at the famous Actor's Studio in New York. While attached to the Playwright's Unit of the Actor's Studio in 1976–77, I attended at least two sessions of the Actor's Unit every week. I observed the Stanislavsky/Method coaching techniques and the work of many of our country's better theatre artists, including the late Lee Strasberg, Vivian Nathan, Ellen Burstyn, Eli Wallach, Frank Corsaro, Elizabeth Ashley, Al Pacino, Michael Moriarty, Jacques Levy, Paul Zindell, Salem Ludwig, Charles Gordone, Martin Oltarsh, and others. The approach to Stanislavsky/Method coaching at the Actor's Studio generally follows nine basic steps:

1. The coach starts a session by announcing that it is beginning—an automatic signal for total silence from the observers. A tape recorder is turned on; all sessions are taped. A large clock is always close to the coach; each actor (or actors if working as a team) receive fifty minutes when they work.

2. Total silence prevails as the actor prepares—*whatever* time is needed for relaxing and concentrating is provided (the time used is part of the fifty minutes). The Studio members believe that discipline is essential and the greatest test of it is both the actor's preparation time and the control required by others to observe it.

3. The scene is performed without interruption.

4. The actor speaks first at the conclusion of the scene (no one ever applauds because it would be a violation of rehearsal/coaching principles).

5. The actor explains his goal in selecting the scene; then he explains his specific, single intention for doing the scene that particular time. He explains exactly what he was trying to accomplish.

6. Observers may then comment on what was seen and heard relative to the stated intention.

7. The coach then asks questions.

8. A general discussion ensues.

9. The coach summarizes with a brief critique and advises on what might be followed as a next rehearsal step.

All scenes are done on a voluntary basis by members of the Actor's Studio. An actor may use successive sessions if no other actor volunteers. During my participation, coaches included Lee Strasberg, Vivian Nathan, Ellen Burstyn, Eli Wallach, and Frank Corsaro. Actors usually perform scenes from plays they are preparing for Broadway or other theatres and cities, as well as films and television. (For example, I saw several scenes coached from early work on a musical which later became a major Broadway success, *The Best Little Whorehouse in Texas*.) Actors also select scenes to work on to sharpen their skills between jobs. No actors are students in the usual sense of that word; all are working professionals who use the Studio to investigate, experiment, seek help, and sustain their craft; risks can be taken and mistakes can safely be made. Members are all proven professionals who have been invited into membership or who have auditioned successfully. For example, actor Christopher Walken was *invited* to membership during my time at the Studio. A half dozen or so new members are also added each year from several hundred applications and many auditions. (Note; the Actor's Studio should not be confused with the Strasberg Institute. The latter is a professional training school for students, utilizing standard admission procedures and tuition fees. The Actor's Studio is reserved as a laboratory for the established professional with membership granted solely by audition and/or invitation.)

While Realism and naturalism (and the tenets of Stanislavsky) remain the foundation of most twentieth-century acting styles, a few other important styles remain to be examined.

Suggested Characters and Plays for Scene Work

Ibsen, Henrik

Hedda Gabler, Eilert Lovborg, Judge Brack, Miss Tesman
   Hedda Gabler
Bernick, Mrs. Bernick
   Pillars of Society
Nora Helmer, Torvald, Mrs. Linde
   A Doll's House
Dr. Stockman, Mrs. Stockman
   An Enemy of the People
Mrs. Alving, Oswald
   Ghosts
Gregers, Hialmar, Gina, Hedvig, Old Ekdal
   The Wild Duck

Shaw, George Bernard

Gloria, Valentine
   You Never Can Tell
John Tanner, Ann Whitfield
   Man and Superman
Barbara, Undershaft
   Major Barbara
Dick Dudgeon, Reverend Anderson, Mrs. Anderson
   The Devil's Disciple

Synge, John M.

Maurya, Nora, Cathleen, Bartley
   Riders to the Sea
Christopher, Pegeen
   Playboy of the Western World

O'Casey, Sean

Fluther, Mrs. Gogan, Nora
  The Plough and the Stars
Juno, Joxer, Boyle
  Juno and the Paycock

Turgenev, Ivan

Natalya, Vera, Adam, Alexey
  A Month in the Country

Gogol, Nikolai

Khlestakov, Osip, Anton, Anna, Marya
  The Inspector General

Zola, Emile

Thérèse Raquin, Laurent
  Thérèse Raquin

Chekhov, Anton

Masha, Olga, Irina, Natasha, Kulygin, Vershinin, Tusenbach
  The Three Sisters
Nina, Trigorin, Treplev, Irina
  The Seagull
Madman Renevsky, Lopahin, Anya, Varya, Gaev, Trofimov, Firs
  The Cherry Orchard
Yelena, Sonia, Serebryakov, Uncle Vanya, Ostrov
  Uncle Vanya

Strindberg, August

Miss Julie, Jean
  Mis Julie
Laura, The Captain
  The Father

Gorky, Maxim

Luka, The Baron, The Actor, Satin, Vassilisa, Natasha
  The Lower Depths

Molnar, Ferenc

Liliom
  Liliom
All characters
  The Guardsman

Actor Checklist *Realism and Naturalism*

Voice	Lifelike, more precise articulation and projection in Realism; more vocal pointing used in Realism; emphasis on dialects; unusual use of silence and pauses; conversational mode, but more heightened in Realism; use of full vocal scale; expressive speech; motivated speech; intonation and imaginative coloring.

Movement	Motivated by thoughts, feelings, and speech; total and controlled body response; considerable physical interaction with others; some selective movement imposed in Realism, seemingly none in Naturalism; all stage areas used; all body positions used; totally representational.
Gestures	Related to inner experience; natural and spontaneous; full use of the entire body; lifelike; more selective in Realism.
Pantomimic Dramatization	Costuming and properties integrally related; extremely inventive; detailed in Naturalism; more selective in Realism; lifelike; motivated; closely tied to environment and scenery, especially in Naturalism.
Character	Rooted in inner psychology and believable human emotion; multidimensional; tied to environment, particularly in Naturalism; subjective, internal use of observation, imagination, senses, and personal experience; highly motivated, particularly in Naturalism; Super-Objective clear; ensemble important.
Emotion	Complex; rooted in human psychology; use of affective or emotional memory; motivated; closely tied to physical action and speech; audience identification and empathy strong.
Ideas	Strong social orientation in Realism; strong human orientation in Naturalism; related to experiences in daily living, problems of environment, and heredity.
Language	Lifelike prose; often rich in symbolism and imagery; more selective in Realism.
Mood and Atmosphere	Closely tied to character, situation, and environment; not superimposed for theatrical purposes; mixed and varied; lifelike.
Pace and Tempo	Unusually varied.
Special Techniques	Full use of Stanislavski system: (1) personalization, (2) Magic If, (3) given circumstances, (4) concentration, (5) tempo-rhythm, (6) observation, (7) imagination, (8) the senses: affective memory or emotion memory, (9) role analysis: Super-Objective and Through Line of Actions.

Suggested Readings

Actors Discuss Vakhtangov. Compiled by H. Khersonski, Moscow-Leningrad, 1940.

Antoine, Andre. *Memories of the Theatre Libre.* Translated by Marvin Carlson. Coral Gables, Fla.: University of Miami Press, 1964.

Arvin, Neil E. *Eugene Scribe and the French Theatre, 1815–60.* Cambridge, Mass.: Harvard University Press, 1924.

Buford, W. H. *Chekhov and His Russia.* London: Keegan Paul, 1947.

Carter, Lawson A. *Zola and the Theatre.* New Haven, Conn.: Yale University Press, 1963.

Clark, Barrett, and Freedley, George. *A History of Modern Drama.* New York: Appleton-Century-Crofts, 1947.

Cole, Toby. *Acting: A Handbook of the Stanislavski Method.* New York: Crown Publishers, 1949.

Durbach, Errol. Ed. *Ibsen and the Theatre: The Dramatist in Production.* New York: New York University Press, 1980.

Edwards, Christine. *The Stanislavsky Heritage.* New York: New York University Press, 1965.

Emeljanow, Victor. Ed. *Chekhov: The Critical Heritage.* Boston: Routledge & Keegan Paul, 1981.

Gorchakov, N. M. *The Directorial Lessons of K. S. Stanislavsky.* Moscow: Iskusstvo, 1950.

———. *The Vakhtangov School of Stage Art.* Moscow: 1960. Translated by G. Ivanov-Mumjier.

Hapgood, Elizabeth R., ed. and trsl. *Stanislavsky's Legacy.* New York: Theatre Arts Books, 1958.

Hethman, Robert H. (ed.) *Strasberg at the Actor's Studio.* New York: The Viking Press, 1965.

Hoover, Marjorie. *Alexander Ostrovsky.* Boston: Twayne Publishers, 1981.

Houghton, Norris. *Moscow Rehearsals: An Account of Methods of Production in the Soviet Theatre.* New York: Harcourt Brace Jovanovich, 1936.

———. *Return Engagement: A Postscript to "Moscow Rehearsals."* New York: Holt, Rinehart, and Winston, 1962.

Lavrin, Janko. *Ibsen, an Approach.* New York: Russell & Russell, 1969.

Lewis, Robert. *Method or Madness?* New York: Samuel French, 1958.

Lucas, F. L. *The Drama of Ibsen and Strindberg.* New York: Macmillan Co., 1962.

Magarshack, David. *Chekhov the Dramatist.* New York: Hill and Wang, 1950.

Marowitz, Charles. *The Method as Means.* London: Herbert Jenkins, 1961.

———. *Stanislavsky and the Method.* New York: Citadel Press, 1964.

Melcher, Edith. *Stage Realism in French Between Diderot and Antoine.* Bryn Mawr, Pa.: Bryn Mawr College, 1928.

Moore, Sonia. *The Stanislavski System.* New York: Viking Press, 1974.

Mortensen, Brita, and Downs, Brian. *Strindberg, An Introduction to His Life and Work.* New York: Cambridge University Press, 1949.

Moscow Art Theatre, The. ed., N. Chushkin. Moscow: Iskusstvo, 1955.

Munk, Erica, ed. *Stanislavski and America.* New York: Hill & Wang, 1966.

Norvell, Lee. "Stanislavsky Revisited." *Educational Theatre Journal,* March 1962, pp. 29–37.

Northam, John. *Ibsen's Dramatic Method: 6 Studies of the Prose Dramas.* London: Faber & Faber, Ltd., 1953.

Redgrave, Michael. *The Actors Ways and Means.* London: Heinemann, 1953.

Simmons, Ernest J. *Chekhov, A Biography.* Boston: Little, Brown, 1962.

Simonov, Reuben. *Stanislavsky's Protege: Eugene Vakhtangov.* Transl. by Miriam Goldina. New York: DBS Publications, Inc., 1969.

Slonim, Marc. *Russian Theatre from the Empire to the Soviets.* Cleveland: The World Publishing Company, 1961.

Sondel, Bess S. *Zola's Naturalistic Theory with Particular Reference to the Drama.* Chicago: University of Chicago Libraries, 1939.

Sprigge, Elizabeth. *The Strange Life of August Strindberg.* New York: Macmillan Co., 1949.

Stanislavski, Constantin. *Actor's Handbook,* 1963; *An Actor Prepares,* 1936; *Building a Character,* 1949, *Creating a Role,* 1961; *My Life in Art,* 1952. Translated by Elizabeth R. Hapgood. New York: Theatre Arts Books.

Stein, Jack M. *Richard Wagner and the Synthesis of the Arts.* Detroit: Wayne State University Press, 1960.

Stone, Edward. *What Was Naturalism? Materials for an Answer.* New York: Appleton-Century-Crofts, 1959.

Strindberg, August. *Open Letters to the Intimate Theatre.* Seattle: University of Washington Press, n.d.

Styan, J. L. *Chekhov in Performance: A Commentary on the Major Plays.* London: Cambridge University Press, 1971.

Tammany, Jane Ellert. *Henrik Ibsen's Theatre Aesthetic and Dramatic Art.* New York: Philosophical Library, 1980.

Tennant, P. F. D. *Ibsen's Dramatic Technique.* London: Albert Saifer, 1962.

Valency, Maurice. *The Flower and the Castle.* New York: Macmillan Co., 1963. (About Ibsen and Strindberg.)

Volbach, Walther. *Adolph Appia, Prophet of the Modern Theatre.* Middleton, Conn.: Wesleyan University Press, 1968.

Waxman, S. M. *Antoine and the Theatre Libre.* Cambridge, Mass.: Harvard University Press, 1926.

Weigand, Hermann. *The Modern Ibsen: A Reconstruction.* New York: E. P. Dutton, 1960.

Williams, Raymond. *Drama From Ibsen to Eliot.* London: Chatto & Windus, Ltd., 1952.

Willis, Ronald. "The American Lab Theatre," *Tulane Drama Review,* Fall 1964, pp. 112–16.

Suggested Filmography

1. *Caesar and Cleopatra.* 1945. U.A. Playwright-G. B. Shaw. Director-Gabriel Pascal. With Claude Rains, Vivien Leigh.
2. *A Doll's House.* 1973. Playwright-Henrik Ibsen. Director-Joseph Losey. With Jane Fonda.
3. *An Enemy of the People.* 1978. English. Playwright-Ibsen. Based on the adaptation by Arthur Miller. With Steve McQueen.
4. *Hedda.* 1975. (*From Hedda Gabler.*). Playwright-Ibsen. Director-Trevor Nunn. With Glenda Jackson.
5. *The Inspector General.* 1949. Warners. Playwright-Nikolai Gogol. Director-Henry Koster. With Danny Kaye.
6. *Juno and the Paycock.* 1930. British. Playwright-Sean O'Casey. Director-Alfred Hitchcock.
7. *The Power of Darkness.* 1922. German film. Director-Conrad Wiene. With Players of the Moscow Art Theatre.
8. *Riders to the Sea.* 1935. MGM. Playwright-J. M. Synge. Director-B. D. Hurst.
9. *The Sea Gull.* 1968. Warners. Playwright-Anton Chekhov. Director-Sidney Lumet.
10. *The Three Sisters.* 1970. British. Playwright-Chekhov. Director-Laurence Olivier. With Olivier, Joan Plowright.

The Wild Duck

by *Henrik Ibsen*

from
Act III   *Translated by Frances Archer*

Characters   Gregers Werle, friend of Hialmar Ekdal
Hedvig, daughter of Gina, age 14
Hialmar Ekdal, photographer
Gina, wife to Hialmar

Scene   The sitting room next to a garret in the modest home of Hialmar Ekdal; the
sitting room serves as Hialmar's photographic studio.

Situation   Hialmar Ekdal, a poor retoucher of photographs, lives a happy life with his wife,
Gina, and daughter, Hedvig. However, an old friend, Gregers Werle, enters his
life determined to force Hialmar to drop his romantic illusions and live an ideal
life based on truth. Gregers knows that Hedvig was probably the daughter of
another man (Gregers' own father, in fact). In this scene, Gregers works to gain
the confidence and trust of Hedvig.

GREGERS   Did the wild duck sleep well last night?

HEDVIG   Yes, I think so, thanks.

GREGERS   *(turning towards the garret)* It looks quite different by day from what
it did last night in the moonlight.

HEDVIG   Yes, it changes ever so much. It looks different in the morning and in
the afternoon; and it's different on rainy days from what it is in fine weather.

GREGERS   Have you noticed that?

HEDVIG   Yes, how could I help it?

GREGERS   Are you, too, fond of being in there with the wild duck?

HEDVIG   Yes, when I can manage it——

GREGERS   But I suppose you haven't much spare time; you go to school, no doubt.

HEDVIG   No, not now; father is afraid of my hurting my eyes.

GREGERS   Oh; then he reads with you himself?

HEDVIG   Father has promised to read with me; but he has never had time yet.

GREGERS   Then is there nobody else to give you a little help?

HEDVIG   Yes, there is Mr. Molvik; but he is not always exactly—quite——

GREGERS   Sober?

HEDVIG   Yes, I suppose that's it!

GREGERS   Why, then you must have any amount of time on your hands. And in
there I suppose it is a sort of world by itself?

HEDVIG   Oh, yes, quite. And there are such lots of wonderful things.

GREGERS   Indeed?

HEDVIG   Yes, there are big cupboards full of books; and a great many of the
books have pictures in them.

GREGERS   Aha!

HEDVIG   And there's an old bureau with drawers and flaps, and a big clock with
figures that go out and in. But the clock isn't going now.

GREGERS   So time has come to a standstill in there—in the wild duck's domain.

HEDVIG   Yes. And then there's an old paint-box and things of that sort, and all the books.

GREGERS   And you read the books, I suppose?

HEDVIG   Oh, yes, when I get the chance. Most of them are English though, and I don't understand English. But then I look at the pictures.—There is one great big book called "Harrison's History of London." It must be a hundred years old; and there are such heaps of pictures in it. At the beginning there is Death with an hour-glass and a woman. I think that is horrid. But then there are all the other pictures of churches, and castles, and streets, and great ships sailing on the sea.

GREGERS   But tell me, where did all those wonderful things come from?

HEDVIG   Oh, an old sea captain once lived here, and he brought them home with him. They used to call him "The Flying Dutchman." That was curious, because he wasn't a Dutchman at all.

GREGERS   Was he not?

HEDVIG   No. But at last he was drowned at sea, and so he left all those things behind him.

GREGERS   Tell me now—when you are sitting in there looking at the pictures, don't you wish you could travel and see the real world for yourself?

HEDVIG   Oh, no! I mean always to stay at home and help father and mother.

GREGERS   To retouch photographs?

HEDVIG   No, not only that. I should love above everything to learn to engrave pictures like those in the English books.

GREGERS   H'm. What does your father say to that?

HEDVIG   I don't think father likes it; father is strange about such things. Only think, he talks of my learning basket-making and straw-plaiting! But I don't think that would be much good.

GREGERS   Oh, no, I don't think so either.

HEDVIG   But father was right in saying that if I had learnt basket-making I could have made the new basket for the wild duck.

GREGERS   So you could; and it was you that ought to have done it, wasn't it?

HEDVIG   Yes, for it's my wild duck.

GREGERS   Of course it is.

HEDVIG   Yes, it belongs to me. But I lend it to father and grandfather as often as they please.

GREGERS   Indeed? What do they do with it?

HEDVIG   Oh, they look after it, and build places for it, and so on.

GREGERS   I see; for no doubt the wild duck is by far the most distinguished inhabitant of the garret?

HEDVIG   Yes, indeed she is; for she is a real wild fowl, you know. And then she is so much to be pitied; she has no one to care for, poor thing.

GREGERS   She has no family, as the rabbits have—

HEDVIG   No. The hens, too, many of them, were chickens together; but she has been taken right away from all her friends. And then there is so much that is strange about the wild duck. Nobody knows her, and nobody knows where she came from either.

GREGERS   And she has been down in the depths of the sea.

HEDVIG   (with a quick glance at him, represses a smile and asks) Why do you say "depths of the sea"?

GREGERS   What else should I say?

HEDVIG   You could say "the bottom of the sea."[2]

GREGERS   Oh, mayn't I just as well say the depths of the sea?

HEDVIG   Yes; but it sounds so strange to me when other people speak of the depths of the sea.

GREGERS   Why so? Tell me why?

HEDVIG   No, I won't; it's so stupid.

GREGERS   Oh, no, I am sure it's not. Do tell me why you smiled.

HEDVIG   Well, this is the reason: whenever I come to realize suddenly—in a flash—what is in there, it always seems to me that the whole room and everything in it should be called "the depths of the sea."—But that is so stupid.

GREGERS   You mustn't say that.

HEDVIG   Oh, yes, for you know it is only a garret.

GREGERS *(looks fixedly at her)*   Are you so sure of that?

HEDVIG *(astonished)*   That it's a garret?

GREGERS   Are you quite certain of it?

(HEDVIG *is silent, and looks at him open-mouthed.* GINA *comes in from the kitchen with the table things.*)

GREGERS *(rising)*   I have come in upon you too early.

GINA   Oh, you must be somewhere; and we're nearly ready now, anyway. Clear the table, Hedvig.

(HEDVIG *clears away her things; she and* GINA *lay the cloth during what follows.* GREGERS *seats himself in the armchair and turns over an album.*)

GREGERS   I hear you can retouch, Mrs. Ekdal.

GINA *(with a side glance)*   Yes, I can.

GREGERS   That was exceedingly lucky.

GINA   How—lucky?

GREGERS   Since Ekdal took to photography, I mean.

HEDVIG   Mother can take photographs, too.

GINA   Oh, yes; I was bound to learn that.

GREGERS   So it is really you that carry on the business, I suppose?

GINA   Yes, when Ekdal hasn't time himself——

GREGERS   He is a great deal taken up with his old father, I daresay.

GINA   Yes; and then you can't expect a man like Ekdal to do nothing but take pictures of Dick, Tom, and Harry.

GREGERS   I quite agree with you; but having once gone in for the thing——

GINA   You can surely understand, Mr. Werle, that Ekdal's not like one of your common photographers.

GREGERS   Of course not; but still——

(*A shot is fired within the garret.*)

GREGERS *(starting up)*   What's that?

GINA   Ugh! now they're firing again!

2. Gregers here uses the old-fashioned expression "havsens bund," while Hedvig would have him use the more commonplace "havets bund" or "havbunden." [Translator's note.]

GREGERS   Have they firearms in there?

HEDVIG   They are out shooting.

GREGERS   What! *(at the door of the garret)* Are you shooting, Hialmar?

HIALMAR *(inside the net)*   Are you there? I didn't know; I was so taken up——
   (to HEDVIG) Why did you not let us know? *(comes into the studio)*

GREGERS   Do you go shooting in the garret?

HIALMAR *(showing a double-barrelled pistol)*   Oh, only with this thing.

GINA   Yes, you and grandfather will do yourselves a mischief some day with that
   there pigstol.

HIALMAR *(with irritation)*   I believe I have told you that this kind of firearm is
   called a pistol.

GINA   Oh, that doesn't make it much better, that I can see.

GREGERS   So you have become a sportsman, too, Hialmar?

HIALMAR   Only a little rabbit-shooting now and then. Mostly to please father,
   you understand.

GINA   Men are strange beings; they must always have something to pervert
   theirselves with.

HIALMAR *(snappishly)*   Just so; we must always have something to divert
   ourselves with.

GINA   Yes, that's just what I say.

HIALMAR   H'm. *(to* GREGERS) You see the garret is fortunately so situated that no
   one can hear us shooting. *(lays the pistol on the top shelf of the bookcase)*
   Don't touch the pistol, Hedvig! One of the barrels is loaded; remember that.

GREGERS *(looking through the net)*   You have a fowling-piece, too, I see.

HIALMAR   That is father's old gun. It's no use now; something has gone wrong
   with the lock. But it's fun to have it all the same; for we can take it to pieces
   now and then, and clean and grease it, and screw it together again.—Of
   course, it's mostly father that fiddle-faddles with all that sort of thing.

HEDVIG *(beside* GREGERS)   Now you can see the wild duck properly.

GREGERS   I was just looking at her. One of her wings seems to me to droop a bit.

HEDVIG   Well, no wonder; her wing was broken, you know.

GREGERS   And she trails one foot a little. Isn't that so?

HIALMAR   Perhaps a very little bit.

HEDVIG   Yes, it was by that foot the dog took hold of her.

HIALMAR   But otherwise she hasn't the least thing the matter with her; and that
   is simply marvellous for a creature that has a charge of shot in her body and
   has been between a dog's teeth——

GREGERS *(with a glance at* HEDVIG)   ——and that has lain in the depths of the
   sea—so long.

HEDVIG *(smiling)*   Yes.

GINA *(laying the table)*   That blessed wild duck! What a lot of fuss you do make
   over her.

HIALMAR   H'm;—will lunch soon be ready?

GINA   Yes, directly. Hedvig, you must come and help me now. (GINA *and* HEDVIG
   go out into the kitchen.)

(END)

Scene from *The Wild Duck* by Henrik Ibsen. Directed by Robert Loper. Designed by Wendell Cole. Stanford University. (Pat Crawford as Hedvig; Jerry L. Crawford as Old Ekdal; David O'Brien as Hailmar.)

The Three Sisters by Anton Chekhov. At The University of Wisconsin-Milwaukee. Directed by Jewel Walker. Scenery by R. H. Graham. Costumes by Maura Smalover. Photograph by Alan Magayne-Roshak.

The Three Sisters

by *Anton Chekhov*

Translated by Constance Garnett

*from
Act III*

Characters

Irina, the youngest sister, 24
Olga, the eldest sister, a schoolteacher, 28
Masha, the middle sister, married to Kuligin, a schoolmaster, but in love with
    Vershinin, a married army colonel
Andrey, brother to the three sisters
Natasha, domineering wife to Andrey
Ferapont, an old servant

Scene

An upstairs bedroom of Olga and Irina, in the Prozoroff home in the Russian
provinces, far from Moscow.

Situation

Over a year after their father's death, three sisters live their days without purpose,
longing to return to their childhood home and happiness in Moscow. Weary and
alone as a fire rages in the town, the sisters express the tortures of their existence
and confess their desires and problems.

IRINA   Yes, how petty our Andrey has grown, how dull and old he has become
    beside that woman! At one time he was working to get a professorship and
    yesterday he was boasting of having succeeded at last in becoming a member
    of the Rural Board. He is a member, and Protopopov is chairman. . . . The
    whole town is laughing and talking of it and he is the only one who sees and
    knows nothing. . . . And here everyone has been running to the fire while he
    sits still in his room and takes no notice. He does nothing but play his
    violin . . . *(nervously)*. Oh, it's awful, awful, awful! *(Weeps)*. I can't bear it
    any more, I can't! I can't, I can't!

*(*OLGA *comes in and begins tidying up her table.)*

IRINA *(sobs loudly)*   Turn me out, turn me out, I can't bear it any more!
OLGA *(alarmed)*   What is it? What is it, darling?
IRINA *(sobbing)*   Where? Where has it all gone? Where is it? Oh, my God, my
    God! I have forgotten everything, everything . . . everything is in a tangle in
    my mind. . . . I don't remember the Italian for window or ceiling . . . I am
    forgetting everything; every day I forget something more and life is slipping
    away and will never come back, we shall never, never go to Moscow. . . . I see
    that we shan't go. . . .
OLGA   Darling, darling. . . .
IRINA *(restraining herself)*   Oh, I am wretched. . . . I can't work, I am not going
    to work. I have had enough of it, enough of it! I have been a telegraph clerk
    and now I have a job in the town council and I hate and despise every bit of
    the work they give me. . . . I am nearly twenty-four, I have been working for
    years, my brains are drying up, I am getting thin and old and ugly and there is
    nothing, nothing, not the slightest satisfaction, and time is passing and one
    feels that one is moving away from a real, fine life, moving farther and farther

away and being drawn into the depths. I am in despair and I don't know how it is I am alive and have not killed myself yet. . . .

OLGA   Don't cry, my child, don't cry. It makes me miserable.

IRINA   I am not crying, I am not crying. . . . It's over. . . . There, I am not crying now. I won't . . . I won't.

OLGA   Darling, I am speaking to you as a sister, as a friend, if you care for my advice, marry the baron!

(IRINA *weeps.*)

OLGA (*softly*)   You know you respect him, you think highly of him. . . . It's true he is ugly, but he is such a thoroughly nice man, so good. . . . One doesn't marry for love, but to do one's duty. . . . That's what I think, anyway, and I would marry without love. Whoever proposed to me I would marry him, if only he were a good man. . . . I would even marry an old man. . . .

IRINA   I kept expecting we should move to Moscow and there I should meet my real one. I've been dreaming of him, loving him. . . . But it seems that was all nonsense, nonsense. . . .

OLGA (*puts her arms round her sister*)   My darling, lovely sister, I understand it all; when the baron left the army and came to us in a plain coat, I thought he looked so ugly that it positively made me cry. . . . He asked me, "Why are you crying?" How could I tell him! But if God brought you together I should be happy. That's a different thing, you know, quite different.

(NATASHA *with a candle in her hand walks across the stage from door on right to door on left without speaking.*)

MASHA (*sits up*)   She walks about as though it were she had set fire to the town.

OLGA   Masha, you are silly. The very silliest of the family, that's you. Please forgive me (*a pause*).

MASHA   I want to confess my sins, dear sisters. My soul is yearning. I am going to confess to you and never again to anyone. . . . I'll tell you this minute (*softly*). It's my secret, but you must know everything. . . . I can't be silent . . . (*a pause*). I am in love, I am in love. . . . I love that man. . . . You have just seen him. . . . Well, I may as well say it straight out. I love Vershinin.

OLGA (*going behind her screen*)   Leave off. I don't hear anyway.

MASHA   But what am I to do? (*Clutches her head.*) At first I thought him queer . . . then I was sorry for him . . . then I came to love him . . . to love him with his voice, his words, his misfortunes, his two little girls. . . .

OLGA (*behind the screen*)   I don't hear you anyway. Whatever silly things you say I shan't hear them.

MASHA   Oh, Olya, you are silly. I love him—so that's my fate. It means that that's my lot. . . . And he loves me. . . . It's all dreadful. Yes? Is it wrong? (*Takes* IRINA *by the hand and draws her to herself.*) Oh, my darling. . . . How are we going to live our lives, what will become of us? . . . When one reads a novel it all seems stale and easy to understand, but when you are in love yourself you see that no one knows anything and we all have to settle things for ourselves. . . . My darling, my sister. . . . I have confessed it to you, now I'll hold my tongue. . . . I'll be like Gogol's madman . . . silence . . . silence. . . .

(*Enter* ANDREY *and after him* FERAPONT.)

ANDREY (*angrily*)   What do you want? I can't make it out.

FERAPONT (*in the doorway, impatiently*)   I've told you ten times already, Andrey Sergeyevitch.

ANDREY   In the first place I am not Andrey Sergeyevitch, but your honour, to you!

FERAPONT   The firemen ask leave, your honour, to go through the garden on their way to the river. Or else they have to go round and round, an awful nuisance for them.

ANDREY   Very good. Tell them, very good. (FERAPONT *goes out*). I am sick of them. Where is Olga? (OLGA *comes from behind the screen*.) I've come to ask you for the key of the cupboard, I have lost mine. You've got one, it's a little key.

(OLGA *gives him the key in silence*; IRINA *goes behind her screen; a pause*.)

ANDREY   What a tremendous fire! Now it's begun to die down. Hang it all, that Ferapont made me so cross I said something silly to him. Your honour . . . (*a pause*). Why don't you speak, Olya? (*a pause*) It's time to drop this foolishness and sulking all about nothing. . . . You are here, Masha, and you too, Irina—very well, then, let us have things out thoroughly, once for all. What have you against me? What is it?

OLGA   Leave off, Andryusha. Let us talk to-morrow (*nervously*). What an agonising night!

ANDREY (*greatly confused*)   Don't excite yourself. I ask you quite coolly, what have you against me? Tell me straight out.

(VERSHININ'S *voice*: "Tram-tam-tam!")

MASHA (*standing up, loudly*)   Tra-ta-ta! (*To* OLGA) Good night, Olya, God bless you . . . (*Goes behind the screen and kisses* IRINA.) Sleep well. . . . Good night, Andrey. You'd better leave them now, they are tired out . . . you can go into things to-morrow (*goes out*).

OLGA   Yes, really, Andryusha, let us put it off till tomorrow . . . (*goes behind her screen*). It's time we were in bed.

(*END*)

The Three Sisters by Anton Chekhov. Monique Morgan as Masha, Deborah Eckols as Olga, and Suzanne Leslie Stark as Irina at The Hilberry Theatre, Wayne State University. Translation by Tyrone Guthrie and Leonid Kipnis. Directed by N. Joseph Calarco. Scenery by Elizabeth Anne Roush. Costumes by Helen Markovitch. Lighting by James A. Hatfield.

17 Early Twentieth-Century Nonrealism

Distortion—A New Reality

Scene: The steward's box of velodrome during a bicycle race. Jewish gentlemen, stewards, come and go. They are all alike; little animated figures in dinner jackets, with silk hats tilted back and binoculars slung in leather cases. Whistling, catcalls and a restless hum from the crowded tiers of spectators unseen, off right. Music. All the action takes place on the platform.

Stage Direction   Scene Five *From Morn to Midnight* by George Kaiser

If life is a dream, then a drama is a dream of dream, even though you have employed it as reality.

Instructor   *The Isle of the Dead* by August Strindberg

Because Realism and Naturalism were so entrenched, rebellion by certain playwrights and poets who believed that the theatre should reflect abstract and intangible values finally occurred. These artists rejected science as a valuable life force. The symbolists lead a late nineteenth century nonrealistic movement in the theatre and, in the early twentieth century, the Expressionists also forged a nonrealistic trail. (See working explanations of Symbolism and Expressionism on pages *308-309* and pages *309-313*.) While pure Expressionist plays are rarely performed today, their influence in terms of playwriting, design, and acting has remained strong in the theatre during the twentieth century. It is important for an actor to study the Expressionist acting style as preparation for work in such acting styles as Epic (chapter 18), Absurd (chapter 19), and Eclectic (chapter 20).

Overview of Nonrealism

I am especially indebted to Linda McCollum for her contributions to Chapters 17, 18, and 19. By 1900, the naturalistic movement had reached its peak and gave way to nonrealistic forms and styles. Many European playwrights turned away from Realism and Naturalism and adopted techniques of symbolic and nonrealistic drama. In his later years, Ibsen wrote plays such as *The Master Builder, Rosmersholm, John Gabriel Borkman,* and *When We Dead Awaken* which used symbols and abstractions in an integral way. Gerhart Hauptmann, from Germany, turned from Naturalism (*The Weavers*) to Symbolism. Hauptmann's *The Sunken Bell* is a highly successful play in the symbolic style. Strindberg abandoned Realism around the turn of the century. Although his later plays were forerunners of Eclecticism (see chapter 20) in which at least three styles—Realism, Naturalism, and Expressionism— were combined, Strindberg's later dramatic work utilized Expressionistic techniques.

Maurice Maeterlinck, from Belgium, favored symbolistic technique in all of his plays. *The Intruder, The Blind, The Blue Bird,* and *Pelléas and Melisande* are his best-known works. Maeterlinck espoused the belief that most dramatic moments onstage should be static and silent, with thought, introspection, mystery, and intuition revealing the secrets of existence. His plays are famous for sound interspersed with silence, frequent vocal repetition, and dreamlike color combinations in lighting. The plots and characters in Maeterlinck's plays are not based on realistic circumstances. His characters live on another plane—on a mystical level where they communicate with a "higher world." In a world beyond reality, characters appear to move through a dream in which personification and symbolism take precedence.

It is tempting if not totally accurate to think of Maeterlinck as a kind of Impressionistic dramatist in the tradition of Impressionistic painting. That is, as an example, the artist Renoir painted people and nature with a gentle stroke, slightly blurred at the edges, as though life had been caught in a static reflection, remembered as a soft and gentle impression left lingering in the mind and senses. (See Renoir's famous painting of *Monet Working in His Garden in Argenteuil*, 1873.) Plays by Maeterlinck contain this same feeling of a gentle, slightly blurred, static quality (see *Pelleas and Melisande*).

During the 1890s, Alfred Jarry, from France, wrote *Ubu Roi*, a play that had far-reaching impact on playwrights of the twentieth century. Because of his extreme dependency on Symbolism and caricature distortion, Jarry was in a sense an early Surrealist and Absurdist[1] (absurd drama is discussed in chapter 19).

The Symbolists reacted violently against the popular notion of a writer's scientific duty to propound social problems in political terms. The basic tenet of Symbolism stresses the autonomy of art, measured entirely in terms of aesthetic standards. Authors used symbols to transcend what was normally considered "realistic" in everyday life. They hoped that the symbols would take them beyond the truth which heretofore had been expressed only directly and explicitly (as in Realism). Characters were created in poetic terms. Ideas were expressed in sophisticated form and term, as opposed to the naturalistic simplicity of, for example, Maxim Gorky. Note that while Gorky also deploys symbols in his play, *The Lower Depths,* and Chekhov does the same in his naturalistic plays, the form, structure, environment, and characters are very life-like in essence and behavior, unlike that of the Symbolists (e.g., Maeterlinck as an example) who rather created an abstract rather than a real world. Symbolists firmly believed that literature should not be used as a weapon for social reform. (Conversely, most Expressionists desired social reform.)

The Symbolists delved deeply into the world of the subconscious mind. Existence of the subconscious human mind has been thought probable since ancient times. In explaining the subconscious, ancient men spoke of Pandora's box. According to this legend, the god Mercury left a box in the cave of Pandora with a warning not to open it. Curiosity got the better of Pandora. She opened the box and allowed all the evils and sufferings of the world to escape. According to mythology, if forces of the subconscious mind were given free expression, universal chaos would result.

However, there is another aspect of subconsciousness. Pandora's box also contained the spirit of hope which sustains and uplifts mankind. The

---

1. In 1917 a movement known as Dadaism (*dada* means "hobby horse" in French) proposed to free the plastic and graphic arts, as well as the verbal arts, from traditional ways of seeing and feeling. The Dadaists took their lead from the nihilistic works of Tzaraz. The work was political, revealing disillusion with World War I, traditional conventions and aesthetics. Dada stresses the unpredictable. Dadaism was followed in the 1920s by a movement called Surrealism. Its leader, Guillaume Apollinaire, coined the term *Surrealism* in the preface to his play *The Breasts of Tiresias* (subtitled "Drama Surrealisti"). Dadaism and Surrealism promised to free the mind of rational control by exposing the subconscious mind of man. The literature and plays provided audiences with vague scenery, fragmentary and unmotivated characters, minimal conscious activity, disjointed events, and in general a chaotic universe. These philosophical forerunners of the Absurd movement preached a new psychology based on combining the dreaming state with the waking state. The goal was to find a new reality, a kind of *sur* ("above") reality.

subconscious is a reservoir of individual and collective wisdom, just as Pandora's box promised "all gifts" to those who possessed it. It is possible to take all that we have seen and heard from our subconsciousness and bring it into harmony with our consciousness (see discussion of dormant emotion and experience in chapter 5, page 45.)

The most direct knowledge of subconsciousness comes from the study of dreams. Symbolists and other nonrealists of the twentieth century were particularly influenced by dreams. Although Sigmund Freud provided the definitive modern analysis of dreams in the nineteenth century, the ancients also recognized the power of the subconscious mind. Alexander the Great was always accompanied by men versed in dream interpretation. On the night before he lay siege to the city of Tyre, he dreamed of a satyr dancing in victorious triumph. The sages foretold that Alexander would take the city, and Tyre fell before the Macedonians as was predicted.

Artemidorus lived during the time of Emperor Hadrian (A.D. 76–138). His theory of dreams was modern in tone. According to Artemidorus, a dream "happens in that instant when the affections are so vehement that they ascend up to the brain during our sleep and meet with the more watchful spirits." Thus, Artemidorus recognized the presence of conflict in dreams, anticipating Freud's modern theories.

Prior to Artemidorus, Plato stated, "In all of us, even in good men, there is a lawless, wild beast nature, which peers out in sleep."

A fourth-century writer, Synesius of Cyrene, emphasized a value in dreaming beyond that of providing a safety value for man's animal nature. He remarked, "We do not sleep merely to live, but to learn to live well."

When we sleep, we escape from the outer world. Dreaming proves that while we sleep our mind is active. Our mind reacts in a specific way while we sleep. It creates strange events from both reality and fantasy. Although we forget most dreams soon after waking, other dreams remain with us for a long time.

Freud's psychological theory of dreams focused on wish fulfillment, that is, a wish appearing in a dream travels from the subconscious mind (i.e., the *id*) to the conscious mind (i.e., the *ego*). Since the id constantly demands satisfaction from the ego in terms of fulfilling its wishes, a dream often presents a conflict situation. Since the subconscious operates differently from the conscious, perception of the subconscious alters perception of the conscious and distortion in the conscious mind arises. Material is condensed and displaced in illogical patterns and structures.

Expressionism was and remains a loosely used term, and confusion often arises as to what exactly the term means. Expressionism had its roots in a German political movement. It was philosophically oriented against mass industrialization and dehumanized mechanization. Its predominate methodology was to transform nature rather than imitate it. The result of the transformation was often distortion. Thus, robots replace people in *R.U.R.* by Josef and Karel Capek. Expressionism as a movement began with artists such as Edvard Munch and Oskar Kokoschka. As early as 1892 Munch was on exhibit in Germany as a leading Expressionist. Kokoschka would follow suit early in the 1900s, before turning to landscape work. Kokoschka also wrote plays of political importance. These artists turned observed reality to distorted reality in order to make both political and social points. Their art was not merely an imitation of reality, but a transformation of it.

In literature, Franz Kafka and James Joyce developed a style of Expressionism through the technique of "stream of consciousness" writing. The Expressionists, like the Cubists in art, tried to depict a conceptualization of the mind's total understanding of what it grasps. Cubism is the total understanding of the two-dimensional plane. Expressionists in theatre attempt this when they show how a simple object may take on gigantic proportions because the viewer sees it as such (e.g., Mr. Zero's view of the adding machine and the Judge's stand in Elmer Rice's *The Adding Machine*).

Dramatic artists became increasingly disenchanted with scientific study of man and his environment. Since the material of science must have a cultural base to give it human significance, many German writers perceived man and his value system as a reflection of a mechanical, contrived, stifling, intellectually oppressive society. Georg Kaiser was a leader in Germany's influential Expressionistic drama. (See *From Morn to Midnight*, *Gas I*, *Gas II*, and *The Coral*.) As noted earlier, the Swedish playwright Strindberg was one of the first major authors to traverse the confines of Naturalism by exploring symbolistic and expressionistic techniques in several of his later plays. In the preface to his *A Dream Play*, written in 1911, Strindberg said he wanted to follow the pattern of dreams in which anything

Scene from *A Dream Play* by August Strindberg. Directed by Philip Benson. Scenery designed by Thad Torp. Scenic projections by Hal Howe. Lighting design by David Thayer. Costumes by Margaret Hall. The University of Iowa.

seemed possible, in which time and space had no reality. In other words, he began to explore the subconscious mind through the forces of the conscious mind in the Freudian tradition. Strindberg believed that by using imagination in combination with memory, fantasy, absurdity, and improvisation a dramatist could create new patterns of existence. Characterization was not to be based in reality. Instead, characters split, doubled and multiplied, vanished and reappeared in a dramatic structure held together by the consciousness of the Dreamer (i.e., the central character who often represented the author). Strindberg advocated a new dramatic form based on artistic subjectivity as opposed to Naturalism which was based on objectivity. Strindberg's dream world was also created from an imaginative "soul." His characters were never fixed, and changed according to his subjective, introspective whims. Strindberg was devoted to interpreting life using spiritual methods and to discovering the secrets of the subconscious mind. His most famous plays utilized the transformation techniques of Expressionistic concepts (e.g., see *To Damascus* (a trilogy), *A Dream Play*, and *The Ghost Sonata*—all variations on the mind of a dreamer).

In Expressionism fantasy and symbolism are combined, as well as fragments of Realism and Naturalism (as do the dream sequences of the human mind). A playwright's subjectivity is necessarily affected by his emotional, political, philosophical, and aesthetic experiences which in turn affect his view of the world. Hence, distortion in stage conceptualization occurs. Characters are more or less representative of states of mind, comparable to dreams, deliriums, or opinions, in which appearance, time, and space lose continuity. A playwright, then, "objectifies the subjective"—that is, he puts onstage the happenings inside the head, in the mind. Because in expressionistic plays fantasy and reality alternate in remarkable elusiveness, characters *at times* appear to be robots or dream figures and at other times to be real (the appearance of robotlike characters are reflections of a mechanized society). In expressionistic plays, people are usually not bound by traditions of duty, morality, society, or family. Man is not represented as an individual nor classified in a specific role. Characters often have generalized names such as Mother, Worker, and so on. The playwright transcends the individual to reveal all of mankind, or the playwright emphasizes human values and polarizes an individual at odds with a collective entity (see German Expressionism). Expressionism was consciously primitive and simplified in order to penetrate man's universality.

Expressionism and its techniques as applied to art spread throughout central Europe and beyond after 1912. In utilizing expressionistic techniques, playwrights aligned themselves with contemporary painters such as Munch and Kokoschka, as well as Emile Nolde, and Paul Klee. In music, Expressionism was fostered by such composers as Arnold Schoenberg and Alban Berg. Following a war with France (Franco-Prussian War) and facing the probability of another war, artists (of theatre, music, literature, and art) experienced the afteraffects of revolt on social and political values. In addition to Kaiser, several great expressionistic playwrights emerged, such as Walter Hasenclever (*The Son, The Seduction*), Ernst Toller (*Man and the Masses*), Franz Wedekind (*Spring's Awakening*), and the Capek brothers, Josef and Karel (*R.U.R., The World We Live In* or *The Insect Comedy*). By using fluid scenes, condensation of reality, situations and characters abstracted by symbolism, intensified distortion, illogical patterns, and lyricism, these authors wrote Expressionist plays. Generally, language was compressed into a staccato or telegram style. Juxtaposed against these abstractions was occasional interpolation of long monologues. Continuity of action was lost in dream sequences.

Some expressionistic plays have one or two acts with large numbers of scenes, and in other plays acts are missing altogether in favor of many scenes or tableaux. Sometimes physical action in expressionistic plays is so dominant that language becomes unnecessary (when this occurs, the actor must focus on pantomimic dramatization).

In many plays women and men were social equals. A woman served as a comrade or friend to a man. She loved with complete understanding. To the Expressionist, love was absolute, a way to escape the restrictions and compromises of the world. Sexual passion was not usually a major theme. Since Expressionism depicted the worthiness of mankind, characters were drawn with pathos. They also had a definite social point of view which usually represented the view of the author.

Expressionistic plays require kaleidoscopic outdoor and indoor settings. Scenic units and props are symbolic. For example, in *A Dream Play* note the scenic transformation of the flower bud on the roof which opens into a gigantic chrysanthemum (usually accomplished onstage by lighting or slide projection). Settings are used to support the main thought of the play. For example, in *Gas I* and *Gas II* by George Kaiser, spacious concrete domes with massive girders and wire apparatus, fanning out from a central platform, suggest the functional industrial architecture of an age of mass production and mechanization. Little or no naturalistic detail is included. Light and shadow contrast frequently to create spectacle (i.e., to create visual wonder and excitement). Music and sound effects are integrated much like music and sound in a film. A "total theatre" approach is used—that is, balanced integration of all theatrical elements.

As the twentieth century began, Stanislavski's system was the dominate acting style. He had opened his studio workshop in 1905 and invited Meyerhold back to experiment with nonrealistic styles, realizing that one approach could not work for every play. Stanislavsky became interested in Hindu philosophy, especially the Toga system of abstract meditation and mental concentration. At the end of 1914, Stanislavski explored further the sphere of the subconscious to discover other methods of stimulating activity. He subsequently conceptualized and wrote his theory of emotion memory. Meyerhold helped "modernize" Stanislavski's style of acting. Uncomfortable with a theatre designed to mirror life, Meyerhold advocated a presentational theatre experience whereby actors and audiences encountered one another with mutual recognition. Meyerhold labeled his acting theories "biomechanics" (see discussion that follows).

Fantastic and imaginative costume designs for *The Insect Comedy* by Josef and Karel Capek. "Lisping Snails!" (Moon snails provided the inspiration for this design by Ellis M. Pryce-Jones.)

To perform expressionistic drama, approach your interpretation of character with the techniques of Stanislavski in order to provide a human base. However, when the human elements of character give way to nonrealistic and dehumanized elements, Meyerhold's technique of biomechanics may be used to great advantage. Biomechanics was an idea focused on efficiency and economy of means. Finding new forms in an industrial society resulted in the external reflex action of biomechanics. The economic necessities in Russia after the revolution resulted in the inexpensive scenic design known as constructivism (see Glossary). On such a set, movement became superior to speech in that "gesture" could often communicate more than dialogue. (Meyerhold was particularly famous for staging a Lovborg-Hedda scene in Ibsen's *Hedda Gabler* in which Meyerhold used a hot, flaming punch rather than a cold liquid to help depict the "fire" and intensity of Hedda in the scene, thereby revealing the action better than through mere dialogue.) Biomechanics were kinetic and often mechanical, utilizing gymnastics, circus movement, ballet, dance, and acrobatics. Such mechanics were usually superimposed upon the actor by a strong director. Meyerhold believed that such activity could best be performed on platforms, ramps, trapezes, cylinders, and scaffolding (e.g., the "constructivism" noted above).

However, there is far more to biomechanics than mere gynmastics and dance. With proper training, the external reflex action can trigger emotional/psychological states in actors with a new efficiency and economy— reflective of a new society.

The acting style was highly theatrical and for the most part in a new direction from the work of Meyerhold's mentor, Stanislavsky. Meyerhold rejected psychological Realism in favor of the science of biomechanics. He believed that movement was superior to speech. He also borrowed heavily from Oriental acting style and staging techniques (Oriental acting is discussed in chapter 18 and in Appendix E, page 491.) Under Meyerhold, actors studied in three phases: a period of movement, a static period of posing, and a so-called realistic period related to lifelike mimicry. Meyerhold was devoted to grotesque satire. Despite this devotion, he retained some of the influence of Stanislavski in his actor coaching, allowing truthful human feeling to be expressed when needed.

Voice

Although three major nonrealistic styles are discussed in this chapter (Symbolism, Expressionism, and biomechanics), the major focus is on Expressionism because it was most influential on the work of the twentieth century.

Vocal work in symbolist drama primarily utilizes the tenets of Stanislavski and Realism, with heightened use of silence and static intonation. Also, in some passages in symbolic plays poetic lyricism is necessary.

The dialogue in expressionistic plays modulates between realistic language, nonrealistic, staccato language, and lengthy, at times, poetic monologue (poetic in imagery though usually written in prose).

The key quality of expressionistic language is its clipped repartee mixed with staccato sounds. Generally, linguistic or literary conventions are disregarded and the language is concise and direct. Articles are often omitted, verbs are usually separated and forged into strange union, and nouns are frequently arranged in a series of lines. Alliteration is used abundantly, and continuous repetition of one sound is frequent. Crescendos heighten the impact of theme. As a result, your speaking is rhythmic and intense, rather than natural and fluid. When the script calls for dehumanized behavior, you may chant and intone or shout and bark to produce noise rather than words. Vocal sounds and noise have direct emotional impact on other characters and the audience. You may lapse into spiritual ecstasy; suddenly you may burst into wild screaming. For example, in the plays of the German playwright Hasenclever wild noise in combination with telegram-style language is often used. At times the sound is just short of a yell, other times it is a lyrically ecstatic cry, or it may be simply a wild, piercing yell. Verse is frequently used to increase the emotional intensity of the play and to heighten the mysticism and the imagination of both participant and viewer. The playwright often creates fables in order to transcend the material world and enter the realm of the imagination. For example, people become robots or insects.

To deliver expressionistic language you need wide vocal range, flexible vocal quality, and varied vocal rhythmic patterns. The staccato or vocal telegram segments require exceptional vocal clarity, breath control, and emotional intensity. Rhythmic variety and control are equally important to all your vocal and physical work in this style, especially in the robot and dream segments.

Exercise 1 Voice—Early Twentieth-Century Nonrealism

1. Practice the following speech aloud. In the speech staccato, expressionistic dialogue is emphasized, with articles omitted, words separated by dashes—all in a machine-gun-like manner. The effect should be somewhat mechanical and dehumanized.

This Lady from Florence—who claims to come from Florence—has a vision like that ever visited you in your cage before? Furs—perfume! The fragrance lingers—you breathe adventure. Superbly staged. Italy . . . enchantment—fairy-tale—Riviera—Mentone—Prodighera—Nice—Monte Carlo—where oranges blossom, fraud blooms too.

Scene One *From Morn to Midnight* Georg Kaiser

The two passages in Exercise 1 are from *From Morn to Midnight* by Georg Kaiser. In *Introduction to Drama* edited by Robert C. Roby and Barry Ulanov, McGraw-Hill Book Company. Reprinted with permission of Robert C. Roby and Barry Ulanov.

2. Practice the following speech aloud. The speech emphasizes the lyric monologue also found in expressionistic, symbolic, and nonrealistic drama. The effect may be somewhat ethereal, human, but elevated to a dream quality.

> Why did I hesitate? Why take the road? Whither am I bound? From first to last you sit there, naked bone. From morn to midnight, I rage in a circle . . . and now your beckoning finger points the way . . . whether?

> Scene Seven   *From Morn to Midnight*   Georg Kaiser

3. Invent or imitate a variety of nonhuman sounds, such as those used by insects, birds, and animals. Practice these sounds and cries as intermittent vocal effects within the speeches of appropriate plays selected from the list at the end of this chapter.

Movement

Movement serves to represent ideas of most realistic plays and less frequently the actor's personal motivation or the character's motivation. Movement helps define character relationships; movement also helps clarify emotional and symbolic attitudes. For example, expressionistic plays require you to fill stage space with pantomimic dramatization and curious dances as others speak or during long periods of silence. At times you perform theatrical acrobatics (as called for in Michel de Ghelderode's *Christophe Colomb* and *Pantagleize*). Movement is often enhanced by strange lighting and weird music. Around you the "drift of dream" or the "mechanics of routine" prevails in an essentially naked environment.

The key problem in nonrealistic movement is "to leave much of your real world behind"—that world of logical, organized action relatively free from chaos and surging passion. A nonrealistic play carries you into a world in which reality and dream abstractions mingle. Action is often only symbolic stereotype resulting from the nightmares and mental distortions/transformations of the playwright. Actions are fragementary and disconnected and take place within symbolic forms or open spaces. Characters often wear symbolic masks and makeup in order to generalize the concept of mankind (exemplified in Eugene O'Neill's *The Great God Brown*). Frequently the realistic base of movement is dehumanized and distorted. In the manner of a marionette, movements are either slow and ephemeral (dreamlike) or mechanical and robotlike. Gestures are graceful, free, and fluid or abrupt, studied, and stilted. As you enter the world of distortion and transformation, conventional logic disappears. Nonetheless, your movement must retain some semblance of realism because realism is part of a dream, and a dream is in part true to observed, experienced reality. Yet, the overall projection of nonrealistic movement (especially expressionistic movement) must be distorted, transformed, and incongruous with everyday life.

Meyerhold's biomechanics work extremely well for nonrealistic acting. Imaginative gestures, gymnastic and acrobatic activity reinforce the mechanical aspects of movement. Ballet and dance are effective for ephemeral dream movement.

Exercise 2   Movement—Twentieth-Century Nonrealism

Following is a list of exercises which will enable you to practice nonrealistic movement.

1. Construct a facial mask which typifies a stereotype attitude, emotion, or character (possibly you can purchase a mask from a party shop). Wear the mask and study it in a mirror. Then practice movement which exemplifies the countenance of the mask. Explore many types of physical action. For example, move in slow motion, move rapidly across the room, move mechanically, move grotesquely, and so on.
2. Imagine you are a puppet. Move according to the strings controlling your arms, legs, head, back, and torso.
3. Imagine you are an insect. Move according to the type of insect you choose to be.
4. Imagine you are a robot. Move according to how a robot behaves.
5. Imagine you are any kind of modern machine (for example, an adding machine, a typewriter, a washing machine, a telephone, and so on). Move according to the actions of the machine.
6. Imagine you are a snowflake, a cloud, rain, lightning, wind, a leaf, a feather, or any similarly lightweight or fragile thing. Move according to the activity of the object in motion.
7. Invent and practice imaginative gestures, gymnastics, circus tricks, acrobatics, ballet movements, and expressive dance activity for application to speeches selected from the plays listed at the end of this chapter.

Character and Emotion

To perform early twentieth-century expressionistic and nonrealistic styles use Stanislavski's character premise that acting is like living, and then counter and balance the style by using Meyerhold's biomechanics. At times believability in role creation is needed in expressionistic and other nonrealistic acting styles, while at other times a formalized or mechanical design and shape is needed to accomplish some of the actions and movements of characters. The actor and director have the important task of careful script analysis to determine which factor is operative at any given moment (e.g., is it Stanislavski's realism? is it Meyerhold's biomechanics?). Combined properly, realism and biomechanics define character and emotion in expressionistic and nonrealistic acting styles. This mix produces a range of character and emotion complexity from simplistic to multidimensional. For example, the mix of realism and biomechanics can be applied clearly and effectively in Kaiser's *From Morn to Midnight*. The Teller (or the Cashier as he is sometimes called) is the central character. In part I, scene 1, the Teller is totally immersed in mechanical routine. Kaiser provided over twenty-four stage directions for the Teller without one word of dialogue. Most of the stage directions involve counting money or rapping on the Teller's window ledge. Analysis quickly reveals how dehumanized the Teller's life in the bank is. Finally, at the end of scene 1, the Teller chokes out the words,

A scene from *Spring's Awakening* by Frank Wedekind. At the Julliard School, New York. Directed by Liviu Ciulei.

"Fetch—glass of water!" The Teller is little more than a robot in the assembly line of the banking business. In this scene, highly formalized robot action and speaking dictate the acting style.

However, in scene 3, the Teller is alone in a snow-covered field near a single tree. As the sun casts bluish shadows on the snow, the Teller begins a long monologue in which he explores the change in his life now that he has stolen money and run away. As the scene and speech progress, a storm develops. The Teller is engulfed in a dreamlike trance, his eyes scanning the field. He murmurs, "snow, snow, sun, silence." His words and movements glide into the ethereal formality of slow motion. As the wind and storm increase, the dream becomes a nightmare. The tree takes on the shape of a human skeleton with grinning jaws. In dream and nightmare fashion, the Teller converses with the tree. In this scene, highly formalized dream movement and speaking dictate the acting style, contrasting vividly with the earlier robot or mechanical style. Of course, both of these formalized elements are constantly contrasted with the real or human element at the base of the character, that of a man with a home, a mother, a wife, daughters, a job, and so on. As the play moves toward its conclusion, the Teller becomes increasingly humanized, discarding his robot and dream natures. By the final scene of the play, the Teller has achieved self-understanding as well as understanding of the world he lives in. No longer a robot or a dreamer, he sees himself and the world clearly. In this scene, the Teller must be performed with genuine warmth and naturalness; the best of Stanislavski realism can be applied here to enhance audience identification and empathy with the pathetic, martyred Teller. Realistic acting should prevail throughout his confession speech. Then, as the play concludes with his death, the audience both observes and feels the loss of a sacrificial human being.

The journey of the Teller provides a solid example of the mixture of styles necessary for successful work with character and emotion in expressionistic acting. Careful role and play analysis determine when to use Realism and when to use biomechanics (either as the unreality of a robot or as a dream).

Exercise 3   Character and Emotion—Early Twentieth-Century Nonrealism

1. Perform the following brief improvisations, first as a mechanical robot, second, as a sleepwalker midst a dream or nightmare, third, as any insect of your choice, and fourth, as any modern machine of your choice. Be certain to define the circumstances prior to performing the improvisation. Keep each of the four phases of the improvisation under five minutes.
    1. A woman serves breakfast to her husband.
    2. A bank teller receives money from a customer.
    3. A woman pleads with her dead son to lay down in his grave and be still.
    4. A man and a woman hoard food by piling it in a cellar.
    5. A man stands lost on a street corner on Madison Avenue, New York City, as people rush by.
    6. An accountant adds columns of figures as his boss observes him.
    7. A man lost in a thick jungle thinks the trees are horrifying figures of fear.

2. Repeat the seven improvisations from Exercise 3, #1 above in a natural, believable, realistic style. Finally, perform them with selective use of both realistic and nonrealistic character and emotional behavior.

In a lighter vein, nonrealistic acting techniques also assist with presenting comic fantasies, such as the popular *Peter Pan* by Sir James M. Barrie. While fundamental realism carries most of the action in this delightful fantasy, the techniques described in this chapter prove applicable to segments in *Peter Pan* dealing with the dog, Nana, the crocodile, and the antics of Captain Hook, the Indians, and the pirates. Such acting techniques are also well utilized in many children's theatre plays and fantasies, such as *Reynard the Fox, Winnie the Pooh, The Great Cross Country Race,* and others.

A clear understanding of nonrealistic acting techniques is vital if you are to make the playwright's philosophic premise clear. The universality of these styles usually rests with the playwright's emphasis on human values, on love, and on spiritual brotherhood. Understanding these styles and the stylistic writing techiques of early twentieth-century nonrealists, the actor applies a mix of realistic and biomechanic acting techniques to fulfill the intentions of the author.

While so-called pure Expressionism and similar nonrealistic movements in theatre disappeared by the mid-1920s, their influence on writing, design, and acting style has continued. When combined with Stanislavski's system of Realism and Naturalism, the styles of the nonrealists led to the unique innovations of Bertolt Brecht and the Absurdists which finally culminated in the contemporary Eclectic theatre.

Suggested Characters and Plays for Scene Work

Stringberg, August

Father Indra, Indra's daughter, Officer, Lawyer
  A Dream Play
Hummel, The Student, The Milkmaid, The Lady in Black, The Mummy
  The Ghost Sonata

Kaiser, Georg

Gentleman in White, The Clerk, The Engineer, The Billionaire's Son
  Gas Part I
Cashier, Salvation Lass, The Lady, The Son
  From Morn to Midnight

Shaw, Irwin

Bess, Schelling, Joan, Levy, Julia, Morgan, Katherine, Driscoll, Martha, Webster
  Bury the Dead

Rice, Elmer

Mr. Zero, Mrs. Zero, Daisy, Shrdlu
  The Adding Machine

O'Neill, Eugene

Brutus Jones, Henry Smithers, The Little Formless Fears
  The Emperor Jones
Yank, Mildred Douglas, Paddy
  The Hairy Ape
Dion Anthony, Margaret, Lillian Brown, Cybel
  The Great God Brown

Capek, Karel

Harry Domin, Sulla, Marius
  R.U.R.

Capek, Karel and Josef

Parasite, Chrysalis, Vagrant, Mr. Beetle, Mrs. Beetle, Fly, Larvae
  The Insect Play

Maeterlinck, Maurice

Pelléas Golaud, Melisande
  Pelléas and Melisande
Boy, Girl, Fairy, Light, Night
  The Blue Bird

Jarry, Alfred

Ubu Roi (King Turd)
  Ubu Roi

Wedekind, Frank

Melchoir, Wendla, Moritz
  Spring's Awakening

Toller, Ernst

The Woman, Nameless One
  Man and the Masses

Connelly, Marc, and Kaufman, George S.
Composer, Girl
Beggar on Horseback

Barrie, Sir James M.
Peter Pan, Wendy, Nana, Captain Hook, John
Peter Pan

(Also see the many children's theatre plays and fantasies utilizing nonrealistic and nonhuman characters and devices.)

Actor Checklist *Early Twentieth-Century Nonrealism*

Voice	Extensive range; lyrical when appropriate; staccato when appropriate; extensive use of pause and silence; varied rhythms; when appropriate, extensive use of chant, intonation, yells.
Movement	Motivated by idea, social function, and theme; when appropriate, distortion through robotlike, puppetlike dehumanization; when appropriate, distortion through slow and ephemeral dream quality; mix of presentational and representational mode; varied.
Gestures	Graceful, free, fluid, as appropriate; or abrupt, studied, stilted as appropriate; more selective in dehumanized moments; full use of entire body.
Pantomimic Dramatization	Use of masks; oriental techniques; acrobatics, strange dances; gymnastics; extremely inventive.
Character	Human reality base; distorted through dehumanization when appropriate, for example, mechanical and dreamlike; symbolic, clear social universality; combination of personalization and role identification and biomechanic formalism; when appropriate, analogous to inaminate objects, machines, animals, insects, and so on.
Emotion	Simplistic in dehumanized moments; complex in human moments; closely tied to social, thematic concepts.
Ideas	Strong philosophical and social orientation against machine age and modern technology; antiscientific; oriented to the common masses.
Language	Mix of prose and verse; mix of staccato and telegramlike dialogue and lyrical monologue.
Mood and Atmosphere	Closely tied to idea and social theme; generally serious; mix of reality and fantasy.
Pace and Tempo	Unusually varied.
Special Techniques	Careful analysis necessary to combine Stanislavski realism and Meyerhold biomechanics; unusual flexibility in physical activity.

Fantasy! A style of non-realism. Peter Pan, Tinkerbell, Captain Hook, and The Alligator in *Peter Pan* by Sir James M. Barrie as graphically illustrated by Ellis M. Pryce-Jones.

Suggested Readings

Arnold, Paul. "The Artaud Experiment." *Tulane Drama Review,* Winter 1963.

Artaud, Antonin. *The Theatre and Its Double.* Translated by Mary C. Richards. New York, Grove Press, 1958.

Balakian, Anna E. *Surrealism: The Road to the Absolute.* Rev. ed. New York: E. P. Dutton & Co., 1959.

Benedikt, Michael, and Wellwarth, George, eds. *Modern French Theatre: The Avant-Garde, Dada, and Surrealism.* New York: E. P. Dutton and Co., 1964.

Braun, Edward, ed. *Meyerhold on Theatre.* New York: Hill & Wang, 1969.

Breton, Andre. *What Is Surrealism?* London: Faber & Faber, Ltd., 1936.

Brockett, Oscar G. and Findlay, Robert R. *Century of Innovation: A History of European and American Theatre and Drama Since 1870.* Englewood Cliffs, N.J.: Prentice-Hall, 1973.

Chiari, Joseph. *Symbolism from Poe to Mallarme.* 2d. Ed. New York: Gordian, 1970.

Cornell, Kenneth. *The Symbolist Movement.* New Haven: Yale University Press, 1951.

Dahlstrom, C. E. W. L. *Strindberg's Dramatic Expressionism.* New York: Benjamin Blom, 1930.

Fowlie, Wallace. *Age of Surrealism.* Bloomington, Ind.: Indiana University Press, 1960.

Garten, H. F. *Modern German Drama.* New York: Essential Books, 1959.

Gorchakov, Nikolai. *The Theatre in Soviet Russia.* Transl. Edgar Lehman. New York: Columbia University Press, 1957.

Kenworthy, B. J. *Georg Kaiser.* London: Oxford University Press, 1957.

Lehman, Andrew G. *The Symbolism Aesthetic in France, 1885–1895.* London: Oxford University Press, 1950.

Lumley, Frederick. *Trends in Twentieth Century Drama: A Survey Since Ibsen and Shaw.* 2d ed. London: Barrie and Rockliff, 1960.

Ossar, Michael. *Anarchism in the Drama of Ernst Toller.* Albany: State University of New York Press, 1980.

Palmieri, Anthony F. R. *Elmer Rice: A Playwright's Vision of America.* East Brunswick, N.J.: Fairleigh Dickinson University Press, 1980.

Patterson, Michael. *The Revolution in German Theatre.* Boston: Routledge & Kegan Paul, 1981.

Rischbeiter, Henning. *Art and the Stage in the 20th Century.* Greenwich, Conn.: New York Graphic Society, 1968.

Roose-Evans, James. *Experimental Theatre: From Stanislavsky to Today.* Rev. Ed. New York: Universe, 1973.

Samuel, Richard and Thomas, R. H. *Expressionism in German Life, Literature and the Theatre (1910–1924).* London: Cambridge University Press, 1959.

Schmidt, Paul, ed. *Meyerhold at Work.* Trnsl. by Paul Schmidt, Ilya Levin, and Vern McGee. Austin: University of Texas Press, 1980.

Segal, Harold B. *Twentieth-Century Russian Drama.* New York, 1979.

Stein, Jack M. *Richard Wagner and the Synthesis of the Arts.* Detroit: Wayne State University Press, 1960.

Valency, Maurice. *The Flower and the Castle: An Introduction to Modern Drama.* New York: Grosset & Dunlap, Inc., 1963.

Willett, John, *Expressionism.* New York: McGraw-Hill, Inc., 1970.

Suggested Filmography

1. *The Adding Machine.* 1969. British. Playwright-Elmer Rice. With Milo O'Shea, Phillis Diller.
2. *The Emperor Jones.* 1933. U.A. Playwright-Eugene O'Neill. Director-Dudley Murphy. With Paul Robeson.
3. *The Hairy Ape.* 1944. U.A. Playwright-O'Neill. With Wm. Bendix, Susan Hayward.
4. *The Long Voyage Home.* 1940. United Artists. Director-John Ford. With John Wayne. Adapted from Eugene O'Neill's sea plays: *Bound East for Cardiff, In the Zone, The Long Voyage Home,* and *Moon of the Caribbees.* Noteworthy for use of dream-like, expressionistic techniques rather than the expected strict naturalism.
5. *Pelleas and Melisande.* 1913. Universal-Bison. Playwright-Maurice Maeterlinck. With Constance Crawley.
6. *Peter Pan.* 1925. Famous Players-Lasky. Playwright-James M. Barrie. Director-Herbert Brenon. With Betty Bronson.

From Morn to Midnight

by Georg Kaiser

Translated by Ashley Dukes

from
scene i

Manager
Porter
Lady
Serving Maid
Cashier

Characters

Interior of a small bank, Germany.

Scene

An anonymous cashier works in robot fashion in the deadly routine of his job. The soft alure of a beautiful foreign woman prompts him to break his dehumanized state, embezzle funds, and embark on a strange search for happiness and identity.

Situation

MANAGER   This lady from Florence—who claims to come from Florence—has a vision like that ever visited you in your cage before? Furs—perfume! The fragrance lingers—you breathe adventure. Superbly staged. Italy . . . enchantment—fairy-tale—Riviera—Mentone—Pordighera—Nice—Monte Carlo—where oranges blossom, fraud blooms too. Swindlers—down there every square foot of earth breeds them. They organize crusades. The gang disperses to the four winds—preferably small towns—off the beaten track. Then—apparitions—billowing silks—furs—women—modern sirens. Refrains from the sunny south—*o bella Napoli!* One glance and you're stripped to your undershirt—to the bare skin—to the naked, naked skin. (*He drums with a pencil on the* CASHIER's *hand.*) Depend upon it, this bank in Florence knows as much about the lady as the man in the moon. The whole affair is a swindle, carefully arranged. And the web was woven not in Florence, but in Monte Carlo. That's the place to keep in mind. Take my word for it, you've just seen one of the gadflies that thrive in the swamp of the Casino. We shall never see her again. The first attempt missed fire; she'll scarcely risk a second! I joke about it but I have a keen eye—when you're a banker—I really should have tipped off the police! Well, it doesn't concern me—besides, banks must be discreet. Keep your eye on the out-of-town papers—the police news. When you find something there about an adventuress, safe under lock and key— then we'll talk about it again. You'll see I was right—then we'll hear more of our Florentine lady than we'll ever see of her and her furs again.

(*Exit.* CASHIER *seals up rolls of bank notes.*)

PORTER (*enters with letters, hands them to* CLERK)   One registered letter. I want the receipt.

(CLERK *stamps receipt form, hands it to* PORTER. PORTER *rearranges glass and waterbottle on the table, and goes out.* CLERK *takes the letters into* MANAGER's *room, and returns.*)

LADY (*reenters; comes quickly to the counter*)   I beg your pardon.

(CASHIER *stretches out his hand, without looking at her. Raps.*)

LADY (*louder*) If you please! (CASHIER *raps on the counter.*) I don't want to trouble the Manager a second time. (CASHIER *raps on the counter.*) Please tell me—would it be possible for me to leave you the letter of credit for the whole sum, and to receive an advance of three thousand in part payment? (CASHIER *raps impatiently.*) I should be willing to deposit my diamonds as security, if required. Any jeweler in the town will appraise them for you. (*She takes off a glove and pulls at her bracelet.* SERVING MAID *comes in quickly, plumps down on sofa, and begins rummaging in her market-basket.* LADY, *startled by the commotion, looks round. As she leans on the counter her hand sinks into the* CASHIER'S. CASHIER *bends over the hand which lies in his own. His spectacles glitter, his glance travels slowly upward from her wrist.* SERVING MAID, *with a sigh of relief, discovers the check she is looking for.* LADY *nods kindly in her direction.* SERVING MAID *replaces vegetables, etc., in her basket.* LADY, *turning again to the counter, meets the eyes of the* CASHIER. CASHIER *smiles at her.* LADY *drawing back her hand*) Of course I shall not ask the bank to do anything irregular. (*She puts the bracelet on her wrist; the clasp refuses to catch. Stretching out her arm to the* CASHIER) Would you be so kind? I'm clumsy with the left hand. (CASHIER *stares at her as if mesmerized. His spectacles, bright points of light, seem almost to be swallowed up in the cavity of his wide-open eyes. To* SERVING MAID) You can help me, mademoiselle. (SERVING MAID *does so.*) Now the safety catch. (*With a little cry*) You're pinching my flesh. Ah, that's better. Thank you so much. (*She bows to the* CASHIER *and goes out.* SERVING MAID *coming to the counter, planks down her check.* CASHIER *takes it in trembling hands, the slip of paper flutters and crackles; he fumbles under the counter, then counts out money.*)

SERVING MAID (*looking at the pile of coins*) That isn't all mine.

(CASHIER *writes.* CLERK *becomes observant.*)

SERVING MAID (*to* CLERK) But it's too much! (CLERK *looks at* CASHIER. CASHIER *rakes in part of the money.*) Still too much!

(CASHIER *ignores her and continues writing.* SERVING MAID *shaking her head, puts the money in her basket and goes out.*)

CASHIER (*hoarsely*) Get me a glass of water! (CLERK *hurries from behind the counter; comes to table.*) That's been standing. Fresh water—cold water— from the faucet. (CLERK *hurries out with glass.* CASHIER *goes quickly to electric bell, and rings.* PORTER *enters from the hall.*) Get me fresh water.

PORTER I'm not allowed to go so far from the door.

CASHIER (*hoarsely*) For me. Not that slime. I want water from the faucet.

(PORTER *seizes waterbottle and hurries out.* CASHIER *quickly crams his pockets with bank notes. Then he takes his coat from a peg, throws it over his arm, and puts on his hat. He lifts a flap in the counter, passes through, and goes out.*)

MANAGER (*absorbed in reading a letter, enters from his room*) Here's the letter of advice from Florence, after all!

(CLERK *enters with a glass of water.* PORTER *enters with a full waterbottle.*)

MANAGER (*looking up*) What the devil . . . ?

(*END*)

"Formless Fears" in a scenic design by Ellis M. Pryce-Jones as they might appear to characters such as The Cashier in Georg Kaiser's *From Morn to Midnight* or Jones in *The Emperor Jones* by Eugene O'Neill.

18 Brecht and Epic Style

Didacticism

PHILOSOPHER   The other day I met my
    audience
In a dusty street
He gripped a pneumatic drill in his fists.
For a second
He looked up. Rapidly I set up my theatre
Between the houses. He
Looked expectant.
Today
I brought it off again. Outside the station
With brass bands and rifle butts I saw him
Being herded off to war.
In the midst of the crowd
I set up my theatre. Over his shoulder
He looked back
And nodded.
    "Buying Brass," from *Poems on the Theatre*
              by Bertolt Brecht

. . . don't show him too much
But show something. And let him observe
That this is not magic but
Work, my friends.

              Bertolt Brecht
     from Kenneth Tynan, *Curtains.*

Of all works, my favourite
Are those which show usage.
The copper vessels with bumps and dented
    edges,
The knives and forks whose wooden
    handles are
Worn down by many hands; such forms
To me are the noblest.

              Bertolt Brecht
     from Kenneth Tynan, *Curtains.*

MOTHER COURAGE   I won't have my war
all spoiled for me! It destroys the weak,
does it? Well, what does peace do for
'em? Huh?
(She sings her song)
So cheer up, boys, the rose is fading
When victory comes you may be dead
A war is just the same as trading
But not with cheese—with steel and lead!
    Christians, awake! The winter's
        gone!
The snows depart, the dead sleep on.
And though you may not long survive
Get out of bed and look alive!
    Mother Courage by Bertolt Brecht

Overview of Brecht Epic Theatre—From Illusion to Fact and Social Action

It is told that shortly after the death of Bertolt Brecht in 1956, the late Lotte Lenya, a principal actress in the Berliner Ensemble, was speaking in Iowa. According to the story of this incident, she related a personal account about Brecht to a group of university students. Lotte was having great difficulty understanding Brecht's acting theories as they applied to a role she was playing in one of his plays. Upon asking Brecht how she was to interpret her role to achieve a performance faithful to his Epic theories, Brecht supposedly patted her reassuringly on the shoulder and said she should simply "follow her instincts" and "go about the business of acting." This was Brecht's way of admitting that his famous theories can be taken only so far, that ultimately traditional acting craft must also be part of the work necessary to present his plays effectively. In other words, there is a vast distinction between Brecht's theories and Brecht's practice.

Since 1956, the ideas of Brecht have revolutionized playwriting, production techniques, and acting methodology. Ironically Brecht's theatre concepts had far-reaching impact only after his death. Brecht wrote his first play *(Baal)* in 1918 and formulated his writing style during the 1920s. *(A Man is a Man* and *The Threepenny Opera).* When the Nazis began their rise to power in 1933, Brecht left Germany and settled in Scandinavia. While in exile, he wrote several major works: *The Private Life of the Master Race, Mother Courage, Galileo, The Resistible Rise of Arturo Ui,* and *The Good Woman of Setzuan.* Later, he left the northern countries of Europe for the United States, making his home in Santa Monica, California until the end of World War II. One of Brecht's most famous plays was written during this time, *The Caucasian Chalk Circle.* Although Brecht had become a convert to Marxism, he did not return to the Eastern Sector of Berlin immediately after the war. He spent some time in Switzerland in 1947, finally settling in East Berlin in 1948. After his self-imposed exile, the name and work of Bertolt Brecht found acceptance and acclaim throughout Europe, the United States, and England.

German theatre during the 1920s received its inspiration from the director Erwin Piscator. Upon founding the First Epic Proletarian Theatre, Piscator formed an alliance with Brecht. Both men were interested in treating subjects in strictly intellectual, didactic terms. They opposed the traditional late nineteenth-century and early twentieth-century focus on Realism, Naturalism, and orientation toward "suspension of disbelief" with its emotional element and its escape-into-make-believe quality. Piscator and Brecht favored a social activist theatre in which the audience remained aware that they were in a theatre absorbing messages and ideas. They documented plays by prefacing scenes with electronically or mechanically projected captions explaining themes and exhorting action. The expressionistic technique of constructing a series of disjointed, episodic scenes was used as a desirable method for abolishing suspense, which was an emotional and undesirable characteristic of traditional theatre. Music was used to neutralize emotion rather than to intensify it. Atmospheric lighting was rejected in favor of general illumination. Actors wore everyday dress; property items were used as blatant theatre props to assist in making an idea clear rather than in reinforcing an emotional "reality." Scenery was constructivistic in design, using stairs, levels, scaffolding, treadmills, and revolving stages. Films, used as background scenery, projected images of places and people from a variety of historical periods and subjects on screens, all for the purpose of better explaining present social circumstances (this technique, later known as *historification*, is explained in detail later in this chapter). Piscator dominated the Berlin theatre of the 1920s and provided an important function by creating a milieu for Brecht's plays.

However, before the 1920s ended, Piscator and Brecht ended their collaboration. Although both men sought enlightenment and education of the masses, the means of achieving that end became a source of contention between them. The young Brecht felt the only true means of achieving social action in the theatre was elimination of all emotion from the stage. Piscator did not want to banish emotion completely; instead, he tried to correlate fictional dramatic story and real contemporary world (e.g., surrounding the play with contemporary slide projections and films from real contemporary society). However, the tempo of the times in Germany (i.e., the concentrated rise of Fascism) proved to Brecht that Epic Theatre had to heighten and intensify didacticism in order to change the social, economic, and political conditions of the country. Piscator's desire to combine traditional emotionalism and didacticism was seen by Brecht as a weakening of their work. Brecht began to explore the pragmatics of didacticism and materialism. Brecht hoped to unify the thinking of his audience members and provoke them into strong, direct social action.

The Epic play presents historical subject matter from the viewpoint of a single storyteller. Sections of dialogue and narration are interspersed throughout the play. Changes in time and place are frequent, and time is bridged by a sentence or a brief passage. In Epic Theatre the sweep of a specific historical period is presented similar to the manner in which Homer wrote his poetic narration, *The Iliad.* Since Epic plays narrate or report many experiences, audiences have little opportunity to identify with the action onstage. Few Brechtian characters gain audience empathy. (Although the Epic actor consciously demonstrates, suggests, and describes behavior, rather than realistically create the inner truth of a role, Piscator would not have denied that emotion is an integral element of characterization. As Lotte Lenya's story indicates, in later years Brecht came to agree!) To counteract emotion onstage, Epic Theatre provides a narrator whose primary function is to *observe* the action and *report* events. The actors, in conjunction with the narrator, attempt to arouse the capacity for social action in an audience. The actors propose arguments, hoping to force decisions involving change in social conditions. To futher clarify the didactic elements of the play, Epic staging often includes use of general illumination of both the

Two-photo sequence of Galileo by Bertolt Brecht. (1) Lype O'Dell as Galileo, Martin Molson as Federzoni, Marshall Borden as Andrea Sarti, and Arthur Inman as Little Monk at The Hilberry Theatre, Wayne State University. Directed by Leonard Leone. Scenery by Richard Spear. Costumes by Robert Pusilo. Lighting by Gary M. Witt.

Two-photo sequence of Galileo by Bertolt Brecht. (2) Marshall Borden as Andrea and Lype O'Dell as Galileo at The Hilberry Theatre, Wayne State University. Directed by Leonard Leone. Scenery by Richard Spear. Costumes by Robert Pusilo. Lighting by Gary M. Witt.

stage and the auditorium, elimination of act curtains, use of blatant scene-shifting with revolves, and use of slide and film projections. The main thesis in Epic Theatre is that human beings can be altered, are capable of change; from moment to moment, man makes many decisions affecting social and economic circumstances.

By the late 1920s, in his theoretical writing Brecht began to explore and expand his concept of Epic Theatre. He also wrote poems, aphorisms, stories, essays, polemics, and novels. However, his greatest achievements were his forty plays and adaptations. In 1948, Brecht published his theoretical writings. Chief among this work was "Small Organum for the Theatre." Thereafter, he turned from the concept of Epic Theatre to theatre oriented more toward didacticism. Although most of Brecht's theories may be categorized under the term *Epic*, his plays tend to transcend the limitations of this label. His plays are a rich mixture of Realism and Expressionism embellished by new and special techniques.

The Brechtian era initiated a change in drama and theatrical production. Brecht viewed the old dramatic theatre as a rigid structure that presented fixed, unchangeable events. Historical subjects were treated in historical terms. Past and present remained separated. Audiences were accustomed to watching events which mirrored their own emotional or psychological makeup, and their sensibilities had been lulled into acceptance of and passivity toward the old order of events. Brecht did not intend to pacify audiences; his plays were meant to arouse, shock, and "make strange" (i.e., alienate audiences by making them *think* and, hopefully, *act* to change society).

The subject matter of Brecht's plays is always based on history. He emphasizes the past in order to place the present in perspective. Brecht believed an audience should see the present through the past. In this manner an audience can view both present and past objectively, unemotionally, and with detachment. The present, then, offers a spectator alternatives for positive action. Brecht labeled this philosophy or technique "historification," a concept dependent on psychological behaviorism. Analysis is possible at any given moment by the thrust of a man's action in a particular circumstance. The primary subject of Brecht's plays is the relationship between men. Instead of watching modern man relate to the present, we study his behavior as he reacts to the past. Or the process is reversed and we watch historic figures react to the present (e.g., St. Joan in a Chicago stockyard, Hitler in an American gangster environment, and so on). The didactic lesson of historification can be likened to a Medieval morality play or to the biblical style of writing in parables. In effect, historification is a kind of propaganda made palatable by quality theatricalism.

An integral element of the process of historification is the concept of *verfremdungseffekt* or *alienation*. The literal translation of *alienation* is "to make strange" (to make actions strange). Objectivity is implied in the theory of alienation. An audience does not identify or empathize with strange events that take place in a blatantly theatrical way. Such events take precedence

The Private Life of the Master Race by Bertolt Brecht. Scott Beers, Megan Anderson, and Myron Freedman at The University of Nevada, Reno. Directed by Bob Dillard. Designed by J. Amburn Darnall. National Finalist winner, American College Theatre Festival, John F. Kennedy Center for the Performing Arts, Washington, D.C. Photograph by David Droes.

over character and emotional depth. To this end Brecht employed a number of shock-making theatrical devices: visible theatre mechanics; scenery changed in view of the audience; musicians participating in stage events; fragmentary, practical sets designed only *to indicate* the place of the scene. Piscator's theatre set the tone for Brechtian production by using multiple treadmills rotating in opposite directions, lifts to hoist actors, and screens to project documentary films. (Documentary films usually confirm or contradict what the characters say by showing *real*life figures in support of or in contrast to *created* characters onstage.) Films show similar events simultaneously in different places, thereby revealing the world in flux. The Epic scenic design can be easily constructed and does not impede the action of the story or the flow of actors onstage. The set is often lighted in flat, white light, and no attempt is made to represent different moods or shades of meaning. Illusion is frequently assaulted by the open use of visual mechanics on the stage.

Brecht also used music as a means to further objectify stage action. He used dissonant music to aid in communicating the text. In Brecht's plays, music helps to eliminate meaning by delineating moral attitude. Songs comment on the action; they become means of arousing social consciousness.

Brecht used satire, comic dance and mime in his plays for both theatrical diversion and didactic purposes. His plays were studded with satiric and farcical elements in the tradition of the witty fool and the circus clown—laughter tinged with irony, sadness, pratfalls, and jokes. Brecht deliberately added comedy to his plays to reveal the ludicrous nature of man's helplessness in a corrupt capitalist world. (It was also fun and entertaining!) Shocking and strange devices were used at every turn: for example, long presentational songs with dissonant music *(The Caucasian Chalk Circle)*; signs from the ceiling proclaiming War Is Evil *(Mother Courage)*; a man standing in a 1930 business suit speaking with a Chicago accent as a motion picture reveals Hitler speaking in the same manner *(The Resistible Rise of Arturo Ui)*; an American flier surrounded by Chinese coolies *(The Good Woman of Setzuan)*; unmasked peasants surrounded by masked tyrants *(The Caucasian Chalk Circle)*; an actor throwing away a moustache and costume to speak as himself rather than as a character (at the final moments of *The Resistible Rise of Arturo Ui*).

Oriental Influence on Brecht

The virtuosity of Brecht's Epic Theatre is allied to ancient Asiatic or Oriental theatre (mainly of India, Indonesia, China, and Japan).

Early Indian plays were primarily dance and music set to plays written in Sanskrit. Later Indian plays were very romantic and highly symbolic—for example, Kalidasa's *Shakuntala*.

Indonesia was famous for its shadow puppet plays and its dance drama.

Mainland China produced two types of drama, Southern drama and the Northern drama. Today, the Peking Opera is the center for classical Chinese drama, a highly symbolic combination of dance and music oriented toward civil and military stories.

Scene from *A Man's A Man* by Bertolt Brecht. At the Julliard School, New York. Directed by Gene Lesser.

Japanese drama has been the most influential of the Eastern dramas. Japan has produced three major theatrical forms: Noh plays, puppet theatre, and Kabuki dramas. Noh is essentially dance drama whose plays are brief and deal with gods, warriors, women, spirits, and demons. The actors are all male. Japan's puppet theatre is internationally famous and centers around a group called Bunraku. Kabuki is the most flexible and most popular Japanese drama. The three types of Kabuki drama are historical and domestic plays and dance dramas. Kabuki plays are inordinately long, running as much as five or more hours. The material is both comic and serious. The American occupation of Japan produced a new kind of theatre called Shingeki, in which Western plays are adapted to the Japanese language.

Acting is the key to all Oriental dramatic forms. The performer, be he dancer, singer, or actor, uses highly complex symbolic systematic gestures emanating from every part of the body. Oriental audiences recognize and immediately understand the system. Oriental acting emphasizes body control and discipline, focusing primarily on movement, gesture, pantomimic dramatization, mood, and use of intricate masks, costumes, and makeup. Character and language are subordinate to the theatrical elements just listed. However, speaking, chanting, and singing are nonetheless important. The vocal work combines with the musical accompaniment of the drama and requires unusually clear, precise diction. Character is primarily symbolic and far less complex and psychological than in Western drama. The presentational mode dominates in Oriental acting. The overall effect is colorful and blatantly theatrical. Brecht found this effect appealing because Oriental acting style provided practical models for his acting theories. Of particular importance to Brecht was the disciplined physical prowess of Oriental actors. Movement is graceful, forceful, and rhythmic. Basically the Chinese use three types of walking, each distinguished by prescribed movements:

1. The roll-walk, in which the hips rotate as the feet move carefully from the ball of the foot onto the heel
2. The flat-walk, in which there is no hip movement and the entire foot lands flat at each step
3. The kick-walk, a goose step in which the lower leg is thrust forward at each step

Gestures are fluid, full, mimetic, and descriptive, and their action and attitude are also symbolic. For example, to indicate a door opened forcefully, an actor raises both hands in front of him and then separates them violently. Some other prescribed gestures are these:

1. An action to repulse, in which one arm is thrust forcefully sideways
2. An action of resolution, in which one arm is thrust forcefully high above the head and the other arm is thrust down and backward at the side

3. An action to conceal, in which the back of the hand is placed across the eyes
4. An action for weeping, in which the fingers are moved up and down in the conceal position

All of these and other important gestures used in the Oriental theatre are accentuated by manipulation of *watersleeves* worn at the wrists of most costumes. Watersleeves are long, dangling scarflike draperies that create lovely, flowing images during movement. (The feet are as important as the hands to gesture. In fact, every part of the body is used for precise, meaningful communication.)

Oriental drama, like that of Spain and England, has always made interesting use of fans on stage. A distinct "language" of the fan has developed over the centuries, with subtle variations between countries. The essence of "fan language" on stage may follow the guidelines suggested below:

With handle to lips:	kiss me.
Carrying in the right hand in front of face:	follow me.
Carrying in the left hand:	desirous of acquaintance.
Placing it on left ear:	you have changed.
Twirling it in left hand:	I wish to get rid of you.
Drawing across forehead:	we are watched.
Carrying in right hand:	you are too willing.
Drawing across cheek:	I love you.
Drawing through hand:	I hate you.
Twirling in right hand:	I love another.
Closing it:	I wish to speak to you.
Drawing across eyes:	I am sorry.
Letting it rest on right cheek:	yes.
Letting it rest on left cheek:	no.
Open and shut:	you are cruel.
Dropping:	we are friends.
Fanning slowly:	I am married.
Fanning fast:	I am engaged.
Open wide:	wait for me.

In Oriental theatre, action is enhanced by vocalization. Emotion is indicated by symbolic body gestures coupled with either dissonant or lyrical vocal qualities. At times, the voice is clipped, staccato, or monotone. The depth of the emotion is indicated by ascending or descending emphasis on the combined effect of body and vocal elements. Diction is always precise and clear.

Music is an integral part of Oriental theatre. However, it is used for supportive purposes rather than for independent value. Whereas Brecht wanted music to stand as an independent element in the drama, in Oriental theatre it is used to create mood and to reinforce thought.

The total theatrical effect of Oriental theatre is substantially less didactic than Brecht's theatre. In spite of his admiration for it, Brecht found Oriental theatre too hypnotic. However, he enthusiastically favored the transparent power and grace of Chinese acting techniques. Brecht discovered a well of social communication within the mimetic and gestural expression of the Chinese theatre. He soon discovered that his actors could clarify and define social relationships if they performed in a detached manner, as though observing their own actions. Thus, both performer and audience became observers. This is the identifying characteristic of Brecht's theatre.

Voice

One of the most striking features of Brecht's plays is the language. Brecht wrote "colloquial-poetry" which has sensual simplicity. His poetry contains melancholy, tenderness, sadness, malice, wit, lyricism, logic, and paradox. When an actor first encounters the plays of Brecht, he may continually make the mistake of fighting the theory that "factual statements claiming reason over emotion" must dominate textual analysis. The language of Brecht is filled with poetry and emotion. The songs (generally set to music by Kurt Weill) are the epitome of Brecht's poetic diction.

Vocal work in Brecht's plays is a selective combination of believable human speech and overtly theatrical, detached, or even dehumanized speech. In other words, both Realism and nonrealism are at work in the Epic plays of Brecht. His is not a pure form. Elements of Realism, Naturalism, Symbolism, and Expressionism can be identified in his scripts. As a result, your voice must be pliant, flexible, and lively to achieve subtle variations of meaning, as well as overt variation of style. Constant attention should be paid to vowels and consonants. National and regional dialects are common in Brechtian plays and must be handled perfectly. Class distinctions are also written carefully into the language. The voice must be used economically. When characterization is multidimensional, as for Grusha in *The Caucasian Chalk Circle*, vocal nuances should reflect the best of Stanislavski's realistic vocal training. On the other hand, when the speech is mechanical and theatrical, as for the Iron Soldiers in *The Caucasian Chalk Circle*, vocal work should reflect the best of the nonreal expressionistic techniques discussed in chapter 17. A large vocal range is of aid to an actor in Brecht's Epic plays. When they are appropriate, dissonant singing, chanting, and intonation in the expressionistic and Oriental manners are valuable assets. Occasionally, lyrical passages require harmonious, pleasant vocal delivery. Sometimes, with very little transition, such passages are followed by disconnected, dissonant, strange-sounding segments. A disciplined, fully trained vocal mechanism is essential for effective delivery of Brecht's plays.

Exercise 1 Voice—Brecht Epic Theatre

Practice the speech from *Mother Courage* given at the beginning of this chapter, emphasizing the following techniques.

1. Believable, human, realistic delivery
2. A variety of regional and national dialects (e.g., British, Japanese, Italian, Irish, Swedish, and American Southern)
3. A variety of class distinctions (e.g., British royalty, common Cockney, American Midwestern middle class, Southern hillbilly, and so on)
4. Robot or mechanical
5. Dreamlike ephemeral
6. Singing, chanting, and intonation
7. Opposite emotional values from those which *seem* apparent in the speech.

Note: Both men and women should practice this speech. Actresses may impersonate male roles, and vice versa.

Movement

Movement, gesture, and pantomimic dramatization in Brecht again require combining several kinds of techniques, namely, realistic, biomechanical, expressionistic, and Oriental. Careful script analysis by you and your director will lead you to the correct determination of which to employ, and when. Such variety of movement necessitates a totally trained body, a body whose muscles must remain loose and flexible for maximum control. Acrobatics, dance, mime, imaginative gestures, and gymnastic training are highly effective in acting Brecht.

Exercise 2 Movement—Brecht Epic Theatre

1. Again using the speech from *Mother Courage* appearing at the beginning of this chapter, invent movement, gestures, and pantomimic dramatization to accommodte each of the vocal deliveries used in all seven of the techniques in foregoing Exercise 1.

2. Practice the following Oriental techniques of movement described in this chapter:
   a. The roll-walk
   b. The flat-walk
   c. The kick-walk
   d. The gesture to repulse
   e. The gesture of resolution
   f. The gesture to conceal
   g. The gesture for weeping
   h. The fluid mixture and combination of all of the above, a-g.

Exercise 3 The Fan—Brecht Epic Theatre

Practice all the "fan language" descriptions listed above under *Oriental Influence on Brecht* page 334. If possible, attach makeshift watersleeves to your wrists when performing.

Rebecca Renfroe in a scene from *The Threepenny Opera* by Bertolt Brecht with music by Kurt Weill. At the College Conservatory of Music, Cincinnati, Ohio. Directed by William Shorr. (Photo by Sandy Underwood.)

Character and Emotion

Except when creating key three-dimensional roles such as Grusha in *The Caucasian Chalk Circle* and Mother Courage in the play of the same name, you usually will not create complex characterization. A certain objectivity or detachment in performance reveals the *actor* as well as the *character*. In theory, most of Brecht's characters do not grow or develop onstage (in practice, growth sometimes takes place in spite of Brecht and his theory). You often encounter your audience directly and honestly; similarly, you often encounter your fellow actors in the same manner. The play and the acting are not disguised by illusion. Your objective is to provoke examination of social issues and raise questions for the viewers. You must frequently increase the spectator's awareness of being in the theatre by revealing your total consciousness in performing your role. In theory, your audience will then concentrate on ideas and action, rather than on emotion and character. (In practice, audiences still seem to respond best to emotion and character in Brecht, rather than to ideas.)

In his plays, Brecht provides you with devices to enhance the concept of alienation such as overt prologue, epilogue, narration, direct address, reference to the author, episodic scene progress, and didactic trial argument. Brecht also outlined a series of specific acting techniques related to character and emotion which can help you discover how to accomplish some of his theory.

1. Perform with an awareness of being watched.
2. Look at the floor and openly calculate movement.
3. Separate vocalization from gesture (in other words, make vocal and physical timing strange and disconnected).
4. Remain uninvolved with other actors, physically and emotionally.

5. Stand and move in a simple, loosely held together group (removed from your colleagues, you are free to change the course of action and make independent decisions).

6. In order to better instruct your audience, freely acknowledge their diversity by speaking to the various collective units as well as to individuals within the units. For example, isolate a group of businessmen by focusing your eyes on the group, and then focus on each member in turn within the group. Similarly, recognize other groups and then each individual within a group until you have contacted the entire audience.

7. Address the audience directly from center stage in full-front presentational fashion.

8. Speak your lines as if they were a quotation and in the manner of delivering a speech in the third person.

9. Occasionally speak stage directions aloud to intensify unemotional acting.

10. Be critical of your character, as though all of your actions had occurred in the past.

11. Change roles with other actors during rehearsals and even during performances to purify and conceptualize ideas and to remain unattached to any role.

12. Stand in front of a mirror and meticulously study your movements and gestures.

13. Employ robot, mechanical, dreamlike, and other nonrealistic techniques learned in Chapter 17.

14. Utilize an acting style absolutely opposite to what you normally would use for the scene in order to create fresh values. For example, do a modern war scene in the style of Restoration comedy.

Total attention to the concept of alienation can produce theatre generally free from emotional, empathic response from viewers. Do not strive for feeling and passion. Express excitement in terms of symbolism and ritual. Emotional portrayal is decorously exemplified and economically projected (for example, to indicate disdain or aloofness, simply turn your back on other actors). The emotional response of your audience need not correspond to the economic emotions of the character portrayed (for example, a spectator may laugh when you are angry). One of the most effective means of heightening alienation in Brecht Epic Theatre is to follow the Oriental example of using white makeup on your face. For example, a curtain opens to reveal you sitting on the stage. Your body is completely still; you rest your head in your hands. Slowly, with much ceremony, your head comes up, revealing a stark white face and traces of the makeup on your hands. No one in the audience misses the point. You are an actor in a theatre! All subsequent action should be tied to that theatrical beginning, even if you later remove the makeup.

In Brecht Epic Theatre, emotional power over an audience is frequently muted, leaving the actors and characters free to perform thought-provoking action. To protect the intellectual content of his plays, Brecht also uses some expressionistic techniques involving robot or mechanical and dreamlike action. Characters frequently and suddenly burst into song or formal commentary. Characters often become grotesque and unreal (e.g., Hitler as a marionette in *The Resistible Rise of Arturo Ui*). With practice and experience, you can adjust to these unusual techniques and provide the appropriate response—such as "dropping character" and singing a song that has nothing to do with the emotion of action and everything to do with the intellectual message or performing in a dehumanized, robot manner as for The Iron Soldiers in *The Caucasian Chalk Circle*.

Exercise 3   Character and Emotion—Brecht Epic Theatre

1. Using the scene at the end of this chapter from *The Caucasian Chalk Circle*, practice the fourteen techniques for character and emotion described above.

2. Practice the scene again with only selected items from the fourteen techniques, appropriately combining realistic, biomechanical, expressionistic, and Oriental techniques.

3. Perform the scene in a totally realistic, natural, believable style. Finally, orchestrate the scene from this reality base with selected use of "Epic techniques."

In concluding the discussion of Brecht's acting theories, I must caution that, paradoxically, any totally faithful application of Brecht's theories to his or other Epic plays (see the work of Peter Weiss, Rolf Hochhuth, and Max Frisch, for example) is doomed to almost certain failure. Audiences have generally rejected rigid use of alienating and didactic techniques.

Scenic design for *Mother Courage* by Bertolt Brecht. The exact scene in the play is seen projected (or hung); note other "Epic" elements revealed in the design.

The problem is how to reconcile Brecht's theory with Epic plays and sustain audience interest. Edward Payson Call, an American director, has provided one of the keys to solving this problem. His analysis and directing of highly successful productions of Brecht plays have captivated audiences. Call uses Brechtian acting theory with discretion and pinpoint selectivity. Apart from Brecht's Epic theories and some use of expressionistic, biomechanical, and Oriental techniques, Call permits certain actors in key roles to perform in a traditional, realistic style, creating emotion and empathy (again, Grusha in *The Caucasian Chalk Circle* and Mother Courage must be played this way). As a result, the eclectic *mix* of the Epic, the nonreal, and the real creates palatable Brecht onstage and also imparts the appropriate didacticism. Perhaps Brecht's advice to Lotte Lenya (given at the beginning of this chapter) best guides your acting: *Once aware of and rehearsed in the Epic techniques, follow your instincts and play the role without worrying about the theory.* Brecht's plays probably present adequate opportunity to achieve his intention without inordinate application of all his acting theories.

Suggested Characters and Plays for Scene Work

Brecht, Bertolt

Azdak, Grusha, The Ironshirt, Ludovica, The Governor's Wife
> *The Caucasian Chalk Circle*

Shen Te/Shui Ta, Mr. Shu Fu
> *The Good Woman of Setzuan*

Arturo Ui, Givola, Roma, Dogsborough, Docdaisy
> *The Resistible Rise of Arturo Ui*

Galileo, Andrea
> *Galileo*

Mother Courage, Swiss Cheese, Catherine, Eilif, Yvette
> *Mother Courage*

Polly, Macheath, Peachum, Lucy
> *The Threepenny Opera*

Joan
> *St. Joan of the Stockyards*

Any role
> *A Man's a Man*

Any role
> *The Private Life of the Master Race*

See also the list of characters and plays at the end of chapter 20 for playwrights influenced by Brecht Epic Theatre, such as Weiss, Hochhuth, and Frisch.

Actor Checklist   *Brecht Epic Theatre*

Voice	Selective combination of human and dehumanized; pliant, flexible; lively; unusual attention to vowels and consonants; national and regional dialects; class distinction; dissonant singing, chanting, intonation, and lyrical, as appropriate.

Movement	Appropriate mix of realistic, biomechanical, expressionistic, Oriental; loose and flexible muscle control; some use of acrobatics, dance, mime, and gymnastics; ranges from graceful to forceful; mix of presentational and representational mode.
Gestures	Varied; at times full use of entire body; highly inventive; at times use of specific Oriental techniques; descriptive; fluid; isolated body gestures.
Pantomimic Dramatization	Unusual use of mask, makeup, music, costume, particularly for Oriental; highly inventive; theatrical; rhythmic.
Character	Combination of real and nonreal; combination of historical and fictional; ranges from simple to complex; oriented toward social issues and themes; clear; controlled; realized with a mix of alienation devices and human behavior; diversified and theatrical.
Ideas	Unusually important; clear; didactic; socially, politically, and philosophically oriented; directed to the masses.
Emotion	Ranges from simple to complex; ranges from human to nonhuman; ranges from full empathy to no empathy.
Language	Colloquial-poetic; sensual simplicity; diversified; unusual use of songs.
Mood and Atmosphere	Clear; controlled; tied to idea, social, and political purpose; combination of real and nonreal; combination of serious and comic.
Pace and Tempo	Unusually varied.
Special Technique	Selective use of alienation devices and Oriental techniques; unusual vocal and physical flexibility; unique character and emotional analysis and execution.

Suggested Readings

Brecht, Bertolt. *Brecht on Theatre*. Translated by John Willett. New York: Hill & Wang, 1964.

Brockett, O. G. *History of the Theatre*. 4th ed. Rockleigh, N.J.: Allyn & Bacon, 1982.

———. *The Theatre: An Introduction*. 3rd ed. New York: Holt, Rinehart, and Winston, 1974.

Esslin, Martin. *Brecht: The Man and His Work*. Rev. ed. New York: Doubleday & Co., 1971.

Gray, Ronald. *Brecht*. New York: Grove Press, 1961.

Innes, C. D. *Erwin Piscator's Political Theatre*. New York: Cambridge University Press, 1972.

Ley-Piscator, Maria. *The Piscator Experiment: The Political Theatre*. New York: James H. Heineman, Inc. 1976.

Munk, Erica. Ed. *Stanislavsky and America*. New York: Hill & Wang, 1966. See Eric Bentley article, "Stanislavsky and Brecht," pp. 116–23.

Needle, Jan, and Peter Thomson. *Brecht.* Chicago: University of Chicago Press, 1981.

Willett, John. *The Theatre of Bertolt Brecht.* New York: New Directions Pub. Corp., 1959.

———. *Erwin Piscator.* New York: 1979.

Weideli, Walter. *The Art of Bertolt Brecht.* New York: New York University Press, 1963.

Suggested Filmography

1. *Galileo.* 1975. British-Canadian. American Film Theatre. Playwright-Bertolt Brecht. With Topol, Edward Fox.
2. *The Threepenny Opera.* 1931. German. Playwright-Brecht. Director-G. W. Pabst. With Carola Neher.
3. *The Threepenny Opera.* 1962. Playwright-Brecht. With Curt Jurgens, Sammy Davis, Jr.

The Caucasian Chalk Circle
by *Bertolt Brecht*

Bertolt Brecht

English version by Eric Bentley and Maja Apelman

from
Part Two, 1

The Story Teller	Shauwa	*Characters*
Chorus	The Blackmailer	
Azdak	The Innkeeper	
The Invalid	Ludovica	
The Limping Man	The Stableman	
The Doctor	An Ironshirt	

A makeshift Court of Justice in a Caucasian city. *Scene*

The civil war in a country turns a drunken rascal into a powerful judge who is   *Situation*
asked to decide on the custody of a governor's son. Should the child go to his
actual mother, who abandoned him, or to his adopted mother, who cared for him?
Prior to the crucial decision, Azdak, the judge, engages in comic trials and
decisions with a variety of cases.

THE STORY TELLER
>   And there was civil war in the land.
>   The ruler was unsafe.
>   And Azdak was made a judge by the Ironshirts.
>   And Azdak remained a judge for two years.

THE STORY TELLER AND CHORUS
>   Conflagration's heat, and blood in every street,
>   And cockroach and bug in every town.
>   In the castle, fànatics. At the altar, heretics.
>   And Azdak wearing a judge's gown.

(AZDAK *sits in the judge's chair, peeling an apple.* SHAUWA *is sweeping out the hall.*
On one side an invalid in a wheelchair. Opposite, a young man accused of
blackmail. An IRONSHIRT *stands on guard, holding the Ironshirt's banner.*)

AZDAK   In consideration of the large number of cases, the Court today will hear
two cases at a time. Before I open the proceedings, a short announcement—I
accept—(*He stretches out his hand. The* BLACKMAILER *is the only one to produce*
any money. He hands it to AZDAK.)—I reserve for myself the right to punish
one of the parties here for contempt of court. (*He glances at the* INVALID.) You
(*To the* DOCTOR) are a doctor, and you (*To the* INVALID) are bringing a complaint
against him. Is the doctor responsible for your condition?

THE INVALID   Yes. I had a stroke because of him.

AZDAK   That would be professional negligence.

THE INVALID   More than negligence. I gave this man money for his studies. So far,
he hasn't paid me back a cent. And when I heard he was treating a patient
free, I had a stroke.

AZDAK   Rightly. (*To a* LIMPING MAN) And you, what do you want here?

THE LIMPING MAN   I'm the patient, your honor.

AZDAK   He treated your leg for nothing?

THE LIMPING MAN   The wrong leg! My rheumatism was in the left leg, and he operated on the right. That's why I limp now.

AZDAK   And you got it free?

THE INVALID   A five-hundred-piaster operation free! For nothing! For a God-bless-you! And I paid for this man's studies! (*To the* DOCTOR) Did they teach you to operate free?

THE DOCTOR   Your Honor, it is actually the custom to demand the fee before the operation, as the patient is more willing to pay before an operation than after. Which is only human. In the case in question I was convinced, when I started the operation, that my servant had already received the fee. In this I was mistaken.

THE INVALID   He was mistaken! A good doctor doesn't make mistakes! He examines before he operates.

AZDAK   That's right. (*To* SHAUWA) Public Prosecutor, what's the other case about?

SHAUWA (*busily sweeping*)   Blackmail.

THE BLACKMAILER   High Court of Justice, I'm innocent. I only wanted to find out from the landowner concerned if he really had raped his niece. He informed me very politely that this was not the case, and gave me the money only so I could pay for my uncle's studies.

AZDAK   Hm. (*To the* DOCTOR) You, on the other hand, can cite no extenuating circumstances for your offense, huh?

THE DOCTOR   Except that to err is human.

AZDAK   And you are perfectly well aware that in money matters a good doctor is conscious of his responsibility? I once heard of a doctor who made a thousand piasters out of one sprained finger: he discovered it had something to do with blood circulation, which a less good doctor might have overlooked. On another occasion he made a real gold mine out of the careful treatment of a somewhat disordered gall bladder. You have no excuse, Doctor. The corn merchant, Uxu, had his son study medicine to get some knowledge of trade, our medical schools are so good. (*To the* BLACKMAILER) What's the name of the landowner?

SHAUWA   He doesn't want it known.

AZDAK   In that case I will pass judgment. The Court considers the blackmail proved. And you (*to the* INVALID) are sentenced to a fine of one thousand piasters. If you get a second stroke, the doctor will have to treat you free. Eventually he will have to amputate. (*To the* LIMPING MAN) As compensation, you will receive a bottle of rubbing alcohol. (*To the* BLACKMAILER) You are sentenced to hand over half the proceeds of your deal to the Public Prosecutor to keep the landowner's name secret. You are advised, moreover, to study medicine—you seem well suited to that calling. (*To the* DOCTOR) You are acquitted in consideration of an unpardonable error in the practice of your profession! Next cases!

THE STORY TELLER AND CHORUS

> With a pound you're on firm ground (no one is willing for a shilling)
>> And the law is a cat in a sack.
> But one whelp brings help to the many for a penny.
>> The name of this rascal? Azdak.

(*Enter* AZDAK *from the caravansary on the highroad, followed by an old bearded innkeeper. The judge's chair is carried by a stableman and* SHAUWA. *An* IRONSHIRT, *with a banner, takes up his position.*)

AZDAK   Put it here. Then we'll get some air and maybe a good breeze from the lemon grove over there. It does justice good to be administered in the open: the wind blows her skirts up and you can see what she's got underneath. Shauwa, we've eaten too much. These official journeys are very exhausting. (*To the* INNKEEPER) Where's your daughter-in-law?

THE INNKEEPER   Your Worship, it's a question of the family honor. I wish to bring an action on behalf of my son, who's on business on the other side of the mountain. This is the offending stableman, and here's my daughter-in-law.

(*Enter the Daughter-in-law, a voluptuous wench. She is veiled.*)

AZDAK (*sitting down*)   I accept . . . (*Sighing, the* INNKEEPER *hands him some money.*) Good. Now the formalities are disposed of. This is a case of rape?

THE INNKEEPER   Your Honor, I caught the fellow in the act. Ludovica was already in the straw on the stable floor.

AZDAK   Quite right, the stable. Beautiful horses! I particularly liked the little roan.

THE INNKEEPER   The first thing I did, of course, was question Ludovica. On my son's behalf.

AZDAK (*seriously*)   I said I particularly liked it.

THE INNKEEPER (*coldly*)   Really? Ludovica confessed the stableman took her against her will.

AZDAK   Take your veil off, Ludovica. (*She does so.*) Ludovica, you please the Court. Tell us how it happened.

LUDOVICA (*well-schooled*)   When I entered the stable to see the new foal the stableman said to me on his own accord: "It's hot today!" and laid his hand on my left breast. I said to him: "Don't do that!" But he continued to handle me indecently, which provoked my anger. Before I realized his sinful intentions, he had got much closer. It had already taken place when my father-in-law entered and accidentally trod on me.

THE INNKEEPER (*explaining*)   On my son's behalf.

AZDAK (*to the* STABLEMAN)   Do you admit you started it?

THE STABLEMAN   Yes.

AZDAK   Ludovica, do you like to eat sweet things?

LUDOVICA   Yes, sunflower seeds!

AZDAK   Do you like to lie a long time in the bathtub?

LUDOVICA   Half an hour or so.

AZDAK   Public Prosecutor, drop your knife—there—on the floor. (SHAUWA *does so.*) Ludovica, go and pick up the knife. (LUDOVICA, *swaying her hips, does so.*) See that? (*He points at her.*) The way it moves? The rape is now proven. By eating too much—sweet things, especially—by lying too long in warm water, by laziness and too soft a skin, you have raped that unfortunate man. Do you imagine you can run around with a behind like that and get away with it in court? This is a case of intentional assault with a dangerous weapon! You are sentenced to hand over to the Court the little roan which your father liked to ride "on his son's behalf." And now, come with me to the stables, so the Court may inspect the scene of the crime, Ludovica.

When visiting your neighbor sharpen up your ax,
For Bible texts and sermons are trivial knickknacks.
What miracles past believing the ax's edge can do!
Sometimes Azdak believed in miracles too.

(*END*)

The Caucasian Chalk Circle by Bertolt Brecht. Don Blakely (seated) as Azdak, Barbara Meek as The Governor's Wife, David Falk as The Governor's Son, and Phyllis Somerville as Grusha at The Hilberry Theatre, Wayne State University. English version by Eric Bentley. Music Score by Herbert Pilhofer. Directed by Leonard Leone. Scenery by Timothy R. Dewart. Costumes by Judith Haugen. Lighting by Gary M. Witt. Musical Direction by Alvin H. Yungton.

Absurd 19

Beyond Reason

. . . We are here as on a darkling plain,
Swept with confused alarms of struggle
    and flight
Where ignorant armies clash by night.
> Matthew Arnold
> from James H. Clancy, "Beyond Despair:
>   A New Drama of Ideas," in Morris
>   Freedman, *Essays in Modern Drama.*

ORATOR He faces the rows of empty chairs;
he makes the invisible crowd understand
that he is deaf and dumb; he makes the
signs of a deaf-mute; desperate efforts to
make himself understood; then he coughs,
groans, and utters the gutteral sounds of a
mute: He, mme, mm, mn. Je, gou, hou, hou.
Heu, heu, go, fou, gueue.
> *The Chairs* by Eugene Ionesco

Berenger as he sees himself in *Rhinoceros* by Eugene Ionesco.

As Arnold so poetically notes, modern man frequently finds himself immersed in a dark and confusing struggle. A case in point was World War II. It was in many ways an unreasonable and devastating war in which innocent people, ranging from the victims of the atrocities of Nazi concentration camps to those of atomic bombs dropped on densely populated cities, were slaughtered. Such devastation renders humanity insensitive; the meaning of life deteriorates; communication fails. As with Ionesco's Orator, the confusion leads to meaningless sounds and groans. After this war, man needed to rediscover himself and his world and the universe in which he lived. Philosophers, poets, and playwrights were once again the leaders in the search.

Overview of the Existential, the Absurd

The actor playing the role of Vladimir (Didi) in Samuel Beckett's play *Waiting for Godot* came despondently into the Little Theatre at the University of Nevada, Las Vegas, and approached the director. "I can't go on with this. You'll have to let me out. This character—this play—I'm really depressed. The way Didi thinks, his habits—they're getting to me. I feel worthless— a bum. Eating a radish—putting on my boots—everything debilitating. I feel like Didi—I need a belt strong enough to hang myself!" At that moment the director removed his own belt, handed it to the actor, and grinned. A general burst of laughter relaxed the very honest and serious actor. The laughter was important for more than one reason. To act Absurd drama, you must find the humor "relief value" in the script and in the role, or audiences may find the negative, existential philosophy of these plays totally unpalatable. Similarly, you must retain and utilize a sense of humor in rehearsal to relieve the inevitable tension. Such is the power of the strange but effective contemporary dramatic genre labeled Theatre of the Absurd.

Originating in the philosophical ideas of Existentialism as expounded by the great French philosopher-author Jean-Paul Sartre (1905–1980), this genre burst impressively upon the theatre world in the early 1950s in the work of such playwrights as Beckett, Eugene Ionesco, and Jean Genet. The genre made a steady, pure contribution to world theatre for more than ten years, and its influence continues to the present day. (Some of the ideas found in the essays, novels, and plays of the French writer, Albert Camus, 1913–1960, are also valuable in understanding the philosophy inherent in most existential, Absurd plays, although Camus essentially rejected the label of existentialist.

How considered Absurd? In what way, Absurd? What does the word mean in the context of drama and acting?

The answers to these questions begin with examination of *Existentialism* as employed by one of the main precursors of Absurd drama, Jean-Paul Sartre. Other forerunners of the Absurd include Alfred Jarry (discussed in chapter 17) and Luigi Pirandello (1867–1936). Jarry often distorted human character to the level of cartoon figures to make a negative point concerning existence.[1] Pirandello was an Italian dramatist who emphasized that truth was a matter of personal viewpoint. Pirandello's plays, such as *Six Characters in Search of an Author*, *Right Your Are*, and *Masks*, depict grotesque conflict between illusion and reality.

Existentialism refers to a particular view of the nature of man's existence. The existentialist believes that man starts life with nothing. His life is made up of acts; through the process of acting man becomes conscious of his original nothingness. By choosing to act, man passes into the arena of human responsibilitty which makes him the creator of his own existence. However, the existence inevitably ends with death. Man returns to his original state of nothingness. This existential notion eliminates the Western concept of man's exalted nature. Life becomes meaningless and useless—a condition which is in essence "absurd." Man's only freedom in this condition is the exercise of his conscious mind. However, consciousness means conflict—between man's awareness of the absurdity of his existence and his need for justification of his human action.

The Sartrian existentialist sees man as adrift in the world. There is no God or religion; man is a quirk of environmental accident and development, "absurdly" (meaning unreasonably) thrust into special consciousness beyond his animal relatives due to the persecuting factors of mind and voice (e.g., thinking and speaking). What man is left with is the tedious condition of waiting to die, whereby he evaporates into nothingness in an empty or meaningless universe. However, if man can recognize and accept the simultaneous existence of his absurdity and his responsibility to give himself definition through choice and action, *there may be hope.*

The chief twentieth-century exponents of existential philosophy were the late Jean-Paul Sartre and the late Albert Camus (albeit Camus denied the label and albeit Sartre and Camus differed on their precise view of human existence.) Sartre, a playwright as well as a novelist, dramatized existential man struggling to cope with a meaningless world. Orestes, in *The Flies*, acts as a free man devoid of emotional attachments in a corrupt world. Although Orestes takes full and, in his view, courageous responsibility for his actions, freedom serves only to isolate him. Absurdity again triumphs. Meaningful existence is only as valuable as man views it to be in light of the demands he places on himself. Since God does not exist (if He did exist, the world would not be in chaos), values are created on the basis of individual decision alone. Most of Sartre's plays focus on a character faced with moral choices or struggles (e.g., *The Flies* and *No Exit*).

Camus' characters are usually repulsed by their existence and violently attack their world (e.g., *Caligula*). The importance of Camus as a playwright rests on his rejection of a didactic premise for his plays in favor of presenting the world as a chasm of frantic, aimless activity. Camus was the first writer to use the term *absurd* in describing the senselessness of the

---

1. See the cartoon figure, Ubu Roi, depicted on the title page of this chapter.

human condition. (See his *Myth of Sisyphus* for a full definition and discussion of his concept of the word, "absurd.") By abandoning the rational approach to life, the existential man must attempt to find values in a world devoid of values; he must attempt to find order in a world gone mad (as opposed to Brecht, whose characters do not accept absurdity, but rather look to social change for a more purposeful, rational world).

The nonrealistic theatre movements discussed in chapter 17 and the work of Brecht were well known by Sartre and Camus. These movements had considerable influence upon their *theatrical* thinking.

Another important influence on the Theatre of the Absurd came from Antonin Artaud (1895–1948), a French theatrical genius whose work began in the 1920's. His theatre experimentations proposed to cure the ills of the traditional Western theatre which he believed was deadening the lives of its members as well as of its audiences. Artaud described theatre in terms of ritual and myth, expecting the audience to experience trance and inspiration. His work attempted psychologically to remove the audience from the present to a primitive past by eliminating words and reliance upon script. Influenced by the Balinese dances and Eastern theatre, Artaud bore witness to a theatre of mystifying spectacle where words had no power and language became incantation. Artaud felt that the Western theatre was a slave to words, to text, and to realistic imitation. Instead, he wanted the Western theatre to utilize aspects of the Eastern theatre and create a shock force which would jar audiences from the complacent conditions of everyday life. Artaud used mechanical devices to create visible and audible frenzy. Light, sound, and physical movement and dance were used to tyrannize or assault the sensibilities of the audience. The overall effect was similar to the impact of Oriental theatre wherein gestures, signs, postures, and sounds were compressed and symbolized.

Artaud called his dramatic theory the Theatre of Cruelty. He saw life and theatre as a "double," one reflecting the other. In his concept of *cruelty* a bloodless state was implied. Artaud defined cruelty as a psychological purging of man's soul, freeing him from the bondage of logical and verbal experience. To effect a reevaluation of our lives, Artaud used shocking, violent, and often pornographic techniques to stimulate a vision that reached beyond ordinary reality. He wanted the subconscious mind to probe the mysteries of existence. The idea of cruelty was comparable to the high priest (actor) disrupting the logical response of the congregation (audience) to subject them ruthlessly to emotional and primitive response.

Absurd plays depict man tyrannized by nonman, by the intractable universe. Life is a "waiting period" which is at best painful and monotonous. For escape, man is left routine and fantasy. In the concept of good and evil each cancels the other out—nothing is absolute—everything is relative. The Absurdists frequently obliterate the distinction between human and nonhuman (for example, men and animals are interchangeable, speech is often disconnected and noncommunicative). References to God's abandoning man to isolation and alienation are frequent. There are no more Western myths or illusions about an Omnipresent Being holding sway over man. Without hope, time and space are meaningless references. Within the concept of time, everything has happened before. Man can only perpetuate the art of game-playing to pass the insidious factor of time. Idle songs may be sung, dances danced, jokes exchanged—violence, sex, and simple hygiene may take on hedonistic excess—inanimate objects may take on life and inordinate significance. If man is strong enough to face reality, he is left to the only certain escape, namely, death, via what may be man's only possibility for a heroic act—suicide—through willful choice.

The Absurdists force us to look over the precipice into the abyss defined by the existentialists. We may reach that precipice through our subconsciousness and our dreams. We may doubt our reality, our traditional and usually abstract values such as love, family, art, science, occupation, religion, education, and so on. These are narrow confines and are rendered meaningless and beyond communicative possibility. An occasional laugh is the most convenient relief from living in such fantasy (and perhaps more meaningful than any of the traditional values). Pain comes with the knowledge that a vast difference separates what we are from what we might be.

How do the existential Absurdists justify the creation of art (plays) if they philosophically view all activity as ultimately meaningless? The playwright invariably justifies the writing as being merely *his* particular fantasy, *his* escape, and thereby *validates* the philosophy. Ask him to explain his philosophy and he may reply, "The forceps of birth lead directly to the shovel of death." To the Absurdist, the surgeon becomes the gravedigger merely by exchanging instruments. In between birth and death is only an absurd or unreasonable existence, voided forever by the only certain end of any living existence: death in an eternal anonymity. Paradoxically, while the Absurdist view of life seems negative (chaotic, disintegrated, and despairing), he may find hope in man's effort to abandon his illusions and confront the truth of his existence. Recognizing his limitations gives man strength to go beyond reality and confront the intangible—a test of ultimate reality. In 1968 the challenging intellectual and emotional impact of these plays reached its zenith when the Nobel Prize was awarded to Samuel Beckett. His "forcept-gravedigger" image stands as one of the clearest symbols of the entire Absurdist movement in theatre.

Now that the viewpoint of existential Absurd drama has been briefly clarified, it is easy to sympathize with the plight of the actor playing the role of Didi. To perform a role in one of these plays, you should retain a sense of humor and adhere to your life values. It is distracting and pointless (possibly even dangerous) to become overinvolved in existential philosophy, expecially if you find yourself agreeing with that philosophy. Your task is to understand the point of view and then, as always, turn to the vital work of creating your role honestly, truthfully, and in the appropriate style.

In *The Theatre of the Absurd*, Martin Esslin, the acknowledged leading critic of Absurd Theatre, discusses the leading playwrights of the Absurdist movement. Chief among them are Eugene Ionesco (1912–), Samuel Beckett (1906–), and Jean Genet (1910–). It is enlightening to consider the fact that most of the "Absurdist" playwrights (i.e., Ionesco, Beckett, and Genet in particular) were *not* involved with theatre when they developed their ideas about life, man, and existence. In fact, they revolted against theatre and its conventions (such as Ionesco calling his scripts "anti-plays"). Sartre and Camus had based their revolt on a philosophical tenet; Beckett, Genet, and others revolted as much against traditional theatre techniques as they did against traditional philosophic premises.

While Harold Pinter (1930–), Edward Albee (1928–), Tom Stoppard (1938–), and others have also been considered Absurdists by some critics, they are perhaps better classified as contemporary Eclectics. As such, they are discussed in chapter 20. As noted above, Ionesco called his plays "antiplays"—plays lacking traditional action, characters, and dialogue. His plays are emersed in fantastic hallucination, secret desires, and pulverizing fears. On the surface, Ionesco's plays resemble light comedies; further examination reveals serious social implication aligned with existential thought. Ionesco usually uses a conventional middle-class drawing room for his setting and conventional clichés for his dialogue (taken from a language primer). The result is a "put-on" with serious intent. Characters are carried away by words, changing identity, and farcical activity (such as having no head, as in *The Leader*, or laying eggs, as in *The Future Is in Eggs*). In *The Bald Soprano*, the banalities of their clichéd dialogue serve to make two middle-class British families appear mad. In *Rhinoceros*, a man seems to change into a rhinoceros. The images created by Ionesco are immediate and strange, comparable to those experienced in a dream or by primitive man. Images evolve with the irrational but compulsive logic of a dream. A corpse grows in a bedroom and Ionesco makes it seem perfectly normal (e.g., *Amedée*). Human beings are displaced by the proliferation of objects (e.g., furniture in *The Tenants*; chairs in *The Chairs*). Displacement such as this is a common occurrence in our lives. Do not material possessions often govern our thoughts and actions? In these plays everything appears to make sense, yet paradoxically is beyond reason. Nightmares are staged in the most unpredictable, irrational, abrupt manner. Dialogue is rendered meaningless by use of countless puns, speech inversions, sonic associations, non sequitors, purposeless nouns, and so on.

Yet, beneath the structure of the game-playing, the automatized language, the mimetic action, and the farcical antics smolders a curious disenchantment. Ionesco sees the individual consciousness isolated in an absurd universe. His characters are generally clowns and marionettes who ape man. The mechanical forces inhibiting man only provoke our laughter, making us nostalgic for the human element.

Early in the 1950s, Samuel Beckett, who is Irish, began to publish frequently in Paris. *Malloy, Malone Dies, The Unnamable,* and *Waiting for Godot,* all originally written in French, were published between 1950 and 1952. Sixteen remarkable years later Beckett was awarded the Nobel Prize for Literature—a prize which recognized the man as a renowned playwright and the Absurd movement as a major force in the world of literature. Early in the Absurd movement, Beckett was usually associated with Ionesco, a fact which severely limited the importance of Beckett. For Ionesco, absurdity meant uproarious farce; for Beckett, absurdity meant a life lived in isolation and despair. Hence, Beckett's vision of the world is not as irrational and unpredictable as is the world depicted by Ionesco. Beckett's unique contribution to the Absurd movement is his view that man's absurdity is simply an outgrowth of his self-conscious condition. As man approaches the end of the game (i.e., life), he remains, above all, rational and precise. The best man can do is pass the waiting time as painlessly as possible. He can plot his life and calculate his actions, making himself "sane" by repetitious patter and vaudeville calamities (e.g., pratfalls and collapsing trousers). This is both the worst and the best that can befall man. The best that man can hope for! The comic and tragic merge in Beckett's plays. *(Endgame, Happy Days, Krapp's Last Tape, Play.)* Any line spoken in a Beckett play can provoke either reaction. Actions, characters, dialogue, and business are a tragicomic commentary on the infinite complexities of our daily lives.

Jean Genet is primarily interested in exploring the spatial and optical possibilities of the theatre. His plays are renderings of ceremonies and rituals created to depict a universe in the throes of annihilation. In this sense they are reflective of an influence from Artaud. For Genet, the theatre is the ultimate exorcist of man's fantasies. Characters are reflections of something other than themselves, prisoners of their own imagination (e.g., *The Balcony* and *The Maids*). What appears to be truth is simply an illusion. The real meaning of life lies in the opposite of what is expected: black is white, white is black; evil is good, good is evil; the criminal is virtuous, the virtuous is criminal *(The Blacks)*. Again, we see the relation to Artaud and his concept of the theatre and its double, the theatre and life, the theatre and cruelty. Ritual is the means devised to perpetuate some semblance of order in a chaotic universe. In keeping with the Absurdist concept of purposeless existence, Genet heightens and grotesquely shapes his so-called order and puts it on display. As members of the audience, we are confronted by our own image in shattered glass—an image distorted and horrifying. According to Genet, we wear black suits, yellow shoes, excessive makeup, clashing and gaudy colors; we wear patched garments and incorrect masks (we are black, not white; we are white, not black—what is *color?*). We use highly artificial language, often eloquent and poetic; yet we steal from the language of the gutter. We curse and scream. No action onstage justifies our outcast existence. We are all alienated, although we pretend not to be. Agree with it or not, Genet presents a highly effective treatise on the decadence of the individual isolated in society doomed to a meaningless death.

Waiting for Godot by Samuel Beckett. Max Wright as Vladimir and Phillip Piro as Estragon at The Bonstelle Theatre, Wayne State University. Directed by Russell Smith. Scenery by Russell Smith. Costumes by Judith Haugen. Lighting by Gary M. Witt.

Voice

It is interesting that words and language in Absurd plays are frequently considered part of the spectacle. That is, words are frequently used as sound and noise (therefore, spectacle) rather than for purposes of logical communication. In a way, words are transparent, revealing only immediate meaning. Language seems to "participate" in the theatrical activity, similar to properties and scenery. On the surface, speech is frequently confusing and nonsensical. However, you should play against the emptiness of the stereotyped language. In other words, you must speak the words with energy, variety, and certainty, even when they seem to be meaningless. Silences and pauses are vital in handling language in Absurd plays. Your vocal tools must function exceptionally well to vary your speech patterns, vocal rhythms, and speaking-singing range. Language is often redundant and monotonous. As a result, many audience members reject the material if actors are not especially effective at providing vocal variety to alleviate the monotony. (Of course, you must be selective in providing variety because if it is overdone, you may violate the philosophical intention of the playwright who has deliberately established the tedium of the language.) When the characters and action involve nonreal, dehumanized activity, you should apply the vocal techniques for such behavior discussed in chapters 17 and 18. However, since most Absurd characters are based on reality, you begin with the tenets of vocal delivery for Realism (see chapter 16). Careful script analysis by you and your director will clarify whether to apply realistic or nonrealistic vocal techniques.

Exercise 1   Voice—Absurd

    1. Select one of the longer speeches by Estragon or Vladimir in the scene from *Waiting for Godot* at the end of this chapter (the speeches work effectively for both men and women). Practice the speech applying the following techniques:

1. As realistic prose
2. As nonsense gibberish through use of strange pauses, inflections, intonations, and so on
3. As an ephemeral dream
4. As a mechanical robot
5. As a didactic message
6. As primitive, ruthless rage
7. As philosophic reflection

Finally, practice the speech with an appropriate mix of any or all of the above foregoing techniques. (Ionesco's *The Bald Soprano* or any of his other plays are also particularly well suited to this exercise.)

    2. Study and observe the traditional rituals practiced by various churches, lodges, clubs, social organizations, judicial systems, and so on. Select facets of these rituals to use in performing the language of the ritualistic segments in plays by Genet, Beckett, Ionesco, and others of the Absurd style. (For example, the use of incense, candles, and gavels can provide interesting, valid activity for use with many speeches in plays by these authors.)

Movement

Absurd plays are unusually antiliterary and frequently nonverbal because they are linked to ritualistic ceremony, circus activity, and routines and techniques used by commedia dell'arte, itinerant jugglers, mime troupes, music hall burlesques, acrobatics, and silent films (including those of Buster Keaton, Charlie Chaplin, the Keystone Cops, Laurel and Hardy, and the Marx Brothers). In all of these activities complex physical dexterity and precise timing are stressed (the timing is even more important when coordinated with dialogue and sounds). These activities are closely tied to what we think of as popular entertainment, that is, visual escape entertainment which is often used as a device to pass time. Hence, these activities relate closely to the philosophical premise of the material (e.g., meaningless routine and the passing of hours, days, weeks, months, and years).

    Your body should be relaxed, disciplined, and nimble. You should be as agile as the old-time vaudeville burlesque comedians. Recall the deft fingers of these comedians as they toss several hats into the air with ease and precision. The entertainment style of the Irish pub humorists, the English dance-hall performers, and the American burlesque entertainers provide a unique ingredient required for mastery of movement in the Absurd style of acting. Again, a combination of the techniques of movement discussed in chapters 16, 17, and 18 are effectively employed.

Exercise 2 Movement—Absurd

1. Everyone become involved in silently arranging twenty chairs in the room. Once arranged, completely rearrange them. Continue rearranging them for a full five minutes.

2. After five minutes of Exercise 1, relieve the monotony by performing a variety of the following activities. Interchange activities at will, always being certain that between each activity you return to some rearrangement of the chairs.

    a. Remove your shoes, shake them out, put them on again.

    b. Practice a soft-shoe shuffle.

    c. Practice juggling two or more objects.

    d. Practice a series of gymnastic or acrobatic exercises.

    e. Rearrange the chairs in the speeded-up tempo of a silent film being run at fast speed.

    f. Vary your tempo in all of these activities by using mechanical robot movement, ephemeral dreamlike movement, Epic alienation techniques, and primitive assault techniques.

3. Return to the rituals studied and practiced in Exercise #1 above. Perform them pantomimically, void of all dialogue and sound.

Character and Emotion

Character and emotion in Absurd plays range from one-dimensional and lack of feeling to multidimensional and sensitive feeling. For example, Berenger in Ionesco's *Rhinoceros* is a full-dimensional, human characterization which permits the use of Stanislavski's techniques. On the other hand, the characters in Ionesco's *The Bald Soprano* are fundamentally one-dimensional stereotypes. Berenger passes through a gamut of emotion, whereas *Soprano's* characters seem relatively free of feeling. In view of the fact that Absurd characters frequently seem involved in pointless activity devoid of traditional plot action, it is best not to ask, What has happened in the past and What comes next? but rather, What is happening *now*? Neither the actor nor the audience can rely on cause and effect and logical sequence of motivated action. We can only be amused or shocked by the often grotesque nature of the spontaneous movement.

Most characters in Absurd plays are based on realism. However, at some point in the play the authors usually distort reality by dehumanization or by having inanimate objects take on life. Absurdist playwrights utilize many of the alienating techniques of Epic Theatre. In fact, some critics believe Absurdist playwrights are more effective alienists than was Brecht (by use of the proliferation of objects, changes in identity, and repetition of language and action).

Absurd material also lends itself well to the primitive assault techniques of Artaud. For example, Absurd characters assault the sensibilities of an audience by such activity as "urinating" onstage and crudely mastigating food (see Beckett's *Krapp's Last Tape*). An actor can perform these activities alternately as realistic behavior or as ritualistic behavior. The latter is germane to Artaud's intentions. For example, peeling and eating a piece of fruit can be performed as primitive man's discovery of nourishment.

At times, the nonrealistic distortion of robot and ephemeral dreamlike behavior can also be used effectively in Absurd theatre. For example, Lucky and Pozzo in *Waiting for Godot* seem almost to be dehumanized robots of power and slavery. In the same play, Didi and Gogo (Vladimir and Estragon) speak of living in a dream. In these moments the actors can permit the characters to react as in a dream state.

Line-by-line textual analysis will help you find the correct style and mood and provide the appropriate interpretation. Absurdist playwrights have a tendency to carry poetry, farce, dialogue, and cabaret activity to excess. When a conflict exists between realistic and nonrealistic characterization and emotion, you are usually well advised to play the humor arising from the incongruity. It is this safety valve of humor which makes the Absurd character palatable to most audiences. At such moments you generally

Design for *Waiting for Godot* by Samuel Beckett (with an Edwardian interpretation in the costumes) by Ellis M. Pryce-Jones.

need not rely upon the realistic techniques of Stanislavski for motivation or probe for deep emotion. Simply perform the immediate action. An appropriate combination of laughter and despair will usually follow naturally. If you follow the principle that emotion and empathy are used during realistic moments and restricted during nonrealistic or ritualistic moments, you will usually find the appropriate performance level.

Creating Absurd characters and emotion requires acute awareness of your own personality and physical and mental resources. The Absurd acting style is a sensitive combination of several preceding styles (e.g., Realism, Naturalism, Expressionism, and Epic, plus vaudeville humor). Its execution necessitates using an inordinate amount of your own personality traits and your own behavioral habits and routines. Once again, personalization is the key to success—ability to skillfully observe your world, sensitive and active perception of your own sensory equipment, vivid imagination, and active knowledge of how your body rhythms fluxuate as you pass the time or engage in routine life activities.

Above all, understand the intentions of the playwright. Do not lose yourself in the interchangeable nature of his vision of the universe. The last and the next moment onstage are unimportant in light of the question, What is happening *now?* Your task is to penetrate both the internal and external realities of action *moment by moment.*

Exercise 3   Character and Emotion

1. Select a monologue from a character of your choice from one of the Absurd plays given in the list at the end of this chapter. Perform the monologue after analysis, incorporating the types of character and emotion just discussed (e.g., realistic, expressionistic, Epic, and cabaret or vaudeville). Your character and emotion should range from multidimensional and real to simplistic and nonreal. For the purpose of the exercise, do not hesitate to superimpose some of these stylistic techniques for the sake of practice. However, you should note that an effective mix of styles cannot usually be accomplished in a single monologue (an exception might be Lucky's unique monologue from *Waiting for Godot*).

2. Using the famous monologue by Lucky from Act One of *Waiting For Godot*, create and perform a series of rituals which help reveal the complex character and emotion revealed by Lucky in this ideal personification of the Absurd effectively dramatized.

In the 1960s the Absurd movement splintered. The final style for our examination is the natural extension of the combination of techniques used in Absurd drama. Playwrights ranging from Eugene O'Neill at the beginning of the twentieth century to such contemporary artists as Harold Pinter intermingle the stylistic considerations prevalent in the last eighty or more years. Our remaining study is of the proliferation of eclectic, stylistic acting techniques of the last three decades. Also, contemporary innovative theatrical groups and movements must be examined (see Appendix B, pages 468-478).

Suggested Characters and Plays for Scene Work

Camus, Albert

Caligula, Caesonia, Scipio
: *Caligula*

Sartre, Jean-Paul

Goetz, Heinrich, Nasti, Tetzel, Hilda, Cathrine
: *The Devil and the Good Lord*

Kean, Soloman, Anna, Amy, Eleana
: *Kean*

Estelle, Inez, Garcin
: *No Exit*

Orestes, Electra, Aegistheus, Clytemnestra
: *The Flies*

Jarry, Alfred

Ubu Roi
: *Ubu Roi*

Pirandello, Luigi

Mother, Father, Stepdaughter, Son
: *Six Characters in Search of an Author*

Beckett, Samuel

Vladamir, Estragon, Lucky, Pozzo
: *Waiting for Godot*

Krapp
: *Krapp's Last Tape*

Winnie, Willy
: *Happy Days*

Nagg, Nell, Hamm, Clove
: *Endgame*

Ionesco, Eugene

Mr. Smith, Mrs. Smith, Mr. Martin, Mrs. Martin, The Firechief
: *The Bald Soprano*

Old Man, Old Woman
: *The Chairs*

Pupil, Professor
: *The Lesson*

Berenger, Daisy, Jean
: *Rhinoceros*

Genet, Jean

Claire, Solange
: *The Maids*

Green Eyes, Maurice, Lafranc
: *Deathwatch*

The Bishop, Irma, The Chief of Police, The Judge
: *The Balcony*

Archibald, Deodatus, Adelaide, Newport News, Augusta, Felicity, Diouf
: *The Blacks*

The playwrights included in this list were early leaders of Absurd drama. Later and related dramatists are discussed in chapter 20.

Voice	Words, sound, and noise as spectacle; energy; variety; certainty; unusual use of silence and pause; rhythmic; monotone; wide range; combination of real and nonreal techniques.
Movement	Mix of realistic, nonrealistic, ritualistic, circus, commedia, acrobatics, silent films; dexterity and precise timing; muscles relaxed; disciplined and nimble; vaudeville and dance activity; balance of presentational and representational mode.
Gestures	Inventive; disciplined; fluid; considerably oriented to hands and feet.
Pantomimic Dramatization	Inventive as appropriate to routine behavior of life, combined with theatrical and entertainment techniques; see Movement, above.
Character	Combination of multidimensional and complex with stereotype and simplistic; heavily oriented to action of the moment; real to nonreal.
Emotion	Same combination as described for Character, above; special use of primitive, ritualistic Artaud techniques.
Ideas	Clear and usually relevant to Existentialism.
Language	Part of theatrical spectacle; often illogical; often immediate meaning only; often stereotyped and clichéd; combination ranging from prose to lyric poetry; philosophical—usually Existentialism.
Mood and Atmosphere	Extremely varied; at times, moment-to-moment combination of serious and comic.
Pace and Tempo	Generally used in consistently fast or consistently slow tempo.
Special Techniques	Cabaret or vaudeville activity; soft-shoe and tap dancing, pratfalls, tumbling, juggling, magic, balancing, sight gags, and slapstick.

Suggested References

Abel, Lionel. *Metatheatre.* New York: Hill and Wang, 1963.

Artaud, Antonin. *The Theatre and Its Double.* Trnsl. Mary Caroline Richards. New York: Grove Press, 1958.

Barnard, G. C. *Samuel Beckett: A New Approach.* New York: Dodd, Mead & Co., 1960.

Brustein, Robert. *The Theatre of Revolt: An Approach to Modern Drama.* Boston: Little, Brown and Co., 1964.

Chiari, Joseph. *The Contemporary French Theatre: The Flight from Naturalism.* London: Barrie and Rockliff, 1958.

Cohn, Ruby, ed. *Casebook on Waiting for Godot.* New York: Grove Press, 1967.

———. *Just Play: Beckett's Theatre.* Princeton, N.J.: Princeton University Press, 1979.

Esslin, Martin. *Absurd Drama.* London: Penguin Books, 1965.

———. *The Theatre of the Absurd.* Rev. ed. Garden City, N.J.: Doubleday & Co., 1969.

Foreman, Richard, et al. *The Theatre of Images.* Ed. Bonnie Maranca. New York: Drama Book Specialists, 1977.

Grossvogel, David. *Brecht, Ionesco, Beckett, Genet: Four Playwrights and a Postscript.* Ithaca: Cornell University Press, 1962.

Guicharnaud, Jacques. *Modern French Theatre from Giraudoux to Beckett.* New Haven, Conn.: Yale University Press, 1961.

Innes, Christopher. *Holy Theatre: Ritual and the Avant Garde.* New York: Cambridge University Press, 1981.

Killinger, John. *World in Collapse: The Vision of Absurd Drama.* New York: Dell Publishing Co., 1971.

Kostelanetz, Richard. *The Theatre of Mixed Means.* New York: The Dial Press, Inc. 1968.

Ragusa, Olga. *Pirandello: An Approach to His Theatre.* New York: Columbia University Press, 1980.

Schechner, Richard. *Environmental Theatre.* New York: Hawthorn, 1973.

Styan, J. L. *The Dark Comedy: The Development of Modern Comic Tragedy.* Cambridge: The University Press, 1962.

Valency, Maurice. *The End of the World: An Introduction to Contemporary Drama.* New York, 1980.

Suggested Filmography

1. *The Balcony.* 1963. Continental. Playwright-Genet. Director-Joseph Strick. With Shelley Winters and Peter Falk.
2. *The Maids.* 1975. British-Canadian. American Film Theatre. Playwright-Jean Genet. Director-Christopher Miles. With Glenda Jackson.
3. *Rhinoceros.* 1974. American Film Theatre. Playwright-Eugene Ionesco. With Zero Mostel, Gene Wilder.

Waiting for Godot
by *Samuel Beckett*

*from the
final scene*

Characters	Estragon (Gogo) Vladimir (Didi)
Scene	An unidentified country road, by a tree.
Situation	Two tramplike men wait wearily for an unknown figure known as Godot to come to them. They pass their time in idle routine and fanciful games and activities. A man named Pozzo drives a slave named Lucky past them and later the two return and the master-slave roles are reversed. Finally, alone as they began, Estragon and Vladimir continue consideration of their dilemma.

ESTRAGON   Why don't we hang ourselves?

VLADIMIR   With what?

ESTRAGON   You haven't got a bit of rope?

VLADIMIR   No.

ESTRAGON   Then we can't.

(silence)

VLADIMIR   Let's go.

ESTRAGON   Wait, there's my belt.

VLADIMIR   It's too short.

ESTRAGON   You could hang on to my legs.

VLADIMIR   And who'd hang on to mine?

ESTRAGON   True.

VLADIMIR   Show all the same. (ESTRAGON *loosens the cord that holds up his trousers which, much too big for him, fall about his ankles. They look at the cord.*) It might do at a pinch. But is it strong enough?

ESTRAGON   We'll soon see. Here.

(They each take an end of the cord and pull. It breaks. They almost fall.)

VLADIMIR   Not worth a curse.

(silence)

ESTRAGON   You say we have to come back to-morrow?

VLADIMIR   Yes.

ESTRAGON   Then we can bring a good bit of rope.

VLADIMIR   Yes.

(silence)

ESTRAGON   Didi.

VLADIMIR   Yes.

ESTRAGON   I can't go on like this.

VLADIMIR   That's what you think.
ESTRAGON   If we parted? That might be better for us.
VLADIMIR   We'll hang ourselves to-morrow. *(Pause)* Unless Godot comes.
ESTRAGON   And if he comes?
VLADIMIR   We'll be saved.

(VLADIMIR *takes off his hat* [LUCKY'S], *peers inside it, feels about inside it, shakes it, knocks on the crown, puts it on again.*)

ESTRAGON   Well? Shall we go?
VLADIMIR   Pull on your trousers.
ESTRAGON   What?
VLADIMIR   Pull on your trousers.
ESTRAGON   You want me to pull off my trousers?
VLADIMIR   Pull ON your trousers.
ESTRAGON   *(realizing his trousers are down).* True.

(He pulls up his trousers.)

VLADIMIR   Well? Shall we go?
ESTRAGON   Yes, let's go.

(They do not move.)

(END)

Waiting for Godot by Samuel Beckett. The Acting Company on Tour for the John F. Kennedy Center. Directed by Alan Schneider for the Twenty-fifth Anniversary Production of *Waiting for Godot.* The Acting Company Artistic Director, Alan Schneider, directed the United States premiere of this and all plays by Samuel Beckett. Photograph by Martha Swope.

20 Eclectic
Intermingling

. . . conglomerations of past and present
stages of civilizations, bits from books and
newspapers, scraps of humanity, rags and
tatters of fine clothing, patched
together. . . .

August Strindberg discussing plays and
characters in *Preface to Miss Julie*

I can sum up none of my plays. I can
describe none of them, except to say: That
is what happened. That is what they said.
That is what they did.

Harold Pinter
from a speech by Harold Pinter
at The University of Hamburg,
June 4, 1970.

Overview of Eclectic

Theatre in the Western hemisphere in the 1960s, 1970s, and 1980s has been somewhat diffused. The mixing of styles that followed the nonrealistic movements were embellished by new contributions from Brecht and the Absurdists. However, in the past three decades, playwrights have generally written in various styles to produce an extremely Eclectic drama and, as a result, an extremely Eclectic style of acting. *Eclectic* refers to material drawn from several sources, much as just described by Strindberg. The result is plays that are difficult to categorize or label. As Pinter noted at the beginning of this chapter, often the plays cannot be summed up nor described. They merely happen.

What are the results of the eclectic intermix of Realism, nonrealism, Brecht Epic Theatre, and Absurd drama? Several groupings of dramatists need to be discussed.

The most important playwrights influenced by Brecht Epic Theatre include Max Frisch, Rolf Hochhuth, and Peter Weiss. Each of these authors used history as the basis for interpretation of the present. Also, dramatic structure, use of music, and other staging techniques in their plays clearly illustrate Epic influence. However, each author modifies that influence and creates fresh theatrical experience which is best categorized as Eclectic. Also, they tend to use less Oriental material, although Frisch does use the technique in *The Chinese Wall*. Also their plays have more emotional content and less focus on Didacticism. *The Firebugs* is one of the most important plays by Frisch. *The Deputy* by Hochhuth is a modern landmark of controversy because of its attack on the Catholic church and Pope Pius XII. Hochhuth's *Soldiers* is similarly controversial because of its attack on Winston Churchill. Weiss's *Investigation* and *Marat/Sade* are exciting theatrical pieces in the Epic tradition. Again, Weiss differs from the theory of Brecht, particularly in premises which elicit emotional rather than intellectual response from an audience.

The most important contemporary playwrights influenced by the Absurd drama of the 1940s and 1950s includes Harold Pinter, Edward Albee, Tom Stoppard, Arthur Kopit, David Storey, Boris Vian, Jack Gelber, Fernando Arrabal, Jack Richardson, and Francois Billetdoux, among others. Of these, Pinter, Albee, Stoppard, and Kopit, are frequently produced in the United States. Each of these playwrights has written plays directly in the Absurd vein, but perhaps with an even greater sense of humor than the early European leaders of the movement. Some of these authors have also written plays that are distinctly entrenched in other forms and styles such as Realism, Symbolism, and Epic. For example, Albee's *Zoo Story, The American Dream,* and *Tiny Alice* are Absurdist, but *Who's Afraid of Virginia Woolf?* is closely related to Realism and Symbolism. Kopit's *Oh, Dad, Poor Dad* is Absurdist, but *Indians* is in the Epic manner. Stoppard's plays are the most consistently Absurdist, but have fresh, contemporary humor. Storey's plays are considerably more realistic than Absurd.

Two-photo sequence of
You Can't Take It with You
by George S. Kaufman
and Moss Hart. Pat
Hingle as Grandpa at the
University Theatre,
Kansas University.
Directed by Jack B.
Wright. Designed by
Greg Hill. Costumes by
Chez Haehl. Photograph
by Andrew Tsubaki.

Two-photo sequence of
You Can't Take It with You
by George S. Kaufman
and Moss Hart. Pat
Hingle as Grandpa at the
University Theatre,
Kansas University.
Directed by Jack B.
Wright. Designed by
Greg Hill. Costumes by
Chez Haehl. Photograph
by Andrew Tsubaki.

Pinter's plays are especially unique in use of character, environment, language, and silence. In Pinter's plays, characters handle the menace of the unknown and unspoken with comic fright. Unable to come to grips with reality, they dwell miserably in a room which becomes their entire world. Settings have only realistic overtones; conversations begin with comic realism. With varying rhythm, comedy reveals the hidden menace that threatens the characters. The colloquial pattern of London speech degenerates into repetition, staccato rhythm, and, finally, silence. Minds wander through vague recollection with no certainty about what happened or what is happening (*Old Times* and *No Man's Land*). In his early plays, the menacing quality climaxes in violent action (such as when Bert Hudd attacks a blind Negro in *The Room*). After *The Caretaker* and *The Birthday Party*, Pinter used sex as the prime force in the breakdown of an individual (e.g., *The Homecoming, Old Times* and *Betrayal*).

In contrast to Pinter, Albee uses vicious comic dialogue to reveal the serious-tragic aspect of human experience. Albee's serious drama does not grow out of the comedy (as does Pinter's). The serious intent of Albee's characters, their motivation, and their underlying justification force action to be immediately serious, although occasionally sentimental. Albee's biting, satirical, highly intense dialogue leaps at an audience (e.g., *Who's Afraid of Virginia Woolf?*). Recently, he has written plays in the manner of the Eclectic playwrights who mix several styles (e.g., *A Delicate Balance, All Over, Seascape, Tiny Alice, Malcolm, The Ballad of the Sad Cafe, Everything in the Garden, Listening, Counting the Ways,* and *The Lady From Dubuque*).

Both Pinter and Albee reject the Absurd label. They consider their plays to be highly personal forms of symbolic Realism and basically comic.

Other leading authors of Eclectic drama in recent years include Arthur Miller, Tennessee Williams, Robert Bolt, Jean Anouilh, Jules Feiffer, Peter Ustinov, John Guare, David Rabe, the late Joe Orton and Friedrich Durrenmatt, among others. Still other contemporary authors were or are more inclined toward straight dramatic realism, although several of them deviate from that style in certain plays. These writers include Clifford Odets, Lillian Hellman, William Inge, Neil Simon, Jason Miller, Paul Zindel, Leonard Gershe, Frank Gilroy, John Osborne, Robert Anderson, Jean Kerr, Lanford Wilson, William Gibson, Michael Cristofer, David Mamet, the late Preston Jones, Albert Innaurato, Milan Stitt, Jerry L. Crawford, Terry Miller, Edward EmanuEl, Ray Carver, Frank Gagliano, Sam Smiley, John Orlock, John Kirk, Chris Moe, Omar Paxson, Christopher Durang, Terence Rattigan, John Bishop, Corrine Jacker, A. R. "Pete" Gurney, Howard Sackler, Alan Ayckbourn, D. L. Coburn, Hugh Leonard, James Leonard, Bernard Slade, Michael Weller, Ernest Thompson, Marsha Norman, John Ford Noonan, Martin Sherman, Ronald Ribman, Simon Gray, Anthony Shaffer, James Lapine, William Mastrosimone, Peter Shaffer, Bernard Pomerance, Ira Levin, Kevin Wade, Brian Clark, Bill C. Davis, Sam Shepard, and Beth Henley, among others. Earlier in the century, Eugene O'Neill, James Thurber, George S. Kaufman, Moss Hart, and Thornton Wilder wrote plays in

Eccentricities of a Nightingale by Tennessee Williams. At the University Theatre, Kansas University. Directed by Jack B. Wright. Designed by Del Unruh. Costumes by Chez Haehl. Photograph by Andrew Tsubaki.

such a variety of styles that in an overall view of their work they may best be called Eclectic. American authors such as Sherwood Anderson, Elmer Rice, Paul Green, Carson McCullers, Mary Chase, William Saroyan, and others have contributed a generally Eclectic drama whose roots are in realism with branches in nonrealism. In France, Jean Cocteau and Jean Giraudoux did much the same thing, with some effort at a return to Classicism. Maxwell Anderson, T. S. Eliot, Christopher Fry, Federico García Lorca, Archibald MacLeish, and others led the way into modern poetic verse drama.

Perhaps O'Neill, Williams, Miller, Albee, Wilson, and Shepard can be considered the most successful and popular American dramatists of this century. Their plays combine many styles which draw material from many sources. Because of this, it is difficult to place their work in an overall category. For example, Miller's *Death of a Salesman* and Williams' *The Glass*

Look Back in Anger by John Osborne. Malcolm McDowell and Lisa Banes at the Roundabout Theatre, New York City. Gene Feist and Michael Fried, Producing Directors. Photograph by Martha Swope.

Menagerie exemplify detailed Naturalism mixed with Expressionism. At times, pure stylistic form was used principally by O'Neill. For example, O'Neill's *Lazarus Laughed* is Epic in nature; *The Hairy Ape, The Great God Brown,* and *Emperor Jones* are all Expressionism; *Beyond the Horizon* is Realism; *Long Day's Journey into Night* is Naturalism; *Mourning Becomes Electra* is based on the classical Greek *Oresteia;* and *Strange Interlude* is an intermix of several styles. O'Neill's canon of plays envelops a mixture of forms and styles probably unparalleled in dramatic history. Most of the plays of O'Neill, Williams, Miller, Albee, Wilson, and Shepard permit the Naturalism approach to character creation as determined by role analysis (see chapter 10), personalization, and Stanislavski techniques (see chapter 16). Nonetheless, the varied Eclectic influence of the nonrealists on these authors at times obligates an actor to draw from other style sources ranging from Absurd techniques to Epic and Expressionism techniques. For example, such plays as Miller's *The Creation of The World and Other Business* and *After the Fall,* Williams' *Camino Real* and *The Milk Train Doesn't Stop Here Anymore,* Albee's *Tiny Alice* and *Seascape,* Wilson's *The Rimers of Eldritch* and *The Mound Builders,* and Shepard's *Operation Sidewinder, The Tooth of Crime* and *Seduced* all require a combination of acting styles dependent upon careful analysis. Accordingly, an actor is best trained to handle the Eclectic body of work offered by these six great American authors *after* training in all the other major twentieth-century acting styles.

In recent years, the motivation of many of the new Eclectic theatre artists was primarily nonverbal. They created basically out of improvisational techniques and modern dance under the direction of an artist-leader rather than of a director. The artist-leader differed from a director in that he was often a creative performer onstage with the actors, rather than a backstage re-creative interpreter who assists actors. Much of the Eclectic theatrical expression centered on group efforts. The groups were closely united by common goals and strong social and political commitments. Their goal was a total theatre activity aimed at bringing the masses into the theatre again.

As discussed in chapter 19, Artaud championed the concept of total theatre, which correlates with Eclectic theatre. This concept became highly influential in theatre movements of the 1960s and beyond. Artaud believed that theatre should be an interplay and synthesis of music, movement, voice, scenery, and lighting—a convergence of the arts as sensory modalities, transmitting information through integrated effects. The controlling factor in this theatre was the emotional ordering of what is often called "multimedia scenography." Artaud's theatre was nonliterary and emphasized dance, sound, and light as the primary expressions of language. Movement became highly stylized similar to ancient hieroglyphic writings in which one sign (e.g., gesture or movement) combined many different meanings in a single prealphabetical symbol or emblem. Ideally, the space where a performer worked was unlimited and thereby no restrictions were placed. Marshall McLuhan, the late modern media theorist, saw this theatre as a "retribalization" of culture that focused on participation, tactility, and sculptural values. Artaud wanted a return to an archaic, primitive, ceremonial mode of expression. He wished to rediscover the "other" or intangible meaning of our existence, the deeper perceptions of the sensory and abstract. Artaud was too far ahead of his time to have significant impact. His was a theatre of the future—a theatre of dynamic forms and colors, filled with chaotic but expressive movement (e.g., jugglers, dancers, and gymnasts). Thirty years early, Artaud established the foundation for the Eclectic theatre of the 1960s and beyond.

The artist-leader attempted to elicit a group expression with didactic purposes (social, political, and religious) in the Brechtian tradition. As a result, the improvisational actor of the sixties became a performer of tasks rather than a creator of roles. The performer's own personality provided some characterization—but impersonation in much of this theatre activity was a dead issue. The goal was a compatible group effort in a highly charged theatrical presentation. Actual audience participation in the theatrical event was encouraged by some groups (see Appendix B). Note that Brecht did not desire audience participation in the theatre event itself. He and Artaud wanted audiences to think and proceed to social action after the event.

Leading contemporary experimental theatre groups, companies, and artists are discussed in Appendix B.

Inadmissible Evidence by John Osborne. Susannah York and Paul Shenar at The Roundabout Theatre, New York City. Gene Feist and Michael Fried, Producing Directors. Photograph by Martha Swope.

Starting in the 1960s and continuing into the 1980s, there was a tremendous upsurge in Eclectic theatrical innovation in an attempt to explore new dramatic expressions in which the written word was reexamined and reshaped. The innovation also produced a new kind of actor, playwright, director, and scene designer, as well as a new kind of audience. The world of the sixties, seventies and eighties evolved in flux, changing and adapting to a new society whose ethics and values produced a new liberalism in social, political, and cultural patterns. The new dramatists rejected many of the concepts of Realism and Naturalism, particularly in stage scenery and environment. Since Realism and Naturalism perpetuated the traditional social order in which humanity was emphasized and man's quest for freedom repressed, they were not harmonious with the political atmosphere of the times. Theatre innovators of the sixties and early seventies shared the Absurdist playwrights' distrust of the written word, of language, of dialogue. They limited the meaning and structure of words, and they communicated ideas with imprecision and inaccuracy. Late in the seventies, a trend returned toward traditional literary and scripted plays. In the eighties, a vast blend of theatre activity burgeoned, including revivals of earlier plays, productions of standard, realistic plays, performances of experimental plays, and productions of innovative works such as *Sweeney*

Inadmissible Evidence by John Osborne. Nicol Williamson and Andrea Weber at The Roundabout Theatre, New York City. Gene Feist and Michael Fried, Producing Directors. Photograph by Martha Swope.

Todd, *Evita*, the multi-hour "canvas" of the adapted Charles Dickens piece, *Nicholas Nickleby*, Michael Bennett's musical success, *Dream Girls* and Kopit's musical based on a Felini film, *Nine*. Extravagant musicals continue to dominate box office success, such as *Cats*.

Voice

It is obvious that vocal training for the Eclectic drama of the late twentieth century requires a totally trained mechanism. The intermingling of styles requires extensive range, effortless articulation and projection, and flexible variation. However, it is unsettling to note the fact that many contemporary American actors are generally regarded to be deficient in vocal execution. According to the critics involved in the American College Theatre Festival competition, voice and diction are glaringly deficient areas of ability. Perhaps this is the result of the great emphasis in the 1960s upon nonverbal, physical, improvisational activity. Nonetheless, in later years a new concern developed for emphasis upon vocal training for both collegiate and professional actors. With the emphasis on production of musical theatre it was necessary that an aspiring actor put concerted effort into vocal training. Most theatre departments in American colleges and universities added specialized courses in stage voice to their curriculums.

The Winslow Boy by Terence Rattigan. Ralph Clanton, David Haller, and Remak Ramsay at The Roundabout Theatre, New York City. Gene Feist and Michael Fried, Producing Directors. Photograph by Martha Swope.

Exercise 1   Voice—Eclectic

1. Create an improvisation based on a job interview. Define your circumstances clearly. Perform the improvisation in three different ways.
   a. With no human speech, relying solely on sounds and noises
   b. With no human speech, relying soley on gibberish which, unlike sounds and noises, includes use of consonants and vowels
   c. Using human speech with good range, articulation, projection, and variety

2. Select a song from a modern musical of your choice and within your vocal range and acting type. Prepare and practice the song without and with musical accompaniment. (Ideally, use a pianist to accompany you.)

Movement

Eclectic drama in the late twentieth century has been unusually oriented toward movement and physical, nonverbal activity. The experimental groups of the 1960s were particularly outstanding for their focus on movement. These troupes went so far as to eliminate standard theatrical environment, frequently leaving the performer with only his body as the means of communication. It follows that the contemporary actor working in Eclectic drama must possess a totally trained physical apparatus. In today's theatre, dance training is almost a necessity. Academic and professional training centers also stress fencing, weight training, gymnastics, acrobatics, mime, Oriental techniques (such as those found in the Tai Chi Chuan system of movement), the Laban theory of movement (a system of spatial movement), and improvisational games.

Exercise 2 Movement—Eclectic

1. Imagine that you are encased in a transparent ice cube.[1] Explore the confines of your rigidly defined space. Perform this exploration with every part of your body. Be aware that the area is extremely cold. Eventually permit your body heat to melt the cube and free you.

2. Select several interesting photographs of people in unusual physical positions. Practice moving from an aligned standing position into the physical positions shown in the photographs. From each position, move into another unusual physical position which evolves naturally from your sense of the space you occupy.

3. Position your body in an unusual way, for example, in a squatting position. Explore kinesthetic movement patterns emanating from particular parts of your body. Begin with extensive arm activity, varying movement in direction and tempo. Continue the kinesthetic experience with movement of the head. Continue the exercise by altering the position while using movement from other parts of the body; for example, recline upon your back, lift your legs in the air, and explore space with them.

4. Create an improvisation related to the Garden of Eden. Define your circumstances. Perform the improvisation without language, using movement and sound as the sole means of telling the story

5. Select a solo and a group dance number from a modern musical play. Prepare and practice the number with musical accompaniment of some sort, ideally with a pianist and drummer.

Ice Cube exercise.

Character and Emotion

In acting the contemporary Eclectic style of drama careful textual analysis is necessary. Actors must play the realistic elements when character demands it, perform Brechtian techniques in Epic and intellectual segments, utilize Absurd stand-up cabaret or vaudeville humor at moments, use Artaud assault techniques when appropriate, use improvisation when required, combine nonrealistic and realistic techniques, and generally work with the fundamental of effective personalization. In other words, character and emotion in Eclectic drama range from simplistic to multidimensional, from stereotype to uniquely individual.

As Joseph Chaikin has noted, "When working on character, it isn't enough just to imitate. What a person says is not as important as where he sees from."

The contemporary actor should be familiar with and capable of using techniques ranging from Stanislavski to Brecht to Artaud to Grotowski to Chaikin to Bob Fosse to Michael Bennett to Tommy Tune to Hal Prince.

1. The origin of this exercise is found in the kinesphere concepts of Rudolf Laban—the spatial area around the body in which one moves the whole body or part of it.

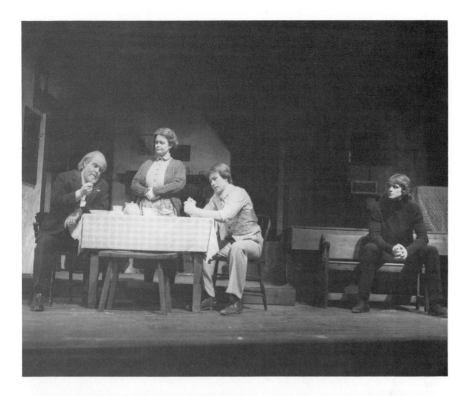

Philadelphia, Here I Come!
by Brian Friel. Wm.
Gregory Etter as S. B.
O'Donnell, Elizabeth
Gulick Eastman as Madge,
Mark Tymchyshyn as Gar
in Public, and Andrew
Barnicle as Gar in Private,
at The Hilberry Theatre,
Wayne State University.
Directed by Robert T.
Hazzard. Scenery by John
Whitting. Costumes by
Jackie Durbin. Lighting
by Marc Riske. National
Finalist winner, American
College Theatre Festival,
John F. Kennedy Center,
Washington, D.C.

*A Funny Thing Happened
on the Way to the Forum* by
Larry Gelbart and Burt
Shevelove, Music and
Lyrics by Stephen
Sondheim, originally
produced on Broadway
by Harold S. Prince. Pat
Cronin as Pseudolus at
The Lyric Theatre of
Oklahoma. Directed by
Lyle Dye, Jr. Music
Director and Conductor:
Joel Levine. Scenery and
Lighting by Randell
Greenlee. Costumes by
James Jay.
Choreographer: Randy
Hugill. Photograph by
Zinn Unlimited/Terry
Zinn.

The actor should understand human emotion and know when and how to use it or restrict it. The contemporary actor is often called upon to be playwright, director, and performer. In other words, full personalization is at work. It is probably to the credit of contemporary theatre with its Eclectic base that the art of the actor in terms of character, emotion, movement, and voice seems to be moving to the forefront of dramatic activity. Also, much of the drama in recent years requires skill in audience participation techniques, use of partial or full nudity, use of abusive, profane language, and heightened sexual activity. The so-called Power Plays are examples of such drama (see *The Drama Review*, vol. 14, no. 4, September 1970). Much of this activity carried into film acting in the 1970s and 1980s.

Exercise 3 Character and Emotion—Eclectic

1. Review the character and emotion exercises given in chapters 11 through 19.

2. Create an improvisation whose setting is a cocktail party. Define your circumstances clearly. Begin the cocktail party in a human form. Slowly, begin to change from being human to being nonhuman. Continue the improvisation until the last nonhuman has left the party.

3. Two people perform an improvisation in which there are two clearly defined characters (e.g., an impolite salesman and an irate customer). At various points throughout the improvisation, your instructor or director will call for reversal of roles. Attempt to change roles easily and smoothly in the improvisation.

4. Four people perform an improvisation in which there are four clearly defined characters involved in a specific activity (e.g., four neighborhood women getting ready for a Fourth of July party). When the director so indicates, change acting styles in the following sequence:
   a. Realism
   b. Expressionism
   c. Epic
   d. Absurd

5. Using the ideas of David Craig (see end of chapter 7 for reference guide to ideas of David Craig), prepare a song and dance from a contemporary musical play in which you must *act* the song and dance, creating believable character and emotion. It may prove helpful to review the instructions in chapter 9 related to "Musical Theatre Auditions."

The contemporary theatre offers a continually expanding experience for actors. The demands imposed upon the actor are astonishing. He should not only study his role (à la Stanislavski), but also relate his own psychical and physical beings to those of a character. Further, he should learn how to work "detached," as in Brecht, often combining all these techniques in one Eclectic, complex performance. The excitement generated by contemporary acting evolves around the attempt to extend a character into life in an organic structure. It is an ongoing experiment. The search to discover an ultimate medium for playing the impulses of a character and yet make

LuAnn Hampton Laverty Oberlander by Preston Jones. At The Kansas Repertory Theatre (Summer), Kansas University. Directed by Jack B. Wright. Designed by Tony Taylor. Costumes by Ellen Wright. Photography by Andrew Tsubaki.

Fallen Angels by Noel Coward. Valerie French, Stephen Schnetzler, and Carol Teitel at The Roundabout Theatre, New York City. Gene Feist and Michael Fried, Producing Directors. Photograph by Martha Swope.

that character functional for the stage takes an extraordinary degree of intelligence, discipline, and concentration.

At this point, it may be justifiably asked: What does the contemporary dramatic scene mean in terms of the growth and development of an actor? Where is the training to take place? What is the specific training? And how does the actor train for a theatre in which audience participation is sometimes an integral part of the action onstage?

If university theatre departments, studio schools, and repertory workshops and training programs do not provide the necessary courses in textual analysis, dance, movement, voice, and improvisational techniques, if tors must still fight the concept of the master director who demands complete control in all areas of production and training, I can then only direct actors toward a new way of *thinking* about contemporary acting. Perhaps traditional *conceptions* (too often stereotyped) can be altered to encompass what acting in the theatre *should* be—*an important and respected art.*

Misalliance by George Bernard Shaw. Phillip Bosco and Patricia Elliot at The Roundabout Theatre, New York City. Gene Feist and Michael Fried, Producing Director.

Suggested Characters and Plays for Scene Work

Wilde, Oscar

Algernon, Cecily, Gwendelon, John Worthing, Lady Bracknell
  The Importance of Being Earnest

O'Neill, Eugene

Jamie, Edmund, Mary, Tyrone
  Long Day's Journey Into Night
Melody, Sarah
  A Touch of the Poet
Nina, Dr. Darrell, Sam, Charlie
  Strange Interlude
Christine, Lavinia, Ezra, Adam, Orin
  Mourning Becomes Electra
Nat, Essie, Richard, Muriel, Lilly, Sid
  Ah, Wilderness!
Hickey, Harry, Larry, Don, Pearl, Margie, Lora
  The Iceman Cometh
Anna, Chris, Mat
  Anna Christie

Miller, Arthur

Chris, Ann, Keller
  All My Sons
Willy, Biff, Happy, Linda
  Death of a Salesman
Eddie, Catherine, Rudolfo, Beatrice
  A View From the Bridge
Proctor, Abigail, Elizabeth, Reverend Hale, Danforth
  The Crucible
All characters
  The Creation of the World and Other Business
All characters
  The American Clock

a

b

c

d

Nicholas Nickleby by Charles Dickens, adapted by David Edgar.

a. Christopher Benjamin and Roger Rees in The Royal Shakespeare Company production. Directed by Trevor Nunn and John Caird. Assisted by Leon Rubin. Scenery by John Napier and Dermot Hayes. Costumes by John Napier. Lighting by David Hersey. Music by Stephen Oliver. Photographs by Chris Davies, London.

b. "The gathering."

c. Lila Kaye, Jule Peasgood, John McEmery, Vincent Crummley, and Roger Rees.

d. "The Milliners."

Williams, Tennessee

Amanda, Laura, Tom, The Gentleman Caller
    The Glass Menagerie
Blanche, Stella, Stanley, Mitch
    A Streetcar Named Desire
Alma, John
    Summer and Smoke
Reverend Shannon, Maxine, Hannah
    The Night of the Iguana
Maggie, Brick
Big Daddy, Big Mama
    Cat on A Hot Tin Roof
All characters
    The Rose Tattoo
All characters
    Small Craft Warnings
All characters
    Eccentricities of a Nightingale

Pinter, Harold

Bert, Rose, Mr. Kidd, Mr. Sands, Mrs. Sands
    The Room
Max, Sam, Lenny, Joey, Teddy, Ruth
    The Homecoming
Sarah, Richard
    The Lover

Anna, Kate, Deeley
Old Times
Mich, Aston, Davies
The Caretaker
Meg, Stanley, Petey, Lulu, Goldberg, McCann
The Birthday Party
All characters
No Man's Land
Jerry, Emma, Robert
Betrayal

Kopit, Arthur

Jonathan, Rosalie, Madam Rosepettle, Commodore
Oh, Dad, Poor Dad, Mamma's
Hung You in the Closet and
I'm Feelin' So Sad
Buffalo Bill, Sitting Bull, Wild Bill Hickok
Indians
Emily Stilson, Amy, Billy, Mr. Brownstein, Mrs. Timmins
Wings
All characters
Nine

Stoppard, Tom

Rosencrantz, Guildenstern, The Player
Rosencrantz and Guildenstern Are Dead
Moon, Birdboot, Felicity, Cynthia, Hound
The Real Inspector Hound
George, Dorothy, Archie, Bones, Crouch
Jumpers
Henry Carr
Travesties
All characters
Dirty Linen and
New-Found-Land
All characters
Night and Day

Albee, Edward

Jerry, Peter
The Zoo Story
Martha, George, Nick, Honey
Who's Afraid of Virginia Woolf?
Mommie, Daddy, Grandma, Mrs. Barker, Young Man
The American Dream
Nancy, Charlie, Leslie, Sarah
Seascape
Tobias, Agnes, Claire, Julia
A Delicate Balance
Miss Alice, Julian, Lawyer, Cardinal
Tiny Alice
The Wife, The Mistress, The Son, The Daughter
All Over
All characters
The Lady From Dubuque

Gagliano, Frank

All characters
    Father Uxbridge Wants to Marry
Jeremy, Indian, Narrator
    Big Sur
Sis, Brother, William Saroyan O'Neill
    The City Scene: Paradise Gardens East
Yam, Jesus
    The City Scene: Conerico Was Here To Stay

Simon, Neil

Barney, Elaine, Bobbi, Jeanette
    The Last of the Red Hot Lovers
Felix, Oscar
    The Odd Couple
Mel, Edna
    Prisoner of Second Avenue
Willy, Al
    The Sunshine Boys
Evy, Polly
    The Gingerbread Lady
Corrie, Paul
    Barefoot in the Park
All characters
    Plaza Suite
All characters
    The Good Doctor

A scene from *Jacques Brel Is Alive and Well and Living in Paris* by Eric Blau and Mort Shuman. At the Showboat Majestic, Cincinnati, Ohio; directed by Worth Gardner.

All characters
God's Favorite
All characters
California Suite
All characters
Chapter Two

Inge, William

Elma, Grace, Bo, Cherie
Bus Stop
Doc, Lola
Come Back, Little Sheba
Howard, Rosemary, Hal, Madge
Picnic
All characters
The Dark At The Top of the Stairs

Bolt, Robert

Sir Thomas More, Henry VIII
A Man for All Seasons
Mary, Elizabeth
Vivat! Vivat! Regina!

Wilder, Thornton

Sabina, Mr. Antrobus, Mrs. Antrobus
The Skin of Our Teeth
Emily, George, Stage Manager
Our Town
Dolly, Barnaby, Cornelius, Minnie, Vandergelder
The Matchmaker

Anouilh, Jean

Becket, Henry
Becket
Antigone, Creon
Antigone

Rabe, David

Harriet, Ozzie, David, Ricky
Sticks and Bones
Ardell, Pavlo
The Basic Training of Pavlo Hummel
Chrissy, Eric, Susan, Al
In the Boom Boom Room
Martin, Richie, Carlyle, Billy, Roger, Cokes, Rooney
Streamers

Feiffer, Jules

Patsy, Marjorie, Carol, Alfred, Reverend Dupas
Little Murders
All characters
Knock, Knock

Storey, David

Harry, Jack, Marjorie, Cathleen
Home

The Athletes
The Changing Room
Ewbank, Claire, Maurice, Kay, Marshall
The Contractor

Miller, Jason

Tom, George, James, Phil, Coach
That Championship Season

Guare, John

Artie, Bunny, Ronnie, Bananas
The House of Blue Leaves
All characters
Marco Polo Sings A Solo
All characters
Bosoms and Neglect

Weller, Michael

The Students
Moonchildren
Paul, Susan
Loose Ends

Zindel, Paul

Beatrice, Tillie, Ruth, Nanny
The Effect of Gamma Rays on Man-In-The-Moon Marigolds
Cathrine, Anna, Ceil
And Miss Reardon Drinks a Little
All characters
The Private Affairs of Mildred Wild

A scene from *Zoot Suit* by Luis Valdez. Presented by the Center Theatre Group/ Mark Taper Forum at the Aquarius Theatre in Hollywood.

Gershe, Leonard
Don, Jill, Mrs. Baker, Ralph
  Butterflies Are Free

Barry, Julian
Lenny
  Lenny

Gilroy, Frank
John, Timmy, Nettie
  The Subject Was Roses

Frisch, Max
Biedermann, Babette, Sepp, Will
  The Firebugs
The Contemporary, The Maskers
  The Chinese Wall

Durrenmatt, Friedrich
Claire, Anton, Teacher
  The Visit
Newton, Einstein, Mobiles
  The Physicists

Hochhuth, Rolf
Father Riccardo, Gerstein, Pope Pius XII
  The Deputy
Churchill, Dorland, Bell, Helen
  Soldiers

Weiss, Peter
DeSade, Marat, Charlotte
  Marat/Sade
All characters
  The Investigation

Wasserman, Dale
MacMurphy, Nurse, Ratched
  One Flew Over the Cuckoo's Nest
Don Quixote, Sancho, Aldonza
  Man of La Mancha

Ayckbourn, Alan
Jane, Sidney, Ronald, Marion, Eva, Geoffrey
  Absurd Person Singular
All characters
  The Norman Conquests
All characters
  How the Other Half Loves
All characters
  Bedroom Farce

Stein, Joseph
Tevye, Motel, Golde
  Fiddler on the Roof

Costume design for the character, Knight of the Mirrors, *Man of La Mancha*, musical play by Dale Wasserman, based on the novel, *Don Quixote* by Cervantes. Design by Ellis M. Pryce-Jones for production at the University of Nevada, Las Vegas, directed by Jerry L. Crawford.

Macleish, Archibald
Zuss, Nickles, J. B., Sarah
   J. B.

Wilson, Lanford
The People, The Residents
   The Hot L Baltimore
Prof. Howe, Cynthia, Kirsten, D. K. Eriksen, Dan and Jean Loggins, Chad
   The Mound Builders
All characters
   The Fifth of July
Sally, Matt
   Talley's Folly
All characters
   A Tale Told
All characters
   Balm in Gilead
All characters
   The Rimers of Eldritch
All characters
   The Gingham Dog
All characters
   Lemon Sky

Hopkins, John
Julian, David, Alan, Jacqueline
   Find Your Way Home

Stop the World I Want to Get Off by Anthony Newley and Leslie Bricusse. Ben Carney as Littlechap at The University of Missouri Summer Repertory Theatre. Directed by Stephen Archer. Musical Direction by Patricia Gallagher. Choreography by Vance Fulkerson. Scenery by James Hooks. Costumes by Hazel Hall.

Shaffer, Peter

All characters
Equus
Antonio Salieri, Wolfgang Amadeus Mozart, Constanze Weber
Amadeus

van Itallie, Jean-Claude

Applicants, Interviewers
Interview
Hal, Susan, George
T.V.
Motel-Keeper, Man, Woman
Motel
The Group
The Serpent

Anderson, Robert

Gene, Margaret, Alice, Tom
I Never Sang for My Father
Muriel, Herbert
I'm Herbert
Tom, Laura
Tea and Sympathy

Terry, Megan

The Group
Viet Rock
He, She
Comings and Goings

May, Elaine

All characters
   Adaptation

Lawrence, Jerome and Lee, Robert E.

All major characters
   Inherit the Wind
All major characters
   First Monday in October

McNally, Terrence

Two Soldiers
   Botticelli
All characters
   Tour
   Next
   The Ritz
Otto, April, Roy, Dr. Pepper, Hiram, Dolly
   Bad Habits
Tommy, Greta, Nedda, Bunny, Ben, Arnold the Dog
   Where Has Tommy Flowers Gone?

Shepard, Sam

All characters
   Operation Side-Winder
Hoss, Crow, Cheyenne, Becky Lou
   The Tooth of Crime
All characters
   Suicide in B Flat
All characters
   Buried Child
All characters
   Curse of the Starving Class
All characters
   La Turista
All characters
   True West
All characters
   Tongues
All characters
   Savage Love
All characters
   Seduced
All characters
   The Unseen Hand

Shange, Ntozake

All characters
   For Colored Girls Who Have Considered Suicide When the Rainbow is Enuf

Jones, LeRoi (Imamu Amiri Baraka)

Clay, Lula
   Dutchman
Grace, Walker, Easley
   The Slave

Hanley, William
Glas, Randell, Rosie
  Slow Dance on the Killing Ground

Baldwin, James
Richard, Meridian, Lyle, Parnell, Juanita
  Blues for Mister Charlie

Hansberry, Lorraine
Ruth, Walter, Beneatha, Mamma, George, Bobo
  A Raisin in the Sun

Gordone, Charles
Johnny, Gabe, Cora, Shanty, Sweets
  No Place to Be Somebody

Mason, Judi A.
All characters
  Livin' Fat

Bullins, Ed
All characters
  The Electronic Nigger
All characters
  Goin' A Buffalo

Sherwood, Robert
Abe, Ann
  Abe Lincoln in Illinois

Gibson, William
Jerry, Gittle
  Two for the Seesaw
Will, Anne, Meg, Kemp
  A Cry of Players
All characters
  The Miracle Worker

Odets, Clifford
Joe, Mr. Bonaparte
  Golden Boy
All characters
  Awake and Sing!

Osborne, John
Jimmie Porter, Alison, Helena, Cliff
  Look Back in Anger
All characters
  The Entertainer
All characters
  Luther
All characters
  Inadmissible Evidence
All characters
  Epitaph For George Dillon

A scene from the hit musical, *The Robber Bridegroom* by Alfred Uhry and Robert Waldman, adapted from a novella by Eudora Welty. At the Edinburgh Fringe Festival, 1978. Rio Hondo College.

Gurney, A. R., Jr.

All characters
 Children
 The Middle Ages
 The Golden Fleece
 The Dining Room

McCullers, Carson

Bernice, Frankie
 Member of the Wedding

Kaufman, George S., and Hart, Moss

Penelope, Essie, Grandpa, Mr. DiPina, Ed
 You Can't Take It With You

Saroyan, William

Tom, Joe, Kitty, Kit Carson
 The Time of Your Life

Hellman, Lillian

Martha, Karen
 The Children's Hour
Regina, Oscar, Ben, Birdie, Horace, Leo, Alexandria
 The Little Foxes

Anderson, Maxwell

Mio, Miriamne
 Winterset

Behan, Brendan

Meg, Pat, Monsewer, Miss Gilchrist, Leslie, Terresa
The Hostage

Ustinov, Peter

The Unknown Soldier, Wife, Archbishop, General
The Unknown Soldier and His Wife

Solzhenitsyn, Alexander

Nemor, Kostya, Lyuba
The Love-Girl and the Innocent

Leonard, Hugh

Charlie Now, Da, Oliver, Mother, Young Charlie, Mary Tate, Drumm, Mrs. Prynne
Da
Dolly, Drumm, Mary, Kearns
A Life

Dean, Phillip Hayes

Paul Robeson, Lawrence Brown
Paul Robeson

Cristofer, Michael

The Interviewer, Joe, Steve, Maggie, Brian, Mark, Beverly, Agnes, Felicity
The Shadow Box

Ross, Judith

Irene, Dan, Jerry
An Almost Perfect Person

Crowley, Mart

All Characters
The Boys in the Band
Loraine, Teddy, Michael
A Breeze From The Gulf

Goldman, James

All characters
The Lion in Winter

Moore, Edward J.

Gertrude, Harry
The Seahorse

Jones, Preston

All characters
A Texas Trilogy (The Last Meeting of the Knights of the White Magnolia; LuAnn Hampton Laverty Oberlander; The Oldest Living Graduate)

Allen, Woody

Allan, Nancy, Bogart, Sharon, Vanessa, Linda, Dick, Gina, Barbara
Play It Again, Sam
All characters
Don't Drink the Water

Ribman, Ronald

Fredrich, Richard, Miss Mudurga, Joseph
  Cold Storage

Gray, Simon

All characters
  Butley
Simon, Dave, Stephen, Jeff, Davina, Wood, Beth
  Otherwise Engaged

Patrick, Robert

Wanda, Sparger, Carla, Rona, Mark, Bartender
  Kennedy's Children

Pinero, Miguel

Juan, Longshoe, Clark, Cupcakes, Ice, El Raheen, Blanca, Mr. Nett, Gypsy, Omar,
Paco, Mr. Brown, Sgt. Morrison, Capt. Allard
  Short Eyes

Innaurato, Albert

Fran, Francis, Lucille, Bunny, Herschel, Judity, Randy
  Gemini
Benno, The Old Man, The Girl
  The Transfiguration of Benno Blimpie

Athayde, Roberto

Miss Margarida, Student-Actor
  Miss Margarida's Way

Mamet, David

Robert, John
  A Life in the Theatre
Charles, Rita, Morton, Lawrence, Mrs. Varec, Mr. Wallace, Bernie, Dave
  The Water Engine
Mr. Happiness
  Mr. Happiness
Bobby, Teach, Donny
  American Buffalo

Durang, Christopher

All characters
  The Vietnamization of New Jersey
All characters
  A History of the American Film
Prudence, Bruce
  Beyond Therapy

Coburn, D. L.

All characters
  The Gin Game

Friel, Brian

Gar (Private and Public), Madge
  Philadelphia, Here I Come!

Shaffer, Anthony

Bartholomew, Stenning, Elizabeth, Millie
Murderer

Osborn, Paul

Theodore Swanson, Cora Swanson, Ida Bolton, Aaronetta Gibbs, Esther Crampton, David Crampton
Morning's At Seven

Lapine, James

All characters
Table Settings

Parnell, Peter

Stephen Hurt, Christine, William, Liz
Sorrows of Stephen

Mastrosimone, William

Rose, Cliff
The Woolgatherer

Clark, Brian

Ken Harrison, Dr. Emerson, Dr. Scott, Mrs. Byle, Nurse
Whose Life Is It, Anyway?

Pomerance, Bernard

Frederick Treves, John Merrick, Mrs. Kendal
The Elephant Man

Davis, Bill C.

Father, Tim Farley, Mark Dolson
Mass Appeal

Wade, Kevin

Michael, Philip, Lisa
Key Exchange

Levin, Ira

Sidney Bruhl, Myra Bruhl, Clifford Anderson, Helga, Porter Milgrim, Drop
Deathtrap

Noonan, John Ford

Maude, Hannah
A Coupla White Chicks Sitting Around Talking

Cryer, Gretchen and *Nancy Ford*

All characters
I'm Getting My Act Together and Taking It On the Road

Sharman, Martin

All characters
Bent

Norman, Marsha

All characters
Getting Out

Giovanni, Paul

All characters
  The Crucifer of Blood

Deane, Hamilton and John L. Balderston

All characters
  Dracula

Fugard, Athol

All characters
  Blood Knot
All characters
  A Lesson From Aloes
All characters
  Master Harold and the Boys

Doctorow, E. L.

Edgar, Joan
  Drinks Before Dinner

Thompson, Ernest

Norman, Ethel, Charlie, Chelsea, Billy Rae
  On Golden Pond

Slade, Bernard

All characters
  Same Time, Next Year
All characters
  Tribute
All characters
  Romantic Comedy

Hirson, Roger O. and Stephen Schwartz

Pippin, Charles, Fastrada, Berthe, Catherine, Leading Player
  Pippin

Jacobs, Jim and Warren Casey

All characters
  Grease

Simon, Neil, Burt Bacharach, Hal David
(based on a screenplay by Billy Wilder)

All characters
  Promises, Promises

Simon, Neil, Marvin Hamlisch, Carole Bayer Sager

All characters
  They're Playing Our Song

Furth, George and Stephen Sondheim

All characters
  Company

Kirkwood, James, Marvin Hamlisch, Nicholas Dante, Edward Kleban

All characters
  A Chorus Line

Wheeler, Hugh and Stephen Sondheim
(based on a version of *Sweeney Todd* by Christopher Bond)

All characters
> *Sweeney Todd*

Rice, Tim and Andrew Lloyd Webber

All characters
> *Evita*

Edgar, David (adapter; based on the book by Charles Dickens)

All characters
> *The Life & Adventures of Nicholas Nickleby*

Eyen, Tom and Henry Krieger

All characters
> *Dream Girls*

Actor Checklist *Eclectic*

Voice	Extensive range; effortless articulation and projection; flexible variation; intermix of many stylistic techniques.
Movement	Total body as communicator; dance, mime, gymnastic, acrobatic, Oriental, Tai Chi Chuan, Laban, spatial activity, improvisational; mix of presentational and representational mode; combination of many stylistic techniques.
Gesture	Inventive; varied; flexible.
Pantomimic Dramatization	Inventive; varied; flexible; improvisational theatre; limited use of objects, properties, and costumes.
Character	Ranges from stereotype to uniquely individual and multidimensional; intermingling of many stylistic techniques; at times includes audience contact, nudity, and profanity.
Emotion	Ranges from simplistic to complex; ranges from human to void.
Ideas	Usually complex; oriented heavily to social and political activity; at times extremely Freudian and sexual base.
Language	De-emphasized in some plays; intermingling of many stylistic forms.
Mood and Atmosphere	Varied; experimental theatre oriented to the serious and grotesquely humorous; commercial theatre oriented to comedy and music.
Pace and Tempo	Varied; experimental theatre unusually slow; commercial theatre unusually rapid.
Special Techniques	Analysis and application of intermix of characteristics; diversified grasp of contemporary experimental theatre.

Note: Because of the wide scope of contemporary Eclectic acting styles, the suggestions given in this list must be adapted individually according to the particular author, play, and role being acted.

Suggested Readings

Baxandall, Lee. "Spectacles and Scenarios: A Dramaturgy of Radical Activity." *TDR The Drama Review,* Summer 1969.

Bentley, Eric. *The Playwright as Thinker: A Study of Drama in Modern Times.* New York: Harcourt Brace Jovanovich, 1946.

———. *In Search of Theatre.* New York: Alfred A. Knopf, 1953.

Brecht, Stefan. "Family of the f.p. Notes on the Theatre of the Ridiculous." *TDR The Drama Review* 13 (1969):117–41.

Brockett, Oscar G. *Perspectives on Contemporary Theatre.* Baton Rouge, La.: Louisiana State University Press, 1971.

Brook, Peter. *The Empty Space.* New York: Atheneum Publishers, 1968.

Brustein, Robert. *The Third Theatre.* New York: Alfred A. Knopf, 1969.

Burton, Hal. *Acting in the '60's.* London: BBC, 1970.

———. *Great Acting.* New York: Hill and Wang, 1967.

Chaikin, Joseph. "The Open Theatre." *Tulane Drama Review,* Winter, 1964, pp. 191–97.

———. *The Presence of the Actor.* New York: Atheneum, 1972.

Cheney, Sheldon. *The New Movement in the Theatre.* New York: Benjamin Blom, 1914.

Clark, Brian. *Group Theatre.* New York: Theatre Arts Books, 1971.

Cohn, Ruby. *Currents in Contemporary Drama.* Bloomington, Ind.: Indiana University Press, 1969.

Corrigan, Robert W. *The Theatre in Search of a Fix.* New York: Dell Publishing Co., Delta Books, 1974.

Croyden, Margaret. *Lunatics, Lovers, and Poets: The Contemporary Experimental Theatre.* New York: McGraw-Hill, Inc., 1974.

Dean, Joan F. *Tom Stoppard: Comedy as a Matrix.* Columbia: University of Missouri Press, 1981.

Elsom, John. *Post-War British Theatre.* London: Routledge & Kegan Paul, 1979.

Drama Review, The. No. 71. September, 1976. (Acting in the 1970's.)

Esslin, Martin. *Reflections: Essays in the Modern Theatre.* New York: Doubleday & Co., 1969.

———. *The Peopled Wound: The Work of Harold Pinter.* Garden City, N.Y.: Doubleday & Co., Inc., 1970.

Estrin, Mark W. *Lillian Hellman: Plays, Films, Memoirs: A Reference Guide.* Boston: G. K. Hall and Co., 1981.

Farber, Donald. *Actor's Guide.* New York: Drama Book Specialists, 1971.

Fowlie, Wallace. *Dionysus in Paris.* Gloucester, Mass.: Peter Smith, 1960.

Freedman, Morris. *Essays in the Modern Drama.* Boston: D. C. Heath, 1964.

Friedman, Philip and Gail Eisen. *The Pilates Method of Physical and Mental Conditioning.* New York: Warner Books, 1981.

Fuchs, Georg. *Revolution in the Theatre.* Translated by C. C. Kuhn. Ithaca, N.Y.: Cornell University Press, 1959.

Funke, Lewis, and Booth, John E. *Actors Talk About Acting.* New York: Avon, 1961.

Gardner, R. H. *The Splintered Stage.* New York: Macmillan Co., 1965.

Gassner, John. *Directions in Modern Theatre and Drama.* New York: Holt, Rinehart and Winston, 1965.

———. *Form and Idea in the Modern Theatre.* New York: Holt, Rinehart, and Winston, 1956.

———. *Theatre at the Crossroads: Plays and Playwrights of Mid-Century American Stage.* New York: Holt, Rinehart, and Winston, 1960.

———. *The Theatre in Our Times: A Survey of the Men, Materials and Movements in the Modern Theatre.* New York: Crown Publishers, 1954.

Goldman, Michael. *The Actor's Freedom: Towards A New Theory of Drama.* New York: Viking, 1975.

Goorney, Howard. *Theatre Workshop Story*. London: Eyre Methuen, Ltd., 1981.

Green, Charles. *Edward Albee: An Annotated Bibliography 1968–1977*. New York: AMS Press, 1980.

Green, Stanley. *The World of Musical Comedy*. San Diego: A. S. Barnes & Co., 1980.

Grossvogel, David I. *Twentieth Century French Drama*. New York: Columbia University Press, 1961.

Grotowski, Jerzy. *Towards a Poor Theatre*. New York: Simon & Schuster, 1968.

———. "Holiday." *TDR The Drama Review*, June 1973.

———. "Interview" by Richard Schechner. *TDR The Drama Review*, Fall 1968.

Haues, William. *The Performer in Mass Media*. New York: Hastings House Pub., 1978.

Hayman, Ronald. *Contemporary Playwrights: Harold Pinter*. London: Heinemann Educational Books, 1968. In same series: Samuel Beckett and John Osborne.

Hinchcliffe, Arnold P. *Harold Pinter*. Rev. Ed. Boston: Twayne Publishers, 1981.

Houghton, Norris. *The Exploding Stage: An Introduction to Twentieth Century Drama*. New York: Weybright & Talley, 1971.

Kerr, Walter. *God on the Gymnasium Floor and Other Theatrical Adventures*. New York: Dell Publishing Co., Delta Books, 1974.

Kirby, Michael. *Happenings*. New York: E. P. Dutton & Co., 1965.

———. "The New Theatre." *Tulane Drama Review*, Winter 1965, pp. 30–34.

———. *The New Theatre: Performance Documentation*. New York: New York University Press, 1974.

Kitchin, Laurence. *Drama in the Sixties: Form and Interpretation*. London: Humanities Press, 1966.

Little, Stuart W. *Off-Broadway: The Prophetic Theatre*. New York: Dell Publishing Co., Delta Books, 1974.

Londre, Felicia Hardison. *Tom Stoppard*. New York: Frederick Ungar Publishing Co., 1981.

Mann, Paul. "Theory and Practice." *Tulane Drama Review*, Winter 1964, pp. 84–96.

Marowitz, Charles. "Notes on the Theatre of Cruelty." *TDR The Drama Review* 1 (1966):152–72.

Marranca, Bonnie, Ed. *American Dreams: The Imagination of Sam Shepard*. New York: Performing Arts Journal Publications, 1981.

Mitchell, Loften. *Black Drama*. New York: Hawthorn Book, Inc., 1967.

National Directory of Grants and Aid to Individuals in the Arts. 3d. ed. Daniel Millsaps. Washington, D.C.: Washington Arts Letter, 1978.

Neff, Renfreu. *The Living Theatre: USA*. New York: Bobbs-Merrill Co., 1970.

Newquist, Roy. *Showcase*. New York: Morrow, 1960.

O'Connor, Garry. *French Theatre Today*. New York: Pitman Publishing Corp., 1975.

Orzel, Nick, and Smith, Michael, eds. *Eight Plays from Off-Off Broadway*. New York: Bobbs-Merrill Co., 1966.

Pasolli, Robert. *A Book on the Open Theatre*. New York: Bobbs-Merrill Co., 1970.

Patterson, Michael. *German Theatre Today*. New York: Pitman Publishing Corp., 1976.

Price, Julia. *The Off-Broadway Theatre*, Metuchen, N.J.: Scarecrow Press, Inc., 1962.

Probst, Leonard. *Off Camera*. New York: Stein and Day, 1975.

Roberts, Vera Mowry. *The Nature of Theatre*. New York: Harper & Row, Publishers, 1971.

Ross, Lillian and Helen. *The Player*. New York: Simon and Schuster, 1962.

Rostagno, Aldo; Beck, Julian; and Malina, Judith. *We, the Living Theatre*. New York: Ballantine Books, 1970.

Schechner, Richard. *Public Domain: Essays on the Theatre*. Indianapolis: Bobbs-Merrill Co., 1969.

————. "Audience Participation." *TDR The Drama Review,* Summer 1971, pp. 73–89.

————. *Environmental Theatre.* New York: Hawthorne Books, Inc., 1973.

————. "Guerrilla Theatre: May 1970." *TDR The Drama Review,* May 1970, pp. 163–68.

Schevill, James. *Breakout! In Search of New Theatrical Environments.* Chicago: University of Chicago Press, 1972.

Smith, Cecil and Glenn Litton. *Musical Comedy in America.* Rev. Ed. Theatre Arts Books, 1981.

Smith, Michael. "The Good Scene." *Tulane Drama Review,* Summer 1966, pp. 159–76.

Theatre Profiles/Latest number available. A Resource Book of Non-profit Professional Theatres in the United States. Marsue Cumming, Ed. New York: Theatre Communications Group, Inc., most recent year.

Van Itallie, Jean-Claude. "Playwright at Work: Off-Off Broadway." *Tulane Drama Review,* Summer 1966, pp. 154–58.

Weales, Gerald. *American Drama Since World War II.* New York: Harcourt Brace Jovanovich, 1962.

Wellworth, George, and Benedickt, Michael. *Theatre of Protest and Paradox.* 2nd ed. New York: New York University Press, 1968.

Woodbury, Lael. *Mosaic Theatre.* Provo, Utah: Brigham Young University Press, 1976.

Ziegler, Joseph. *Regional Theatre: The Revolutionary Stage.* New York: Da Capo Press, 1973.

Suggested Filmography

1. *All My Sons.* 1948. Universal. Playwright-Arthur Miller. Director-Irving Reis. With/Edward G. Robinson, Burt Lancaster.
2. *Anna Christie.* 1923. Th. H. Ince-First National. Playwright-Eugene O'Neill. Director-John Griffith Wray. With/Blanche Sweet.
3. *Anna Christie.* 1930. MGM. Playwright-O'Neill. Director-Clarence Brown. With/Greta Garbo.
4. *The Birthday Party.* 1970. Playwright-Harold Pinter. Director-Wm. Friedkin. With/Robert Shaw.
5. *Bus Stop.* 1956. 20th. Playwright-William Inge. Director-Joshua Logan. With/Marilyn Monroe.
6. *The Caretaker.* 1963. Playwright-Pinter. Director-Clive Donner. With/Robert Shaw, Alan Bates, Donald Pleasence.
7. *Cat on a Hot Tin Roof.* 1958. MGM. Playwright-Tennessee Williams. Director-Richard Brooks. With/Elizabeth Taylor, Paul Newman.
8. *Craig's Wife.* 1936. Columbia. Playwright-George Kelly. Director-Dorothy Arzner. With/Rosalind Russell.
9. *Death of a Salesman.* 1952. Columbia. Playwright-Arthur Miller. Director-Laslo Benedek. With/Fredric March.
10. *The Desperate Hours.* 1955. Paramount. Playwright-Joseph Hayes. Director-Wm. Wyler. With/Humphrey Bogart, Fredric March.
11. *Detective Story.* 1951. Paramount. Playwright-Sidney Kingsley. Director-Wyler. With/Kirk Douglas.
12. *The Fugitive Kind.* 1959. U.A. Playwright-T. Williams. Director-Sidney Lumet. (From *Orpheus Descending*.). With/Marlon Brando, Anna Magnani, Joanne Woodward.
13. *Golden Boy.* 1939. Columbia. Playwright-Clifford Odets. Director-Rouben Mamoulian. With/Wm. Holden.

14. *I Never Sang For My Father.* 1969. Columbia. Playwright-Robert Anderson. Director-Gilbert Cates. With/Gene Hackman, Melvyn Douglas.
15. *The Importance of Being Earnest.* 1952. Universal. Playwright-Oscar Wilde. Director-Anthony Asquith. With/Michael Redgrave, Edith Evans.
16. *The Last of the Mobile Hot Shots.* (Also known as *Blood Kin.*). 1970. Warners. Playwright-Williams. (From *The Seven Descents of Myrtle.*). Director-Lumet. With/James Coburn, Lynn Redgrave, Robert Hooks.
17. *The Little Foxes.* 1941. RKO. Playwright-Lillian Hellman. Director-Wyler. With/Bette Davis.
18. *Long Day's Journey Into Night.* 1962. Embassy. Playwright-O'Neill. Director-Lumet. With/K. Hepburn, Ralph Richardson, Jason Robards, Dean Stockwell.
19. *Look Back in Anger.* 1959. Warners. Playwright-John Osborne. Director-Tony Richardson. With/Richard Burton.
20. *Marat/Sade.* 1967. U.A. Playwright-Peter Weiss. Director-Peter Brook. With/Glenda Jackson.
21. *Night Must Fall.* 1937. MGM. Playwright-Emlyn Williams. Director-Richard Thorpe. With/Robert Montgomery, Ros. Russell.
22. *The Odd Couple.* 1968. Paramount. Playwright-Neil Simon. Director-Gene Saks. With/Jack Lemmon, Walter Matthau.
23. *Our Town.* 1940. U.A. Playwright-Thornton Wilder. Director-Sam Wood. With/William Holden.
24. *The Petrified Forest.* 1936. Warners. Playwright-Robert E. Sherwood. Director-Archie Mayo. With/Bette Davis, Bogart, Leslie Howard.
25. *The Philadelphia Story.* 1940. MGM. Playwright-Philip Barry. Director-George Cukor. With/K. Hepburn, Cary Grant, James Stewart.
26. *Picnic.* 1955. Columbia. Playwright-Inge. Director-Logan. With/William Holden, Kim Novak.
27. *A Raisin in the Sun.* 1961. Columbia. Playwright-Lorraine Hansberry. Director-Daniel Petrie. With/Sidney Poitier.
28. *Salome.* 1922. U.A. Playwright-Wilde. Director-Charles Bryant. (Settings, costumes based on drawings by Aubrey Beardsley.). With/Nazimova.
29. *Strange Interlude.* 1932. MGM. Playwright-O'Neill. Director-Robert Z. Leonard. With/Norma Shearer, Clark Gable.
30. *A Streetcar Named Desire.* 1951. Warners. Playwright-T. Williams. Director-Elia Kazan. With/Marlon Brando, Viv. Leigh.
31. *A View From the Bridge.* 1961. Playwright-A. Miller. Director-Lumet. With/Raf Vallone, Maureen Stapleton.
32. *Watch on the Rhine.* 1943. Warners. Playwright-Hellman. Director-Herman Schumlin. With/Bette Davis, Paul Lukas.
33. *Who's Afraid of Virginia Woolf?* 1966. Warners. Playwright-Edward Albee. Director-Mike Nichols. With/Burton, Taylor.
34. *Winterset.* 1936. RKO. Playwright-Maxwell Anderson. Director-Alfred Santell. With/Burgess Meredith.
35. *You Can't Take It With You.* 1938. Columbia. Playwrights-George S. Kaufman and Moss Hart. Director-Frank Capra. With/Jean Arthur, James Stewart.

Strange Interlude
by *Eugene O'Neill*

from
Part I, Act IV

Nina, age 22 years
Darrell, age 28 years

Characters

The study in the home of Professor Henry Leeds; evening; New England, a
small university town; autumn.

Scene

Nina Leeds loved a man who was killed in the war. She marries a professor,
becomes pregnant, but has an abortion, fearing that an insanity streak in the
family might affect the child. She decides to strike a bargain with Dr. Darrell
to father a child with her. (Indented dialogue represents the inner thoughts of
each character which when spoken cannot be heard by the other character.)

Situation

NINA (*enters silently. She has fixed herself up, put on her best dress, arranged her
hair, rouged, etc.—but it is principally her mood that has changed her,
making her appear a younger, prettier person for the moment.* DARRELL
*immediately senses her presence, and, looking up, gets to his feet with a smile
of affectionate admiration. She comes quickly over to him saying with frank
pleasure*)   Hello, Ned. I'm certainly glad to see you again—after all these
years!

DARRELL (*as they shake hands—smiling*)   Not as long as all that, is it? (*thinking
admiringly*)

> Wonderful-looking as ever . . . Sam is a lucky devil! . . .

NINA (*thinking*)

> Strong hands like Gordon's . . . take hold of you . . . not like Sam's . . .
> yielding fingers that let you fall back into yourself . . .

(*teasingly*) I ought to cut you dead after the shameful way you've ignored us!

DARRELL (*a bit embarrassedly*)   I've really meant to write. (*his eyes examining
her keenly*)

> Been through a lot since I saw her . . . face shows it . . . nervous tension
> pronounced . . . hiding behind her smile . . .

NINA (*uneasy under his glance*)

> I hate that professional look in his eyes . . . watching symptoms . . .
> without seeing me . . .

(*with resentful mockery*)   Well, what do you suspect is wrong with the
patient now, Doctor? (*She laughs nervously.*) Sit down, Ned. I suppose you
can't help your diagnosing stare. (*She turns from him and sits down in the
rocker at center.*)

DARRELL (*quickly averting his eyes—sits down—jokingly*)   Same old unjust
accusation! You were always reading diagnosis into me, when what I was
really thinking was what fine eyes you had, or what a becoming gown, or—

NINA (*smiling*)   Or what a becoming alibi you could cook up! Oh, I know you!
(*With a sudden change of mood she laughs gaily and naturally.*) But you're
forgiven—that is, if you can explain why you've never been to see us.

DARRELL   Honestly, Nina, I've been so rushed with work I haven't had a chance to go anywhere.

NINA   Or an inclination!

DARRELL *(smiling)*   Well—maybe.

NINA   Do you like the Institute so much? *(He nods gravely.)* Is it the big opportunity you wanted?

DARRELL *(simply)*   I think it is.

NINA *(with a smile)*   Well, you're the taking kind for whom opportunities are made!

DARRELL *(smiling)*   I hope so.

NINA *(sighing)*   I wish that could be said of more of us—*(then quickly)*—meaning myself.

DARRELL *(thinking with a certain satisfaction)*

   Meaning Sam . . . that doesn't look hopeful for future wedded bliss! . . . *(teasingly)* But I heard you were "taking an opportunity" to go in for literature—collaborating with Marsden.

NINA   No, Charlie is only going to advise. He'd never deign to appear as co-author. And besides, he never appreciated the real Gordon. No one did except me.

DARRELL *(thinking caustically)*

   Gordon myth strong as ever . . . root of her trouble still . . . *(keenly inquisitive)* Sam certainly appreciated him, didn't he?

NINA *(not remembering to hide her contempt)*   Sam? Why, he's the exact opposite in every way!

DARRELL *(caustically thinking)*

   These heroes die hard . . . but perhaps she can write him out of her system. . . .

   (persuasively) Well, you're going ahead with the biography, aren't you? I think you ought to.

NINA *(dryly)*   For my soul, Doctor? *(listlessly)* I suppose I will. I don't know. I haven't much time. The duties of a wife—*(teasingly)* By the way, if it isn't too rude to inquire, aren't you getting yourself engaged to some fair lady or other?

DARRELL *(smiling—but emphatically)*   Not on your life! Not until after I'm thirty-five, at least!

NINA *(sarcastically)*   Then you don't believe in taking your own medicine? Why, Doctor! Think of how much good it would do you!—*(excitedly with a hectic sarcasm)*—if you had a nice girl to love—or was it learn to love?—and take care of—whose character you could shape and whose life you could guide and make what you pleased, in whose unselfish devotion you could find peace! *(more and more bitterly sarcastic)* And you ought to have a baby, Doctor! You will never know what life is, you'll never be really happy until you've had a baby, Doctor—a fine, healthy baby! *(She laughs a bitter, sneering laugh.)*

DARRELL *(after a quick, keen glance, thinking)*

   Good! . . . she's going to tell . . .

   (meekly) I recognize my arguments. Was I really wrong on every point, Nina?

NINA *(harshly)*   On every single point, Doctor!

DARRELL *(glancing at her keenly)*   But how? You haven't given the baby end of it a chance yet, have you?

NINA *(bitterly)*   Oh, haven't I? *(then bursts out with intense bitterness)* I'll have you know I'm not destined to bear babies, Doctor!

DARRELL (*startledly*)

        What's that? . . . why not? . . .

(*again with a certain satisfaction*)

        Can she mean Sam? . . . that he . . .

(*soothingly—but plainly disturbed*) Why don't you begin at the beginning and tell me all about it? I feel responsible.

NINA (*fiercely*)   You are! (*then wearily*) And you're not. No one is. You didn't know. No one could know.

DARRELL (*in same tone*)   Know what? (*thinking with the same eagerness to believe something he hopes*)

        She must mean no one could know that Sam wasn't . . . but I might have guessed it . . . from his general weakness . . . poor unlucky devil . . .

(*then as she remains silent—urgingly*) Tell me. I want to help you, Nina.

NINA (*touched*)   It's too late, Ned. (*then suddenly*) I've just thought—Sam said he happened to run into you. That isn't so, is it? He went to see you and told you how worried he was about me and asked you out to see me, didn't he? (*as* DARRELL *nods*) Oh, I don't mind! It's even rather touching. (*then mockingly*) Well, since you're out here professionally, and my husband wants me to consult you, I might as well give you the whole case history! (*wearily*) I warn you it isn't pretty, Doctor! But then life doesn't seem to be pretty, does it? And, after all, you aided and abetted God the Father in making this mess. I hope it'll teach you not to be so cocksure in future. (*more and more bitterly*) I must say you proceeded very unscientifically, Doctor! (*then suddenly starts her story in a dull monotonous tone recalling that of* EVANS' *mother in the previous act*) When we went to visit Sam's mother I'd known for two months that I was going to have a baby.

DARRELL (*startled—unable to hide a trace of disappointment*)   Oh, then you actually were? (*thinking disappointedly and ashamed of himself for being disappointed*)

        All wrong, what I thought . . . she was going to . . . then why didn't she? . . .

NINA (*with a strange happy intensity*)   Oh, Ned, I loved it more than I've ever loved anything in my life—even Gordon! I loved it so it seemed at times that Gordon must be its real father, that Gordon must have come to me in a dream while I was lying asleep beside Sam! And I was happy! I almost loved Sam then! I felt he was a good husband!

DARRELL (*instantly repelled—thinking with scornful jealousy*)

        Ha! . . . the hero again! . . . comes to her bed! . . . puts horns on poor Sam! . . . becomes the father of his child! . . . I'll be damned if hers isn't the most idiotic obsession I ever . . .

NINA (*her voice suddenly becoming flat and lifeless*)   And then Sam's mother told me I couldn't have my baby. You see, Doctor, Sam's great-grandfather was insane, and Sam's grandmother died in an asylum, and Sam's father had lost his mind for years before he died, and an aunt who is still alive is crazy. So of course I had to agree it would be wrong—and I had an operation.

DARRELL (*who has listened with amazed horror—profoundly shocked and stunned*) Good God! Are you crazy, Nina? I simply can't believe! It would be too hellish! Poor Sam, of all people! (*bewilderedly*) Nina! Are you absolutely sure?

NINA (*immediately defensive and mocking*)   Absolutely, Doctor! Why? Do you think it's I who am crazy? Sam looks so healthy and sane, doesn't he? He fooled you completely, didn't he? You thought he'd be an ideal husband for me! And poor Sam's fooling himself too because he doesn't know anything about all this—so you can't blame him, Doctor!

DARRELL (*thinking in a real panic of horror—and a flood of protective affection for her*)

God, this is too awful! . . . on top of all the rest! . . . how did she ever stand it! . . . she'll lose her mind too! . . . and it's my fault! . . .

(*Getting up, comes to her and puts his hands on her shoulders, standing behind her—tenderly.*) Nina I'm so damn sorry! There's only one possible thing to do now. You'll have to make Sam give you a divorce.

NINA (*bitterly*)   Yes? Then what do you suppose would be his finish? No, I've enough guilt in my memory now, thank you! I've got to stick to Sam! (*then with a strange monotonous insistence*) I've promised Sam's mother I'd make him happy! He's unhappy now because he thinks he isn't able to give me a child. And I'm unhappy because I've lost my child. So I must have another baby—somehow—don't you think, Doctor?—to make us both happy? (*She looks up at him pleadingly. For a moment they stare into each other's eyes—then both turn away in guilty confusion.*)

DARRELL (*bewilderedly thinking*)

That look in her eyes . . . what does she want me to think? . . . why does she talk so much about being happy? . . . am I happy? . . . I don't know . . . what is happiness? . . .

(*confusedly*) Nina, I don't know what to think.

(*END*)

The Homecoming

by Harold Pinter

*from
Act II*

Ruth, wife of Teddy, in her early 30s
Teddy, a professor in an American college, middle 30s
Max, father of Teddy and Lenny, 70
Lenny, a pimp and hustler, early 30s

Characters

The old home of Max, in North London; a large living room.

Scene

Teddy is ending the uncomfortable homecoming with his male family to return to
America to teach. However, his father and brothers have asked Teddy's wife,
Ruth, to remain with them as a mother-prostitute figure. Ruth encounters Max
and Lenny who make the proposition.

Situation

(RUTH *comes down the stairs, dressed. She comes into the room. She smiles at the
gathering, and sits. Silence.*)

TEDDY   Ruth . . . the family have invited you to stay, for a little while longer. As
a . . . as a kind of guest. If you like the idea I don't mind. We can manage
very easily at home . . . until you come back.

RUTH   How very nice of them.

(*pause*)

MAX   It's an offer from our heart.
RUTH   It's very sweet of you.
MAX   Listen . . . it would be our pleasure.

(*pause*)

RUTH   I think I'd be too much trouble.
MAX   Trouble? What are you talking about? What trouble? Listen, I'll tell you
something. Since poor Jessie died, eh, Sam? we haven't had a woman in the
house. Not one. Inside this house. And I'll tell you why. Because their mother's
image was so dear any other woman would have . . . tarnished it. But you . . .
Ruth . . . you're not only lovely and beautiful, but you're kin. You're kith.
You belong here.

(*pause*)

RUTH   I'm very touched.
MAX   Of course you're touched. I'm touched.

(*pause*)

TEDDY   But Ruth, I should tell you . . . that you'll have to pull your weight a little,
if you stay. Financially. My father isn't very well off.
RUTH (*to* MAX)   Oh, I'm sorry.

MAX   No, you'd just have to bring in a little, that's all. A few pennies. Nothing much. It's just that we're waiting for Joey to hit the top as a boxer. When Joey hits the top . . . well . . .

(*pause*)

TEDDY   Or you can come home with me.
LENNY   We'd get you a flat.

(*pause*)

RUTH   A flat?
LENNY   Yes.
RUTH   Where?
LENNY   In town.

(*pause*)

But you'd live here, with us.
MAX   Of course you would. This would be your home. In the bosom of the family.
LENNY   You'd just pop up to the flat a couple of hours a night, that's all.
MAX   Just a couple of hours, that's all. That's all.
LENNY   And you make enough money to keep you going here.

(*END*)

The Deputy
by Rolf Hochhuth

Translated by Richard and Clara Winston

from
Act IV

Characters

Father Riccardo, a priest
Cardinal
Pope Pius XII
Fontana, Riccardo's father

A throne room in the Papal Palace, the Vatican, Rome.

Scene

Father Riccardo, a young and conscious-stricken priest, can no longer tolerate
the silence from the Pope concerning the European slaughter of the Jews. He
confronts the Pope to appeal for a public, specific statement against the genocide.

Situation

RICCARDO   Holy Father . . .

(*He bows to the* CARDINAL, *who coldly refers him to the* POPE.)

POPE   We are delighted with you, Riccardo, and contemplate your zeal with
affection. He who defends the persecuted, always speaks as We would wish.
But—We have just heard with dismay that you or Bishop Hudal in Our name
has protested the arrest of the Jews. Is that so? Eminence—please send for the
Father General.

(CARDINAL, *at the door, gives a command to the* SWISS GUARD.)

RICCARDO (*still not understanding, very politely*)   I? No, Your Holiness, I heard
from my liaison man in the SS that Your Holiness through Bishop Hudal has
threatened to protest.

POPE (*angered*)   What have you arrogated to yourself—to conspire with the SS?

CARDINAL (*malignantly*)   The Holy Father, you know, has just heard the first
word of his alleged statement.

POPE   I am speaking to him, Eminence!

RICCARDO (*crushed, turns to his father, but does not lower his voice*)   So—after
all—nothing whatsoever has been done! (*He still cannot believe it.*) But Your
Holiness did threaten a protest. I do not understand . . . (*However, he has
understood; he says passionately, almost crying out.*) Your Holiness, the Jews
are being shipped out, murdered.

CARDINAL   Be still!

POPE (*smiling*)   Why, no, Your Eminence . . . God bless you, Riccardo. Speak,
your heart is good. Only you must not negotiate with the SS. The Father
General will tell us what has happened. Hold yourself back! At your age
modesty alone honors one.

RICCARDO   I am not concerned about my honor, Your Holiness. I am concerned
for the honor of the Holy See, for that is dear to me . . .

FONTANA   Riccardo!

(*The* POPE *remains silent; the* CARDINAL *answers swiftly for him.*)

Eclectic   405

CARDINAL   Aha, he is concerned for the honor of the Curia! And have you never heard that we have set up whole bureaus, offices and committees, solely in order to help, to rescue—why, you know, it seems to me that we have several times discussed that very matter, haven't we?

RICCARDO *(more and more losing his self-control)*   Such assistance reaches only some Jews in Italy, Your Eminence. That too has been discussed often enough. *(He now turns to the* POPE.*)*But the terror rages in the other countries! In Poland alone one million eight hundred thousand Jews have already been slaughtered! Since that figure, Your Holiness, was confirmed last July, and officially communicated by the Polish ambassador in Washington to the Papal Legate there—God cannot wish Your Holiness to ignore it!

CARDINAL *(indignantly)*   Leave at once! What language in the Holy Father's presence! Count, say something to your son . . .

(During RICCARDO's *last words the* POPE *had risen, but he sits down again. A moment passes before he is able to speak, with utmost effort.)*

POPE   "Ignore!" We do not intend to account for Our actions to Riccardo Fontana—does his father make no comment? Nevertheless, We would be pleased if We might also be permitted to speak a word on the matter. *(with mounting bitterness, attempting to change the subject)* Do you know, for example, my young man, that weeks ago we were already prepared to help the Jews of Rome, who were threatened with arrest, out of their predicament with gold, considerable gold. Hitler's bandits offered the Jews freedom for a ransom. They attempted to extort from Us a sum that was no longer realistic. *Nevertheless* we would have paid it!

RICCARDO *(has turned, aghast, to his father; now speaks softly to the* POPE)   Then Your Holiness has already known—for weeks—what the SS here intended to do to the Jews?

POPE *(agitated, evasively)*   What are you saying! Father General can bear witness to all that has already been accomplished. The monasteries stand open . . .

(END)

No Place to Be Somebody by Charles Gordone. Linda Ramsay as Dee and Roosevelt Johnson as Johnny at The Bonstelle Theatre, Wayne State University. Directed by Von H. Washington. Scenery by Blair Vaughn Anderson. Costumes by Elizabeth Gulick Eastman. Lighting by Joseph P. Grigaitis. Sound by Dean Egnater. Properties by David H. Kuykendall.

No Place to Be Somebody
by Charles Gordone

Gabe, young black narrator-author of the "play"
Johnny, young black owner of the bar
Shanty, young Caucasian musician-drummer-worker
Dee, a young Caucasian woman
Evie, a young black woman

Johnny's Bar, New York City.

Gabe introduces life in a run-down New York bar where the pain and struggle
of black life in white America unfolds.

GABE   Excuse me. Forgot you were out there. My name is Gabe. Gabe Gabriel,
to be exact. I'm a writer. Didn't mean to lose my temper. Something I've been
working on all my life. Not losing my temper. (*Takes out marihuana
cigarette. Lights it. Inhales it. Holds smoke in.*) Right now I'm working on a
play. They say if you wanna be a writer you gotta go out an' live. I don't
believe that no more. Take my play for instance. Might not believe it but I'm
gonna make it all up in my head as I go along. Before I prove it to you, wanna
warn you not to be thinkin' I'm tellin' you a bunch'a barefaced lies. An' no
matter how far out I git, don't want you goin' out'a here with the idea what
you see happenin' is all a figment of my grassy imagination. 'Cause it ain't!
(*He picks up Bible from table. Raises it above his head. Without looking turns
pages.*) "And I heard a Voice between the banks of the U'Lai. And it called,
Gabriel! Gabriel! Make this man understand the vision! So He came near
where I stood! And when He came, I was frightened and fell upon my face!"

(*He closes Bible. As he exits, lights dim out, then come up on* SHANTY, *at jukebox.
Jazz is playing.* SHANTY *takes out his drumsticks. Begins to rap on bar.* JOHNNY
enters. Hangs up raincoat and umbrella.)

JOHNNY   Cool it, Shanty.
SHANTY   Man, I'm practicing.
JOHNNY   Damned if that bar's anyplace for it. Git on that floor there.
SHANTY (*Puts drumsticks away. Takes broom.*)   Ever tell you 'bout the time I
went to this jam session? Max Roach was there. Lemme sit in for him.
JOHNNY   Said you played jus' like a spade.
SHANTY   What's wrong with that? Ol' Red Taylor said wasn't nobody could hold
a beat an' steady cook it like me. Said I had "the thing"! Member one time we
played "Saints." For three hours, we played it.
JOHNNY   Had to git a bucket'a col' water an' throw it on you to git you to quit,
huh?
SHANTY   One these days I'm gonna have me a boss set'a skins for my comeback.
Me an' Cora was diggin' a set up on "Four-Six Street." Sump'm else ag'in.
Bass drum, dis'pearin' spurs, snares, tom-toms. . . .

JOHNNY   Gon' steal 'em?

SHANTY   I been savin' up. Gonna git me them drums. Know what I'm gonna do then? I'm gonna quit you flat. Go for that. Sheee! I ain't no lifetime apron. That's for damned sure.

JOHNNY   Yeah, well meantime how 'bout finishin' up on that floor? Time to open the store. (DEE *and* EVIE *enter. Hang coats up.*) You broads let them two ripe apples git away from you, huh?

DEE   Don't look at me.

EVIE   Aw, later for you an' your rich Texas trade.

DEE   Just gettin' too damned sensitive.

EVIE   Sensitive my black behin'! Excuse me, I mean black ass. (*Goes to jukebox. Punches up number.*)

DEE   Last night we bring those two johns up to her pad. An' like, Jack? One with the cowboy hat? Stoned? Like out of his skull. And like out of nowhere he starts cryin'.

EVIE   All weekend it was "Nigger this an' Nigger that."

DEE   Never bothered you before. I didn't like it when he started sayin' things like "The black sons a'bitches are gettin' to be untouchables! Takin' over the country!"

EVIE   Bet he'll think twice before he says sump'm like that ag'in.

DEE   That lamp I gave her? One the senator brought me back from Russia? Evie goes an' breaks it over his head.

JOHNNY   What the hell'd you do that for?

EVIE   Sure hated to lose that lamp.

JOHNNY   Wouldn't care if they b'longed to the Ku Klux Klan long's they gimme the bread. (*He goes into* DEE's *purse.*)

SHANTY   Sure had plenty of it too! When they was in here, they kept buyin' me drinks. Thought I was the boss.

JOHNNY   Crackers cain't 'magine Niggers runnin' nothin' but elevators an' toilets.

DEE   Leave me somethin', please.

EVIE   Ain't gon' do nothin' with it nohow.

JOHNNY (*Finds pair of baby shoes in* DEE's *purse*)   Thought I tole you to git rid'a these?

DEE   I forgot.

JOHNNY   Save you the trouble. (*He starts to throw them away.*)

DEE   Don't you do that, you black bastard. So help me, Johnny.

EVIE   Aw, let 'er have them things, Nigger! Wha's the big deal?

JOHNNY   'Tend to your own business, bitch. Ain't a minute off your ass for messin' it up las' night.

EVIE   Excuse me. Didn't know you was starvin' to death.

JOHNNY (*Goes for* EVIE *but quickly checks himself when she reaches for her purse. He turns back to* DEE.)   Look'a here, girl. I ain't gon' have no harness bulls knockin' down yo' door.

DEE   All of a sudden you worried about me.

JOHNNY   Jus' git rid'a that crap. Worrin' over sump'm pass, over an' done with.

(*END*)

No Place to Be Somebody by
Charles Gordone.
Anthony Lucas as Gabe,
Clifford A. Reed as
Sweets, and Roosevelt
Johnson as Johnny at The
Bronstelle Theatre,
Wayne State University.
Directed by Von H.
Washington. Scenery by
Blair Vaughn Anderson.
Costumes by Elizabeth
Gulick Eastman. Lighting
by Joseph P. Grigaitis.
Sound by Dean Egnater.
Properties by David H.
Kuykendall.

Interview
From America Hurrah
by *Jean-Claude van Itallie*

from
beginning of play

Characters   First Interviewer
First Applicant
Second Applicant
Third Applicant
Fourth Applicant (a Lady's Maid)

Scene   A basically empty stage with a few blocks to sit on; two subway stairs at the back.

Situation   A group of job applicants come before an interviewer for questioning in this improvisationally created script.

FIRST INTERVIEWER (*standing*)   How do you do?
FIRST APPLICANT (*sitting*)   Thank you, I said, not knowing where to sit.

(*The characters will often include the audience in what they say, as if they were being interviewed by the audience.*)

FIRST INTERVIEWER (*pointedly*)   Won't you sit down?
FIRST APPLICANT (*standing again quickly, afraid to displease*)   I'm sorry.
FIRST INTERVIEWER (*busy with imaginary papers, pointing to a particular seat*)
    There. Name, please?
FIRST APPLICANT   Jack Smith.
FIRST INTERVIEWER   Jack what Smith?
FIRST APPLICANT   Beg pardon?
FIRST INTERVIEWER   Fill in the blank space, please. Jack blank space Smith.
FIRST APPLICANT   I don't have any.
FIRST INTERVIEWER   I asked you to sit down. (*pointing*) There.
FIRST APPLICANT (*sitting*)   I'm sorry.
FIRST INTERVIEWER   Name, please?
FIRST APPLICANT   Jack Smith.
FIRST INTERVIEWER   You haven't told me your MIDDLE name.
FIRST APPLICANT   I haven't got one.
FIRST INTERVIEWER (*suspicious but writing it down*)   No middle name.

(SECOND APPLICANT, *a woman, a Floorwasher, enters.*)

FIRST INTERVEWER   How do you do?
SECOND APPLICANT (*sitting*)   Thank you, I said, not knowing what.
FIRST INTERVIEWER   Won't you sit down?
SECOND APPLICANT (*standing*)   I'm sorry.
FIRST APPLICANT   I am sitting.

FIRST INTERVIEWER *(pointing)* There. Name, please?

SECOND APPLICANT *(sitting)* Jane Smith.

FIRST APPLICANT Jack Smith.

FIRST INTERVIEWER What blank space Smith?

SECOND APPLICANT Ellen.

FIRST APPLICANT Haven't got one.

FIRST INTERVIEWER What job are you applying for?

FIRST APPLICANT Housepainter.

SECOND APPLICANT Floorwasher.

FIRST INTERVIEWER We haven't many vacancies in that. What experience have you had?

FIRST APPLICANT A lot.

SECOND APPLICANT Who needs experience for floorwashing?

FIRST INTERVIEWER You will help me by making your answers clear.

FIRST APPLICANT Eight years.

SECOND APPLICANT Twenty years.

(THIRD APPLICANT, a Banker, enters.)

FIRST INTERVIEWER How do you do?

SECOND APPLICANT I'm good at it.

FIRST APPLICANT Very well.

THIRD APPLICANT *(sitting)* Thank you, I said, as casually as I could.

FIRST INTERVIEWER Won't you sit down?

THIRD APPLICANT *(standing again)* I'm sorry.

SECOND APPLICANT I am sitting.

FIRST APPLICANT *(standing again)* I'm sorry.

FIRST INTERVIEWER *(pointing to a particular seat)* There. Name, please?

FIRST APPLICANT Jack Smith.

SECOND APPLICANT Jane Smith.

THIRD APPLICANT Richard Smith.

FIRST INTERVIEWER What EXACTLY Smith, please?

THIRD APPLICANT Richard F.

SECOND APPLICANT Jane Ellen.

FIRST APPLICANT Jack None.

FIRST INTERVIEWER What are you applying for?

FIRST APPLICANT Housepainter.

SECOND APPLICANT I need money.

THIRD APPLICANT Bank president.

FIRST INTERVIEWER How many years have you been in your present job?

THIRD APPLICANT Three.

SECOND APPLICANT Twenty.

FIRST APPLICANT Eight.

(FOURTH APPLICANT, a Lady's Maid, enters.)

FIRST INTERVIEWER How do you do?

FOURTH APPLICANT I said thank you, not knowing where to sit.

THIRD APPLICANT I'm fine.

SECOND APPLICANT Do I have to tell you?

FIRST APPLICANT Very well.

FIRST INTERVIEWER Won't you sit down?

FOURTH APPLICANT   I'm sorry.
THIRD APPLICANT *(sitting again)*   Thank you.
SECOND APPLICANT *(standing again)*   I'm sorry.
FIRST APPLICANT *(sitting)*   Thanks.
FIRST INTERVIEWER *(pointing to a particular seat)*   There. Name, please?

(FOURTH APPLICANT sits.)

ALL APPLICANTS   Smith.
FIRST INTERVIEWER   What Smith?
FOURTH APPLICANT   Mary Victoria.
THIRD APPLICANT   Richard F.
SECOND APPLICANT   Jane Ellen
FIRST APPLICANT   Jack None.
FIRST INTERVIEWER   How many years' experience have you had?
FOURTH APPLICANT   Eight years.
SECOND APPLICANT   Twenty years.
FIRST APPLICANT   Eight years.
THIRD APPLICANT   Three years four months and nine days not counting
    vacations and sick leave and the time both my daughters and my wife had the
    whooping cough.
FIRST INTERVIEWER   Just answer the questions, please.
FOURTH APPLICANT   Yes, sir.
THIRD APPLICANT   Sure.
SECOND APPLICANT   I'm sorry.
FIRST APPLICANT   That's what I'm doing.

(SECOND INTERVIEWER, a young man, enters and goes to inspect APPLICANTS. With the entrance of each INTERVIEWER, the speed of the action accelerates.)

SECOND INTERVIEWER   How do you do?
FIRST APPLICANT *(standing)*   I'm sorry.
SECOND APPLICANT *(sitting)*   Thank you.
THIRD APPLICANT *(standing)*   I'm sorry.
FOURTH APPLICANT *(sitting)*   Thank you.

(END)

Last of the Red Hot Lovers
by Neil Simon

*from
beginning of Act II*

Barney, runs a fish and seafood restaurant, age 47 years
Bobbi, a young, attractive woman, about 27 years

Characters

The apartment of Barney's mother, New York City, in the East Thirties; late afternoon, August.

Scene

Suffering from middle-age insecurity, Barney has decided to have an extramarital affair. Having failed in his first attempt, he now encounters a young woman he had met the day before. A pleasant but nervous man, Barney hopes to seduce the girl who *appears* to be innocent and uncomplicated.

Situation

BARNEY   Well, hello.

BOBBI   Oh, thank God, air conditioning. Do you know it's a hundred and forty degrees outside? I swear. I mean it gets hot in California but nothing like this. Hi. Bobbi Michele?

BARNEY   Yes, yes. Come in, I'll close the door. It's cooler. *(She comes in; he closes the door)*

BOBBI   I was wandering up and down the hall. All these apartments look alike. *(looks quickly)* Oh, this is nice. I like this. I'm not disturbing you now, am I? I mean you're not busy or anything?

BARNEY   No, no. I was expecting you. Remember I said—

BOBBI   I wasn't sure I'd be here on time. I just got through with my audition.

BARNEY   No, you're fine. Remember I said three o'clock—

BOBBI   It's got to be a hundred and ten, right? *(crosses to the air conditioner)* I mean forget about breathing, it's over. *(stands with her back to the air conditioner)* You sure I'm not disturbing you? I could come back later.

BARNEY   No, I'm positive. I'm clear till five. *(He smells his fingers.)* Can I get you a cool drink?

BOBBI   I love this neighborhood. I knew this street looked familiar. I once had a girl friend who lived on this block. Forty-seventh between First and York.

BARNEY   This is Thirty-seventh.

BOBBI   Thirty-seventh. Of course. Then she couldn't have lived on this block. Ohh, that's better. The Shubert Theatre was a sauna bath. Oh, listen, my accompanist *did* show up, which I have you to thank for because you were so sweet in the park yesterday and I want you to know I have not forgotten it, but here I am talking and talking and I really haven't said hello yet. Hello.

BARNEY   Hello.

BOBBI   Hello. Here I am.

BARNEY   So I see.

BOBBI   Oh, God, I talk a lot when I get nervous. Have you noticed that? I'll try and stop it if I can. You'll have to forgive me.

BARNEY   Are you nervous?

BOBBI   Well, I'm not nervous now. I was nervous before. I just had a terrible experience with a cab driver. Well, I don't want to go into it. Ohh, God, I just wilt in the heat. If I pass out on the floor, I'm just going to have to trust you.

BARNEY   (smiles)   You don't have to worry.

BOBBI   Well, you're not a cab driver. You wouldn't try something like that.

BARNEY   Like what?

BOBBI   He wanted to make it with me under the Manhattan Bridge during his lunch hour. Listen, can we forget about it, it's over now. I must look awful.

BARNEY   Not at all. You look lovely.

BOBBI   Oh, poof, I don't.

BARNEY   You do. You do.

BOBBI   Give me three minutes, I'll dazzle you. Did you get shorter?

BARNEY   Shorter? Since yesterday?

BOBBI   Why do you look shorter?

BARNEY   I can't imagine why I should look shorter. (He sits next to her.)

BOBBI   Oh, flats.

BARNEY   Flats?

BOBBI   I was wearing flats yesterday. I put on heels for the audition today. I got taller. Actually, you're not really short. Well, you know that.

BARNEY   Yes, well, sometimes when a person has large bones—

BOBBI   You know, I couldn't make out your handwriting. I thought I had the wrong address. 432 East Thirty-seventh?

BARNEY   No, that's the right address.

BOBBI   Well, I should hope so. Otherwise where am I and who are you? (She laughs; he tries to.) Oh, that's silly. If I'm goofy today, it's the heat.

BARNEY   You're not goofy at all.

BOBBI   I am. I'm goofy, let's face it.

BARNEY   I think you're charming.

BOBBI   Oh, I know I'm charming but I'm also goofy which I think is part of my charm. That's a terrible thing to say, isn't it?

BARNEY   Not at all. Sometimes frankness can be—

BOBBI   It's terrible, I can't help it. I'm so open about things. That's why I'm always getting myself into trouble, you know what I mean?

BARNEY   What kind of trouble do you get—

BOBBI   My God, I didn't even notice it. You shaved your moustache.

BARNEY   What moustache?

BOBBI   Didn't you have a moustache yesterday?

BARNEY   Me? No.

BOBBI   You *never* had a moustache?

BARNEY   Never. I don't look good in a moustache. It doesn't grow in thick on the left side.

BOBBI   Who am I thinking of? Who did I meet yesterday with a moustache?

BARNEY   That I couldn't tell you.

BOBBI   Well, I can't think straight. I'm still a nervous wreck over that cab incident. I've been back in New York three days and look what happens. I just want to forget about it.

BARNEY   Certainly. How about a drink? I have J&B Scotch, Wolfschmidt vodka . . .

BOBBI   I wrote the cabbie's name down. Max Schoenstein. I was going to report him to the police but he started to cry. Tears pouring down his face, I thought his cigar would go out. Then he pleaded with me he's married twenty-seven years with one son in Vietnam and another son in medical school and that he didn't mean any harm and I felt sorry for him and I said all right, I wouldn't report him, so he thanked me and asked me to reconsider going under the Manhattan Bridge. *(brushes her hair and poses)* How do I look? Better?

BARNEY   Marvelous. Gee, that's terrible.

BOBBI   Oh, it happens to me all the time. Coming in on the plane from California. The man sitting next to me kept feeling me up all during the movie. Well, I don't want to go into that. *(looks around)* This is the kind of place I'm looking for. Does it have a terrace?

BARNEY   No, no terrace. He was *feeling* you?

BOBBI   Well, he said he was looking for the dial to turn up the volume but he didn't even have the headset plugged in his ears . . . Nice view.

BARNEY   Why didn't you say something to him?

BOBBI   Well, he was Chinese, I didn't want to seem bigoted. Then he has the nerve to call me, in the middle of the night. Some strange Chinaman.

BARNEY   How'd he get your number?

BOBBI   I don't know. I must have given it to him or something. What's the difference? Look, it's over, let's forget it. Am I talking too much? I haven't given you a chance to say anything.

BARNEY   I'm fascinated. Those are incredible stories.

BOBBI   How do you mean incredible? You don't believe them?

BARNEY   I do. I do believe them.

BOBBI   Because they're true.

BARNEY   That's the fascinating part.

BOBBI   Maybe to you. They were terrifying to me.

BARNEY   To me too.

BOBBI   Could I have a drink?

BARNEY   What a good idea. J&B? Vodka?

BOBBI   I don't provoke these things. They just happen.

BARNEY   I'm not surprised. You're such a pretty girl.

BOBBI   I don't know why they single me out. I'm always getting these obscene telephone calls.

BARNEY   Well, there's an awful lot of that going on.

BOBBI   I get them wherever I go. Once I wasn't home, he left an obscene message.

BARNEY   My goodness.

BOBBI *(looking at the photos on the table)*   And the language. I never heard such filth. I once got a call where this psycho actually described vile and indecent acts for over fifteen minutes.

BARNEY   FIFTEEN MINUTES!

BOBBI   Listen, if you don't shut me up I'll never stop talking. What time is it?

BARNEY   A quarter after three.

BOBBI   Oh, God, I've got to make a call. May I? I don't have one on me.

BARNEY   Yes, certainly.

BOBBI   Is this where you write those sea stories you were telling me about?

BARNEY   Yes, I work here during the day. Actually it's my mother's apartment.

BOBBI   I knew this writer in California. A registered weirdo. He used to write these underground movies you see on Eighth Avenue. You know, *Sex Family Robinson, Tom Swift and His Incredible Thing* . . . I thought I was in love with him until I found out he was deranged. I mean the things he wanted me to do.

BARNEY   Like what?

BOBBI   Oh, God, I couldn't repeat them.

BARNEY   That's all right. You can repeat them.

BOBBI *(dials the phone and listens)*   She hears the phone. She's just a lazy bitch.

BARNEY   But like what? What kind of things did he want you to do?

BOBBI   I couldn't tell you. I told my analyst, he went into cardiac arrest . . . Can you believe this? I could wait here twenty minutes.

BARNEY   You mean things together or alone? What kind of things?

BOBBI   If I tell you this man had his teeth sharpened, can you fill in the rest?

(She inspects the photos on the table)

BARNEY   His teeth? My God!

BOBBI   The man was psychotically inclined. *(smiles at a photo)* This is adorable. Your mother?

BARNEY *(shakes his head)*   No, it's me. But did you ever do any of them? These things he wanted?

BOBBI   Me? No! Never! Of course not . . . Some. I had to do some otherwise I was afraid he would kill me. Is this you and your father?

BARNEY   Yes . . . He actually forced you to do these things?

BOBBI   You don't play it cool with a man who had his teeth sharpened.

(END)

That Championship Season
by Jason Miller

from
Act I

Characters

Coach, retired high school basketball coach
George, the local Mayor
James, brother of Tom, in local politics and a junior high school principal
Phil, a local businessman
Tom, an alcoholic
All the men are in their forties except the coach, who is past sixty.

Scene

The living room of the coach, somewhere in the Lackawanna Valley, Pennsylvania.

Situation

Members of a former state championship basketball team meet for a reunion in the home of their old coach. Generally disappointed and frustrated men, their charismatic coach enters to meet them and begin the reunion.

COACH   All right. Line it up. Shape it. Twenty laps around the room. Too much fat in the ass around here. I want my boys lean and mean. *(great laughter)* A voice from the past boys, the old gunner can still bray with the best. *(pouring whiskey)* Hit those boards hard, Romano . . . And you, Sikowski, don't just stand there with your finger up you know where, move! . . . And you, Daley, have a drink. . . . *(laughs)* And you big Daley [JAMES], hustle some of this whiskey into you. Imported. Jamison. Boil your brains, this stuff!

GEORGE   You haven't changed in twenty years.

COACH   I haven't changed in sixty years. I can take the four of you around the court till you drop, run you into the ground. *(proudly)* Even one eighty-five. Weighed that in 1940. *(gets down and does ten quick push-ups)* And that's after having my belly cut open, twenty stitches. *(opens shirt)* Look at that sonofabitch. Belly looks like a baseball.

JAMES   What's the secret?

COACH   "Walk softly and carry a big stick." *(Pause. Great joy, shy almost)* Oh, Christ, boys, Christ, it's so good . . . the joy in my heart to feel you around me again, *(he pats, feels, whacks them all)* together again, can't find words to say it. . . . Magnificent! My boys standing around me again! A toast to the 1952 Pennsylvania State High School Basketball Champions! *(they drink)* You were a legend in your time, boys, a legend. Never forget that, never.

GEORGE   We owe it all to you, Coach.

(MEN *ad lib agreement.*)

COACH   I used to tell people you boys were like a fine watch. My very expensive and fine watch that kept perfect time. You froze the ball against Tech for three minutes. Fantastic. Stay in shape. Lean and mean. You're in your thirties and that's the heart-attack season, boys. Most important muscle in your body, boys . . . the heart . . . keep it in shape, work it out!

GEORGE   Bought one of those exercise bikes. Keeps the stomach flat.

PHIL   But your ass is still down around your knees.

GEORGE   That's it, start on me, the old scapegoat.

TOM   You love it.

GEORGE   Yeah.

COACH   Drink up, boys, put it away, night's young. Take off your jackets, relax.

GEORGE   Chicken is in the stove.

COACH   You're working on your third chin yourself, Phil.

PHIL   I'm an executive.

COACH   James, you're starting to sag a little too, you look tired.

JAMES   I haven't been sleeping well, Coach.

COACH   Why?

JAMES   My teeth.

COACH   What's the matter?

JAMES   They're gone.

COACH   Gone.

JAMES *(embarrassed)*   They took them out last month.

COACH   You got plates?

JAMES   Yeah.

COACH   Let's see. Open your mouth. Uh-uh. Good job. They look almost real.

PHIL *(laughs)*   Never had enough Vitamin C in your diet!

JAMES *(half-smile)*   Try feeding five kids.

COACH   You didn't feed them your teeth, did you? You need iron in your blood. . . . *(opens mouth)* I got twenty-seven originals.

(MEN *laugh*)

JAMES   Actually they've recently completed studies proving that nerves can cause severe damage to teeth.

COACH   Really! Maybe you should have gotten your nerves out! *(laugh)* Have another shot and relax, James.

COACH   Better put that chicken on low, George. Tom, . . . *(Hugs him; they touch glasses and drink.)* I'm so goddam happy, so grateful you're back with us again. Doesn't he look wonderful, boys?

TOM *(pouring)*   Nothing keeps the old gunner down, either.

COACH   You were a thing of rare . . . beauty, boys. Life is a game and I'm proud to say I played it with the best. We were one flesh twenty years ago; never forget that as long as you live! *(pause)* Ten seconds left on the clock . . . we were down by one point . . . remember . . . unbelievable!

GEORGE *(quiet intensity)*   I passed inbounds to Tom.

TOM   I brought the ball up.

PHIL   Passed to me in the corner.

COACH *(urgent)*   Six seconds left!

PHIL   I hit James coming . . .

JAMES   Across the court and I saw . . .

COACH   Three seconds left!

JAMES   Martin at the foul line . . .

GEORGE   Martin caught the ball in mid-air . . . he went up . . .

JAMES   Up . . .

COACH   One second . . .

GEORGE   *(jumping up)*   Yes!

COACH   State Champions! They said we couldn't do it, boys. We beat a school
three times our size. We beat them in Philadelphia. We performed the
impossible, boys, never forget that, never. Jesus, remember they had an
eight-foot nigger, jumped like a kangaroo. *(proudly)* There's the trophy, boys.
Fast, Jesus, fast, you were a flash of legs . . . gone, like lightning!

GEORGE   Martin was a pressure ballplayer.

COACH   He thrived on it . . . loved it.

JAMES   He had a great eye.

COACH   Priceless.

GEORGE   The perfect ballplayer.

COACH   Not a flaw. He made it all go . . . magnificent talent! *(pause. quietly)*
Yeah. Not a word in twenty years. Let's say a little prayer for him, boys, a
prayer that he's safe and happy and still a champion. *(They lay their hands
together. Moment of silence)* We never had a losing season, boys; there's not
many that can say that. . . .

(*END*)

That Championship Season
by Jason Miller. Biff
McGuire and Ronny
Graham at The Seattle
Repertory Theatre.
Directed by Duncan Ross.

Father Uxbridge Wants to Marry

by Frank Gagliano

*from
the middle of the play*

Characters

Morden
Debden, his mistress
Angel, Debden's young daughter
Father Ongar, a new-breed priest who, in this scene, is a presence in Morden's
    mind.

Scene and Situation

The play is a series of dissolves that unfold in the fragmenting mind of Morden;
whose Faith, loves and even employment are taken away from him bit by bit.
Beginning in an elevator where he's told he's being fired as operator to be
replaced by an Otis automatic, Morden's mind—and the elevator walls—crack
open and Morden wanders through a series of tragicomic, out-of-sequence
flashbacks; each one distorted; each heightened by intrusions of sound, Bach
arias and the pursuing presence of a young, new-breed priest named "Ongar"
who, finally, brings Morden to the edge of the abyss. . . . In the following
scene Morden fights to hold on to the two people he loves most.

(DEBDEN *enters from the shadows, wheeling in a small table-on-casters with a suitcase on
it.* DEBDEN *recites as she packs*)

DEBDEN   Sometimes there's a terrible scream inside.

MORDEN *(From the shadows)* Debden.

DEBDEN   Why couldn't God make me the type to get that scream out?

MORDEN *(From the shadows)* Debden.

DEBDEN   It would be such a satisfying scream. Long . . . sustained . . . full of
    rocks and sand and broken glass. Ripping. Burning. Forcing me to spit up
    blood, perhaps. But that couldn't stop it. Even if my throat was being ripped
    out by that scream, that scream wouldn't stop.

MORDEN *(From the shadows)* Debden.

DEBDEN   A monumental scream! A scream to end all screams! And it would yank
    out—drag out—wriggling, like tin cans and obscenities—my heart, liver,
    uterus, bones, and breath. Finally cleaning me out. Leaving me a limp,
    wrinkly skin; some huge, punctured, mustard-colored balloon, shriveled in
    the dirt.

(*Picks up sheet of paper*)

That was from a play I wrote, Morden. Self-indulgent. All monologue, as I
recall. Still, I won a prize for that play in my undergraduate days. I was
considered quite a writer. With a brilliant future.

The nightmare prologue from the West Virginia University production of Frank Gagliano's, *Father Uxbridge Wants to Marry*, directed by the playwright.

(She rips up the paper)

Curtain.

(She lets the pieces flutter to the floor)

MORDEN *(From the shadows)* Debden.

DEBDEN *(Picking up a hand mirror)* How is it possible for a woman my age to have acne.

MORDEN *(Entering from the shadows)* Debden, don't leave me.

DEBDEN My period has never been regular. My mother had beautiful skin. I guess her's was.

MORDEN Debden, your face has a scar and you limp.

DEBDEN No! *(She limps away, then moves about)*

MORDEN You were in an accident that left you with a scar and a limp. I took care of you. If you leave me, no one else will.

DEBDEN Don't be cruel, Morden. Please. I'm trying to face reality. But don't make me face it all at once. I'm not strong enough for that. Not yet.

MORDEN I don't want to be cruel, but what about me? What will I do if you leave me?

DEBDEN   You'll do what you always do—exist! . . . Oh, Morden. I'm sorry. I
                didn't mean that. Well, I mean I *did* mean that but I didn't mean it to sound
                so bitter. I'll try it another way: You'll do what you always do . . . *(with
                compassion)* exist. *(She embraces him)*
MORDEN   *(While still in the embrace)*   There's got to be someone.
DEBDEN   *(Letting him go)*   Morden, there were people who believed in me. I've got
                to get involved with my own kind again. I've sat here feeling sorry for
                myself, allowing you to take care of me—
MORDEN   *And* Angel! I've taken care of her, too. Don't forget that. Or have you
                even thought about her? What about her? . . . You're not taking her? . . .
                You *are* taking her.
DEBDEN   *(Calls)*   Angel! *(To* MORDEN*)* She's mine. Of course I'm taking her. *(Calls)*
                Angel! *(To* MORDEN*)* I'll provide for her. *(Calls)* Angel, put those scissors away
                and come help Mommy pack.
MORDEN   Provide? *(*FATHER ONGAR *brings* ANGEL *on)* Oh, I see. Once away from me,
                you'll be free to go about your "business."
DEBDEN   Oh, no . . . not *that* again.
MORDEN   Bring your customers right to the house.
DEBDEN   Angel, come here! Don't listen!

*(*FATHER ONGAR **rushes** ANGEL *over to* DEBDEN. DEBDEN *covers* ANGEL'S *ears with* ANGEL'S *own
hands.* FATHER ONGAR *exits)*

MORDEN   Haven't I seen it? Haven't I visited such filthy bitches? Haven't I been
                taken on right under the same roof with the bitch's kid? And sooner or later
                the kid becomes useful—Mommy's little helper—
DEBDEN   *(Showing her wrists. They are bandaged)*   Morden, I tried to kill myself! Are
                you trying to make me do it again!?!?

(Second's freeze. Then, realizing what she's done. DEBDEN *tries to pull back her wrists. But
* MORDEN *rushes to her, falls to his knees and kisses one bandaged wrist)*

MORDEN   Mommy's hurt, Angel. You, too. You kiss the hurt.

(Angel kneels to kiss DEBDEN'S *other bandaged wrist, but before she can,* DEBDEN *pulls both
* ANGEL *and* MORDEN *to her)*

DEBDEN   Morden. Morden. Let us go.
MORDEN   Why? Why did you do this, Debden? Why?
DEBDEN   *(After a pause. Drained. Quiet)*   I'm a witch, Morden. I can make people die
                by wanting it badly enough. Just before the car accident. I knew I wanted
                my husband to die. And he did. And I never stopped blaming myself. Now
                . . . lately . . . I've been feeling the same about you. And I despaired.

(A beat)

MORDEN   Jesus, Debden, that's a terrible sin. I mean, no matter how bad it all is,
                you should never try to kill yourself. *(Rising)* No no no. You're staying.
                (Helps ANGEL *to rise. Takes* ANGEL *with him as he moves away from* DEBDEN*)* Angel,
                you and me—we'll take care of Mommy because Mommy isn't strong
                enough to go.
DEBDEN   Not strong? I wasn't when I tried this. *(shows wrists again)* But I've since
                had some expert guidance. Now I know that I have a right to live, Morden.
                No matter how hurt you are, have a right to leave, if I choose. And I do
                choose. I'm going, Morden.

(Begins to move toward ANGEL*)*

MORDEN *(Protecting* ANGEL. *Stepping back)* What expert guidance? No, you can't. I won't—Angel, you agree with me. Right? And you want to stay here with me. Don't you? *(Beat.* ANGEL *nods)* You see, Debden. She wants to stay with me.

DEBDEN *(A beat.)* Angel. You want to be with Mommy wherever she goes. Don't you?

*(*ANGEL *looks back and forth between the two people she really loves. Hesitates. Then runs to her mother.)*

All right, dear. Go play until we're ready to leave.

*(*ANGEL *goes off into the shadows. Pause.* DEBDEN *resumes packing)*

MORDEN Don't take Angel away from me. I know she's not really my child, but she's become mine. And—I don't know how I know this, but—I'll never have a child of my own. *(Pause)* Things are good now. My mother's gone. My old marriage has been annulled and I'm working. There—there—thats the main thing. I've got a steady job and I *can* provide.

DEBDEN Not for long.

MORDEN What?

DEBDEN They're replacing you with an automatic elevator.

MORDEN How do you know? I don't know that. Where did you hear that? Huh?

DEBDEN At the rectory.

MORDEN Father Uxbridge. But you only met him once. With me.

DEBDEN I've been back.

MORDEN *(moving in on her)* Why? You didn't even like him.

DEBDEN *(uncomfortable)* That's right. But there was no one else and I had to talk to someone.

MORDEN What did he tell you?

DEBDEN Nothing.

MORDEN WHAT DID HE TELL YOU!?!

DEBDEN *(Moves away from the suitcase)* Nothing! I only saw him once. When I went back the next time, he was giving a lecture. I looked in. Saw you sitting on a stool.

MORDEN I got money for that. Anyway, I don't go anymore. But *you* went back. Why? *Why?!!*

DEBDEN I had to talk to someone. I called Father Uxbridge again. But he was leaving. They were sending him on a lecture tour. Something about "the new clergy."

MORDEN New. Yes. New's right. You knew than and you know now.

DEBDEN What?

MORDEN That Father Uxbridge wants to marry.

DEBDEN No.

MORDEN You must have. Everyone knew. That's why I stopped seeing him. Disgusting.

DEBDEN He advocates marriage for priests. So what? A lot do now.

MORDEN I don't care what a lot of 'em advocate. *He* wants to marry. That's the upsetting thing. There was an article—in a magazine. By a Father X. Well, it didn't take some of the ladies in the Parish long to figure out who Father X was. Mrs. Bethnal—Green herself—yes, my employer—high up in the Church because of her donations—herself, reached that conclusion. Uxbridge—even the first time I talked to him, he talked about it. Then he had no opinion, he said. Then he said he took the middle road. The middle road—sure. Right to a lady's middle. I'll bet he was after yours.

DEBDEN   I only saw him once. And Father Ongar—

MORDEN   Who?

MORDEN'S VOICE (Over)   Bang. Bang. Bang. Bang. Bang. . . .

DEBDEN   The priest I've been seeing.

MORDEN   Ongar? I know that name. What about him?

(The "Bangs" crescendo under the following)

DEBDEN   My counselor . . . *he* replaced Father Uxbridge.

MORDEN   And this Father Ongar—*he* wants to get at your middle.

DEBDEN   Nobody wants to get at my middle!

MORDEN   I do! I do! What about that? I need it. What will I do without it?

DEBDEN   There are others. There are always others.

MORDEN   No. There won't be. Anyway, I want you.

DEBDEN   But . . . but I don't . . . want you.

MORDEN   Suddenly! Suddenly!

DEBDEN   No. Yes. What's the difference? Now I know.

MORDEN   What? WHAT!?!?

DEBDEN   THAT YOU'RE BENEATH ME!

(The "Bangs" are brought down very low. Then the sound crescendoes again under the following.

FATHER ONGAR *enters. He moves in front of* DEBDEN *and faces* MORDEN. DEBDEN *turns so that she's standing back to back with* FATHER ONGAR.)

DEBDEN   I know it's cruel. But sometimes you've got to be cruel. It's over, Morden. We're through. I've found others who aren't beneath me; whom I can look up to, stretch my mind up to. Morden, my brain has atrophied with you.

MORDEN   Beneath you. Who told you to think that? This new one? This Father Ongar?

*(FATHER ONGAR *quickly moves aside and* DEBDEN *turns to face* MORDEN)*

You scarred cripple. I could kill you. KILL YOU! God, isn't it right to kill that cruelty? I'll bet there's something in The Book that gives you that o.k. You're smart, Debden. Quote me something from The Book.

DEBDEN   Please. Morden.

MORDEN   There must be something. When they nailed him to the cross. No! That part forgives. Some part that gives me the right to—

DEBDEN   Morden! Don't do anything to me! Please.

(The "bangs" quieten. ONGAR *moves back to the edge of the shadows)*

MORDEN   No. I won't do anything to you. Because this is how it's going to be. You're going to stay here. And you can have all the customers you want. HERE! Right in this house. You can diddle away here for the rest of your life. I don't care. Just as long as you diddle me once in awhile. And I don't even care anymore if you keep on laying stiff as a stick under me. But I'll take care of Angel. I'll give her all my love. I'll be her father and mother. Because no slut should be. Agreed?

(The "bangs" crescendo again)

DEBDEN   No! *(Shouts off)* Angel! *(To* MORDEN*)* No!

*(*FATHER ONGAR *reaches into the shadows and pulls on* ANGEL. ONGAR *then quickly moves off into the shadows)*

DEBDEN *(To* ANGEL*)*   Come on, darling. We're going now.

*(*MORDEN *grabs* ANGEL*)*

MORDEN   You're not taking her anywhere!

*(*FATHER ONGAR *returns with the scissors and places them in* MORDEN'S *hand. He raises* MORDEN'S *hand)*

DEBDEN   Morden!
MORDEN   She's mine! I love her so much I'll kill her rather than let her go!

*(*FATHER ONGAR *gestures. The "bangs" come up very loud)*

DEBDEN   Don't, Morden! *(She screams.* MORDEN *lets* ANGEL *go)*
MORDEN   How can I kill her with so much noise? And it's getting worse.

*(*FATHER ONGAR *takes the scissors from* MORDEN. *He exits.* MORDEN *covers his ears.)*

The thing is—it had stopped. You know? All the while I was sure of you. Now . . . wait! A movie! Once I saw this movie! . . . they had a scene—I think it was a movie. Maybe I dreamed it? . . . Anyway, in it, they were nailing Him to the cross.

(The "bangs" stop)

And the thing about it, you see, was that the men doing the nailing were simple fellows, you know. Carpenters, I guess. That sort. And they're chatting like you do when you work together with someone all the time. You know? And I remember that one of them keeps a large—very large—nail in his teeth all the while he's talking. And at the same time he's talking—with that nail in his teeth—he's arranging the arm, you see. Straightening it out on the cross and forcing open the hand. Palm up. . . . And that's something in itself. You can't see his face—the one who's being nailed. I mean. But he's putting up a struggle. You can tell that by the way those two fellows are having trouble keeping his arm straight and the palm open, face up. In fact—yes—one of them has to put his knee on the arm to keep it down. And you figure, that's strange because he knows there's nothing he can do about it—the one who's being nailed, I mean. In fact, he's known it all along. Even before he was born. Right? In fact, that's what he was born for. But that doesn't seem to matter. I mean, from the struggle he's making, you can see that he doesn't want to die. Imagine. . . . Anyway, the one with the nail between his teeth takes it out. Looks at it. It's a shiny, new nail. He looks around, puts the shiny one in his pocket and takes out an old, rusty one. "Sure. What the hell," the other one—his friend—says. "Why waste a new one?" Then he looks at the palm—face up—and he places the old, rusty nail right smack in the center of that face-up palm and the beam right underneath that palm—just with his eye. And bang! One fast shot and the nail is through. But it's messy. I mean, blood spurting out all over. And that's a shock, too. In all the pictures where you saw the hole in the palm, I remembered it was always clean. Neat. Just a little round shaft from front to back. Oh, maybe a little blood just around the rim. But neat. Dried and neat. But here—well, when you stop to figure it, the nail *has* to smash through veins and little bones and arteries before it catches in the wood. I mean, in true life where there's a pain, it does. . . . Anyway, there's this funny little part where fingers on the face-up palm jerk in. You know, like a reflex to cover the hurt as soon as the nail tears through. And the carpenter gets annoyed. And so he makes a face—a funny face, the carpenter does, as if to say, "Dear God, all I want to do is my job and look at this! There's no cooperation." So what he does is, he pries back the fingers and begins to hammer down the rusty nail in the center of that face-up palm into the wooden beam. . . . And *that's* when it happened to me . . . RIGHT! . . . Throughout the whole thing, I was pretty much out of it. I mean—oh—it was terrible and all, but I really couldn't side with any of them. You never saw his face, the one who was being nailed, I mean. And the carpenters . . . well, I guess they were too skilled for me to really feel any kinship with. But I was there somewhere. I knew that. And you know where? You know *what* I was in that scene? I was the bangs!

(The sound of "bang, bang, bang" begins again)

MORDEN I suddenly recognized the sound. Those bangs. My voice. Those bangs were my voice. My voice was those bangs. And you know how they do in movies. They turn up the sound. Bang, bang, bang! My voice banging away at that rotten nail into the face-up palm! I thought they'd all recognize me, those people sitting in the movie house. And the one thing I wanted more than ever at that moment was to be an invisible giant; go up to the screen with a giant knife, stab it at the top and hack down. Then stab it at the side and slash across. Then rip those flapping sections right out of that mouth, forever opened and black, and I looked down in it after slashing out that silver membrane and got dizzy, dizzy. The invisible giant was about to fall into—nothing! Debden!

(The "bangs" stop)

Debden? . . . Angel?

(He frantically looks around)

Debden! . . . Debden.

(Beat. DEBDEN and ANGEL are gone. That fact sinks in)

Debden. You used to like it when I dipped my fingers in the ice cube tray and touched your burning scar.

(Pause)

Father Ongar. Ongar! I'll kill him!

(END)

When You Comin' Back, Red Ryder?

by *Mark Medoff*

from
Act I

Characters

Angel, well into her 20s; an overweight, pleasant waitress.
Teddy, 3–35; long hair, intelligent and rough, unruly, yet with a controlled and
    charming "surface" at times; a deep, smouldering violence within him.
Cheryl, 20; pretty in a straight-haired, unwashed, no makeup way. She wears
    jeans, a tank top (braless).
Clarisse, late 30s; attractive; well dressed; carries a violin case; reserved.
Richard, early 40s; attractive; well dressed; confident.
Lyle, early 60s; a brace on one leg; proud; handsome; wears work clothes and a
    hat.

Scene

A diner on the desert in southern New Mexico. Six stools, three tables, a
jukebox. The diner is clean, but "its day has gone."

Situation

A typical morning in a roadside diner is interrupted by the troubling presence
of an intense stranger and his girl friend. The stranger begins to menace the
staff and customers.

ANGEL Good mornin.

(TEDDY *is silent a long moment. He turns to smile at* CHERYL.)

TEDDY *(Affecting a stereotyped southwestern accent.)* Mornin, neighbors.

(TEDDY *starts upstage, between the counter and the booth inside the door. When he is
abreast of* CLARISSE, *he suddenly stops and turns to her.)*

    Pardon me, m'am, but aren't you. . . .

(CLARISSE *looks up at him. She obviously does not know him.* TEDDY *holds fleetingly on
her and then averts his gaze. . . .)*

'Scuse me.

(. . . *as if he's trying to suggest that he doesn't recognize her when in fact he really
wants to suggest that he does.* CLARISSE *and* RICHARD *exchange bewildered glances, and a
strange dormant seed is planted in* RICHARD'S *mind.)*

    Well, now . . . who runs that yere fillin station next door?

(TEDDY *glances at* CLARISSE, *who is looking at him. She averts her eyes.)*

LYLE Right here. Lyle Striker, owner proprietor, and janitor.

TEDDY   Well, sir, need a rebuilt generator for a VW van.

LYLE   Nothin open today. Sunday.

TEDDY   Sunday, is it?

LYLE   Ever'body sleepin it off or out prayin forgiveness for it.

TEDDY   Tell ya what I had in mind. Thought maybe in a town such as yours a man with a service station, and a good-natured crippled man to boot, would be in a position to call up a parts store on a Sunday mornin and get a part anyhow.

LYLE   (Pause.) S'pose I could.

TEDDY   We surely would appreciate it.

LYLE   Let's have a look at your van first and make sure—

TEDDY   (Accentless.) Don't have to look at the van.

LYLE   Wouldn't want ya to spend—

TEDDY   (Accentless.) Generator's gone, sir. If you'll be kind enough to get us a rebuilt, I'll install it myself.

LYLE   Well, that sounds like a tough offer to beat. (He meets TEDDY's eyes and then has to avert his gaze.) I'll just go on over to the station and see who I can rouse up.

TEDDY   Mighty accommodatin of ya.

LYLE   (Rising.) Back in a jiffy, Angel. Don't auction off my eggs now.

(LYLE winks at ANGEL, then turns and exits with a glance at CHERYL's bosom and a small follow-up smile at her face.)

ANGEL   (As LYLE exits.) What do I hear for Mr. Lyle Striker's eggs?

(TEDDY and CHERYL sit at the booth inside the door. CHERYL is noticeably nervous and has been since they entered.)

TEDDY   How are y'all this mornin?

ANGEL   Just fine. How're you folks?

TEDDY   Just fine. How you?

ANGEL   Fine.

TEDDY   That's fine. (Slapping dust from his pants.) Y'all seem to have the dust market pretty well cornered out here. (Looking to STEPHEN, who is staring at him.) How you, kid?

STEPHEN   I'm okay, dad.

TEDDY   Gladda hear it. (To himself.) Boy's got a sense of humor, gonna think about puttin him on T.V. (To the ETHREDGES.) And how bout you nice lookin folks. How you this mornin?

RICHARD   Excellent, thanks.

TEDDY   Excellent! (To CHERYL.) Ever'body here's fine or okay or excellent. Whadduya thinka that?

CHERYL   (Quickly, quietly.) Stop it.

TEDDY   The call has gone out for me to "stop it." All y'all in favor, kindly signify by raisin your hands.

CHERYL   (To ANGEL.) Do you have some coffee?

TEDDY   (To himself.) Looks like it's gonna be a close vote.

ANGEL   (To CHERYL.) To go or to drink here?

CHERYL   Jesus—to drink here. Where are we gonna go?

ANGEL   Two?

CHERYL   (*To* TEDDY *who stares at* STEPHEN *who stares right back.*) Will you cut it out! Do you want coffee?

TEDDY   (*Turning away from* STEPHEN.) Yeah.

CHERYL   Two.

ANGEL   Where you folks from?

TEDDY   Istanbul. (*Pause, then sings the rest.*) Used to be Constantinople—

STEPHEN   You got California plates.

TEDDY   (*Squinting at* STEPHEN, *gaming.*) Just who are you, mister?

(STEPHEN *sucks his teeth.*)

ANGEL   Where ya headed?

TEDDY   *Mexico.*

ANGEL   Oh, that's nice down there.

TEDDY   Get around a lot, do ya?

STEPHEN   Shee! She never been outta the state a New Mexico. She don't know.

ANGEL   I know more'n you think, Stephen. I see books and I meet a lotta nice people've been there.

STEPHEN   Sure ya do.

ANGEL   (*Staring at* STEPHEN, *then turning to* TEDDY *and* CHERYL.) You folks wanna order something to eat?

TEDDY   Don't mind if we do.

ANGEL   Steak and eggs is our specialty.

TEDDY   Steak and eggs it is then. And home fries ya sliced up with your own little fingers?

ANGEL   Stephen's fingers.

TEDDY   Well, hell, I'll take a chance.

ANGEL   M'am?

CHERYL   Yeah—fine.

TEDDY   Now, over easy on them eggs, darlin, med-jum on that beef.

ANGEL   How bout you, m'am?

CHERYL   Any way—it doesn't matter.

TEDDY   You surprise her, darlin.

(ANGEL *retreats to her grill.*)

Where you nice looking folks from San Diego in that Cadillac car headin?

RICHARD   Do you know us? You know, I got the feeling when you came in—

TEDDY   (*Winking, whispering.*) Saw the San Diego State Faculty sticker on the bumper.

RICHARD   On—that's my wife's.

TEDDY   Uh-huh. Thought for a second there she was my cousin Faye.

(TEDDY *and* CLARISSE *stare at each other a moment.*)

Headin back to San Diego are ya?

RICHARD   New Orleans.

TEDDY   New Orleans. (*Nodding at the violin case.*) Packin a submachine gun?

RICHARD   Only a violin, I'm afraid.

TEDDY Prefer a submachine gun, would ya?

RICHARD *(Laughing.)* I didn't mean I was literally afraid—

TEDDY Yes, m'am, I don't mind sayin that you tend to remind me a whole helluva lot of my cousin Fern.

(Again, TEDDY and CLARISSE'S eyes hold a moment.)

That must be a mighty fine fiddle to get took to breakfast with ya.

RICHARD It's a Guarnerius. *(Smiling.)* Sometimes I think my wife has an added appendage.

TEDDY Lady playin the hoe-down circuit, is she?

CLARISSE No, I'm—

(RICHARD stops her from answering by touching her shoulder.)

RICHARD She's going to be with the New Orleans Philharmonic this summer.

TEDDY Uncle Clyde Bob and Aunt Cissy must be mighty proud of you, Cousin Freda. *(To RICHARD.)* And you just goin along to anwer the tough questions for her? Just livin off the little woman's residuals, as it were?

RICHARD Not quite.

TEDDY Not quite. Doctor, lawyer, or Indian chief?

(RICHARD smiles indulgently.)

Don't mean to be nosey.

RICHARD No?

TEDDY Just curious. Just makin a little roadside diner conversation. Pass the time. Hope ya don't mind.

RICHARD As of yet I don't.

TEDDY But at some future date you might. . . . Gonna jot that down here.

RICHARD That accent you're affecting seems a form of condescension aimed at all of us.

TEDDY Surely not. No law against havin fun, is there? Leastways, not yet.

(TEDDY smiles broadly at RICHARD who smiles coolly back and goes on with his breakfast.)

RICHARD No. Not yet.

TEDDY May I ask, sir what *do* you do?

RICHARD I am in the *im*port business.

TEDDY *im*port. Well well. And just what do you im*port?*

RICHARD *Textiles.*

TEDDY *Textiles.* Had you figured for an osteopath. *(To himself.)* Never have been able to figure what folks got against osteopaths. *(To CHERYL.)* Doctor here imports *textiles.*

(CHERYL nods uncomfortably.)

(To himself.) Got me on a called third strike on that one, all right. Thought it was a fast ball comin at my head and then she suddenly dives down across the plate and I'm left alookin. Live and learn. *(Turns to STEPHEN.)* And how bout my little buddy in the corner there? My, my, but I like your hair style. I'll bet that look'll be back before ya know it. Girls'll be climbin all over ya. Rolled up sleeves, the works. What do you do, buddy?

(STEPHEN stares at TEDDY.)

ANGEL *(When* STEPHEN *does not answer.)* He works the graveyard shift here.

TEDDY The graveyard shift. That must be a might important position. Eh, buddy?

STEPHEN Stinks.

TEDDY *(Putting a hand to his ear.)* Didn't quite catch that.

ANGEL *(When* STEPHEN *doesn't repeat himself.)* He said it stinks—workin the graveyard shift.

TEDDY You his agent, honey? What's the boy's long suit?

ANGEL What do ya mean?

TEDDY Well, I mean what's the boy *do* that's so impressive that an agent of your reputation took him on as a client?

ANGEL I don't know. What's your long suit, Stephen?

*(*STEPHEN *stares at her with fire in his eyes.)*

TEDDY Lad doesn't talk much, does he?

ANGEL You should hear him when no one's around.

TEDDY When no one's around or just when someone like me's not around?

(Pause.)

   (To himself.) Like to listen in one of these days on a coversation between my little buddy there and my cousin with the fiddle.

CLARISSE I wasn't aware I was under any obligation to carry on a conversation.

*(*LYLE *enters.)*

LYLE Well I don't mind confessin that our parts store fella wasn't tickled pink, but he'll have it up here inside fifteen minutes.

TEDDY Obliged. Yessir, deeply o-bliged.

LYLE Service is the name of the game.

TEDDY I can believe it.

LYLE Product lists at thirty-seven fifty, but he was in such an almighty hurry to get himself out on the lake before all the fish is gone, that I jewed him down to thirty-five.

TEDDY Doggone if that ain't a bargain.

LYLE Well I always say two and a half dollar is two and a half dollar.

TEDDY I'll tell ya the truth, neighbor: I hope ya don't say it too often, you'd like to bore folks right outta their minds.

LYLE *(Laughing.)* Wouldn't be a bit surprised.

TEDDY *(Laughing.)* No sir, I wouldn't either. *(He stops laughing.)* I surely wouldn't.

(END)

The Auction Tomorrow
by *Jerry L. Crawford*

*from the
latter part of Act II*

Characters

Carla Sullivan, 44, an ex-secondary sociology teacher, now a "Hostess" at the
Sands Hotel in Las Vegas. Bright, attractive, and intense. She hides a
vulnerable gentleness beneath a facade of glib sarcasm and biting wit. She
wears an attractive suit or dress, a bit conservative for her as she has just
come from her mother's funeral.

Tony Sullivan, 46, Carla's brother; a Professor of English at a Mississippi
college for girls. He is attractive in a "rumpled" way; intelligent;
brooding; he often wears dark glasses; his suit is dark and a bit old.

Jeff Thornton, 46; a successful small town Iowa banker; trustee and
administrator of the estate of Carla's and Tony's mother. He has arranged
the auction; he is prematurely grey, handsome, and intelligent.

Alice Thornton, Jeff's wife; 48; attractive and vital; very direct; a "talker";
beneath her pleasant exterior, she harbors fear of Carla relative to Jeff.

A scene from *The Auction
Tomorrow* by Jerry L.
Crawford. At the
Hartman Theatre,
Stamford, Connecticut.
(Left to right) Patricia
Englund as Alice,
Stephen Joyce as Tony,
Charles Bateman as Jeff,
and Carol Mayo Jenkins
as Carla. Directed by Del
Tenney; scenery by James
F. Tilton; costumes by
Sarah Nash Gates;
lighting by Rick Butler;
stage manager—J.
Thomas Vivian. (Photo by
Gerry Goodstein.)

The living room of the old Sullivan home in a small town in north-central Iowa; the present August.

Scene

A brother and sister, once close and happy in this small Iowa town, are reunited after many years of alienated separation. They meet on the occasion of their remaining parent's funeral. The family home and all the antique furnishings are to be sold at public auction. Intense conflicts exist between the two and their old friend, Jeff. In this scene, Jeff brings his wife to the house to pick up Carla and Tony for dinner. This reunion also turns toward conflict.

Situation

(JEFF and ALICE *appear—talking, walking slowly up on the porch. The doorbell rings.* TONY *shakes his head in exasperation at* CARLA, *turns, and goes to the door.* ALICE *and* JEFF *enter the hallway.* CARLA *picks up her drink and drifts into the dining room.*)

TONY Hi, hi, come in, come in.

JEFF Tony, you remember Alice? Alice . . . Tony.

TONY Of course, of course. *(Shaking her hand)* How are you, Alice? Good to see you.

ALICE Fine, thank you.

(She hugs him fully-he is a bit taken-aback.)

Oh, how wonderful to see you, Tony!

TONY *(Recovering)* Well, come in the living room. Carla's here. *(They enter)* Carla, it's Alice and Jeff. You two remember each other, don't your?

(CARLA *reaches out to shake* ALICE'S *hand, but* ALICE *stuns her by going straight into her arms and embracing her like a long lost friend.*)

ALICE Of course, of course. How are you, Carla my dear?

CARLA *(Looking over* ALICE'S *shoulder at* TONY *with abject horror.)* Fine, thank you.

ALICE I'm so sorry about your mother. *(She kisses* CARLA *on the cheek—*CARLA *is almost ready to push her away)* It's so . . . so difficult to know what to say . . . under these circumstances.

CARLA *(Freeing herself, moving away quickly)* That's quite all right. There's nothing need be said. It's over.

ALICE *(Following her)* I hope Jeff explained about my not making the funeral. The children—especially the twins. Six is such an age—into everything. All my sitters were tied up. You know how it is.

CARLA *(Turning, cornered, feeling no choice but to begin a small counterattack)* No, I'm afraid I don't.

(ALICE stops in her tracks)
(Beat)

JEFF Well, I don't know about the rest of you, but I'm starved. Better get going, it's a good half hour drive.

CARLA I'll tell you what. I'm feeling a little under the weather. Headache. It's been a day. Why don't you three run along without me? Give me a raincheck?

ALICE Oh, Carla, come on. Food will do you good. A thick, juicy T-bone? Iowa beef? At times like this, you need your strength-protein!

CARLA *(Beat)* Protein? *(Beat)* Thank you, Alice, I'll settle for some aspirin.
     (Glancing unbelievingly at JEFF *who was obviously not expecting this from* ALICE*)*
     And maybe one more drink. Then I'll lie down.
TONY For God's sake, don't have another drink. It'll only make it worse.
CARLA Wrong. Really wrong, Anthony. According to a recent survey, nine out
     of ten leading doctors everywhere recommends vodka for tension. . . .

*(*JEFF *and* ALICE *laugh,* ALICE *a bit too long and loud)*

ALICE Well, why don't we all have a drink and then if Carla feels better, we
     can go eat?
JEFF Alice, it's late—already dark. It's still quite a drive over there.
ALICE Oh, don't be a fuddy-duddy, Jeff. I'd like a drink myself.

(To TONY *and* CARLA*)*

     He always holds me down at home—you know, in front of the kids. I get
     absolutely bored eating at six every night. What do you say, Tony?
TONY One more. OK. Two beers, two vodkas. Tonic OK, Alice?
ALICE Do you have any orange juice?
TONY 'Fraid not. And I'm out of limes.
ALICE Tonic will be fine. At the Country Club, everyone drinks tonic—tonic
     and vodka, tonic and gin, tonic and rum—but it *is* good for you—all that
     quinine. . . .

*(*JEFF *shoots her a private look and exits suddenly to the kitchen, followed by* TONY, *who
grins broadly.)*

CARLA *(Before* ALICE *can begin again)* Well, Alice, tell me about the twins.
ALICE The twins. Let's see. Well, they start first grade next month. Johnny's
     taller than Jimmy, but Jimmy's heavier. They look like their father. I have
     a picture *(Opens purse, then wallet—shows photo;* CARLA *nods approvingly.)*
     They're happy and healthy and boys are much more difficult to raise than
     girls, just as they say.
CARLA You have a girl, too?
ALICE Yes, Angela. Named after my mother.
CARLA Angela . . . Walker?
ALICE Yes . . . did you know her?
CARLA No. I recall the name, that's all—perhaps my mother knew her.
ALICE Oh, my, no.

(Awkward silence)

CARLA Tell me, Alice, did you marry Jeffrey right after high school?
ALICE No, we waited til we both finished college. Jeff worked in the bank
     while I commuted to Iowa Falls.
CARLA I see. Let me guess. Education major, Home Ec minor.
ALICE Other way around.
CARLA Well, close. . . .
ALICE *(laughing)* Yes, close. . . .
CARLA But close only counts in horse shoes.
ALICE *(laughter subsiding)* Does it?
CARLA How old is Angela again?
ALICE Twelve.

CARLA My, waited awhile for the first one. . . .

ALICE (*Now aware she has lost her initial footing—she is with a master and finds herself on the defensive now.*)

Yes, well, we wanted to do some traveling, get the house clear. . . .

CARLA Oh, of course. Good old Jeffrey. Careful, thorough, reliable. . . .

ALICE Well, they are virtues, you know, Carla.

CARLA Oh, I know, I know. Absolutely. Yes-sir-ree-bob. No argument. I agree. (*beat*) So, Angela is in seventh grade.

ALICE Yes.

CARLA Good marks.

ALICE Yes. A very bright young lady.

CARLA And I bet she looks like you.

ALICE Well, of course I like to think so. She has Jeff's coloring, but most people do think she looks like me.

CARLA Isn't that something? Would you have ever thought it way back when? Jeffrey Thornton, father of three? He used to kid us, Alice, that he wasn't the marrying kind.

ALICE Oh, yes, I remember him in those days, too. (*beat*) You don't recall me at school, do you, Carla?

CARLA Let me see. No, I'm mortified to admit it, darling, but I don't believe I do. Let's see, what were you, a freshman when Tony and Jeff graduated?

ALICE Yes, one year behind you.

(TONY *and* JEFF *enter*)

CARLA Heavens, I should be able to recall you, shouldn't I? Anthony, do you remember Alice as a freshman?

TONY Yes, of course I do.

CARLA Jeffrey, how about you? Do you recall Alice as a freshman?

JEFF Oh, I think I can recall Alice as a freshman, yes. Damn cute girl with long black hair.

CARLA In pigtails?

JEFF No, full to the shoulders.

CARLA You're sure it was the shoulders?

JEFF The shoulders. (*He pops his beer can loudly; beat*)

CARLA You always did have an amazing memory, Jeffrey. Have you noticed that, Alice? What an amazing memory your husband has? It's what makes him such a successful businessman, don't you think? Class treasurer all through high school. That old eagle eye on the Jolly-Green-Jesus. Or on girls with long black hair, full to the shoulders.

ALICE (*quickly*) Tony, you're looking wonderful! That easy, Southern life must really agree with you.

TONY It's all right, Alice, once you become accustomed. (*Quite naturally; in no way showing off*) "The readiness is all—Let be."

ALICE Beg pardon?

CARLA Shakespeare, Alice. He can't help himself.

ALICE Well, I should say. What a wonderful writer.

CARLA (*A throw-away as she moves off some*) Fair to midling, no question. . . .

ALICE Tony, we go every summer to that Guthrie Theatre in Minneapolis. Fantastic plays. A Shakespeare play every year.

TONY It's a fine theatre.

ALICE   What was the name of that thing we saw last summer, Jeff? (*Before he can answer.*) *Macbeth!* That was it!

CARLA   "Twenty four silver dollars and a box of Mars bars to that lady! Now, Dr. I.Q., I have a question from a gentleman in the balcony!"

(*They all laugh some*)

ALICE   The actor was . . . Claude . . . Claude . . . whatever—oh, you know, he's always on Merv Griffith . . . Griffin?

TONY   Some people should drink with harness on their throats.

CARLA   Are you insinuating that I am a bit high with vodka and should sober up and shut up?

TONY   I am insinuating nothing. I am stating as a fact that you have had enough to drink. (*Quickly to* JEFF *and* ALICE) Let's go.

CARLA   Wait a minute, here, friends and neighbors. No one accuses Carla Marston of alcoholic insobriety. Of God's creatures, I am one of the best at maintaining control to the point of absurdity. Leave us put me to the test.

TONY   Oh, for God's sake, cut it out. Let's go!

CARLA   No way, brother love. I have been insulted. As Alice and Jeffrey as my witnesses, I have been insulted. I demand a test.

TONY   All right, stay here then. Alice, Jeff, come on. (*The three turn to go*)

CARLA   Hey, you!

(*Silence; everyone stops in their tracks;* ALICE *turns around and confronts* CARLA.)

ALICE   Are you addressing me?

CARLA   That's right. (*With a sweeping change of manner; smiling, pleasant*) I owe you an apology. I owe you all an apology. Can't imagine what came over me, getting all bitchy like that. Please forgive me. It has to be the vodka, no question about it. Goodness, my head's just whirling. Let me sit down a moment and then we'll go. I'll buy you all a lovely big meal, what'cha say?

(*They hesitate, then relax*)

ALICE   Well, all right. I know what a headache can do, Carla.

CARLA   I'll bet you do, Alice.

ALICE   Well, we all get headaches, Carla. Mississippi, Nevada, even Iowa.

CARLA   Well, it's all that bank work . . . all that church work in between tennis matches at the country club. Ah, those clubs. Playboy Club, Jockey Club—such quality places! What you have to do, Alice, is get out and let your hair down, to coin a phrase.

ALICE   Oh, we do that, too . . . every Saturday night . . . after the weekly bath.

(*They all laugh, the men uneasily*)

CARLA   My, my, Jeffrey—she's all right. A-OK. (*Still laughing some*) Well, thank God it's not Saturday.

ALICE   Oh, I don't know, Carla. In some ways it *feels* like Saturday.

(*They stare at one another a moment*)

CARLA   I'll just go rest a moment—and get ready for Saturday night.

(*END*)

Vanities
by Jack Heifner

from
Act II

Characters

Joanne, in Act II, a senior and sorority girl in a Texas college. A happy, somewhat shallow, plain but "breezy" girl intent on a typical life. She wants to marry her high school-college sweetheart, raise a family, and never lose her close friendship with Mary and Kathy.

Mary, in Act II, a senior and sorority girl in a Texas college. A sensual and attractive girl intent upon freedom and independence. She wants to explore the world, meet lots of men, and live a carefree, unrestrained life.

Kathy, in Act II, a senior and sorority girl in a Texas college. Attractive and well disciplined, she is a master organizer. She is uncertain about life, her goals, and herself.

Scene

A sorority house, spring, 1968. Boxes form the shape of twin beds. A casual room.

Ann Floor, Amy Marie Rose, and Jacque DeJohn in *Vanities* by Jack Heifner. At The University of Utah. Directed by Bud Coleman. Lighting by Josanne W. Alexander and Costumes by Bud Coleman. Photograph by Robert Clayton.

Three seniors prepare for the events of their final weeks of college prior to graduation, revealing their hopes and uncertainties, and the beginning of lives which will eventually separate them as friends.

JOANNE   This spring will kill me yet. With rush and graduation and this wedding, I'm going to make Ted do some of the work. We've got to find an apartment.

MARY   Why not keep Ted's place?

JOANNE   Oh, it's awful. Boys don't care what they live in. If I had to live in that dump, I'd just scream. It doesn't even have a pool.

MARY   What would you do?

JOANNE   Mary, I just don't know. I really don't.

KATHY   I hadn't even thought about a place to live after graduation.

JOANNE   We want a place near Law School. That way Ted can walk to class. Why not get an apartment next door to us?

KATHY   I don't see much sense in staying near campus. I'm not going to graduate school.

JOANNE   Well, Ted has to. I mean if he doesn't stay in school he'll get drafted. If he went to Vietnam, I'd die.

KATHY   I guess I'll get an apartment close to my job. Wherever that is.

JOANNE   I hope it's not too far away. With Ted in school, I'll need someone to talk to. I want you both nearby.

MARY   I'm not making any plans past Europe.

JOANNE   We'll get together here for homecoming and football games. The sorority will need us to make sure things are done right. What would the Kappas do without you, Kathy?

KATHY   I don't know. But, after they hand you that diploma, you're expected to get out there, do something, be someone.

MARY   I plan to do something . . . someone.

JOANNE   I just won't listen to this talk. You're both acting childish.

MARY   We're not all as grown-up as you, Joanne.

KATHY   Remember when you were a little girl and people would ask, "What do you want to be when you grow up?"

MARY   Sure. I wanted to be a nurse, then a stripper, then a psychologist.

JOANNE   I always wanted to be a wife. Just a wife and mother.

KATHY   But what else?

MARY   We all wanted to be pretty.

JOANNE   I think the two of you are pretty. Me? I'm just attractive.

MARY   And popular.

JOANNE   We are popular.

MARY   And cheerleaders and sorority girls.

JOANNE   Whew! We've done it all. We ran the gamut.

KATHY   But didn't you want more?

MARY   Well, I wanted to leave home. God, more than anything, I wanted some freedom.

KATHY   More than anything?

MARY   Well, yes. More than anything, I wanted to do as I like.

KATHY   What about you?

JOANNE   More than anything?

KATHY   Yes.

JOANNE Well, Ted, of course.

MARY Of course.

JOANNE (To KATHY) Did you want Gary more than anything? Or should I ask? Is it too painful?

MARY I'll bet more than anything you want to teach.

JOANNE Oh, I know. More than anything you wanted to be head cheerleader in college. You should have been.

(A pause)

MARY I give up.

JOANNE Me, too. We've told you what we wanted. Now, you tell us.

KATHY I can't.

JOANNE There you go with those secrets again.

KATHY I mean I can't, because I don't know.

MARY Haven't a clue?

KATHY Not an idea.

JOANNE Well, I think you should have been the interior decorator. Look at all you can do with decorations.

MARY I wish I could organize like you. I would have studied urban planning or planned parenthood.

KATHY What will I do?

JOANNE You'll teach.

MARY Jesus, Kathy, if you're going to get upset at all this, let's just drop the subject.

JOANNE Look on the bright side, Kathy.

MARY Who knows what will happen?

JOANNE Life's full of surprises.

MARY All this worry is for nothing.

KATHY I really hate my life.

JOANNE How dare you talk like that! It's been fun. Just think, we could have turned out like all those girls in high school who weren't popular.

KATHY How did they turn out?

JOANNE Well, I don't know. I guess unpopular.

MARY They're all probably married with a bunch of kids.

JOANNE There's nothing wrong with that.

KATHY I'm just saying that after school ends, my life is going to be awfully lonely.

JOANNE It never has been. Why will it be now?

KATHY Because in the last ten years, I'll bet the three of us haven't been apart for a day.

MARY That's not true. Remember the summer you taught at that girl's camp, Joanne went to summer school because Ted went to summer school and I went to Mexico?

JOANNE We didn't see each other for three months and in the fall we were closer than ever before.

MARY Being apart didn't change things.

JOANNE Absence makes the heart grow fonder.

KATHY But I have to face a whole new life alone. I don't even have a plan for it.

JOANNE   Well, let's make a plan. We'll meet every Wednesday afternoon. That's our schedule now. Kappa officers' meeting every Wednesday. So why change? Mary, when you come back you'd like to see Kathy every week, wouldn't you?

MARY   Just as soon as I'm back, I'll be there every Wednesday.

JOANNE   We can go to movies and shop. I wouldn't know how to buy anything if you weren't with me. Isn't that right, Mary?

MARY   Joanne's always depended on your taste.

JOANNE   You can decorate for all my parties. And we'll join a country club. You can teach us golf and tennis. Mary and I should learn to play. Well, say something Mary.

MARY   It's time I got into sports.

JOANNE   No matter what happens, Kathy, we three have each other. *(She chants)*

KKG

KKG

KKG

Eternally.

MARY   Don't worry, Kathy. Joanne's right. We all love each other.

JOANNE   Cheer up. Let's all get out and go somewhere. I'd kill for a pizza.

KATHY   Don't you have to meet Ted?

JOANNE   He told me to get lost this afternoon. He's going to some kind of demonstration. Ugh, politics.

KATHY   Oh, I wish they'd stop protesting. You can't go anywhere on this campus without someone pushing a picket sign into your face.

JOANNE   I told Ted I didn't understand why he had to get involved. The Viet Cong aren't bombing the campus.

MARY   I protested when they decided to start closing the student center snack bar at midnight. It had always stayed open to one.

JOANNE   Well, that was a good cause. It directly affected you. But Ted says he's protesting because the war bothers his conscience. That he can't stand the needless killing of women and children. And I said, "Ted, for heaven's sake, control your conscience. You don't even know those people."

MARY   You didn't say that.

JOANNE   Of course, I did. Don't be stupid.

KATHY   Well, I'm glad I'm not going to be around to see the destruction of this campus.

JOANNE   It's the flower children. Pot . . . everywhere I look I smell pot. I don't want the Kappa house to turn into a hippie commune.

MARY   Hippies couldn't afford this house, Joanne.

KATHY   The way things are going it's going to be a fight to keep this sorority together.

JOANNE   What we need is an interesting activity calendar for this spring. Enough social events to keep the girls' minds off current events.

KATHY   We'll rush those pledges like we've never rushed before.

JOANNE   We're losing ten good girls, including ourselves, at graduation. We need ten more "perfect" people to fill in. Keep Kappa forty strong.

KATHY   Ten noble women. That's what KKG is all about. Noble, noble women with the key to the kingdom of God. KKG.

ALL I'm a noble, noble woman
       With the key to the kingdom of God.
       Kappa the key.
       Kappa the kingdom.
       Gamma of God.

JOANNE Kappa Kappa Gamma.

KATHY I don't want to see it end. I'm scared.

MARY It's easy to be scared.

KATHY Are you?

MARY Scared? Why do you think I'm going to Europe?

KATHY To see the world.

MARY To avoid it. I'm running scared.

KATHY I wish I could run.

MARY I wish you could, too. But you, Kathy, have always done what's right. What's expected. I can't. I never could. Don't worry, Kathy. For once stop planning. Let life happen. Don't think about it.

JOANNE I agree, Kathy. Mary's right. Don't think. I've always found it's better not to think.

(They freeze, the music begins, the lights fade on the playing area and come up on the vanities. The girls go to their dressing tables and prepare for Scene Three.)

(END)

Oh Dad, Poor Dad, Mamma's Hung You in the Closet and I'm Feelin' So Sad

by *Arthur Kopit*

*from
scene iii*

Characters   Jonathan Rosepettle, a 17-year-old boy who dresses like a child of 10
Rosalie, a 19-year-old girl, very sensual, but dressed in sweet girlish pink
Two Venus'-Flytraps,* enormous carnivorous plants
Rosalinda the Fish,* a silver piranha fish in a bowl

Scene   A hotel room in Havana, Cuba.

Situation   Emerging from his hiding place, after listening to strange stories told by his mother, Jonathan begins to rebel against her suffocating and strange domination by killing her man-eating plants and killer-fish. In this comic but frightening play, Jonathan travels with his bizarre mother who keeps his dead father's body hanging in the closet wherever they travel. A seductive girl named Rosalie returns to see Jonathan, bent on seducing him in his journey toward manhood, freedom, madness, murder, sanity, or insanity. This is a philosophically perplexing, **self-mocking theatre piece in the Absurd style. (Other plays by Kopit are better included under the classification of Eclectic—see chapter 20.)**

JOHNATHAN *emerges from behind the* VENUS'-FLYTRAPS. *He runs to the door, puts his ear to it, then races back to the balcony and stares down at the street below. Carnival lights flash weirdly against the night sky and laughter drifts up. The* VENUS'-FLYTRAPS *reach out to grab him, but somehow he senses their presence and leaps away in time.*

VENUS'-FLYTRAPS (*gruffly*)   Grrrrrr! (*He walks dazedly into the living room.*)

ROSALINDA THE FISH   (*Snarlingly.*) Snarrrrrrl! (*The* VENUS'-FLYTRAPS *have grown enormous. Their monstrous petals wave hungrily in the air while they growl.* JONATHAN *stares at them fearfully, the laughter below growing stronger all the while. Suddenly he runs to the wall and smashes the glass case that covers the fire axe. He takes out the axe. He advances cautiously toward the* FLYTRAPS. *He feints an attack, they follow his movements. He bobs, they weave. It is a cat-and-mouse game of death. Suddenly* JONATHAN *leaps upon them and hacks them apart till they fall to the floor, writhing, then dead.* JONATHAN *stands above them, victorious, panting, but somehow seeming to breathe easier. Slowly he turns and looks at the fish bowl. His eyes seem glazed, his expression insanely determined. He walks slowly toward the fish bowl. . . . There are three knocks on the door. He does not hear them. He raises his axe.*)

* Typically cast with either actors or actresses.

The door opens. ROSALIE *enters. She is dressed in an absurdly childish pink dress with crinolines and frills—the picture of innocence, the picture of a girl ten years old. Her shoes are black leather pumps and she wears short girlish-pink socks. Her cheeks have round circles of rouge on them—like a young girl might have who had never put on makeup before.*

ROSALIE   Jonathan! Jonathan! What *have* you done? [JONATHAN *stops. He does not look at her but stares at the fish bowl.*] Jonathan! Put down that silly axe. You might hurt yourself. [*He still does not answer but stares at the bowl. He does not lower the axe.*] Jonathan! [*Slowly he turns and faces her.*]

JONATHAN   I killed it.

ROSALIE   Ssh. Not so loudly. Where'd you put her body?

JONATHAN   (*pointing to the* PLANTS)   There.

ROSALIE   Where? I don't see a body. Where is she?

JONATHAN   Who?

ROSALIE   Your mother.

JONATHAN   I haven't killed my mother. I've killed her plants. The ones I used to feed. I've chopped their hearts out.

ROSALIE   (*with an apologetic laugh*)   I thought you'd . . . killed your mother. (*The* PIRANHA FISH *giggles.* JONATHAN *turns and stares at it again. He starts to move toward it, slowly.*)

ROSALIE   Jonathan, stop. (*He hesitates, as if he is uncertain what to do. Slowly he raises the axe.*) Jonathan! (*He smashes the axe against the fish bowl. It breaks. The fish screams.*)

ROSALINDA THE FISH   (*fearfully*)   AAIEEEEEEEEEEEEEEEE!

ROSALIE   Now look at the mess you've made.

JONATHAN   Do you think it can live without water?

ROSALIE   What will your mother say when she gets back?

JONATHAN   Maybe I should hit it again. Just in case. (*He strikes it again.*)

ROSALINDA THE FISH   (*mournfully*)   UGHHHHHHH! (JONATHAN *stares in horror at the dead* FISH. *He drops the axe and turns away, sickened and weak.* ROSALIE *walks over and touches him gently, consolingly, on the arm.*)

ROSALIE   There's something bothering you, isn't there? (*pause—coyly.*) What's-a matter, Jonathan? (JONATHAN *does not answer at first but stares off into space frightened, bewildered.*)

JONATHAN   (*weakly*)   I never thought I'd see you again. I never thought I'd talk to you again. I never thought you'd come.

ROSALIE   Did you really think that?

JONATHAN   She told me she'd never let you visit me again. She said no one would *ever* visit me again. She told me I had seen enough.

ROSALIE   But I had a key made.

JONATHAN   She . . . she hates me.

ROSALIE   What?

JONATHAN   She doesn't let me do anything. She doesn't let me listen to the radio. She took the tube out of the television set. She doesn't let me use her phone. She makes me show her all my letters before I seal them. She doesn't—

ROSALIE   Letters? What letters are you talking about?

JONATHAN   Just . . . letters I write.

ROSALIE   To *whom?*

JONATHAN   To people.

ROSALIE   *What* people?

JONATHAN   Oh . . . various people.

ROSALIE   Other girls? Could they be to other girls, by any chance?

JONATHAN   No. They're just to people. No people in particular. Just people in the phone book. Just names. I do it alphabetically. That way, someday, I'll be able to cover everyone. So far I've covered all the "A's" and "B's" up to Barrera.

ROSALIE   What is it you say to them? Can you tell me what you say to them . . . or is it private? Jonathan, just what do you say to them!?

JONATHAN   Mostly I just ask them what they look like. *(Pause. Suddenly he starts to sob in a curious combination of laughter and tears.)* But I don't think she ever mails them. She reads them, then takes them out to mail. But I don't think she ever does. I'll bet she just throws them away. Well if she's not going to mail them, why does she say she will? I . . . I could save the stamps. Why must she lie to me? Why doesn't she just say she's not going to mail them? Then I wouldn't have to wait for letters every day.

ROSALIE   Guess why I had this key made.

JONATHAN   I'll bet she's never even mailed one. From Abandono to Barrera, not one.

ROSALIE   Do you know why I had this key made? Do you know why I'm wearing this new dress?

JONATHAN   She doesn't let me stand in the window at noon because the sun is too strong. She doesn't let me stand in the window at night when the wind is blowing because the air is too cold. And today she told me she's going to nail shutters over the windows so I'll never have to worry about being bothered by the sun or the wind again.

ROSALIE   Try and guess why I'm all dressed up.

JONATHAN   She tells me I'm brilliant. She makes me read and reread books no one's ever read. She smothers me with blankets at night in case of a storm. She tucks me in so tight I can't even get out till she comes and takes my blankets off.

ROSALIE   Stop talking about that and pay attention to me!

JONATHAN   She says she loves me. Every morning, before I even have a chance to open my eyes, there she is, leaning over my bed, breathing in my face and saying, "I love you, I love you."

ROSALIE   Jonathan, isn't my dress pretty?

JONATHAN   But I heard everything tonight. I heard it all when she didn't know I was here. *(He stares off into space, bewildered.)*

ROSALIE   What's the matter? *(He does not answer.)* Jonathan, what's the matter?

JONATHAN   But she must have known I was here. She *must* have known! I mean . . . where could I have gone? *(Pause.)* But . . . if that's the case . . . *why did she let me hear?*

ROSALIE   Jonathan, I do wish you'd pay more attention to me. Here, look at my dress. You can even touch it if you like. Guess how many crinolines I have on. Guess why I'm wearing such a pretty, new dress. *Jonathan!*

JONATHAN *(distantly)*   Maybe . . . it didn't make any difference to her . . . whether I heard it or not.

(END)

Grease
by Jim Jacobs and Warren Casey

Kenickie: Second in command of the Burger Palace Boys. Toughlooking, tattooed, surly, avoids any show of softness. Has an offbeat sense of humor.

Sonny: Italian-looking, with shiny black hair and dark oily skin. A braggart and wheeler-dealer who thinks he's a real lady-killer.

Frenchy: A dreamer. She's good-natured and dumb. Heavily made-up, fussy about her appearance—particularly her hair. She can't wait to finish high school so she can be a beautician.

Doody: Youngest of the guys. Small, boyish, open, with a disarming smile and a hero-worshipping attitude toward the others. Plays the guitar.

Danny: The leader of the Burger Palace Boys. Well-built, nice-looking, with an air of cool, easygoing charm. Strong and confident.

Teen Angel: A good-looking, falsetto-voiced, Fabian look-alike. A singer who would have caused girls to scream and riot back in 1958.

(Chorus/Choir of standard teen-age "types.")

It is evening in front of the Burger Palace. 1959.

Grease by Warren Casey and Jim Jacobs. At the University Theatre, Kansas University. Directed by Jack B. Wright. Designed by Greg Hill. Scenery and costumes by Greg Hill. Photograph by Andrew Tsubaki.

Situation   Frenchy is pacing around, magazine in hand, looking at sign on Burger Palace window: "Counter Girl Wanted." After a few moments Sonny, Kenickie and Doody enter with weapons: Doody with a baseball bat, Sonny with a zip gun, Kenickie with a lead pipe and chain. They wear leather jackets and engineer boots. The kids are preparing for a "rumble" with the Flaming Dukes!

KENICKIE   Hey, Sonny, what Cracker Jack box ja' get that zip gun out of, anyway?

SONNY   What do ya mean, I made it in shop. (*Seeing* FRENCHY) Hey, what's shakin', French? You get out of beauty school already?

FRENCHY   Oh . . . I cut tonight. Those beauty school teachers they got working there don't know nothin'. Hey, what's with the arsenal?

DOODY   We gotta rumble with the Flaming Dukes.

FRENCHY   No lie! How come?

KENICKIE   Remember that scurvy broad I took to the dance?

FRENCHY *looks blank.*

DOODY   (*Helpfully*) Godzilla!

DOODY and KENICKIE   (They *do imitation of* CHA-CHA *and* EUGENE *dancing*) "One-two-cha-cha-cha!"

FRENCHY   Oh! Y'mean Cha-Cha Dee Garage-io . . . the one Danny won the dance contest with?

SONNY   Well, it turns out she goes steady with the leader of the Flaming Dukes. And she told this guy Danny got in her silks.

KENICKIE   If he did, he musta been makin' a bug collection for Biology.

ALL GUYS *laugh.* KENICKIE *joins in, laughing at his own joke.* DANNY *enters jogging, wearing a white track suit with a brown and green number four on his back. The trunks are white with a thin green and brown stripe running vertically on each side.* HE *has a relay-race baton.*

FRENCHY (*Seeing* DANNY)   Hey look . . . ain't that Danny?

DOODY   Hey, Danny!

FRENCHY   What's he doing in his underwear?

DOODY   That's a track suit! Hiya, Danny.

DANNY *stops.* HE'S *panting.* GUYS *gather around him.*

KENICKIE   Jesus, Zuko, where do you keep your Wheaties?

DANNY (*Reaching in front of jock strap and pulling out a crumpled pack of Luckies*)   Ha-ha. Big joke. (HE *lights a cigarette*)

SONNY   Hey, it's a good thing you're here. We're supposed to rumble the Dukes tonight!

DANNY (*Alarmed*)   What time?

KENICKIE   Nine o'clock.

DANNY (*Annoyed*)   Nice play! I got field training till 9:30.

KENICKIE   Can't ya sneak away, man?

DANNY   Not a chance! The coach'd kick my ass.

SONNY   The coach!

DANNY   Besides, what am I supposed to do, stomp on somebody's face with my gym shoes? (HE *puts cigarettes back in jock*)

KENICKIE   Ahh, c'mon, Zuko, whattaya tryin' to prove with this track team crap!?

DANNY   Why? Whatta you care? Look, I gotta cut. I'm in the middle of a race right now. See ya later.

SONNY   You got the hots for that cheerleader or somethin'?

DANNY   How'd you like a fat lip, Sonny? Nine o'clock, huh? I'll be back if I can get away. Later! (*Silence.* DANNY *stands glaring at the* GUYS *for a moment and then* HE *runs off, cigarette in his mouth*)

SONNY Neat guy, causes a ruckus and then he cuts out on us!

KENICKIE Jeez, next thing ya know he'll be gettin' a crew cut!

DOODY He'd look neater with a flat top.

KENICKIE C'mon, let's go eat. (HE *and* SONNY *start toward Burger Palace*)

SONNY Hey, Kenicks, you wanna split a superburger?

KENICKIE Yeah. All right.

SONNY Good. Lend me a half a buck.

SONNY *and* KENICKIE *exit into Burger Palace, stashing their weapons in a painted oil drum used for garbage.*

DOODY Hey, Frenchy, maybe I'll come down to your beauty school some night this week . . . we can have a Coke or somethin'.

FRENCHY *(Uncertain)* Yeah . . . yeah, sure.

DOODY *smiles and, depositing his baseball hat in the same oil drum, exits into the Burger Palace.*

(To her movie magazine) Jeez! What am I gonna do? I mean, I can't just tell everybody I dropped out of beauty school. I can't go in the Palace for a job . . . with all the guys sittin' around. Boy, I wish I had one of those Guardian Angel things like in that Debbie Reynolds movie. Would that be neat . . . somebody always there to tell ya what's the best thing to do.

Spooky angelic guitar chords. FRENCHY'S *Guardian* TEEN ANGEL *appears.* HE *is a Fabian-like rock singer. White Fabian sweater with the collar turned up, white chinos, white boots, a large white comb sticking out of his pocket.* HE *sings "Beauty School Dropout." After the first verse, a chorus of* ANGELS *appears: a group of* GIRLS *in white plastic sheets with their hair in white plastic rollers, arranged in a halo effect.* THEY *provide background doo-wahs.*

TEEN ANGEL

> Your story's sad to tell:
> A teenage ne'er-do-well,
> Most mixed-up non-delinquent on the block,
> Your future's so unclear now.
> What's left of your career now?
> Can't even get a trade-in on your smock.
> (ANGEL CHORUS *enters*)
>
> Beauty school dropout,
> No graduation day for you.
> Beauty school dropout,
> Missed your midterms and flunked shampoo.
> Well, at least you could have taken time
> To wash and clean your clothes up
> After spending all that dough to have
> The doctor fix your nose up.
> Baby, get movin',
> Why keep your feeble hopes alive?
> What are you proving'?
> You got the dream but not the drive.
> If you go for your diploma you could join a steno pool
> Turn in your teasing comb and go back to high school.

Beauty school dropout,
Hangin' around the corner store.
Beauty school dropout,
It's about time you knew the score.
Well, they couldn't teach you anything,
You think you're such a looker,
But no customer would go to you
Unless she was a hooker.
Baby, don't sweat it,
You're not cut out to hold a job.
Better forget it,
Who wants their hair done by a slob?
Now your bangs are curled, your lashes twirled,
But still the world is cruel.
Wipe off that angel face and go back to high school.

At the end of the stanza the TEEN ANGEL *hands* FRENCHY *a high school diploma, which* SHE *uncurls, looks at, crumples up and throws away. The* TEEN ANGEL *and* CHOIR *look on.* FRENCHY *walks away.*

Baby, ya blew it.
You put our good advice to shame.
How could you do it?
Betcha Dear Abby'd say the same.
Guess there's no way to get through to you,
No matter who may try.
Might as well go back to that malt shop in the sky.

The TEEN ANGEL *and* CHOIR *exit.*

(END)

Grease by Jim Jacobs and Warren Casey. Kurt Ford as Doody, Curtis Shaw as Roger, Mark Fauser as Kenickie, Brent Briscoe as Sonny, and Daryl D. Vaughan as Danny at the University of Missouri: University Theatre and the Department of Music. Directed and Choreographed by James M. Miller. Musical Direction by Harry S. Morrison. Scenic and Lighting by Patrick Atkinson. Costumes by Carmen Slider.

Tribute

by *Bernard Slade*

from
Act I
Scene 2

Characters Sally Haines: a beautiful girl in her early twenties.
Jud Templeton: Scottie's twenty-year old son. Shy, intelligent, awkward and intense.

Scene The living room of Scottie Templeton's townhouse in New York City. The present.

Situation Sally and Jud spread a blanket on the floor of the living room and proceed to have a "picnic" from a shopping bag full of food. It is, in effect, their "first date." Jud is an unsure young man trying to deal with his anguish with his father, a father who is dying and trying to affirm a loving relationship with his son after alienating him by botching the marriage he had with Jud's mother. Sally is a happy, loving girl intent on opening a relationship with Jud.

SALLY You sure your father won't mind us turning his place into a picnic
　　ground?
JUD It'll probably make his day.
SALLY *Starting to put food on blanket* There—this is going to work out just fine.
JUD Well a lot better than your original idea. If it had rained we'd have been
　　soaked.
SALLY Your father must be pretty successful to afford a place like this.
JUD Not really.
　　She looks at him.
　　His partner—his boss really—is an old friend of his. He owns the building.
　　A somewhat awkward pause
　　I've always liked the name Sally.
SALLY Yeah? I didn't but I finally came back to it.
JUD You had other names?
SALLY Dozens.
　　She continues to set out food
　　My father was a construction engineer and we moved around a lot so I was
　　always the new girl in town.
　　She takes a bite from a pastrami sandwich
　　I was kind of a shy, scruffy-looking kid so it was tough making friends.
　　She holds the sandwich for him as he takes a bite
　　Here, try this pastrami—it's terrific. Anyway, I hit on this dumb idea. I used
　　to take the first name of the most popular girl from the last school. Believe it
　　or not, for about three months, I was actually named Corky.
JUD I can't imagine you ever being unattractive or shy.
SALLY Well, I got over it.
JUD How?
SALLY *Matter of factly* I grew tits.
JUD *Deadpan* Funny, that didn't work for me.
　　She looks at him, notices him staring at her

SALLY   What is it?

JUD   Oh, nothing, I just can't get over your being here.

SALLY *Puzzled*   You invited me.

JUD   I know. It's just—
Happily—blurting
Well, you're my first pickup!
She is too surprised to say anything. A slight pause
I guess this is a good time to tell you that my nickname is 'El Blurto.'
Awkwardly
I didn't mean to sound offensive. It's just that I've never been very good at—
meeting girls and I'm very pleased you're here.

SALLY *Amused*   Yeah, well don't get too carried away. I practically had to tackle
you around the knees to stop you leaving the Museum.
She hands him a bottle of pickles to open
Why didn't you talk to me the first time I approached you?

JUD   I didn't know what to say.

SALLY   You have trouble talking to people?

JUD   I got out of practice.

SALLY   You were a monk?

JUD   I used to stutter. When that cleared up I had trouble—getting the hang of it
again.
Awkwardly
It's not as strange as it sounds.

SALLY *Grinning*   Wanta bet?
They smile at one another
You see how well this is all working out? You're holding up your end of the
conversation beautifully.

JUD   You want to hear something hysterical? Well, interesting maybe.
He tries to open the bottle without success
My father's very—you know—glib. No—socially adept. Very gregarious—
you'd like him—everybody does. He's not at all like me.
He gives up on the bottle
Anyway, during the winter, I used to carry around this exercise book so I
could jot down amusing things to say when I saw him in the summer. I tried
it a couple of times but then I gave up.

SALLY   Why?

JUD   A certain look of panic comes into people's eyes when they're confronted
by a fourteen-year-old Henny Youngman.
He turns the jar top the opposite way and it unscrews easily
Why'd you want to meet me anyway?

SALLY   Oh, I'm always attracted to eccentrics.
Sitting back
Do you visit your father every summer?

JUD   No, I used to but I haven't seen him for a couple of years.

SALLY   Why not?

JUD *Shrugs*   I had summer jobs—one thing and another—you know.

SALLY   What made you decide to see him this summer?

JUD *Evasively*   Oh, a lot of reasons.

SALLY   You don't like to talk about anything personal, do you?

JUD *Half kidding*   Yeah—well, I don't know you very well. Here—
He gives her a cushion for her back. She looks at him for a moment

SALLY   Thanks. Can I have a bite of your pickel?

JUD *Indicating*   There's one right here.

SALLY   No, I want a bite of yours.

JUD *Offering it*   Here, have a whole pickel.

SALLY No, just a bite.

She takes a fairly large bite

There—now we've shared a pickle.

JUD I noticed that.

SALLY So now we know each other a lot better and you can tell me anything.

He looks at her for a moment

JUD Okay—I wanted to tie up some loose ends.

She doesn't understand

I realized my father and I were both getting older and that this was probably the last chance we'd have to—reach some understanding.

SALLY See, was that so hard?

She leans over and kisses him lightly. They gaze at one another

You really *hated* me taking a bite of your pickle, didn't you?

JUD *Earnestly* It was nothing personal. I don't like *anybody* touching my food.

SALLY *Teasing* And you don't think *that's* weird?

He looks at her for a moment and then impulsively kisses her.

(END)

Pippin

by Roger O. Hirson and Stephen Schwartz

from
Scene 7: The Hearth

Characters

Leading Player: Often performed by a black actor, a dynamic singer, dancer, performer—head of a troupe of theatrical actors from an undetermined period. A trifle cynical and caustic, but appealing.
Pippin: a young, handsome, earnest fellow; a fine singer and dancer. Striving to "find himself" and "his place" in the world. He is falling in love with Catherine.
Catherine: somewhat older than Pippin, more mature, pretty, and a widow with a young son. In love with Pippin.
Theo: Catherine's young son; a bright, precocious child (could be played by a very youthful, but older actor for scene study purposes).
Players (may be cut for scene study purposes)

Scene:

The forestage area; a warm, cozy locale such as Catherine's bedroom (often played with her large bed upstage). The downstage area should have the feeling of being played in front of a warm fire in a fireplace. The time of Charlemagne.

Situation:

Pippin and Catherine have been in love for some six months and they sing happily of that fact. However, the intrusion of Theo, Catherine's cooking, and other domestic concerns prompt Pippin to search for escape.

Pippin by Roger O. Hirson and Stephen Schwartz. Leslie Bauer, Daryl D. Vaughan, and Susan Krobot at the University of Missouri—the University Theatre and the Department of Music. Directed and Choreographed by James M. Miller. Musical Direction by Harry S. Morrison. Scenery and lighting by Patrick Atkinson. Costumes by James M. Miller. Photograph by David Rees.

LEADING PLAYER   Listen, I think we're gonna skip part of this. Nothing much
     really happens. A little bit of this, a little bit of that . . . *(And then referring to
     the bed upstage)* . . . a whole lot of *that.* (PIPPIN *and* CATHERINE *come around the
     bed now, and start to move downstage)* But, the season changed as it always
     does, and the days were filled with those everyday things. Seeds to be sown
     . . . fences to be mended . . . and, finally, of course, a love song to be sung.
     (CATHERINE *and* PIPPIN *are seated on the floor center stage. The* LEADING PLAYER
     goes)
PIPPIN   *(Sings)*
Sitting on the floor and talking 'til dawn
CATHERINE   *(Sings)*
     Candles and confidences
PIPPIN   *(Sings)*
     Trading old beliefs and humming old songs
CATHERINE   *(Sings)*
     And lowering old defenses
PIPPIN   *(Sings)*
     Singing a
BOTH   *(Sing)*
     Love song—la la la la la la la la la la
     Love song—la la la la
PIPPIN   *(Sings)*
     Private little jokes and silly pet names
CATHERINE   *(Sings)*
     Lavendar soap and lotions
PIPPIN   *(Sings)*
     All of the clichés and all of the games
CATHERINE   *(Sings)*
     And all of the strange emotions
PIPPIN   *(Sings)*
     Singing a
BOTH   *(Sing)*
     Love song—la la la la la la la la la la
     Love song—la la la la la
PIPPIN   *(Sings)*
     They say the whole is greater
BOTH   *(Sing)*
     Than the sum of the parts it's made of
PIPPIN   *(Sings)*
     Well if it's true of anything
BOTH   *(Sing)*
     It's true of love
PIPPIN   *(Sings)*
     Cause how can you define a look or a touch?
CATHERINE   *(Sings)*
     How can you weigh a feeling?
PIPPIN   *(Sings)*
     Taken by themselves now they don't mean much
BOTH   *(Sing)*
     Together they send you reeling
PIPPIN   *(Sings)*
     Into a

BOTH *(Sing)*
    Love song—la la la la la la la la la la la
    Love song—la la la la la
    La la la la la la la la la
    La la la la la la la la la
CATHERINE *(Speaks)*
    Close your eyes.
PIPPIN Why?
CATHERINE Because we've got a surprise for you.
    (THEO, *who has entered quietly, now runs to* PIPPIN *and throws his arms around*
    PIPPIN'S *neck)*
THEO We've got a surprise!
    The tree-unit revolves, and this time the bed has been converted into a dining room
    table set with dishes and food. From the wings, a few of the PLAYERS *enter with*
    stools and place them around the table. After this is done, they exit.
    CATHERINE *helps* PIPPIN *up and leads* PIPPIN *to the table.* THEO *clings to* PIPPIN)
CATHERINE Keep your eyes closed, Pippin. Now no peeking.
PIPPIN I usually don't like surprises.
CATHERINE Well, you'll like this one.
    (They have reached the table, and CATHERINE *and* THEO *help* PIPPIN *to a seat)*
PIPPIN Can I open my eyes, please?
CATHERINE Yes, now you can. (PIPPIN *opens his eyes.* CATHERINE *uncovers a dish and*
    lights the contents) Quince pudding flambé! Oh, I haven't made it for years
    . . . but I thought that for this special occasion . . .
PIPPIN What special occasion?
CATHERINE Well . . . six months ago today . . . *(Pause)* . . . you arrived here. So
    Theo and I thought that we would celebrate with a little party. So I made
    this . . . and Theo made you a flute . . .
THEO *(Handing the flute to* PIPPIN) Here.
PIPPIN Oh, Theo . . . it's beautiful. Thank you. I don't know what to say.
CATHERINE Well let me say something then. *(Pause)* In the six months that you've
    been with us, you've come to mean a great deal to me . . . to us . . . to our
    very ordinary lives. So, I just want to say for me . . . for Theo . . . we're
    glad you're here. And now . . . well, now we have so many good years
    ahead of us . . . *(She and* THEO *move* PIPPIN *to the head of the table.* PIPPIN *sits*
    very reluctantly) Well, isn't anybody going to eat my pudding?
THEO I am!
    (CATHERINE *starts to dish out the pudding.* PIPPIN *rises suddenly, and goes*
    downstage)
PIPPIN I've got to get out of here.
CATHERINE *(Going to him)* . . . Pippin, what's the matter?
PIPPIN I just can't stay here.
CATHERINE I don't understand.
PIPPIN I've got to go.
CATHERINE Why?
PIPPIN Because this isn't enough. Life is more than ducks that die . . . and
    leaking roofs . . . and flaming quince pudding!
CATHERINE Are you sure?
PIPPIN Yes I'm sure. And I am not going to be stuck doing the same damn thing
    every day . . .
CATHERINE . . . and night?
PIPPIN Don't you see, there has to be something more than this. There has to be.
CATHERINE Maybe there isn't any more.

(END)

Pippin by Roger O. Hirson and Stephen Schwartz (Music and Lyrics). Lori Zabriskie, Kevin Harris, Maria Tirabassi; Charan Levitan, Michael Ruud, and Jon Buffington at the Pioneer Memorial Theatre, The University of Utah. Directed by James Prigmore. Scenery by George Maxwell. Costumes by Elizabeth Robinson Novak. Photograph by Robert Clayton.

Buried Child
by Sam Shepard

from
Act II

Shelly: Vince's girl friend; a 19 year old, beautiful girl with black hair. She wears tight jeans, high heels, purple T-shirt, and a short rabbit fur coat. She's a "road-wise" girl.
Vince: Tilden's son and the grandson of Dodge and Halie. He is about 22 year's old, nice looking, wearing a plaid shirt, jeans, dark glasses, and cowboy boots. He carries a black saxophone case.

Characters

It is night; a cold rain falls. The battered old front room and screened-porch of Dodge's Illinois farmhouse. The present.

Scene

Vince and Shelly arrive for Vince's "homecoming;" he has decided to stop and see his grandparents on a trip toward Arizona where he hopes to be reunited with his father. Vince is unaware that his father is in fact home in Illinois. It has been several years since Vince has been home.

Situation

SHELLY *and* VINCE *appear up left outside the screen porch door sharing the shelter of* VINCE'S *overcoat above their heads.* SHELLY *is about nineteen, black hair, very beautiful. She wears tight jeans, high heels, purple T-shirt and a short rabbit fur coat. Her makeup is exaggerated and her hair has been curled.* VINCE *is* TILDEN'S *son, about twenty-two, wears a plaid shirt, jeans, dark glasses, cowboy boots and carries a black saxophone case. They shake the rain off themselves as they enter the porch through the screen door.*

SHELLY: *(laughing, gesturing to house)* This is it? I don't believe this is it!

VINCE: This is it.

SHELLY: This is the house?

VINCE: This is the house.

SHELLY: I don't believe it!

VINCE: How come?

SHELLY: It's like a Norman Rockwell cover or something.

VINCE: What's a'matter with that? It's American.

SHELLY: Where's the milkman and the little dog? What's the little dog's name? Spot. Spot and Jane. Dick and Jane and Spot.

VINCE: Knock it off.

SHELLY: Dick and Jane and Spot and Mom and Dad and Junior and Sissy!
She laughs. Slaps her knee.

VINCE: Come on! It's my heritage. What dya' expect?
She laughs more hysterically, out of control.

SHELLY: "And Tuffy and Toto and Dooda and Bonzo all went down one day to the corner grocery store to buy a big bag of licorice for Mr. Marshall's pussy cat!"
She laughs so hard she falls to her knees holding her stomach. VINCE *stands there looking at her.*

VINCE: Shelly will you get up!
She keeps laughing. Staggers to her feet. Turning in circles holding her stomach.

SHELLY: *(continuing her story in kid's voice)* "Mr. Marshall was on vacation. He had no idea that the four little boys had taken such a liking to his little kitty cat."

VINCE: Have some respect would ya'!

SHELLY: *(trying to control herself)* I'm sorry.

VINCE: Pull yourself together.

SHELLY: *(salutes him)* Yes sir.

>*She giggles.*

VINCE: Jesus Christ, Shelly.

SHELLY: *(pause, smiling)* And Mr. Marshall—

VINCE: Cut it out.

>*She stops. Stands there staring at him. Stifles a giggle.*

VINCE: *(after pause)* Are you finished?

SHELLY: Oh brother!

VINCE: I don't wanna go in there with you acting like an idiot.

SHELLY: Thanks.

VINCE: Well, I don't.

SHELLY: I won't embarrass you. Don't worry.

VINCE: I'm not worried.

SHELLY: You are too.

VINCE: Shelly look, I just don't wanna go in there with you giggling your head off. They might think something's wrong with you.

SHELLY: There is.

VINCE: There is not!

SHELLY: Something's definitely wrong with me.

VINCE: There is not!

SHELLY: There's something wrong with you too.

VINCE: There's nothing wrong with me either!

SHELLY: You wanna know what's wrong with you?

VINCE: What?

>SHELLY *laughs.*

VINCE: *(crosses back left toward screen door)* I'm leaving!

SHELLY: *(stops laughing)* Wait! Stop. Stop! (VINCE *stops*) What's wrong with you is that you take the situation too seriously.

VINCE: I just don't want to have them think that I've suddenly arrived out of the middle of nowhere completely deranged.

SHELLY: What do you want them to think then?

VINCE: *(pause)* Nothing. Let's go in.

>*He crosses porch toward stage right interior door.* SHELLY *follows him.*

SHELLY: I mean I'll do anything you want. I'll pretend anything. I'm good at pretending. I can pretend I'm a Senator. How 'bout that?

>*They disappear from view behind the solid door.* VINCE *knocks on the door.* VINCE *and* SHELLY'S *voices are heard without being seen.*

VINCE'S VOICE: Just do whatever you want! I don't care what you do.

SHELLY'S VOICE: I could tell them I'm a busboy. That's not so far fetched.

VINCE'S VOICE: Don't tell them anything, okay? Just let me do the talking.

>*The stage right door opens slowly.* VINCE *sticks his head in. Calls out toward staircase.*

VINCE: Grandma!

>SHELLY *breaks into laughter, unseen behind* VINCE. VINCE *pulls his head back outside and pulls door shut. We hear their voices again without seeing them.*

SHELLY'S VOICE: *(stops laughing)* I'm sorry. I'm sorry Vince. I really am. I really am sorry. I won't do it again. I couldn't help it.

VINCE'S VOICE: It's not all that funny.

SHELLY'S VOICE: I know it's not. I'm sorry.

VINCE'S VOICE: I mean this is a tense situation for me! I haven't seen them for over six years I don't know what to expect.

SHELLY'S VOICE: I know. I won't do it again.

VINCE'S VOICE: Can't you bite your tongue or something?

SHELLY'S VOICE: Just don't say "Grandma," okay? *(she giggles, stops)* I mean if you say "Grandma" I don't know if I can stop myself.
VINCE'S VOICE: Well try!
SHELLY'S VOICE: Okay. Sorry.

(END)

Buried Child by Sam Shepard. At Circle Repertory Company, New York City. Marshall W. Mason, Artistic Director. Photograph by Gerry Goodstein.

Talley's Folly

by *Lanford Wilson*

from
*The Beginning of the
play*

Characters   Matt Friedman: 42 years old, dark, and rather large. He is warm and unhurried, and has a talent for mimicry. He has a slight German-Jewish accent.
Sally Talley: 31 years old, light, thin, quite attractive, but in no way glamorous or glamorized. She is straightforward, rather tired, and angry as she enters. She has a pronounced Ozark accent, except when she concentrates to overcome it.

Scene   A Victorian boathouse, constructed of louvers, lattice and lots of Gothic Revival gingerbread. The riverside is open to the audience. A canopy above; weeds and willows nearby. Sunset. July 4, 1944; The Talley place, Lebanon, Missouri.

Situation   Matt has driven down from St. Louis to talk to Sally's father, but really to see her. Sally's brother has just run Matt out of the house and down to the boathouse, outraged by Matt's liberal, progressive ideas. Sally is angry that Matt will make things even more difficult with her concerning her family, a family that Sally already has difficulty living with day to day. There begins an evening's association which blossoms into a gentle romance.

Talley's Folly by Lanford Wilson. Judd Hirsch and Trish Hawkins at the Circle Repertory Company, New York City. Marshall W. Mason, Artistic Director. Photograph by Gerry Goodstein.

SALLY: *(Off, yelling)* Matt? (MATT *is silent. He almost holds his breath)* Matt? *(The houselights begin to dim. The sunset and reflection from the river begin to appear; we hear the sound of the river and birds)* Matt?

MATT: *(Softly, to the audience)* This is a waltz, remember. One-two-three, one-two-three . . .

SALLY: *(Off)* Are you in that boathouse? I'm not going to come down there if you're not there 'cause that place gives me the creeps after dark. Are you down there?

MATT: No.

SALLY: *(Coming closer)* I swear, Matt Friedman, what in the devil do you think you're doing down here? *(Coming through the tall weeds and willow)* Oh, my—everything is soaking wet here. Buddy said he chased you off with a shotgun. I thought, good, we're maybe rid of you. I saw your car parked up there, I could not believe my eyes! *(She enters)* Not even you! And there you sit. Wiping your glasses. (SALLY TALLEY *is thirty-one. Light, thin, quite attractive, but in no way glamorous or glamorized. Straightforward, rather tired, and just now quite angry. In this state she has a pronounced Ozark accent, but when she concentrates on what she is saying, the accent becomes much less pronounced)*

MATT: The better to see you with, my dear.

SALLY: Don't even begin with me, Matt, I'm in no mood.

MATT: Were you hiding behind the window curtains when I was out in the yard talking to your brother? You like to hide from me so much.

SALLY: I got home five minutes ago. You know what time I get off work. Rachel and Ida dropped me out front, we could hear Buddy cussin' all the way out to the road.

MATT: You talk to your Aunt Charlotte? How did you know I'd be here?

SALLY: I was inside that house exactly thirty seconds. I walked in the door, Momma and Buddy lit in on me like I was ten years old, screaming about the Communist traitor infidel I'd let in the house. Buddy said he run you off with a shotgun.

MATT: He had a large two-barreled weapon, yes, with apertures about like so.

SALLY: If they knew you were still on the place, they'd have Cliffy on you.

MATT: You want the sheriff, all you have to do is keep yelling. Your sister-in-law called him. He's probably at your house right now.

SALLY: *(Near whisper)* Whatever possessed you to come down here and get into a fight with my brother? You know I can't stand livin' there as it is.

MATT: Sally, one of us had better go for a walk and cool off. Both of us can't be angry.

SALLY: What better happen is you better march right back up there to your car and head back to St. Louis.

MATT: No, see, the way they build those things now they require gasoline to really get them running good. Especially Plymouths.

SALLY: Matt Friedman, you did not run out of gas.

MATT: You want to go try it? See if you can get it to catch?

SALLY: Oh, if that isn't just . . . typical.

MATT: That's what saves it, I think. I was just thinking that that was typical.

SALLY: That car is gonna kill me. I mean, I'm a strong person, but that car is gonna do it. Not one time has that car gone from one place to another place without breaking down.

MATT: Sally, you don't deprecate a man's car. A man's car reflects his pride in himself and his status in society. Castigate my car, you castigate me.

SALLY: Well, good. And you may be full of hot air on most things, but you are right about that. That—that—haybailer!—is a good reflection of you.

MATT: Boy, you get angry, you really are a mountain daughter, aren't you? Where's the still? I was looking for the still you said was down here.

SALLY: Matt, I'm exhausted. I've been up since five. I was at the hospital at six-thirty. I don't want to argue. The still was right there. They busted it up—broke it up.

MATT: Your dad get raided by Cliffy?

SALLY: Cliffy wasn't sheriff then, McConklin was sheriff. Him and Dad were half-partners in the still. They broke it up to sell for scrap after the repeal. Matt—

MATT: They were runnin' liquor, were they?

SALLY: Is the only thing keeping you here a gallon of gas for your car? 'Cause we have a can in the pump house.

MATT: Better wait till it gets a little darker if you're gonna start stealing Buddy's gas.

SALLY: You've alienated Buddy. You've almost paralyzed Olive.

MATT: (Snapping his fingers) Olive! Olive! I could not think of your sister-in-law's darn name! I'm thinking pickled herring, I'm thinking caviar, I'm thinking boiled egg. I knew she was on a relish tray.

SALLY: Why are you always barging in places?

MATT: No, ma'am. I wrote you how many times I'd be down today.

SALLY: You barge into a person's home, you barge into where they work!

MATT: I telephoned your house here. I had a nice Missouri telephone chat with your Aunt Charlotte.

SALLY: Aunt Lottie would invite the devil into the parlor for hot cocoa.

MATT: Actually, I came here to talk to your father. That's the way I've been told these things are done in the South.

SALLY: You're not in the South. You're in the Midwest.

MATT: Sally, I've been all over the country, and there is New York City, isolated neighborhoods in Boston, and believe me, the rest is all the South.

(END)

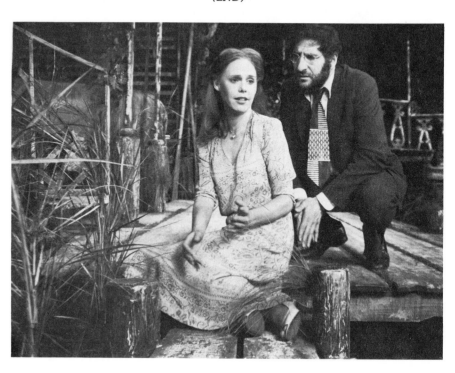

Talley's Folly by Lanford Wilson. Trish Hawkins and Judd Hirsch at the Circle Repertory Company, New York City. Marshall W. Mason, Artistic Director. Photograph by Gerry Goodstein.

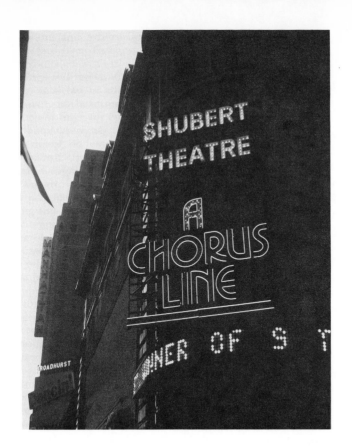

Broadway! Still the dream of most actors. This excellent photograph of the famous Shubert Theatre on W. 44th Street flashes its lights in honor of one of New York's greatest musical hits, *A Chorus Line.* (Photo by Ruth Pearson.)

Epilogue
Quo Vadis?

The contemporary approach to acting as described by Brecht, Artaud, Grotowski, Beck, Chaikin, and others does not ask the author to avoid illusion on the stage. Actors must recognize that *everything* in the theatre is illusion. They should be guided, provoked, stimulated, and occasionally even yielded to in order for them to realize a personalized performance. Actors must run the risk of penetrating the inner self. By using improvisation, actors must move away from lifelessness onstage and open themselves to creative impulses and thereby respond to truth instantly. Perhaps for the first time actors must realize that they have the vital responsibility to economize when creating a character. Actors must be capable of self-detachment and personal objectivity to discover the clichés and hollowness lurking in preconceived value systems. The concern of an actor should be to live fully in mind and body, giving himself over completely to really personalizing, not merely performing, through his dexterity and expertness. Sincere, honest, dedicated art comes also from the unconscious state of the artist. Surface description makes for imitation and destroys spontaneity. Once he is in complete control of his mental, emotional, and physical faculties, an actor should be able to personalize onstage with confidence and with discipline. The late Lee Strasberg and many great actors and teachers of acting in this century personify just such personalization, confidence, and discipline in their art and in their instruction. Having discovered the ability to unmask himself, an actor has found the means to interest an audience, lower its defenses, and provide it with awareness of the complex levels inherent in both existence and in art.

> The mask which an actor wears
> is apt to become his face.
> > Plato

Separate your analysis into four major sections as follows. Effective play analysis must be written out. It is not merely mental activity. The acronymn PASTO, used throughout these instructions, stands for preparation, attack, struggle, turn, and outcome.

Section One

In this section list the following important facts about the author of the play and its production.
1. Brief author information.
2. Brief information on the initial production of the play if known.
3. Brief information on any *vital* or *unusual* subsequent production if known.

Section Two

This is a specific discussion encompassing your overall analysis of the *form* of the play and its structural components which you are to accomplish by completing twenty-three separate paragraphs, numbered 1 through 23, in the following sequence.

1. Identify and clarify the *Preparation* section of the play by specifying the pages and page numbers of your script used for this aspect of the PASTO.

2. Identify and clarify the *Point of Attack* in terms of the earliest incident in the play that exposes the basic conflict of the play. State the nature of the basic conflict—who is it between or what is it between, what it is, and page number of *Attack*.

3. Identify and clarify the *Major Dramatic Question*—MDQ—of the play.

4. Identify the *protagonist* of the play and give a brief justification for your identification.

5. Identify the chief *antagonist* of the play and state a brief justification for your identification.

6. Identify who or what resolves the conflict (i.e., the *Deciding Agent*) and state briefly how and where in the play the resolution occurs (give page number of the conflict resolution).

7. Identify and clarify the *Struggle* section of the play by specifying the pages and page numbers of your script used for this aspect of the PASTO. NOTE: You need to identify the key *Complications* of the play in paragraph 7 after you have clarified the pages and page numbers used for the *Struggle*. Simply list them in the order they occur: for example, p. 16, the protagonist's brother suddenly arrives from California; p. 27, the brother is discovered murdered in the library; and so forth. These complications should be numbered Complication No. 1, and so on.

8. Identify and clarify the major crisis or *Turn* of the play. Where and how does it take place? Give the page number of your script on which it occurs.

9. If a *Climax* can be distinguished from the major crisis, identify and clarify it. Where and how does it take place? Give the page number of your script on which it occurs.

10. Identify and clarify the denouement or *Outcome* section of the play by specifying the pages used for this aspect of the PASTO and by briefly clarifying what gets wrapped up in this section.

11. Identify and clarify the subject *Issues* of the play. List them as one-word subjects or as subject-and-issue questions or as both, as you prefer. List them in priority of importance (e.g., justice, revenge, and so on).

12. Identify and clarify the *key Drives* (nervosity) or character desires for all the characters in the play. List these in priority of importance for each character.

Also list the characters in order of importance in the action of the play. Thus, Hamlet's *Drives* would be listed in order of their importance first; then Claudius' *Drives* would be listed in order of their importance; and so on.

13. Clearly state the *major Theme* or central idea of the play in one complete sentence. Then list any important subordinate themes in order of importance.

14. In one succinct paragraph comment on the quality of the author's skill with the *Plot* in the play (for example, is it strong with Suffering and Discovery, but weak with Reversal? How well is the story organized? Etc.).

15. Repeat number 14 relative to *Character*. For example, are the personalities clear and well distinguished from one another? Are they believable? Are they of full dimension? Do they possess emotion and thought?

16. Repeat number 14 relative to *Thought*. For example, comment on the overall intellectual content of the play: Is it shallow? Is it philosophical? Does it have a theme or themes?

17. Repeat number 14 relative to *Language, Diction,* or *Dialogue*. For example, does the play employ iambic pentameter verse? How good is it? Is it naturalistic American prose? How good is it? Is it good "heard" language?

18. Repeat number 14 relative to *Melody* and *Music*. For example, are the lines conducive to musical effect? Is there use of actual instrumentation? of singing? How good are all these effects?

19. Repeat number 14 relative to *Spectacle*. For example, are all the visual and aural effects theatrical? Are they handled well? evocative? static? What are their outstanding qualities? Do certain technical effects of spectacle tend to dominate the play? For example, is there constant use of drum sounds? Is lighting particularly vital to the play? If so, how? What do the costumes contribute? the scenery? etc.

20. Clarify the meaning of the title of the play.

21. Categorize the *overall Mood* of the play. For example, does the overall mood of the play express the emotion and feeling of sexual heat or frustration? What are the dominate emotions and feelings that make up the overall mood of the play? Relate your discussion of mood to a few key specifics from the acutual play.

22. Categorize the *overall Rhythm* of the play. For example, are the rhythmic surges of the play similar to a gathering thunderstorm? If so, explain how. Relate your brief discussion directly to major action incidents of the play that clarify your discussion of the rhythm. Categorize the overall *tempo* of the play (*speed*-of-movement factor). *Rhythm* evolves from a *combination* of tempo or speed, mood, and emotion.

23. As a categorizing label, state precisely what the *Style* (type or kind) and the *Form* of the play are, based on the foregoing twenty-two points of analysis (e.g., Classic Greek Tragedy; 19th Century Melodrama; Turn-of-the-Century Farce; Expressionistic Serious Drama; etc.). As needed for further clarification, elaborate upon the label: for example, an Expressionistic Farce in the French tradition, an Elizabethan tragedy in the Aristotelian sense influenced by the Roman plays of Seneca, and the like. (Remember that there are only two basic or pure *forms* of drama, namely, tragedy and comedy. All other forms are derivates or amalgamations of those basic two, such as, farce, satire, melodrama, tragicomedy, and so on.)

Section Three

In this section you are to record the following important information on the script itself, in this manner.

1. Cut out the actual script and paste or mock it up on large sheets of paper with openings cut so that both sides of the script can be read. Standard-size acting scripts pasted on 8½-by-11-inch paper is the usual procedure.

2. Include on the script, written in the margins, both your *Literal* and *Metaphorical* analyses. Use separate Comment Sheets for lengthy comments and insert the sheets in proper order among the script pages.

3. On the script designate all *French Scenes* as they occur. Include both your *Literal* and *Metaphorical* titles for each French Scene.

4. On the script designate all major *Complications* as set down earlier in number 6, section 2.

5. On the script categorize the *Tempo* (rate of beat) for each French Scene (e.g., rapid to slow, etc.).

6. On the script identify the *Mood* of each French Scene (e.g., violence, anger, gentle love, etc.).

Note: In section 3, analysis of some items covered previously in section 2 (e.g., complications, major crisis, attack, MDQ, etc.) are usually repeated.

Section Four

Make the conclusion of your play analysis succinct. The conclusion should explicate the play's *Commanding Image* and should be stated in a clear, complete sentence which begins: The play is like . . . Base your conclusion on the *Metaphorical Analysis* noted in the script margins as directed in section 3. For example: The play is like the eye of a hurricane.

Note: Your analysis should be the result of your *own* thinking. If you include the views of critics or scholars in any way, they must be properly acknowledged or footnoted. However, play analysis is *not* research. It should be individual creative play analysis in preparation for acting or directing the play, and it should originate with you.

Seventeen specific steps in role analysis are given in chapter 10.

The Happening

One of the first adventures into new theatrical expression in the 1960s was the Happening. A Happening consisted of creating and projecting visual or aural images into a large open space (such as a field) through open-ended, task-oriented activities. The image projected had no preset meaning; performers improvised in a number of artistic mediums such as painting, sculpture, dance, and music. Each individual addressed himself to the task at hand and participated in an activity focused on a theme, a chance combination, a game, or a trip. Happenings were sometimes staged performances (e.g., dance or multimedia) and sometimes work activities (e.g., building a fence with blocks of ice). Sometimes, Happenings had ceremonial significance (e.g., Allan Kaprow's *Overtime*, 1968). The general aim of a Happening was to consume energy and talent. Happenings were literally exercises in mass consumption. The individual role diminished significantly due to the communal aspect of the task-oriented project. Often, actors were not needed at all when Happenings were strictly technological or work oriented. By the 1970s the Happening was no longer a viable theatrical form. The ultraliberalism of both the theatre and society of the 1960s was joined in a return to structure and conservatism in the 1970s.

The Happening disappeared, leaving a considerable contribution. The Happening explored possibilities for new relationships between participants and spectators, reevaluated and infused life into habitual routines and habits, and made us more aware of the process of creating art. The Happening was powerfully antiliterary, antiactor, antidirector, and antidesigner. The concept was literally divorced from all traditional types of theatre experience. It existed somewhere between the theatricalism of Artaud and the alienation of Brecht and gave little recognition to the theatre of Stanislavski. However, the Happening did open the door to concrete experimentation in communication, body movement, concentration, emotion, and audience participation. Because of the importance of Stanislavski's methodology in twentieth-century theatre, it was very difficult for modern critics and artists to ignore his influence. The Happening helped to break that influence. Surface truth was revealed to be as important as inner truth in view of the fact that it was not always possible for the spectator to experience the same feelings as the actor. However, it was possible for the actor to affect an audience, sometimes involuntarily. The test for truthfulness was not always possible in the realm of intense and authentic personal feeling. The Artaudian actor, on the other hand, could shape feeling into a communicative image by gesture, movement, and a sequence of actions.

Polish Laboratory Theatre

In 1959, Jerzy Grotowski began his unusual study of acting. Grotowski was influenced by Stanislavski (particularly his work on physical actions), Meyerhold (his work on biomechanical training), Vakhtangov (his concept of the actor's central position in a theatre company), Artaud (his Theatre of Cruelty), and Delsarte (his investigations of centrifugal reactions). In addition, Grotowski was sensitive to Oriental theatre (particularly the Peking Opera, the Kathakali, and the Noh theatre of Japan). Grotowski has also worked closely with Joseph Chaikin. Grotowski probed the spiritual nature of the actor by penetrating the psychic and physical faculties of man. To enter Grotowski's training program, actors must be willing to devote several years of selfless service. All training is precise, disciplined, and intensely physical. The central effort of Grotowski's work is exploration of the confrontation which takes place between the performer's mask (i.e., his role) and his self and how the two relate to the written text. Grotowski sees the performer's mask (or role) as a system of signs designed to reveal the man behind the mask. If the actor is in a spiritual state (i.e., disciplined psyche and body), the signs will be rhythmically articulated and artistically formed through acting, dancing, and singing.

How does the actor reveal the man behind the mask? behind the role?

In the Polish Laboratory Theatre, Grotowski's actors embark on a concentrated training program of self-exploration. They work first within the context of personalization. The core of their studies include exercises in concentration and psychophysical body movement. The initial step involves unblocking the conscious and subconscious processes by evoking silence. Silence turns attention inward toward complete concentration. (Incidentally, Grotowski rejects Yoga exercises for concentration because the Yoga aspect of breath control becomes too excessive, thereby blocking expressiveness. However, Yoga exercises are helpful for relaxation and confidence to facilitate natural adaptation to space.) Once the mind and body are at rest and unified, senses can be put to creative use. Grotowski urges reliance upon free personal impulses instead of upon manipulated and calculated moves, looks and thoughts. Actors become "resigned to doing" what they do not want to do. Thoughts and associations flow evenly and freely. They are disarmed and defenseless and have no need to hide behind clothes, ideas, signs, or intellectual concepts.

After the discovery of inner freedom, Grotowski turns to externals. Again personalization is used to project impulses and associations; the character evolves and comes to the actor through his psyche. In this step, the actor finds his "secure self" by learning how to create while being controlled by others and how to create without the security of awareness. The goal is an authentic creation of role through actor (i.e., the role comes to him in the context of his own experiences). Grotowski also trains a well-developed vocal apparatus. During this process, Grotowski cautions actors to remain private by eliminating external friendliness among actors, a social activity which only reintroduces the mask behind which an actor can hide (recall Dustin Hoffman's point on actor relationships in chapter 8, page 89.) Grotowski actors use no makeup or regular theatre costumes. Lighting and sound effects are not provided (except illumination of both actors and spectators). Few properties if any, are used. Grotowski prefers that actors "transform" objects through action and gesture such as treating a plain table as though it were an ornate religious confessional. The stripping away of all theatrical "luxuries" (i.e., lighting, costumes, and so on) explains the term *poor theatre*. Grotowski's productions are inexpensive to produce and to attend—are truly poor theatre.

Grotowski's theatre environment is shaped by the confrontation between actors and their subsequent transformation of space (which implicates the audience physically). Hence, the audience shares all space with the actors. Movement is free, but not random. The cubic space is designed to provide easy and free movement through the audience. Grotowski's early experimentation with audience participation failed. His actors forced audiences into a false position by applying pressure on them to perform with the actors. His rejection of this approach led to the idea of having spectators perform the "role of spectators" naturally and freely within the context of the play's action. Grotowski designed his theatre to include flexible seating arrangements adjusted to the needs of the play (e.g., seats were partially eliminated, or spectators viewed the action from above, or seating changed during a performance, depending on the action). Thus, space, time, and events are unified by the ability of both actors and audience to negotiate with the environment.

Grotowski prefers to have his actors perform classical works (for example, Shakespeare, Sophocles, Calderón) because he believes that the classics allow actors to confront "great actions" by exchanging personal actions with those of great characters. It is precisely this kind of exchange between the actor as human being and the role as art which produces theatre. The transformation between actor and role sometimes makes textual alteration necessary. If certain actions do not conform to personal impulses or are not harmonious with the group, then text may be rearranged or sections omitted. However, Grotowski keeps such changes to a minimum. The literary work remains substantially intact.

In effect, the poor theatre of Grotowski is a way of life (see his book *Towards a Poor Theatre.*) It is mostly a training program; few productions reach an audience. When they do, less than one hundred spectators are permitted to watch. Clearly, this is the antithesis of commercial theatre. The discipline of Grotowski's theatre is designed to initiate the process of revealing the actor. The actor "sacrifices" himself as a gift to the art and to the spectators. In this sense, Grotowski calls his theatre a "holy theatre" that relinquishes all but its humanity.

The Living Theatre

An exciting and noteworthy group of performers calling themselves The Living Theatre also had an important influence on the theatre of the 1960s. The impetus for The Living Theatre (organized in 1959 by Julian Beck and Judith Malina) is their commitment to political revolution as a means of destroying capitalism. The group is a nomadic community of continually travelling social-political artists. Their philosophical intent is similar to that of Artaud. Acting is living in the moment; it is a magical, vigorous creation dedicated to a lucid consciousness and to the joy and pain of creation. The theatre is the ultimate experience, a rebirth. The Living Theatre became famous for its insistence upon audience participation. During the transformation of spectator to participant, the actors give the audience a transfusion by assaulting them with sound, nudity, sexuality, mechanical and programmed gestures, incantation, and frenetic activity.

The Living Theatre is influenced by the stylized movements of the Oriental theatre. Artaud's concept of the theatrically spectacular integration of the arts is also an influence. For example, in plays such as *Mysteries, The Chord, Frankenstein,* and *The Bacchae* a mixture of Pop Art, mythology, science fiction, and the "Late Late Show" creates a strange type of total theatre experience. Plays are relatively unstructured (sometimes only a synopsis is used). All action is directed toward reinforcing political dogma and moral polemics. The plays are kinetically executed with animal energy. They frequently verge on political anarchy in their quest for communal freedom.

In 1964, The Living Theatre left the United States for Europe, exiled because they refused to pay "back" taxes to the federal government. As their art, ideology, and collective existence gained importance in Europe, their popularity increased in the United States. The Becks were instrumental in introducing Eastern religious and philosophical ideas into the theatre. The establishment of the community and communal experience was essential to the fulfillment of their spiritual essence. Yoga was used to help the actors accelerate breathing patterns in order to create different levels of energy. The discovery that breathing can control organic function including blood circulation had far-reaching effect on the emotional status of Beck's company. They learned that sound is a manifestation of certain vibratory energy and that different audience moods can be created by effecting chemical changes in the bodies of the spectators. Tangential to all of their work is the belief that every man is a universe unto himself, that once bodily truth is known universal truth is known. Physical contact between actors and between actors and spectators is central to the theatrical technique of The Living Theatre. Beck's actors use space, a scenario, themselves, and the audience to create a theatre experience in which the actor or performer is the controlling agent.

All plays produced by The Living Theatre are created collectively. In an effort to make theatre a living experience, theatrical speech is rejected because of its artificial nuances and regality. Instead, they use natural or impromptu speech projected by a total vocal effort. More important, they attempt to communicate without words through physical and sensory experiences.

In 1968, The Living Theatre returned to the United States to perform their most important work, *Paradise Now*. Since returning, their energies have dissipated somewhat due to ever-increasing emphasis on political ideology at the expense of good theatre technique. At the August 1972 American Theatre Association Convention in San Francisco, Beck stated that theatre is only a means to their political ends. The Living Theatre's contribution to the new theatre movement has been extensive.

Off-Off Broadway

During the 1960s experimental theatre was produced in coffee houses away from both the Broadway theatrical center and the original Off-Broadway theatres. This endeavor, which was called Off-Off Broadway, produced a conglomeration of plays written by new playwrights performed by actors trained in improvisation and directed by both directors and artist-leaders.

The objective of the original Off-Broadway movement was to enable new playwrights to have their plays produced with less financial risk.

The watchwords of the Off-Off Broadway café theatres were freedom, economy, and intimacy. The general attitude was that professional theatre procedures were inadequate to foster theatrical experimentation, give new playwrights ample opportunity to have their plays produced, and elevate the political consciousness of the public. The most well-known and important theatres were Café Cino, under the direction of the late Joe Cino; Café La Mamma, operated by Ellen Stewart (who sponsored such directors as Jacques Levy); The Judson Memorial Theatre, under the direction of playwright Al Carmines; the Genesis Theatre, under the direction of Ralph Cook; and the Theatre of the Ridiculous under the direction of John Vaccaro (see Appendix B).

Most of the café theatres operate workshops for actors and playwrights. The artists-in-residence rediscover the premise that theatre can be an effective collaborative art experience. Plays take shape from exploratory improvisation, focusing on social and political conditions of the day. Acting exercises are shaped into spontaneous audience events. Dream, myth, and poetry are explored and funneled into spiritual and political commitments. Most of the plays rely on Artaud, Brecht, and Absurdist techniques to make their political or social comment. Each café acting company researches and reexamines the role of every type of person in our culture. Great effort is made to explore the unlimited potential for expression of human sensibility. Disciplined movement training is stressed, but voice becomes a matter of untrained individual expression for the actor. The workshop setting provides actors with the opportunity to work on dance and improvisational techniques. Here the work of the actor and director overlap. The actor finds he must have a director's knowledge of how to elicit specific responses from an audience, and the director realizes that he needs an actor's knowledge of how to create a performance.

The café Off-Off Broadway Theatre stresses nonillusionistic techniques and audience interaction with the theatrical event. Few of the plays are conventional expressions of Realism or Naturalism. They are usually ironic, self-mocking, and unsentimental. Costumes, sets, lighting effects, and casts are kept at a minimum because of the low production budget. The list of playwrights and plays from these small theatres is indeed impressive: Sam Shepard's *Chicago* and *Operation Side-Winder*; Jean-Claude van Itallie's *America Hurrah* and *The Serpent*; Joel Oppenheimer's *The Great American Desert*; Rochelle Owen's *Futz*; Le Roi Jones' *The Dutchman*; Paul Foster's *Tom Paine* and *Balls*; Megan Terry's *Viet Rock* and *Calm Down Mother*; Terrence McNally's *Apple Pie* and *Next*; Maria Irene Fornes's *The Successful Life of 3*; Frank O'Hara's *The General Returns from One Place to Another*; Kenneth Brown's *The Brig*; Al Carmines's *Promanade*; and many others.

In recent years, Off-Off Broadway has become a proving ground for Broadway. Joining the major regional theatres in this regard, Off-Off Broadway has provided the impetus for such hits as *A Chorus Line, For Colored Girls Who Have Considered Suicide When the Rainbow is Enuf, Ain't Misbehavin', Da, The Elephant Man,* and *On Golden Pond.* Leaders in this area have included Joseph Papp at the Public Theatre, Lynne Meadow at the Manhattan Theatre Club, and Craig Anderson at the Hudson Guild Theatre now headed by David Henry Keefner).

The Open Theatre
(Note: in the fall of 1976 in New York City, Joseph Chaikin personally assisted me with the revision of the following material.)

Perhaps the most well-received and well-known experimental theatre in America was Joseph Chaikin's The Open Theatre. Established in the first half of 1963, Chaikin's theatre was organized to help actors deal with nonrealistic material. Influenced by Nola Chilton and Stanislavski's method, Chaikin began his studies around a "sound-and-movement" procedure. Chaikin's innovations in the area of kinetic responses were instrumental in breaking traditional ties between artistic forms and fixed doctrines of naturalistic representation and emotional expressiveness.

Early in his career when he was concerned with his own acting, Chaikin turned to Brecht and the Absurd playwrights. However, during the middle sixties, he moved into exploratory areas of avant-garde literature which subsequently demanded new acting techniques. The central thrust of most avant-garde plays is the paradoxical use of simplicity and clarity to dramatize complexity and confusion. How can the actor-performer make the complex and chaotic visibly simple and clear to an audience and thereby give it the necessary impetus to participate in developing similar perceptions? Chaikin's answer was to develop new deeply penetrating techniques of improvisation. He led his actors to the discovery of their own intuition, their own inner dimension. Chaikin's actors explored their inner lives (somewhat similar to the creating of subtext, except without verbalization). Chaikin learned that inner emotions are rarely externalized. He knew, in fact, that external behavior often contradicts inner feeling. (In the play *Interview* by Jean-Claude van Itallie, the Politician speaks realistically to the people while they speak to him in sounds and movements reflecting the inner feelings of the earlier external action.) Chaikin also utilized many of the techniques of theatre games. The easy structure of games helps actors free themselves from over-reliance on Stanislavski techniques. Games help actors use their bodies, their inventiveness, and their sensory experience in task-oriented exercises (e.g., walking in space, molding objects, mirroring images, exploring the interrelated parts of a machine; exploration of machines is an important aid in examination of social roles in society—since machines are analogous to society, the various machine parts are analogous to the people who make up society). In his search for a "communal dynamic," Chaikin was also influenced by his work with The Living Theatre and, above all, by Grotowski and the Polish Laboratory Theatre. Chaikin conducted exercises in breathing and talking together, in starting and stopping in unison, in trusting one another (by creating, for example, a trust circle; see chapter 4, page 36), in orchestration and musical conducting, and in chord harmony (all actors inhale breath and hum in unison to affirm the collective identity). Improvisational investigation led to the study of "perfect people" whose social behavior is predictable and deadening. Chaikin's actors were sensitized to the idea of being alive in the world and to the possibilities of communication through nonverbal behavior. Chaikin's work attacked social taboos and social conflicts. Improvisations developed into short nonstructured scenes based on political and social satire.

In 1964–1965, The Open Theatre began to perfect performance techniques. The start-and-stop exercises and the transformation concept tightened discipline (e.g., improvising reversal of roles or places; changing from human to nonhuman form; changing styles, lines of texts, or brief dialogue). A collaborative play between Megan Terry and The Open Theatre actors called *Comings and Goings* evolved.

Further gains were made by Chaikin's company when Grotowski visited the United States. Grotowski provided new artistic control through exercises in seeking spiritual privacy, in experiencing emotion physically, and in sharing space with an imaginary "partner-in-security." (See Grotowski's *Towards a Poor Theatre* for exercises on the Cat, Big Tower, Small Tower, headstands, somersaults, and so on.) Under the direction of Lee Worley, The Open Theatre pursued further innovation through unusual work with masks. The result was the company's final collaborative effort of director Jacques Levy and playwright Jean-Claude van Itallie—a striking play called *The Serpent*.

The Open Theatre gave its final performance in Santa Barbara, California. Chaikin stated at the conclusion of the last tour: "Intuitively we feel that it's time to disband. We can no longer be transitional and in progress without becoming an institution. . . ." The legacy that Chaikin and his company willed to the American theatre scene has proved invaluable in expanding the concept of what theatre should be and in re-establishing a broader, deeper inner experience (linked with the mysterious and sacred). The Open Theatre's major contribution was probably in providing the playwright with a new role, that of functioning as a member of an acting company collectively involved in creating a play. Playwrights such as van Itallie and Terry helped devise a new concept of playwriting by fitting words to actor impulses (as opposed to dictating those impulses). Actors became interpreters of the collective vision of a particular company.

Chaikin's group was not the only ensemble unit doing radical or ritual theatre in the 1960s. However, it was the most effective instrument for demonstrating that an American ensemble company *could* be a *poor theatre* (in the Grotowski sense) and a *holy theatre* (in the sense of the contemporary British experimental director Peter Brook). Chaikin is currently acting, directing, coaching, and teaching in New York, as well as abroad. Recovered from serious heart surgery, he is also planning new programs and ideas in the advancement of his art. For example, he has recently worked on the creation of new plays with Sam Shepard. *Tongues* is the result of one such mutual effort between these two outstanding American theatre artists.

Guerrilla Theatre

Guerrilla Theatre began with people who generally lacked training. A number of companies composed of dedicated amateurs sprang up throughout the United States. Anyone with a burning desire to teach and demonstrate social and political doctrines could join this theatre. It had no home but the streets. Performances were usually conducted outdoors on grassy areas, in public parks, in clean middleclass residential suburbs, in dilapidated ghettos, and in urban renewal projects. Guerrilla Theatre was established on the principles of guerrilla warfare and its action was symbolic of guerrilla tactics. The how-to manuals and handbooks on the procedures necessary to conduct Guerrilla Theatre state that tactics should be simple and that mobility is imperative, that groups should be small, that social weakness should be pressured from all sides, and that the element of surprise must be utilized. Guerrilla Theatre reveals a problem and urges the audience to solve it (the Viet Nam War was a prime target for Guerrilla Theatre troupes). Actors perform in Guerrilla Theatre much like a commedia dell'arte troupe, complete with colorful masks, music, and mime. A backdrop and platform are set up for a performance and removed as the company changes location. Guerrilla plays are usually simple in design, utilizing the general format of morality play, burlesque, rock show, modern dance, vaudeville, and circus. The longevity of Guerrilla Theatre/action theatre is minimal

Guerrilla theatre in action on the streets.

and sporadic. Such theatre activity quickly dissipates when the revolutionary spirit subsides. However, the San Francisco Mime Troup continues to work successfully in sociopolitical Guerrilla Theatre activities. The Provisional Theatre Group in Los Angeles is another successful organization specializing in sociopolitical themes.

Bread and Puppet Theatre

Bread and Puppet Theatre.

Peter Schumann and his Bread and Puppet Theatre use the theatre as a pulpit to preach, sermonize, and ritualize life on a level of purity and ecstasy. Performances in which puppets and/or masked figures dramatize social and political expressions are given in the streets (much like Guerrilla Theatre.) These inanimate figures scream and dance, displaying life in highly stylized, ritualized stories. The action is simple and dancelike and requires specialized gestures. Ten-foot rod-puppets (each puppet having a different construction) are used as replacements for live actors. The puppet show uses imaginary characters—gods, monsters, legendary animals, magicians, and the like—to enlarge the basic theme of the play. Individual characterization and motivation are not used. A number of dramatic sequences are performed using noise, music, narration, speech, and modern dance. Emotions, meanings, and attitudes are expressed entirely through strong movements and gestures. The effect is an enlarged, almost grotesque picture of parading puppets and puppeteers who have taken to the streets to celebrate a ceremony called *Life.*

Ethnic Theatre

In the late 1950s and early 1960s, the Southern American black began to agitate for liberation. The Free Southern Theatre was established by Len Holt, Gilbert Moses, and John O'Neal. These and many other artists joined in a collective movement aimed at influencing the shape of black folklore and black psychology, ultimately cutting through the fear of white aggression. Organized in a church basement, the Free Southern Theatre preached the gospel and sang spirituals as freedom songs. Political rhetoric was used to energize black people. Unfortunately, the Free Southern Theatre was unable to establish a continuity of meaningful Black Theatre. Neither did it communicate the needs of blacks. The overall program failed to sustain a unified understanding concerning problems of black people, nor did the program propose solid solutions to the problem of identifying the cultural dynamic. Beset by arguments over the black-white composition of the group, the members of the Free Southern Theatre saw their work as merely another extension of white Western drama. They disbanded. The black movement desperately needed to discover a black heritage rooted solely in black people.

This alternative to Western dramatic tradition appeared on the American theatre scene in the late 1960s and early 1970s. The soul and spirit of the black experience surfaced in the writings of Ed Bullins *(In the Wine Time),* Le Roi Jones (Imamu Amiri Baraka) *(Dutchman and The Slave),* Jimmy Garett *(And We Own the Night),* Ben Caldwell *(The King of Soul),* N. R. Davidson *(Eli Haji Malik),* James Baldwin *(Blues for Mister Charlie),* Lorraine Hansberry *(A Raisin in the Sun),* Lonnie Elder III *(Ceremonies in Dark Old Men),* Charles Gordone *(No Place to Be Somebody),* Joseph A. Walker *(The River Niger),* and Douglas Turner Ward *(The Reckoning).* Ossie Davis *(Purlie Victorious)* and Ted Shine *(Contribution)* are also active black playwrights of note, as are Carlton and Barbara Molette *(Rosalee Pritchett),* Judi A. Mason *(Livin' Fat),* and Phillip Hayes Dean *(Paul Robeson).* Others of promise include Richard Wesley, Adrienne Kennedy, Ron Milner, and Melvin van Peebles. Charles Fuller won the 1982 Pulitzer Prize for drama with his fine play, *A Soldier's Play.* Plays reveal the world as it is—a world seeking to transcend reality into a world as it can be or should be. The major characteristics of modern black plays are their allegorical character, melodramatic action, and simple language. The most important work being done in the area of Black Theatre is that of the Negro Ensemble Company in New York, a group devoted to producing the work of black playwrights and providing a training ground for black actors.

The Chicano theatre groups, particularly the groups in California, represent another movement in Ethnic Theatre. For example, Luis Valdez has developed the Teatro Campesino into a viable, exciting company that champions the cause of Chicanos. Additionally, Valdez has written an important play, *Zoot Suit*.

Theatre of the Ridiculous and the Liquid Theatre

A unique alternative to the revolutionary and social experimental theatre groups was the Theatre of the Ridiculous led by John Vacarro. By erotic, self-assertive, playful, imaginative means, the Theatre of the Ridiculous held public authority up to ridicule. The main purpose of this highly bizarre theatre was to dramatize the fictitious nature of our illusions. The plays attempted to prevent escape into those illusions by forcing us to look at our ridiculous reality. The Happenings influenced the direction of the Theatre of the Ridiculous, as did Spolin's improvisational games and Grotowski's confrontation and disarming techniques. This theatre was a format for task-oriented activities. Lacking characters and logical plot organization, actors simply displayed their own personalities or created clichéd stereotypes.

Using the format of the Theatre of the Ridiculous, the Liquid Theatre sought to present a similar barrage of theatricality, utilizing active audience participation. It now appears to have been a short-lived experiment.

Theatre of Fact

A more stimulating and seemingly lasting experience known as the Theatre of Fact evolved in the late 1960s. Originating in Germany from the Brecht influence and led by Rolf Hochhuth and Peter Weiss (see chapter 20), the movement developed drama based on factual history. Later Heiner Kipphard in his play *In the Matter of J. Robert Oppenheimer* raised ethical questions concerning the conflict between science and humanity. The actor in the Theatre of Fact operates in an environment similar to Brecht's Epic Theatre. He has full intellectual knowledge of the subject matter being presented and a heightened consciousness of all action. In effect, he is "standing in" for a particular person who cannot be there to speak for himself. The actor's task is to create a believable, historic human being and yet to keep the didactic polemic operative (see the plays *Pueblo, The Trail of the Cantonsville Nine,* and *Are You Now or Have You Ever Been,* the latter by Eric Bentley). Jerry L. Crawford has also written a treatment of the last day in the life of President Lyndon B. Johnson which intermingles fact and fiction; the play is titled, *The Last President.*

Performance Group

In 1968 Richard Schechner organized an experimental group in a converted New York garage devoted to what he termed *environmental theatre.* He called the troupe the Performance Group. Schechner believed that his concept of theatre was placed somewhere between a Happening and traditional theatre presentation. The actors used all the space in the theatre including audience area and stage. The total environment was involved. Any space could be converted into a production area. Schechner's group at times used a text, but generally worked improvisationally. His most important productions were *Dionysus 69, Makbeth,* and *Commune.*

The Public Theatre

Joseph Papp has introduced more new American playwrights than any other producer in recent years through his efforts for a free public theatre in New York City, particularly in Central Park. *Hair*—a landmark rock musical presentation—was produced by Papp. Later, plays by such promising playwrights as Charles Gordone and Jason Miller were produced under the auspices of Papp, as were the successful plays, *For Colored Girls Who Have Considered Suicide When the Rainbow Is Enuf*, and *A Chorus Line*. For several years, Mr. Papp also produced at the Lincoln Center.

Other Groups and Regional Theatres/
College and University Theatres/
Professional Schools and Studios

Other important experimental theatre companies included Andre Gregory's Manhattan Project, Robert Wilson's Byrd Hoffman School, Ernie McClintock's Afro-American Studio Theatre in Harlem, Herbert Blau's various groups, Lee Breur's Mabou Mines, Richard Foreman's Ontological-Hysteric Theatre, Michael Cullen's Travel Light Theatre (in Chicago), Al Carmine's theatre at the Judson Memorial Church, Harvey Lichtenstein's Brooklyn Academy of Music and Dodger Theatre at BAM, Theatre Genesis at St. Marks Church, and Michael Hadge's Theatre at St. Clement's. (Not all of these companies survived, but each made significant contributions to contemporary theatre.) The noted director and teacher, Terry Schreiber, continues to do exemplary work at all levels of New York theatre activity. A variation upon the "experimental" theatre is represented in New York by the work of Christopher Martin who produces, directs, acts, and designs at the Classic Stage Company, specializing in classics from the Greeks to Shakespeare to modern "masterpieces."

Experimental theatre reached its apex during the civil rights and antiwar movements of the middle 1960s. The early efforts of most of these groups have faded, but their influence remains in some Off-Off Broadway activity. The character of this theatre changes almost weekly. Recently, Off-Off Broadway entered a period of consolidation. The "company" idea has given stability to Off-Off Broadway and has enabled small groups of actors and directors to control their artistic destiny. The emphasis on Off-Off Broadway has shifted from the script and the playwright to the artistic cohesiveness of the company. Experimental theatre is no longer identified strictly with youth and rebellion; the 1970s altered the focus and expanded it in multidirections.

The 1970s also saw a decentralization of American professional theatre away from New York which resulted in highly successful regional theatre, most of which fostered important new plays and playwrights.

Leaders among the regional theatres include the Barter Theatre, Virginia (Rex Partington); the Oregon Shakespeare Festival, Ashland, Oregon (Jerry Turner); Center Stage, Baltimore, Maryland (Stanley Wojewodski); the Studio Arena Theater, Buffalo, New York (Neal Du Brock); the Champlain Shakespeare Festival, Burlington, Vermont (Edward J. Feidner); the Goodman Theater Company (Gregory Mosher); the St. Nicholas Theater Company, Chicago, Illinois (Steven Schacter); Playhouse in the Park, Cincinnati, Ohio (Michael Murray); The Cleveland Play House, Cleveland Ohio (Richard Oberlin); Dallas Theater Center, Dallas, Texas (Paul Baker); Hartford Stage Company, Hartford, Connecticut (Paul Weidner); Alley Theater, Houston, Texas (Artistic Director, TBA); Indiana Repertory Theater, Indianapolis, Indiana (Edward Stern); Missouri Repertory Theater, Kansas City, Missouri (Patricia McIlrath); Center Theater Group; Ahmanson Theater, Los Angeles, California (Robert Fryer) and Mark Taper Forum, Los Angeles, California (Gordon Davidson); Actors' Theater of Louisville, Louisville, Kentucky (Jon Jory); Milwaukee

Repertory Theater Company, Milwaukee, Wisconsin (John Dillon); The Guthrie Theater Company, Minneapolis, Minnesota (Artistic Director, TBA); Long Wharf Theater, New Haven, Connecticut (Arvin Brown); Yale Repertory Theatre, New Haven, Connecticut (Lloyd Richards); McCarter Theater Company, Princeton, New Jersey (Nagle Jackson); Trinity Square Repertory Company, Providence, Rhode Island (Adrian Hall); Loretto-Hilton Repertory Theater, St. Louis, Missouri (David Frank); American Conservatory Theater, San Francisco, California (William Ball); Seattle Repertory Theater, Seattle, Washington (John Hirsch); Hartman Theater Company, Stamford, Connecticut (Artistic Director, TBA); American Shakespeare Theater, Stratford, Connecticut (Michael Kahn); Syracuse Stage, Syracuse, New York (Arthur Storch); Utah Shakespeare Festival, Cedar City, Utah (Fred Adams); Arena Stage, Washington, D.C. (Zelda Fichandler and David Chambers); John F. Kennedy Center: Eisenhower Theater, Washington, D.C. (Roger L. Stevens); Eugene O'Neill Theater Center, Warterford, Connecticut (Lloyd Richards); The Cricket Theatre, Minneapolis, Minnesota (Louis Salerni); The Children's Theatre Company, Minneapolis, Minnesota (John Clark Donahue); The Acting Company, New York City based, primarily on tour (John Houseman); Old Globe Theatre, San Diego, California (Jack O'Brien); The Rainbow Children's Theatre Company, Las Vegas, Nevada (Jody Johnston and Brian Kral); The Empty Space, Seattle, Washington (M. Burke Walker); South Coast Repertory, Costa Mesa, California (David Emmes); PAF Playhouse, Huntington Station, New York (Jay Broad); Colorado Shakespeare Festival, Boulder, (Daniel S. P. Yang); Denver Theatre Center, Denver, Colorado (Edward Payson Call); A Contemporary Theatre, Seattle, Washington (Gregory Falls); Karamu House, Cleveland, Ohio (Mike Malone); National Theatre of the Deaf, Waterford, Connecticut (David Hays); Williamstown Theatre Festival, Williamstown, Maine (Nikos Psacharopoulos); Virginia Museum Theatre, Richmond, Virginia (Tom Markus); Asolo State Theatre, Sarasota, Florida (Richard G. Fallon); New Jersey Shakespeare Festival, Madison, New Jersey (Paul Barry); The Magic Theatre, San Francisco, California (John Lion); Great Lakes Shakespeare Festival, Lakewood, Ohio (Vincent Dowling); California Actors Theatre, Los Gatos, California (Sheldon Kleinman); and Arizona Theatre Company, Tucson, Arizona (Gary Gisselman). New Professional theatres are being founded every year.

In New York City, leaders in the production of new plays include the Circle Repertory Company, the Manhattan Theatre Club, The Hudson Guild Theatre, The American Place Theatre, and Playwright's Horizon, among others.

American colleges and universities are also exerting new thrust and leadership in all facets of contemporary theatre. Notable among these are the drama and theatre departments at Yale University, Carnegie-Mellon, Penn State, The University of Texas at Austin, Kansas University, The University of Iowa, Louisiana State University, Wayne State University, the University of Michigan, The University of Wisconsin at both Madison and Milwaukee, the University of Georgia, the California Institute of the Arts, California State University at Fresno/Los Angeles/Sacramento/Fullerton/Long Beach, Los Angeles City College, University of California, Irvine/Los Angeles/Berkeley/Davis/San Diego, U.S.C., the University of Nevada, Las Vegas and Reno, Stanford University, the University of Utah, the University of Hawaii, the University of Arizona, Indiana University, the University of Minnesota, Ohio State University, the University of Illinois, Northwestern University, the University of Oklahoma, the University of Washington, Hunter College, New York University, Brandeis University, the University of South Florida, the University of Florida, Temple University, the University of Montana, the University of Colorado, the University of Missouri, Wisconsin State University at Stevens Point, Drake University, the University of Tulsa, Oklahoma State University, Iowa State University, the University of Arkansas at both Fayetteville and Little Rock, the University of Nebraska at both Lincoln and Omaha, Cornell University, Otterbein College, Oberlin College, Kenyon College, Illinois State University, Illinois Wesleyan

University, Central State University (Oklahoma), Brigham Young University, Utah State University, Texas Tech University, Arizona State University, Northern Arizona University, Evansville University, Prairie View A & M University, Hanover College, Northern Iowa University, Eastern Illinois University, Western Illinois University, University of Alaska, Oregon State University, University of Oregon, Portland State University, Rio Hondo College (California), Western Reserve University, Baldwin Wallace University, Bowling Green University, Grambling State University, Cameron University (Oklahoma), University of Tulsa, Southern Illinois University at Carbondale, Occidental College, Oklahoma State University, Kansas State University, San Joaquin Delta College (California), Tulane University, University of New Orleans, Michigan State University, University of New Mexico, Mexico State University, Panamerican University, University of North Carolina, North Carolina State University, University of South Carolina, University of Vermont, State University of New York at Purchase and Buffalo, University of Maine, University of Idaho, Idaho State University, University of Wyoming, Colorado State University, Princeton University, Dartmouth College, University of Alabama, Auburn University, University of Kentucky, University of Tennessee, Ohio University, Miami University (Ohio). University of Miami, University of Akron, University of Mississippi, West Virginia University, University of Virginia, University of Pittsburgh, and San Angelo State University. Such a listing, of course, can only be incomplete; most land grant state universities house good drama and theatre departments, as do most of our private institutions. I provide the list above as a mere indication of the growth and development of drama departments in our major colleges and universities. One of the most successful programs in theatre at the educational level is the American College Theatre Festival. Sponsored by the American Theatre Association and headquartered in Washington, D.C., this program has become an exciting and valuable addition to the country's dramatic activity in just a few years. The American Oil Company is an outstanding corporate sponsor of ACTF with particular advantages offered the student playwright through the Michael Kanin Playwrighting Award, the Norman Lear Award for Comedy, the David Library Award for plays on American themes (adjudicated by Ezra Stone), and many other special awards. Also, college and university acting is enhanced by the Irene Ryan Acting Awards, another outstanding feature of ACTF. This entire enterprise is housed at the John F. Kennedy Center for the Performing Arts, where the annual national festival is held under the auspices of Roger Stevens. David Young serves as Producing Director.

There are also many professional schools or studios offering quality training for the actor. Leaders among these include the American Conservatory Theatre in San Francisco, the Joseph Bernard Acting Studio in Las Vegas, the Strasberg Institute in New York and Los Angeles, the Neighborhood Playhouse in New York, the American Academy of Dramatic Art in New York and Pasadena, the Herbert Berghof Studios in New York, and the distinguished Julliard School in New York. Additionally, most of the major regional theatres listed above conduct classes and training programs for actors. Finally, many outstanding individuals teach, coach, and tutor privately. These people are listed in the major trade papers and in the drama section of the Sunday New York *Times*. Recommendations concerning tutors and schools may be found in valuable source books, such as Rebecca Nahas' *Your Acting Career* and Robert Cohen's *Acting Professionally*. Perhaps the best advice and recommendations of all come from "word of mouth"—the suggestions of colleagues working in the field.

"Observations and Advice for Actors (and Directors)—Comments Most Frequently Heard from Teachers, Coaches and Directors"

Appendix C

Good things *will* repeat. One must go back and work on it again and again. Like a dancer, musician, or athlete.

Don't move your head much when you speak.

Don't push or force for emotion and character. Be patient. Often let the lines do it—trust the playwright.

When in doubt, do less—even nothing.

Don't sermonize, posture, and play so much subtext you forget the text.

Don't frame every moment in emotion—it becomes pretentious and tedious. Don't show the art.

The key is to lean on yourself for that within you which wants to reach out to people. Doing this, you're less likely to act. However, once you tap yourself and use it, be it humor or pain, the thing must be crafted. *It* can't work *you.*

If you just let emotion pour out, it will use you up.

Risk yourself on stage. If *you* "hide," it will lead to mediocre acting.

In early rehearsals, explore *yourself*, not your role; dare to take risks. Later, learn craft. Mechanical actors and directors *begin* with craft. They allow no room for exploration and risk. The result is safe, mediocre, and boring theatre.

Be you for awhile; let the role come to you, be you.

Don't get with the role and lines too quickly (which is the initial risk!—avoiding that safety factor!). Don't run to "hide" too quickly in character and emotion.

"Not enough time" is always a "cop-out." Use well and use properly whatever time you have.

Faith begins with faith in self.

If you don't have the time to do something well, prepare it well, and strive for greatness, don't do it at all.

Working alone in a monologue should be more relaxed than working with someone else because one need worry only about oneself.

Never cry over criticism; only cry over failure to work purposefully and hard.

If you know it is not working in rehearsal, stop. Begin again.

Score a scene in terms of what your character *sees* and *hears.*

Ala Stanislavsky, do your homework and find the "why"—the past history—the motivation; *however*, it is even better to analyze the "what for"—the present *situation* and the future goal.

Subtext requires improvisation, not mere mental invention.

Never try to become an "actor;" try to become a fuller person. Keep your feet on earth, pavement, and wood.

Acting is serious business, but one can approach it too seriously and become grim.

Don't *feel* everything to the sacrifice of craft.

Too many actors are emotional rather than dramatic.

Don't "indicate." Don't move or speak as though saying, "Look! I'm moving! I'm speaking!"

Learn to *locate* as an actor. Know where you are—to whom you speak! And why! And what for!

Speak to me first as you, later as the character.

Let punctuation lead you to rhythm. Acting is all rhythm finally.

One can't act carrying self-criticism in one's head. Don't make clinical decisions. Just do.

Act one thing at a time—always use single intentions. Like a butcher, put one piece of meat on the wax paper at a time.

Use pauses, not holes.

Use opposite values.

You don't know the precise age of your character? Well, that's "spur-of-the-moment" acting for you.

Use of private moments is a risk actors must learn to take.

Don't be too dependent upon a director; respect him, but never be his slave or puppet. Most actors survive in spite of directors.

Good directors often listen to suggestions from actors; great directors even use the suggestions now and then.

Watch great actors over and over again. Watch Olivier, Tracy, Hepburn, Burstyn, Pacino, DeNiro.

Use real liquor in a drinking scene once in a rehearsal—never again.

You can't stand still on stage? Do the scene once with your back constantly against a wall.

The clearer and simpler the imrov, the better it will be.

Don't suppress nervousness—channel it and use it.

Look—see—react. Brecht said that and so did Stanislavsky.

Play clichés honestly—let the audience discover they are clichés. Don't lead them by indicating.

Don't fret about results. Leave it to directors and critics. Just act one intention at a time. When you get to the last one, there will be the results.

Never panic in the face of time and throw out necessary work to get to results.

If you scream and get hysterical, you'll get screaming, hysterical theatre.

Analysis, discussion, and exploration are more important than learning lines and blocking. The latter stuff will actually take care of itself. Of course, you'll never know that or believe that unless you try it.

To dwell on learning lines and blocking is to kid yourself; that isn't work. Technicians do that, not artists.

Musicians know what it takes to play a note—to execute. Why shouldn't actors?

Affective memory work (emotion memory) should be done at home, alone, if done at all. Homework should appear *in* the rehearsal, not *at* the rehearsal.

You have to be yourself before you can be any character. Acting is use of self.

Speak out. If you're angry, say so. Don't sulk and brood. Get rid of it. Then rehearse. Speaking out also builds confidence.

Drill cannot accomplish what improvisation can.

Don't show; do.

The supreme accomplishment is to get thinking and impulses to coincide. (Self coincides with character.)

Eventually get around to selecting and discarding. *Then* set it and polish it. What in hell is there to set and polish from the first week of a rehearsal devoted to line and blocking memorization?

Late in rehearsals, go ahead and repeat blocking and movement patterns. But never repeat inner reaction. Keep those fresh (especially if some fool director is "blocking" you).

If your director is a traffic cop, follow his law like any good citizen, but put essence (yourself) under it.

Don't imitate—recreate.

If a director says, "Drop the organic and Method crap and just do it—do what I tell you!" smile and do it, but do even more homework later by yourself.

Remember the lesson of the baseball hitter—every pitch is a bit different—you can't always hit the same way. React a bit differently—go with the pitch. The logic is the same—the territory—not the reaction/action.

Habit just leads to imitation. Add "Will" and "Adaptation."

Have only one intention at a time, even when you're doing many things at once. Instinct and craft must weld. You need both.

Don't act from the negative ("I will resist"). Use the positive ("I will triumph").

Some actors need "will" in their emotional flow to maintain control; others need no "will" and still have little emotion—the latter aren't really actors.

The other paradox: acting is indeed mental and the key approach to it is through the mind, but the actor cannot do a lot of thinking in the usual sense of that word while on stage performing. Instinct and some mystery are involved.

Trust cannot be bargained or requested—only earned via work.

An actor has to have a studio; a lab; a classroom—to just work in production and performance will make actors lazy and drive them insane.

You always have time for homework. No actor or director can do it all at rehearsal.

Prepare or get out.

Stop acting *before* you come on stage.

When you deny, you hide.

Don't do facile, easy things. If you rein everything in, you can't get "naked" up there. Think in physical terms, not emotional terms.

Stop coming to conclusions about your own work.

Don't let a director *force* you to do anything. You *find* a way to do it.

Don't be defensive about yourself or your character. Avoid personal negativism. Open up and let them at you.

Don't "pump up." Go to the toilet, then walk on and just say the lines. Stop having Dostoevsky seizures.

Note the weather you just left every time you come on.

Find some pleasure in yourself. It leads to confidence.

You have to be heard and understood.

Later in rehearsals, do you have the courage to face craft? *Then* accept direction, even commands?

A rare role will allow you to just personalize throughout. But no role will deny you starting with it.

Don't "glide" verbally. Speak.

Be patient—must you see the end of the journey at the start? Cool it and take it moment by moment.

Never play for laughs—it's not believable and it's undisciplined, exhausting, and unprofessional.

Artificial bellowing always leads to the same thing: losing your voice.

Goethe said an artist's career develops in public—but talent develops in private.

Let's struggle with your talent, but not applaud it yet.

Success often kills development. It's easy to get bought in this society. It's our profession's fatal trap. Why do you think most film and television actors feel guilty?

Be sure to bow beautifully in the face of your greatest calamities. The bow should say, "I did my best—for now."

Show me worlds within me I did not know existed.

The great actor has the emotion always *there*—but the greatness will not hold without continual practice and use.

A monologue must be done with an audience—even if unseen, it must be to someone. Thus, there is no such thing as a monologue. They are always to someone.

Always play action and situation; also, wait for your cue.

Learn to compress your preparation; tighten cues; establish a proper environment; nail down business specifically; use what you have, no matter the pain or discomfort.

With Pinter, don't worry about the mystery and menace and silence—all that stuff—just make your selections and do them. The Pinter stuff takes care of itself. If you play at his oddities, you'll drown in them. Just do solid, motivated acting. You don't have to understand all of it—search, think, select, and do.

Trust your playwright; remember, playwriting is not a collaborative process; production is, but not playwriting.

Good improvs should always be set up so that each actor is unaware of what all the other actors know.

Is there a great audience out there waiting and wanting art and artistry? Probably not. Most actors do it for each other and themselves. That's ok.

Most actors have to act; it is more real up there. That is what is meant by the power of acting. Do not fear it; most actors don't really act for money and fame and satisfaction. No, most hold to it for personal survival. No wonder George C. Scott says: "Don't." Nobody should be *encouraged* to be an actor.

Want to do a grim scene with depth? Then sing a happy song just before doing the scene. (Comb it the other way, in other words. That's what we often do in life—do something else to escape our pain and vulnerability. Naturally, then, the actor should do the same thing.)

If you are mechanical in movement patterns, play the scene once in the dark. Have someone put obstacles around. See what happens, but don't get hurt. (This is called, "Reacting honestly.")

Don't show your preparation *in* the scene. That's acting. Rather, use it *under* the scene, or throw it away before entering.

To freshen an entrance, have at least four places to enter. In early rehearsals, never let the other actor know which one you'll use. (Fresh reactions!)

When acting poetry, learn first what you are doing physically—then add the poetry.

Never huff and puff a soliloquy.

Few can act well out of mere instinct and inspiration (George C. Scott—maybe). It leads to emotional posturing. Leave all that to the geniuses.

Act under the influence of the passion and in character, but don't act *in* a passion.

Try being deaf all morning; blind; without smell; without taste; without being able to touch.

Don't be a "Method Mutant"—an "Organic Ostrich." That is, don't just use feeling. Eventually, get to the craft, too.

Don't just approach a scene through its language—go into it via intentions. What is the situation—what do you want to win? How do you win? And what for?

Don't anticipate.

Animal work is often good. A monkey is terrific for use.

With great acting, the "thing" is still there after it's done. It should never just be over. Try to act so you leave something behind.

Remember, a director is just an ideal audience of one. (Good ole Tyrone Guthrie! Or was it Arthur Hopkins?)

A director does not know everything, but should have authority whenever he tells the truth.

The best actors have a secret. Good directors get to know their actors well and allow those secrets to emerge.

Avoid the rap of opportunism as actors. Hold to your integrity as you do commercials and other such jobs. The times ahead will be morally dangerous for actors; no matter your work, can you also do it as a service to people? To better Mankind?

Any one idea from an actor is worth more than four ideas from a director. Why? Because the actor is personally involved in a way no director can hope to match.

A good director will never tell you what to do, he will just tell you what not to do.

The hardest thing about acting is to not seem to know what is going to happen next. (Good ole Lee Strasberg!)

The key director's task is to discover what is unique about each of his actors.

"Blocking" an actor is the curse of actor creativity. So is forced line memorization.

A director must be careful of creative selfishness. Beware of the director who claims to have "a great idea or concept" about the play.

Good acting reveals a collision of values.

Your character's spine or super objective or motivating force should plug into why the play was written.

Do not try to just "create a character;" just try to play action and situation. Let other characters "create" you though their response to your action.

Never play as direct to an audience as you play to another character. (This includes playing Brecht and soliloquies.)

As Zen said, begin with an empty cup. Fill it slowly and carefully and only to the rim. (Bottle is a good metaphor as well as cup.)

Some things cannot be acted; they can only be earned, as in life. Such a thing is dignity.

The best playwrights write for actors, not audiences.

A new play, one untried and unproven, is the most beneficial vehicle for actors to experience.

Ask the Charles Dickens question of your character: "Will he be the victim of his life or become the hero of it?"

No director that one might admire "blocks" a play. The groundplan takes care of that, as does actor instinct and the playwright. It is best to create a ground-plan through director-actor collaboration; after that, the designer should enter the collaboration.

It was Chekhov who noted that the most important thing in acting is the placement of the furniture.

An actor must allow himself to be ambushed by his character's thoughts and, of course, by the thoughts of other characters and other actors. (Ambush = surprise!)

Good directors rarely use adjectives, adverbs, and directives *early* in rehearsal. To do this is to force actors to play qualities rather than action. Do not create barriers for actors by commanding them at the very start. This is the time barriers must come down. Trust them awhile and let them work on their own a bit.

The key to good directing is understanding people.

Good directors let actors evolve organically at their own pace toward some point *late* in rehearsals. *Then* the director steps in to command, edit, refine, polish, set, and clarify.

Pace and speed are two different things. Pace is the rate at which a good moment follows another good moment. A play can be performed and spoken at great speed and still be slow.

Pace cannot be a director's concern until *late* in rehearsals. Never tell an actor early in rehearsal to "speed up" or "pace it faster" or "move it more quickly." A good actor should only answer such commands with this question: "Faster with *what?*"

Always look to opposites. Always look for the tragic in the comic and the comic in the tragic. Shakespeare, Moliere, and Chekhov, to name but three playwrights, always mixed opposites. (To do *The Miser*, first learn where Harpagon is *generous.*)

Style is mostly the mix of the tragic with the comic. Style does not imply that an actor has to do a lot of "performing." That is merely boring.

The key to directing is *through* actor work. First treat the actor as a person, then an artist. Finally, the actor will become more responsible for the play than the director and that is good.

Actors often save directors, rarely does a director save an actor.

"Block" a play, if you must, during the *final* two weeks of rehearsal.

The key is to free the actor early on, not rein him in like some wild thing. Line memorization is mere self-discipline. Leave it to the actor. Freedom does not mean anarchy. Free actors are profoundly disciplined.

To those who say we have no time to work organically, reply that the challenge is theirs to take up or reject. To resist is to repeat the same bad habits again and again. A class in directing should not create models of the director who is teaching the class.

If your theatre program is in too much of a hurry to work properly, try doing just one play a year well, not five or six poorly. Or do the five or six without quite finishing them in order to train actors better.

In America, especially in colleges and universities, we have tremendous facilities and better budgets than we care to admit. Yet we rarely free actors to create.

The readiness to respond to accidents and build on them is the key to good acting and directing.

Create chains of unbroken moments.

Authority belongs only to the teller of truth.

Create group ensembles; no one person is larger than the play, including the director.

Use passion; why am I doing this role and this play? Find out and be passionate about it.

Watch other actors.

Avoid a "production concept." Just stage the action.

Be certain your director works more than once with you alone, as an individual.

If you discover the style of the play, keep quiet about it.

Edit your own excessive ideas. Remember again that less is more.

(A special Third Edition "tip of the hat" to my good friends, Barry Kyle and Robert Benedetti, for many of the ideas stated above. These two directors are in fact coaches, not directors because they understand the art of directing, that is, of promoting actor creativity in an organic fashion.)

Oh, yes, one more thing to repeat:

Entering into acting is entering Purgatory. Good luck. And get on with it.

"SHORT-FORM ROLE ANALYSIS DOCUMENT." (Name of actor: _____)
(Name of role: _____)

(You are advised to duplicate this two page form/document and use it for each role you create in scene practice, auditioning, and stage production.)

Each actor/actress is asked to complete this and return it. Whenever possible, all answers or comments are to be based strictly on information about your character supplied in the actual text! When this is not possible, you may create answers or comments provided they are *logically related* to information in the text. Your director will discuss your responses with you later, as needed. Note: this is in no way an "academic" assignment; it is rather an opportunity for fresh, original actor creativity, provided in an organic framework for directing and acting which permits and encourages artistic individuality as well as artistic collaboration.

Name of actor/actress _____ Name of character _____ Age of character _____ Precise birthdate of character _____ Astrological sign _____ What significance, if any, to this sign _____
_____
Generally, how "physically active" is your character? (Describe in a sentence):
_____
_____

Name an animal* which in appearance, movement, or manner seems analogous to your role: _____ What is it about this animal that most specifically relates to your role: _____
_____

Can you name a person close to you, family or friend, who seems to be a good deal like your character? If so, name him or her _____
_____ (relationship) _____
Can you name a famous person who seems to be a good deal like your character? If so, name him or her _____ Vocally, is your character generally quiet and demure or loud and flamboyant? _____ If neither, how would you describe your character's vocal nature? _____
Basically, how would you describe the way your character likes to dress (casual, tailored, sloppy, neat, colorfully, etc.) _____ Basically, how would you describe the way your character likes to wear or comb his/her hair?
_____ Select the three or four *major* emotions your character seems to experience the most (Fear, love, hate, anger, etc.)
_____ Give an example *from the text* in which each of the examples you listed are revealed: (use back of page if necessary) _____
_____
_____
_____

What is the MF or Motivational Force (spine) of your character (for example, in *Death of a Salesman*, "Willy wants Biff to love him again." State the MF of your character by beginning with the name of your character and the word, "wants . . ." If possible, the spine or "want" should relate to another character or characters in the play.) _____
_____
_____

What is the major beat of action (or key moment of activity and/or decision/choice) in the play for your character (the most important moment in the play for your character):
_____
_____

*A bird may also be used, although animals usually provide more humanlike characteristics.

page 2 ROLE ANALYSIS FORM for _____

Name of actor/actress _____

_____

List 5 to 10 *major* subtext events in your character's life *prior* to the beginning of the play (these may be revealed by the text or you may have to create them from imaginary biography, provided they are logically related to known facts in the text); examples of the kind of life events that might be included as major are events of family (names of parents, brothers, how old you were when and if they died, etc.), education (how much, where accomplished), marriages and children (if any), divorces, major illnesses, etc. Again, list 5 to 10 *major* subtext events: (just use short phrases, not full sentences) _____

_____

_____

_____

_____

Briefly describe the *major* activities your character engaged in during the day of action of the play (from rising, up to the first entrance on stage): (just use short phrases, not full sentences) _____

_____

_____

_____

Briefly describe the *major* activity your character engages in during all offstage time after every exit made during the action of the play: (just use short phrases, not full sentences) _____

_____

_____

_____

Create a brief list of *major* character "idiosyncrasies, likes and dislikes" for your character (for example: likes cheeseburgers and french fries, suffers from insomnia, reads mystery novels, likes Dustin Hoffman movies, hates John Wayne movies, etc.): (use at least 5–8 items) _____

_____

_____

_____

_____

_____

Add any other pertinent notes or comments about your character that you have noted (not covered somehow above), if any:

NOTE: Your director *advises* but does not require that each of you keep a rehearsal and performance "log" or diary for totally personal observations, insights, problems, etc. Later, you will be amazed at the record of growth, development, and human interest you will have caught in your log. (You are at liberty to share this log with your director at any time if you feel it might help your work in any way.) A good log often closes with a personal self-evaluation statement.

"SHORT-FORM ROLE ANALYSIS DOCUMENT." (Name of actor: _____)
(Name of role: _____)

*ACTUAL STUDENT
ACTRESS SAMPLE:
"POORLY DONE."*
(Completed in haste with
inadequate analysis.)
(Contrasting sample well
done by the same actress
follows in this appendix.
Compare and contrast the
two samples as a guide to
the correct approach in
using this document.)

Each actor/actress is asked to complete this and return it. Whenever possible, all answers or comments are to be based strictly on information about your character supplied in the actual text! When this is not possible, you may create answers or comments provided they are *logically related* to information in the text. Your director will discuss your responses with you later, as needed. Note: this is in no way an "academic" assignment; it is rather an opportunity for fresh, original actor creativity, provided in an organic framework for directing and acting which permits and encourages artistic individuality as well as artistic collaboration.

Name of actor/actress __Julie Tjaden__ Name of character _____ Age of character __35__ Precise birthdate of character __July 2, 1904__ Astrological sign __Cancer__ What significance, if any, to this sign __"eyebrows distinctly marked"__

Generally, how "physically active" is your character? (Describe in a sentence): __She isn't physically active__

Name an animal* which in appearance, movement, or manner seems analogous to your role: __Butterfly__ What is it about this animal that most specifically relates to your role: __She flits from man to man__

Can you name a person close to you, family or friend, who seems to be a good deal like your character? If so, name him or her __Can't think of anybody__ (relationship) _____
Can you name a famous person who seems to be a good deal like your character? If so, name him or her __Valerie Bertenelli__ Vocally, is your character generally quiet and demure or loud and flamboyant? __loud and flamboyant__ If neither, how would you describe your character's vocal nature? _____
Basically, how would you describe the way your character likes to dress (casual, tailored, sloppy, neat, colorfully, etc.) __1930s style__ Basically, how would you describe the way your character likes to wear or comb his/her hair? __Like a prostitute__ Select the three or four *major* emotions your character seems to experience the most (Fear, love, hate, anger, etc.) __love, hate__ Give an example *from the text* in which each of the examples you listed are revealed: (use back of page if necessary) _____
__Love - when she says she loves him__
__Hate -__

What is the MF or Motivational Force (spine) of your character (for example, in *Death of a Salesman*, "Willy wants Biff to love him again." State the MF of your character by beginning with the name of your character and the word, "wants . . ." If possible, the spine or "want" should relate to another character or characters in the play.) _____
__She wants to be romantic and fall in love with a doctor__
What is the major beat of action (or key moment of activity and/or decision/choice) in the play for your character (the most important moment in the play for your character):
__When she dances with the cop__

*A bird may also be used, although animals usually provide more humanlike characteristics.

page 2 ROLE ANALYSIS FORM for _____ _Julie Tjaden_
Name of actor/actress _____

List 5 to 10 *major* subtext events in your character's life *prior* to the beginning of the play (these may be revealed by the text or you may have to create them from imaginary biography, provided they are logically related to known facts in the text); examples of the kind of life events that might be included as major are events of family (names of parents, brothers, how old you were when and if they died, etc.), education (how much, where accomplished), marriages and children (if any), divorces, major illnesses, etc. Again, list 5 to 10 *major* subtext events: (just use short phrases, not full sentences) _____

_____ Family lived on a farm _____

_____ She went to San Francisco _____

Briefly describe the *major* activities your character engaged in during the day of action of the play (from rising, up to the first entrance on stage): (just use short phrases, not full sentences) _____
_____ Washing her face _____

_____ Drinking coffee _____

Briefly describe the *major* activity your character engages in during all offstage time after every exit made during the action of the play: (just use short phrases, not full sentences) _____
_____ Crying with Tom _____

_____ Dressing up. _____

Create a brief list of *major* character "idiosyncrasies, likes and dislikes" for your character (for example: likes cheeseburgers and french fries, suffers from insomnia, reads mystery novels, likes Dustin Hoffman movies, hates John Wayne movies, etc.): (use at least 5–8 items) _____

_____ Likes to dress up. Likes men. _____

_____ Likes watching TV. _____

Add any other pertinent notes or comments about your character that you have noted (not covered somehow above), if any:

NOTE: Your director *advises* but does not require that each of you keep a rehearsal and performance "log" or diary for totally personal observations, insights, problems, etc. Later, you will be amazed at the record of growth, development, and human interest you will have caught in your log. (You are at liberty to share this log with your director at any time if you feel it might help your work in any way.) A good log often closes with a personal self-evaluation statement.

"SHORT-FORM ROLE ANALYSIS DOCUMENT." (Name of actor: _T̲j̲a̲d̲e̲n̲_ [Julie])
(Name of role: _K̲i̲t̲t̲y̲ D̲u̲v̲a̲l̲_)

ACTUAL STUDENT ACTRESS SAMPLE: "WELL DONE." (Completed carefully after thorough analysis. See poorly done sample by same actress earlier in this appendix.) (Compare and contrast the two samples in this appendix as a guide to the correct approach in using this document.)

Each actor/actress is asked to complete this and return it. Whenever possible, all answers or comments are to be based strictly on information about your character supplied in the actual text! When this is not possible, you may create answers or comments provided they are *logically related* to information in the text. Your director will discuss your responses with you later, as needed. Note: this is in no way an "academic" assignment; it is rather an opportunity for fresh, original actor creativity, provided in an organic framework for directing and acting which permits and encourages artistic individuality as well as artistic collaboration.

Name of actor/actress _J̲u̲l̲i̲e̲ T̲j̲a̲d̲e̲n̲_ Name of character _K̲i̲t̲t̲y̲ D̲u̲v̲a̲l̲_ Age of character _2̲4̲_ Precise birthdate of character _J̲u̲l̲y̲ 2̲, 1̲9̲1̲5̲_ Astrological sign _C̲a̲n̲c̲e̲r̲_ What significance, if any, to this sign _"̲R̲o̲m̲a̲n̲t̲i̲c̲ a̲n̲d̲ i̲m̲a̲g̲i̲n̲a̲t̲i̲v̲e̲ w̲h̲e̲r̲e̲ t̲h̲e̲ a̲f̲f̲e̲c̲t̲i̲o̲n̲s̲ a̲r̲e̲ c̲o̲n̲c̲e̲r̲n̲e̲d̲."̲_
Generally, how "physically active" is your character? (Describe in a sentence): _I̲ m̲o̲v̲e̲ s̲l̲o̲w̲l̲y̲, w̲e̲a̲k̲l̲y̲, e̲v̲e̲n̲ f̲a̲i̲n̲t̲l̲y̲ a̲t̲ t̲i̲m̲e̲s̲, b̲u̲t̲ w̲/f̲l̲a̲s̲h̲e̲s̲ o̲f̲ q̲u̲i̲c̲k̲n̲e̲s̲s̲ a̲n̲d̲ e̲x̲t̲r̲e̲m̲e̲ e̲n̲e̲r̲g̲y̲ — a̲l̲l̲ d̲u̲e̲, p̲e̲r̲h̲a̲p̲s̲, t̲o̲ m̲a̲l̲n̲u̲r̲t̲r̲i̲t̲i̲o̲n̲._
Name an animal* which in appearance, movement, or manner seems analogous to your role: _A̲l̲l̲e̲y̲ c̲a̲t̲_ What is it about this animal that most specifically relates to your role: _W̲h̲i̲l̲e̲ s̲t̲a̲l̲k̲i̲n̲g̲, I̲ m̲o̲v̲e̲ w̲/a̲ l̲i̲g̲h̲t̲, s̲o̲f̲t̲ s̲t̲e̲p̲. I̲'m̲ a̲l̲s̲o̲ v̲e̲r̲y̲ w̲a̲r̲y̲ o̲f̲ p̲e̲o̲p̲l̲e̲ — m̲y̲ m̲u̲s̲c̲l̲e̲s̲ a̲r̲e̲ f̲u̲l̲l̲ o̲f̲ t̲e̲n̲s̲i̲o̲n̲. W̲h̲e̲n̲ I̲ d̲o̲ r̲e̲l̲a̲x̲, m̲y̲ w̲h̲o̲l̲e̲ b̲o̲d̲y̲ — e̲v̲e̲r̲y̲ m̲u̲s̲c̲l̲e̲ — r̲e̲l̲a̲x̲e̲s̲ T̲o̲t̲a̲l̲l̲y̲._
Can you name a person close to you, family or friend, who seems to be a good deal like your character? If so, name him or her _T̲e̲r̲e̲s̲a̲ G̲i̲l̲m̲o̲r̲e̲_ _____ (relationship) _F̲r̲i̲e̲n̲d̲_
Can you name a famous person who seems to be a good deal like your character? If so, name him or her _J̲u̲l̲i̲e̲ C̲h̲r̲i̲s̲t̲i̲e̲_ Vocally, is your character generally quiet and demure or loud and flamboyant? _N̲e̲i̲t̲h̲e̲r̲_ If neither, how would you describe your character's vocal nature? _s̲h̲a̲r̲p̲ - f̲r̲a̲g̲i̲l̲e̲_
Basically, how would you describe the way your character likes to dress (casual, tailored, sloppy, neat, colorfully, etc.) _C̲l̲a̲s̲s̲y̲_ Basically, how would you describe the way your character likes to wear or comb his/her hair? _F̲r̲e̲e̲ f̲l̲o̲w̲i̲n̲g̲ a̲n̲d̲ l̲o̲n̲g̲_ Select the three or four *major* emotions your character seems to experience the most (Fear, love, hate, anger, etc.) _S̲a̲d̲n̲e̲s̲s̲, A̲n̲g̲e̲r̲, F̲e̲a̲r̲_ Give an example *from the text* in which each of the examples you listed are revealed: (use back of page if necessary) _S̲a̲d̲n̲e̲s̲s̲: "I̲ d̲o̲n̲'t̲ l̲i̲k̲e̲ t̲h̲i̲s̲ l̲i̲f̲e̲."/ A̲n̲g̲e̲r̲: "Y̲o̲u̲ c̲a̲n̲'t̲ p̲u̲s̲h̲ m̲e̲ a̲r̲o̲u̲n̲d̲."/ F̲e̲a̲r̲: "I̲ w̲i̲s̲h̲ I̲ c̲o̲u̲l̲d̲ t̲e̲l̲l̲ y̲o̲u̲ h̲o̲w̲ i̲t̲ m̲a̲k̲e̲s̲ m̲e̲ f̲e̲e̲l̲ T̲o̲ b̲e̲ a̲l̲o̲n̲e̲."_

What is the MF or Motivational Force (spine) of your character (for example, in *Death of a Salesman*, "Willy wants Biff to love him again." State the MF of your character by beginning with the name of your character and the word, "wants . . ." If possible, the spine or "want" should relate to another character or characters in the play.) _____
_I̲ w̲a̲n̲t̲ t̲o̲ h̲o̲o̲k̲ J̲o̲e̲._
What is the major beat of action (or key moment of activity and/or decision/ choice) in the play for your character (the most important moment in the play for your character): _____
_M̲y̲ c̲o̲n̲f̲e̲s̲s̲i̲o̲n̲ t̲o̲ J̲o̲e̲ t̲h̲a̲t̲ I̲'m̲ a̲f̲r̲a̲i̲d̲ t̲o̲ l̲e̲a̲v̲e̲ t̲h̲e̲ s̲t̲r̲e̲e̲t̲s̲ f̲o̲r̲ t̲h̲e̲ s̲a̲k̲e̲ o̲f̲ T̲o̲m̲. (B̲u̲t̲ f̲o̲r̲ J̲o̲e̲, y̲e̲s̲!?̲)_

*A bird may also be used, although animals usually provide more humanlike characteristics.

page 2 ROLE ANALYSIS FORM for _Kitty Duvall_ "The Time of Your Life"
Name of actor/actress _Julie Tjaden_

List 5 to 10 *major* subtext events in your character's life *prior* to the beginning of
the play (these may be revealed by the text or you may have to create them from
imaginary biography, provided they are logically related to known facts in the
text); examples of the kind of life events that might be included as major are
events of family (names of parents, brothers, how old you were when and if they
died, etc.), education (how much, where accomplished), marriages and children
(if any), divorces, major illnesses, etc. Again, list 5 to 10 *major* subtext events:
(just use short phrases, not full sentences) _No formal education - At 13, Papa
died - At 14, brother Louie Killed - At 15, brother Stephen ran away - At 16,
Mama died - Grew up on a farm near Van Wert, Ohio - Struggled in
Chicago w/sister Mary - Got to San Francisco - Left Mary -
Cousin Taught me street walking._

Briefly describe the *major* activities your character engaged in during the day of
action of the play (from rising, up to the first entrance on stage): (just use short
phrases, not full sentences) _Kicked out drunken sailor asleep on
my bed - Wrote Mary a long letter - Walked the streets -
Fed stray cats._

Briefly describe the *major* activity your character engages in during all offstage
time after every exit made during the action of the play: (just use short phrases,
not full sentences) _Act I: Revealed pieces of my life to Tom/Act III:
Relived my childhood - watched sun set - Danced and drank the
night away w/ Joe and Tom / Act V: Moved to St. Francis Hotel -
Bought new dresses - Said goodbye to the streets_

Create a brief list of *major* character "idiosyncrasies, likes and dislikes" for your
character (for example: likes cheeseburgers and french fries, suffers from insomnia, reads mystery novels, likes Dustin Hoffman movies, hates John Wayne movies, etc.): (use at least 5–8 items) _Loves champagne - hates cigarette
smoke - loves toys - likes beer - hates bums - loves daydreaming - hates authority - hates big cities - loves to
dance - loves big shepherd dogs - loves brick homes -
loves fireplaces - loves the ocean - loves fog_

Add any other pertinent notes or comments about your character that you have
noted (not covered somehow above), if any: _Must be careful to
not be too sweet and likeable and weak. Am a
predator who survives - on scraps maybe - but
survives. Must explore why I return to bar in
last act. Am a street - smart predator._

NOTE: Your director *advises* but does not require that each of you keep a rehearsal
and performance "log" or diary for totally personal observations, insights, problems, etc. Later, you will be amazed at the record of growth, development, and
human interest you will have caught in your log. (You are at liberty to share
this log with your director at any time if you feel it might help your work in
any way.) A good log often closes with a personal self-evaluation statement.

Special thanks to actress Julie Tjaden, and her husband, director Todd Tjaden, for
their contributions to this Appendix.)

This book necessarily deals with acting in the drama and theatre of the Western Hemisphere. The primary users of this book speak English and the experience of its author has been fundamentally restricted to English speaking drama and theatre. Nonetheless, as the chapter on Epic/Brechtian drama proves, the influence of Oriental/Eastern drama and theatre on certain facets of Western drama and theatre is undeniable. The dramatic activity of China, Japan, India, Korea, and Southeast Asia presents key lessons to the Western actor in terms of *discipline* and *lengthy, intensive training*. Oriental drama and theatre have always focused on dance and music, puppets and dolls, and inordinately symbolic action. For example, the Japanese Noh plays stress indirectness, suggestion, simplicity, and restraint; Japanese Kabuki drama represents a mixture of Oriental dramatic and theatrical conventions and is the most popular of all Oriental dramas.

Line delivery and movement in Oriental drama are totally controlled by conventions. There are established prescriptions for vocal timbre and pitch; strict rhythm and tempo are deployed; everything is highly stylized; much of the script material is chanted and sung. All movement is related to dance and is characterized by rhythmical, mimetic, and symbolic action. There are literally hundreds of codified gestures for the *entire* body. Specific walks are learned for specific types of characters. All activity is tied to elaborate, ritualistic costuming and makeup (complete to the art of face painting). Training for Oriental acting begins when a child is only seven or eight years of age and continues into adulthood. It is long, intensive training, complete to circus-like tumbling and stunts. Breathing and concentration exercises are fundamental to Oriental acting training.

Such Western producers as Meyerhold, Vakhtangov, Brecht, and Artaud led the way for the Oriental influence on Western acting, drama, and theatre. However, the influence is not widespread enough to signify Oriental productions in most of our professional and academic theatres. Similarly, most acting programs and books justifiably do not deal with Oriental acting techniques. Nonetheless, these facts may change in the years ahead. Certainly, some drama and theatre departments in American colleges and universities are beginning to develop Oriental programs. For example, see the programs at the University of Hawaii, Kansas University, and Pomona College at Claremont, California, to cite but three. Without question, all Western actors should respect the breathing/concentration techniques, physical training, and discipline practiced by Oriental actors.

Appendix E
Acting in Oriental
Drama and Theatre

Glossary

Above. To be or go behind something or someone. The general area farther away from the audience.

Acoustics. The qualities that govern the transmission of sound.

Action. Any change of form or condition on the stage which forcibly affects the mind or senses of the spectator; physical movement; a lively series of stimulations causing a feeling of suspense; a rapid progression of arresting ideas. Action when conceived as the movement of sensory stimuli may be expressed by the voice of the actor as well as by his body.

Ad lib (from Latin *ad libitum*, "at pleasure"). To add, especially to improvise, words or gestures.

Affective memory (Emotion memory or recall; Sensory memory or recall). Recollection of details and situations that have deeply moved an actor to assist him in achieving an inner justification that lets him enter into the character's experiences. Important to the Stanislavski system of acting (popularly called the Method in the United States).

Agon. In Classical Greek drama, a dramatized debate or argument.

Alarum. An offstage sound effect of trumpets, drums, and guns in Elizabethan drama.

Alienation effect (German, ver Fremdungseffekt). Theatrical devices in Brecht's Epic plays designed to estrange the audience from excessive emotional response; to "make strange" action in order to respond to it intellectually.

Antagonist. The person, group, or force in opposition to the central character (hero or protagonist).

Antecedent events. Part of *exposition* in a play; the important actions which have occurred *before* the play begins.

Apron. The part of the stage extending beyond the proscenium curtain line toward the audience.

Arena. A playing space for actors which is surrounded by spectators; in England, a playing space with audience on three sides and a wall at the back of the players. In the United States, the latter is usually called *horseshoe* or even *thrust* staging.

Arras. A curtain. A common term in Elizabethan drama.

Aside. Dialogue intended for the audience with the accepted convention that other characters cannot hear it.

Attack. *See* **Point of attack.**

Audience. The viewers and hearers of a theatre performance.

Audition. A demonstration of performance ability, usually competitive, usually prepared. Many directors distinguish an audition from a *tryout* by designating the latter as a reading without memorization or preparation.

Auditorium. The theatre area usually designated for the audience; often called the *house.*

Auxesis. A rhetorical device used on occasion in verse drama (especially Elizabethan drama) in which ideas are intensified via repetition.

Awareness. A state of sensory alertness; a preparedness to respond to sight, sound, taste, touch, and odor. A sensitive recognition of other stage presences.

Backdrop or Back cloth. A flat, screen, curtain, canvas, or scrim hanging behind the performers, usually painted with a sky or scene.

Backstage. All of the theatre back of the stage proper including the wings, shop, dressing rooms, and so forth.

Balance. The equilization of attention onstage (as between actors, between stage set properties, etc.).

Barnstorm. To tour in a play performing in makeshift theatres.

Baroque. Usually associated with art and architecture, in theatre the term may be associated loosely with eighteenth-century drama, with its elaborate and ornate patterns of language. For example, the work of some of the English sentimentalists and even the work of Sir Richard B. Sheridan.

492

Batten.   A wooden or metal stiffener used behind stage cloth or canvas or as a mount for lighting instruments.

Beats.   A term employed by actors of the Stanislavski system meaning the distance from the beginning to the end of a character's intention, whether explicitly stated in the dialogue or not.

Below.   To be or go in front of something or someone. The stage area closest to the audience in a proscenium theatre.

Blackout.   A sudden extinguishing of all stage lighting; usually used for a theatrical effect at the end of a scene.

Blank Verse.   Any form of unrhymed verse with a regular metric pattern (usually associated with iambic pentameter).

Blocking.   To work out all movement of actors.

Bombast.   Ranting, loud, ornate dramatic speech.

Book.   The nonmusical segments of musical plays.

Borderlights.   *See* **Striplights.**

Bourgeois drama.   Serious plays with middle-class characters, particularly popular in the eighteenth and nineteenth centuries, as in George Lillo's *The London Merchant*, 1731.

Box.   In some theatres an isolated seating area for four to six persons.

Box office.   A place usually at the front of a theatre where tickets are sold.

Box set.   Scenery representing an interior, usually realistic, with three walls, ceiling, doors, and windows.

Broadway.   A famous avenue in the theatre district of New York City. By popular concept, the heart of commercial theatre.

   Off-Broadway.   The more artistic, less commercial *avant-garde* theatre performed in improvised theatres in New York City.

   Off-Off Broadway.   Usually considered the true standard-bearer of Off-Broadway drama since Off-Broadway has become very commercialized.

Build.   The increase of emotion, tension, or energy directed toward a peak or climax.

Burla.   Comic jokes, dialogue, and activity in Commedia dell'Arte.

Business.   Minor physical action, often with the hands, by a performer (includes facial expression).

Cadence.   The measure or beat of any rhythmic motion, as in verse, dance, and music.

Caesura.   A pause or break in verse.

Call.   (1) An announcement listing cast, rehearsals, and performances. (2) Readiness to do anything in the theatre.

Canon.   The undisputed work of an author.

Cast.   (1) Performers in a play. (2) To assign roles to actors.

Catharsis (Katharis).   The purging of emotion and suspense which occurs at the end of a tragedy; experienced by the audience and, at times, by the characters as well.

Center stage or stage center.   A position approximately in the middle of the acting area.

Character.   One of the dramatis personae; the personality of such a figure. The agent(s) of the plot. One of the six key elements of a drama according to Aristotle.

Character role.   Normally an elderly or an eccentric character.

Cheat.   To move or turn slightly to provide more space for other actors or to improve the compositional stage picture. To pretend you can see someone onstage as you speak to him when in reality you cannot. To project the voice more to the audience than to the character you are addressing.

Chorus.   In Greek drama, a group of performers who play a role (in modern drama, the chorus is often supplanted by a narrator). In musical theatre, a group of dancers and/or singers.

Classical. In ancient times, used to designate an author of the "first class." Today, term commonly means an author or work whose greatness is universally recognized.

Clean up. (1) To polish, work, or rehearse a scene to perfect it. (2) To move slightly to afford other actors space and provide a better compositional picture onstage.

Climax. The moment of highest interest in a play which leads to the answer to the MDQ and resolution of the conflict. The climax can be the *major crisis* or *turn,* or it can occur later. In *Hamlet* the *turn* occurs at the end of the play-within-a-play scene in act 3, and the *climax* occurs in the duel scene in act 5. In *Death of a Salesman* the *turn* and *climax* occur together after Biff cries in Willy's arms and Willy exits to commit suicide.

Close. To turn away from the audience.

Clown. A comic figure present in much drama. At times the clown merges with the *Fool,* a *jester* having unique wisdom.

Comedy. One of the two central forms of drama (tragedy is the other). Broadly, comedy is anything that amuses, movement from unhappiness to happiness, or action that excites mirth.

Communion. The connection between actors established primarily through eye contact, listening, touching, and reaction.

Community Theatre. A theatre operated by and for the entertainment and edification of local people of a town or city.

Company. A group of actors who perform together. Also called a troupe.

Complication. An incident which alters the direction of a play's action line (turns the action in a new direction). For example, Hamlet's killing Polonius is a major complication.

Concentration. Complete attention to something as concentration on a task. A key element in effective acting.

Confidant. A character in whom a principal character confides (as Horatio to Hamlet).

Conflict. Forces of opposition, central to the action of most plays.

Constructivism. A scenic and staging movement associated with Meyerhold and Tairov in Russia in which painted realistic scenery was rejected in favor of ladders, platforms, and other constructed items.

Convention. An unrealistic device that the public agrees to tolerate or accept. (For example, it is a convention that one actor cannot hear another speak an aside.)

Counter. To shift position to compensate for the movement of another actor to maintain an effective compositional picture.

Couplet. In verse drama, a pair of poetic lines with end rhyme, usually providing a complete thought.

Cover. To hide from view of the audience, often deliberately, so as not to make obvious some necessary action of artifice.

Crisis (Major crisis). *See* **Turn.**

Cross. A movement onstage from one area to another.

Cue. A signal, usually a word or a gesture, to which an actor or member of the crew must respond.

Curtain. A drapery used to conceal part of the stage. Sometimes the term is used to denote the end of a scene or an act.

Curtain call. The appearance by the cast at the end of a play to receive applause. Generally considered a professional courtesy, it also provides the cast with the opportunity of acknowledging the audience. It is usually self-indulgent rudeness to forgo a curtain call.

Cyclorama, or Cyc. A shell-shaped structure at the rear of the stage, curved at the sides, usually made of cloth. Properly lighted, it gives the illusion of depth and of sky.

Deciding agent. The person or event in a play that resolves the conflict between the forces (between protagonist and antagonist). Often the deciding agent is a third person (such as a girl choosing between male rivals for her hand in marriage), or it is the will and decision of the protagonist (e.g., Hamlet is the deciding agent as well as the protagonist).

Denouement. Unknotting or resolution of the main plot. The end of a play; usually follows the climax.

Designer. One who makes the plans from which scenery, costumes, and the like are constructed.

Deus ex machina. In classical Greek plays a god lowered in a machine or basket to provide an ending for the play. Today, an improbable device used to conclude a work.

Dialogue. Speech between characters; speech of a single character.

Diction. Choice of words or wording in a play. Language. Today, a performer's manner of speaking including pronunciation and phrasing. One of the six key elements of a drama according to Aristotle.

Director (Régisseur). The coordinator of all artists and technicians working on a theatre production.

Double. To play more than one role in a single production. In films, to stand in place of another performer, as for dangerous stunts.

Downstage. Toward the audience on a proscenium stage.

Dramatis personae (Latin, "masks of the play"). The characters in a play.

Drame. A solemn but not tragic play; associated with eighteenth-century bourgeois drama.

Dress the stage. (1) To move slightly to provide more space for other actors and to improve the compositional stage picture. (2) To furnish props and items to hang on the scenery to improve the appearance of the stage.

Drive (Nervosity). The dramatic thrust of character desires in a play. The emotional hungers or nervosity of each character.

Dumb show. A scene having action without words; used frequently in Elizabethan drama.

Emotion. Feelings; impulses manifested outward from within (as grief, joy, anger, etc.).

Emotion memory or recall. *See* **Affective memory.**

Empathy. The projection of one's feelings into a perceived object. Distinguished from *sympathy:* we empathize if we feel *with* a character; we sympathize if we feel *for* a character.

Emphasis. Accent or special focus on an action, line, person, or word.

Ensemble acting. Presentation in which the performance of the group, rather than the individual, is stressed.

Entrance. (1) Act of entering the stage in view of the audience. (2) An opening in a set through which actors may enter.

Epic. The label given to Bertolt Brecht's plays whose aim was to arouse an audience's detached thought. Usually instructive episodic drama in the structural mode of Homer's Epic poems or narratives.

Epilogue. An appendix or concluding address in a play.

Exit. (1) Departure from a stage area. (2) An opening in a set through which actors may leave.

Exposition. The essential information provided the audience to begin the action of a play, or given later to clarify action.

Extra (Supernumerary). One with so small a role in a play that he need have no training or talent (as a court guard who merely stands by the door in a trial-scene).

Farce. A form of comedy that relies on artificial plot contrivance and slapstick or "low," physical activity, as opposed to wit and character depth, for its humor.

Flat. A light wooden or metal frame covered by canvas and used for scenery.

Flies. The area above the stage used for hanging scenery, lighting equipment, and so on.

Floodlight. A lensless lamp that provides broad illumination.

Floor plan (Ground plan). An outline drawing of a stage setting as it would look from above.

Fluff. A blunder or error onstage.

Focal point. The point of greatest interest onstage at any given moment.

Foil. (1) A character who sets off another, as Laertes and Fortinbras set off Hamlet. (2) A piece of fencing equipment.

Folio. A book made of sheets folded once, each sheet providing two leaves or four pages. Shakespeare's plays were first published as a folio in 1623.

Fool. *See* **Clown.**

Footlights. *See* **Striplights.**

Fop. A comic male character from Restoration drama, given to eccentricities and excesses of dress, vanity, and manner. (Such behavior is often played as mere femininity; this is a mistake and contrary to the key factor of *excess.*)

Form. *See* **Play form.**

French Scene. That stage action contained between the entrance and exit of any character in a play.

Gallery. An area above and at the rear of theatres; called a balcony today.

Genre. Type or kind of play (such as, revenge tragedy, Gothic melodrama, and so on).

Gestalt. The synthesis of separate elements of emotion, experience, and the like to constitute an organic whole.

Give. To move a bit to provide space for another actor. To respond or offer emotion, energy, or activity onstage. To provide greater emphasis to someone else onstage.

Given circumstance. A Stanislavski term referring to any dramatic occurrence which affects an actor's playing of a scene.

Greasepaint. Stage makeup. Coloring-matter mixed with grease in sticks or tubes used as base to help the features look natural under artificial illumination.

Greenroom. The traditional name for a theatre lounging room for performers and their guests. (From the actor tradition of waiting on the green or lawn.)

Grid. The framework of beams above the stage area in the flies.

Grotesque. A term in drama referring to the ludicrous or comic (associated with the work of Victor Hugo and Luigi Piradello, as examples).

Ground plan. *See* **Floor plan.**

Ground row. A flat or scenic piece with an irregular profile, usually used as a wall, mountain, hedge, or the like, often used to mask lighting instruments.

Groundlings. The patrons who stand in front of a stage to see a play, particularly in an Elizabethan theatre.

Ham. An incompetent performer who overacts.

Hamartia. A Greek-based word referring to the error in judgment of the hero in tragedy.

Heads up! A stage warning that something (usually scenery) is being lowered (or falling) onstage.

Heavens (Shadow). The canopy area over the stage in Elizabethan drama where an actor could hide from view from other characters or where musicians resided.

Heavy. A solemn major character, especially a villain.

Hero, or Heroine. The central character or protagonist; the leading romantic character.

Hold. To stop or delay action onstage (usually because of laughter or applause.)

Hubris. A Greek-based word for excess pride, the most common form of hamartia.

Humor. The quality of being amusing.

Humour. In ancient physiology, one of the four principal bodily fluids—blood, phlegm, choler (yellow bile), and melancholy (black bile). These humours were believed to influence health and temperament.

Iambic pentameter. A verse form consisting of ten syllables (five iambic feet) to the line. (See Chapter Thirteen.)

Iambia trimeter. A verse composed of three measures, consisting of three dipodies (six feet) in ancient or classical Greek dramatic poetry.

Imagination. The process of forming mental images. The reproduction of images from memory. The mental ability to create original and striking images and concepts. A key element in effective acting.

Imitation (Greek, *mimesis*, "to imitate or imitative"). Not a pejorative term in the theatre. It implies "making" or "re-creating" or "representing" in the theatre.

Impersonate. To invest with personality; to personify; to assume or act the person or character.

Improvisation. Invention of lines and stage business by performers.

In. To the center of the stage.

Ingenue. (1) The role of an innocent young woman. (2) The actress who plays such a role.

Intention. A Stanislavski term for an actor's real reason for being in a scene, regardless of the actor's dialogue. *See* **Subtext.**

Interlude. Light entertainment, usually musical, while scenery is being shifted. In sixteenth-century England, a short farce play.

Intermission. A period between scenes or acts permitting audiences to go to the theatre lobby.

Intuition. Immediate comprehension or knowledge of something without the conscious use of reasoning.

Irony. A condition in plays in which the truth is the reverse of what the participants think. Irony is usually more fully understood by the audience than by the characters.

Jester. *See* **Clown.**

Jig. A short farce, sung and danced at the end of some Elizabethan plays.

Kill. To spoil by accident or deliberately cease any activity onstage.

Kinesics. The study of body motions as related to the nonverbal aspects of interpersonal communication.

Lazzi. Comic business in the Commedia dell'Arte.

Lead. A principal role.

Legitimate drama. In eighteenth-century England, a play performed in a *licensed* theatre. Today, a play, in contrast to a musical, vaudeville, film, and the like.

Libretto. The text or "book" of the dialogue and lyrics for a musical play.

Lighting. Illumination of the theatre, especially of the stage. Today, the province of artistic designers and technicians.

Limelight. (1) A stage lighting device of the nineteenth century which produced illumination by directing an oxyhydrogen flame against a piece of lime. (2) Today, to give special focus or attention.

Line. (1) A rope or wire used to hang scenery. (2) Dialogue in a play.

Living Newspaper. A cinematic dramatic form in the United States in the 1930s in which factual data and dramatic vignette were integrated. Part of the brief Federal Theatre Project headed by Hallie Flanagan Davis (1890–1969), the Living Newspaper produced such works as *Triple A Plowed Under* in 1936.

Lobby. The lounge area for spectators in a theatre, usually at the front of the building.

Major crisis. *See* **Turn.**

Major Dramatic Question (MDQ). The question upon which the action of a play focuses. Usually the MDQ is not presented as a direct question in the script, but is recognized to be the key action factor by the audience. For example, the audience ponders whether Hamlet will revenge his father's murder and restore order to the Kingdom.

Make up. To disguise one's face by using cosmetics, false hair, nose putty, and the like.

Makeup. Materials applied to disguise the face.

Malapropism. The mistaken use of a word in place of another of similar sound. (See Mrs. Malaprop in Sir Richard Sheridan's *The Rivals*.) Example: *it will percussion the blow* for *it will cushion the blow.*

Marionette. A doll controlled from above or below by rods, wires, or strings.

Mask. A face-covering worn by many actors, especially in Greek drama and commedia dell'arte.

Masque. An entertainment of the Renaissance using lavish scenery and costumes.

Matinee. (from French, *matin*, "morning"). An afternoon (and, rarely, a morning) performance.

MDQ. *See* **Major dramatic question.**

Melodrama. A form of serious drama that uses artificial plot contrivances, stock characters, unexpected reversals, happy endings with "poetic justice," and sensational effects. (A valid and respectable form of drama although one type of it is "kidded" as comedy, such as *The Drunkard.* A higher form of it is a play such as *The Desperate Hours.*)

Melody, or Music. (1) Actual music in a play. (2) Any melodic element such as an arrangement of words. One of the six key elements of a drama according to Aristotle.

Method. An American adaptation of the Stanislavski system that focuses on inner motivation, whose chief exponent is an American school of acting, the New York Actor's Studio.

Mezzanine. The front or first balcony in a theatre.

Mime. An ancient dramatic entertainment in which acrobats, jugglers, singers, dancers, actors, and actresses perform. *See also* **Pantomime.**

Mise-en-scène. The stage setting including the scenery, lighting, and arrangement of actors.

Mono-Drama (Mono-Acting). (1) A piece for one actor. (2) One performer doing several roles.

Monologue. (1) A long speech delivered by one character. (2) A performance by a single actor.

Mood. The dominant atmosphere created by a production—usually a combination of tempo, imagery, rhythm, sound, lighting, scenery, costuming, acting, and so forth.

Motivating Force (MF; Spine; Super-Objective). The central emotional hunger or drive of a character; what the character wants above all, usually expressed relative to other characters. For example, the MF or spine of Willy Loman is that he wants to regain the love of his son, Biff; that is Willy's Super-Objective.

Motivation. Ground in character and situation that make behavior plausible.

Multiple setting (Simultaneous setting). A stage that displays at one time several locales.

Musical comedy (Musical theatre). A piece in which songs and dances are integrated to form a story.

Narrator. One who tells a story rather than enacting it. (See the Stage Manager in Thornton Wilder's *Our Town*.)

Naturalism. A heightened style of realism. "A slice of life."

Neoclassicism. New or revived classicism. (As in the 17th Century French theatre and the late 17th, early 18th Century English theatre.)

Neon acting. Overacting; performing everything with great emphasis. Usually a very ineffective kind of performance unless varied.

Nervosity. *See* **Drive.**

Obligatory scene (Scene a faire). (1) A scene in a play which an audience foresees and desires and whose absence it may, with reason, resent. (2) The necessary and most dramatic confrontation between two characters.

Observation. (1) The act of studying something closely. (2) The act of learning by observing (in acting, for the purpose of imitation). A key element in effective acting.

Off-Broadway. *See* **Broadway.**

Off-Off Broadway. *See* **Broadway.**

Offstage. The part of the stage out of view of the audience.

Onstage. The acting area of a stage in view of the audience.

Open. To turn more toward the audience.

Organic. Acting made up of systematically interrelated parts; theatre work which promotes actor creativity; working from within a group with a common goal; guided acting rather than commanded.

Out. A direction away from the center of the stage, often toward the audience.

Out Front. Refers to the auditorium, house, or audience.

Overlap. To move or speak slightly ahead of cue.

Overplay. To act with more exaggeration than is needed.

Oxymoron. A thing is described in terms of its opposite. ("A wise fool.") A favorite device of Shakespeare.

Pace (Pacing; Tempo). The speed with which a play or actor moves.

Pantomime. An ancient dramatic performance featuring a solo performer who gestures and dances without using dialogue. *See also* **Mime.**

Parallel movement. When two or more actors move in the same direction at the same time.

Pathos. A quality that evokes pity.

Peripeteia (from Greek for "reversal"). A plot term indicating a sudden change in conditions, usually in tragedy.

Personalization. A process whereby the actor discovers and explores in himself characteristics, qualities, and attributes which are legitimate dimensions of the role he is creating.

Pickup. To increase the playing pace or to shorten the interval between cues.

Pin. *See* **Rail.**

Pit. An area at the front of the stage where the orchestra sits.

Pity and Fear. The chief emotions inspired by tragedy (according to Aristotle).

Places! A command for actors to get in position to begin a rehearsal or performance.

Plant. A device to call attention to something which will have special significance later in a play.

Play. (1) A story communicated by impersonators. (2) To act.

Play doctor. One called in to patch up a play's weaknesses by rewriting, cutting, and adding.

Play form. The characteristic nature of play such as tragedy, comedy, farce, melodrama, and the like (as opposed to play type, which refers to the stylistic mode of the play, e.g., Realism, Expressionism, etc.).

Play type. The stylistic mode of a play such as, realistic, expressionistic, and the like (as opposed to play form such as tragedy, comedy, farce, melodrama, etc.).

Play up (Plug). To emphasize a key moment.

Playhouse. A theatre.

Play-Within-A-Play. A representation of a drama within the drama itself (as in *Hamlet*, act 3, scene 2).

Plot. Story organization. The most important ingredient in a play according to Aristotle—*the* key element in the six elements of a play.

Plug. *See* **Play up.**

Poetic drama. A play whose language is metrical.

Poetic justice. A term denoting reward of the virtuous and punishment of the vicious, coined by Thomas Rymer in 1678.

Point of attack. The earliest incident in a play that arouses strong audience interest and exposes the basic conflict of the play; the point at which an author chooses to begin the story.

Practical. A functioning prop or piece of scenery which can actually be *used* by the actor and which is not merely decorative or ornamental (as a window that can actually be opened).

Precast. To select actors for roles prior to auditions or tryouts. A very unpopular and infrequent practice, particularly in educational and amateur theatre.

Preface. A statement by the dramatist that serves as an introduction to the play.

Premiere. The first public performance of a work.

Presentational. The style of performance which is openly theatrical and delivered directly to the audience. (A nonrealistic device.)

Preview. A tryout before an audience of a play previous to the performance considered "the opening."

Producer. In England and Ireland, the director, but in the United States, the entrepreneur chiefly concerned with raising money. The person who often hires the artistic staff.

Production. (1) A dramatic entertainment onstage. (2) The process of getting the work onstage.

Project. To accentuate or intensify vocal delivery, volume, or articulation; to accentuate or intensify movement and emotion as well.

Prologue. A preface or introduction.

Prompter. One who reminds forgetful actors of their lines. Often the assistant director-assistant stage manager.

Property, or Prop. An object or article used in a play and called for in the script.
>   **Hand props.** Props used by the characters in a play.
>   **Set props.** Furniture and other standing props; often unused by the characters in a play.
>   **Trim or Dress props.** Objects hanging on the walls of a set.

Proscenium arch stage. A playing area framed in the front and thus separated from the audience.

Protagonist (from Greek for "first contender"). The chief figure in a play.

Puppet. A doll that can be manipulated. The operator places his hand into the body of a puppet to manipulate it.

Pun. A play on words; one word suggests another that is pronounced similarly but with different meaning. (Hair; hare.)

Quibble. An elaborate pun (see above). Especially popular with Elizabethan playwrights.

Quarto. A book made of sheets folded twice, each sheet supplying four leaves or eight pages. (Shakespeare's plays were issued in quartos before they were collected in a folio.)

Rail (Pin; Tie-Off; Trim). Part of the flies and grid system used to hang scenery in a theatre; related to sandbag and counterweight flying systems.

Raillery. Witty banter and repartee.

Raisonneur. A character in a chorus; any character who serves as a "mouthpiece" for the author.

Raked stage. A playing area that slopes upward toward the rear wall. In present-day theatre, the rake is usually under the spectator area, rather than under the acting area.

Ramp. A sloping platform used in the manner of a step unit.

Rant. Wild, violent language.

Realism. A style like life; carefully selected or crafted to represent life believably.

Régisseur.   In Germany and Russia, the director of a play.

Rehearsal.   A practice performance of a dramatic work or part of the work. Rehearsals: reading, line-check, blocking, working, polishing, technical, run-through, dress and costume.

Relaxation.   An unstrained but prepared state of readiness. A key element in effective acting.

Repartee.   Witty remarks and clever, unexpected answers, usually in rapid delivery.

Repertory (Repertoire).   The body of dramatic works a company is trained to perform in turn or frequently. A *Repertory Company* performs a number of plays daily, weekly, or monthly rather than a single play for an extended run.

Response (Respond).   A player's manifest reaction to another presence on the stage. Especially, a particular reaction called forth by a particular act.

Representational.   The style of performance which is illusory and represents life with fidelity; delivered only between characters who ignore the audience whom they pretend is nonexistent (or hiding behind an imaginary "fourth wall").

Return.   A flat set parallel to the audience at the downstage edge of the set jutting into the wings just above the tormentor. Any similar flat attached to a larger piece of scenery.

Reversal.   (See Peripeteia.)

Revival.   A production of a play usually long unperformed.

Revue.   A loose collection of musical numbers, skits, comic bits, and the like.

Rhythm.   The combination of tempo, emotion, mood; imagery, stress, beat, sound, accent, motion, and so forth, that creates a pattern of activity. A play has a rhythm; a production has a rhythm; an actor and his role have a rhythm.

Ritual.   A ceremonial act.

Routine.   Specially rehearsed stage actions, lines, songs, and dances.

Run.   (1) The period during which a company performs a play. (2) To run through a scene or act without interruption from the director.

Satire.   A work ridiculing aspects of human behavior, usually socially corrective in nature and intended to provoke both laughter and thought.

Scansion.   Determining the meter of verse by analysis of metric feet, syllables, and accents.

Scenario.   A detailed outline of a dramatic entertainment.

Scene.   A subunit of an act or a play.

Scène à faire.   (See Obligatory Scene.)

Score.   To determine character activity, business, and pantomimic dramatization. To score a role.

Scrim.   (1) A loosely woven gauzelike fabric. (2) A theatre drop. When lighted from the front, a scrim becomes visible, almost opaque, and when lighted from the back it becomes semitransparent, nearly disappearing. A scrim with a scene painted on it is called a *transparency*.

Script.   The text of a dramatic work.

Sensory memory or recall.   *See* **Affective memory.**

Set speech.   A device where a long speech accomplishes many points without another character interrupting.

Shadow.   *See* **Heavens.**

Share.   Equal attention for two or more actors.

Show.   A theatrical entertainment.

Side.   A sheet containing an actors lines, cues, stage directions, and so forth.

Sight line.   The line of vision from any seat in the spectators' area to the stage.

Simultaneous setting.   *See* **Multiple setting.**

Sketch (Skit).   A short comic entertainment.

Slapstick.   A board used by comics in classical plays to strike other characters in buffonery. Broad, physical farce action.

Soap Opera. Domestic melodrama on radio and television.

Soliloquy. A speech wherein a character utters thoughts aloud while alone; usually delivered directly to an audience and less frequently as self-meditation given aloud.

Sonnet. A form of lyric poetry (see the work of Shakespeare). A regularized form of fourteen lines with a set rhyme scheme.

Soubrette. (1) A minor young female role, usually a maid. (2) An actress who plays such a role.

Sound effect. An imitative sound, often performed offstage. Can be produced "live," on record, on tape, and by machinery.

Spectacle. *All* that is seen or heard onstage, including the actors. Today, that which appeals to the eye, such as lavish scenery. One of the six key elements of drama according to Aristotle.

Speech tag. The name of the speaker in a play, or, the stage directions.

Spine (Super-Objective). *See* **Motivating force (MF).**

Stage business. *See* **Business.**

Stage center. *See* **Center stage.**

Stage left. Left of stage center; on the actor's left facing the audience.

Stage manager. The person who coordinates the efforts of the producer, director, playwright, actors, technicians, and the like. He "runs" the production during performances.

Stage right. Right of stage center; on the actor's right facing the audience.

Stage time. The running time of a play. (Dramatic time is the fictional time covered by the action of the play.)

Star. A leading performer whose appeal is so great that his name may precede the title of the play.

Static. Little or no movement; a slow pace.

Steal. When one actor draws attention to himself at the expense of other actors (a practice greatly frowned upon when not called for in the script).

Stichomythia. In classical tragedy, individual lines of verse dialogue assigned to alternate speakers.

Stock character. Any traditional, stereotypical character (such as Harlequin).

Stock company. A repertory group attached to a theatre which commonly changes plays weekly, as in summer stock (the straw-hat circuit).

Straight role. A role without marked characterization; not very particularized or eccentric (normally a young man or young woman).

Straw-Hat circuit. *See* **Stock company.**

Striplights. A lighting unit consisting of a row of lamps. When on the floor at the front of the stage called *footlights*. When suspended on iron pipes overhead called *borderlights*.

Strong. High attention value.

Struggle. The major action line of complication in a play. The longest segment of a play (its body).

Style. (1) The mode of expression. (2) The essence or truth of a particular reality. (3) The total work of art: its material, its language, its historical era, its customs, and the like. (See Introduction to Part Two of this book for a full discussion of style.)

Subject issues. The basic subject matter and questions raised by a play, usually expressed by a single word such as incest, murder, or justice.

Subordinate. To restrict focus or emphasis.

Subtext (Intention). A term common to both the Stanislavski system and the Method. Refers to the meaning underlying dialogue and stage directions. Subtext may include invented autobiographical material about a character provided that it is clearly related to the text and not merely arbitrary.

Subtitle. The second or alternate title used for some plays.

Suffering. *Any* emotion felt by a character. Part of Plot, according to Aristotle.

Supernumerary. *See* **Extra.**

Surrealism. A literary, dreamlike style in theatre promulgated as a reaction against realism. (See the plays of Alred Jarry.)

Symbolism. A late nineteenth century antirealistic movement in theatre focused on the spiritual, symbolic, and mystical. (See the work of Maurice Maeterlinck.)

Synopsis. A summary of a play's action.

Tableau. A picture presented on stage by motionless actors.

Tag line. The final line before an exit, before the end of a scene, act, or play, or at the end of a joke.

Take stage. To achieve prominent emphasis or to command a scene or situation.

Teaser. Scenic mask (a drop) at the top of the stage.

Telescope. To overlap the reading of lines or execution of business.

Tempo. *See* **Pace.**

Tetralogy. A group of four plays, each complete, but which tell a larger story. (Such as Shakespeare's *Richard II, Henry IV, Part I, Henry IV, Part II,* and *Henry V*.)

Text. The dialogue and stage directions of a play without reference to the underlying meaning.

Theatre or Theater. (1) A seeing place; a hearing place. (2) A playhouse. (3) A body of plays.

Theme. The intellectual content in a play. Generally considered to be that idea basic to the thought of the play; the author's central idea. Usually the theme is expressed in one full sentence using an active verb: Pride taken to excess causes destruction. *See also* **Thought, or Idea.**

Thesis play. A play in which the dramatist argues a point of view, such as Ibsen's, *A Doll's House.*

Three Unities. Unity of time, place, and action; a prescriptive theory of drama and play action constructed by Renaissance Italian and French critics; often *mistakenly* attributed to Aristotle.

Thought, or Idea. The intellectual content of a play including its theme or central idea. One of the six key elements of a drama according to Aristotle.

Throw away. To deliberately underplay a line or business. Often used to place greater emphasis elsewhere.

Thrust stage. *See* **Arena.**

Tie-Off. *See* **Rail.**

Timing. The art of delivering words or performing movement at the effective instant.

Tirade. A long declamatory speech.

Top. To emphasize a line or an action to make it more emphatic than the preceding dialogue.

Tormentor. Scenic mask at the sides of the stage.

Tragedy. One of the two major forms of drama (the other is comedy). It involves suffering and frequently death and contains universal truths. For Aristotle, a tragedy was a dramatic imitation of action of high and serious importance.

Tragic flaw. (See Hamartia.)

Tragicomedy. A play which mixes tragic and comic material to a suitable balance, or, which emphasizes tragedy but ends happily.

Transparency. A gauze theatre drop with a scene painted on it. *See also* **Scrim.**

Trap. Door or opening cut into the floor of the stage for access to the cellar or area below.

Trilogy. A unit of three works. For example, *Oresteia* by Aeschylus.

Trim. *See* **Rail.**

Tryout. *See* **Audition.**

Turn (Crisis, or Major crisis). The high point of suspense when a decision or action occurs which turns the rising action of a play toward an immediate or eventual climax and denouement (ending). The key turning point of a play.

Type. *See* **Play type.**

Type casting. A theatre practice in which performers are cast according to their age and physical and personality characteristics.

Underplay. To deliberately restrict or de-emphasize emotion when acting. To de-emphasize delivery and stage action.

Understudy. One who prepares a role normally performed by another in order to substitute in the role when necessary.

Upstage. Away from the audience in a proscenium theatre.

Vaudeville. (1) A stage entertainment of song, dance, acrobatics, skits, trained animal acts, and the like. (2) A series of speciality acts. (3) A short comic play or skit.

Vehicle. A play especially suited to exhibit the acting skills of a performer or company.

Villain. A type of character predisposed to evil or doing harm. (The villain is featured as a figure of evil in melodrama.)

Walk-on. A small role without lines. *See* **Extra.**

Wardrobe mistress. The person who collects, cares for, and stores costumes.

Weak. Low attention value or weak position onstage.

Well-made play. A play with suspense that relies on a tight, cleverly constructed plot, as in the plays of Scribe, Sardou, and Ibsen.

Willing suspension of disbelief. Samuel Coleridge's phrase to identify the basis upon which "poetic faith" is operated in the theatre. An audience usually does this to appreciate and "believe" the play being enacted before it.

Wing. The space offstage right or left of the acting area.

Wit. (1) Knowledge, sagacity, good sense. (2) The sudden ingenious association of ideas and words, often amusing.

Zanni. Comic characters (usually servants) in Commedia dell'Arte.

Altman, George, et al. *Theatre Pictorial: A History of World Theatre as Recorded in Drawings, Paintings, Engravings, and Photographs.* Berkeley: University of California Press, 1953.

Archer, William. *Masks or Faces.* New York: Hill & Wang, 1957.

Arnott, Peter. *The Theatre and Its Time: An Introduction.* Boston: Little Brown and Company, 1981.

Barton, Lucy. *Historic Costume for the Stage.* Boston: Walter H. Baker Co., 1940.

Benedetti, Robert L. *The Actor At Work.* 3d Ed. Englewood Cliffs, N.J.: Prentice-Hall, 1981.

Blunt, Jerry. *The Composite of Acting.* New York: Macmillan Co., 1966.

Bowman, Walter P., and Ball, Robert H. *Theatre Language: A Dictionary of the English of the Drama and Stage from Medieval to Modern Times.* New York: Theatre Arts Books, 1961.

Brockett, Oscar G. *The Essential Theatre.* (Condensed version.) New York: Holt, Rinehart, and Winston, 1976.

———. *The Theatre An Introduction.* 4th Ed. New York: Holt, Rinehart, and Winston, 1979.

———. *History of the Theatre.* 4th Ed. Boston: Allyn and Bacon, Inc., 1982.

Brockett, Oscar G., and Findlay, Robert. *Century of Innovation: A History of European and American Drama Since 1870.* Englewood Cliffs, N.J.: Prentice-Hall, 1973.

Brockett, Oscar G.; Becker, Samuel; and Bryant, Donald. *A Bibliographical Guide to Research in Speech and Dramatic Art.* Chicago: Scott, Foresman and Company, 1963.

Bronner, Edwin J. *The Encyclopedia of the American Theatre, 1900–1975.* New York: A.S. Barnes & Co., 1980.

Cartnell, V. H., ed. *Plot Outlines of 100 Famous Plays.* New York: Doubleday, 1926.

Chinoy, Helen Krich and Linda Walsh Jenkins, eds. *Women in American Theatre: Careers, Images, Movements.* New York: Crown Publishers, 1981.

Clark, Barrett H., ed. *European Theories of the Drama.* New. rev. Henry Popkin. New York: Crown Publishers, 1965.

Clay, James H., and Krempel, Daniel. *The Theatrical Image.* New York: McGraw-Hill Book Co., 1967.

Clayes, Stanley A. *Drama and Discussion.* 2d. ed. Englewood-Cliffs, N.J.: Prentice-Hall, 1978.

Clurman, Harold. "Actors in Style—and Style in Actors." *New York Times Magazine,* 7 December 1952, pp. 26–38.

Cohen, Robert. *Theatre.* Palo Alto: Mayfield Publishing Co., 1981.

Cole, David. *The Theatrical Event.* Middletown, Ct.: Wesleyan University Press, 1975.

Corey, Irene. *The Mask of Reality: An Approach to Design for the Theatre.* Anchorage, Ky.: Anchorage Press, 1968.

Corson, Richard. *Stage Makeup.* 6th Ed. Englewood Cliffs, N.J.: Prentice-Hall, 1981.

Coquelin, Constant. *The Art of the Actor.* New York: Crown Publishers, 1953.

Corrigan, Robert W. *Comedy: Meaning and Form.* 2d. Ed. New York: Harper & Row, 1981.

———. *Tragedy: Vision and Form.* 2d. Ed. New York: Harper & Row, 1981.

Dezseran, Louis. *The Student Actor's Handbook: Theatre Games and Exercises.* Palo Alto: Mayfield Publishing Co., 1975.

Diderot, Denis. *The Paradox of Acting.* New York: Hill & Wang, 1957.

Dramatic Index (1909–1949). Boston: F. W. Faxon, Inc., 1910–1950.

Duerr, Edwin. *The Length and Depth of Acting.* New York: Holt, Rinehart and Winston, 1962.

Dukore, Bernard F. *Dramatic Theory and Criticism. Greeks to Grotowski.* New York: Holt, Rinehart, and Winston, 1974.

Dury, F. K. W. *Dury's Guide to Best Plays.* New York: Scarecrow Press, 1953.

Emery, Joy. *Stage Costume Technique.* Englewood Cliffs, N.J.: Prentice-Hall, 1981.

Elam, Keir. *The Semiotics of Theatre and Drama.* New York: Methuen, 1980.

Ganz, Arthur. *Realms of the Self: Variations on A Theme in Modern Drama.* New York: New York University Press, 1980.

Farber, Donald C. *Producing Theatre: A Comprehensive Legal and Business Guide.* New York: Drama Book Specialists, 1981.

Gassner, John. *Masters of the Drama.* 3rd ed. New York: Dover Publications, 1954.

Geisinger, Marion. *Plays, Players, and Playwrights.* New York: Hart Publishing Co., 1971.

George, Kathleen. *Rhythm In Drama.* Pittsburgh: University of Pittsburgh Press, 1980.

Gilman, Richard. *The Making of Modern Drama.* New York: Hill & Wang, 1975.

Gillette, A. S. and J. Michael Gillette. *Stage Scenery.* 3d. Ed. New York: Harper & Row, 1981.

Gillette, J. Michael. *Designing With Light: An Introduction to Stage Lighting.* Palo Alto: Mayfield Publishing Co., 1978.

Goodman, Randolph. *Drama on Stage.* 2d ed. New York: Holt, Rinehart, and Winston, 1978.

Gradus, Ben. *Directing: The Television Commercial.* New York: Hastings House, 1981.

Guthrie, Tyrone. *Tyrone Guthrie on Acting.* New York: Viking Press, 1971.

Hansen, Henry Harold. *Costumes and Styles.* New York: E. P. Dutton & Co., 1956.

Hapgood, Elizabeth R., ed. *Constantin Stanislavski: Stanislavski's Legacy.* London: Eyre Methuen, 1981.

Hartnoll, Phyllis, ed. *The Oxford Companion to the Theatre.* 2nd ed. London: Oxford University Press, 1957.

Hatlen, Theodore. *Orientation to the Theatre.* 3d. Ed. Englewood Cliffs, N.J.: Prentice-Hall, 1981.

Heinig, Ruth and Lyda Stillwell. *Creative Drama For The Classroom Teacher.* 2d. Ed. Englewood Cliffs, N.J.: Prentice-Hall, 1981.

Hodgins, Gordon W. *The Broadway Musical. A Complete LP Discography.* Metuchen, N.J.: Scarecrow Press, 1980.

Jeffri, Joan. *The Emerging Arts: Management, Survival, and Growth.* New York: Praeger, 1980.

Johnston, Keith. *Impro: Improvisation and the Theatre.* New York: Theatre Arts Books, 1979.

Jones, Margo. *Theatre-in-the-Round,* New York: Harper & Row, 1951.

Kalter, Joanmarie. *Actors on Acting. Performing in Theatre & Film Today.* New York: Sterling Pub. Co., 1980.

Kernodle, George R. "Style, Stylization, and Styles of Acting." *Educational Theatre Journal,* December 1960, pp. 251–61.

King, Nancy. *A Movement Approach to Acting.* Englewood Cliffs, N.J.: Prentice-Hall, 1981.

Kislan, Richard. *The Musical. A Look at the American Musical Theatre.* Englewood Cliffs, N.J.: Prentice-Hall, 1980.

Knapp, Bettina. *Theatre & Alchemy.* Detroit: Wayne State University Press, 1980.

Kuritz, Paul. *Playing. An Introduction to Acting.* Englewood Cliffs, N.J.: Prentice-Hall, 1982.

Leese, Sue and Moira Packer. *Creative Dance For Schools.* Boston: Plays, Inc., 1981.

Levine, Mindy with Off-Off Broadway Alliance (OOBA). *New York's Other Theatre: A Guide to Off-Off Broadway.* New York: Avon/Discus, 1981.

Long, Beverly and Mary Hopkins. *Performing Literature: An Introduction to Oral Interpretation.* Englewood Cliffs, N.J.: Prentice-Hall, 1981.

Lounsbury, Warren. *Backstage from A to Z.* Seattle: University of Washington Press, 1959.

Lucas, F. L. *Tragedy: Serious Drama in Relation to Aristotle's Poetics.* Totowa, N.J.: Barnes & Noble, 1981.

Machlin, Evangeline. *Teaching Speech for the Stage: A Manual for Class Instruction.* New York: Theatre Arts Books, 1980.

Mersand, Joseph, ed. *Guide to Play Production.* New York: Appleton-Century-Croft, 1953.

Molinari, Cesare. *Theatre through the Ages.* Tr. Colin Hamer. New York: McGraw-Hill, 1975.

Murry, J. Middleton. *The Problem of Style.* London: Oxford University Press, 1968.

Nagler, Alois M. *Source Book of Theatrical History.* Orig. title: *Sources of Theatrical History.* New York: Dover Publications, 1952.

Nicoll, Allardyce. *The Development of the Theatre.* 5th ed. New York: Harcourt Brace Jovanovich, 1966.

Nicoll, Allardyce. *World Drama from Aeschylus to Anouilh.* New York: Harcourt Brace Jovanovich, 1949.

Oxenford, Lyn. *Design for Movement.* New York: Theatre Arts Books, 1951.

Prisk, Berneice, and Byers, Jack A. *The Theatre Student: Costuming.* New York: Richards Rosen Press, 1970.

Rae, Kenneth, ed. *International Dictionary of Technical Terms.* New York: Theatre Arts Books, 1900.

Redgrave, Michael. *Mask or Face.* New York: Theatre Arts Books, 1958.

Reinhardt, Paul D. "Movement in Period Plays." *Educational Theatre Journal,* March 1962, pp. 50–55.

Roberts, Vera Mowry. *On Stage: A History of Theatre.* Rev. ed. New York: Harper & Row, 1974.

Rossi, Alfred. *Astonish Us in the Morning.* (Tyrone Guthrie) Detroit: Wayne St. U., 1981.

Russell, Douglas. *Period Style for the Theatre.* Boston: Allyn and Bacon, Inc., 1980.

Saint-Denis, Michel. *Theatre: The Rediscovery of Style.* New York: Theatre Arts Books, 1969.

Shank, Theodore, ed. *A Digest of 500 Plays.* New York: Crowell-Collier, 1963.

Stern, Lawrence. *School and Community Theatre Management: A Handbook for Survival.* Boston: Allyn and Bacon, Inc., 1979.

Stevenson, Isabelle. *The Tony Award.* New York: Crown, 1980.

Stuart, Donald C. *The Development of Dramatic Art.* New York: Dover Publications, 1928. Paperback reprint.

Styan, J. L. *Drama Stage and Audience.* Cambridge: University Press, 1975.

Theatre and Stage: An Encyclopedic Guide to the Performance of All Amateur Dramatic, Operatic, and Theatrical Work. (Two volumes.) Ed. by Harold Dawms. Westport, Ct.: Greenwood Press, Inc., 1978.

Van Laan, Thomas F. *The Idiom of Drama.* Cornell University Press, 1970.

Vaughn, Jack. *Drama A to Z. A Handbook.* New York: Ungar, 1978.

————. *Early English Dramatists: From the Beginnings to 1900* (World Dramatists.) New York: Ungar, 1981.

Wagenknecht, Edward. *Seven Daughters of the Theatre.* New York: Da Capo Press, Inc., 1964.

Way, Brian. *Audience Participation: Theatre For Young People.* Boston: Walter H. Baker Co., 1981.

Wickham, Glynne. *Early English Stages 1300 to 1600: Volume Three, Plays and Their Makers to 1576.* New York: Columbia University Press, 1981.

Wilmeth, Don. *The Language of American Popular Entertainment: A Glossary of Argot, Slang, and Terminology.* Westport, Ct.: Greenwood Press, 1981.

Wilson, Edwin. *The Theatre Experience.* Rev. Ed. New York: McGraw-Hill Book Co., 1980.

Wilson, Garff B. "What Is Style in Acting?" *Quarterly Journal of Speech.* April 1955, pp. 127–32.

508

Rolf Hochhuth. From *The Deputy*. Reprinted by permission of Grove Press, Inc. Copyright © 1964 by Grove Press, Inc.

Henrik Ibsen. From *The Wild Duck*. From *Eleven Plays—An Introduction to Drama,* edited by Gerald Weales. Reprinted with the permission of W. W. Norton and Company.

Eugene Ionesco. From *The Chairs*. From *Four Plays*, by Eugene Ionesco. Reprinted by permission of Grove Press, Inc. Copyright © 1958 by Grove Press, Inc.

Jim Jacobs and Warren Casey. From *Grease*. Reprinted by permission of Bridget Aschenberg, International Creative Management, 40 West 57 St., New York, New York 10019.

Copyright © 1971, 1972 by Warren Casey and Jim Jacobs.

International Copyright secured. All Rights Reserved.

Caution: Professionals and amateurs are hereby warned that *Grease,* being fully protected under the copyright laws of the United States, the British Empire including the Dominion of Canada, and all other countries of the Copyright Union, is subject to royalty. All rights, including professional, amateur, motion picture, recitation, lecturing, public reading, radio and television broadcasting, and the rights of translation into foreign languages, are strictly reserved. Particular emphasis is laid on the question of readings, permission for which must be obtained in writing from the author's agent. All inquiries should be addressed to the author's representative, Bridget Aschenberg, International Famous Agency, 40 W. 57 St., New York, N.Y. 10019.

Georg Kaiser. From *From Morn to Midnight*. From *Introduction to Drama,* edited by Robert C. Roby and Barry Ulanov. Reprinted with the permission of McGraw-Hill Book Company, Robert C. Roby, and Barry Ulanov.

Arthur L. Kopit. From *Oh Dad, Poor Dad, Mamma's Hung You in the Closet and I'm Feelin' So Sad*. Reprinted with the permission of Farrar, Straus & Giroux, Inc. from *Oh Dad, Poor Dad, Mamma's Hung You in the Closet and I'm Feelin' So Sad* by Arthur Kopit, Copyright © 1959, 1960 by Arthur L. Kopit.

Mark Medoff. From *When You Comin' Back, Red Ryder?* Reprinted by permission of James T. White & Company.

Arthur Miller. From *Death of a Salesman* by Arthur Miller. Copyright 1949 by Arthur Miller. Reprinted by permission of The Viking Press, Inc.

Jason Miller. From *That Championship Season* by Jason Miller. Copyright © 1972 by Jason Miller. Reprinted by permission of Atheneum Publishers.

All rights reserved. No part of this publication may be reproduced, stored in a retrieval system, or transmitted, in any form or by any means, electronic, mechanical, photocopying, recording or otherwise, without the prior permission of the publishers.

That Championship Season is the sole property of the above-named copyright owners and is fully protected by copyright. It may not be acted by professionals or amateurs without written permission and the payment of a royalty. All rights, including professional, stock, radio, broadcasting, television, motion picture, recitation, lecturing and public reading, are reserved. Inquiries should be addressed to the owner's agent, Earl Graham, 317 West 45th Street, New York, N.Y. 10036. Amateur acting rights to *That Championship Season* are controlled exclusively by The Dramatists Play Service Inc., 440 Park Avenue South, New York, N.Y. 10016, without whose permission in writing no amateur performance of the play may be given.

Molière. From *The Misanthrope*, translated by Henri Van Laun. From *A Treasury of the Theatre,* 3d ed., edited by John Gassner. Reprinted with the permission of Simon and Schuster.

Eugene O'Neill. From *Strange Interlude*. Copyright 1928 and renewed 1956 by Carlotta Monterey O'Neill. Reprinted from *Nine Plays by Eugene O'Neill,* by permission of Random House, Inc.

Harold Pinter. From *The Homecoming*. Reprinted by permission of Grove Press, Inc. Copyright © 1965 and 1966 by H. Pinter, Ltd; also by permission of Methuen and Co. Ltd.

Jean Racine. From *Phaedra*. From *Six Plays by Corneille and Racine,* edited by Paul Landis. Copyright 1931 and renewed 1959 by The Modern Library, Inc. Reprinted by permission of Random House, Inc.

William Shakespeare. From *Hamlet*. Reprinted from *Hamlet,* a Norton Critical Edition, Edited by Cyrus Hoy. By permission of W. W. Norton & Company, Inc. Copyright © 1963 by W. W. Norton & Company, Inc.

Ian Anderson
Bernhard and Williams
Photographers, Inc.
Robert Clayton
Susan Cook
Chris Davies
Steve Droes
Gerry Goodstein
Diane Gorodnitzki
Ken Howard
Louisa Johnson
Hank Kranzler
Beth Odle
Ruth Pearson
Alan Magayne-Roshak
Boyd D. Redington
David Rees
Dave Robbins
Martha Swope
Randy Tunnel
Andrew Tsubaki
Sandy Underwood
Terry Zinn/Zinn Unlimited

Credits for
Professional
Photographers (all
editions)